EMPLOYMENT AND PRICES, 1950–1975

Year	Civilian labor force (millions of persons)	Unemployment (millions of persons)	Unemployment (percent)	Consumer price index (1967 = 100)	Wholesale price index (1967 = 100)
1950	62.2	3.3	5.3	72.1	81.8
1951	62.0	2.1	3.3	77.8	91.1
1952	62.1	1.9	3.0	79.5	88.6
1953	63.0	1.8	2.9	80.1	87.4
1954	63.6	3.5	5.5	80.5	87.6
1955	65.0	2.9	4.4	80.2	87.8
1956	66.6	2.8	4.1	81.4	90.7
1957	66.9	2.9	4.3	84.3	93.3
1958	67.6	4.6	6.8	86.6	94.6
1959	68.4	3.7	5.5	87.3	94.8
1960	69.6	3.9	5.5	88.7	94.9
1961	70.5	4.7	6.7	89.6	94.5
1962	70.6	3.9	5.5	90.6	94.8
1963	71.8	4.1	5.7	91.7	94.5
1964	73.1	3.8	5.2	92.9	94.7
1965	74.5	3.4	4.5	94.5	96.6
1966	75.8	2.9	3.8	97.2	99.8
1967	77.3	3.0	3.8	100.0	100.0
1968	78.7	2.8	3.6	104.2	102.5
1969	80.7	2.8	3.5	109.8	106.5
1970	82.7	4.1	4.9	116.3	110.4
1971	82.7	5.0	5.9	121.3	133.9
1972	86.5	4.8	5.6	125.3	119.1
1973	88.7	4.3	4.9	133.1	134.7
1974	91.0	5.1	5.6	147.7	160.1
1975	92.6	7.7	8.3	161.2	174.9

ECONOMICS
THE WAY WE CHOOSE

ECONOMICS
THE WAY WE CHOOSE

Paul W. Barkley
Washington State University

Under the General Editorship of William J. Baumol, Princeton University

Harcourt Brace Jovanovich, Inc.
New York Chicago San Francisco Atlanta

Illustrations by Eric G. Hieber, eh Technical Services
Cartoons by Sidney Harris
Part-opening and cover art by Jane Sterrett

© 1977 by Harcourt Brace Jovanovich, Inc.
All rights reserved. No part of this publication may be reproduced or transmitted in any form or by any means, electronic or mechanical, including photocopy, recording, or any information storage and retrieval system, without permission in writing from the publisher.

ISBN: 0-15-518812-7
Library of Congress Catalog Card Number: 76-52250

Printed in the United States of America

Preface

Some years ago I accepted my first faculty position, as Instructor in the Department of Economics at Kansas State University. A large, complex textbook was placed in my hands, and I was directed to teach two sections of introductory economics. The book was too hard for the students. By the end of the second week, they had begun to ignore it and rely entirely on a neophyte teacher. This process was repeated later at Colorado State University and again at Washington State University. By then, the problem had become more severe because a number of "easy" books had appeared. But the easy texts were too easy. They failed to carry the main thread of economic science from one chapter to the next. Many were relevant to popular issues, and some were even fun to read, but a student well schooled from these books could not understand the central message of economics and how it related to the problems of a modern industrial society. And with every edition the difficult texts became more difficult. The students lost either way.

Eventually I undertook to write a principles book that would meet the needs of students who were likely to enroll in only one course (or one year) of economics. It was intended to be simple yet complete, modern yet traditional, problem oriented yet based in the comprehensive science of economics. It does not make economics easy, for that cannot be done. But it does make economics tractable. It talks about theory, problems, and policy in a way that can be understood by the beginner, and will also allow consistent and meaningful analysis.

Key definitions, highlighted in color on their first appearance in the book, are all readily accessible in the Glossary at the end. After studying the introductory section on graphing in Chapter 2, readers will find that they are comfortable with graphical illustrations of the topics discussed and will profit from the generous distribution of charts and graphs in all chapters. Sidney Harris read the entire manuscript several times and produced a program of cartoons that show the lighter side of the battle with scarcity. Influential economists throughout the history of the discipline, as well as interesting digressions and pithy clarifications, are introduced in two-column boxes throughout the book. Each chapter ends with a point-by-point summary of the content and a set of exercises for practice, beginning with a review list of the most crucial terms and concepts. Following every chapter there is a Contemporary Problem, a real-world situation to which the theory just learned can be applied.

The Study Guide, prepared by Professor Sam M. Cordes of The Pennsylvania State University, will be an invaluable help to students who use it in working through the lessons of this book. It sets forth learning objectives, summarizes the main concepts to be learned in each chapter, and provides a diversity of self-test questions, exercises, problems, and discussion questions (with answers available for checking) to develop mastery of the principles of economics.

For instructors I have prepared an Instructor's Manual containing suggestions for guiding the discussion of the end-of-chapter exercises in the text and for exploiting the Contemporary Problems as applications of economic theory. I have drawn upon my own experience with the topics students find most difficult or most rewarding in the way of theory, explanations, and examples. Additional references on the material of each chapter are also included.

Many people have helped in authenticating the correctness of the theoretical and problem-oriented portions of this book. Professor William Baumol of Princeton University served as consulting editor and provided extremely helpful guidance in many sections. Outlines and drafts of the manuscript were read and commented upon by Professors Robert Allison of California State University, Fresno; Edgar Bagley of Kansas State University, Manhattan; Edward Coen of the University of Minnesota; Charles Cole of California State University, Long Beach; Michael DePrano of the University of Southern California; David Denslow of the University of Florida; Fred R. Glahe of the University of Colorado; Carl Guelzo of Catonsville Community College; John Kirk of the College of San Mateo; Michael Magura of the University of Toledo; and Joseph Perry of the University of North Florida. My colleagues at Washington State University answered many day-to-day questions, and my administrative officers gave both encouragement and forgiveness. Joanne Buteau played an important role in gathering data as well as in preparing questions for the accompanying Test Booklet. Nancy Wagner, Leslie Poler, Cheryl Peters, and Charlotte Larson helped in typing, making minor changes in the manuscript, and keeping abreast of the large volume of correspondence that is a necessary part of a major writing effort.

Two small groups deserve special thanks. Without them the book would never have gotten beyond the proposal stage. The first of these is the College Editorial staff of Harcourt Brace Jovanovich, Inc. Donald De-Laura started helping when the agreement was first signed and continued through the entire project. He is an excellent trouble-shooter and a good economist, above all a close friend. When Don DeLaura was not available, Gary Burke assisted, also making a contribution to the book. Claire T. Rubin took on the chore of putting the prose in order. In addition to being an accomplished editor, she is a most reasonable person. Tina Norum was copy editor and performed that demanding assignment without any apparent loss of enthusiasm or any lapse in rigor. Arlene Kosarin designed the text. All the people at HBJ have been extremely understanding, helpful, and decent.

Finally, there is my family. Andy spent much time in libraries searching for numbers and articles. Chris found and corrected typographical and grammatical errors. Daniel drew graph after graph. Above all, there was Lela, who typed as many as seven drafts per chapter, maintained her poise, and kept the whole family engrossed in the project. In truth, she should be listed as senior author of this book.

PAUL W. BARKLEY

NOTE: *Economics: The Way We Choose* is published also in two volumes, paperbound, under the titles *Introduction to Macroeconomics* and *Introduction to Microeconomics,* with accompanying Study Guides.

Contents

Preface   v
Suggested Outlines for One-semester Courses   xx

1 CHOICE AND ECONOMICS   1

Scarcity and Choice   3
Something Gained Means Something Lost   6
Systematic Choosing: The Market System   7
About This Book   8

A Contemporary Problem: Energy and Many Choices   10

PART ONE   INTRODUCTION   11

2 THE NATURE OF ECONOMIC SCIENCE   13

Science and Economics   14
   Identifying the Problem   15
   Fact Gathering   16

Generating Principles	16
Making Economic Policy	18
About Graphs	18
Production Possibilities: A Model of Choice	23
Production-Possibility Curves	24
Moving Along the Curve—Opportunity Cost	25
New Curves—Changes in Capacity	26
A Tool for Choosing	28
A Contemporary Problem: Potential and Actual Achievement	31

3 THE CIRCULAR FLOW OF ECONOMIC ACTIVITY 35

Three Major Actors	36
Firms	36
Households	38
Governments	38
Comparative Advantage and Interdependence	40
The Factors of Production	41
The Circular Flow—Households and Firms	43
Government in the Circular Flow	48
Investment, Growth, and Interdependence	49
A Contemporary Problem: California—The Late Great State	51

4 THE MARKET, FEEDBACK SYSTEMS, AND PRECARIOUSNESS 53

A Market System	54
An Automatic Mechanism	55
Market Defects	55
Nonmarket Aspects of the U.S. Economy	56
The Market in Isolation	57
Demand	57
Supply	60
The Supply/Demand Relationship	61
Changes in Supply and Demand	64
The Precariousness of the System	69
A Contemporary Problem: Another View of Market Capitalism	74

PART TWO MACROECONOMICS 77

5 THE ECONOMICS OF A SYSTEM 79

Appropriate Goals for an Economy 81
    Full Employment 81
    Price Stability 84
    Economic Growth 86
    Environmental Protection 87
    Increased Well-being 88
Methods of Goal Attainment 89
    Altering Aggregate Demand 90
    Direct Regulation 92
Limitations on Monetary and Fiscal Policy 93

A Contemporary Problem: Inflation + Recession = Stagflation 94

6 NATIONAL INCOME ACCOUNTING 97

The Major Accounts 98
    Gross National Product 99
    Net National Product 104
    National Income 105
    Personal Income 105
    Disposable (Personal) Income 107
    Summarizing the Accounts 107
The Empirical Record 108
    Deflating a Performance Series 109
    GNP in Current and Constant Dollars 110
    Graphing the Major Accounts 112
Limitations of the National Income Accounts 114
    GNP and Well-being 114
    GNP and Quality 115

A Contemporary Problem: GNP Is Not the Whole Story 118

7 FROM THE CLASSICAL TO THE MODERN MACRO MODEL 121

The Classical Economists 122
    J. B. Say and Say's Law 122
    Say's Law and Savings 124

Limitations of the Classical Model	129
Keynes Challenges the Classical Model	129
The Keynesian Model	130
The Aggregate Consumption Function	134
Aggregate Demand and Equilibrium	135
Aggregate Demand, Equilibrium, and Full Employment	136
Summary of the Keynesian Model	137
A Contemporary Problem: Should Workers Accept Pay Cuts?	139

8 AN EXPANSION OF THE MACRO MODEL 143

The Macro Model, Step by Step	144
Households Only	144
Households and Firms	145
Households, Firms, and Government	147
Summary of the Macro Model	148
Understanding Aggregate Economic Behavior	149
Determinants of Consumer Spending	150
Determinants of Investment	152
Determinants of Government Spending	156
Changing the Level of Equilibrium	158
Altering Consumer Expenditure	158
Altering Investments	159
Altering Government Expenditure	159
A Contemporary Problem: The Dream House in the Suburbs	164

9 CHANGES IN LEVELS OF AGGREGATE INCOME 167

The Average Propensity to Consume or to Save	168
The Marginal Propensity to Consume or to Save	170
The Multiplier	172
A Contemporary Problem: President Ford's Tax Refund Plan	179

10 FISCAL POLICY 181

Deliberately Managing the Economy	182
When to Use Fiscal Policy	183
The Deflationary Gap	184
The Inflationary Gap	185

How Much Should Fiscal Activity Be Changed?	188
Automatic Stabilizers	190
Unemployment Compensation	190
The Progressive Income Tax	191
Discretionary Stabilizers	192
Public Works	192
Welfare Payments	194
Changes in Tax Rates	196
Conclusion	198
A Contemporary Problem: The Defense Budget	200

11 THE PUBLIC DEBT 201

The Public Budget and the Public Debt	202
The Public Debt	203
Why Increase the Debt?	204
The Other Side of the Ledger	206
Problems of the Public Debt	207
The Size of the Debt	207
Repayment	208
Interest	210
Who Sacrifices?	211
A Contemporary Problem: What to Do in Case of Peace	214

12 MONEY, SYMBOL OF MUTUAL TRUST 217

The Evolution of Money	218
Early Forms of Money	219
The Introduction of Paper Money	220
Money Grows	221
Money in the U.S. Economy	221
Coins	222
Paper Money	223
Demand Deposits	223
The Modern Banking System	224
Expanding the Money Supply	225
Weaknesses of a Fractional Reserve System	228
Enlarging the Definition of Money	229
A Contemporary Problem: Government Grants and the Local Bank	232

13 MONEY AND THE PERFORMANCE OF THE ECONOMY — 233

Money and Prices — 234
    The Quantity Theory of Money — 235
    Limitations of the Elementary Quantity Theory — 237
The Desire to Hold Money — 237
    The Transactions Demand — 237
    The Precautionary Demand — 238
    The Speculative Demand — 240
    The Total Demand for Money — 242
The Supply of Money — 242

A Contemporary Problem: How Potent Is Monetary Policy? — 245

14 THE FEDERAL RESERVE SYSTEM — 249

Creation and Organization of the System — 250
Altering the Money Supply — 252
    Changes in the Discount Rate — 252
    Buying and Selling Bonds in the Open Market — 253
    Changing the Reserve Requirement — 256
    Minor Controls — 258
The Federal Reserve System and the U.S. Treasury — 261
The Use of Monetary Policy — 262

A Contemporary Problem: Bank Lending — 264

15 ECONOMIC INSTABILITY AND MACROECONOMIC POLICY — 267

Business Fluctuations and Their Causes — 268
    Exogenous Theories — 270
    Endogenous Theories — 272
Monetary vs. Fiscal Policy — 274
    The Monetarists — 274
    The Keynesians — 277
    The Middle Ground — 279

A Contemporary Problem: Monetarists and Keynesians—The Dispute Continues — 281

16 MACRO POLICY IN ACTION — 285

The Record	288
Growth	288
Price Stability	289
Employment	289
Policy Indications and Responses	291
Fiscal Measures	294
Monetary Measures	295
Conclusion	297
A Contemporary Problem: Recovering from Stagflation	299

PART THREE
MICROECONOMICS — 301

17 THE DEMAND FOR ECONOMIC GOODS — 303

The Market System	304
The Concept of Demand	305
Diminishing Marginal Utility	305
Changes in Demand	307
Individual and Market Demand Curves	308
Elasticity of Demand	310
A Contemporary Problem: Shifts and Changes in Demand	317

18 THE SUPPLY OF ECONOMIC GOODS — 321

Supply and the Costs of Production	322
Classes of Production Costs	323
Marginal Cost and the Supply Curve	327
Supply and Technology	330
Supply and Time	331
Conclusion	333
A Contemporary Problem: Bigger Is Not Always Better	335

19 DEMAND, SUPPLY, AND EQUILIBRIUM — 337

The Market	338
A Change in Equilibrium	340
The Cobweb	343

A Final Comment   345

A Contemporary Problem: Office Space on Manhattan Island   346

20 COMPETITION   349

Firms and Industries   350
The Competitive Industry   351
    Why Are Industries Competitive?   353
    Price for the Industry   354
    Price, Cost, and Firm Supply   355
    Profits or Losses?   356

A Contemporary Problem: Agriculture in a Mechanized Economy   363

21 MONOPOLY   367

Cost and Revenue Structures   368
    What Makes a Monopoly?   368
    The Monopolist as Price Searcher   370
    Optimal Level of Output   372
Controversies About Monopoly   374
    Allocation of Resources   374
    The Distribution of Income   375
    The Advance of Technology   376
The Discriminating Monopolist   378
Antimonopoly Measures   381
    Possible Solutions   381
    Legislation   383
The Natural Monopoly   384

A Contemporary Problem: Monopoly or Not in Hawaii?   386

Appendix: Monopoly, Demand, Revenues, and Costs   388

22 MONOPOLISTIC COMPETITION   391

The Nature of Monopolistic Competition   392
Equilibrium of Firm and Industry   395
Three Peculiarities   398
    Equilibrium   398
    Product Differentiation   401
    Nonprice Competition   401
Advertising the Product   403

A Contemporary Problem: A Tale of Many Tailors   406

23 OLIGOPOLY 409

Why Oligopoly Exists 410
How the Oligopolist Makes Decisions 413
    Oligopoly Prices 414
    The Kinked Demand Curve 415
    Joint Profit Maximization 417
    Price Leadership 420
    Other Explanations of Oligopolists' Behavior 421

A Contemporary Problem: Oligopoly in Oil 424

24 SELLING THE FACTORS OF PRODUCTION 427

The Demand for Factors 428
    The Production Function 428
    Production in Terms of Revenue 430
The Supply of Factors 434
    Land and Natural Resources 435
    Labor 437
Imperfections in the Factor Markets 439
    Land 439
    Labor 440
    Capital 441

A Contemporary Problem: A Young Man Enters the Labor Force 443

25 THE DISTRIBUTION OF INCOME 445

Economists Grapple with the Problem 446
The Functional Distribution of Income 449
The Size Distribution of Income 450
The Effects of Change 453
Perfect Income Equality? 454

A Contemporary Problem: Food Stamps in the U.S. Economy 457

26 WHEN THE MARKET FAILS 459

The Causes of Market Failure 460
Kinds of Market Failure 462
The Economist's View 463

Means of Correcting Market Failures	465
Internalization or Merger	465
Taxes and Subsidies	468
Legal Restrictions	471
Beneficial External Effects	473
A Contemporary Problem: Selling "Pollution Certificates"	476

27 WHEN THERE IS NO MARKET AT ALL   479

Lighthouses—Pure Public Goods	480
The Demand for Lighthouse Services	481
Public Goods and the Free Rider	484
City Sidewalks—Uncollectible Revenues	485
Income Redistribution Programs	486
Making Decisions: Benefit/Cost Analysis	488
Once Produced, Who Pays?	492
A Contemporary Problem: Public Goods and the Budget Crunch	495

28 MICROECONOMIC POLICY   497

What Is Micro Policy?	498
Antimonopoly Policy	500
Protecting Natural Monopolies	503
Protection and Control	503
Protection and Nurture	504
Placing Bounds on Behavior	506
Policies Affecting Households	506
A Contemporary Problem: The Taxis in New York	511

PART FOUR
INTERNATIONAL ECONOMICS   513

29 AN INTRODUCTION TO THE WORLD ECONOMY   515

Trade Among National Economies	517
The United States as a Trading Nation	520
With Whom Does the United States Trade?	524

Problems of World Economics ... 525
    The Expansion of World Trade ... 525
    Population ... 526
    Income Distribution ... 526
    Artificial Barriers to Trade ... 527
    Multiple Currencies ... 528

A Contemporary Problem: A "Trade Visit" from China ... 530

30 WHY NATIONS TRADE ... 535

The Law of Comparative Advantage ... 536
    The Gains from Trade ... 541
    The Rate of Trade ... 543
    Do Nations Specialize? ... 543
Artificial Barriers to Trade ... 544
    Infant Industries ... 544
    Diversified Economies ... 545
    Protecting the Labor Force ... 545
Comparative Advantage and Diminishing Returns ... 546

A Contemporary Problem: Multinational Corporations ... 549

31 MONEY AND INTERNATIONAL TRADE ... 551

British Automobiles and U.S. Machinery ... 552
    The Demand for Foreign Exchange ... 555
    The Supply of Foreign Exchange ... 556
    The Equilibrium Price of Foreign Exchange ... 557
Fixed Exchange Rates ... 559

A Contemporary Problem: Argentina Changes a Fixed Exchange Rate ... 563

32 THE BALANCE OF INTERNATIONAL PAYMENTS ... 565

The Balance of Payments ... 566
    Exports and Imports ... 567
    Remittances ... 569
    Net Government Transactions ... 569
    Net Capital Movements ... 569
    Paying Debts Between Nations ... 570
    Errors and Omissions ... 571
Continuing Balance-of-Payments Disequilibrium ... 571

Recent Developments in U.S. Trade	573
Trade Surpluses	574
Balance-of-Payments Problems	575
Possible Solutions	575
Bringing Order to the Trading World	577
The Bretton Woods Conference	577
The Smithsonian Agreement	578
A Contemporary Problem: The Common Market	580

33 THE LESS DEVELOPED COUNTRIES   583

World Poverty	584
Growth in the LDCs	586
Factors Affecting Growth	588
Land	588
Labor	589
Capital	590
Entrepreneurship	592
Development Strategies	593
The Role of Agriculture	594
Population Control	595
Balanced or Unbalanced Growth?	596
Sources of Capital	598
U.S. Foreign Aid	600
A Contemporary Problem: The Green Revolution	602

34 THE MIGRATION OF LABOR   605

Causes of Migration	606
Patterns of Migration	608
Migrating to a Frontier	608
Rural to Urban Migration	610
Following a Migration Path	611
International Migration	611
The Brain Drain	612
Effects of Migration	613
Emigration	613
Immigration	614
Migration and the U.S. Economy	615
A Contemporary Problem: Trouble Near the Borders	619

Index   621
Glossary   640

Suggested Outlines for One-semester Courses

Chapter	Macro Emphasis	Micro Emphasis	Balanced Emphasis
1. Choice and Economics	x	x	x
2. The Nature of Economic Science	x	x	x
3. The Circular Flow of Economic Activity	x	x	x
4. The Market, Feedback Systems, and Precariousness	x	x	x
5. The Economics of a System	x		x
6. National Income Accounting	x		x
7. From the Classical to the Modern Macro Model	x		
8. An Expansion of the Macro Model	x		
9. Changes in Levels of Aggregate Income	x		x
10. Fiscal Policy	x		
11. The Public Debt	x		
12. Money, Symbol of Mutual Trust	x		x
13. Money and the Performance of the Economy	x		
14. The Federal Reserve System	x		x
15. Economic Instability and Macroeconomic Policy	x		
16. Macro Policy in Action	x		
17. The Demand for Economic Goods		x	x
18. The Supply of Economic Goods		x	x
19. Demand, Supply, and Equilibrium		x	x
20. Competition		x	
21. Monopoly		x	
22. Monopolistic Competition		x	
23. Oligopoly		x	
24. Selling the Factors of Production		x	x
25. The Distribution of Income	x	x	x
26. When the Market Fails		x	
27. When There Is No Market at All		x	
28. Microeconomic Policy		x	
29. An Introduction to the World Economy	x	x	x
30. Why Nations Trade	x		x
31. Money and International Trade			
32. The Balance of International Payments			
33. The Less Developed Countries		x	
34. The Migration of Labor		x	x

1 Choice and Economics

It probably comes as no surprise that no one can have all he or she wants of everything. But that is the first lesson of economics. Things are scarce, and that means that there is choosing to be done. Choices are made on all levels of social organization. Turn the dial on your TV set and you have chosen. You can't watch two programs at the same time. Other choices are not so trivial. Should a family have a new roof or a new car? Should Coca-Cola get into the furniture business? Should New York City have free education or free garbage collection? Should the world use its entire coal supply now or save some for future generations? Choice is an inescapable part of all individual and group behavior. Economics is about choosing and the range of choices.

Redwoods or revenue? On the northern California coast stand many groves of redwood trees, among the oldest and most beautiful of all living things. For generations, people have used redwood for construction, furniture, and adornment. Until very recently, no one objected much to the cutting of the trees. When one grove was cut, there was always another beyond the next mountain ridge, and the lumber business enhanced well-being by generating incomes and jobs.

To raise revenue, the State of California taxes the value of standing trees, just as it taxes the value of business buildings, factories, and homes. A tree that has been cut, however, is not taxed at all. So in addition to an economic system that encourages owners to cut their trees and enjoy the income, there is a tax system that penalizes those who do not. The combined pressures make it absurd to leave trees standing. The redwoods continue to be cut and the country is in danger of losing this beautiful resource.

The threat to the continued existence of redwood trees has aroused intense reaction among conservationists. As a result, in the 1960s Congress created the Redwood National Park and the King Range Conservation Area. No trees within these large preserves can be cut, and people can choose whether or not to visit and experience these trees. In successfully defending this choice, the conservationists closed options for the many people who live among the redwoods and depend upon them for their incomes. Now the woods are still, and loggers, sawyers, truckers, scalers, and scores of others are out of work. Society made an explicit choice in passing the law that created the parks. It saved the trees, and as a result many people have lost their jobs.

Specialization or flexibility? Detroit is the nation's fifth largest city. It is nearly always in the news because it (and its fashionable suburb, Grosse Point) dictates the course of the automobile industry. From Detroit come the shape and style of next year's cars, their cost, and their efficiency in converting gasoline to forward motion. Executives in Detroit also decide which of the industry's plants will open and which will close. In the confines of walnut-panelled board rooms, such decisions are impersonal and related mainly to the profits of the firm. Out on the assembly line, these same decisions mean the difference between work and unemployment; between varied, high-protein diets and inexpensive starchy diets; between new shoes and repaired shoes.

Detroit is a cosmopolitan city complete with museums, private clubs, and symphony orchestras. It is also a one-industry town. Half a century ago, Detroit's industrialists and public officials boasted that their city held great promise because from it would spring America's most important piece of equipment—the family car. Civic leaders and officials holding to this vision cast the city's lot entirely with the auto industry as they decided where houses would be built, where telephone lines would be located, and where factories would dump industrial waste. The city grew in size, income, and importance.

If those same officials had seen Detroit in the winter of 1975, they would have questioned the wisdom of making Detroit a one-industry town. The automobile industry had attracted a large labor force, but the workers were trained to perform very special jobs found only in the auto industry. When the assembly line was moving, people worked. When the line stopped, the labor force was idle. And the auto industry proved vulnerable to every change in the U.S. economy. When business boomed in Alabama, Montana, and New Hampshire, automobile production boomed in Detroit. When business slumped in South Dakota, Illinois, and West Virginia, auto production in Detroit decreased.

The economic stress of the mid-1970s affected many families. And when it came to a choice between new cars and necessities, they did without new cars. As a result, a quarter of a million auto workers were temporarily or "indefinitely" out of work. The city was in turmoil, suffering the harvest of what once had been "correct" decisions made by industrial and civic leaders hoping to bolster the city's economy.

Baby clothes or birthday presents? Ellen and Jack live in the open country near a small metropolitan area. Jack was injured in an industrial accident several years ago and is now unable to work. The couple and nine of their eleven children live on a monthly welfare check of $376. A married daughter lives nearby and is an occasional financial drain on the family's resources when her husband's take-home pay of $58 per week fails to meet household expenses. The recent birth of her first child forced the daughter to rely on Ellen for many baby-care items. The eldest child, a son aged twenty-two, is separated from his wife and presently lives at home. He dropped out of school in the tenth grade and has been unable to find employment since he returned from army duty. The third eldest child, a daughter aged nineteen, recently finished a year-long clerical course at a nearby community college (her educational expenses were paid by special welfare grant), but is unable to find work.

During the last year, Ellen completed a nine-month, college-level clerical and bookkeeping course, using funds from a special federal program. This program provided an income supplement of $75 per month, but it had to be spent in a special way ($55 per month for transportation; $10 per month for books and tuition; $10 per month for child care). For several months Ellen received $26 each month as a representative on a county Human Resources Board. She saved this money for Christmas and birthday gifts and such unplanned items as nursery furnishings for her first grandchild. Ellen and Jack live by making careful decisions about how to buy food and clothing and by going without many of the things their neighbors have.

Scarcity and Choice

The redwood owners, conservationists, Detroit's civic and industrial leaders, and Ellen and Jack have one thing in common: they must continually choose. Economics is concerned with all their decisions—those of the tree owners, the State of California, and the conservationists;

those of the auto company executives, the assembly line workers, the city officials, and the auto buyers in Nebraska; those of Ellen and Jack about how to spend their income. Economics is about choice. The need for choice comes from scarcity. The source of scarcity—time, money, or redwoods—does not really matter. Choosing is always necessary because there is not enough of everything to go around. Some things are always scarce.

The history of humanity is a history of the struggle against scarcity. Early peoples looked for new hunting grounds when game became scarce in the old locale. They found new valleys to farm when their populations outgrew their own lands. Spain sent explorers to the New World because gold was scarce, and the early colonists in North America left England so they could expand the range of their choices in political and religious affairs. The Industrial Revolution was a response to the scarcity of machine-made things like cloth, tools, and power. The more recent revolution in food-producing techniques is a worldwide response to the scarcity of food.

Scarcity is everywhere, and children, students, homemakers, and corporate executives must spend a large part of their lives deciding how to deal with it. Government officials, for example, have heavy demands placed on their time. They receive requests to speak, to discuss problems, or simply to appear at countless numbers of functions. But they also have obligations to their offices and to their families, which also take time. How are they to allocate twenty-four hours each day in such a way as to satisfy their offices, their families, and their public? Time to them is very scarce and they must choose carefully in order to get the most out of each hour.

For Ellen and Jack the problem is the same, but it is written in different terms. Jack and the other adult males in the household are unemployed. Time is no problem for them; they have plenty of it. Money, however, is a problem. With eleven people living on $376 per month, money is scarce and careful choices must be made to insure that each dollar spent purchases those goods that bring a great deal of satisfaction to the family. Their choice process must be geared to getting the most out of each dollar.

The pioneers crossing the great desert between Utah and California faced still another kind of scarcity—water. They left Salt Lake City with casks brimful, but in the absence of rain, this limited supply of water would have to be used for people, cattle, horses, and oxen. As days went by and no rain fell, choices had to be made. Which animals would be allowed to drink the scarce water, and which would die? The water had to be rationed, or *allocated,* among its many possible uses. Certainly, none was used for washing or for cleaning the wagons. Choices were made with only one objective in mind: helping the wagon train across the desert.

The Economist

There are about 65,000 active professional economists in the United States today. Most are employed by universities or at some level of government, but many work for large firms and corporations, forecasting economic conditions and predicting the economic effects of various courses of action.

When the economy is performing well, the economist relaxes. When inflation, unemployment, or recession occurs, the economist becomes very busy. In many ways the economist is like a physician. Doctors might *like* dealing with healthy people all the time, or treating only mild illnesses or superficial wounds. But most doctors spend a lot of their time confronting difficult diseases, mutilated bodies, or incurable illnesses. The economist too would like to study and work with a healthy economy, but seldom has the opportunity.

A very obstinate disease often calls for consultation among a number of medical doctors, and they may disagree on both diagnosis and cure. This is not because the doctors are obstreperous; it merely shows that what we know about the functioning or malfunctioning of the human body is far from complete, and incomplete knowledge leads to variations in diagnosis and prescription. A complex economic system is certainly not fully understood either, so prescriptions for curing economic ills are also likely to differ. To solve a specific economic problem, one economist will urge selling while another urges buying. For another problem, one economist will call for more government spending and another will call for less. In the troublesome years from 1974 to 1976, John Kenneth Galbraith, a noted Harvard University economist, continually recommended *more government activity* to control inflation. At the same time, Secretary of the Treasury William A. Simon was strongly advocating *less government involvement* in national economic affairs!

These differences of opinion, which appear in newspapers and magazines every day, may baffle students beginning the study of economics. Just remember that economists sometimes make inaccurate predictions or are unable to name the cures for particular problems. Like physicians, they deal with complex systems and must be expected—within limits—to make errors.

Something Gained Means Something Lost

The discipline of economics studies the problem of scarcity and shows how choices should be made. It helps in understanding what is gained and what is sacrificed each time a choice is made. Fortunately, most day-to-day choices are nearly automatic and have such insignificant consequences that they do not require extensive study. It may be necessary or even urgent to decide between cereal and eggs at breakfast time, between a ball game and a movie, or between two school subjects that need to be studied, but these are personal choices, involving or affecting only a few people.

Even these simple choices affect other people. Choosing eggs instead of cereal means that somewhere an egg producer sells more eggs and a cereal producer sells less cereal. Usually, as more people become involved in the choice, the process becomes more complex and the result is felt by more people. When a family decides to take a month's vacation, the choice of where to go becomes very hard. Parents want to go where there is peace, quiet, and relaxation; children want to go where there is action and excitement. The choice to go to the shore causes a series of events to unfold as the car is prepared, reservations are made, and equipment is purchased. When the family changes its plans and goes to the mountains rather than the shore, surfboards go unused and skis are purchased; one resort loses business and another gains. If the family decides to use public transportation rather than the family car, the travel agency rather than the service station gains business.

Scarcity is not a phenomenon felt only by individuals and families. In a large industrial firm, the board of directors makes weighty decisions. Will the new plant be built in Ireland or in Arizona? Should a new line of products be started or should the production lines for the old product be modernized? Should branch plants be developed or the home plant enlarged? Should the whole firm be automated to increase profits even though this would leave many laborers unemployed? No choice is easy, but each is necessary because the board of directors has limited amounts of time, money, and skill—the firm cannot do everything.

Towns and cities too are continually forced to make choices. Budgets are limited, existing services become more expensive, and citizens demand more services. City officials are always under pressure. Should they spend money for sidewalks used mostly by the elderly or for downtown parking that would benefit businesses? The answers are neither easy nor obvious, but the choices must be made. Because of scarcity and the need to choose, New York City has been compelled to reduce employment by 2,200 workers, and Minneapolis has recently ended its $80,000 annual subsidy to the city transit company.

The federal government is responsible for producing goods and services like highways, defense, education, and disaster relief, but it also has the awesome responsibility of providing a stable environment in which public and private choices can be made. It chooses between peace and war; it also decides how to battle inflation, how to cope with unemployment and—within limits—how to manage the supply of money. Choices made by the federal government vary in gravity and in effect. Regardless of how difficult or how easy, choices must still be made.

Systematic Choosing: The Market System

Because choice is so pervasive, it is not surprising that a great deal of intellectual effort has gone into studying it. The result of this effort is the field of *economics,* which introduces discipline and system to the process of choosing.

Economics is the study of the allocation of scarce resources among alternative and competing ends.

In less elegant language, economics is the study of how to use what is available to get what is wanted.

Choosing is not done in a vacuum. The process of choice is a part of culture and society, so there are always limits on what can be decided. General Motors cannot choose to increase its profits by burning all the Ford and Chrysler plants. New York City cannot choose to avoid layoffs by defaulting on all its bills, and Ellen and Jack cannot solve their economic problem by robbing a bank. Most personal decisions are made within limits imposed by time and financial budgets; laws, customs, and informal rules provide the framework for other choices.

In the United States, nearly all economic decisions are made in markets where the interaction of buyers and sellers determines what will be traded and at what price. This kind of bargaining is more sophisticated than that found in the bazaars of underdeveloped countries and in suburban garage sales. A customer does not dicker with Safeway or A&P for a better price on the tomatoes. However, if many customers feel the tomatoes are too expensive, they are left on the rack until either the price falls or the fruit spoils. If the price falls, the supermarket manager is responding to information about consumer preferences. If the price stays high, the tomatoes spoil and the store manager does not buy any more; he thus passes a message on to the tomato grower. In this way, the market system gathers information and transmits it to buyers and sellers.

The market system has enabled the American economy to grow, industrialize, and develop. The system, though, has flaws. In an advanced industrial country, a high degree of specialization and interdependence among different parts of the economy means that good choices in one place may yield bad results in another. The entirely wise choice of hundreds of thousands of families not to buy new automobiles in 1974 led to 250,000 auto workers being out of work in early 1975. The very profitable choice of many industries to dump their sewage into Lake Erie caused the "death" of that body of water. Similarly, a market economy does not automatically develop markets for things like police protection, city parks, quiet redwood groves, and clean air. Since people in the United States do want these things, some nonmarket mechanism must be developed to provide them. In each case—that of problems caused by interdependence and that of the need for nonmarket goods—it has been necessary for governments or formal and informal groups of people to try to fill the void.

About This Book

A modern study of economics, then, cannot be limited to the study of individual or even group choice. It must inquire into the framework for choice, the causes of choices, and their effects on the chooser as well as on others in the economy. This book is about the economy, economics, and economists. The main threads—scarcity and choice—begin here in Chapter 1. By the last chapter, these threads will be woven into a cloth that also includes threads dealing with the economic performance of the whole society, government's responsibility in maintaining the economy, the economic role of the household, the economic role of the individual firm, and the way in which the U.S. economy fits in the complex world economy. From time to time a decorative thread will appear in the cloth to show how a single outstanding economist dealt with problems faced by the economy or contributed to the body of thought called economics.

The whole fabric of economics is not yet woven. Even now, as the 1970s come to a close, the economy of the United States and all others in the Western world are encountering new and different problems of choice and scarcity. The old lessons of economics cannot always solve new economic problems. Like officers in the military, economists sometimes seem to be fighting a bygone war. Rather than making the subject obsolete, this characteristic provides the controversies and challenge that have kept economics alive for some 200 years.

The book divides into four major sections. The first section (Chapters 2-4) provides introductory lessons that are necessary for understanding the remaining chapters. Chapters 5-16 deal with macroeconomics and the study of the whole economic system; Chapters 17-28 focus on the problems of choices made by individual firms, industries, and households. Chapters 29-33 relate the U.S. economy to economic problems in the world and discuss such topics as the balance of payments and

A Limitation: Ideologies

The nations of the world have made different decisions about what constitutes the best economic framework. At this time well over half of the people in the world live in nations that use some collective means to make choices. Among these are China, the U.S.S.R., and Cuba. Most European and some of the Eastern Hemisphere countries use a market-oriented framework. Still other countries compromise and try to combine the best of both systems in making their individual and group choices. No system can be described as the best or the worst; none is always good or always bad. Each has advantages and disadvantages. This book considers only a mixed economy like the one present in the United States today—an economy that is basically market oriented but has a bit of collective choice, too.

aid to less developed countries. Chapter 34 brings a number of themes together in a discussion of how people react to economic opportunity.

Summary

1. Individuals, firms, groups, and governments must make choices. The necessity for choices gives rise to the modern science of economics.
2. Economics is the study of scarcity and choice. It shows how to use available resources to attain desired goals.
3. This book studies choices, the framework for choices, and the results of choosing. It is divided into four sections that deal with general topics, the system as a whole, choice making within a firm or household, and international economics.

Exercises

1. Explain these important terms and concepts:
   - choice
   - scarcity
   - the process of choosing
   - market system
   - market interdependence
   - group choice
2. Scarcity and choice are facts of life and together form the backbone of economics. How does each of the following definitions of economics relate to scarcity and choice?
   a. Economics is the study of men in the business of organizing production and consumption activities.
   b. Economics is the study of how to improve society.
   c. Economics is the study of exchange transactions.
   d. Economics is the study of how to use limited resources to achieve what sometimes appear to be unlimited goals.
3. Which of the above definitions do you prefer? Why?

4 When you decided to attend your college or university, your choice was influenced by some scarcities. Name them and show how they affected you.
5 The choice of this college or university closed other options that had been open to you. Can you ever go back and start again? What has changed? Is this an economic problem?

A Contemporary Problem
Energy and Many Choices

One of the most difficult problems facing the nation today is the difficulty of producing enough energy. Oil imports depend on fragile political considerations as well as economic ones, thermal power plants pollute the atmosphere, all the good hydroelectric sites have already been developed, and nuclear energy still does not seem to be truly safe. Society must choose a method of coping with this problem. It may choose simply to raise the price so that people will want to use less energy, it may subsidize domestic oil production, or it may relax environmental standards so that a greater number of polluting power plants can be used. As the choices are made, society will attain some things and give up some others. Make a list of three or four energy-related choices that are now available to the U.S. economic society. How are those related to scarcity (what things are *scarce* in each case)? And what effects will the choices probably have?

"I've been keeping my thermostat down to 14."

2 The Nature of Economic Science

The Biblical record of our ancestors' behavior in the Garden of Eden shows that even they were making choices. In the early millennia of human existence choices were undoubtedly few. As people acquired knowledge and skills, the number of alternatives expanded. Eventually, the need arose for a science devoted to reliable and efficient choosing.

Economics has roots in classical antiquity. Indeed, the word is derived from the Greek phrase *oikos nemein,* which means "to manage a household." But economics as a field of study did not really develop until after the Renaissance, about the beginning of the seventeenth century.

With the coming of the industrial age, the tempo and complexity of life increased. People were exposed to many alternative ways of doing things and satisfying wants, and making choices became so important that some scholars began to examine how we choose and what we gain or lose by choosing one thing over another. The systematic pursuit of these questions was economics and, like other studies of the period, it followed the general method of science. Modern economics emerged by the late eighteenth century as a scientific discipline dealing with people, society, and choice. Economics is a *social science*. The social sciences are those fields of learning concerned primarily with relationships among people and with the institutions people use to guide behavior. Sociology, political science, anthropology, and psychology are among the other social sciences.

As social scientists, economists use the methods of science to gather facts, develop principles, predict behavior, and form policy. This chapter deals with science and economics. It begins with a section on science, then moves to the application of the scientific method to economic problems.

Science and Economics

Science is the never-ending struggle to find truth. You may dismiss this statement as the rambling of an amateur philosopher, but it holds some practical value. Truth is a temporary phenomenon. It is limited by human communication systems, technology, and skill. For example, during the Dark Ages in Europe, the world was perceived as flat. This flatness was acceptable as "truth" because travel and human knowledge of celestial phenomena were so limited that no other concept was needed. A family lived in a small area and confined its activity to a small region. This region appeared to be flat, so for all practical purposes, the earth was flat, too. When travel and exploration became widespread, and especially when ships were able to sail far out on the Atlantic, the vision of a flat earth had to change. Many observations of stars and planets and of ships' movements at sea led to new principles and to a new truth. Those who were in a position to do so could exploit the new truth about the earth's shape and turn it into riches. The Spanish, knowing they would not fall off the edge of a flat earth, found the New World and brought gold and silver back to Spain.

The situation has not changed much since the Dark Ages. Truth is still sought because it has value, and the scientific method remains the most systematic way of pursuing it. The method starts with a problem. Once the problem is well defined, information that might have an effect on it is gathered. The information is sorted and analyzed, and that which is useful is kept—to be used as the basis for general principles. In the social sciences, the principles are often used to help formulate policies. The policies ultimately are aimed at removing the problem and improving people's lives.

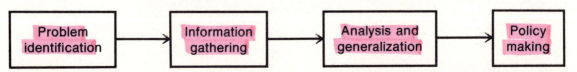

In the 1970s the United States economy began to experience an energy crisis. The problem was identified as a shortage of several kinds of fuel. Economists studying the problem gathered facts about prices, shipping, environmental considerations, alternative forms of fuel, and problems of international diplomacy related to fuel sources. These facts were analyzed to show the costs and the benefits associated with each alternative and a policy emerged: Keep thermostats turned down, build the Alaska pipeline, and continue to search for methods of harnessing solar power. The scientific method led from the problem of fuel scarcity to the understanding that fuel will continue to be scarce and then to a policy of fuel conservation.

In economics (and in the other social sciences), the pursuit of truth is slowed because human behavior cannot ordinarily be subjected to the kinds of controlled experiments that are possible with white rats and guinea pigs. The economist must follow the steps in a search for new truths about economic behavior, but following them is frustrating and often leads up blind alleys. Nevertheless, problems, facts, principles, and policies must be considered in a systematic way.

Identifying the Problem

Economic problems do not occur in a sterile hothouse under conditions of controlled heat and humidity. They arise in the very untidy world of human beings. One difficulty facing economists is knowing how serious an economic problem really is. Is the balance-of-payments problem serious enough to deserve the attention of economists? A local school bond issue may be crucial in Minot, North Dakota, but should the economists of that state give it priority over other problems? In early 1975, 250,000 auto workers were out of work. Although the unemployment was centralized in the region near Detroit, its effects were felt throughout the economy. Should economists address this problem? There are no rules about which economic problems should be studied. In general, economists have always been concerned about issues as large as unemployment in the auto industry. Their concern with issues like local school bond issues has been less frequent.

Several schemes are used to help identify problems that can be studied usefully. One divides issues into *macroeconomic* problems and *microeconomic* problems. The former are matters affecting the whole economy, like unemployment, inflation, the balance of payments, and the national debt; the latter are problems facing individuals or firms, like the price of food, how to use gasoline efficiently, and the profitability of the family store. Another scheme classifies problems according to the way they relate to national economic goals.[1] In this light, problems like inflation, stagnation, and unemployment receive high priority.

---

[1]The goals of the national economy are discussed in Chapter 5. Although there is much conflict over the relative importance of national economic goals, it is generally conceded that they include economic growth, price stability, full employment, economic freedom, and equity in income distribution. In recent years, some policy makers have attempted to introduce environmental considerations into the list of economic goals.

Regardless of classification schemes, the measure of an economist's skill is the ability to identify the real problem rather than a symptom. The mother of a fretful and crying infant recognizes the child's problem to be a temperature of 103°. The pediatrician observes the temperature but recognizes it as only a symptom of a more critical ailment—pneumonia, perhaps. Consumers observe that the price of telephone calls is rising very rapidly. The economist recognizes this price change as a symptom of monopoly power in the hands of the phone company—since it is the only provider of telephone service, it charges what it pleases regardless of the public's welfare.

Fact Gathering

Anyone—scientist, student, or homemaker—should be able to gather facts once a problem is identified. Say that the rapid rise and fall of egg prices at the corner store is making it difficult for consumers to plan meals. Learning all there is to know about the market for eggs is not so simple as it may seem. Observing market prices and quantities sold will not explain how the price of eggs got to be 75 cents per dozen. A more thorough effort requires inquiry into the price of chickens and chicken feed, transportation costs, egg storage, quality control, breakage, anticipations of the future, and scores of other items. Again, anyone can gather these bits of information, but it takes skill to examine them, keep what is relevant, and discard what is not. The skill comes from understanding the structures and operation of the economic system or some of its constituent parts.

Generating Principles

After a problem has been identified and facts have been gathered, generalizations can be made about economic behavior. The generalizations may be called laws, principles, theories, or models. Regardless of the name, they are rules about behavior and can be used to describe or predict events. Staying dry outdoors during a rainstorm is a problem. Facts show that when it rains, more people will purchase umbrellas. A general rule (principle) can then be derived: If it is raining and only one store has umbrellas to sell, that store's business will increase.

An important key to effective generalization is the ability to simplify the problem. Simplification helps to expose regular patterns of behavior. Babies cry for dozens of reasons, but they cry regularly when they are very hungry or very wet. A simplified law of behavior says that babies will probably stop crying if they are either fed or dried. In economics, a common law of behavior is the law of demand, which says that if the price of an item falls, more of that item will be purchased. There are exceptions

to this law. Some goods have appeal only because of their high prices, others—salt, for example—are purchased in fixed quantities regardless of price. But for most goods and for most people, behavior is regular: a drop in price brings increased purchases. And behavior that is so regular allows generalization to an economic law or principle.

Laws, Principles, Theories, and Models

All sciences, whether they be physical, biological, or social sciences, are based on relationships that are so regular that they can generally be depended on. Economics is no exception. In some sciences there are relationships so well tested and well documented that they have the status of *laws*. In physics, the law of gravity tells us that apples will fall from trees at known velocities.

Regularities in economic behavior are sometimes called laws, sometimes principles, sometimes theories, and sometimes models. There is the *law* of demand (Chapter 17), the *principle* of comparative advantage (Chapter 30), the *theory* of international trade (Chapters 29–32), and the Keynesian *model* (Chapters 7–9). The terms are almost interchangeable. All imply some form of causation—one kind of behavior leads to or causes another. All imply that at least something is known about a problem (facts have been gathered), and all imply some degree of confidence about anticipated outcomes.

In many regards, the term *model* is most appropriate in economics. A model is a simplification of the real world. It tells how variables are related to each other and predicts how changes in one variable will in turn affect others throughout the economic system. Although all four terms—*law, principle, theory,* and *model*—are used in this book, *model* will be used most frequently because it is most descriptive of the purpose of economic analysis.

CHAPTER TWO

Making Economic Policy

Economic principles and economic models have one major practical value: they help predict the consequences of various economic decisions. If the response of an economic variable can be predicted, it can also be controlled. Economic policy is used to control, or to prepare for, various contingencies that may arise in the economy. A policy of full employment obligates policy makers to promote those economic activities that increase the size of the domestic economy.

Making economic policy work is not easy. Even though principles and models may be available and reasonably accurate, they are seldom perfect. A policy of growth might be thwarted by devastating weather conditions, the collapse of a foreign government, or the outbreak of war. A policy of full employment may be disrupted if everyone suddenly decides to make the family automobile last one more year.

Inexact as it may be, the process of policy making must go on. The nation has proved that it wants policies to help in the attainment of economic goals. People also seem to realize that policy making is a hazardous task, and policy makers as well as economists have been forgiven for their inability to design plans that meet every conceivable contingency.

About Graphs

Economic facts are almost always in the form of numbers: the price of eggs is 75 cents per dozen; there were 250,000 auto workers unemployed in January 1975; the United States imported 2.4 million autos in 1973; in 1969, 21,000 widowed citizens had net assets valued at between $200,000 and $500,000. Because working with numbers is tedious business, economic facts are often presented in graphic form. Graphs are the economist's counterpart of the architect's scale model and the astronomer's planetarium. They present an instant picture of relationships among kinds of information.

Since it is drawn on a surface having only two dimensions, a graph is limited to showing the relationship between two *variables*.

A variable is a characteristic whose value changes over time or from one context to another. The height of a child is a variable, and so is the number of hours a college student studies per week. The hourly wage paid to plumbers varies from city to city and from year to year, so it, too, is a variable.

On a graph, one variable is measured vertically, the other horizontally. Variables can have positive (plus) values or negative (minus) values, so

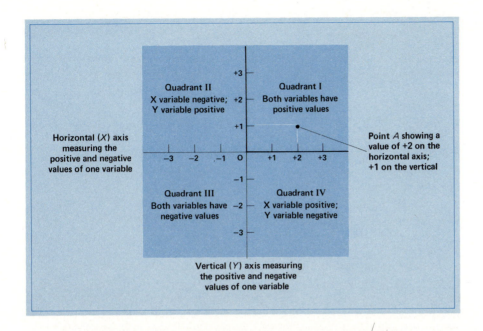

Figure 2-1 The Parts of a Four-Quadrant Graph

a graph may have positive and negative ranges. Over many years, graph makers and graph users have followed the practice of using two *axes* to divide a graph into four quadrants. Examples of axes and quadrants are shown in Figure 2-1. The axes are the heavy lines that cut the square horizontally and vertically. The vertical axis is customarily called the *Y* axis and the horizontal axis, the *X* axis. The point at which they intersect is called the origin (*O*) of the graph—here shown in the center of the square. At the origin, the value of each axis is zero. Above the horizontal axis, all values of the *Y* variable are positive. Below the horizontal axis, the *Y* variable takes negative values. If the temperature in Racine, Wisconsin, is measured on the vertical axis, the July temperature will be positive and will be shown above the center of the graph. The January temperature could easily be below zero, so it could lie below the center of the graph.

To the left of the vertical axis, all values of the horizontal (*X*) variable are negative. To the right, all values are positive. If time is measured on the horizontal axis and if 1900 is assumed to be a "starting place" (origin), all years before 1900 would be shown to the left of the vertical axis and all years since 1900 would be shown to the right of it.

Nearly all the economic data encountered in this book will be positive numbers, so the graphs will almost always be drawn using only the upper right-hand quadrant and will typically look like the one shown in Figure 2-2. The two points, *A* and *B*, are described as *plots* or *plotted variables*.

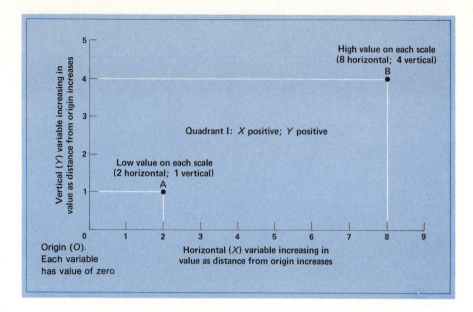

Figure 2-2 The "Typical" Graph for Economic Data

Each represents a known value on the vertical axis *and* a known value on the horizontal axis. Point A shows a relatively low value for each variable (X = 2; Y = 1); point B shows a relatively high value for each variable (X = 8; Y = 4).

The table below shows economic data of a type that is usually graphed. The left-hand column lists each year from 1960 to 1975; the right-hand column shows gross national product (GNP) for each year.

Year	GNP
	billions of dollars
1960	503.7
1961	520.1
1962	560.3
1963	590.5
1964	632.4
1965	684.9
1966	749.9
1967	793.9
1968	864.2
1969	930.3
1970	977.1
1971	1,054.9
1972	1,158.0
1973	1,294.9
1974	1,396.7
1975	1,498.8

Source: *Economic Report of the President*

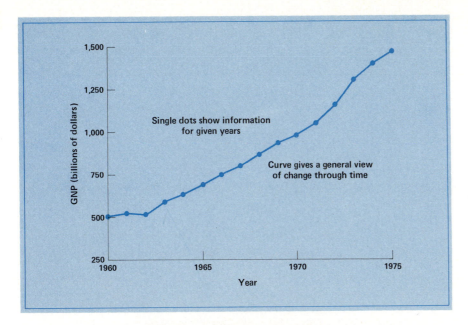

Figure 2-3   GNP, 1960-1975

On a graph, when one variable represents the passage of time, that variable is shown on the horizontal axis. Values of the other variables are then measured on the vertical axis. In Figure 2-3, each dot represents one year's value of GNP. The line connecting the dots is referred to as a *curve* and shows that GNP has increased consistently since 1960. Since the curve rises as it moves to the right, the relationship between time and GNP is positive. If GNP had fallen in each year between 1960 and 1975, the curve would fall from left to right and the relationship would be negative.

Figure 2-4 shows another set of data that can be graphed. The left-hand column in the table beside the graph shows the number of hours a student studies in a week; the right-hand column shows hours spent in

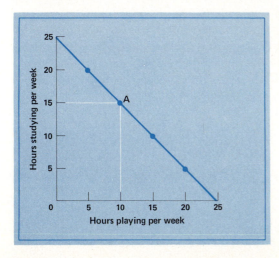

**Figure 2-4
Possible Divisions of a Student's Time Between Study and Play**

Hours studying	Hours playing
25	0
20	5
15	10
10	15
5	20
0	25

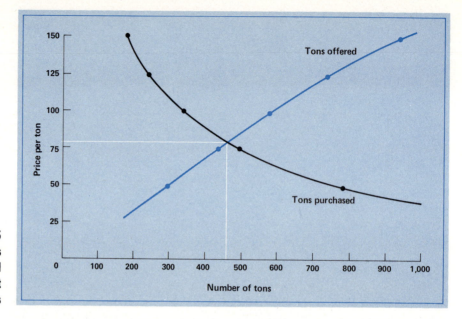

**Figure 2–5
Tons of Beans
Offered and
Purchased at
Different Prices**

recreational activities. The figure assumes that the student has 25 hours per week that can be used for either activity. The student can spend this time on all study and no play, all play and no study, or any combination of study and play that adds to 25 hours. The possible distributions are graphed beside the table. The "curve" is a straight line that intersects the Y axis at the value 25. This point of intersection shows that if all of the student's available time is used for studying, play will be reduced to zero. The curve intersects the X axis at value 25, showing that if all available time is spent in play, none is left for study. The dots along the curve represent several combinations of study and play that are possible. Each exhausts the total hours available. For example, at point A, 15 hours of study plus 10 hours of play use the total 25 hours.

Sometimes two variables relate to the same axes, so two curves can be shown in a single graph. Usually the two combine to form a model of economic behavior. Figure 2–5 shows the quantity of beans purchased and the quantity offered for sale at different prices. The facts are shown below in tabular form. In the figure, the positively sloped curve shows that as the price of beans rises, sellers will offer more for sale. The negatively sloped curve shows that as the price falls, buyers will want to purchase larger and larger quantities of the product.

Price per ton	Tons purchased	Tons offered for sale
$ 50	780	300
75	480	440
100	340	580
125	240	740
150	180	940

The curves together show a model of behavior of the bean market. They intersect when the price is $80 per ton and 460 tons of beans are exchanged. Given the available facts, it can be predicted that if the price of beans deviates from $80 per ton, either buyers will want more beans than sellers are willing to sell or sellers will want to sell more than buyers want to buy. The graph is a simple way to expose these useful relationships.

Production Possibilities: A Model of Choice

The graphs in the preceding section show how facts can be presented visually. Figure 2–4 illustrates that by arranging the axes in a special way, graphs can be used to show the opportunities for choice and the results of choosing. A similar graph shows how a society can use its *resources* to produce desired combinations of food, clothing, gasoline, public parks, winter coats, education, and rug cleaning.

Resources are the things society has available to use in producing the goods it desires. Resources include land, coal, machines, labor, transportation networks, technology, and the other assets that make a society productive.

Resources are sometimes called *factors of production* or *productive inputs.* These two terms will be defined more carefully in Chapter 3. The exact division of society's productive resources is almost too complex to imagine, so the problem must be simplified. A model of choice is shown in Figure 2–6.

The vertical axis in Figure 2–6 represents the quantity of government goods and services. (Remember that "government" is not confined to the federal government. It also includes activities performed by cities, counties, states, school districts, and other organized governmental groups.) The horizontal axis represents the quantity of private goods. Government goods are things like parks, police protection, justice, and education. Private goods include food, clothing, houses, and automobiles.

Most government goods are produced using equipment manufactured in private businesses. A public school uses desks made by Steelcase, books from several publishers, and paper from Crown Zellerbach —all private companies. If resources are used to produce government goods, some private goods must be sacrificed. The same resources cannot be used to produce both.

If all society's resources are used for government goods, the quantity *OA*, measured on the vertical axis, can be produced. If all the resources are used for private goods, the quantity *OB*, measured on the horizontal

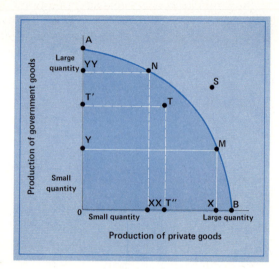

**Figure 2-6
A Production-Possibility
Curve for a Whole Society**

axis, can be produced. Using all resources for one or the other purpose is unlikely. A modern society will more likely decide on some of each.

Point N designates one possible combination. By reducing the production of government goods to *OYY*, and transferring the resources to private goods production, the output of private goods can be increased from zero to *OXX*. By transferring still more resources out of government goods and into private goods, point M (*OY* government goods; *OX* private goods) can be attained. Since almost any distribution of resources between government goods and private goods is possible, an infinite array of combinations of the two types of goods can be produced.

Production-Possibility Curves

The infinite number of combinations of government and private goods can each be shown by a point. If all points are shown at one time, they trace a curve like the one starting in point A, passing through points N and M, and ending in point B. This curve is called a *production-possibility curve.*

A production-possibility curve shows all the possible combinations of government goods and private goods that can be produced by an economy when all its resources are fully employed.[2]

[2] A production-possibility curve can also be used to show attainable combinations of other kinds of output. If agricultural production is measured on the vertical axis and manufactured goods on the horizontal axis, the curve would show tradeoffs between food and manufactured goods.

Most industrial economies do not operate at full capacity. At any given time, some of their available resources are idle. Any point inside the production-possibility curve (that is, any point in the area bounded by the production-possibility curve and the graph's axes) represents a combination of goods that can be produced by using resources at less than their full capacity. Point T is such a point. Point T yields OT' government goods and OT'' private goods, but the output of either kind of goods could be expanded. The combination represented by point S, however, lies outside the production-possibility curve, so it is impossible to attain. Even if all available resources are fully employed, this combination of public and private goods and services cannot be produced. The production-possibility curve, then, divides the graph into attainable and unattainable combinations of goods.

Moving Along the Curve—Opportunity Cost

The real lesson of the production-possibility curve is shown when there is movement from one point on it to another. The curve, as we have seen, shows combinations of goods and services that are possible. As movement from one axis toward the other occurs along the curve, some of one thing is sacrificed in order to obtain more of another. Figure 2–7 shows a curve similar to the one in Figure 2–6. Say that at the outset an economic society chooses to produce at point A. It divides its resources so that OX government goods and OY private goods are being produced. Now, for some reason (perhaps a new government, a natural disaster, or a major technological breakthrough), the economy decides to increase the output of private goods to ON. With full employment of resources this means that the economy will produce at B.

Since all resources are being used when production is at point A, the

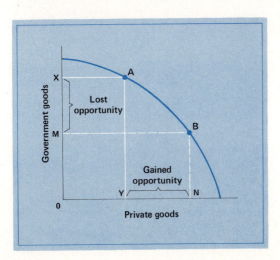

**Figure 2–7
Opportunities Gained and Forgone**

movement from A to B can come only by sacrificing some output of government goods. At B, output of government goods has dropped to OM. The expansion from OY to ON requires that XM government goods be given up. The cost of producing more private goods is the reduction in the output of government goods. This sacrifice is called the *opportunity cost* of the additional private goods, since the cost of producing them includes the loss of the opportunity to produce some government goods.

The opportunity cost of a thing is whatever was given up in order to gain it. Opportunity cost is a crucial concept in economics, since it shows that economic activity is a complex phenomenon in which, usually, one thing can be gained only if another is given up. If all steel is used for automobiles and none for railroads, the opportunity cost of the autos produced is the railroads that are not being produced. Opportunity cost follows choice like a shadow.

When Proctor and Gamble decides to use all its equipment to produce laundry soap, it loses the opportunity to use the same equipment to produce toothpaste. A person who chooses to be a haberdasher loses the opportunity to be a grocer; one who decides to be a dentist loses the opportunity to become an electrical engineer. Each of the things lost is a cost associated with the thing that is chosen.

New Curves—Changes in Capacity

Two important modifications of the production-possibility curve are shown in Figure 2–8. In part a, a "cluster," or "family," of three curves

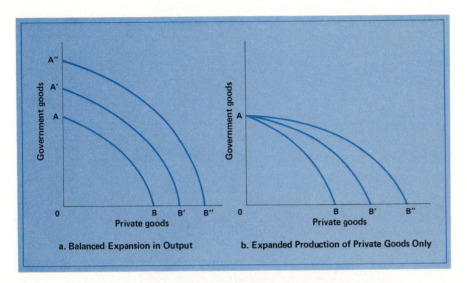

Figure 2-8 Changes of Production-Possibility Curves

is shown. Curve AB, the inside curve, maps the production possibilities for a society capable of producing modest combinations of government and private goods. Curve A'B' shows possibilities that include more of each class of goods, and A"B" shows combinations of still greater amounts. Each successively higher curve portrays an economy that is larger than the one before it. Movement from AB to a higher production-possibility curve requires time, but it can be accomplished in any of several ways. One way would be through technological progress or through acquiring the ability to combine given sets of resources in more efficient ways. If the ability to produce government goods increases at the same rate as the ability to produce private goods, a concentric set of production-possibility curves results.

Figure 2-8b shows a different situation. When production-possibility curve AB is replaced by curve AB' and then by curve AB", society is expanding its capacity to produce private goods but not its capacity to produce government goods. The three production-possibility curves join in point A but diverge to represent three quite different possible collections of private goods. A new technology in private industries might allow this to occur.

Both sets of curves in Figure 2-8 represent extreme cases. No society can vastly increase its ability to produce private goods without enjoying some increase in its potential to produce government goods, too. The major point is that over some time periods the ability to produce different things may increase at different rates. At one time, expansion may occur rapidly along the vertical axis, reflecting tremendously improved capacities to produce government goods. At another time, rapid expansion may occur along the horizontal axis. In the 1930s the U.S. government established numerous programs to serve the aged, the unemployed, and the handicapped. It expanded its capacity to produce government goods. Two decades later, after World War II, the nation switched from producing the government goods needed to prosecute a war to producing private goods to satisfy consumer demand. In the former case, the production-possibility curve bent one way; in the latter case, it bent another. At still another time, expansion may be balanced. There is no set pattern.

A Tool for Choosing

The production-possibility curve provides a useful way of viewing options open to individuals, firms, or entire societies. The axes of the graph might be labeled "two-door sedans" and "four-door sedans" for an automobile manufacturer, or "apricots" and "squash" for a farmer. In the case of the farmer, the production-possibility curve would show the amount of apricots that must be given up in order to allow a specified increase in the output of squash.

The production-possibility curve is a versatile and important tool for conceptualizing the basic problem of economic choice. It shows the maximum amount of production that can be attained if all resources are used for one purpose and it shows the attainable combinations of goods if society's resources are divided between two uses. More important in the 1970s, it can be used to organize thinking about the possible tradeoffs between different combinations of goods and services.

While the production-possibility curve fulfills a useful function in describing the alternatives open for choice, it does nothing to tell what choice *will* be made, or what choice is *best* for an individual, a firm, or a society. In a market-oriented society like the United States, this choosing is done through the market. The market assimilates information about things that are available and things that are desired. This information is eventually translated into relative prices and used as criteria by consumers in deciding whether one good is to be preferred over another and by firms in deciding what to produce, and when and how to produce it. The market mechanism is complicated, but it is essential that we grasp it. The next two chapters provide a good look at the system and how it operates.

Summary
1. Economics is a scientific discipline that uses the method of science to define problems, gather information, develop principles, and formulate policies.
2. Economic information takes many forms. The real skill is to be able to recognize the information that will be useful in problem solving.

3 When regular patterns of behavior are observed, they may be called *laws, principles, theories,* or *models.* The term *model* is preferred; it implies an abstraction or simplification of the real world.
4 Economic information is often presented by using graphs. Graphs use axes to measure two variables and points or curves within the axes to show relationships between the variables.
5 Curves can show positive (upward-sloping) or negative (downward-sloping) relationships between variables. Often, two or more curves are used in the same graph to depict a complex relationship.
6 The production-possibility curve is a special kind of graph that can be used to show tradeoffs between certain outputs. The tradeoffs are the opportunity costs of choosing one activity in preference to another.
7 Production-possibility curves may be altered in shape and location by changes in technology or changes in resource availability. To be most useful, information presented by the production-possibility curve must be supplemented by information on market prices that reflect consumer preferences.

Exercises

1 Explain these important terms and concepts:
   social science
   scientific method
   laws, principles, theories, models
   abstraction of a problem
   economic policy
   variables
   axes of a graph
   production-possibility curve
   opportunity cost
2 Discuss the verity and meaning of this statement: "The method of science is a huge filtering device that sorts truth from nontruth."
3 One reason why "truth" is sought in economics is that it is valuable. How can economic truth be turned into dollars and cents? Does economic truth have other value, in policy making for example?
4 Why is a model a useful way of approaching an economic problem? How does simplification help?
5 Many economists, scientists, and casual observers have noted that the law of gravity is eternal and the laws of thermodynamics are well settled, yet the laws of economics always seem to have many exceptions. Why is this true and what are the consequences of this instability in economic rules?
6 The production-possibility curve is useful in showing how issues involving choice can be analyzed. Two examples may be helpful.
   a Should the United States decrease its expenditures for defense activities so that the funds can be used to satisfy some other important national goal? Place defense expenditure on the vertical axis of a graph, and all other federal expenditures on the horizontal axis.

b Should economic growth be cut back to improve the quality of the environment? This is not an idle question or merely a textbook example. This is one of the most crucial issues in the contemporary United States—indeed, in the world. Put economic growth on the vertical axis and environmental quality on the horizontal axis. Add a steep, downward-sloping curve at random, and you can see that huge cutbacks in growth may be needed to secure only very small increases in quality. If the production-possibility curve is flat, on the other hand, it indicates that only a modest reduction in growth will yield significant improvements in the quality of the environment.

7 The surest way to learn about graphs is to construct some. Label the axes provided and plot the information given in each of the following tables.

(a) Data

Year	Value of U.S. exports (billions of dollars)
1970	52.2
1971	52.2
1972	55.7
1973	66.6
1974	71.6

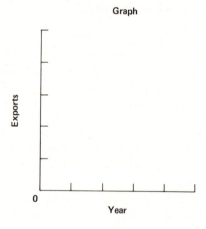

(b) Data

Price of visits to the zoo	Number of visitors annually
$ 0	50,000
.25	45,000
.50	35,000
.75	30,000
1.00	20,000
1.25	9,000
1.50	7,000
1.75	4,000
2.00	1,000

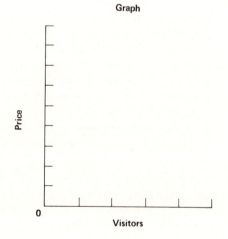

Economists are sometimes criticized because their models do not seem to resemble the real world and their predictions do not seem to come true. While this is unfortunate, it is also understandable. An economy is a rapidly changing set of structures and interconnections. The whole of an economy is so complex that no one individual can hope to understand it. Often, just as understanding of one set of relationships begins to emerge, the structure itself changes, so that the honest efforts of capable scientists are made useless. Moreover, although economics and economic knowledge are steadily improving, many attributes of individual and group behavior are still not clearly understood. Until they are, economics will remain an inexact science.

If people behaved in a rational and consistent way, economics could help society improve the level of available satisfactions. A major part of these satisfactions would derive from the production and consumption of goods and services, but some would also come from simply reading or gazing at beautiful sunsets. No economy has yet been able to consistently maintain such a high level of effort.

If the problems of economies could be correctly perceived and the correct models and policies always developed, the peoples of the world would enjoy ranges of choice close to their potential maximums. The facts from the real world indicate that most of the world's population lives below the maximum attainable level of choice. In general, the availability of many choices indicates a high degree of economic development and the availability of few choices indicates a low level of development. The people of India have low incomes and there are few goods and services available for them to choose among. By contrast, since the United States, Canada, New Zealand, and a number of other countries are developed, their peoples have high incomes and can choose from among thousands of kinds of things. (This example can be carried too far. Increasing the range of choice is desirable when the increasing choices bring more variety and relief to people's lives. The example is not intended to extend down to the paint store, where the variety of colors and textures is enough to cause nervous frustration!)

The diagram on page 32 is a model of human achievement through history. The horizontal axis shows the passage of time; the vertical axis shows the numbers of things (commodities, services, objects, life styles, etc.) over which an individual can exercise some choice or control.

The graph shows three curves over time. The lowest curve shows the range of choices present at the subsistence level of living—the range of choices needed in order merely to survive.[3] The middle line shows the

A Contemporary Problem
Potential and Actual Achievement

---

[3]The subsistence line is shown as rising through time. Some will argue that subsistence is subsistence—that twentieth-century people can subsist on the same number of calories and the same kinds of things as the Neanderthals. Such a view denies that man has evolved from prehistoric times. The view that modern people need more choices than their forebears appears more plausible.

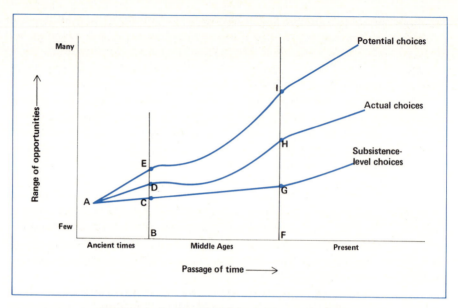

Changes in the Number of Opportunities

actual range of opportunity existing at a given time, and the uppermost line shows the range of opportunities that it would be physically and technologically possible for the human race to attain. The actual and attainable curves show a slight dip during the middle ages, when, for all practical purposes, civilization fell into a deep technological and productive chasm. Evidence shows that during this time the human race lost some of its inventiveness and skill, so that actual and potential opportunities diminished.

In the time period represented by point *A*, people had few choices. They lived in a traditional society and were able to produce only those things needed to sustain life. Before the Middle Ages, people were producing enough things (level *BD*) to permit choices well beyond the subsistence level (now represented by the vertical distance *BC*). If they had worked harder or in a more organized fashion, they could have reached the maximum attainable output (level *BE*) and thus extended their range of choices.

The vertical line (*FGHI*) near the right-hand side of the graph represents the condition of the domestic economy today. The subsistence level of choice (*FG*) is still quite low. The actual range available to most persons (*FH*) is well above subsistence levels but considerably below the attainable level (*FI*).

The discrepancy between actual and potential can be explained in a variety of ways. It may arise because society is inefficient and uses wasteful production processes. Or it may mean that society is in a recession and, because of a temporary failure of the economic system, has many unemployed resources. Another possible explanation is that society consciously chooses to operate at a slow pace, gaining leisure but sacrificing some opportunities that are potentially available.

The middle line shows how the lot of the human race has improved over time. It describes the levels of choice that have been realized and thus shows the pace of economic progress. Between the subsistence level (lowest line) and the attainable level (highest line) is a wide range within which people can and usually do exert considerable control and discretion. They can choose to live near the maximum attainable level or at a level near subsistence. If they choose the former, they may have to work longer hours, employ more machines, and use available resources more rapidly. If the latter, there may be fewer ulcers and heart attacks but more deaths from snake bite and tick fever.[4] Generally speaking, the world's developed nations have chosen to live close to the maximum attainable level of living. Individuals in these nations have a wide range of choice, and as science and technology have unfolded that range has increased.

The less developed countries have struggled to rise above the subsistence level, but even so the people of Bangladesh, Chad, Niger, and Burma have very few choices. They live much as their ancestors did—close to the level of bare subsistence.

The range of choice is a central theme in economics. In this chapter it has been used to show something about models, facts, graph making, and choosing. Each of these themes will be repeated in a variety of ways as the story of economics unfolds in the following chapters.

---

[4]This is not a frivolous comment. If we decide to cut back on the hectic pace of life, we will have to forgo such things as medical research and/or automobiles that rush people to hospitals in times of emergency. Choice making is not confined to brands of canned soup, but includes such demonstrably important issues as how much attention should be paid to the possibility of accidental death. Again, economics—the science of choosing—emerges as an important study.

3

The Circular Flow of Economic Activity

The eighteenth century was a time of rapid change in Western Europe. It is hard to name a single event that made all the difference, but many advances taken together had a huge impact on the way life was lived and the way society was organized. The period is called the Industrial Revolution because of the transformation that came in manufacturing. It could as well have been called a social revolution or an economic revolution.

The keys to the change were mechanization and specialization. Mechanical power supplanted hand labor, and productive activities were brought together in huge factories that specialized in producing cloth or tools or household goods. By specializing, factories were able to increase output by substantially more than the increase in resources used to run them.

Specialization brought a great change in economic organization. Families no longer struggled each day to keep themselves supplied with food, clothing, and shelter. They did only those things they could do best and traded with other families for other necessities. The weaver wove cloth and the farmer grew turnips. By trading with one another each had food and clothing. The weaver also traded to obtain wool and services. The farmer traded with other farmers, with the harness maker, and with the tinsmith. Specialization increased output and it also created the need for a system in which trade could be conducted. What emerged was a set of trade patterns that operate continuously, insuring that food moves from farms to industrial areas and manufactured goods flow back from factory to farm. The system is referred to as the *circular flow of economic activity*.

A complete picture of the circular flow would look much like a picture of the water cycle that sometimes appears in physical and biological science books. In the water cycle, rainfall leads to runoff; runoff leads to storage in lakes, reservoirs, and oceans; storage leads to evaporation; evaporation causes moisture to accumulate in the air. This accumulation leads to rainfall and the cycle begins anew. Each step in the cycle is separate, but each is a part of a larger scheme. Each step can be studied independently, but ultimately all must be studied together.

In the circular flow of economic activity, one person may provide land, a second seed, a third water. Together they produce grain. The grain is harvested, some is sold or traded, some is kept for food, and some is kept for seed. In the next year, the cycle begins again. Just as in the water cycle, the steps are separate but integrated. They can be studied individually, but some knowledge of the whole process is also needed. The purpose of this chapter is to inquire into the circular process of transforming raw materials into finished products and making these products available to consumers. This inquiry will look into the roles of three actors in the process—firms, households, and governments—and then into the ways in which these actors relate to one another.

Three Major Actors

Firms, households, and governments continually interact. In so doing, they determine the course of economic activity among themselves and in the nation. The remainder of this chapter and much of the rest of the book is devoted to describing these three actors and understanding the types, causes, and results of their interaction and interdependence.

Firms

The *firm* is the basic production unit in a modern industrial society. A firm may be as simple as a child's lemonade stand or as complex as Mitsubishi, Japan's international conglomerate.

A firm is any producing unit responsible for making its own decisions about what it will produce, the method of production, and how the finished product will be sold.

The firm purchases land, labor, and materials, then converts these into finished goods and/or services, which it sells. Some firms are highly specialized and produce only a single item. Some farms in Kansas are firms that produce only wheat. Other firms produce wide ranges of products—automobiles, refrigerators, TV sets, and tractors. Giant firms like General Motors carry out varied productive activities all over the world.

Some firms—Sears or the corner grocery, for example—produce service rather than goods. The "product" of these selling firms is actually *convenience* for both consumers and producers. Because the corner grocery exists, Campbell's does not have to sell soup door-to-door. Because the grocery is there, one need not negotiate separately for each item in the grocery cart. General Motors produces automobiles, Exxon produces petroleum products, and Westinghouse produces kitchen ranges. These are tangible items that are easily observed and counted. The local grocery store, the mail-order house, and the lumber yard produce an intangible service but one that is no less important in the conduct of economic affairs.

Regardless of its size or what it produces, a firm is generally thought to behave consistently in pursuit of some goal. It is easiest to think of a business as attempting to maximize its profits. If this is the objective of the firm, the manager of the firm—the *entrepreneur*—has a rigid set of rules to follow, although adherence to them may be automatic. The manager may not be aware of the rules, but the profits of the firm will depend on how closely the rules are followed.

Profit Maximization and Reality

The assumption about profit maximization used in this chapter is surely not without its questionable aspects. Not all firms strive to maximize profits. The charitable hospital is a firm, but it does not usually behave in such a way as to maximize profits. A foundation supporting the fine arts is a firm, but it may never *earn* any profits. A farm operator who can maximize profits only by raising hogs may not raise them because of their unpleasant odor. A craftsman may choose to sacrifice some profits in order to make a high-quality product. Firms may intentionally incur losses in one time period so that profits can be increased in a later period. Very large firms may intentionally reduce profits—by locating in high-cost areas, for example—to improve their public image. These special cases cannot be used as a basis for generalizing or abstracting. In order for the study of economics to proceed, it is necessary to assume (to abstract) that firms attempt to maximize *something*. Some will maximize profits, some quality, and some good will. Regardless of what is maximized, the logic of the analysis remains the same. This logic will be developed as if all firms maximized profits, keeping in mind that some firms conduct these profit-maximizing activities only after considering some other objective.

The number of business firms in the United States is hard to estimate. The very large companies like Standard Oil, General Electric, American Telephone and Telegraph, and Pan American are visible and can be counted simply because of their size. Small businesses, including grandmothers who make doll clothes to pick up "pin money," are almost uncountable. Restaurants come and go without anyone keeping track of them. Service stations open and close or change managers several times per year, and no one counts to see how many actually exist. One estimate reports that there are currently more than 13 million business firms in the U.S. economy.

Households

The household is the basic consuming unit in the economy. It obtains incomes and makes decisions as to how they will be spent. In making expenditure decisions, it is assumed that the household, like the firm (and subject to the same kinds of limitations), attempts to maximize something—usually its own well-being. Given this goal, specific behavioral rules much like those applicable to a firm come into play.

Because the U.S. Department of Commerce conducts a census of the population every ten years, and continually updates its population estimates in between, we have a reasonably accurate notion of the number of households in the United States. The 1970 census counted 63.4 million households, and by 1974 the number had reached 69.9 million. Like businesses, households vary in composition. A household might be a widower living by himself; it might be a husband, wife, and three children; it might be a mother and five small children who have been deserted by the father.

Governments

The mention of "government" may evoke the image of a huge, monolithic force that continually encroaches on the freedom of households and firms to make their own decisions. This is a popular caricature, based on an emotional view, and must be discarded before the role of government can be put in perspective. To begin with, government is not a single entity. There are thousands of groups in the United States that fall into the category of government. Some—like school districts—are very small and have almost no economic power. They can levy taxes for their own purposes and make decisions about the spending of their own funds, but that is all.

Going up the ladder to higher levels of government—from cities to counties to states to the federal government—economic powers and

"... plus federal tax, state tax, city sales tax, and a special tax we have here on 34th Street."

responsibilities become increasingly complex. Small towns keep the fire trucks in working order and maintain the municipal swimming pools. Counties administer welfare programs for the needy, keep county roads passable in bad weather, and operate the sheriff's office to protect county residents. States create large systems of colleges and universities, regulate gambling and the sale of alcoholic beverages, decide where major highways will be located, and operate complex policing and traffic control systems for the highways. The federal government builds a dam in North Dakota to prevent flooding in St. Louis, maintains a system of benefits for veterans of military campaigns, applies nationwide wage and price ceilings when needed, and declares that blue whales cannot be killed in U.S. territorial waters.

The higher the level of government, too, the more complex the question of what goal to seek (what to maximize) and what economic role to play. Different roles are associated with the various levels of government, so there cannot be a uniform set of guiding principles comparable to those appropriate for firm and household behavior. If some national government desired only to maximize its rate of economic growth—a suitable goal for a desperately poor nation—a single set of rules could be established and a single policy could be designed. But an advanced nation may have several goals. It may wish to maintain a "suitably high" rate of growth, and at the same time it may want to insure "minimum" levels of unemployment or "modest" rates of inflation. All this contributes to making government's role in economic affairs ambiguous. "Suitably high," "minimum," and "modest" cannot be defined objectively. Even if these terms had clear meanings, the role of government would still be difficult because officials and policy makers would not be sure how much of one goal to sacrifice in order to satisfy another.

Comparative Advantage and Interdependence

The United States is a nation of specialists. In freeing people from the soil the Industrial Revolution bound them to machines, and the machines have become so complicated that one person generally learns to operate only one or two of them. In today's production processes, one person usually performs a limited number of tasks but performs these very well. This system makes it possible to produce large quantities of goods and services, as well as provide some leisure for workers.

How does one choose a speciality? The law of comparative advantage states that if one person can perform several jobs better than his neighbor, he should select the one in which he enjoys the greatest advantage. A dentist should of course be able to fill teeth better than his receptionist. Suppose, however, that he can also type faster than the receptionist. *Comparative advantage* says that even though the dentist himself is the best typist in the office, he should continue to fill teeth and let the receptionist type. In this way, the output of the office is higher.

Comparative advantage refers to the superior productive capacity of one producer (laborer) compared to all others. The concept is most often used to describe the way nations behave (see Chapters 29–32), but it is equally applicable to individuals and to states or other geographic areas.

Job selection and specialization within the United States are geared toward allowing the law of comparative advantage to work. The system rewards people for developing special skills and applying them to a narrow range of tasks. This sorting process puts dentists in their offices, carpenters beside their tools, drivers in the cabs of trucks, and nurses in the wards of hospitals. Each person has something to sell and by selling it receives income to use in buying the goods and services produced by others.

Specialization increases output, but it also makes people dependent on one another. Robinson Crusoe had very few things but at least he was his own man. He could choose not to fix the leaking roof and he would be the only one to get wet. By contrast, in 1976, more than 700,000 American workers were involved in the production of automobiles alone. Their comparative skills in operating machines, designing parts, and testing the strength of metals led them to this special kind of work. The national economy is better because of this specialization, but these workers—over 10 percent of the entire labor force—depend entirely on the buying habits of the remainder of the population. If automobiles are not sold, these specialists lose their jobs. The price of specialization is interdependence.

The Factors of Production

Although the law of comparative advantage and the problem of interdependence have been considered with reference to labor, labor is only one of the factors (resources) used in the production of goods and services. It is only one of the factors that receive a reward and return income to a household.

The household is the basic building block in economic society. Its members collectively make decisions about where it lives, how it spends its money, and how it interacts with other households. Before these decisions can be made, or before they can have economic meaning, the household must have income at its disposal. It receives this income by selling *factors of production* to producing firms.

Factors of production are any resources that are used in the process of producing a good or service. Today some economists prefer to call them *inputs*. Factors (or inputs) can be as tangible as a lump of coal or as intangible as the thought process of an inventor.

Starting with the earliest writers of economic treatises, it has been customary to divide the factors of production into three general groupings: land, labor, and capital.

Land. Land includes not only surface area but also water, minerals, coal, soil fertility, air, and any other *natural* endowments associated with geographic territory. This factor could as accurately be called *natural resources*.

Labor. Like land, labor is a category that includes a variety of qualities. It refers not only to physical toil but also to skills and talents that differentiate one person from another. Labor includes a worker's ability to execute specialized tasks, to read, and to use past experience in performing a job. A physician's practice of his or her profession is labor just as a construction worker's efforts are labor.

Capital. Capital is produced wealth that is used in further production. A factory is capital. It has been produced by those who built it but is not directly consumed. Rather, it is used to produce other items. Trucks are capital; they contribute to more production. Machines are capital; they are used to make consumer goods. Office buildings and hydroelectric dams are capital. Sometimes this classification is ambiguous. For example, during the week a traveling salesman's car is capital, because it is used in producing a service (marketing), but on the weekend it is used for consumption—for family outings.

Rewards to factors, and entrepreneurship. This three-way classification suffers as do all such schemes in that there are many items—like the salesman's car—that could reasonably be placed in more than one class. It is futile to argue this point except as an intellectual exercise. Usually, some of each factor must be present if production is to take place. Acres of land, hours of labor, and dozens of hoes (capital) are required to produce beans. Some land, much skilled labor, and huge quantities of machinery are required to produce automobiles.

Because the factors contribute to production, they earn rewards when the products are sold. Land earns rent, labor receives wages, and capital receives interest. Households owning much land are in a position to earn high rents. Households possessing skilled labor can earn high wages, and the capital-owning household receives interest on its capital. You might think at first that a tract of land is owned, not by a household, but by the Boeing Company, or that a factory is owned, not by a family, but by General Motors. But remember that both the Boeing Company and General Motors are themselves owned by the thousands of individual households that have shares of stock in these companies. Thus, the shareholding households become owners of buildings, trucks, machines, dams, and other forms of capital. These capital holdings help determine the income of the households.

Grouping factors into three classes was satisfactory for most purposes until the early twentieth century, when economists began to speak of *entrepreneurship,* or management, as a fourth factor of production.

An entrepreneur is one who organizes, manages, operates, and takes the risks associated with a business venture. Entrepreneurship is distinguished from labor because it is a special class of labor that includes the capacity and willingness to take such risks. The returns to a household possessing this quality are called *profits*.

In a developed society, risks must be taken in order to find new ways of combining land, labor, and capital so that they yield more product or a different, more highly valued product. The entrepreneur is the person who perceives needs and opportunities, then gathers factors in order to meet them; the reward for this is profit. The fourfold factor classification scheme, then, can be summarized like this:

Factor	Description	Reward
Land	Any natural resource	Rent
Labor	Toil and/or skill	Wages
Capital	Man-made resources	Interest
Entrepreneurship	Risk taking and organizing	Profit

Ownership

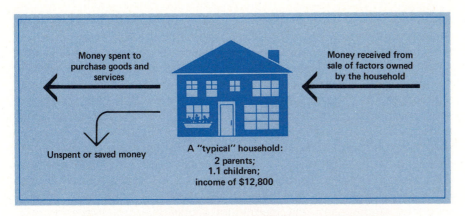

Figure 3-1 Income and Expenses of a Household

The Circular Flow—Households and Firms

Looking at one hypothetical household in isolation gives an idea of the relationship of households to the remainder of the economy. In 1974 the "typical" U.S. household had an income of about $12,800 to spend.[1] This was the quantity of money reaching the household's coffers, as shown on the right-hand side of Figure 3-1. Since the typical U.S. household has only its own labor to sell, nearly all this income comes from wages. If a household is fortunate, it may earn additional income by selling the use of its nonhuman resources, such as land, trucks, or machines. In any case, income is earned as a result of the household's possessing resources that other people—usually entrepreneurs—want and selling them as factors of production.

Income earned by households through the sale of factors is expended to purchase necessities and desirables from firms, as shown in Figure 3-1. The earnings arrow on the right and the expenditure arrow on the left show the economic connection and the interdependence of households and firms.

It is usual for a household not to spend all its earnings, but to hold back some money in the form of savings. This is shown on the left side of the household in Figure 3-1, where the large arrow denotes consumer expenditures and the small arrow represents the part that is not spent but saved. Savings will appear as an extremely important topic in several later chapters.

[1] Of course there is no such thing as a typical household or family (name a family with 1.1 children). When dealing with large populations, though, some method of summarization must be found. One is to describe things as "typical" or "average," a practice followed in this book from time to time.

Once a household has earned income, then, it must choose among limited alternatives. It either spends, saves, or uses some combination of spending and saving, to dispose of its income. Spending and saving patterns can take many forms. The essential point is that the household has income coming in and expenditures flowing out, and must put each of its earned dollars into either the savings or the expenditure category. The amount of money coming into the household is thus always equal to the amount going out.

Concurrent with the economic activity of households is a great flurry of activity by the firms. The firm is the basic producing unit in a free-enterprise, industrial society. Bakeries are firms that produce bread, farms are firms that produce food, the Chrysler Corporation is a firm that produces automobiles, the Menninger Clinic is a firm that produces rehabilitation. Because firms are extremely diverse in both size and function, it makes little sense to discuss a "typical" firm. General Motors and a neighborhood barber shop are both firms, but they are so vastly different that it is difficult to think of them in the same category. Yet even though they do not seem to be comparable, all firms conform to a general pattern: they buy factors of production, transform them into products, and then sell the finished products. Figure 3–2 shows this common process. It is analogous to Figure 3–1, but it relates to the behavior of firms rather than that of households.

Like a household, the firm earns income and spends it. It earns income through the sale of finished goods and services, as shown by the large arrow on the left in Figure 3–2. Many firms obtain their income by selling only one or a few things. (A restaurant sells only meals.) Others earn income by selling an extremely diverse range of goods and services to a worldwide clientele. (General Motors sells thousands of different products to people all over the world.) In either case, some household or some other firm is depended on as a buyer and a source of revenue.

The producing firm must use some land, labor, and capital whether it produces wheat, haircuts, or road graders. These factors must be pur-

Figure 3–2 Income and Expenses of a Firm

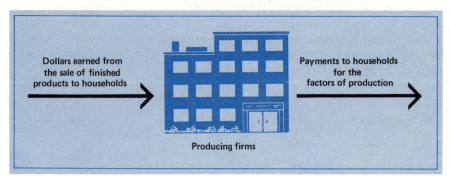

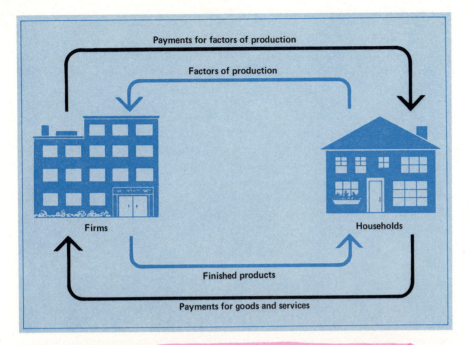

Figure 3-3 The Circular Flow of Economic Activity

chased from the households that own them. The large arrow on the right in Figure 3-2 depicts payments made by firms for factors. The firm, then, depends on households to provide the factors of production as well as to buy its products. Firms are dependent on households just as households depend on firms.

Like the household, the firm must balance its books. Each dollar coming in must eventually find its way to the owner of some factor of production. The firm's income is used to purchase land, labor, and capital. Dollars that are not used in this way are profits and go to the risk takers (entrepreneurs) who own the firm. Profits too are thus a payment for a factor. Like the household, the firm spends exactly as much as it receives in income.

A quick glance at Figures 3-1 and 3-2 might lead to the conclusion that all payments to and from households and firms occur instantly. In reality, transactions between firms and households are *flows* rather than single events. Money flows from households to firms; money flows from firms back to households. And this happens continuously.

The continuous flows between firms and households are graphically pictured in Figure 3-3. All firms are represented by the factory on the left, and all households are represented by the house on the right. At any point in time, factors of production are flowing from households to firms, and goods and services are flowing from firms back to households. These simultaneous and continuous flows occur without explicit instruction from anyone. The circular flow in a free-enterprise economy is automatic. Within limits, households are free to purchase any products they wish and free to sell their factors to any firm that will purchase them. Similarly, firms can elect to produce any product and to use any method they wish to produce it.[2]

The inner ring in Figure 3–3 shows the physical transfer of factors and products. In a barter economy, where labor is traded for bread, and land use is traded for protection, no money is involved and the inner ring would explain the whole system. The U.S. economy, however, is far from a barter economy, and money is used as a facilitator of trade. It is a convenience that eliminates the need to arrange complicated exchanges among all kinds of factors and products. With money as the medium of exchange, the prices of all goods and services can be reckoned in terms of dollars and cents. The outer ring of Figure 3–3 represents flows of money payments from firms to households and from households to firms.[3]

Figure 3–3 shows the overall interdependence among actors in the economy quite clearly, but it fails to capture the complexity of the system. The figure is an abstraction of how factors are transformed into products and how products are exchanged for factors. It does not recognize that households in the economy do not spend all their income on goods and services. In Figure 3–1, nonspending does appear—as savings. Households in the U.S. economy save in a fairly regular way—approximately 7.5 percent of their incomes in an average year. In 1975 this amounted to $75.9 billion.

Funds earned but not spent by households almost always go into savings accounts at banks or savings and loan associations, into government bonds, or to other *financial intermediaries*.

A financial intermediary is an institution that handles money for other people (households or firms). A common function of a financial intermediary is to gather funds from many savers and make these accumulated funds available to borrowers.

The money is then loaned to households wishing to spend more than their current incomes or to firms seeking to expand their productive

---

[2]There are limitations on production and consumption. These limits are imposed by law and prevent, for example, the production or marketing of substances or activities that are harmful to society. Thus, not just anyone can go into business producing drugs, people may not raise chickens in downtown Chicago, and one may not hire oneself out as a professional murderer.

[3]Figure 3–3 can be read in another way. The two flows at the top represent *factor markets*. Land, labor, and capital are traded between firms and households, and the arrows show who is paying and who is receiving. The bottom flows designate *product markets*. In these markets are traded finished goods—the necessities and desirables of life. The study of factor and product markets has always occupied a large portion of economists' time. Some of the reasons for this, and some of the results of this collective study, will appear in Part Three.

An Early Circular Flow Model: France, 1765

Although modern economic thought is often claimed to have begun with Adam Smith in the British Isles about 1776, a group of French thinker–philosophers were dwelling on economic problems several years earlier. The "Physiocrats," as the group was called, developed a highly sophisticated system of economic thinking that included a circular flow of activity. Their actors were (1) the productive class, (2) the proprietary class, and (3) the artisans, among whom were included government functionaries and dignitaries. Since France was an agrarian nation, it is not surprising that the only persons considered productive were those engaged in agriculture or other extractive industries (mining, forestry, and fishing). The Physiocrats presumed that the economy of France could progress only if agriculture produced a surplus of food. They considered the proprietors and the artisans economically sterile. The proprietors, however, since they extracted great rents from the farmers, were to support the government through taxes. Artisans were not "bad," just unproductive. (The Physiocrats themselves would have been counted as artisans.)

The three groups in this scheme coexisted and depended on one another. Their interdependence gave rise to a circular flow like the one shown below. The man primarily responsible for its formulation was François Quesnay (1694–1777), a physician-economist in the court of King Louis XV. With very little accurate numerical information at his disposal, he had to build a rather abstract model. He assumed that half of all workers would be productive, one-fourth would be proprietors, and one-fourth would be artisans. The productive class would produce food on land owned by proprietors and would use ideas provided by artisans. Quesnay's system anticipated the interdependence models that became popular among economists 150 years later.

The Physiocrat's Circular Flow

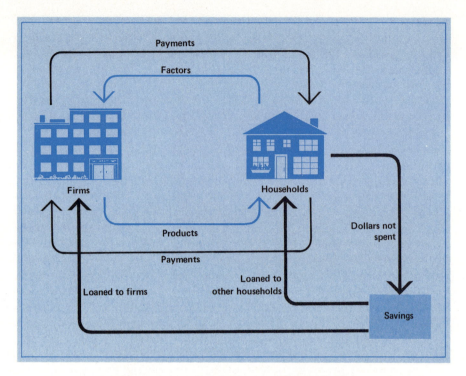

Figure 3-4 Two Savings Relationships

capacity by enlarging or modifying their facilities. Figure 3-4 adds saving and borrowing to the circular flow. The arrow from households to savings represents a continuous flow of dollars. The savings are reinjected into the economic stream by firms' and households' borrowing. Savings are sometimes described as "leakages" out of the system, but as the figure shows, they reenter the flow through two straightforward and common mechanisms.

It should not be implied that saving is practiced only by households. Firms also save. When they do, the process is called *retaining earnings*. A firm engaged in this process will not spend all its revenue to purchase factors, nor will it send all its profits on to the households. Instead it will keep some of its earnings so it can add to its plant, buy new equipment, or start a new line of production. Retained earnings are a form of saving.

Government in the Circular Flow

One more addition to the circular-flow picture is necessary. In the early days of economics, Adam Smith, now generally regarded as the father of modern economic analysis, noted that government was an active force in economic affairs. As time has passed, the role of government has grown to the point that no circular-flow model is complete unless government is given a position as important as those occupied by firms and households. Figure 3–5 shows the relationship of firms and households to government.

The flows in Figure 3–5 show that government uses its taxing powers to obtain funds from households and from firms. Far from being merely a social institution that exists to stifle incentive by taxing away money (and, thus, purchasing power), government is made up of thousands of firm-like institutions, agencies, and branches that use the revenue obtained in taxes to purchase factors of production, which in turn are used to produce things that private firms ordinarily do not find profitable (defense, flood control, city beautification, and streets, to name a few). No new rules need be elaborated here. Flows of income and expenditures exist between governments and the other actors just as flows of income and expenditures exist between firms and households. Governments use their income to purchase valuable factors, and provide useful products and services in return.

Investment, Growth, and Interdependence

If all the income and expenditure in the economy is continually flowing among the three actors, how does the economy grow? The key to growth

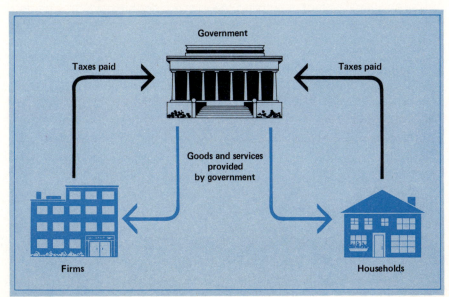

Figure 3–5 Government in the Circular Flow

is *investment,* and investment takes place as part of the ordinary circular flow of economic activity.

Investment is the actual creation or construction of capital facilities. It includes building a new plant, buying a new machine, or constructing a new nuclear power plant. The key to understanding investment lies in the question, Will this action add to the productive capacity of society? If the answer is Yes, investment has occurred.

Households, firms, and governments invest when they make expenditures that increase their future productivity. A household invests when it sends a child to college or when the breadwinner becomes involved in an on-the-job training program. A firm invests when it expands into larger quarters and purchases more sophisticated machinery. The government invests when it dredges a navigation channel in the Ohio River or when it builds rehabilitation clinics for addicts and halfway houses for parolees. Each of these activities adds to future output. Although all three actors do some investing, firms conduct most of the investment activity in any one year. Data are not available to show exactly how the total is divided between firms and households, but in 1974 these two actors spent $209.4 billion on investment.

It is common to think of households "investing" when they purchase shares of common stock in companies. In the language of economics, these purchases are transfers of ownership of existing capital. Since the purchase of the stock does not add to the economy's productivity, it is not investment. These "transfers" will be discussed more fully in Chapter 6.

Diagraming the circular flow among governments, firms, and households is a simple way of describing the interdependence within a modern industrial society. Each of the major actors in the scheme—firms, households, and governments—must be scrutinized separately, but their interdependence is truly the most critical element that must be understood in a study of economics. Interdependence in an economy means that if one person or firm or unit of government changes its behavior, many people are affected. Interdependence allows for increased output but brings with it the risk of failure and instability. An interdependent society is a delicate mechanism whose functioning is always precarious.

Summary

1. In a modern market economy, firms, households, and governments interact to produce goods and services. Their interaction is circular and a continuous circular flow exists among them.
2. Firms are the basic producing units in society. They are assumed to be attempting to maximize their profits.
3. Households are the basic consuming units and are assumed to be acting to maximize their satisfaction.
4. Households sell factors of production—land, labor, capital, and entre-

preneurship—to firms, and in turn use the income received to purchase finished outputs of firms.

5 Households sometimes hold money as savings rather than spend it for consumption.
6 The government, no less than firms and households, is an actor in the circular flow. It taxes firms and households but purchases factors and goods from them.

Exercises

1 Explain these important terms and concepts:

    circular flow of economic activity   labor
    firm   capital
    household   entrepreneur(ship)
    government(s)   interdependence
    comparative advantage   saving
    factors of production   investment
    land

2 The U.S. economy can be described as a huge perpetual-motion machine; it just keeps going. Does interdependence help or hinder the process? What would happen if we were a nation of Robinson Crusoes, each of us totally self-sufficient? Could the circular-flow diagram still be drawn?

3 The insert on profit maximization, on page 37, has many elements that can be used to clarify the explanation of scientific analysis in Chapter 2. What does it say about (a) simplification and (b) models?

4 Most local economies have some characteristics of a circular flow. Draw an imaginary circular-flow diagram for your hometown, city, county, or nearby area. In the box labeled "firms," name the major producers. In the box labeled "households," name the kinds of factors supplied by most local residents.

5 Would it be more realistic to tie your local economy to a larger economy? If so, how would the arrows be drawn? (Hint: What things would come in from outside and what would be sent out?)

A Contemporary Problem
California—the Late Great State

Ever since 1849, when gold was found in the American River near Coloma, California has held a hypnotic attraction for people. When other states foundered, California flourished. Today, about one-tenth of the U.S. population lives there and over 10 percent of the GNP is produced there. In the state the three forces—households, firms, and governments—enjoy a fragile relationship that is sometimes sympathetic, sometimes hostile.

At present, Californians are puzzled about where they want their state to go and what they want it to do. After accepting millions of "immigrants" from other states, the current residents wonder if more will be better. Households are grouping together to make tough environmental laws aimed at protecting the coastal regions from further development and preventing such capital investments as nuclear power plants. Understandably, the people want to keep their state for themselves. But they also want jobs and good government.

The firms in the state are in a frustrating position. They have access to a large and highly trained labor force, but the industrial make-up of the state is heavily oriented toward aerospace, electronics, and agriculture. The aerospace industry suffers ups and downs. It is now in a down period, with foreign nations the only big purchasers. Electronics is picking up after the recession-inflation of the early 1970s. People are again buying TV sets, calculators, and small electric appliances. The condition of agriculture in the state is hard to describe because California grows specialty crops—avocados, almonds, and limes—rather than wheat, corn, and hogs. Many parts of the state are overplanted with the specialties, and the state's vast livestock industry is affected by the weather—a factor of production that remains outside human control.

The third actor, government, is crucial in California. It is a spending state, and even political conservatives find it necessary to endorse expensive welfare and social programs. The current trend is to hold down both spending and the size of the state payroll, but the state is actively participating in the formation of potentially expensive environmental legislation to protect natural areas, prevent certain kinds of development, and impose high taxes on firms locating in the state. A firm that specializes in finding suitable locations for other firms recently ranked California forty-seventh among the forty-eight mainland states. They reasoned that the state was hostile toward business and lacked long-term supplies of energy, and that it had very high and discriminatory tax rates. (In 1975 an electronics firm attempting to locate a plant in the West found it would pay annual taxes of $63,300 in New Mexico, $63,600 in Utah, $84,800 in Arizona and $158,900 in California.)

California is composed of households, firms, and governments that for over a century have worked together in a beautiful geographic area to develop a vital and attractive economy. The state grew because the links among the actors were strong and complementary. In recent years, the state has not been so attractive to outsiders, and the three actors have not seemed to be operating smoothly in the circular flow. The future of California is uncertain. Some forces affecting an economy cannot be controlled, but often the crucial links among actors can be. Firms, households, and governments working together can form a congenial place for economic growth and development. When the three actors are at odds, the business and economic climate is almost never conducive to success.

4 The Market, Feedback Systems, and Precariousness

All societies—rich and poor, large and small, young and old, advanced and primitive—must make decisions about what to produce, how to produce it, and for whom to produce it. Some societies do this by tradition, parents passing on skills to children. Other societies use political force to dictate that some people will farm, some will work in industry, and some will care for young children.

In the United States, the basic economic questions of what, how, and for whom to produce are answered through the *market*.

The market is the stage on which the actors in an economy perform their continuous drama. It is any place where buyers and sellers come into contact with each other for the purpose of trading. A market may be a physical location, like Gimbels or Woolworths, or it may consist simply of all the possible buyers or sellers of a given product. The *market mechanism* is the process by which buyers express what they want to buy and sellers respond by communicating what they are willing to sell. Their combined activities yield the price at which the good or service is exchanged.

Activity in the market is constant because buyers and sellers must continually react to each other and adjust their behavior to reflect new dispositions about what or how much should be bought or sold. The market lies at the heart of all economic activity in the United States. This chapter is devoted to markets and to some of the consequences of using the market method to resolve a society's basic economic questions.

A Market System

A market economy is a sophisticated and complex society. In it, groups of specialists perform the tasks they do best and receive monetary rewards, which they use to purchase goods that they cannot (or do not wish to) produce for themselves. Production is carried out by specialized firms. They place goods on the market, these goods are purchased, and the producing firm uses the money received from sales to buy inputs for the next round of production.

In a market system, consumers' decisions answer the important question, What will be produced? Buyers, operating as individuals and as groups, take their earnings to the market and select the collection of goods that will bring the greatest satisfaction per dollar spent. Surely, there is a hierarchy of purchases. Food is purchased before entertainment; serviceable work clothing is selected before evening clothes. But in each case the consumer decides what to buy and what to reject. In so doing, he signals producers to respond to his wishes. This concept is known as *consumer sovereignty.*

Consumer sovereignty is the ability of the consumer to use his income as he wishes, and thus to influence the kind and the amount of goods produced by firms. A market-oriented society is not effective unless the consumer has this freedom.

In a market economy, the firms are the sellers. Producers and middle men in firms respond to the desire of consumers. They carefully study market information in order to learn what buyers want. In responding to market information, it is up to sellers to answer the question, How will the desired products be produced? They will attempt to produce them in the cheapest way possible. This is not an effort to deceive the consumer by producing shoddy goods. It is an effort by the producing firm to be efficient and to realize the highest possible profit. A producer could manufacture finely tooled wristwatch mechanisms using materials that might last a lifetime or even many lifetimes. A watch of this quality might cost $1,000 or even $1,500. Most buyers do not request this kind of quality from watchmakers. They prefer a $16.95 watch that they may have to repair once or twice, then replace with another $16.95 model. Watchmakers do not use valuable materials or high-cost skills in creating these timepieces. They make the cheapest possible *acceptable* watch. They respond to the market.

The market also decides for whom goods will be produced. Buyers meet sellers to set a price for an item. Buyers who think the price is reasonable and who have the money will buy. Those who think the price is too high or those who do not have the money will not buy. The market and the market system are very severe in this regard. Even if the product is a highly coveted one or is needed for personal survival, the market is strict: Those who can pay obtain the item; those who cannot, go without.

An Automatic Mechanism

The beauty of the market system is that it is automatic. Buyers bring their needs and their money to the marketplace and exchange them for desired goods and services. They do this without instruction, without initiation, and without needless interference. Sellers automatically bring their wares to market and consummate exchanges whenever the opportunity for profit arises.

Self-interest is the driving force behind the actions of both buyer and seller. Each uses what he has to obtain what he wants or needs. The market process consists of a continuous negotiation and reevaluation between buyers and sellers to determine the terms of the various exchanges. This adjustment is fueled by the self-interest of each party. The market system is a self-oriented way of answering the basic questions, What, How, and For whom? It works only in the presence of a high degree of individual freedom and a socioeconomic climate that allows each person to be the judge of what he wants and what he should have. The U.S. economy is essentially a *market economy.*

A market economy is one in which decision making is broadly based and each person—buyer or seller—becomes an active part of the massive marketing apparatus. In such an economy, owners of land, labor, capital, and entrepreneurial skill are free to negotiate with potential buyers, and producers of goods and services are free to negotiate with consumers. The distinguishing characteristic is that most factors, goods, and services are sold after reasonably free negotiations have taken place between buyers and sellers.

Market Defects

The machinery of the market does not always enhance everyone's welfare. Later chapters will be devoted to flaws in the market system that cause economic injury to some people or groups, but some can be mentioned now. The most serious flaw attached to a market system of economic organization is its indifference to those who have no money. Markets answer questions through prices, and the prices are stated in terms of dollars and cents. Only those who have money to spend are a part of the market process.

Because it is a money-oriented process, two kinds of problems arise. First, a market can develop for guns, narcotics, and illegal services just as easily as it can for work clothes and wholesome food. Second, a diabetic with no money cannot purchase insulin, and a defendant with no money cannot hire a lawyer. The market—*as a market*—is indifferent to these problems.

It was the market process that provided impetus for the automobile industry. Buyers wanted the new, convenient machines, and sellers were happy to provide them. Markets urged firms to develop the capacity to produce automobiles and all the related support facilities (freeways, traffic police, garages, filling stations, and motels, to name but a few). Meanwhile, the automobile—a market good—has caused revolting amounts of air pollution around the nation's major cities. Since no one will pay for clean air, the market is indifferent to the need for it.

Nonmarket Aspects of the U.S. Market Economy

Even though most economic activity in the United States is fostered through a market mechanism, the economy is not entirely free of social and political forces or choice-making schemes. It is because of the society and its culture, not the market, that most stenographers are women and most steam fitters are men. Hundreds of years of Western civilization have reinforced the idea that men are breadwinners and women are homemakers. This social fact is reflected and accommodated by the market, but the market does not generate a disposition of its own.

Political forces dictate that we drive cars on the right-hand side of the road, children will complete a certain number of years of schooling, and tax rates will increase as a family's taxable income increases. Moreover, county, state, and federal governments provide roads, bridges, defense, education, justice, fire protection, and other services. This has a profound effect on the market, but in these areas answering the questions What? How? and For whom? is done in legislative halls rather than in the marketplace.

Because the economy of the United States includes these nonmarket aspects, it is often described as a *mixed economy,* combining a bit of socially oriented choice making and a bit of political choice making with a large measure of market choice making.

A mixed economy is one in which some goods and services are produced under private auspices, while others are produced under the control of public mechanisms. The U.S. economy is a mixed economy with about 65 percent of all goods produced in response to market signals and 35 percent produced through government sponsorship.

The market and its strengths, weaknesses, and deficiencies will be considered in many of the following chapters. Our present task is to expand on the operation of the market and to understand how it works to decide the What, How, and For whom.

The Market in Isolation

A market brings buyers and sellers together. It can be a place (the shopping center); it can be a contact made by telephone; it can be the mail-handling room at Sears' or Ward's mail-order outlets. Each of these qualifies as a market since each brings sellers into contact with buyers. The market, however, does other things, too. It aids in exchanging things in surplus for things that are needed, and it helps to define the relative trading values (prices) of the goods and services that are exchanged. The market performs these functions regardless of the degree of sophistication of those who use it and the location of the exchange—whether it takes place in the village square of a primitive community, in the complicated sales machinery of the New York Stock Exchange, or at the college bookstore.

In the remainder of this chapter, markets are described using the basic economic concepts of supply, demand, and equilibrium. We shall also examine how some economic decisions are made without the aid of a market. Demand and supply will be dealt with separately, and then joined to show how prices are established and how equilibrium prices are obtained. As in earlier sections of the book, certain ideas are presented as abstractions and should not be regarded as complete pictures of reality. Simplification is necessary in order to see clearly the major underlying forces operating in the system. Although the relationship under discussion is most often stated as the law of supply and demand, demand will be treated first because it is much the easier concept.

Demand

Webster's Third New International Dictionary lists 16 different meanings for *demand*, and *The American Heritage Dictionary* lists 15. Given so many possible definitions, demand is bound to be a somewhat elusive concept. To an economist, however, the demand for goods and services has a clear and specific meaning.

Demand is a technical term meaning "desire backed by purchasing

"Good news—the price of beef is way up again this week."

power."[1] To want something does not provide demand for it. To want something and to be willing to pay for it does provide demand. Two qualities—desire and willingness to pay—combine to form demand for a product.

This information by itself is not terribly useful. However, information about the way the quantity demanded *changes* in response to other pressures is quite useful. If society knows how demand will change, it can determine how much of each resource input will be needed to produce the demanded items. If society knows that by 1980 the demand for economical, compact automobiles will double and the demand for luxurious, gas-consuming monsters will be halved, resource inputs now used to produce large cars will be diverted into the production of smaller ones.

Most discussions of demand do not center on the switch from one product to another. Instead, they deal with the factors that affect changes in the quantity demanded of a particular commodity. The major influence on the demand for a product is its price. The way in which the quantity demanded responds to a change in price is illustrated in Figure 4–1. In the figure, curve *D* shows how a purchaser responds to different prices for a particular commodity.[2] The figure shows that if a price of $6 per unit

---

[1] In economics, as in any scientific discipline, *technical terms* are terms that take on special meaning. Ordinarily, they are a form of verbal shorthand in which a few words are used to express a somewhat complicated relationship or phenomenon. Technical terms are not confined to science or to professions. A cook uses a *pinch* of salt and lovers go on a *date*. Each word is a simple way of describing a much more complex occurrence.

[2] When a graph is used to show the relationship between price and quantity taken, price is always put on the vertical axis. Any study of demand, supply, or equilibrium prices will make use of this convention. It is also customary to talk of a demand or supply *curve,* even though the graphed lines representing supply and demand may be straight.

Market Capitalism

Market capitalism is the form of economic organization used in most European countries, most of the nations of the Western Hemisphere, and a handful of Asian nations—most notably Japan and the Republic of China. The system apparently developed in northern Europe in the sixteenth and seventeenth centuries—about the same time that Europe was being transformed from a feudal to an industrial region. Market capitalism developed simultaneously with humanism and the notion that each person is the proper custodian for his or her own resources. The system requires that individuals be motivated by self-interest and that this self-interest be reflected in their market behavior. Individuals enter markets to exert demands; producers respond by providing those things that have been demanded.

An economy based on market capitalism will usually have the following characteristics:

1 Very highly commercialized productive activity, with most goods and services sold in organized markets.
2 Heavy reliance on profits and self-satisfaction as guiding principles for decisions.
3 A high degree of risk taking on the part of producers.
4 A highly developed banking and credit system that can be used to facilitate trading.
5 Rapid introduction of technological advances into productive activity.
6 Individual laborers free to choose how much labor they place on the market.

Some economists call this type of economic organization simply *capitalism;* others, *the free-enterprise system;* and still others, *the market system* or *market capitalism.* Regardless of the name, many—though not all—of the nations that have adopted this system have been successful in obtaining high levels of output for their citizens.

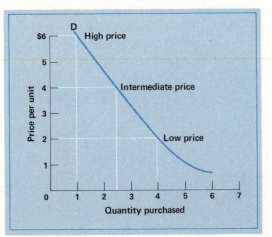

Figure 4-1
A Hypothetical Demand Curve

is asked, a buyer will be interested in buying one unit of the good. If the price drops to $4, two and one-half units will be purchased and at the low price of $2, four units will be taken. The message is obvious: Quantity demanded increases as price falls. But why?

The drop in price means that the consumer can now purchase more of the want-satisfying good without increasing his total expenditure, so he feels free to buy more of the good. When the price of apples falls from 25 cents per pound to 10 cents per pound, the apple buyer has more purchasing power. He can double his purchase of apples from one pound to two pounds and still have 5 cents left over. A drop in the price of apples, therefore, brings with it an increase in the quantity purchased. Put another way, as the price of a good falls, that good becomes a "better buy" relative to other goods and the quantity purchased increases. This theme will become the major topic addressed in Chapter 17.

Supply

In some respects, supply is analogous to, or symmetrical with, demand. In other ways it is an entirely new relationship. Like demand, *supply* is a technical term that has a special meaning in economics.

Supply refers to the quantities of a good, factor, or service that will be placed on the market at each of a series of prices.

While demand expresses the willingness of consumers to buy a good, supply expresses the producers' willingness to provide that good, and is related to the costs that they incur by manufacturing more of it. Supply is producer oriented. As the price of a product increases, more firms can profitably produce it, and the quantity placed on the market increases.

The supply curve is most often an upward-sloping line like the curve S in Figure 4–2. The reason for the upward (positive) slope is obvious. At a very low price, only a few firms are able to earn profits by placing the good on the market. As price increases, those firms that incur higher

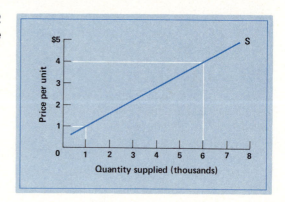

**Figure 4–2
The Supply Curve**

costs in producing the item can earn profits, so they, too, place some of the good on the market. As prices rise more, even firms that are old, outdated and inefficient can cover their costs, so they begin to supply the good. Because different firms require different prices to cover their costs, the supply curve becomes an upward-sloping line. The very efficient firms supply the quantities shown on the left end, and the inefficient firms supply the final quantities represented by the right end. When the price of light bulbs increases from 50 cents to one dollar and then to $1.50, firms other than Westinghouse, Sylvania and GE begin to make them. When the price reaches two and then three dollars per bulb, even oil companies, farmers, and cobblers might be tempted to try their hands at making these extremely valuable items. Because more firms are willing to produce an item as its price rises, the supply curve is an upward-sloping line.

In addition to showing the general relationship between the price of a good and the amount of it that will be put on the market, the supply curve can also provide more specific information about how high the price of a product must be in order to attract a certain quantity onto the market. What price would be necessary to get producers to place 6,000 units of the commodity on the market? The question would need to be asked of all producers who might possibly have some of the commodity to sell. At some price—$4 in the case shown in Figure 4–2—potential sellers would be willing to place the appropriate number of units on the market. This theme will be elaborated in Chapter 18.

The Supply/Demand Relationship

Supply and demand curves are useful devices for inquiry into two separate attributes of the market system, but their real value stems from using them together to show the relationship between quantities demanded and quantities supplied. This relationship helps explain the process of price determination, and prices are the signals that help both producers and consumers make decisions about the use of scarce resources, money, and time.

In Figure 4–3, a supply curve S and a demand curve D are shown on the same price/quantity graph. The intersection of the two curves at point P has special significance. At point P, a price of four dollars per unit is related to a quantity of 5 (the coordinates of point P are $X = 5$ and $Y = 4$). The relationship is important because at the point of intersection —and only at that point—both demanders and suppliers of the good are satisfied. When price is four dollars per unit, suppliers are willing to place 5,000 units on the market, and demanders will buy exactly this quantity. There is no shortage and there is no surplus.

When the price is higher—for example, the six-dollar level illustrated in Figure 4–4—demanders are going to want to buy only 2,000 units, while

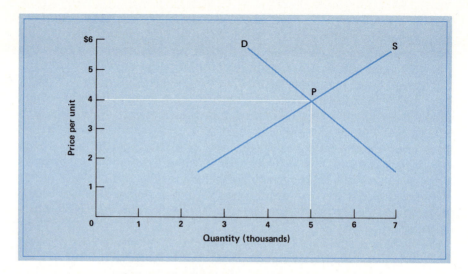

Figure 4–3 Supply, Demand, and Price

suppliers will wish to sell approximately 9,500 units. In this situation, a *surplus* exists, since the quantity supplied exceeds the quantity demanded by 7,500 units.

A surplus is the excess of quantity supplied over quantity demanded at a given price.

In 1975, high prices of automobiles caused purchasers to refuse to buy them, and so a surplus of cars developed.

Figure 4–4 Surpluses and Shortages

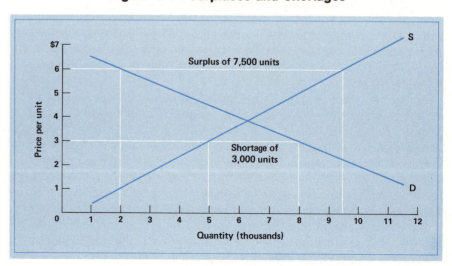

If a surplus develops in a market that is relatively free of hindrances, automatic forces will begin to operate to drive the market price down to the point where supply is equal to demand. These automatic forces are not complicated. If the local store finds it has too much beef on hand, it can sell the beef by dropping the price. Automobile manufacturers responded to 1975 surpluses by offering "cash refunds" of up to $500 to anyone purchasing a new car. The cash refund was nothing more than a reduction in price intended to get suppliers and demanders closer to agreement on the appropriate price for automobiles. Individual actions by stores or producers add together to make the market respond almost automatically by lowering prices when surpluses appear.

Analogous but opposite forces will come into play when the price is *lower* than that corresponding to the intersection of the two curves. In Figure 4–4, at a price of three dollars, demanders will wish to purchase 8,000 units, but suppliers, not earning much profit at this low price, will be willing to supply only 5,000 units. Hence, a *shortage* develops.

A shortage is the quantity by which supply falls short of demand when product prices are very low.

During a shortage, buyers wish to purchase more than sellers are willing to supply. As before, a price adjustment brings buyers and sellers together, and the forces for adjustment are still relatively automatic. A buyer observes that the good is scarce and agrees to pay a higher price rather than go without. Simultaneously, a seller observes the shortage and so raises the price on the remaining quantity. Such adjustments continue until demanders and suppliers agree on how much should be exchanged and what price should be charged.

The price/quantity relationship designated by the intersection of the two curves is called the equilibrium level of price and output or, simply, *equilibrium.*

Equilibrium is the level of price and output at which there is no net force toward changing either price or quantity exchanged. At equilibrium the money that buyers are willing to give up is just equal to the amount sellers are asking for a given quantity of the good or service.

Thus far we have been considering a market operating without interference. It is unlikely that any markets would behave this smoothly or this simply over an extended period of time. Too many things can change or go wrong. Buyers or sellers can gain control of a market and exert undue influence on any others trying to enter the market. A breakdown in communications may make it difficult for buyers to obtain information about what sellers are doing. Advertisers or skilled salespeople may alter the nature of the demand relationship by convincing more people to buy. Any of dozens of other things may happen. In spite of all of these weaknesses and in spite of the fact that the real world is known never to be as tidy as the diagrams show, there are four lessons to be learned from this model of the market system:

1. If more is to be sold, price must be lowered (law of demand).
2. If more is to be supplied, a higher price must be offered to producers (law of supply).
3. An equilibrium price is the only one at which supply equals demand.
4. While the concepts of supply, demand, price, and equilibrium as shown in these simple diagrams are only approximations of reality, they do help to explain the direction and the intensity of many changes occurring in this economy.

This excursion into the world of tools (supply and demand may be regarded as perhaps the most important tools of economic analysis) has given some insight into the workings of the market. Its main purpose, however, has been to provide enough tools so that the precariousness of the circular flow can be understood. Some relationships between the circular flow and the market economy will be elaborated in the next section of this chapter.

Changes in Supply and Demand

The previous section defined demand and supply curves and showed how the quantities demanded or supplied change when the price of a good changes. The purpose of this section is to show how demand and supply may change in response to other forces as well. These other forces do not result in a movement from left to right or right to left along an existing curve. They produce an entirely *new* curve.

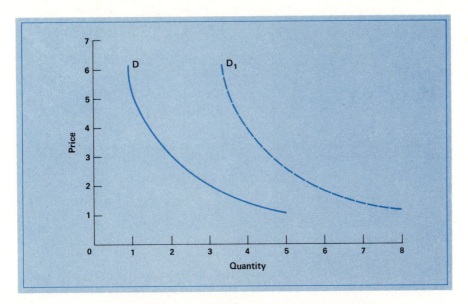

Figure 4-5 A Shift in the Demand Curve

Shifts in demand. The demand curve for a product shows how potential buyers will respond to a change in price, assuming all other factors affecting demand remain constant. It is unlikely that all other factors will remain constant for very long. In a world beset by change, demands for almost any product are bound to respond to changes in consumer incomes, tastes and preferences, availability of substitutes, and a host of other things. A single demand curve for carrots assumes no change other than in their price. But other things do change. Figure 4-5 shows two demand curves, D and D_1. D is a solid line representing the demand for a product at a given time. It is developed from potential buyers who have given incomes. If, after one year, the incomes of all potential demanders doubled, the demand curve would shift out, indicating that with increases in income, buyers will purchase more than before at each level of price. In 1960, very few people in the United States had color TV sets. Since then, incomes have increased demonstrably and now "everyone" has living color in the living room.

A change in the availability of substitutes can also have a demonstrable effect on demand. Throughout the 1950s and 1960s, U.S. scientists were developing more and more versatile and high-quality synthetic fabrics. The demand for these synthetics increased, so from year to year larger volumes were purchased at the same price. At the same time, the demand for wool fabrics decreased. Hypothetical demand curves for these two kinds of fabrics are shown in Figure 4-6. In the left-hand panel, the demand for wool suits is shown to be *shifting* to the

Figure 4-6 Changing Demand for Wool Suits and for Synthetic-Fabric Suits

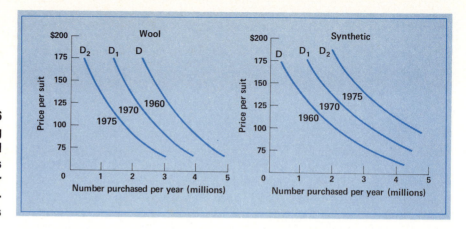

left. Each year fewer suits are being purchased at the original prices. In the right-hand panel, the demand for suits made of synthetic fabrics is shown to be shifting to the right. More of these suits were purchased at $100 in 1970 than in 1960, and the volume sold at this price increased still more between 1970 and 1975.

Shifts in supply. Just as changes in any of several circumstances will cause a shift in demand, changes in methods of production and costs of materials bring about shifts in supply. The original supply curve introduced in Figure 4-2 represented quantities that could be placed on the market at each of several prices provided there were no changes in the cost of production or in methods of manufacture. But changes do occur. If inexpensive electrical power is substituted for expensive steam power, the cost of manufacturing an item may drop, so that each level of output could now reach the market at a lower price. This kind of shift in a supply

Figure 4-7 A Shift in the Supply Curve

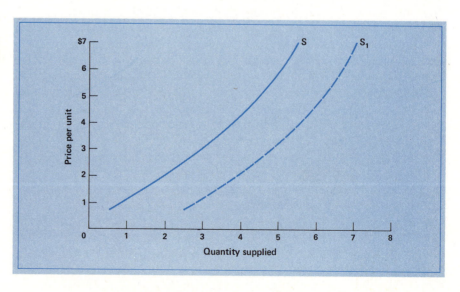

curve is shown in Figure 4–7. The original curve, S, shows one set of quantities being made available at each price. A second supply curve, S_1, shows the result of a switch from high-cost to low-cost power. More is now available at each price; there is a new supply curve.

Shifts and equilibrium. With demand curves and supply curves constantly shifting or rotating in response to dozens of different forces, the equilibrium price of a product cannot be expected to remain constant for very long. Figure 4–8 shows a few of the things that can happen to prices in a changing world. Only one demand curve is shown. This demand curve shows that when the price of a good is $4 per unit, one unit will be purchased; when the price is $1 per unit, five units will be purchased. The original supply curve, S, shows that suppliers will offer two units when the price is $2 and about four units when the price is $4. The original demand and supply curves intersect (come into equilibrium) when the price is about $2.50 and the quantity exchanged is 2.5 units. This equilibrium is shown at point M.

For some reason—perhaps a new method of production—producers begin to respond with respect to supply curve S_1. Now, a price of $1 per unit brings nearly four units to the market and a price of $3 per unit brings nearly six units. Since there has been no shift in demand, the change causes the equilibrium price to drop from $2.50 to $1.50 and the equilibrium quantity to expand from 2.5 units to 4.2 units. The new equilibrium is at point N.

It is important to be aware of the difference between a shift in a curve (as from S to S_1—a "shift in supply"—and a movement along an existing curve (as from M to N)—a "change in the quantity demanded."

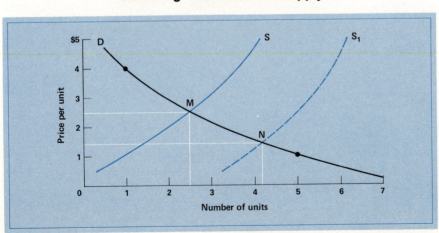

Figure 4–8 Changes in Equilibrium Stemming from a Shift in Supply

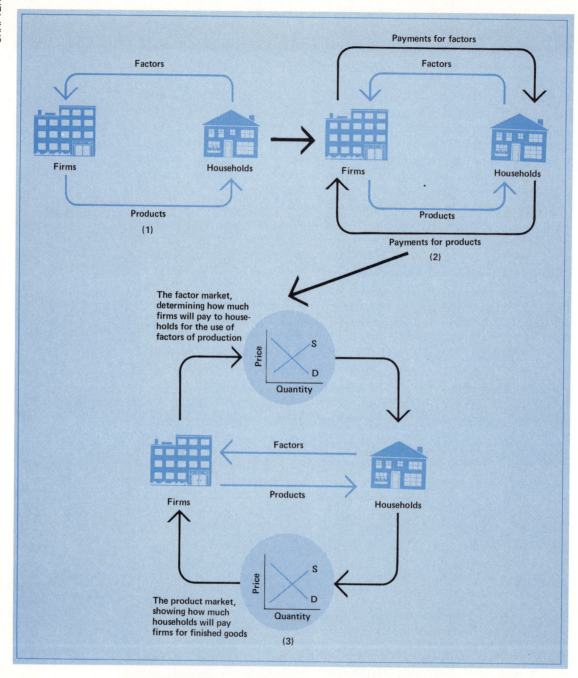

Figure 4-9 Increasing Complexity of the Circular Flow

The Precariousness of the System

In Chapter 3, the roles of actors in the circular flow—firms, households, and governments—were explained and tied together in a framework describing the continuity of economic activity. The bonds tying the actors together were loosely defined flows of funds. The concepts of supply, demand, and equilibrium have now been introduced as analytical tools that can be used to show the fragile interdependence that exists among the actors. The evolution of the analysis appears in the three sections of Figure 4–9, showing (1) the crude circular flow, (2) the introduction of money flows, and (3) the supply and demand structures in each market. Government activity is omitted from this figure for the sake of simplicity. Moreover, government decisions are often made through mechanisms other than the market.[3] Part (3) of Figure 4–9 gives an idea of how delicately balanced a market system can be. It is expanded and redrawn as Figure 4–10.

Firms demand factors; households supply them. At any moment, a price is established for factors, and at the established price, certain quantities of factors move from households to firms in exchange for given amounts of money (the price per unit times the number of units transferred). This market-transaction process may result in $100 million transferring from firms to households. The $100 million received by the households provides them with funds to purchase finished goods and services from firms. Households enter the product market with $100 million in purchasing power and demand goods supplied by firms. In the product market, a price/quantity relationship is established, and transactions take place, resulting in a flow of money from households back to firms. If the flow is equal to $100 million, the system is in equilibrium and all participants are satisfied.[4] It is unlikely that the system will remain in equilibrium for very long, because many forces are continually changing the demand and supply for factors and products. As long as changes are modest, the system can usually absorb them. Fluctuations in businessmen's inventories, for example, are an indication of the system absorbing some mistakes. Short periods of unemployment during which people relocate into new jobs reflect the system's ability to absorb errors in

---

[3]Examples of nonmarket decision making and allocations are not hard to find. Public education—primary, secondary, and (to a lesser extent) higher—is provided by government, although there is no market for public education in the same sense that there is a market for beans. Taxes are collected by law, and allocations are made by the appropriate public decision-making body. This theme is elaborated in Chapters 26 and 27.

[4]Equilibrium of the system is a new concept. It refers to equilibrium among households, firms, and governments. This kind of equilibrium is the subject of the next section of the book (Chapters 5–16).

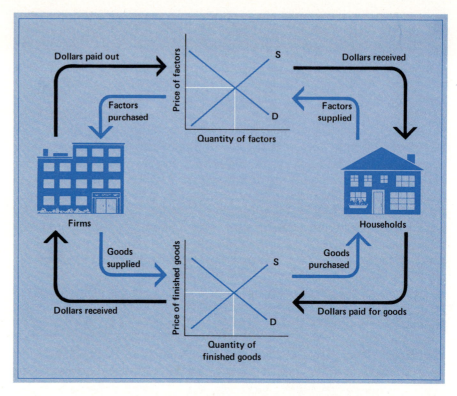

Figure 4–10 The Circular Flow, Factor Markets, Product Markets, and Equilibrium

planning. If, however, sudden large-scale changes occur in either the factor or the product market, the flow of funds from one actor to another may be badly distorted, causing severe disruption of economic activity. A sudden drop in demand—for whatever reason—may reduce the flow of monies from households to firms to, say, $75 million. Firms that have paid out $100 million to purchase factors and receive only $75 million in return are likely to respond by reducing their demand for factors. Such an action would lead to serious reductions in the amount of money available to households for the purchase of finished goods and services. Similarly, firms may rapidly increase purchases of factors, giving households more purchasing power, only to find that they cannot produce goods fast enough to keep up with the increase in demand. As a result, prices of goods already on the market would rise and the economy would experience *inflation.*

Inflation is a condition characterized by general rises in prices of most commodities. Inflation is dreaded by economists and by consumers because prices rise at different rates. Thus, some groups are hurt more than others.

In either situation—or in any of a dozen more—the market economy is placed in a very precarious position. The firms depend on the households and the households depend on the firms. As long as changes are modest, the system is accommodating and resilient—it can respond. Once the changes become too large, however, the system shudders and threatens to break. More than once in its 200-year history, the basic economic structure of the United States has threatened to collapse. Such periods include the years immediately following the Civil War, the closing years of the nineteenth century, and the Great Depression of the 1930s.

In sum, the decentralized characteristic of a market economy is at once its genius, its strength, and its weakness. The genius lies in the automatic way in which markets signal buyers and sellers regarding shortages and surpluses. Through these signals, resources are reallocated and products reselected, so that buyers can purchase what they want and sellers can produce what is profitable. The strength lies in the specialization that permits tremendous increases in output. The weakness is in the fragile interdependence between buyers and sellers that

In the Beginning There Was Adam Smith

"[If all other] systems . . . are taken away, the obvious and simple system of natural liberty establishes itself of its own accord. Every man, as long as he does not violate the laws of justice, is left perfectly free to pursue his own interest his own way, and to bring both his industry and capital into competition with those of any other man. . . ."

The writer was Adam Smith; the year, 1776. Adam Smith is universally acknowledged as the founder of modern Western economics. Born in Scotland in 1723, he had the "standard" education of the well-to-do of his era. He chose to specialize in understanding why some nations were rich and others were poor. After many years of study and ten years of writing, he published *An Inquiry into the Nature and Causes of the Wealth of Nations*. The book was encyclopedic; it drew together the best thinking of a century of economists, then presented its major message: A society of individuals motivated by their own self-interests will automatically arrange itself in such a way as to maximize the well-being of its citizens.

With this as a major theme, Adam Smith wrote at length on specialization, trade, the division of labor, the cause (source) of value, capital, savings, and scores of other themes that still dominate economics.

Adam Smith was a champion of the free, unregulated market, but he was not, as many of his followers seem to suggest, antigovernment. He saw government playing an important role in providing a framework of rules for the conduct of trade and in providing many facilities, such as highways, bridges, communication lines, and accurate scales, that facilitate trading. His main cause was economic growth, and he set a handsome stage for the generations of economists that followed him.

comes with specialization. If one party changes its behavior, the other parties must change their behavior too. When buyers do not buy enough, sellers must make drastic adjustment; when sellers do not provide enough, buyers must make drastic adjustment.

Adam Smith, the earliest modern economist, wrote very freely about the virtues of market-oriented economies. He described all the characteristics—specialization, exchange, interdependence—that have been focal points and problem areas in this chapter. Smith summarized the market economy as one depending on an "invisible hand"—the combined forces of supply and demand. The main message of this chapter has been that the invisible hand is at work in the mixed market economy of the United States. Even though this is true, many uncertainties continually arise. These uncertainties cause a very fragile and precarious relationship to exist between buyers and sellers, which might lead one to speculate that an industrial market economy is guided by an unsure, rather than an unseen, hand.

Summary

1 All societies must choose what to produce, how to produce it, and for whom to produce it. The U.S. economy uses a market system to answer these questions. When the market works well, each household uses its income to purchase those things that will maximize its satisfactions.

2 The market is an automatic mechanism that brings buyers into contact with sellers.

3 The U.S. economy is a mixed economy because some decisions are made through nonmarket channels—custom and government, for example.

4 Demand is one of the two major forces in a market. It is the combined desire and purchasing power of buyers. The other major force is supply, the response of producers.

5 The forces of demand and supply join to form an equilibrium price. The equilibrium price is the single price that leaves both buyers and sellers satisfied.

6 The relationship between buyers and sellers is the same as that between firms and households. One group cannot act without affecting the other. Thus, the relationship between actors in an economic system is a precarious one.

Exercises

1 Explain these important terms and concepts:

    the market   law of supply and demand
    market economy   surpluses
    consumer sovereignty   shortages
    market defects   equilibrium
    mixed economy   equilibrium in the system
    demand   movement along a curve

    market capitalism   shift in a demand or supply curve
    supply   inflation

2 Why is the U.S. economy sometimes referred to as a "mixed economy?" What things are being mixed? As the decade of the 1970s comes to a close, do you think that a mixed economy is a good idea? Better than an economy that depends only on markets or only on governments?

3 In rough terms, the market helps to answer the questions, What will be produced? How will it be produced? For whom will it be produced? How does the market go about answering these questions?

4 Given this price and quantity-purchased information, draw a demand curve for beefsteak:

Price per pound	Pounds purchased per week
$10.00	0.0
7.50	1.0
5.00	2.0
2.50	4.0
2.00	5.0
1.50	7.5
1.00	9.5
.50	11.0

5 How would the location of the demand curve in question 3 change if
    a family income doubled?
    b the price of chicken dropped to one-third its present level?
    c the U.S. Department of Health, Education, and Welfare discovered that eating large quantities of beef increases the amount of cholesterol in the human body?

6 Here are data on a firm's response to increases in the price of the good it manufactures. Draw a supply curve for this firm.

Price per unit	Quantities made available
$ 5.00	1,000
6.00	5,000
7.00	8,500
8.00	10,500
9.00	12,000
10.00	13,000

7 What will happen to the supply curve in question 5 if
    a a new technology allows costs to be cut in half?
    b the cost of labor doubles?

8 A producer of phonograph records finds that in December 1976 he can sell as many records at $4.95 each as he could in December 1975 at $3.95 each. What has happened to the demand curve?

9 Retailers know that the price of electric irons has remained quite stable for several years. They also know that the arrival of permanent-press fabrics has changed the demand curve, and changes in costs borne by manufacturers has shifted supply. If both demand and supply have shifted, how can prices remain the same? (Hint: there is no trick here. Draw the price/quantity quadrant, put in a horizontal line to designate a stable price, then show how demand and supply could both shift.)

A Contemporary Problem
Another View of Market Capitalism

Karl Polanyi was long a critic of the market mechanism. The following excerpt comes from an article appearing in *Commentary* in 1947. Even though the article was written thirty years ago, its message is still important, and it provides a worthwhile perspective on the market system in the United States.

The first phase of the Machine Age has run its course. It involved an organization of society that derived its name from its central institution, *the market.* This system is on the downgrade. Yet our practical philosophy was overwhelmingly shaped by this spectacular episode. Novel notions about man and society became current and gained the status of axioms. Here they are.

As regards *man,* we were made to accept the heresy that his motives can be described as "material" and "ideal," and that the incentives on which everyday life is organized spring from the "material" motives. Both utilitarian liberalism and popular Marxism favored such views.

As regards *society,* the kindred doctrine was propounded that its institutions were "determined" by the economic system. This opinion was even more popular with Marxists than with liberals.

Under a market-economy both assertions were, of course, true. *But only under such an economy.* To overcome such doctrines, which constrict our minds and souls and greatly enhance the difficulty of the life-saving adjustment, may require no less than a reform of our consciousness.

[The free market] economy, this primary reaction of man to the machine, was a violent break with the conditions that preceded it. A chain-reaction was started —what before was merely isolated markets was transmuted into a self-regulating *system* of markets. And with the new economy, a new society sprang into being. The crucial step was this: labor and land were made into commodities, that is, they were treated *as if* produced for sale. Of course, they were not actually commodities, since they were either not produced at all (as land) or, if so, not for sale (as labor). Yet no more thoroughly effective fiction was ever devised. By buying and selling labor and land freely, the mechanism of the market was made to apply to them. There was now supply of labor, and demand for it; there was supply of land, and demand for it. Accordingly, there was a market price for the use of labor power, called wages, and a market price for the use of land, called rent. Labor and land were provided with markets of their own, similar to the commodities proper that were produced with their help. The true scope of such a step can be gauged if we remember that labor is only another name for man, and land for nature. The commodity fiction handed over the fate of man and nature to the play of an automaton running in its own grooves and governed by its own laws.

Nothing similar had ever been witnessed before. Under the mercantile regime, though it deliberately pressed for the creation of markets, the converse principle still operated. Labor and land were not entrusted to the market; they formed part of the *organic structure* of society. Where land was marketable, only the determination of price was, as a rule, left to the parties; where labor was subject to contract, wages themselves were usually assessed by public authority. Land stood under the custom of manor, monastery, and township, under common-law limitations concerning rights of real property; labor was regulated by laws against beggary and vagrancy, statutes of laborers and artificers, poor laws, guild and municipal ordinances. In effect, all societies known to anthropologists and historians restricted markets to commodities in the proper sense of the term.

Market-economy thus created a new type of society. The economic or productive system was here entrusted to a self-acting device. An institutional mechanism controlled human beings in their everyday activities as well as the resources of nature. This instrument of material welfare was under the sole control of the incentives of hunger and gain—, or, more precisely, fear of going without the necessities of life, and expectation of profit. So long as no propertyless person could satisfy his craving for food without first selling his labor in the market, and so long as no propertied person was prevented from buying in the cheapest market and selling in the dearest, the blind mill would turn out ever-increasing amounts of commodities for the benefit of the human race. Fear of starvation with the worker, lure of profit with the employer, would keep the vast establishment running.[5]

The world of the late 1970s is quite different from that of 1947. The important question is, Does Polanyi's argument still apply? If the answer is affirmative, what is it that Polanyi dislikes? Can his argument be restated in terms of "dehumanization," "indifference," or "exploitation"? With these objections in mind, what arguments can be marshalled *in favor of* a market system? Do the words *automatic and efficient* provide clues?

---

[5]"Our Obsolete Market Mentality," *Commentary* 3 (1947) 109–17. A modern treatment of the same theme can be found in E. F. Schumacher, *Small Is Beautiful: Economics as if People Mattered* (New York: Harper & Row, 1973). An opposing view, and a more erudite one, is Friedrich von Hayek, *The Road to Serfdom* (Chicago: University of Chicago Press, 1944).

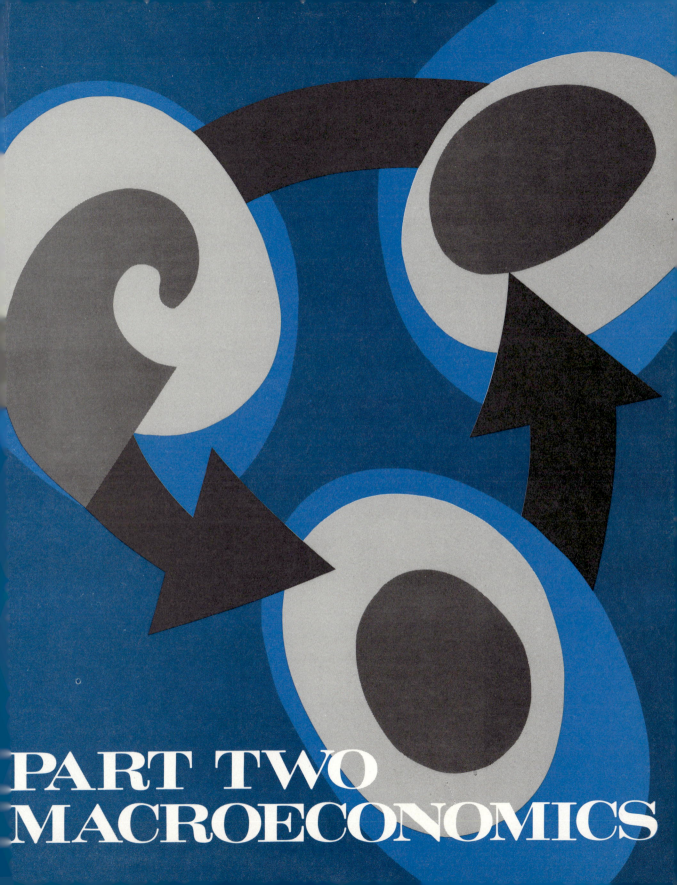

5 The Economics of a System

In 1787, the framers of the U.S. Constitution wrote a document intended to guarantee certain freedoms to citizens of the young nation. In their zeal to allow citizens as much freedom as possible, participants in the Constitutional Convention were explicit in permitting a number of activities forbidden in other countries. Later, interpreters of the Constitution were forced to limit some of these freedoms. In general, the citizens of the United States may enjoy their many freedoms only if in pursuing them they do not infringe upon the rights and freedoms of others.

The Constitution is not strictly an economic document, but it does have many economic consequences and implications. It is interesting to compare individual freedom as guaranteed by the Constitution and economic freedom as suggested by Adam Smith's recommended policy of *laissez faire*.

Laissez faire is a French phrase meaning literally "let them do." Adam Smith used the term to describe a self-regulating, market-oriented economy operating without interference from government.

When freedom to bear arms results in too many deaths in the neighborhood, the right to bear arms must be curtailed. The same is true of economic freedom. In general, participants in the capitalistic economies of the Western world are free to conduct economic affairs with little threat of interference. When, on occasion, the economic behavior of one person, firm, or group inhibits or drastically diminishes the economic capabilities of another person, firm, or group, government has the power and the obligation to intercede on behalf of the injured party. More than this, the nation's central government is responsible for maintaining a generally healthy economic atmosphere in which individuals can—to a large degree—realize their potentials as producers and consumers. Government has the power to carry out many activities in order to maintain this atmosphere. At any one moment, however, very few of these powers are likely to be in use. Like the national defense mechanism, the economic powers of government are intended to be available but used only when needed.

Early chapters of this book concentrated on circularity and interdependence within the economic system. Part Two describes the obligations of government with respect to these themes. Government is responsible for maintaining the circular flow of economic activity—expanding it when necessary, contracting it when necessary. Government also has vast responsibility in adjusting for interdependencies—helping disadvantaged groups, maintaining high levels of employment, keeping prices stable, insuring economic growth, and solving questions of *equity*.

Equity has two major meanings in economics. One has to do with ownership—a shareholder has a certain equity in a company. The second meaning is older and is related to fairness or equal treatment—an equitable wage is a fair and just wage.

It is the second meaning that is used here.

The chapters in Part Two deal with macroeconomics. The prefix *macro* is used to indicate that the study concentrates on large units. The output demanded by the whole society, the indebtedness of the entire nation, and the percentage of the whole labor force that is employed or unemployed are all attributes of the macroeconomy. The behavior of single individuals and of single firms will not be far from the surface, but the emphasis will be on studying collective behavior.

Studying the macrosystem is very different from analyzing individual firms, commodities, or consumers. Interdependencies and circularities in the macroeconomic system are strong enough to give the system a force of its own. Just as very large masses—especially large celestial bodies—acquire gravitational pulls all their own, so the economic system, once millions of individual elements are intertwined in it, acquires a force and an action of its own. This system and its force must be understood because it provides the framework for all forms of economic activity. It provides the institutional factors—laws, regulations, habits, money, and information—needed for orderly production and exchange. If the

Microeconomics Defined

Although the study of microeconomics is delayed until Chapter 17, it needs definition so that its focus can be distinguished from that of macroeconomics. Microeconomics, or simply "micro," is the study of individual decision-making units. Micro inquires into how a firm or a household decides to buy or sell. Micro places great emphasis on logic and on the process of choice making. It shows how firms or households respond to change and, in turn, how they accomplish change. In this book, macroeconomics is studied first because the macroeconomy provides the framework within which micro units carry out their economic activities.

macrosystem fails, the individual (micro) components of the market economy will not be able to function effectively. The task of macroeconomics is to study the performance of an economic system and to make policy recommendations aimed at promoting advantageous microeconomic behavior in the system.

Appropriate Goals for an Economy

How is "desirable performance" of the macroeconomy to be recognized? The U.S. government does not have explicit goals for its economy. Citizens, politicians, planners, and policy makers have a number of expectations or implicit goals in mind but attach different weights to them, making it difficult or impossible to describe "the goals" of the U.S. economy. Many people will agree to five commonly held expectations for the economy. These are full employment, price stability, economic growth, environmental protection, and increased well-being for individual citizens.

Full Employment

In a strict sense, full employment would mean that 100 percent of the labor force is employed, that everyone who wants to work is working. In practice, a highly developed economy cannot ever attain this goal because people are constantly "unemployed" as they move from job to job or because of health problems, and because changing technology forces some jobs to close while others open. In recent years, economists

"What's unemployment?"

have reasoned that the U.S. economy is performing well whenever unemployment drops below 4 percent of the civilian labor force.[1]

The government of the United States is required to maintain maximum employment. This requirement was made law in 1946 when the Employment Act was passed by a Congress that did not want the nation to experience a post–World War II depression similar to the one experienced after World War I. The act made it the responsibility of the federal government to ". . . promote maximum employment, production and purchasing power." The difference between maximum employment and full employment has never been made clear, but they probably have nearly the same meaning to most interpreters. The difference between *promoting* and *insuring* full employment is equally vague. In spite of its occasional obscurity, most observers take the act to be a specific instruction that the federal government take major responsibility to eliminate unemployment.

[1]The definition of unemployment is sometimes further refined by calling one kind of unemployment *frictional,* another kind *structural.* Frictional unemployment is caused by individual workers changing jobs because of layoffs, personal reasons, or the magnetic force of a more attractive job offer. Structural unemployment is more serious. It results from drastic changes in the make-up of society, the relocation of industry, and the uneven advance of technology. The invention of the mechanical cotton picker caused structural unemployment for millions who had previously found work harvesting this valuable crop. The slowdown in space contracts caused severe structural unemployment in the Pacific Northwest and in the Los Angeles area in the early 1970s.

Even though government is required by law to become directly involved in maintaining full employment, the record of its effectiveness is far from perfect. Figure 5–1 shows unemployment as a percent of the labor force in each year since 1950. The faint horizontal line at 4 percent shows a level of unemployment that would be "acceptable" to most economists. In 1954, the nation had a spectacular record with only 2.9 percent of the labor force out of work. A year later, after defense spending for the Korean War had been lowered, the record was poor—5.5 percent of the labor force was unemployed. The high for the two and one-half decades was reached in early 1975, when more than 9.1 percent were unemployed—hardly a notable record for a nation consciously attempting to keep its labor force working. The magnitude of unemployment is, however, only one aspect of the problem. In the twenty-five-year period shown on the graph, unemployment rose 10 times and fell 14 times. The rises were most often quite sharp, and the behavior of the whole series is extremely erratic. The battle against unemployment may have been joined but it is far from won. If the nation is to meet its legal and moral responsibility to keep people employed, it will have to find more effective ways of adjusting the performance of the macroeconomy. Methods of dealing with this problem will be a recurrent theme in the following chapters.

Figure 5–1 Unemployment as a Percentage of the Civilian Labor Force, 1950–1975

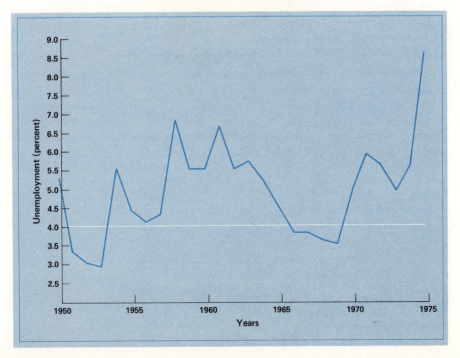

Source: *Economic Report of the President*

Price Stability

The record in maintaining price stability—a second economic objective of society—is even less attractive than the employment record. Consumer prices increased by more than 90 percent between 1950 and 1975. As this is being written, the newspapers are filled with articles about rising prices—chicken prices up by 10 percent in a year; beef up by 6 percent in a month; rent up by 18 percent in a decade; and natural gas up by as much as 73 percent, if certain gas-producing and delivery firms are granted their requests. Prices of all retail commodities increased by an average of 12.2 percent in 1974.

Increasing prices have been the rule for many years in the United States. As long as prices rose gradually no one seemed to notice, but when sharp increases began to occur, individuals and groups began to raise questions about whether or not direct government interference should be used to control price levels. The desire to limit price increases stems from two important and visible problems:

1. Rising prices erode the purchasing power of money. In a time of rising prices, people get less for their money, as each dollar buys fewer things.
2. More important, rising prices have demonstrably different effects on different people, depending on whether their incomes change with the *cost of living*.

Cost of living is a summary term used to describe changes in the total cost of goods and services a representative household will consume in a year's time. Changes in the cost of living are often measured by the Consumer Price Index—a single number that compares consumer prices in one year with prices paid by consumers in previous years. A rise in the index means prices are higher than before; a drop means they are lower. The CPI is kept up to date and published at frequent intervals by the Bureau of Labor Statistics—a part of the U.S. Department of Labor.

Some people earn wages that are very responsive to price changes. When the cost of living goes up by 10 percent, a clause in their wage contract insures that their wages will go up by 10 percent, too. Such wage earners are not burdened by increasing prices because their purchasing power is not eroded. Another group of people—those who are salaried or who work under wage contracts negotiated at infrequent intervals—are adversely affected by rising prices. Many families with little or no economic or political power have fixed incomes and lose purchasing power during periods of rising prices. Pensioners, for example, are on fixed incomes and most often cannot find any supplemental sources of income. Welfare recipients receive fixed amounts and cannot alter their earnings. Employees of state and county governments are

"The way prices are rising, I'd say our salaries are now only 120 years ahead of the cost of living."

often working within pay scales that are adjusted infrequently. These groups and many others are particularly vulnerable during periods of rising prices, since the purchasing power of their fixed incomes erodes.

Families living on their accumulated savings are also adversely affected by a rise in prices. During periods when prices are rising, the purchasing power of money in savings accounts declines. If inflation is rapid, a dollar that could have purchased five loaves of bread when it was saved may buy only two when it is taken out of savings a few months or years later. Inflation thus has an insidious, two-pronged effect on those who have low and unchangeable incomes. It diminishes the purchasing power of current income, and it reduces the value of earnings that may have been kept for years in a safe deposit box or in a savings account.

Periods of dropping prices have the opposite effect. Those with fixed incomes now benefit, since their fixed incomes buy more goods than formerly, whereas those on incomes tied to the cost of living find their wages dropping along with prices. Their purchasing power is maintained but not increased by the price decrease. This question of relative gains associated with general price decreases seems somewhat academic, however, since there has not been a general drop in prices in the United States for over forty years.

Although there is no overall legislation similar to the Employment Act giving the federal government responsibility to insure price stability, such action has long been recognized as a primary objective of economic policy. In times of emergency, there has been little hesitation on the part of government in intervening to stabilize prices. Unfortunately, govern-

"Times of Emergency"

When the federal government makes a conscious effort to control prices, the controls are most often carried out by a special board or agency created in response to conditions that might arise in the following manner:

1. A major international conflict requires complete mobilization of the nation's industrial capacity for military purposes.
2. Mobilization to produce war materials provides employment for everyone—men and women, low- and high-skilled persons. The tremendous increase in employment creates new purchasing power and increases the demand for consumer goods and services.
3. The shift to production of war goods, however, requires reducing the output of ordinary consumer goods. Although the consuming public has more money to spend, fewer goods are available for them to purchase. So consumers bid against each other for the privilege of buying the limited quantities of goods. Prices of available consumer goods rise rather sharply—the law of supply and demand in operation.
4. Government responds to this undesirable and somewhat artificial increase in prices by creating an agency to regulate prices. Federal efforts of this kind have included the creation of price administering agencies like the Office of Price Administration (1941–1946) and the Office of Price Stabilization (1950–1953), and, more recently, a series of "price boards" and "pay boards" created by President Richard M. Nixon in the early 1970s.

---

ment bodies involved in regulating prices often have no guidelines to use other than, simply, "stop the increase." They cannot make effective adjustments in *relative prices* so that prices of one group of commodities maintain a reasonable relationship to prices of other groups of commodities. And if the correct price relationships cannot be maintained, the market will not necessarily be efficient when it signals resources out of one activity and into another. The price-setting board or agency must perform all the functions of a market in a deliberate rather than an automatic way. Mistakes are bound to happen. Price setting is at times a necessary part of government activity, but it is highly controversial and difficult to accomplish.

Economic Growth

Not too many years ago, the goal of economic growth was easily defined.[2] It meant a higher output of goods and services, or perhaps an increase in the variety of things being produced. More food meant fewer hungry people; more automobiles meant a more mobile public; more

---

[2]Today, if 200 economists were asked what they meant by economic growth, 200 different definitions would emerge. Some would be complex and would relate to the cause of growth or to the result of growth. Others would build only on the number of things available for

movies meant escape for the populace from workaday routines. In point of fact, more of almost anything yielded a happier and healthier economy.

In recent years, the definition of growth has been questioned by most economists and citizens. Two major forces have caused this questioning. On one hand there is the question of distributing the fruits of economic growth. Growth for whom? Should the economy produce more to satisy the insatiable demands of the wealthy for conspicuous goods, or should the nation redirect its productive efforts so that the poor, the elderly, and the disfranchised can have more of the necessities of life? On the other hand, there is the very difficult problem of the environmental costs of growth. Processes that produce basically good things—frozen pies, radial tires, permanent-press shirts, and electricity—leave appallingly bad things in their wake—pollution, smoke, slag, noise. This tradeoff between growth and pollution makes it more difficult to assess the desirability of growth and has caused many economists to shrink from once well-established societal goals. While growth remains an important goal, then, and all economists, politicians, and political scientists must acknowledge it, reasonable people may disagree about what constitutes growth and how it should be achieved. This problem will be addressed briefly in the next section and in some detail in Chapters 26 and 27.

Environmental Protection

With growing concern for the environment and growing public realization that no single firm can be expected to clean up its own mess consistently and unilaterally, various government agencies have taken responsibility for environmental protection. There is, however, no general agreement on the attributes of an environmentally and ecologically sound society. Moreover, protection of the environment is often at odds with efforts to achieve economic growth. The public is unsure about how much quality should be sacrificed for how much growth.

To be sure, maintenance of the environment is not a strictly economic goal of society. However, environmental protection has so many effects on economic behavior that it must be treated along with the more explicit economic objectives such as full employment and stable prices. The formal environmental impact statements that must now accompany any industrial development in natural areas bear testimony to government's intention to make environmental quality a part of the framework within which economic activity is conducted. If economic activity is expanded, the public must be sure it knows in advance of any environmental degradation that will likely result.

---

each person to enjoy. Older definitions centered on output, however measured, per capita. More recent criteria include the range of choice or the qualitative aspects of the collected goods. The only point of agreement is that economic growth has to mean *more* of something.

Increased Well-being

No one will argue against the view that increased well-being is a commendable goal for an economy but, as in the case of environmental quality, there is no widely accepted definition of well-being. Interest in the general well-being of a society can be traced to Jeremy Bentham, a British Humanist of the late eighteenth century. Bentham's view was that society should seek the greatest good for the greatest number. On the surface this may sound like a laudable prescription. It is not, however, an operational concept, since no one can effectively define the greatest good and no one knows who is included in the greatest number!

In spite of the difficulties surrounding the idea, increasing the general well-being has become an informal economic objective of contemporary U.S. society. Many policies undertaken to achieve the greatest possible good have noticeable economic consequences. Mandatory education for all children is not an economic policy, but it has economic consequences in the cost to the public of building and operating schools and in the greater productivity of high school and college graduates. Welfare programs (Social Security, Aid to Families with Dependent Children, and Aid to the Blind, to name but a few) are intended to promote the greatest good. The policies they represent are not economic policies, but they have the economic consequence of requiring money to be taxed from some people and transferred to others. Such programs redistribute income and purchasing power.

A Very Fine Line

Conscientiously trying to sort every government program into its appropriate micro or macro box would be a futile and unrewarding task. Is an education program macro because through it the government places $10.8 billion in the hands of its citizens? Or is it micro because the decisions about how the money is used are made by individuals or local school boards? Is the space program macro because it redirects $3.2 billion through the whole economy? Or is it micro because colleges, research institutes, and private firms use the money to purchase factors and produce products? In each case, the answer is, It is some of both.

In general, if the purpose of a program is to affect the economy's total spending or its level of prices or its rate of unemployment, that program is a macro program. Thus, when Congress decides to spend $275 billion, it is making a macro decision. When the $275 billion is divided among many purposes—highways, welfare, space, education, and the like—numerous micro decisions result.

These five objectives—full employment, price stability, economic growth, environmental protection, and increased well-being—are major goals of various levels of government in the United States. Knowing these objectives helps to show why it is necessary for government periodically to become directly involved in economic affairs.

Methods of Goal Attainment

When a government deems it essential to intervene in its country's economic affairs, it has two main tools at its disposal. It can attempt to alter *aggregate demand,* or it can impose regulations.

Aggregate demand refers to the total quantity of all goods and services demanded and purchased by an entire economy in a given period of time. Since aggregate demand includes literally thousands of goods and services—tin cups, lawn mowers, encyclopedias, trip hammers, and gas-filled balloons—the only reasonable way to express it is in dollar terms. Aggregate demand in the United States in the mid-1970s was more than $1 trillion annually.

Aggregate demand can be altered by using the taxing and spending powers of government or by changing the amount of money available in a society. The first of these is called *fiscal policy;* the second is *monetary policy.* There is no question that fiscal policy is a policy of and by the government. State, local, and federal governments levy taxes and arrange spending programs. In so doing, they change the extent, quality, and distribution of economic activity. Monetary policy is not so distinctly a property of government. Many public and private agencies, boards, commissions, and administrative offices have an influence on monetary policy. The links between monetary authorities and government are quite visible, but monetary authorities—those who manage the Federal Reserve Bank and those who are appointed to superintend the U.S. Treasury—do not always have to clear each aspect of their behavior with the legislative and executive branches of government or even with other authorities responsible for monitoring the quantity of money. Because of this, monetary policy is not wholly controlled by elected officials. Monetary policy is, however, a conscious policy. It can be described as selective private policy conducted within a close web of government supervision. Monetary and fiscal policy will be introduced briefly in the remainder of this chapter, and elaborated on in Chapters 6–14.

Direct regulation of the economy is used to make either very severe changes or very minor changes that the market system will not effect by itself. Thus, regulations may be used to prevent runaway inflation—a severe imposition on the market system—or to prevent hunters from killing the last of the mountain lions that roam the Plains and Western states—an almost insignificant imposition on the market. Several types of direct regulation will be mentioned in this chapter. Because they are so diverse, they will be elaborated on at various places in the book.

Altering Aggregate Demand

Fiscal policy. Fiscal policy is a deliberate attempt to influence the behavior of the macroeconomy through the use of taxing and spending programs. The support of public schools is a large taxing and spending item in most county and local budgets. Local cemetery districts levy taxes and make decisions about spending money on fences, lawns, and upkeep. These decisions are deliberate choices about taxing and spending and might appear to be fiscal policy. Neither is fiscal policy, however, since neither has the express intention of changing the level of *macroeconomic* variables like the rate of inflation or the level of unemployment. Deliberate fiscal policy is the domain of the federal government.

The fiscal activities and policies of the federal government are neither automatic (like local school budgets) nor insignificant (like cemetery districts). The federal government now has a budget of about $280 billion per year. By making choices about whom to tax and where to spend, the federal government can have a pronounced effect on economic activity.

Fiscal policy of the federal government can speed, slow, or redirect economic activities in the U.S. macroeconomy. An economy experiencing high levels of unemployment might seek to expand economic activity—and, hence, employment—by increasing government expenditures. This increase in spending would increase purchases made from firms, which would in turn increase purchases of factors from individual households. When the federal government decides to construct a commercial supersonic transport, it places money in the hands of two or three large aircraft companies. They in turn hire workers, buy material, and rent land. The accumulation of thousands of such activities (building highways, putting men on the moon, cleaning up Yellowstone National Park, planting trees in strip-mined areas, and the like) puts people to work and eventually relieves the unemployment problem.

A similar effect can be achieved by lowering taxes. This leaves more purchasing power in the hands of households which, in all likelihood, will spend most of this "added income" on consumer goods. Their expenditures encourage firms to increase output, and in doing so, firms are forced to employ more factors. Hence, the tax reduction ameliorates the unemployment problem.

A government in the midst of inflation can use fiscal policy as a means of mitigating rapid price increases. The remedy for inflation is to slow, rather than to speed, economic activity. Fiscal authorities therefore attempt to take purchasing power away from households and to persuade businesses not to make any added expenditures. In this way, pressures on demand are eased and prices are not bid up so rapidly. Contractionary fiscal policy is quite simple in principle: Take money away from people! The difficult question is how much to take from whom.

Unfortunately, economic life is never simple or well behaved. Because this is so, simple and well-behaved fiscal policies cannot easily be designed and carried out. In the 1970s it has been quite common for general inflation to appear simultaneously with socially unacceptable levels of unemployment. This sounds contradictory and, indeed, it is hard to explain. But that does not reduce government's responsibility to act. It does require that the tools of fiscal policy be used with care, because any successful effort to combat inflation is likely to aggravate the unemployment problem. To combat inflation, purchasing power and demand must be reduced, yet reducing purchasing power and demand increases unemployment. Authorities responsible for managing a modern economy indeed walk a tightrope.

Monetary policy. The second major means available to alter aggregate demand is by expanding or contracting the money supply. Policy that accomplishes this is called *monetary policy.*

Monetary policy is conscious policy of government and/or banking authorities to alter the supply of money, the availability of loanable funds, or interest rates.

The supply of money in the U.S. economy is not controlled by a group of men making arbitrary choices about who is to be given money and who is not. The money supply changes in response to changes in the policies of the nation's commercial banks, the Federal Reserve System, and the federal Treasury. It also responds to pressures from the executive and legislative branches of government. Regardless of who is responsible for the policy, when the money supply is expanded, business activity speeds, because more money is available to course through the circular flow. When the supply of money is reduced, economic activity slows, since fewer dollars are then available to be spent on goods and services.

A notable characteristic of monetary policy is its essentially voluntary characteristic. The banking system can make money easy to obtain, but if no one wishes to obtain it the effort is futile. Similarly, the banking system can make money very difficult to obtain, and still some households and some firms will pay dearly to obtain it. While fiscal authorities must constantly take care not to do either too little or too much, monetary authorities face the possibility that no one will heed their efforts to control macroeconomic activity. They can offer a change, but there is no assurance that society will respond.

Direct Regulation

Because of possible inadequacies in fiscal and/or monetary policy, more selective measures are occasionally used to direct the movement of the economy. These measures may include, for example, price controls, to cool a steaming economy, or rationing, to allocate a particularly scarce resource. Selective measures may also encourage economic activity. A *subsidy* may be paid to an industry or to a firm; and toll roads may give special rates to cars with more than one or two passengers.

A subsidy is a form of financial assistance used to encourage production that otherwise would not occur because it is basically unprofitable. For years subsidies have been paid to airlines to insure that air transport would be available to smaller cities. Transportation, communication, defense-related and food-producing industries have been major recipients of government subsidies.

An economy that is experiencing rapid increases in prices but at the same time has high rates of unemployment among minority groups and young people might develop a selective training and education program aimed at those two groups and at the same time impose price controls on consumer goods. This is roughly what occurred in 1971 and 1972 when President Nixon imposed the Phase I, Phase II, and Phase III economic policies, the most recent attempts to use direct regulation.

As the economy itself becomes more complex, efforts needed to control the macroeconomy must also increase in complexity. In earlier years, macroeconomic policy could be a broad—even blunt—attack on a few of the economy's diseases. Now it must be sharpened. It must become more incisive in order to maintain a stable structure in which private markets can perform their allocative functions.

"This place is all right. Two more weeks, and I'll be a molecular biochemist."

Limitations on Monetary and Fiscal Policy

In Chapter 3 it was pointed out that "Government spending" included expenditures made by all levels of government. However, the range of governments significantly involved in fiscal and monetary policies is much narrower. In the United States, only the federal government has a central banking and monetary system. Individual states are forbidden from engaging in efforts to expand or contract the supply of money and from attempting to alter interest rates charged on loanable funds. Therefore, no state can have a monetary policy. Certainly state and local areas have "fiscal policies," since they all engage in taxing and spending. The fiscal activities of state and local governments are, however, limited in scope. No state can expect to influence the pattern of economic activity in the nation as a whole, and it is unlikely that at one time all 50 states could be convinced to follow a pattern of fiscal activities that would be consistent with some single national economic goal. Managing the economy at the macro level is a federal responsibility that cannot be taken over by smaller units of government.

Even within the federal government there is a dispersion of responsibility that sometimes leads to confusion and even to contradictory policies. Monetary and fiscal activities are controlled and conducted by separate parts of the federal government. Monetary policy is controlled by the central bank—the Federal Reserve System—which in turn is responsible to a board made up of members appointed by the President. However, the board has no direct obligation to behave in any way dictated by the President or any other elected officials.

In most cases, fiscal activities originate in the executive branch of government but must be approved by the legislative branch. Some checks and balances are exerted by the two branches interacting with each other, but generally they argue about how much to spend (or not spend) rather than about whether or not a particular function should be performed at all.

The checks-and-balances system is a necessary part of a democratic society, but the time consumed in deliberation often weakens the capacity of macroeconomic policy to correct specific problems associated with maintaining a suitable climate for other, private, economic activity. In a 1973 speech Secretary of the Treasury George P. Shultz said

Economic policy issues seldom present themselves to the policy maker in disembodied terms. If they did, economic policy would be handled by statisticians and computer experts—no doubt for the lasting benefit of all. Rather, those issues are served up to the policy maker by a variety of political and economic forces outside his direct control. In addition, the time horizon for resolving a policy issue is usually short: an economist's "lag" may be a politician's catastrophe.[3]

[3]George P. Shultz, "Reflections on Political Economy," *Challenge* (March/April 1974): 6.

Summary

1. A modern industrial economy requires strong support and frequent regulation from government authorities.
2. An economic society may have several goals that are clearly economic—full employment, price stability, and growth—and some goals that are not strictly economic but have profound effects on the economy—environmental quality and increased well-being.
3. In order to achieve these goals, a society may choose to use fiscal, monetary, or direct regulatory policies. Fiscal policy operates to alter characteristics of the circular flow by rearranging tax and spending activities. Monetary policies seek to alter aggregate demand by changing the quantity of money available for use. Direct economic controls make rules about how economic behavior is to be conducted.

Exercises

1. Explain these important terms and concepts:
   - laissez faire
   - equity
   - macroeconomics
   - microeconomics
   - full employment
   - cost of living
   - economic growth
   - aggregate demand
   - fiscal policy
   - monetary policy
   - subsidy
   - direct regulation

2. This chapter repeatedly makes the point that the federal government must act to maintain a stable economy in which private decisions can be made with assurance and ease. What is the government doing now to fulfill this obligation?

3. In what ways might the five stated economic objectives of the society conflict with one another? Does environmental protection conflict with economic growth? Does full employment conflict with price stability? Does increased well-being conflict with any of the others?

4. Monetary policy and fiscal policy are often used to cure national economic problems. What is the difference between the two? Who is responsible for each, and how does each affect the average person?

5. Many citizens are concerned about the size of government in the United States. This concern is seldom made explicit, so that "size" remains a vague concept. It could relate to the size of the federal budget, the number of people employed, or the range of activities performed. Some people argue that limits on size, however measured, should be imposed. Would such limits aid or hinder the conduct of monetary and fiscal policy? Which of the two would be more severely affected?

Inflation + Recession = Stagflation

Common sense says that when things are in surplus, their prices will fall. This rule should be applicable in factor markets as well as product markets. Historically, it has not been a bad rule. During recessions—

particularly the 1890s and the 1930s—factors have been unemployed and prices of factors have dropped, encouraging factor users to expand their purchases. The 1970s have brought another problem to the U.S. economy. There has been widespread unemployment (up to 9.1 percent of the labor force), but prices have continued to rise—sometimes at a rate exceeding 10 percent per year. The unemployment may be characteristic of *economic stagnation*—the condition of an economy that refuses to grow. The inflation may be the result of an on-again, off-again wartime economy or the result of increasing scarcity of some essential industrial inputs—especially those related to energy production. Regardless of cause, the result is a peculiar hybrid, *stagflation*.

Government officials are responsible for keeping the economy on the right track and for maintaining high levels of employment. They make decisions based on a tradeoff between inflation and unemployment. This tradeoff is described by a "Phillips curve" like the one shown below. (The Phillips curve is an important tool in macroeconomic analysis.) Although the placement and the slope of the solid curve in the figure are arbitrary, the curve shows that at high rates of inflation the rate of unemployment will be quite low. A 20 percent annual rise in prices will be accompanied by rates of unemployment that are below 2 percent of the labor force. This sounds reasonable. High rates of inflation mean a superactive economy and this intense activity means that all resources, human and non-human, can be easily employed. The lower right-hand end of the solid curve is equally reasonable: A low rate of price increase (or a price decrease) indicates a supercool economy in which very little is happening. Factors cannot find employment, so unemployment rates soar. The curve shows the tradeoff between them.

During the summer of 1975, the U.S. economy was operating at point

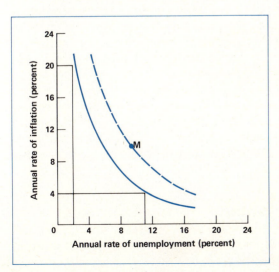

Hypothetical Phillips Curve

M—9.1 percent unemployment, 10 percent annual price rise. Policy makers assumed this point to be on a Phillips curve like the dotted one in the figure. Those authorities generally charged with stopping inflation were fearful that their actions would only exacerbate an already intolerable unemployment problem. Those officials concerned with alleviating unemployment were equally stymied because they knew their efforts could touch off added rounds of inflation.

In the end, all policy makers seemed to agree that unemployment was worse than inflation. President Ford suggested a government fiscal policy that would place much additional purchasing power in the hands of consumers. A tax refund gave each taxpaying family a minimum refund of $100 on its income tax, and interest rates on home mortgage loans began to be lowered. Both these actions were deemed necessary, but it was recognized that each could intensify inflation. Policy makers were responding to a Phillips curve.

It is quite possible that a large segment of the population thinks inflation is a more serious problem than unemployment. If this group had influence on policy, what measures might be taken? Via what mechanisms would these measures affect prices and unemployment?

6 National Income Accounting

In 1975, the U.S. economy performed the phenomenal feat of producing goods and services having an aggregate value of $1,499 billion. This was accomplished in response to market forces and without extensive planning by any central agency.[1] Even though production was carried out without a great deal of direct interference by government, productive activity was watched and carefully recorded by agencies within the U.S. Department of Commerce. These agencies—particularly the Bureau of Economic Analysis—have the responsibility of collecting data on the economy's performance and compiling them into the national income accounts. These accounts provide information needed to determine whether the economy is growing or standing still; whether it is investing too much or too little; whether employment levels are too high or too low. In short, these accounts are needed in order to keep track of and to understand the macroeconomy.

The Department of Commerce began collecting economic data in the 1930s. Since few changes have been made in the original data-collecting and processing methods, detailed records are now available to show

---

[1]This is not to deny that much planning went into the production effort—for indeed it did—but only to say that the planning was decentralized among households and firms. It was not done, or even extensively coordinated, by any government planning agency.

the performance of the U.S. economy over the last forty years.[2] This chapter will explain several measures of performance and show how they are interrelated, using actual data from the national income accounts. This will be done in major sections dealing with the accounts themselves, which are *empirical evidence* related to the economy's performance.

Empirical evidence is information based on fact or observation rather than on theory or speculation. Empirically, the wage rate earned by plumbers in Anchorage, Alaska, is $13.09 per hour. Theoretically, this rate should fall if more plumbers move to Anchorage.

Finally, we shall consider some limitations on the use of the national income accounts.

The Major Accounts

Five major series are included in the national income accounts. These include:

1. Gross national product (GNP)
2. Net national product (NNP)
3. National income (NI)
4. Personal income (PI)
5. Disposable (personal) income (DI or DPI)

In this chapter, the largest account, gross national product, is discussed first, followed by the others as they appear in the list. Starting with GNP, the total value of all society's output, this sequence shows what needs to be deducted to arrive at each of the other accounts in the list. The series ends with DI, the amount left in the hands of households to use as they wish.

It would be simple to talk about the income accounts if there were only one approach to measuring an economy's performance. There are, however, two approaches, each giving the same result. Both come directly from the circular flow illustrated in Chapter 3, where goods and services valued at some specific amount pass from firms to households, while factors of production with specific values pass from households to firms. These two flows are repeated in Figure 6–1. The bottom flow (from households to firms) represents payments going to the firms in return for their output. The top flow shows payments going from firms to households. Since households pay out income they have received from firms

---

[2]A specialist would complain about the oversimplification implied by this statement. In a strict sense, thousands of changes have been made in data-gathering and processing methods. The point here is that the *results*—the several major accounts—do form a reasonably consistent record spanning nearly forty years.

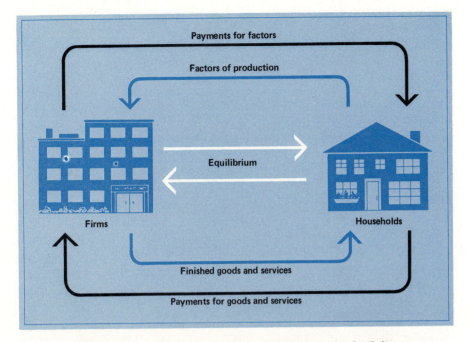

Figure 6-1   The Circular Flow of Economic Activity

and firms then pay out what has been received from households, the values of the two flows (top and bottom) are equal. Because they are equal, either flow can be used to measure the volume or value of economic activity. If the bottom flow is used, performance is measured by adding up the values of things that have been produced. This method of counting is called the *product approach* or the *expenditure approach*. If the top flow is studied, performance is measured by adding up the income earned by factors and the method is called the *income approach*. The product approach is usually easier to understand, so in discussing gross national product we shall begin with it.

Gross National Product

Gross national product (GNP) measures the money value of all final goods and services produced in an economy in one accounting period—usually a year.

The value of GNP is simply the price of beans times the quantity of beans plus the price of drill presses times the quantity of drill presses plus the price of haircuts times the quantity of haircuts . . . plus . . . plus . . ., until all final goods and services produced by the entire economy in one production period have been included.

> ### Another Convention
>
> Throughout the definitions of the national income accounts, the terms *year, production period,* and *accounting period* are frequently used. This raises a sometimes confusing point. Most people are comfortable talking about a calendar year: January 1 to December 31. A few U.S. citizens spend so much time dealing with school systems that they begin to think in terms of academic years, beginning in September and ending in June. People acquainted with government are used to the federal fiscal (or accounting) year. For a long time the federal fiscal year ran from July 1 through June 30, but it has recently been changed. Fiscal year 1977 began on October 1, 1976, and henceforth the federal accounting period will run from October 1 through September 30. Which "year" should the national income accountants use in the measurements of the economy's performance? They try to satisfy everyone! Data are normally kept on a quarterly (three-month) basis, although most of the oldest data are available only on a calendar-year basis.

The product approach. Although this approach to GNP is easy to grasp, it carries with it the dangerous possibility that some goods may be counted twice. The danger of double counting creeps in because of the temptation to include in GNP the value of *all produced goods,* even those which are not final products but intermediate goods that will be used in producing other things. Counting all products would measure output in the automobile industry by adding the value of glass to the value of rubber to the value of steel to the value of upholstery fabric to the value of the finished automobile. But values of the *intermediate products*—glass, rubber, steel, and upholstery fabric—*are all included* in the value of the final product—the automobile. Only the value of the automobile, then, should be counted in calculating GNP.

Defining GNP as the value of all goods and services produced in one time period omits two complicating features of the accounting system. The first arises when an economy produces more than it consumes in a single period. This is fairly common, since producers sometimes miss in their guesses about how much they can sell. When producers produce too much, the overproduction adds to the nation's output but does not pass through the circular flow from firms to households. This surplus, since it was produced, is counted as part of GNP, and it is retained in the inventories of the firms that produced it.

Inventories held by firms are defined as part of *investment*.

Investment is production that will add to further productive capacity and, hence, to the capacity to satisfy wants in the future.

In this respect, adding to inventories is like manufacturing a machine. Removing stocks (of miniskirts, for example, or narrow ties) from inventories so that they will not be sold is called *disinvestment,* since it reduces the capacity of the economy to satisy demands in the future. A positive net change in inventories means that some output produced in one year was not sold in that year but will remain available for future sale to consumers. A net reduction in inventories means that households want to purchase more than firms are able or willing to produce in one year's time. Firms disinvest, drawing down inventories of finished goods, to meet this demand. The amount by which business inventories are reduced is deducted from GNP when the product method of calculation is used. Sales from inventory do not represent current production, so they are not added to the account that measures current output.

A second complication related to the measurement of GNP comes from foreign trade. Exports from the United States to other nations represent production carried out by U.S. firms. The value of this output is added to GNP, since it does represent the outcome of productive activity, and it could be channeled into domestic use. Imports, on the other hand, are not produced by the domestic economy, so any expenditures on them must *not* be counted when measuring the performance of the U.S. economy. The value of imports into the economy is, then, subtracted from the estimate of GNP.

Using the product approach, the GNP of the United States was calculated to be $1,499 billion in 1975. This figure represents the value of all final goods and services produced by the U.S. economy in that year. The possibility of double counting has been removed, the figure has been corrected to allow for goods moving into and out of inventories, and allowances have been made for United States-produced goods that move in international trade and for foreign-made goods that enter the domestic economy.

The product approach is also called the expenditure approach to GNP because it measures how much is spent on goods and services—that is, the value of all final goods and services is determined by the amounts paid for them. When viewed as an accumulation of expenditures, GNP becomes the sum of expenditures made for consumption, expenditures made for investment, expenditures made by all units of government, and the net product of U.S. exchanges with other economies. This relationship is often written in symbolic form.

$$GNP = C + I + G + (X - M)$$

where C = consumption expenditures
I = expenditures on investment (including inventories)
G = government expenditures
$(X - M)$ = value of exports less the value of imports

In 1975, the empirical record showed (in billions of dollars):
$1,498.8 = $963.8 + $182.6 + $331.2 + $21.2.

The income approach. Results identical to those found using the product

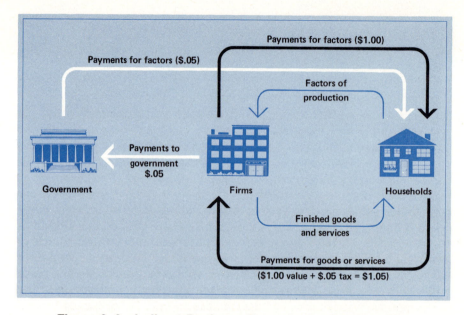

Figure 6-2 Indirect Business Taxes in the Circular Flow

or expenditure method can be obtained by inquiring about incomes received through transactions in the upper half of the circular flow (Figure 6-1), which designates markets for factors of production. As factors are sold, households receive payments. In the circular flow, the total payment for factors must offset payments made for finished goods and services, so the sum of factor payments must equal the value of output. If GNP is the value of output, it must also be the value of input. It is, . . . almost. In addition to the payments made to factors, GNP includes two items not represented in Figure 6-1—indirect business taxes and depreciation.

Indirect business taxes are taxes levied on persons but collected by businesses. A sales tax is a good example. The sales tax is levied on the purchaser of a commodity, but it is collected by the business firm (seller) and then turned over to the state or city. The sales tax causes a feedback loop to open in the circular flow as shown in Figure 6-2. In the transaction represented by this figure, an item valued at $1.00 is sold by a firm to a household. Because of a 5 percent state or city tax, the household must pay $1.05 to the firm. The firm, having turned over the $.05 tax to the government, has only $1.00 to pay back to the household for the purchase of factors of production. The transfer of $.05 to the government has opened a feedback loop, since it causes households to pay out more than they receive in turn. The open feedback loop is closed when the government that finally collects the indirect tax uses the funds to purchase factors of production for producing government services. The white line at the top of Figure 6-2 shows this payment.

A second problem associated with the income approach to estimating GNP is *depreciation*.

Depreciation is the loss in value or productive capacity of a capital asset. It is usually associated with aging, physical deterioration, destruction, or obsolescence. A machine depreciates as it wears out.

A producing firm must prepare for the fact that capital assets like machines wear out and must be replaced. To do this, a firm may establish a depreciation fund.[3] Out of each dollar collected from buyers of goods and services, it may set 10 cents aside in the depreciation fund and use 90 cents to purchase factors for current production. This diversion of funds interrupts the circular flow in a process identical to the interruption caused by indirect business taxes. Depreciation thus causes factor payments to be less than expenditures on finished goods. But since this depreciation is, indeed, a cost of doing business, it must be counted as part of GNP. The process is shown in Figure 6–3. A household purchases a $1.00 item from a firm. The firm divides its $1.00 receipt into two parts. One part ($.90) is used to purchase factors of production that are used in the current production process. A second part ($.10) leaves the circular flow and enters the firm's depreciation fund. This interrupts the circularity of the system and leaves a feedback loop open. The loop is closed when the firm uses its depreciation fund to purchase new capital—a process shown by the white line across the top of the figure.

[3]If there are 1,000 producing firms in a city, there are surely 1,000 different ways of preparing for depreciation and replacement of capital assets. These manifold ways are related to tax laws, technology, the labor force, and dozens of other things. Here, the emphasis is on the fact that there is depreciation, not on the method used to calculate it. The point is, the value of some output is retained in the firm and does not cross immediately to the household side of the circular flow.

Figure 6–3 Depreciation in the Circular Flow

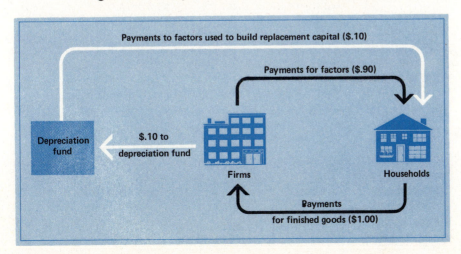

"Depreciation already? You just invented it."

A calculation of GNP using the income approach is shown in Table 6–1.

Table 6–1 Income Approach to Calculating GNP, 1975
(billions of dollars)

Rent	$ 21.1
Interest	81.6
Wages and salaries	921.4
Profits	185.6
Total return to factors	1,209.7
Indirect business taxes	137.1
Depreciation	152.0
Gross national product	**$1,498.8**

Results using either the expenditure method or the income method are always the same. Regardless of how it is counted, GNP is a measure of the value of all final goods and services produced by the economy in one year's time.

Net National Product

Net national product (NNP) is found by subtracting depreciation allowances from GNP.

NNP has not received the public attention given to GNP, and it does not yet generally appear on the business page of every major paper. This is unfortunate, since NNP provides a superior indication of what is available to satisfy the demands of over 200 million consumers. GNP includes all output of the society. NNP is more refined because it measures output after allowance has been made for depreciation. Depreciation payments are made to replace worn-out facilities, to *maintain* productive capacity. They are not used to add to the stock of goods and services available for consumption or to increase the productive capacity of society.

An increase in NNP from one year to the next indicates that economic society has replaced all its worn-out machines and still has more goods, services, or machines than it had in the past. Movements in NNP thus tell a bit more than changes in the cruder measure associated with GNP. In 1975, NNP was $1,346.8 billion. It was found by subtracting depreciation ($152.0 billion) from that year's GNP ($1,498.8 billion).

National Income

National income (NI) is the return to the factors of production sold by households.

NI is the value expressed by the top flows in Figures 6-1 and 6-2 and is often thought of in connection with the income approach to GNP. Rents, wages and salaries, interest, and profits are included in this flow. National income is found by subtracting depreciation and indirect business taxes—neither of which is a direct payment for a factor—from GNP. These two items opened feedback loops in the circular flow and thus caused expenditures on goods and services to be temporarily in excess of factor payments. Removing these loop-opening expenditures shows the exact amount earned by factors in any single accounting period. In 1975, NI was calculated as shown in Table 6-2.

Table 6-2 Calculation of National Income, 1975
(billions of dollars)

Method I			Method II	
Gross national product	$1,498.8		Rent	$ 21.1
less depreciation	− 152.0		Interest	81.6
Net national product	1,346.8	or	Wages and salaries	921.4
less indirect business tax	− 137.1		Profits	185.6
National income	$1,209.7		**National income**	$1,209.7

Personal Income

Personal income (PI) is a measure of what *factor owners* receive, as distinguished from what *factors* earn. It shows the total income persons receive from all sources.

Understanding PI requires understanding of corporations and the fact that they have "wills" of their own. A corporation, while owned by thousands of stockholders, carries out economic activities as if it were a person. It saves. It spends. It invests. The stockholders own the land, labor, and capital that the corporation uses, but these stockholders do not always get full payment for the corporation's use of the factors because

1. The corporation may decide to keep some of its profits to be used at a later time. These retained earnings are called *undistributed corporate profits* and are often used to expand the activities of the corporation.
2. The corporation, like an individual, must pay income taxes. The money taxed away is not available for distribution to stockholders, so it cannot become a part of the incomes of households.
3. The corporation—and even most unincorporated business firms—must make payments to the social security program operated by the federal government. These payments, like corporate income taxes, are siphoned away and do not make their way immediately into the pockets of factor owners.

In 1975, the true earnings of factors (NI) were reduced by $23.8 billion of undistributed corporate profits, $45.7 billion of corporate income taxes, and $108.3 billion of social security payments. Because of these reductions in payments, only 85.3 percent of national income reached the pockets of factor owners who had provided productive services.

This portion of NI is not, however, the total amount of money available to households. Like Ellen and Jack in Chapter 1, many families receive *transfer payments* as a part of their incomes.

"Are you interested in a growth stock, high dividends, a share in America's future, or do you just want to make a buck?"

Transfer payments are expenditures that involve an exchange of money but do not give rise to an increase in the production of goods or services. All pensions and welfare payments are transfers, since they are not connected with current output. The purchase of a used car is also a transfer payment because the transaction does not increase the nation's stock of automobiles.

Although transfer payments do not reflect current productive activity, they certainly influence a family's income. PI, as a measure of households' incomes, must include transfers, even though they do not appear in the accounts related to current productivity (GNP, NNP, and NI).

Table 6–3 shows a calculation of personal income for 1975.

Table 6–3 Calculation of Personal Income, 1975
(billions of dollars)

National income	$1,209.7
less undistributed corporate profits	− 23.8
less corporate profits tax	− 45.7
less social security tax	− 108.3
plus public and private transfers	+ 214.0
Personal income	**$1,245.9**

Disposable (Personal) Income

The smallest member of the income account family is *disposable income* (DI or DPI).

DI measures how much households have available to spend on the output of the economy. DI includes only those dollars over which the family has direct control.

It is calculated by subtracting personal taxes (state and federal income taxes and individual contributions to social security, for example) and values such as the estimated rental value of owner-occupied houses from personal income. In 1975, disposable income was estimated at $1,076.7 billion.

Summarizing the Accounts

These five accounts—GNP, NNP, NI, PI, and DI—form the backbone of the national bookkeeping system. The next section shows how each of these series has behaved in recent years, but first, a summary of the accounts is warranted. Table 6–4 presents an overall picture of the accounts. GNP is shown using both the expenditure method and the income method of calculation. The other accounts have only one method of calculation and so are shown only once.

Table 6–4 Calculation of the National Income Accounts, 1975
(billions of dollars)

Gross National Product			
Expenditure method		Income method	
Consumption	$963.8	Rent	$ 21.1
Investment	182.6	Wages and salaries	921.4
Government spending	331.2	Interest	81.6
Net exports	21.2	Profits	185.6
		Total return to factors	1,209.7
		Indirect business taxes	137.1
		Depreciation	152.0
GNP	**$1,498.8**	**GNP**	**$1,498.8**

Gross national product	$1,498.8
less depreciation	− 152.0
Net national product	1,346.8
less indirect business taxes	− 137.1
National income	1,209.7
less undistributed corporate taxes	− 23.8
less corporate income taxes	− 45.7
less social security contributions	− 108.3
plus transfers	+ 214.0
Personal income	1,245.9
less personal taxes	− 169.2
Disposable income	$1,076.7

The Empirical Record

The circular-flow diagram in Figure 6–1 provides the analytic lessons needed to understand the income accounting system. It is interesting, though, to examine the economy's actual performance record to see how the major economic indicators have behaved since consistent data first became available in the 1930s. It would be easy merely to show how GNP has changed from 1930 to the present time. Because substantial price changes have occurred, however, the data for various years are not comparable in terms of purchasing power. Comparability is obtained by "deflating" the individual series.

Deflating a Performance Series

The income accounts are designed to measure productivity. Since "productivity" includes everything from apples to oranges, wine barrels, visits to the chiropractor, windshield wipers, and denim shirts, the most obvious common denominator—money value—must be used for all comparisons. The needed money values are obtained by multiplying prices by quantities of goods.

Once prices of individual commodities enter the calculation, a real danger emerges, since continual shifts in supply and demand yield constantly changing sets of prices and, hence, constantly changing total values. Thirty-cent apples, two-dollar windshield wipers, and 12-dollar denim shirts in 1975 must be compared with the five-cent apples, 65-cent windshield wipers, and one-dollar denim shirts of 1938. A further problem arises when inflationary (or deflationary) pressures are present in the economy. In a period of general inflation, all prices tend to rise. Using a constantly increasing set of prices to measure *real* increases in output will overestimate the productivity of an economy. Ten apples sold for 10 cents each in a period of low prices constitute the same physical output as ten apples sold for 50 cents each in a later period of high prices. In the former case, the apples contribute one dollar to GNP, however, while in the latter, they contribute five dollars. Regardless of their cause, price changes mean that each year the multitude of items being counted for income-accounting purposes are evaluated using a measuring rod of a different size. It is much like trying to draw a road map using different scales of miles in different areas.

This problem is solved in the simplest possible way. A single year is chosen as a "base." Prices paid by consumers in that year are used to evaluate goods and services produced in each of the years being studied. If 1970 is chosen as the base year, then the values of all apples, oranges, wine barrels, windshield wipers, and denim shirts produced in 1950 or 1961 or 1975 are measured using 1970 prices. Thus, if it is desirable to learn how the value of the output of oranges changed between 1950 and 1970, the price of any single year in this time interval can be applied to physical output in each year. The 1970 price may be chosen or the 1952 price may be chosen, but selecting a single price means that measurements are made using a yardstick of constant size. (Note: A *single* base year is not an essential part of the deflating process. An average of several years may be chosen. For decades, prices of agricultural commodities were related to a base period that used average prices in the 1910–1914 era. This period was chosen because during it agriculture enjoyed relative prosperity.)

This process is called "deflating" a series of values. When it is used —and it invariably is—two sets of figures appear in the national income accounts. One series is reported in *current dollars* to reflect the prices in effect when the product was produced. The second series is reported in *real dollars,* or, *constant dollars,* to reflect (or remove) changes in the purchasing power of the dollar. Because of inflated prices, the value of U.S. economic output in the mid-1970s is likely to be slightly exaggerated —the purchasing power of the dollar has decreased. A series presented in current dollars will make the economy appear more productive than the same series in dollars of constant purchasing power.

GNP in Current and Constant Dollars

Figure 6–4 charts changes in GNP over the past quarter century. The data are shown in current dollars and in constant 1958 dollars. The constant-dollar curve is the most useful record of changes in the total value of output. Because 1958 is the year chosen as the base year for correcting prices, the two curves cross at that year. Prior to 1958, the current-dollar curve is below the constant-dollar curve, indicating that

Figure 6–4   Gross National Product in Current and 1958 Dollars, 1950–1975

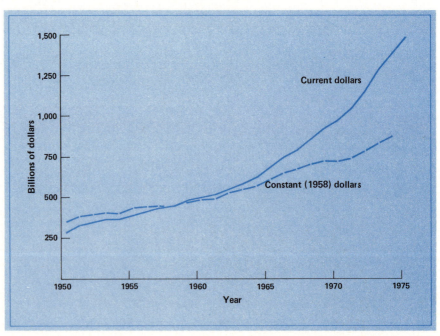

Source: *Economic Report of the President*

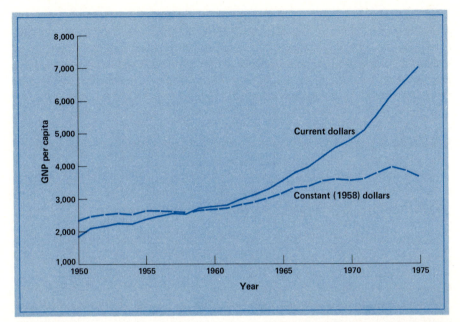

Source: *Economic Report of the President*

Figure 6-5 **Per Capita GNP in Current and 1958 Dollars, 1950–1975**

before 1958 the purchasing power of the dollar was generally higher than it was in 1958. After 1958, the opposite is true: dollars have gradually lost their capacity to purchase goods and services, so the current-dollar curve rises above the constant-dollar curve.[4]

Despite the convergence, then divergence, of the curves, they do show the same ups and downs in short periods. In the early years of the series, GNP was very low. But growth in current-dollar GNP has been nearly continuous since 1960. GNP corrected to reflect changes in the dollar's ability to buy goods and services had the same general path of ups and downs as the current value series until the 1970s. In 1970, the real value of GNP dropped, then recovered, and continued to grow through 1975.

Certainly GNP—in current *or* constant dollars—tells an interesting story. While GNP was rising dramatically from 1950 to 1975, however, the population was also growing. Figure 6-5 shows *per capita GNP* (GNP divided by population) in current and in 1958 dollars for the twenty-five-year period beginning in 1950. The increase in GNP per capita is impres-

---

[4]Most modern series of economic data do, in fact, have 1958 as a base year. In 1958, many older series that had a number of different base years were brought up to date. It is quite likely that a more recent year will soon be chosen and existing time series will be rewritten.

sive. It shows that even when population is growing rapidly, the nation's enormous productive capacity can still provide more goods and services for each person in nearly every year. As illustrated in Figure 6–5, the record of per capita GNP shows modest ups and downs along the way, but the constant-dollar curve shows an increase from $2,342 per capita in 1950 to $3,637 per capita in 1975.

Graphing the Major Accounts

The five major accounts are graphed—in current dollars only—in Figure 6–6. The fact that these series move together so consistently permits the accounts to be used almost interchangeably in discussions of the long-run performance of the economy. It is perfectly acceptable to talk of the tremendous change in either national income or gross national product when referring to progress over long periods of time. The two series—as well as the other three—show nearly the same rates of change.

Figure 6–6 The Five Major Accounts in Current Dollars, 1950–1975

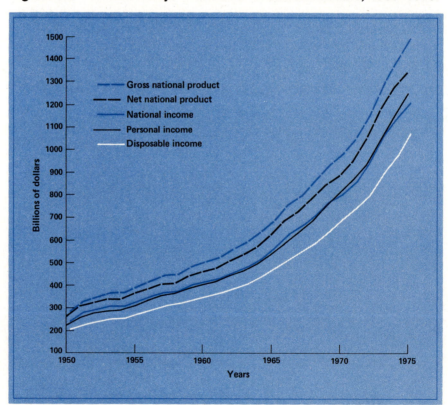

Source: *Economic Report of the President*

The Three Components of GNP

The three actors introduced in Chapter 3 share the nation's GNP, and each is responsible for spending some part of it. The households spend on consumer goods, the firms make investment expenditures, and the governments make their own kinds of purchases. In 1975, consumer expenditures purchased 64.3 percent of GNP, investment used 12.2 percent, government expenditures accounted for 22.1 percent, and the remaining 1.4 percent found its way into international trade. Each of these components is expanded below.

Consumption expenditures. Consumption expenditures are expenditures made by households for finished goods and services. Consumers purchase durable goods such as refrigerators, automobiles, and TV sets; soft goods like food and clothing; and personal services (of the doctor, the gardener, and the hairdresser). In 1975, households spent an estimated $963.8 billion on consumer goods.

Investment expenditures. Investment expenditures are expenditures on items that will be used in further production. Common investment expenditures include a contractor purchasing a dump truck, a small manufacturer buying new machines, and the Ford Motor Company buying land and materials to build a new assembly plant. Generally, about one-sixth of the nation's output is purchased by firms investing in capital. In 1975, firms in the nation invested approximately $182.6 billion. Not all of this was used to purchase new machines or to expand the nation's physical plant. Some was used to replace worn-out machines. The $182.6 billion investment expenditure includes both replacement and expansion components of business expenditures. Only net investment is spent for expansion. The difference between gross investment and net investment is depreciation and amounted to $152.0 billion in 1975. (Note: The difference between gross investment and net investment is depreciation—the same as the difference between GNP and NNP. This is not coincidence. In each case, gross expenditure describes the total spent, but net expenditure describes the gain or change made available by the expenditure.)

Government purchases. Whenever government is mentioned without a qualifier, *all* levels of government are being discussed. The federal government has an annual budget that makes the budgets of other levels of government pale by comparison. Nevertheless, the 50 states, 3,000 counties, hundreds of incorporated cities, countless school districts, mosquito control districts, and rural fire departments are also included in the government category. Governments purchase labor (teachers, road maintenance crews, secretaries) as well as ships for the navy, paper clips for offices, fire trucks, and thousands of other things required to make governments operate effectively. In 1975, the federal government plus all the state and local governments spent approximately $331.2 billion in order to conduct their activities.

Net sales to other countries. Although the three actors mentioned above account for nearly all of GNP, approximately $147.7 billion worth of United States-produced goods and services were sold in foreign countries in 1975. The revenues generated from these sales were used to purchase foreign-produced goods valued at $126.5 billion. The surplus of exports over imports—$21.2 billion—represents net U.S. production that is properly counted as part of GNP.

"How do we get in on that gross national product?"

Limitations of the National Income Accounts

The national income accounts have been presented as refined and reliable indicators of an economy's behavior. What they tell is important, but it is not the whole story. An industrial society produces many "goods," but also many "bads" (smog, industrial waste, noise, occupational diseases, and the like) that are not reflected in the value of goods produced.

GNP and Well-being

The U.S. economy (and other economies as well) now seems to be turning from its decades-old dedication to expanding production toward a set of priorities that places more emphasis on the quality of life. The usefulness or the *completeness* of GNP and its companion accounts may well be questioned in the face of such new concern. For example: Does an increase in GNP automatically bring an increase in well-being? GNP was designed to measure the nation's productivity—its output of material goods and services. For generations, any increase in the output of goods and services *was* an increase in well-being. Most people were living so close to subsistence that any increase in output was automatically a welfare-increasing activity. In recent years, especially since 1960, there has developed a great interest in other aspects of the quality of life, in the natural environment, and in the possibility that growth as measured by GNP cannot be sustained for long. There has been considerable concern that GNP does not measure well-being and that recent increases in GNP may actually have been accompanied by decreases in well-being. Although in some respects the question is unfair—since GNP was not designed as an indicator of the quality of life—this critical view is not hard to support.

Take the case of the cigarette. Cigarettes are made from tobacco and paper. Producing tobacco and paper requires factors of production, and payments for these factors are included in GNP. But only a very few companies produce cigarettes. To maintain their shares of the market, these companies must advertise strenuously. It is a moot point whether the huge advertising outlays actually increase smoking or influence buyers' preferences, but even though it may not add anything to the product, the cost of advertising is included in GNP. As advertising increases, so does GNP.

Smoking is a messy activity. When many smokers gather in a confined space, ashes must be carried away, wrappers and cigarette butts must be cleaned up, and sometimes air must even be filtered to protect non-smokers. All of these processes add to GNP. Cigarette smoking has been known to contribute to the incidence of respiratory diseases, many of which require expensive medical services. The costs of the medical care are added to GNP in exactly the same way that the value of more food and more wool socks is added to GNP. To carry this example of the perversity of GNP calculations to an extreme, consider the smoker who accidentally sets the bed afire. The values of his new bed, new chair, and new rug are added to GNP, and so are all the costs to the taxpayers of putting out the fire. In short, GNP includes the costs of producing millions of goods and performing millions of services, but it does not distinguish which of the activities add to well-being.

Some headway is being made with this problem. A number of economists are suggesting that a new "social progress" accounting system be developed to show the distinction between activities that add to well-being, those that attempt to maintain well-being, and those that actually decrease well-being. There are major stumbling blocks, but progress is coming through separating accounting systems so that those activities producing "goods" are distinct from those producing "bads." The two can be aggregated to yield a conventional measure of GNP.

GNP and Quality

A second serious problem with the present accounting system is its inability to reflect changes in the quality of individual goods and services. Again, relying solely on price as an indicator of quality is responsible. Advances in technology have improved the quality of thousands of household items—light bulbs, automobiles, batteries, plastic combs, bicycle tires, and bed sheets, to name a few—yet the prices of these items have not risen drastically in the past forty years. Improved quality cannot be reflected in the present income accounts. Surprisingly, this problem has attracted very little attention—much less than the quality-of-life issue mentioned earlier. No one seems interested in attempting to change accounting techniques so that the effects of quality improvements can be recognized.

In sum, the national income accounting system used in the United States provides a forty-year record of the performance of the economy. Performance is, however, a limited term in that it measures only the total production of goods and services; it does not distinguish between products that add to the quality of life and products that detract from it. As interest in the quality of life, the natural environment, and the relationship between economic growth and the condition of nature continues to grow, economists will be forced to modify their measuring sticks.

Summary

1. The national income accounting system is a massive bookkeeping service that keeps track of the economy's productivity. Through its use, the United States has been able to maintain nearly five decades of consistent records on how much is being produced and how the output is distributed among actors in the society.

2. *Gross national product (GNP)* is the total value of all final goods and services produced in one year. Intermediate goods are not counted, as that would lead to counting some things more than once.

3. *Net national product (NNP)* is GNP less depreciation. NNP measures the value of goods and services available to society after all machines worn out in the production process have been replaced.

4. *National income (NI)* is the return to land, labor, capital, and entrepreneurship. NI measures the volume of money flowing from firms to households. It is found by subtracting indirect business taxes from NNP.

5. *Personal income (PI)* is the total amount of money available to households. To find PI, corporate taxes, withheld corporate earnings, and social security taxes are subtracted from NI, then transfers of money earned in previous periods are added.

6. *Disposable (personal) income (DI or DPI)* is personal income less the money households must pay to governments in the form of taxes. DI is exactly what the name implies—the amount of money households can use in any way they please.

7. Because of the long span of years involved in the national accounting record, price changes can grossly distort measures of productivity. This problem is solved by choosing a "base year" and relating all production to prices charged in that period.

8. The output of all things—good and bad—is included in the accounts.

They contain no provision for distinguishing between products and services that add to well-being and those that do not.

9 There are no easy ways of reflecting changes in the quality of goods being produced. The only measure in the system is a mechanical counting of monetary values of the economy's output.

Exercises

1 Explain these important terms and concepts:
   national income accounts   investment
   product approach   depreciation
   income approach   transfer payment
   final product   deflating a price series
   intermediate product   current and constant dollars

2 The national income accounting system was designed to describe the performance of the economy. Investment expenditures, made to increase the potential (future) productivity of the economy, constitute an important part of the accounts. Determine which of the following are investment expenditures:
   a Exxon Corporation developing a new port facility in Chesapeake Bay.
   b The Hughes Tool Company discarding worn-out machines valued at $10 million and replacing them with new machines costing the same. Does the response differ if the new machines cost $20 million? (Hint: Be careful of differences between gross and net investment.)
   c A family breadwinner cajoling the boss into a $100 per month raise. Half of the added income is used for consumption; the other half goes to the stockbroker's, where it is used to purchase stocks, bonds, and securities.

3 Personal income and disposable income remain after some things have been deducted from national income, but they also *include* some transfer payments. Transfers add to family income but do not increase national output. Which of the following are transfers?
   a A pension check from a railroad retirement fund.
   b A check from the neighbors for caring for their yard while they were on vacation.
   c A payment for a used car.
   d An insurance payment made to a local hospital.

4 Why is the following statement true? If all sales made in an economy in one year were added together, the value would exceed GNP.

5 A very tiny and primitive economy uses crude tools to produce yams. The yams are its only food and it conducts no trade with other economies. Last year, the nation's "national income accounts" showed the following:

yams for consumption	$10,000
yams for seed	5,000
digging tools	1,000

During the year, old tools valued at $500 had to be discarded. Calculate GNP and NNP for this economy.

6 The year is 1960. The economy is recovering from a moderate recession and no foreign entanglements seem to be threatening. You have this information (in billions of dollars):

Personal consumption expenditures	$333.0
Indirect business taxes	45.2
Undistributed corporate profits	20.0
Corporate income tax	29.9
Personal saving	17.0
Depreciation	43.4
Corporate social security contributions	20.7
Transfers to families	57.0
Personal tax payments	50.9

Calculate each of the five major accounts—GNP, NNP, NI, PI, and DI. (Hint: Start with the small account and recognize that a family can only do two things with its money—spend and save.)

A Contemporary Problem
GNP Is Not the Whole Story

GNP is a market-oriented measure designed to record the performance of a market-oriented economy. While many economists have spoken out against the measure, Arthur M. Okun, a highly regarded member of President Johnson's Council of Economic Advisers, defended it. His comments, made before a group of federal employees responsible for maintaining the income accounts, are at once a succinct expression of what the accounts can do and a very understanding commentary on their limitations. In part, Okun said:

The national accounts system is a great accomplishment of modern quantitative economics; it supplies an intelligible, integrated, and invaluable body of information about the functioning of the nation's economy. Its big summary number—the gross national product—has become a household word. . . .

Yet, even as your numbers are receiving greater use and attention than ever before, they also are receiving more criticism. The fundamental criticism is that, even after correction for price and population change, the gross national product does not necessarily [show] that the nation has become better off. This diagnosis may be followed by either of two prescriptions: (1) ignore GNP, or (2) fix GNP so that it does measure social welfare.

I know you will not ignore the GNP. . . . I urge that you not try to "fix" it—to convert GNP into a purported measure of social welfare. You are doing your job so well that people are asking you to take on a different and bigger job. Resist at all costs, for you can't do that job; indeed, nobody can. Producing a summary measure of social welfare is a job for a philosopher-king. . . . To suggest that GNP could become the indicator of social welfare is to imply that an appropriate price tag could be put on changes in all of these social factors from one year to the next. This would hardly be a minor modification of the national accounts. . . .

What you can and do measure as national income statisticians is the output resulting from market-oriented activity. The key to market-oriented activity is the presence of price tags—the essential ingredient in an objective standard of measurement. Price tags enable you to sum up physicians' prescriptions and phonograph records and pounds of steak and packages of beans, or all the things that money can buy. . . .

As we have known for decades, the guiding principles still leave some fuzzy boundary areas. Some of the questions about where to draw lines are terribly perplexing. . . . You should continue to think about the difficult boundary-line issues. But you should not . . . introduce major changes in the concept of productive activity, the boundary lines between final and intermediate product, and the evaluation of externalities. Let me run through some examples of changes you should not make.

Imputation of the Value of Housewives' Services and of Leisure

For good reasons, you violate the normal institutional boundary between business and consumers when you include in GNP the imputed rental value of owner-occupied housing. You do this because the owner-occupant is short-circuiting the market that tenants go through. You do the same for the food farmers produce and consume within their own households rather than sending to market. Why, so the argument goes, should you not similarly treat the housewife as short-circuiting the market by providing services that other families obtain by hiring domestic workers? I find it a compelling argument that a housewife is not a maid—and that this difference is of a higher order than the difference between the title to a house and a lease. The valuation of the housewife's hourly services by the wage rate of maids, or any multiple thereof, would not really translate her activity into dollars and cents.

I have never been disturbed by the well-known paradox that when the bachelor marries his cook, the national product goes down. The GNP measures the output of market-oriented activity, and the market-oriented activity is reduced by the cook's marriage. . . .

"Regrettable Necessities"

It is obvious that many of the things consumers buy are not intended for pure enjoyment, but are rather a means of avoiding discomfort or preventing deterioration of physical and human capital. Yet you count them all as final product. You have been urged to try to eliminate "regrettable necessities" from final product and thus to classify them as a cost of living rather than a source of satisfaction. Don't start down that path. . . . Costs of physicians' services and other medical care are obviously regrettable necessities. So are the services of lawyers, policemen, firemen, sanitation workers, and economists (including national income statisticians). So are heating and air-conditioning outlays. Except for the few people who live to eat rather than eating to live, food is a regrettable necessity. Indeed, it is hard to imagine any output that clearly serves the purpose of pure, unmitigated enjoyment. But even if you could invent some arbitrary definition that kept final-product consumption from falling to zero, the exclusion of regrettable necessities would make no sense. It would deny the distinction between meeting one's needs and failing to meet them. . . .

The GNP is not the whole story of our society or even of our economy, and no conceivable redefinition can turn it into the whole story. You can help in many ways to put together some of the other pieces required to develop the whole story about social performance. But you would not assist by compromising on the proposition that GNP is not a measure of total social welfare. The beauty of your present practice is that no sensible person could mistake it for such.[5]

In large measure, the Okun article declares its own message. The only tasks remaining are (1) to sharpen understanding about the relationships among priced articles, nonpriced articles, and GNP; and (2) to devote more thought to the usefulness of a welfare indicator broader than GNP—perhaps one that approaches the measurement of social well-being.

---

[5]Arthur M. Okun, "Social Welfare Has No Price Tag," *Survey of Current Business* 51, no. 7, part II (July 1971): 129–33.

7 From the Classical to the Modern Macro Model

Nobody can yet explain fully why an economy behaves as it does. In recent decades, however, economists have made substantial progress toward understanding the workings of a macroeconomic system. Some have been content to describe the macroeconomy's behavior, using graphs of GNP, NNP, gross investment, and other measures. Others have not been content with description and have tried to construct models to explain *why* GNP rises and falls; *why* gross private investment exceeded depreciation in most years but fell short of depreciation during the Great Depression of the 1930s and again during the 1940s; *why* inventories and employment levels rise and fall.

This chapter describes the evolution of an important contemporary model of the macroeconomy. The model did not rise Phoenix-like from the ashes of some burned-out system of thinking. It evolved slowly with the economists who followed Adam Smith and ended with John Maynard Keynes, perhaps the greatest economist of this century. To aid in understanding the contemporary view, this chapter first describes the classical model, then singles out Jean Baptiste Say and Say's Law—one of the longest-lived of all explanations of macroeconomic behavior. From here discussion turns to Keynes's objections to classical economics and the model he devised as a replacement.

The Classical Economists

After Adam Smith had made his famous inquiry into why some nations were wealthy and others poor, economics—then called "Political Economy"—became a recognized field of study. In its early years it attracted a number of scholars who made such a lasting impression that they are known as the classical economists. They brought discipline to the study of economics and in doing so brought discipline to the process of choosing. Prominent among them were Thomas Robert Malthus (1776–1834), who worried about the relationship between population growth and the availability of food; David Ricardo (1772–1823), who was concerned with public policy and how it might affect economic activity; James Mill (1773–1836), who was especially concerned with England's economic relationship to her colonies; Nassau Senior (1790–1864), who was concerned about the source of funds needed for investment purposes; and John Stuart Mill (1806–1873), son of James Mill, who was preoccupied with the causes and effects of economic growth and development.

As individuals, these men were concerned with a vast number of problems that still occupy the attention of economists. They built logical systems to explain the source of value; they wondered whether adding too many factors of production would eventually cause the productivity of these factors to drop, and whether public policies might adversely affect exactly those groups they were intended to aid.

In addition to these varied concerns, the classical economists shared an interest in the overall working of an economic system. How would the system grow? Would growth have the same impact on all parts of the economy? Could public policy affect the performance of the system? Could the system become stagnant and not do its job? Jean Baptiste Say (1767–1832) was perhaps the best qualified to answer questions about the performance of the macroeconomy.

J. B. Say and Say's Law

Jean Baptiste Say was a solid member of the classical economists. Born and trained in France, he was influenced more by the Physiocrats than many of his British colleagues. He preferred to think of economics as a natural science, and he developed a particular abhorrence of any form of government involvement in economic affairs. Unlike Adam Smith, who encouraged many forms of publicly sponsored economic activity, Say believed that *all* government interference was bad and that a smoothly functioning market system could take care of anything.

Say's steadfast belief in the capacities of a market-oriented system gave him the key to formulating what was to become the dominant nineteenth-century view of the macroeconomy. Say held the prevailing view

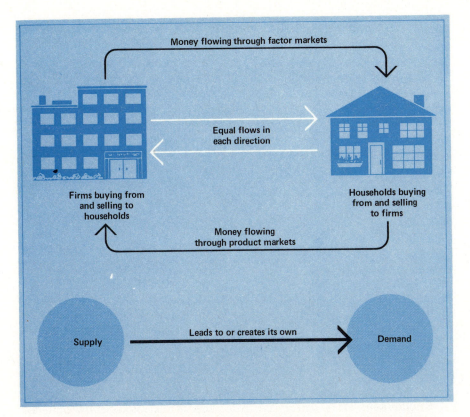

Figure 7-1 Modification of the Circular Flow to Show the Operation of Say's Law

that the production process took factors from households, transformed them into finished goods and services, then returned these goods to the households. The refinement that he introduced was based on exchange relationships in the factor and product markets. In Say's scheme, the producer of one product buys factors and in doing so releases enough purchasing power that the finished product can be bought. The process of production thus creates sufficient demand to clear the market. If activity in the factor market guarantees an equal volume of activity in the goods-and-services market, the upper and lower loops of the circular flow should always be in equilibrium.

Say's Law is a commentary on this symmetry between the factor and product flows and is usually stated simply as "supply creates its own demand."

The workings of this law are graphed in Figure 7-1, using a slight modification of the familiar circular-flow diagram.

Say was not so naive as to think that the circular flow could continue week after week and year after year without change or error. He recognized that producers would occasionally overestimate market demand and buy a large quantity of factors only to find that no one wanted to purchase what was being produced. Say reasoned that even in the face of gross errors, the laws of supply and demand would eventually solve allocation problems by signaling producers to adjust factor purchases and production plans to fit the persuasion of the market. In the end, equilibrium would be maintained. When the grocer laid in too large a supply of turnips, his customers would point out his error by not buying all he had. The grocer, taking this hint, would change his behavior in anticipation of the turnip grower's next visit.

As long as market signals keep buyers and sellers perfectly informed, and as long as all prices (factor as well as product) move up and down in response to changes in market forces, Say's conception of economic processes insures that all factors of production will be fully employed. A surplus of machines causes the price of machines to drop. Prices drop until the machines are bought. The purchase of machines increases purchasing power that is used to buy the economy's output. Similarly with labor. If laborers are unemployed, the price of labor drops until all who want work are actually working. Once all willing workers are employed, their wages give them sufficient purchasing power to clear the market of the goods and services they have labored to produce. Say's Law, coupled with flexible prices, provides a seemingly rational explanation of how a macroeconomy should maintain itself in equilibrium at full employment. The only missing feature is an explanation of what happens when there are savings that are not used to purchase goods and services.

Say's Law and Savings

When households obtain incomes above the subsistence level, they make choices about how this income is to be spent. In addition to a wide choice of consumer goods, a household also has the choice of keeping some of its income in the form of savings. When saving occurs, some of the income that has passed through the circular flow from firms to households is drained out of the flow and is not used for purchasing goods and services. This possibility is shown in Figure 7–2.

Any act that absorbs part of a household's income reduces its purchasing power. It also means that some goods produced by the economy will not be purchased. Certainly, saving is a voluntary act of the household; nonetheless, it reduces the household's capacity to buy goods and services. Say realized this, so he and his followers expanded the basic conception of Say's Law to explain how savings *reentered* the economic system. Given Say's disposition toward markets, it is not surprising that his explanation was simply a market for savings.

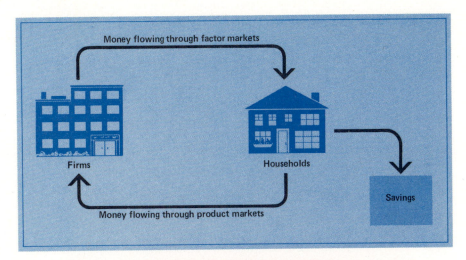

Figure 7-2 **Savings Disrupting the Circular Flow and Interfering with the Operation of Say's Law**

In the U.S. economy, many people save, but very few are able to save more than a modest sum. Because the amounts saved are small, no purchaser of savings (borrower) will be interested in buying them.[1] Banks, savings and loan associations, credit unions, and many other types of institutions serve the useful purpose of gathering savings of individuals into salable lots, then marketing the collected funds.

An important question is, Who buys savings? or Who absorbs the savings and reinserts them into the circular flow? Firms wishing to expand their productive capacity; dentists, lawyers, and plumbers who need more space or new equipment; and industrial firms seeking to retool will all want to "buy" savings. The market for savings can be depicted as having a supply-and-demand relationship similar to that for any other commodity or service. Figure 7-3 has the same meaning as Figure 4-3 in Chapter 4, but some changes in labeling have appeared. The vertical axis measures the rate of interest—the special price of borrowed money. The horizontal axis measures units of funds available for loans (loanable funds). Since the economy produces vast amounts of savings, the horizontal axis is registered in millions of dollars. In Figure 7-3, equilibrium (E) in the market for loanable funds occurs when the interest rate is 8.5 percent per year and when $4.5 million is loaned.

Suppliers of loanable funds (mainly households) respond to changes in the price, or interest rate. Low rates of interest are unattractive to

---

[1] This peculiarity is not unique to the savings market. Producers of small quantities of eggs and milk, single airplanes, or a few panes of glass simply cannot find buyers without the help of a middleman or broker.

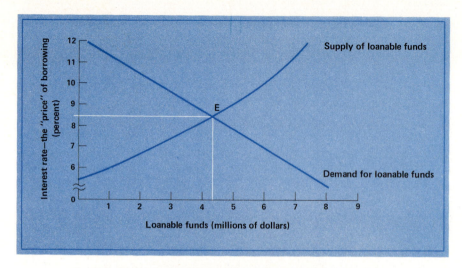

Figure 7-3 The Classical Conception of the Market for Loanable Funds

savers, so that when the interest rate is low, little is saved. As the rate increases, saving becomes more attractive, so more savings emerge. The result is a positively sloped supply curve for saving.

The market for loanable funds is also well behaved on the demand side. At high rates of interest, little is borrowed; the cost is simply too high. However, as the rate falls, more investors will be enticed to borrow money. Thus, the demand curve maintains its characteristic downward slope.

As an example of the working of the theory, in 1973 and 1974 the interest rate soared to unprecedented levels. Among the highest rates paid were those offered by the federal government for savings used to purchase short-term government securities. The rates attracted millions of dollars that in earlier years might have been saved in banks. The high rate thus induced a change in the location of saving. The supply side of the market was working as predicted—savings were shifted from institutions paying low rates of interest to institutions paying high rates. At the same time, interest rates paid by users of funds also soared. Prospective home builders and prospective automobile buyers were deterred by the extremely high interest payments that would be incurred if they borrowed. Borrowers, too, were responding in the way predicted by the theory.

At one price the quantity of savings supplied is exactly equal to the quantity of savings demanded by investing firms. In Figure 7-3, a rate of 8.5 percent causes savers to save $4.5 million and investors to invest $4.5 million. Householders open a feedback loop when they drain the $4.5 million savings out of the economic system. If the market for loanable funds is operating perfectly, the rate of interest will shift rather continuously to insure that all these savings are used by investors and are, thus, reinjected into the circular flow. This process of reinjection automatically closes the feedback loop.

Say was an advocate of the market as a powerful allocative force. He firmly believed in a market for saved and borrowed funds that worked as simply and as surely as the market for fish or the market for linen. The working of this market, he reasoned, would insure that all savings drawn out of the system (that is, all income not currently spent on goods and services) would be automatically rechanneled back into the circular flow and equilibrium would be restored. Even though savings appeared to be disrupting the flow, supply would still create its own demand. Funds flowing through the factor market and through the saving mechanism would always create enough purchasing power to permit households to purchase the entire output of a society.

This more complete picture of Say's Law is shown in Figure 7–4. The familiar circular flow is supplemented by the market for loanable funds.

Figure 7–4 **The Circular Flow Expanded to Include the Market for Loanable Funds.**

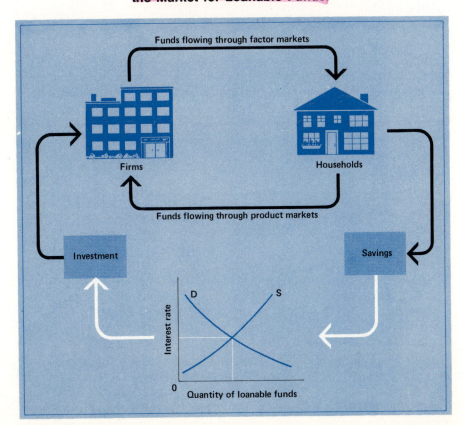

"The educational network is doing Shakespeare this week—all that nonsense about 'neither a borrower nor a lender be'."

Savings drained off the household side are purchased by investors and reinjected on the firm side.

Say's Law gave economists of the nineteenth and early twentieth centuries a reassuring view of the macro system. The system did not always operate to perfection, but the assurance that ultimately supply would create its own demand, together with complete reliance on a flexible market system, led scholars and policy makers of that era to conclude that any disruption of the circular flow was purely temporary. If markets were left to themselves, the disruptions would soon end, and prosperity and full employment would be restored.

Who Saves and Who Invests?

For the sake of clarity it has been implied here that in a market-oriented economy, households do the saving and firms do the investing. It is true that households are the biggest savers in the economy. Each year they save between 7 and 8 percent of their disposable incomes. Firms, however, also save by retaining profits from stockholders. The savings accumulated by both are available for investors to use.

In the same way, firms conduct most but not all the economy's investment activities. Households are investing when they build new houses or add garages to the old ones. These possibilities have not been included in the more general picture of saving and investing in Figure 7–4. The point remains the same regardless of who does the saving and investing.

Limitations of the Classical Model

The classical economists built an impressive macro model. By all appearances it should have worked. Freely operating markets, with prices—including those of loanable funds and labor—moving up and down in response to changes in demand and supply, should have guaranteed a generally healthy economy characterized by generally full employment. But the performance record through the postclassical years (roughly 1850–1940) shows quite different behavior. Starting at the time of the Civil War, the U.S. economy (which was essentially a market-oriented economy and should have behaved as Say suggested it would) went through an almost endless series of ups and downs. First prices, employment, and output would rise, making prosperity available to most citizens. Then prices, output, and employment would fall, resulting in a depression or recession that could last for a number of years. Major periods of prosperity occurred in the 1870s, 1880s, 1900s, and 1920s. Major periods of economic tribulation appeared in the late 1870s, the 1890s, 1907, the early 1920s, and the entire decade of the 1930s. But even these "major" periods of good and bad fortune were interspersed with shorter swings in economic activity that ran counter to the general trend. The 1890s were generally rather troublesome and depressed, but in 1895 there was a quick spurt of economic activity that must have given hope to many people. It lasted only a few months. By 1896, the economy was again in the doldrums. The economists were adamant; leave the market alone and these problems will certainly moderate even if they do not disappear completely.

Meanwhile, workers, craftsmen, and farmers were suffering the burden of not knowing if and when they could work, if and when they could sell their products, and what prices they might receive for their efforts. The economy was erratic and it was hard on everyone.

Keynes Challenges the Classical Model

By the 1930s a few economists were beginning to question the classical model and the automatic regulation described by Say's Law. Their questions were brought together in the thinking of John Maynard Keynes, who challenged the classical model and prepared the way for an up-to-date method of economic analysis and policy making.

Keynes's major attack centered on the market for loanable funds. He was not satisfied with the classical explanation of either the supply of or the demand for these monies. On the supply side of the market, he reasoned, certainly households do save and the quantity saved varies from time to time, but *probably not always in response to changes in the interest rate.* Some households are likely to save money as a residual —that is, they save only that part of their incomes that is left over after all bills are paid. Other households save in order to be prepared for some contingency that might demand more dollars than current income provides. In either case, the rate of interest in itself does not determine a household's behavior. An individual saver is pleased if interest rates go up, but the rising rate alone will not call forth large amounts of added savings.

Keynes postulated that the case was similar on the demand side of the loanable-funds market: investors are probably responsive to changes in interest rates, but they are more likely to be concerned with the general economic outlook or with business expectations. If the prospect seems very good, they will go about their investment activities even if rates of interest are very high. As in the case of the supply of loanable funds, the rate of interest may not be a major determinant.

If neither the supply of savings nor the demand for loanable funds responds in any regular way to "price," the market for loanable funds is imperfect and the classical notion of automatic linkages between savers and investors is broken. Funds saved by households and drained out of the circular flow may or may not be borrowed by investors; they may or may not be reinjected into the circular flow. If they are reinjected, circularity is maintained; if they are not, the leakage causes factors to be unemployed and the equilibrium level of economic activity to fall.

The Keynesian Model

If questioning the classical notion regarding behavior of the market for loanable funds had been Keynes's only contribution, he would not be an overwhelmingly interesting figure in the history of economics. But Keynes also constructed a new model to describe the macro behavior of a market economy. His model was comprehensive enough to explain why an economy could have many of its factors unemployed and still appear to remain in equilibrium for a long period of time. It offered an alternative to the classical notion that full employment is the automatic resting place for the macroeconomy. Keynes's theory explained why an economy could fall into a depression and not recover. It explained why inflation could occur year after year without individual markets automatically correcting the situation.

The new model centered on demand. While the model can be expanded to include demands of business and governments, it is best understood in terms of the *aggregate demand generated by households*.

The aggregate demand of households is the total value of all goods and services purchased by all households during a year's time.

Keynes reasoned that as a household's disposable income increases, its expenditures on consumer goods also increase but not as rapidly. A household with an extremely low income may dip into previous savings to find the funds needed for current expenditures. As its income rises, past savings are no longer dipped into, but all current income is used to purchase necessities. With further increases in income the household will surely spend more on goods and services, but some of the increased income can be saved. This increase in income opens the feedback loop that Say closed by assuming that supply creates its own demand. In Keynes's model, rising income brought higher levels of living and increased consumption, but it created the problem posed by more savings leaking from the system.

But the problem only begins with increased saving. Since there is no automatic mechanism like Say's market for loanable funds to reinject savings into the income stream, an economy composed of high-saving households could find itself in the predicament of never wanting to buy all its own output. Such an economy might, as a result, suffer perennially from unemployment or underemployment of capital and labor. The argument is described graphically in Table 7-1 and Figure 7-5. The hypothetical household represented in Table 7-1 behaves as many millions of U.S. households surely do. At low levels of disposable income, consumption expenditure is actually higher than income, since the family is not earning enough to live as it feels it must. As income rises, so do consumption expenditures, but not as fast as income. When the household's disposable income is $5,000, expenditure and income are equal. As income continues to rise, some is directed to savings. When disposable income reaches $10,000 per year the household spends more than it ever has on goods and services, but it also diverts $2,500 to savings. The household uses its factors to produce revenue of $10,000, but the household itself returns only $7,500 to the income stream.

The same information is shown in Figure 7-5. The solid line labeled

Table 7-1 Hypothetical Schedule of One Household's Income and Expenditure

Disposable income	Consumption expenditure	Saving
$ 3,000	$4,000	$ − 1,000
4,000	4,500	− 500
5,000	5,000	0
6,000	5,500	500
7,000	6,000	1,000
8,000	6,500	1,500
9,000	7,000	2,000
10,000	7,500	2,500

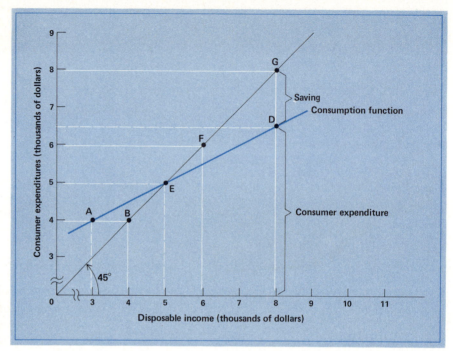

Figure 7-5 Household Consumption Function

"consumption function" tells the same story as the numbers in Table 7-1. Point A corresponds to the low-income family that earns $3,000 (read on the horizontal axis) but spends $4,000 (read on the vertical axis). Point E shows the family with disposable family income of $5,000 spending the entire amount on consumer goods and services. Point D shows the family earning $8,000 but using only $6,500 to purchase goods and services.

The black line emanating from the graph's origin (O) provides a special frame of reference: situations in which all income is returned to the circular flow. Since it rises from the origin at a 45-degree angle, and since the graph's two axes are measured using the same units (dollars), every point along the line represents equality between income and expenditure. At point B, income and expenditure are equal at $4,000. At point F the two are equal at $6,000, and point G shows income and expenditures equal at $8,000. This 45-degree reference line will be used somewhat extensively through several chapters in this book. The blue line showing the behavior of the hypothetical family is called the *consumption function*.

The consumption function is the relationship between disposable income and total expenditure on consumer goods and services. As income rises so does expenditure, but the rise in expenditure is not as rapid as the rise in income. The consumption function is an important tool used by macroeconomists.

John Maynard Keynes (1883-1946)

No figure has dominated twentieth-century economics more than John Maynard Keynes. Like several other famous modern economists, Keynes studied under the tutelage of Alfred Marshall at Cambridge University in England. Keynes was phenomenal. His training was begun by his father—John Neville Keynes, also a noted economist—and, by the time Marshall had finished with him, Keynes was a qualified mathematician, a diplomat, a successful stockbroker, and a patron of the arts. Early in his career, Keynes began to question the appropriateness of the classical method of studying an economy in terms of the prices of factors, goods, and services. He thought that these were essential but that some way should be found to quickly ascertain the performance of an entire economic system. He chose to look at the economy's performance using levels of *aggregate* income, general price levels, and levels of employment (or unemployment). It took Keynes several years to refine his theories, but they were eventually published in a very cumbersome book entitled *The General Theory of Employment, Interest, and Money.*

This book appeared in 1936 and shook economists no less than the *Wealth of Nations* had done one hundred and sixty years earlier. The main message of Keynes's important work is a complex and technical one, but the policy that stems from it is based on the notion that an advanced industrial economic society can, in the aggregate, be controlled (or manipulated) through judicious use of the public's ability to tax and spend. An economy need not suffer from continual inflation and deflation, from growth and collapse, if only the policy makers will use their powers to adjust the supply of money, the interest rate, and the way in which money is spent.

Keynes provided answers to many important questions. There were, however, and continue to be, two disappointing aspects of the Keynesian system. First, his hypothesis seemed to be easily researchable and thus capable of being proven or disproven. On close examination, though, it turns out that many important aspects of *The General Theory* defy accurate testing. To sort out the effects of a change in interest rates, for example, on the level of employment or on the rate of inflation is almost an impossible task because too many other things are happening at the same time. A second disappointing aspect of *The General Theory* is that it has reinforced the separation between studying economic problems of small units—firms, households, corporations—and studying economic problems of large units—national governments. While giving economists appropriate tools to use in studying and adjusting the performance of the macroeconomy, Keynes also made the gap between microeconomics and macroeconomics almost impossible to bridge. The reason: the economic system has a will of its own and that will cannot be found by adding (aggregating) the behavior of all the economy's parts. To date, no economist has been entirely successful in showing how all the micro units can add together to become the aggregate economic system.

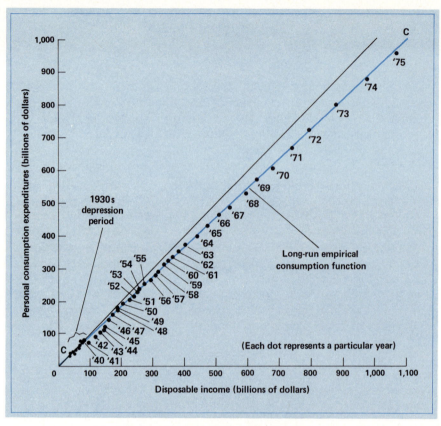

Sources: *Economic Report of the President, Survey of Current Business*

Figure 7-6 Disposable Income and Consumer Expenditures, 1930-1975

The Aggregate Consumption Function

If a consumption function can be drawn for a single household, no special tricks should be required to draw one for a whole society. In fact, a consumption function for the U.S. economy's 69.9 million households would look much like the one in Figure 7-5. It would show poor families living off past savings, at the lower end of the function, and wealthy families adding to their savings at the upper end. Somewhere in the middle-income range would be the household that spends all its disposable income on current consumption.

Unfortunately, the limited information available on savings and consumption expenditures does not permit drawing an aggregate consumption function for the United States in 1977. However, *time series* data for disposable income and consumption expenditures are available for the past forty years.

A time series is a sequence of empirical observations made at regular intervals—weekly, monthly, quarterly, or annually—to show how a particular variable is behaving. A time series of GNP includes GNP for each of the past forty years. A time series of the price of eggs may include daily observations of egg prices for the past five months.

When these time series are plotted against each other, a picture like Figure 7–5 emerges. Figure 7–6 shows an aggregate consumption function using annual data from 1930 to the present.

As disposable income has grown, so has personal consumer expenditure. The large cluster of points at the lower end of the income scale in Figure 7–6 shows that in the 1930s incomes were very low. At these levels of income, all or nearly all DI went for consumption. In 1932 and again in 1933, personal consumption expenditure actually exceeded personal disposable income. As incomes have increased through the 1940s, 1950s, 1960s, and 1970s, the aggregate consumption function has dropped away from the line of equality. Savings have increased with increases in income.

Aggregate Demand and Equilibrium

In macroeconomics, as in all of economics, equilibrium is a position (or situation) in which there is no net force toward change. In the consumer spending model of Figure 7–5, equilibrium is represented by the income level at which income and expenditures are equal. When income and expenditures are equal, the household pays out what it receives; it reinjects everything it takes from the income stream. Consumption expenditure is equal to disposable income where the aggregate demand function crosses the 45-degree line. At this level, households are not exerting any force to disrupt the equilibrium condition.

In Figure 7–7, the equilibrium condition and two other conditions are shown. At condition I, aggregate disposable income is $30 million. Since the aggregate consumption function (C) intersects the reference line at this level of income, all income is restored to the circular flow and the system is in equilibrium. When aggregate disposable income drops to $20 million (condition II), households are very poor and must rely on past savings to maintain themselves. By using savings to help purchase goods and services, these families have a magnifying effect on the macroeconomy. They are injecting more than their disposable income into the circular flow. The increases in incomes to producers act as a signal to them. With the injection from savings there is an increase in sales; firms find it profitable to increase production, and hence incomes, to $30 million—the point where disposable income is just equal to consumer expenditures. The flows in the upper loop and the flows in the lower loop are equal.

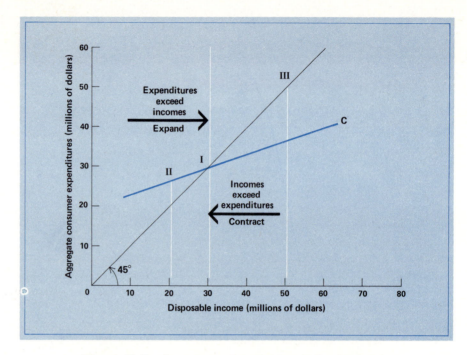

Figure 7-7 Aggregate Demand and Equilibrium

When aggregate disposable income is $50 million (Figure 7-7), condition III arises. Household expenditures fall short of aggregate disposable income. While households earn $50 million from the sale of factors, they purchase goods and services valued at only $37 million. Firms do not sell all they hoped to sell. As a result, laborers are released, plants stand idle, and inventories collect in warehouses. The firms must contract. They contract until their payments for factors equal their incomes or—using terms of this example—they contract until the level of disposable income is offset by (or just offsets) the level of expenditures.

In a simple world where households are the only purchasers of goods and services, the intersection of the consumption function and the 45-degree line shows the equilibrium level of disposable income. Any deviation from this level sets off a chain of events that leads the system back to equilibrium. When the price of eggs is too high, the rules of supply and demand dictate that the price fall to an equilibrium level. Similarly, when aggregate demand exceeds disposable income, the macroeconomy struggles to get itself into equilibrium.

Aggregate Demand, Equilibrium, and Full Employment

Unlike the classical model, the Keynesian model does not insure or even suggest that an economy will find equilibrium at the full-employment level or any other particular level of output. Say's Law was used to argue that the act of securing factors put sufficient revenue in the hands of factor owners to insure that all products could be purchased. Moreover, factor prices, like all other prices, were assumed to be flexible so that any factor—labor included—could be employed merely by offering its services at a lower price. Under these conditions, involuntary unemployment was impossible.

The modern Keynesian argument does not deny that supply creates purchasing power. It only allows that purchasing power may go unused. Further, the modern model suggests that as aggregate income grows, households will be inclined to use a smaller proportion of their income for consumption. There is little assurance that all society's output will be purchased, and much less that equilibrium will be reached at that level which insures that all people eager to work can actually find employment.

Summary of the Keynesian Model

Although Keynes was trained as a classical economist, he developed a model to explain the macro behavior of a modern, industrial society. Over the last few pages, the elements of the Keynesian system have been used to illustrate an economy assumed to include only households as consumers and firms as producers. The Keynesian model differs from the older models in three important ways:

1 The classical model explained the workings of the macro system in terms of the workings of thousands of individual markets for thousands of individual goods and services. The Keynesian model is a model of aggregates. It is built on aggregate demand and the relationship between aggregate income and aggregate demand.

2 The classical model depended on price flexibility in every market; the more modern model recognizes that price flexibility is perhaps desirable but is seldom achieved.

3 The classical model generally assumed that supply would create its own demand and equilibrium would be reached at full employment. The modern model recognizes that the process of supplying does in fact create purchasing power, but asserts that there is no guarantee that all purchasing power will be *used*. If some is not used, the economy will contract to an equilibrium level that may be considerably below the full-employment level. Thus, an economy may persist month after month with high levels of unemployment and not be moving to correct the difficulty. The economy may be in equilibrium at low levels of employment and output.

Building on these themes has given contemporary economists a more complex but a more realistic view of the macroeconomy. But the household-only assumptions of this chapter are too limiting. The investment activities of firms and the buying and selling activities of governments must still be added to the model. That is the task of Chapter 8.

Summary

1. The classical economists thought that the circularity of an economic system could be maintained through orderly markets for goods and services.
2. Jean Baptiste Say developed a model showing that producers always pay factor owners just enough so that the total output of society can be purchased by households.
3. According to Say's model, if households chose to save rather than spend, the saving found its way back into the circular flow through an orderly and well-behaved market in which both savers and users of savings were assumed to respond to changes in the interest rate.
4. Say's conception of the macroeconomy was summarized in Say's Law: Supply always creates its own demand.
5. John Maynard Keynes suggested that neither savers nor borrowers always respond to changes in the interest rate. Savers save what is left over; borrowers borrow more on the basis of profit expectations than the rate of interest.
6. Keynes pointed out that as an economy matures, it is less likely to behave in the fashion suggested by Say. An advanced economy will not automatically spend all its income on consumption.
7. Keynes developed a new model of the macroeconomy. The model centered on the growing gap between aggregate income and aggregate demand.
8. The approach initiated by Keynes and his followers contends that for a mature capitalistic society to survive, massive efforts will at times be required to put savings back into the income stream.

Exercises

1. Explain these important terms and concepts:

   Say's Law   investors
   aggregate demand   the Keynesian model
   loanable funds   consumption function
   savers   time series

2. J. B. Say produced a reasonable explanation of what he thought was economic reality. He was convinced that the purchase of factors valued at $100 would yield products of equal value, and that these products would be purchased at a cost of $100. He "proved" the circular flow. Draw a crude circular-flow diagram and show what might happen to disrupt it. In the process, define savings and develop a concise argument showing how savings can disrupt a circular flow.

3. In Say's system a market glut was impossible. (A market glut is the simultaneous oversupply of a substantial number of goods and commodities. A glut results from large numbers of producers being unable to sell all they have produced.) Why? What made the system automatic?
4. Make lists of the reasons why people save and the reasons why people invest. Which of these are consistent with a well-behaved market for savings? What is the consequence of the savings market not working to perfection?
5. Keynes did not contradict Say's Law. Rather, he developed an alternative theory that depended on aggregate demand and the collective behavior of millions of people. What is aggregate demand? In a graph with consumer expenditures on the vertical axis and disposable income on the horizontal (and with each axis marked with equal units), the aggregate demand curve will intersect the vertical axis at some point above zero but will have a slope of less than 45 degrees. Why? What does this tell you? What relevance does it have with respect to Say's Law?
6. Year after year, the U.S. colleges and universities turn out thousands of teachers, engineers, pharmacists, and home economists. These trained people enter markets to sell their skills and talents. Since 1970, it has been very hard for graduates with degrees in elementary education to find employment. It has been nearly as difficult for engineers and mathematicians. If supply creates its own demand, why can't these highly skilled workers find jobs? Explain this in terms of Say's Law and then in terms of aggregate demand.

A Contemporary Problem
Should Workers Accept Pay Cuts?

The "stagflation," or "slumpflation," of 1974–75 was a curious phenomenon. Not only did unemployment reach the highest levels since the 1930s, but inflation eroded the purchasing power of paychecks earned by those workers who were lucky enough to be employed. Firms paid high prices for things they bought, and watched nervously in hope that one week's output would be sold so they could stay in business the following week. To them Say's Law was a remote fiction. Their production activities did not insure that demand would be generated for their products. Managers in many firms made choices about whom to lay off, but in other firms the choice went to the workers themselves. The following commentary, adapted from *Business Week,* describes the problem:

"The worker is caught between the problem of prices rising at a time when jobs are disappearing," says James F. Searce, deputy director of the Federal Mediation & Conciliation Service. So even when they know that jobs might be saved, workers are often hard-pressed to accept pay cuts.

Despite the problems of the auto industry, where over 25 percent of the production workers have been laid off, UAW members this month received an 11 cents-an-hour cost-of-living wage increase. UAW vice-president Douglas

Fraser says that even Chrysler made no effort to have the increase deferred, "and it wouldn't have done them a damn bit of good if they had." UAW President Leonard Woodcock opposes any pay cuts because he feels they would neither reduce car prices nor increase employment.

Where pay cuts in one form or another have been agreed to, the companies generally have been small, nonunion shops. Hoff Lumber Co. in Idaho, now owned by Boise Cascade Corp.; canceled layoffs when all 350 employees, including executives, agreed to a 10 percent cut in pay. At Wang Laboratories, Inc., a Tewksbury (Mass.) electronics maker, production workers' pay was cut by 13 hours a month.

There has been more response to share-the-work proposals among municipal workers. City employees in Altoona, Pa., agreed to one payless day to stave off layoffs. And New York police have agreed to extra work at the same pay to keep 500 rookies on the force.

Building trades
Even in the deeply depressed housing and construction industries, the signs are mixed. About 1,100 operating engineers who work in residential construction along the Ohio-Pennsylvania border have agreed to a $1.50-an-hour pay cut and have also eased some restrictive work rules in the hope of stimulating construction. It is too early to tell whether the move will have the desired effect. On the other hand, government inflation watchers are deeply worried about this spring's construction contract talks and were alarmed by a settlement in Alaska increasing electricians' wages by $6 an hour to nearly $20.

More common than actual cuts in the hourly wage rate are management-imposed short work weeks for production workers as an alternate to layoffs. One approach, taken by the Chase Brass subsidiary of Kennecott Copper Corp. in Cleveland, is rotating every-other-week layoffs, allowing workers to keep health and other benefits intact.

The AFL-CIO is taking a different approach to the problem. It is lobbying to amend the Fair Labor Standards Act to require payment of overtime to nonexempt employees after 35 hours of work a week rather than 40 as a job-stimulating measure. "I think there will have to be some consideration given to a shorter work week in order to make more jobs," says AFL-CIO President George Meany.[2]

Analysis. Understandably, individual businessmen are skeptical of the working of Say's Law. Their own productive activity generates buying power for the economy as a whole, but there is no guarantee that the money will be used to buy goods and services produced by that particular firm. The employment of thousands will not insure sales of an unwanted good. In the current stagflation, increasing expenditures on labor will not increase sales (note Leonard Woodcock's feelings), so firms have little choice. They must reduce the amount they spend for wages. This can be done by reducing the number of people who are paid or by reducing the amount paid to each person. Keeping more people employed would reduce the need for unemployment benefits, reduce the

---

[2] "Workers' Plight: Pay Cut or Layoff?" *Business Week,* 24 March 1975, pp. 31–32. Reprinted by special permission. © 1975 by McGraw-Hill, Inc.

number of mortgage foreclosures, and give more families the income they need to buy necessities. It would reduce expenditures on luxury items. Reducing the work force but maintaining pay at high levels would mean that fewer things would be purchased but the *range* of things purchased might remain high.

Choosing the "correct" path is not easy. Management has cut its own pay and in some cases has turned over the wage-employment problem to workers. Workers' reactions are mixed. How would you respond? What would be the economic consequences at the household, firm, and macroeconomic levels if your choice were adopted?

8
An Expansion of the Macro Model

Simplicity is at once the beauty and the bane of science. Whether a problem concerns breeder reactors, DNA chains, voting habits, or the delicate ecology of the Alaska pipeline path, that problem must be defined and then simplified before it can be solved. The beauty of science is that it provides a systematic way of doing this; the catch is that often once a problem is simple enough to solve, it is so remote from reality that the answer has no relevance. The classical economists simplified the problem until they found an answer in the perfect working of markets. Keynes simplified too, but since he defined the problem in terms of aggregate demand, it is not surprising that he found a different answer and proposed a different way of managing the macroeconomy.

The Macro Model, Step by Step

Chapter 7 was an exercise in simplicity. It provided the barest outline of the working of a macroeconomy. But its argument depended upon an aggregate demand function that took account of only that demand generated by households. Thus it could not be used to answer the economic questions that arise in a society made up of investors and governments as well as consuming households. This chapter will add detail to the picture outlined in Chapter 7, starting with the activities and behavioral characteristics of investors and governments, and ending with a more comprehensive model of the macroeconomy.

Households Only

Figure 8–1 shows a model that can be used to determine the level of aggregate income in an economy. It uses a 45-degree reference line to show all points of equality between income and spending, and an aggregate consumer expenditure curve or consumption function (C) to describe the collective behavior of households. In this figure, the system is in equilibrium when aggregate consumer expenditure equals aggregate disposable income. Only at this level will consumers purchase all that is produced and return all their income to the circular flow. Equilibrium is shown when disposable income and consumer expenditure are each $20 billion.

Expanding disposable income beyond $20 billion to, say, $30 billion results in surpluses of goods, since consumers do not wish to purchase

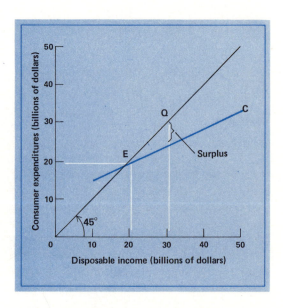

**Figure 8–1
Income Determination with Consumption Only**

"We've done it again. We've disposed of all our disposable income."

all that firms wish to produce. This is known to be true because aggregate consumption *(C)* is below aggregate output (shown on the reference line as point *Q*). Expanding households' disposable income to $30 billion gives them more purchasing power than they wish to spend. Since firms are producing too much, they will want to minimize their losses by purchasing fewer inputs and producing fewer goods. This contraction in output leads the economy back to equilibrium at $20 billion.

The model in Figure 8–1 is called the *income determination model* because the behavior of an actor *determines* the aggregate level of income in the economy.

Households and Firms

Adding firms to the model does not change any rules—it simply adds the kinds of expenditures made by firms to the consumption expenditures of households. The firm's unique expenditures are those made for investment purposes. When they are included, the vertical axis must be changed to reflect both consumption and investment expenditures, and the horizontal axis must represent a measure of the income earned by both households and firms. None of the ordinary income accounts (Chapter 6) is exactly appropriate, since none is designed to show the combined income of consuming households and investing firms. For this reason, the hypothetical and simple *private income* is used. Private income is at least as high as national income, since this is what firms, in aggregate, must pay households for the use of factors. It is likely lower than net national product, however, since firms must pay some taxes before they make their investments and purchase their factors. In 1975,

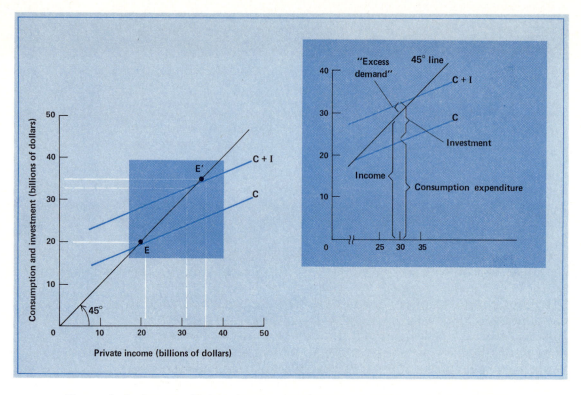

Figure 8-2 Income Determination Using Consumption and Investment

private income would have been somewhere between $1,208.1 billion (NI) and $1,346.9 billion (NNP).

In Figure 8-2, the vertical distance between C and $C+I$ shows the amount of investment purchases made by all private firms taken together. The level of investment is assumed not to vary as private income changes, so the curves C and $C + I$ are parallel. Including investment adds significantly to aggregate demand, for now the demand for new factories, new dump trucks, and new office buildings is being considered in addition to the demand for canned soup, auto tires, and dry cleaning. This additional category of expenditures magnifies the economy and raises the level of private income at which there is equilibrium between aggregate expenditure and aggregate income. The equilibrium level (E) of private income expands from $20 billion to a new level—$35 billion.

Now, a drop in private income to $30 billion immediately disrupts the equilibrium (E') that existed when private income was $35 billion. When private income is $30 billion, consumers will spend $24 billion on consumer goods, and investors will add demand equal to the vertical distance between C and $C + I$—approximately $9 billion. The two sources of demand yield aggregate expenditures of $33 billion. These expenditure plans add up to more than the aggregate income of firms and households. With expenditure exceeding income, some *dissaving* must be occurring to cover expenditures that are larger than revenues.

Dissaving is spending more than current income. Dissaving occurs when money is taken from savings accounts or depreciation funds and used for consumption or investment purposes.

The disequilibrium can be corrected by increasing income—driving private income out toward $35 billion—or by reducing consumption expenditure, investment expenditure, or both. Equilibrium is restored only when private income is equal to consumption plus investment expenditure.

Households, Firms, and Government

The addition of government expenditure, like the addition of private investment, does not change the basic macroeconomic model. Again, however, the diagram undergoes modification. In Figure 8–3, the vertical axis measures expenditures made by households, firms, and governments. The horizontal axis measures all "income" earned by the entire society—net national product (*NNP*). As in the case of investment expenditure, government expenditure is assumed to remain constant regardless of the level of NNP, so it is shown as a constant vertical addition to C and C + I. The curve C + I + G (parallel to and above C and C + I) represents aggregate expenditures made by all three groups of spenders. When expenditures made by governments are added, a new equilibrium level of income and expenditures appears at OP.

All rules about the economy returning to equilibrium remain the same. If NNP increases to levels greater than OP, consumers, investors, and

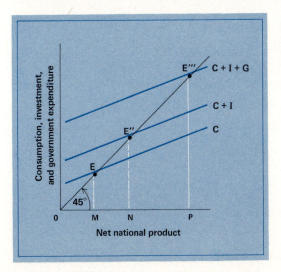

**Figure 8–3
Income Determination Including Consumption, Investment, and Government**

government decision makers will not return the full amount to the circular flow. The high level of NNP cannot be maintained. If NNP falls below *OP*, the three actors will together want to spend more than they are earning. Their use of prior savings will serve to expand the economy until equilibrium is restored.

Summary of the Macro Model

The income-determination model is based on a simple notion: As a capitalistic society expands, its willingness to purchase its own potential output diminishes. If not all output is purchased, producers and businesses are forced to store goods and make unplanned additions to their inventories of finished but unsold items. These same businesses are also forced to decrease the quantity of inputs, including labor, used in the production process, and the economy settles at an equilibrium level, with aggregate expenditures equaling net national product but at a level less than that required for full employment. The simplest model (like the one in Chapter 7) is shown on the left side of Figure 8–4. It includes only the 45-degree reference line and the aggregate consumer expenditure curve. The aggregate expenditure curve has a slope less than the 45-degree line, indicating that as aggregate income increases, households spend a lower proportion of their incomes on consumer goods. If consumer expenditures on goods and services were the only expenditures in the system, the economy depicted by this simple model would be in equilibrium when NNP reached about $35 billion.

Figure 8–4   The Expansion of the Simple Model

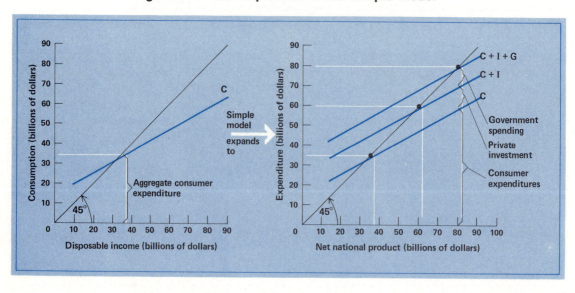

The model shown on the right-hand side of Figure 8–4 is more complicated. Private investment and government spending are added on top of consumer expenditures. When investment is added, the economy is in equilibrium when NNP is approximately $60 billion, and when the activities of government are added, the equilibrium level becomes $80 billion. With NNP at this level, households (consumers), firms (investors), and governments generate enough aggregate demand to clear the market. The circular flow becomes a closed feedback system. At any level of NNP greater than $80 billion, all goods and services will not be sold because the three actors—households, firms, and governments—do not generate sufficient effective demand to repurchase their own output. In such a circumstance, the economy is forced to contract. At any level of NNP below $80 billion, aggregate expenditure exceeds the output of the economy, and automatic forces drive output back up to the $80 billion level.

Understanding Aggregate Economic Behavior

As might be surmised after viewing the expanded income-determination model in the preceding section, it would be very useful to understand what determines the behavior of the three actors in an economy. It is frustrating that no one knows exactly why they behave as they do. It will be useful, however, to discover what *is* known about the behavior of

These "Automatic Forces"

A market-oriented economy is often characterized as having automatic forces that regulate its behavior. The term *automatic force* is a modern economist's version of Adam Smith's invisible hand. The forces are the combined effects of the activities of thousands of businesses that make decisions on the basis of what is happening or what can be expected to happen in the market. In the model shown in Figure 8–4, when NNP exceeds $80 billion, buyers will not show interest in buying all available products. The subsequent loss of sales and increase in inventories automatically causes producers to reduce output, lay off workers, reduce the use of other inputs, and take other steps that will lower NNP. If NNP drops below $80 billion, buyers will compete with one another for available products, and store shelves will be emptied. Consumers will want to purchase more than is being produced. Producers, noticing this, will see opportunities to increase profits and will automatically expand output until aggregate demand and NNP are equal.

consumers, about investment patterns, and about the economic activity of government.

Determinants of Consumer Spending

Quite likely, a good share of consumer behavior is built into social customs and mores. Thus, spending patterns may be expected to vary from one society to another but to remain relatively stable within a given economy. In 1973, consumer expenditures in the United States were divided among products as shown in Table 8–1. Surely many of the expenditures were for necessities and would not change even with changes in income, but some might easily have been shifted among categories or even forgone in favor of savings, according to the whim of the consumers.

Table 8–1   U.S. Consumer Expenditures, 1973

Type of product	Percent of expenditures
Food, beverages, and tobacco	22.2
Clothing, accessories, and jewelry	10.1
Personal care	1.5
Housing	14.5
Household operations	14.6
Medical care	7.8
Personal business	5.6
Transportation	13.6
Recreation	6.5
Other	3.6

Members of a society devoted to the ideal that everyone should eat, drink, and be merry all the time might almost automatically spend all their income. People in a society where children are taught that a penny saved is a penny earned might put a high premium on *not* spending and, hence, not ever return all their earnings to the income stream. In either kind of society, consumption expenditures may be affected by social episodes such as war, severe depressions, or natural disasters. A major war accompanied by complete military mobilization may deprive people of the opportunity to spend because productive resources are used to produce war materials rather than consumer goods. The price of vigilance among nations in the Near East, for example, is a lowered volume of consumer goods among peoples who must use their resources to maintain military preparedness. Similarly, a natural disaster like a tornado, flood, or earthquake may destroy all previously owned consumer goods and force households to expend nearly all their incomes on consumption activities until they again have acceptable stocks of consumer goods in their living rooms and in their cupboards.

Table 8–2 Disposable Personal Income, Personal Outlays, and Outlays as a Percent of DPI, 1930–1975

Year	DPI	Personal outlays*	Outlays as a percent of DPI	Year	DPI	Personal outlays	Outlays as a percent of DPI
	(billions of dollars)				(billions of dollars)		
1930	74.5	71.1	95.4	1955	275.3	259.5	94.3
31	64.0	61.4	95.9	56	293.2	272.6	93.0
32	48.7	49.3	101.3	57	308.5	287.8	93.3
33	45.5	46.5	102.0	58	318.8	296.6	93.0
34	52.4	52.0	99.3	59	337.3	318.3	94.4
1935	58.5	56.4	96.3	1960	350.0	333.0	95.1
36	66.3	62.7	94.6	61	314.4	343.3	94.2
37	71.2	67.4	94.7	62	385.3	363.7	94.4
38	65.5	64.8	98.9	63	404.6	384.7	95.1
39	70.3	67.7	96.3	64	438.1	411.9	94.0
1940	75.7	71.8	94.9	1965	473.2	444.8	94.0
41	92.7	81.7	88.2	66	511.9	479.3	93.6
42	116.9	89.3	76.4	67	546.3	506.0	92.6
43	133.5	100.1	75.0	68	591.2	550.8	93.2
44	146.3	109.1	74.5	69	634.4	593.9	93.6
1945	150.2	120.7	80.3	1970	691.7	634.7	91.8
46	160.0	144.8	90.5	71	746.0	685.8	91.9
47	169.0	162.5	95.7	72	802.5	747.2	93.1
48	189.1	175.8	92.9	73	903.7	829.4	91.8
49	188.6	179.2	95.0	74	983.6	909.5	92.3
1950	206.9	193.9	93.7	1975	1,076.7	987.8	91.8
51	226.6	209.3	92.4				
52	238.3	220.2	92.4				
53	252.6	234.3	92.8				
54	257.4	241.0	93.6				

Source: *Survey of Current Business*

*Includes consumer expenditures on goods and services and interest paid on installment credit.

These examples depend on dire circumstances to explain alterations in households' decisions about how much to spend on goods and services. A more regular determinant of the level of consumer expenditures is, quite simply, the amount of income available to be spent. Table 8–2 shows the level of disposable personal income, the level of personal outlays on consumption, and these outlays as a percent of DPI for each year from 1930 to 1975. DPI has increased in forty-one of the past forty-six years. The only decreases occurred in the early 1930s, when the Great

Engel's Law of Consumer Behavior

In the 1850s, German statistician-economist Ernst Engel (1821–1896) studied 153 Belgian families to learn something of their spending habits. In general, he found that a poor family spends a much greater percentage of its income on food than a wealthy family does. His studies indicated that as income increases, the total *amount* spent on food increases too, but the *percentage* of all income used for food falls. In the 125 years since Engel did his work, dozens of economists have repeated his study in many nations and among many income classes. Results of more recent studies show that

1. The original finding relating to food still applies. As family income increases, the percentage of income spent on food diminishes.
2. As family income increases, the percentage spent on housing remains about constant.
3. As family income increases, the percentage spent on medical care and personal care remains about constant.
4. As family income increases, the percentage spent for most other categories of goods, including savings, increases.

These general behavioral patterns lend weight to the argument that as economic society progresses, total family expenditures may increase but the gap between family income and family expenditure will also increase.

Depression was at its worst. Total personal outlays display nearly the same pattern, indicating that DPI is a reasonable proxy for consumer expenditures.

When outlays are calculated as a percent of income, two lessons emerge. First, as income has increased, there has been a slight decrease in the percentage of DPI used for consumption. This does much to confirm the hypothesis that as a society grows, it becomes increasingly reluctant to purchase all its own output. Second, the series shows a sharp decrease in percentage of DPI used for consumption expenditures during years of World War II (roughly 1941–1944). This confirms the second hypothesis that certain peculiar events can drastically alter an economy's disposition toward consumption expenditures. In sum, consumption expenditure—the largest component of aggregate demand—is hard to predict, but the best clues to its magnitude are estimates of total income. Over any short period of time, an unusual event or series of events can cause exceptions to this rule.

Determinants of Investment

Investment is tool building. It is producing things that will be used in further production. When a society constructs a factory, it invests. When a

"Is this another one of your get-rich-quick schemes, Cosgrove?"

Reproduced by special permission of *Playboy* Magazine; copyright © 1976 by *Playboy*.

construction contractor replaces a worn-out back hoe, it is investing, and when a law firm expands, it invests in new office furniture. The process of investment requires two things—savings and the expectation that the investment will be profitable. Savings provide the means; favorable expectations provide the incentive.

Expectations. If the business community thinks that a certain product will be profitable over the coming years, firms will seek to invest in machines to produce it. If outlook for the product is gloomy, investment, if undertaken at all, will be limited to replacing worn-out machines. But *expectation* and *outlook* are not well defined terms. If a farm operator, for example, is considering planting a sizable acreage of apples, his investment plans might be affected by considerations like these:

1. *Price.* Will the price of apples remain stable or will it fall?
2. *Consumer tastes.* Will consumers continue to buy apples or will they shift their demands to other fruits? Even within the apple industry, will red apples or yellow apples be preferred?
3. *Competition.* Will other parts of the nation suddenly start producing more apples? If so, will these new sources of supply compete with local production?
4. *Market for surplus.* Can apples not sold as fresh fruit be processed into applesauce or cider, or will they have to be discarded?

5 *Technology.* Will new technologies be developed that will either greatly expand productivity or greatly reduce cost?
6 *Vulnerability to severe weather.* Will the next few years bring cold weather severe enough to kill young trees, thus requiring replanting (reinvesting) and setting back the date at which production can start?

Once a decision to invest has been made, funds must be secured to purchase the required inputs. Some firms will have previously earned profits to draw upon (recall undistributed corporate profits in Chapter 6), but others will be forced to borrow money for their investments. In that case, the anticipated return from the investment must be at least as high as the rate of interest paid on the borrowed money. Borrowing money that costs more than it returns would be foolish.

The interest rate. These variables and uncertainties make it very hard to predict the return on a planned investment with any accuracy. Predict one must, however. A firm's managers must make educated guesses about contingencies, then decide how much the firm's profits are likely to increase as a result of an added investment. The estimate of the return on the added investment is called the *marginal efficiency of investment.*

The marginal efficiency of investment (MEI) is the expected rate of return on an anticipated addition to capital. Unless the MEI equals or surpasses the rate of interest on borrowed funds, borrowing for investment purposes is not likely to be profitable.

The rate of interest, then, becomes a determinant of investment

Pay or Earn Interest?

Even firms with large pools of undistributed profits may sometimes have difficulty deciding whether or not to use these accumulated profits for investment purposes. These firms face the same problems as firms that must borrow in determining the marginal efficiency of their investments. They do not have to pay interest to others for borrowing money to invest, but they have to reckon with another kind of cost. Their accumulated profits may have been placed in the local savings and loan association, or they may have been used to purchase government bonds. If the money is recalled from these purposes to be used for an apple orchard, the investing firm must count the interest lost by taking the money out of the savings and loan as a *cost* associated with the new investment. In this way, the interest rate affects both borrowers and users of retained profits. The cost to the investor in the latter case is an opportunity cost (Chapter 1). The opportunity cost of using your own investment funds is the money these funds could have earned if placed in the bank.

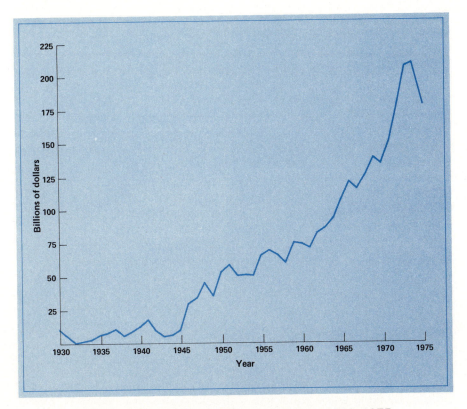

Figure 8-5 Gross Private Investment, 1930-1975

expenditure. If the rate is high enough to exceed the MEI, investment will probably be unprofitable. If the rate is very low, even low profit expectations may be sufficient to induce investment.

The investment record. The uncertainties surrounding the outcome of investments cause great variations in investment spending from year to year. Figure 8-5 shows annual expenditures on private investment in each year since 1930. In fourteen of the forty-six years, private investors were cautious enough about economic prospects to actually reduce investment below the previous year's level. Two of these drops—in 1942 and 1943—occurred during war years, when government regulations and severe shortages of important industrial materials made investment difficult. Eleven other drops in gross private investment expenditures, however, occurred during periods characterized by a generally healthy economy. These decreases were caused by investors' unsettled opinions about the future and their subsequent refusal to commit money to investment purposes. This erratic behavior of individual investors makes aggregate investment very difficult to predict.

In simple models of the economy's behavior, investment expenditures are considered to be independent of income levels. They appear, therefore, as a constant addition to consumer expenditures. If investment is anticipated—*guessed* is a better word—to be $50 billion in a year, this $50 billion expenditure on capital plant and equipment is assumed to remain the same regardless of the level of NNP. Thus, $C + I$ is the same distance above C at all levels of income. The simplicity of this convention hides the more important relationship between changes in investment and changes in income and employment. Although it is assumed that income does not have an effect on investment, investment has a significant effect on income. The U.S. economy uses many of its factors in tool building. When investment drops, some people involved in producing investment goods are out of work. When investment increases, employment does too. The recession of the mid-1970s caused reductions in most kinds of investments. In the building trades, the reduction in investment expenditure caused 780,000 laborers to lose their jobs temporarily. Aggregate demand was not great enough to maintain these workers as part of the employed labor force.

Determinants of Government Spending

Government expenditures have pronounced economic effects, but they do not always have well defined economic *causes*. They are more often affected by factors like the mood of the public, natural disasters, public needs and concerns, and national security. These causes of government spending have varying degrees of predictability. Wars cannot be accurately predicted as to either timing or severity. The mood of the public swings from liberal and high spending to conservative and low spending. Without warning, severe hurricanes occasionally batter the Southeastern states and bring massive and costly destruction.

Some expenditures made for public needs and public goods are subject to conscious manipulation. Funds expended for highways can be increased or decreased. Spending to build dams and national parks can be modified, increased, accelerated, or stopped. Welfare payments to the aged and needy can be manipulated by altering eligibility requirements. All these help to determine the magnitude and variation of government expenditures.

Figure 8-6 shows how expenditures made by governments have varied since 1930. The volume of government expenditure has increased from virtually nothing in the 1930s ($3.3 billion in 1931) to well over $275 billion forty years later. Viewed as a percentage of GNP, government expenditure has grown from less than 15 percent in the early 1930s to approximately 22 percent in the mid-1970s.

The two "humps" in the government expenditure curve coincide with World War II (1941–1945) and the Korean conflict (1951–1954). The

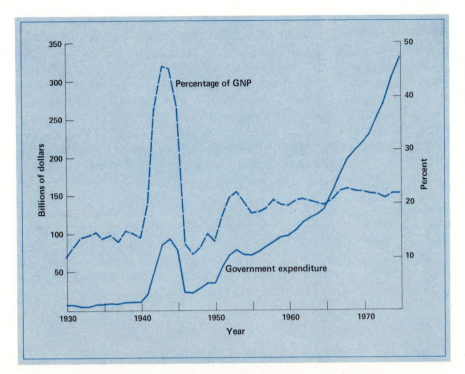

Figure 8-6 Government Expenditure, 1930–1975

massive increase in government expenditure starting in 1960 reflects —to a large degree—the nation's military involvement in Southeast Asia. Even without these tragic and costly wars, the proportion of the nation's output utilized or controlled by some level of government would likely have increased. With increased affluence has come increased demand for things that can be supplied only by governments—roads, recreation areas, flood control, educational facilities, police protection, and income maintenance programs, for example. It is almost inescapable that as a capitalistic society develops, an increasing proportion of its output will be used by government. This is not a reflection of a trend toward taking power and freedom away from people, but rather, an indication that wealth brings with it the capacity and the desire to enjoy different collections of goods and services, many of which must be produced by government. (This topic is developed with more care in Chapters 26 and 27.)

These arguments lead to the conclusion that government expenditures, like consumption expenditures, respond to changes in the level of income. In some respects they do, but not with the same regularity. They also respond to votes, political power, and public moods. It is generally impossible to predict the level of expenditure that will be made by the many units of government in the United States in any one year. Expenditures can be guessed to be at a given level, such as the vertical distance between the *C + I* curve and the *C + I + G* curve in Figure 8-1. As in the case of investment, it is safe to assume that in a given year this vertical distance will be the same regardless of the level of NNP.

The simple income-determination model, then, is mixed in its structure. That part related to consumer expenditure is *behavioral* in the sense that it seeks to describe how people's spending behavior is determined. The investment and government-spending parts, though, are not behavioral. In this model it is assumed that in any one year, either of these elements of aggregate spending may be high or low, but their levels are determined by variables outside the model. They do not depend upon the magnitude of NNP.

The three classes of spending combine to form aggregate spending for the national economy. What is spent must be earned, so the level of spending must equal the level of national output, or NNP. If deviation from this equilibrium condition appears, the economy will struggle to bring itself back to equilibrium—the system will correct an imbalance between income and expenditures.

Changing the Level of Equilibrium

Three spending streams—consumer expenditures, investment, and government expenditures[1]—determine the level of net national product, the measure of performance of an economic society. There is no assurance, however, that the level of output (equilibrium) so determined will be the most desirable for the society. Equilibrium is not an *optimum* condition for an economy, only a *natural* one. If consumer expenditure plus investment plus government expenditure yields an equilibrium output of $400 billion but permits only 70 percent of the labor force to be employed, equilibrium is producing a natural but not an optimum number of jobs.

Altering Consumer Expenditure

To alter the level of output in order to reach some economic goal *other than* the initial or natural equilibrium, the behavior of at least one of the three actors must be changed. It is possible that massive public-

---

[1] Government expenditures are made for both consumption and investment. When the government purchases paper, janitorial services, or food for school lunches, it is consuming. When the federal government builds dams on the Columbia River or helps complete the St. Lawrence Seaway, it is investing. Government activity is so diverse that it is virtually impossible to try to separate its efforts into the two usual categories.

awareness campaigns could induce consumers to behave differently and that in behaving differently consumers could change the level of NNP. In time of war, households in the United States and elsewhere have been persuaded to consume less so that more resources could be devoted to the war effort. This kind of exhortation was particularly effective in the early 1940s when complete mobilization of the nation's industrial capacity was required. In more recent years, however, an intense propaganda campaign against pollution and against products contributing to it has been almost totally ineffective. Political "jawboning" has not saved the economy the pain of inflation. It seems that manipulating consumer behavior is sometimes possible but never reliable. This is probably because decision-making power is widely dispersed and any one consumer or group of consumers can have only a miniscule effect on the total volume of consumer expenditure. There was an important difference between the World War II cutback on consumer expenditures and the experience of the 1960s and early 1970s. In the 1940s, cutbacks in consumption were imposed through an elaborate rationing system. Taxes increased significantly, and strong publicity campaigns appealed to people's emotional involvement in the war, urging them to use their funds to purchase government bonds. More recently, only public urging has been used to change public consumption patterns.

Altering Investments

Investment expenditure is nearly as intractable as consumption expenditure, and any single investor—even an industrial giant—makes up only a small proportion of the nation's total investment in any one year. Trying to control investment is a difficult task. In the early 1970s the banking system was moderately successful in altering investment behavior by increasing interest rates, just as in 1975 President Ford influenced consumption expenditures by lowering federal income taxes. The activities of investors, like those of consumers, can be changed, but the change depends on their individual willingness to respond to suggestion, coercion, and incentive. There are no guarantees.

Altering Government Expenditure

The purchasing and taxing habits of government can be consciously controlled. Because of this, government is the only actor through which aggregate demand $(C + I + G)$ can be easily altered. Regulating the performance and output of the economy, then, not only is the responsibility of government but is a function that *only* government can perform. To suggest this is not to say that government should absorb all economic functions. It means only that the taxing and spending powers of govern-

A Second Approach to the

The equilibrium discussions of Chapters 7 and 8 have been in terms of aggregate demand (expenditures). The economic system is in equilibrium when total income is equal to total expenditures made by households, firms, and governments.

The same argument can be made using savings and investment. The discussion of Say's Law in Chapter 7 noted that in the macroeconomic model of the classical economists, all savings removed from the system would be reinjected, restoring the income flow. This was to take place through investment activities conducted primarily by firms.

Figure A below uses savings and investment to show the equilibrium of an economic system. This graph is somewhat different from those encountered earlier, because its vertical axis extends below its intersection with the horizontal axis, so that the variable measured on the vertical axis can have either positive or negative values. The vertical axis in this graph measures the volume of saving. The horizontal axis shows some measure of national product—most likely NNP.

The savings line shows the volume of aggregate saving occurring at each level of NNP. The positive slope of this curve indicates that as income increases, savings will increase, too. Income in the economy may be so low, however, that families must *dissave* in order to pay their bills. In Figure A, dissaving occurs at all levels of NNP below $2 million.

Savings are a leakage from the income stream. If they are not reinjected into the circular flow, some goods will go unpurchased and, eventually, some factors will go unemployed. Investment is the mechanism used to inject saved income back into the system. When investment is equal to savings, as at $5 million NNP in Figure A,

Figure A   The Determination of Equilibrium Levels of National Income

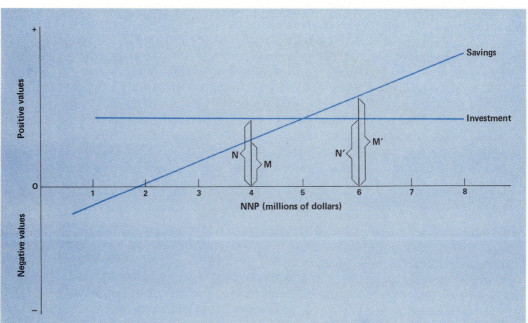

Income-Determination Model

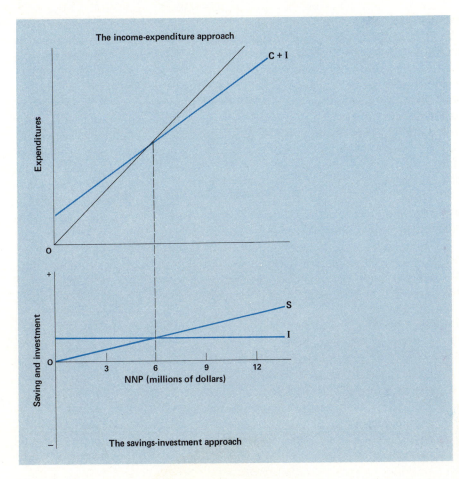

**Figure B
Income
Determination:
Two Approaches**

all saving is used to purchase investment goods and the system is in equilibrium.

If NNP is $4 million, savers extract $M from the income stream while investors pour in $N—a larger sum. The large injection causes expansion, so NNP climbs to the equilibrium level. If NNP is $6 million, savers extract M' and investors inject N'. Because more is taken out than is returned, the economy contracts, eventually settling at the $5 million equilibrium level of NNP.

Figure A tells the same story told by a number of graphs in the past three chapters: At high levels of NNP an economy may be unable (or unwilling) to buy all that it is producing, and at low levels of NNP the same economy may wish to purchase more than it is producing. Figure B combines the savings-investment approach with the income-expenditure approach to income determination. In Figure B, the top graph shows the $C + I$ curve intersecting the 45-degree reference line at $6 million. At this level of NNP, consumers and investors purchase all that is produced. In doing so, they return all income to the circular flow. The lower graph shows that when NNP is $6 million, the savings of households are returned to the income stream by investors.

ment are the only ones that can be relied on to change the aggregate level of performance.

In the 1970s, there is little assurance that private forces will combine to yield an aggregate level of output that will satisfy consumers and producers and still provide for other social goals like full employment, stable prices, economic growth, and an improved quality of life. The role of government must be understood if economists and/or voters are to use government effectively. More than this, government must be increasingly used as a regulator of the economy to insure that its private functions can be safely carried out within a stable and reasonably predictable framework.

Summary

1. The complete model of income determination must include households, firms, and governments—the three major actors in an economy.
2. Households are the consumers. They purchase approximately 63 percent of the value of GNP. As income increases, so do consumption expenditures, but not quite as fast as income. At some high level of income, households will not want to purchase all that firms wish to produce.
3. Firms purchase investment goods valued at approximately 15 percent of the nation's output.
4. Investment activity depends on many subjective judgments and is highly unpredictable. Firms will invest if they sense that the future holds good fortune. Neither economists nor diviners nor soothsayers have been able to ascertain accurately what makes businessmen act the way they do.
5. Government expenditures are unpredictable to some extent because events such as wars and natural disasters, which require government spending activity, are also unpredictable.
6. A significant portion of government spending, however, is subject to conscious control and can be used to influence economic activity.
7. These three kinds of economic activity give rise to the familiar $C + I + G$ classification of aggregate output, which permits an analysis of the equilibrium level of output.
8. There is no assurance that the equilibrium level is the most desirable level from society's point of view.

Exercises

1 Explain these important terms and concepts:
   - income-determination model
   - dissaving
   - determinants of consumer spending
   - Engel's Law
   - marginal efficiency of investment
   - determinants of government spending
   - determinants of investment

2 Draw a graph so that personal expenditures are measured along the vertical axis and disposable personal income along the horizontal. Draw a 45-degree line out from the origin, then perform the following exercises, assuming that all economic activity is conducted by consumers (that is, with no investment and no government spending).
   a Draw an aggregate demand (consumption) function showing that all those in the society always spend all their income.
   b Draw a time-series aggregate demand function related to the last twenty-five years of experience in the U.S. economy.
   c Draw an aggregate demand function for your family or a "typical" family in your town. (The measurements on the axes will have to change.)
   d What are some factors that might cause this whole function to move up? To move down?
   (Comment: Note the similarity between the answers to b and c. Aggregate demand functions are very similar when drawn for a family or for a society. Be sure you know what you are dealing with.)

3 The following table gives information about spending, saving, and investment in an economy.

Disposable income	Consumption expenditure	Planned saving	Planned investment
(billions of dollars)			
$1,200	$1,100	$100	$50
1,125	1,050	75	50
1,060	1,000	60	50
1,000	950	50	50
945	900	45	50

   a What is the equilibrium level of disposable income? How do you "prove" or "support" this answer?
   b Will levels of disposable income above or below this level be stable? Why?

4 The 1960s saw tremendous increases in air travel. By 1965, the major U.S. airlines were well on the way toward completely replacing propeller-driven aircraft with jets. Massive investments were made to obtain the new, fast planes. In the early 1970s, the jumbo jet appeared, and a new round of investment began as the older Boeing 707's and DC8's were replaced by $35-million 747's and DC10's. Now, with increasing costs and decreasing passenger loads, several airlines have announced that they will not purchase more planes for several years. Others are trying to sell planes.
   a How did the purchase of jets, then jumbo jets, affect the investment function?

b If investment is added to consumption, what does investment do to the equilibrium level of output?
c Will the planned moratorium on purchases of planes have any effect on equilibrium output? If so, what will it be?

5 The government of a small country discovers $50 million worth of gold in the back of an old vault. It is rumored that the money was stolen from peasants by a deranged and greedy dictator. The current dictator is more benevolent, and decides to return the money to the people. This can be done by increasing the pensions of survivors of the decadent regime, by building a new highway system, or simply throwing the money to the crowds. Ignoring any question of fairness, decide how each of these measures would affect the country's level of output, and how each should be shown on a diagram.

A Contemporary Problem
The Dream House in the Suburbs

Housing is the most personal of all investments. It qualifies as investment (rather than consumption) because it can be used to generate income from rentals, producing a potential stream of wealth. Housing is a critical issue in the American economy. The nation has not built enough housing units to keep up with the rising population or with the changing desires of its citizens. In spite of the need for more houses, there was a sharp reduction in building activity during the early and mid-1970s. The reason was high interest rates. Interest rates were increased by the banking

Interest Rates and Housing Starts in Fiscal Year 1974

Month	Mortgage lending rate	Housing starts
July 1973	7.87	203,200
Aug. 1973	7.94	199,900
Sept. 1973	8.17	148,900
Oct. 1973	8.13	149,500
Nov. 1973	8.39	134,600
Dec. 1973	8.49	90,600
Jan. 1974	8.52	86,200
Feb. 1974	8.62	109,600
Mar. 1974	8.64	127,200
Apr. 1974	8.67	160,900
May 1974	8.74	150,400
June 1974	8.84	149,400

system in an attempt to prevent too much money from entering an already inflationary economy. An unintended consequence of these high rates was the severe drop in investment in housing. This drop in investment caused unemployment in the building trades and in nearly all economic activity related to construction. A month-by-month sketch of the relationship between housing starts and the interest rate during 1973–74 is shown in the table on page 164. As the interest rate climbed, housing fell, so that by June 1974, housing starts were at levels 25 percent below those of the previous year.

If you were an economist for the government, what would your conclusions be about the housing problem and its possible relationship to national income? Would you advise further increases in the interest rate?

9 Changes in Levels of Aggregate Income

The rivers of North America are particularly susceptible to flooding. They regularly escape their banks, causing destruction and loss of life. One widely used means of averting these disasters is to construct dams, which contain the floodwater and render it harmless. Flood-control reservoirs collect water during wet seasons and release it when flood danger has passed. The level of water in the reservoirs therefore rises during rainstorms and spring thaws, and falls during dry months. The changes are often imperceptibly slow.

In the mountains behind the reservoirs, the scene is different. Brief storms turn creeks into maelstroms, sudden droughts turn verdant valleys into harsh deserts, and a late thaw can upset plans along the lower reaches of the streams. And it is these violently changing and totally unpredictable individual events combined that determine the halting, sometimes imperceptible, but totally predictable behavior of the reservoir.

The economy behaves in much the same way. Local catastrophes make a few families poor, and local windfalls make a few families rich. A tornado ruins the fortunes of an Oklahoma family, and a sudden rise in the price of silver makes a few Idaho families very rich. But these are miniscule events that are hidden by the rather plodding movement of the huge macroeconomy.

Chapter 8 dealt with three streams that contribute to the nation's reservoir of goods and services and determine its level. This chapter will examine the effects of changes in those three individual determinants: consumer expenditures, business investments, and government spending.

In large measure, this chapter explains three technical relationships that affect consumption, saving, investment, and national income. These relationships are the average propensity to consume (or save), the marginal propensity to consume (or save), and the multiplier.

The Average Propensity to Consume or to Save

The average propensity to consume and the average propensity to save are concepts that Keynes himself introduced into the language of economics. The *average propensity to consume* refers to the proportion of a household's income (or a nation's income) that is, on the average, spent for consumption.

The average propensity to consume (APC) is that proportion of disposable income that households generally spend on consumer goods and services.

In 1975, households in the United States had access to disposable income of $1,076.6 billion and purchased consumer goods and services valued at $987.8 billion. When consumption expenditure is calculated as a percentage of disposable income, the average propensity to consume is 91.8 percent. That is, in 1975, households in the United States *on the average* spent approximately 92 percent of their incomes to buy consumer goods and services. They had an average propensity to consume about 92 percent of their disposable income.[1]

Previous chapters have stressed that a household can do only two things with disposable income—spend it or save it. This being the case, there is a simple relationship between the average propensity to consume and the *average propensity to save*.

The average propensity to save (APS) is that proportion of disposable income that households save rather than spend for consumer goods and services.

If an economy, on the average, spends 92 percent of its income on consumer goods, then it must, on the average, save the remaining 8 percent

[1] The average propensity to consume can be, and often is, calculated with reference to GNP rather than DI. Either use is acceptable, but for different purposes one may be preferred to another. Here, since discussion centers on the way a household chooses to use its income, an APC related to disposable income is preferred. This same qualification holds true with the average propensity to save.

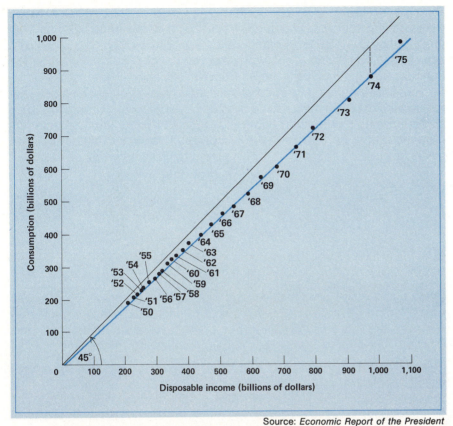

Source: *Economic Report of the President*

Figure 9–1 Relationship Between Disposable Income and Consumption Expenditure, 1950–1975

of disposable income. Since dollars spent plus dollars saved must always add to total income, the average propensity to consume plus the average propensity to save must always add to 100 percent.

Empirical evidence about the average propensity to consume and the average propensity to save is available for the United States and is plotted in Figure 9–1. Disposable income is measured along the horizontal axis, while consumption expenditure is measured on the vertical axis. Each individual dot shows the relationship between these two values for a particular year. In 1955, for example, disposable income was $275.3 billion and consumption expenditure was $254.4 billion. (The average propensity to consume was .924; average propensity to save was .076.) The blue line drawn through the dots shows the general trend in the relationship between consumer income and spending since 1950. If all income had been spent for consumer goods during these years, the blue line would coincide with the 45-degree reference line. Since the dots and the blue line consistently fall *below* the reference line, it follows that some saving took place in each year. The volume of saving is shown by the vertical distance between each dot and the reference line. In 1974, for example, disposable income was $979.7 billion, of which $74.0 billion was saved. The saving is shown by the vertical dashed line between the consumption function and the 45-degree reference line.

The amazing thing about this relationship is its regularity. Notice that a straight line drawn through the dots comes very close to touching them all. Notice also that the percentage of income used for consumption has dropped slightly as incomes have increased. This shows that as society's wealth grows, the share of its income used for consumer goods declines.

The Marginal Propensity to Consume or to Save

While the average propensities to consume and save are important in understanding the general behavior of households, the *marginal propensities* are more useful since they show how an *increase* in income will be divided between increased consumption and increased saving.

The marginal propensity to consume (MPC) is the proportion of any increase in income that is spent on consumer goods and services. The marginal propensity to save (MPS) is the proportion of any increase in income that is saved. Both concepts relate to what is done with additions to income.

If a household is given an additional $100 per month, the marginal propensity to consume reveals what proportion of that $100 is spent and the marginal propensity to save shows what part is saved. The two concepts together describe how a household will respond to a change in its income.

An entire economy as well as a single household has a marginal propensity to consume and a marginal propensity to save. The collective MPC and MPS of 69.9 million households are necessary pieces of information whenever economic planning or policy warrants changing the level of income going to the households. The MPC and MPS will show how that increase is divided between consumer spending and saving.

The average propensities are relatively easy to calculate from data reported by the U.S. Department of Commerce. The marginal propensities to consume and to save are more difficult, however. Intensive studies are required to learn what families do with increases in income. Such studies are more complex than merely going down the street asking, "What would you do with an extra $100 per month?" Most families do not recall what happened to last year's increase in wages; nor do they know for sure what they will do with next year's. Although the MPC (and hence the MPS) will vary with the level of income, some recent estimates of the marginal propensities indicate that under normal conditions the typical U.S. family will spend approximately 90 percent of any increase in income for consumption and will save the other 10 percent. The marginal propensity to consume is then .90; the marginal propensity to save is .10. But the marginal propensity to consume is variable and will change in response to the appearance of rapid inflation and to other influences like changes in tax laws, changes in foreign trade, and changes in the general expectations for the future.

The marginal propensity to consume and the marginal propensity to save apply to the effects of either an increase or a decrease in disposable income. The marginal propensity to consume describes what proportion of each added dollar will be used for consumption and what proportion will be saved. Since a reduction in income reduces both consumption and saving, the MPC also tells how much consumption will be reduced if income is decreased by one dollar. The MPC tells what part of the reduction in income is absorbed by consumer purchases; the MPS tells what part is absorbed by savings. While the marginal propensities are symmetrical concepts that apply to both increases and decreases in income, there is no reason to suspect that the MPC applying to an increase in disposable income will have the same numerical value as the MPC applying to a reduction in income.

"He has this bizarre *system of* spending *10 percent and* saving *90 percent.*"

CHAPTER NINE

The Multiplier

The concepts presented above may sound suspiciously like something put into a textbook only to give the instructor something to use in an examination. It is quite possible that the concepts will appear on a test, but they do have other uses too. The marginal propensity to consume and the marginal propensity to save are important clues needed to define the *multiplier*—one of the most important tools in all of macroeconomics. The multiplier is used to determine or measure the ultimate effect of a change in spending, income, or investment.

Everyone has a common-sense notion closely related to the multiplier. It seems logical to every local resident that the local (and ultimately the national) economy can be stimulated by "keeping money in circulation." This belief apparently stems from the obvious interrelationships that arise among economic actors. The local school district pays the schoolteacher. The teacher then buys from the grocer, who buys from the wholesaler, who buys from the cannery, which buys from farmers, who send their children to school.[2] All these actors pay taxes to support the schoolteacher, and this closes the circle shown in blue in Figure 9-2.

[2]Throughout this section, the "grocer" should be taken to represent all retailers; "wholesaler," all intermediate handlers; and the canner and farmer, all producers. In real life, the entire increase in salary will obviously not be spent at the grocery store.

Figure 9-2 The Multiplier at Work

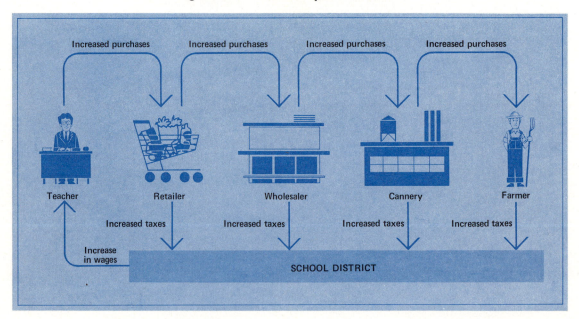

If the teacher's salary is increased, a part of the increase will be used to buy more food from the grocer. That is, the teacher has a marginal propensity to consume more food. The increased purchase from the grocer induces the grocer to purchase more from the wholesaler and the wholesaler to purchase more from the canner who in turn buys more from the farmer. The initial increase in purchases from the grocer *plus* increases for the wholesaler *plus* increases for the canner *plus* increases for the farmer will yield a sum greater than the original increase in the teacher's salary. The salary increase brings an increased expenditure, which is *multiplied* as it moves through the chain of producers and firms supplying the increased goods demanded by the schoolteacher. This is the multiplier effect.

The multiplier is the numerical relationship between an original increase in expenditure and the ultimate change in total income that results as the money is spent and respent through various sectors of the economy.

Describing the multiplier by continual reference to teacher, grocer, wholesaler, canner, and farmer is too cumbersome. A more useful expression of the multiplier stems from the marginal propensity to consume. If the teacher's MPC is .50, he will use half of any increase in salary to purchase consumer goods from the grocer.[3]

Figure 9–3 illustrates a sequence composed of five "rounds" of economic activity. Each person involved in the sequence is assumed to have an MPC of .50. In Round 1, the teacher receives an increase in salary of $100 per month. In the second round, the teacher again receives his $100 and, in addition, $50 of his previous check has been spent and becomes part of the grocer's income. In Round 3, the teacher is still receiving his added $100 and is still spending $50 on groceries. Now the grocer, too, spends half of his $50 on consumer goods, bringing the total money in circulation to $175 above what it was before the increase in the teacher's salary (teacher's $100 raise plus teacher's $50 spending plus grocer's $25 spending). By Round 4, all three of the recipients from the previous round are spending half of their added receipts, so total expenditures swell by $187.50 ($100.00 + $50.00 + $25.00 + $12.50 = $187.50), and in Round 5 the process continues with the total increase in economic activity reaching $193.75. The process does not end with Round 5, since even the recipient of the $6.25—whoever that might be —will move ahead into Rounds 6, 7, and 8, always spending half the new income on consumer goods. In this fashion, the teacher's increase in earnings is passed along through the economy. Even though only half the teacher's increase is spent on consumer goods, the total effect on the economy is greater than the value of the teacher's original increase.

---

[3] An MPC of .50 is much lower than marginal propensities actually observed in the U.S. economy. It is used only for simplicity's sake. The more realistic MPC—.90—could be substituted without changing the argument.

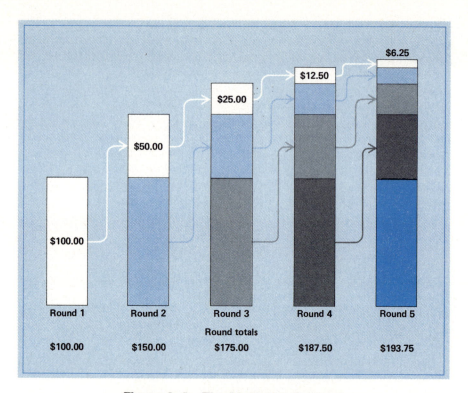

Figure 9-3 The Multiplier Concept

The multiplier can be brought into focus by following a single increase in expenditure as it goes through the five rounds shown in Figure 9-3. The original Round 1 increase is shown as an unshaded bar valued at $100. In Round 2, the $50 increase in expenditures arising from this first $100 is shown as the unshaded square valued at $50. The consequences of the original injection can be traced by following the arrows to the unshaded boxes in subsequent rounds. In this case the original increase led to $50, then $25, then $12.50, then $6.25 more in expenditures as subsequent income recipients each spent half their increase in income on consumer goods.

Illustrations up to this point have been based on the fundamental assumption that each recipient of a raise in income spends half the increase on consumer goods. The MPC has been assumed constant at .50. If the MPC were assumed to be .90, and if each consumer were to spend 90 percent of any increase in income on consumer goods, the numerical difference in the results would be quite large even though the process would remain the same. With MPC at .90, the original recipient of $100 would spend $90 rather than $50 on consumer goods, the Round 2 recipient would spend $81 ($90 received, × .90), and the expenditures of each other participant in this small example would increase correspondingly. As the marginal propensity to spend on consumer goods changes, so does the relationship between the original increase and the aggregate expenditures ultimately made by all actors.

The value of the multiplier is directly related, then, to the magnitude of the marginal propensity to consume. A high marginal propensity to consume means that a high proportion of any increase in income will be spent for consumer goods. With most money being spent, the total effect will be substantial and a high multiplier effect will result. If the MPC is low, only a small portion of any increase in income will be used to purchase goods and services. Since only small amounts of money go from first- to second-, third-, and fourth-round consumers, the multiplier will be small. This is consistent with the popular common-sense notion that keeping money in circulation brings high benefits while keeping money out of circulation has some damaging effects.

Even this graphic portrayal of the multiplier is too cumbersome for everyday use in describing aggregate economic behavior. The multiplier concept can be made more compact by putting it into symbolic form. All that is needed is a way of recognizing the relationship between the MPC and the multiplier. This relationship is not complex. The definition of the income multiplier is given by the relationship:

$$\text{multiplier} = \frac{\text{total (ultimate) change in income}}{\text{original change in expenditures}}$$

One-Shot or Sustained Increases: Differential Multiplier Effects

As long as consumers spend even a part of each addition to their incomes, the multiplier is operating. The effect is different, though, depending on whether the increase is a temporary, one-shot increase or one that will be sustained over a long period of time. A one-time increase in a teacher's income (say, a gift from a benevolent uncle) will increase the incomes of people with whom the teacher does business and, in turn, the incomes of people with whom they do business. If the MPC throughout the economy is .50, each will spend one-half the added income, so $100 would ultimately build to $100.00 + $50.00 + $25.00 + $12.50 + $6.25 + ... = some multiple of the original increase. A one-shot change in consumer income has an immediate effect on the economy, but the subsequent effects become dissipated as the amount spent and respent dwindles.

A continuous or permanent increase has a continuous effect. The original increase is multiplied, so that the subsequent rounds have increased impacts on the total economy. The impact in each round will be permanent and the effect on national income will show no tendency to dwindle.

There is also a simple formula that shows how the multiplier is related to the marginal propensity to consume:

$$\text{multiplier} = \frac{1}{1 - \text{MPC}}$$

and since MPC + MPS = 1, MPS = 1 − MPC and

$$\text{multiplier} = \frac{1}{\text{MPS}}$$

This formula shows that a high MPC leads to a high multiplier, while a low MPC leads to a low multiplier—again confirming the common-sense notion. Indeed, if all income were spent by everyone who received it, the multiplier would expand to infinity

$$(\text{multiplier} = \frac{1}{1 - \text{MPC}} = \frac{1}{1 - 1} = \infty).[4]$$

If the original recipient of new income did not spend any of the new income, the multiplier would have a value of 1

$$(\text{multiplier} = \frac{1}{1 - 0} = \frac{1}{1} = 1)$$

and the aggregate contribution of that person's income to the total economy would be limited to the amount of the increase in income itself.

A final qualifying note must be mentioned in connection with the multiplier. The multiplier operates as income flows through various rounds of economic activity. A "round" represents an indefinite period. It may be a day, a week, or a year in duration, or its length may vary,

[4]The expansion to infinity would require many rounds to accomplish. These rounds would build income in exactly the same fashion as the example of Figure 9–3.

Do Not Take the Multiplier Lightly

The multiplier is not merely an exercise. The early discussions in Chapters 3, 4, and 5 stressed the interdependence and circularity of a modern economic system. That fact has also been explicitly recognized in more recent chapters. The multiplier builds on both circularity and interdependence. It shows that money injected into the system has a capacity to affect total income by more than one might expect, because that money is multiplied as it traces a complex path through the circular flow. The multiplier shows, too, that under certain conditions a small change in income can have a massive effect on the entire economy. This concept must be understood not as an exercise in mechanics but as one of the vital, dynamic forces in the economy and in the formulation of economic policy.

What Kind of Multiplier?

In the late 1930s, the multiplier became a permanent part of economic reasoning. At that time it was applied mostly to investment expenditure. Investment spending was then—as it is now—extremely volatile, and changes in investment brought wide (multiplied) swings in the level of economic activity. As time has passed, the original concept of the "investment multiplier" has been broadened. It is now recognized that *any* increase in spending will have a multiplied effect. An unexpected jump in consumption will be multiplied; so will an increase in defense spending. Unless there is reason to qualify the term, economists now refer simply to "the multiplier."

depending on the season, the age of the income recipient, or even the section of the country. Moreover, one person's spending habits are likely to change quite demonstrably over time. This variability in the length of a "round" has important consequences. It means that, while the direction of a change might be easy to ascertain, the magnitude and the timing of the change are always difficult to estimate. Even though it is known that an increase in teacher salaries will help the local economy, the timing and magnitude of the effect will vary with the circumstances.

In sum, the multiplier is a sophisticated illustration of the bromide "A little goes a long way." The multiplier process shows how increases in income are amplified. They are highly amplified if the MPC is high, modestly amplified if the MPC is low. This behavior is extremely important to policy makers who wish to change the aggregate level of income for the

"Believe me, the whole economy profits. We rob someone of five grand. Then we buy some stuff from a fence. He gives his cut to the mob. They pay off the cops . . ."

whole economy. If a change of $100 million in consumer income is ultimately needed to accomplish some economic goal, a policy that brings about a much more modest initial change should suffice because of the multiplier's effect of expanding any initial change. This aspect of economic behavior will become very important in the next chapter.

Summary

1 The average propensity to consume (APC) is the proportion of income that is—on the average—spent for consumption purposes. In the U.S. economy, the APC is approximately 90 percent of disposable income.
2 The average propensity to save (APS) is the proportion of income that is—on the average—saved by households.
3 The marginal propensity to consume (MPC) describes the proportion of all *increases* in income that will be spent for added consumption.
4 The marginal propensity to save (MPS) tells the proportion of an *increase* in income that will be added to saving.
5 The multiplier concept is a sophisticated version of the common idea that keeping money in circulation is good for the economy. It describes the formal relationship between an increase (or decrease) in purchasing power and the final increase (decrease) in aggregate income after the increase has been spent, respent, then spent again.
6 The multiplier is uniquely related to the marginal propensity to consume. If the MPC is high, the multiplier will be high; if the MPC is low, the multiplier will be low.

Exercises

1 Explain these important terms and concepts:
  average propensity to save
  average propensity to consume
  marginal propensity to save
  marginal propensity to consume
  "keeping money in circulation"
  "round" of economic activity
  the multiplier
  $$\frac{1}{1 - \text{MPC}} = \frac{1}{\text{MPS}} = \text{multiplier}$$

2 The following data apply to a hypothetical economy:

  Consumer expenditure $500 million
  Government expenditure   100 million
  Investment expenditure   200 million
  Marginal propensity to consume .75

  a For some reason, government expenditures double to $200 million. What will be the total effect on GNP?
  b If half the increase had come from investment, would the result be the same?

3 Why does a higher MPC always lead to a higher multiplier? Explain this in words and without reference to mathematical expressions.

A Contemporary Problem
President Ford's Tax Refund Plan

The depressed but inflationary economy of Spring 1975 was vexing to public administrators and politicians as well as to economists. The causes of the problems were not well understood, and if causes are not known, solutions are hard to find. The executive branch of government thought that getting more money into the hands of individual consumers would spur buying and the increase in buying would raise employment. A tax refund was proposed as a measure of increasing buying power. This refund was to be based on a family's taxable income. Low-income families were to receive a proportionately higher refund than high-income families, but in no case would a family's refund exceed $200. Through this refund process, the Ford administration hoped to return some $8 billion to the income stream.

Ford and his advisers hoped the multiplier would swell the $8 million into a much larger sum. Opponents of the measure were afraid it would not work because the refund was too small and refund recipients would use the money to pay off debts or would save it in case the recession became worse. The measure was passed by Congress, and by June 15, 1975, checks had been sent to legitimate claimants.

It is too early to tell if the tax refund had the desired effect. Evaluation of such massive programs must usually wait from three to five years. Some practical questions arising from the refund are (1) If the MPC is .90 (as some economists think), what will be the total effect on the economy? (2) If half the refund goes to savings, what will the effect be? (3) If the refund is divided between saving and debt repayment, what will the effect be?

Analysis. The arguments center on two questions: what proportion of the refund will be spent, and will this expenditure be sufficient to bring the desired result? Only the first is analyzed here. Certainly, the Ford administration had the right idea if increased purchasing power was what was needed. An MPC of .50 would cause multiplier effects to build the refund to $16 billion. However, if the money was used to pay off debts, no new purchases would be made and the infusion of money into the economy would not have the desired employment-building effects. Similarly, if individual families expected the recession to grow more severe, the refund may well have been placed in savings—again failing to bring jobs for the unemployed. Individual refund recipients had three options: spend, pay off debts, and save. Since two of the three would not allow fulfillment of the employment objective, it can be concluded that the Ford administration was acting somewhat dangerously.

10

Fiscal Policy

The macroeconomics of Chapters 7, 8, and 9 is very useful in helping to understand why an economic society behaves the way it does. Aggregate spending—the result of consumption, investment, and government activity—can be too high or too low. If it is too high, potential buyers will compete for the privilege of buying, prices will be forced upward, and some buyers will go without. If it is too low, goods will go unsold, inventories will accumulate, and eventually factors will be idle. Consumer spending, investment spending, and government spending are important explanatory variables. If they can *explain* macro behavior, they can also be used to alter or *control* macro behavior.

Changing the level of aggregate income stems from changing the level of one of its determinants. When the level of income is too high or too low to stimulate healthy activity among the economy's firms and households, government may act to restore a level of economic activity that is conducive to the profitable management of private business affairs. Although thousands of options are open to a government that wants to intervene in economic affairs, most intervention takes place through the use of fiscal policy and centers on changes in the mix of taxing and spending measures. This chapter describes the mechanics of fiscal policy. Chapter 11 will discuss the national debt, a by-product of some kinds of fiscal activity.

Deliberately Managing the Economy

Taxing and spending are powerful tools. Governments the world over and in all times have been forced to use them to provide facilities and perform functions that are not or cannot be left to private sectors of the economy. While nations and lesser governments have always taxed and spent, only in recent decades have they felt compelled to design *fiscal policies*. The distinction between just "taxing and spending" and "fiscal policy" is an important one. Taxing and spending need be nothing more than the bookkeeping activity performed in any organized society. Frequent Biblical references indicate that even in ancient times taxes were collected and governmental disbursements were made. Nations were thus engaged in taxing and spending activity. Fiscal policy, however, is quite another thing, because *policy* implies a plan or objective. An agricultural policy may be geared to increasing the output of food; a welfare policy may be designed to transfer money from rich to poor; a defense policy may be designed to keep the enemy out. A nation's fiscal policy, however, is broader than any of these, since it involves the entire set of taxing and spending policies sponsored by a government. The announced fiscal policy of a nation may be simply to make total tax receipts cover all intended expenditures—to make government income equal government expense. Or it may be the announced policy of a government to tax *more* than it spends, thus reducing the volume of purchasing power (aggregate demand) available to the public. A third option is for the government to spend more than it taxes, in a effort to increase the income entering the circular flow.

For decades, most economists and public policy makers shared one unyielding attitude toward fiscal policy: Budgets should be balanced. It took the devastating, world-wide Great Depression of the 1930s, plus the inventive mind of John Maynard Keynes, to convince nations that the combination of taxing and spending could be varied in order to influence growth, employment, and economic stability. Keynes's notion was deceptively simple. He believed that aggregate economic activity could be described in terms of the three components of aggregate demand—consumer spending, investment spending, and government spending. Of these three, only government spending was amenable to conscious and direct manipulation. If quick changes in economic performance were desired, the way to accomplish them was to manipulate government spending. Once governments understood the power associated with their ability to tax and spend, fiscal policy became a useful method of managing an economy. Government could use the power to tax and spend not only to carry out its traditional role of providing public goods and services, but also to help achieve other important economic and social goals—to eliminate depression, unemployment, or inflation.

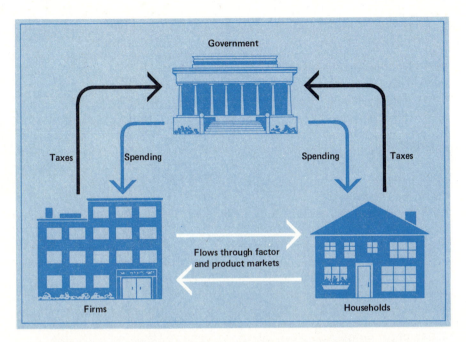

Figure 10-1 Government as an Actor in the Circular Flow

When to Use Fiscal Policy

Fiscal policy can be designed to increase, decrease, or maintain aggregate demand. Regardless of its goal, fiscal activity occurs when government decides either to tax or to spend. The flow diagram in Figure 10-1 omits some of the more elaborate connections seen in earlier chapters, but shows that money can flow to government from households and firms or money can flow from government to these other actors. All relationships can be (and usually are) two-way, with households and firms giving money to government and receiving services in return.

Depending on the needs of the economy, the flows may be into government treasuries or they may be from the government to the households and firms. Similarly, depending on the needs of a particular policy, the flows—in either direction—may be large or small. When there is inflation the appropriate objective of fiscal policy is to reduce purchasing power. This can be done by imposing higher taxes to take money away from firms or households, or by reducing the amount of money spent by government. Either course allows fewer dollars to enter the circular flow—fewer dollars to add further pressure to an inflationary situation or to push up demand for the limited stock of goods.

In a recession, or when unemployment is threatening, the opposite actions are appropriate. Fiscal activities should be used to *increase* the purchasing power of firms and households. This can be accomplished by lowering taxes or by increasing spending. By taxing less, the government leaves more purchasing power in the hands of firms and households. If society's marginal propensity to consume is indeed .90, 90 percent of the additional income will be used to buy goods and services, and so the increases in purchasing power will eventually lead to an expansion in output and a weakening of recession. An increase in government spending will have a similar effect: placing additional income in the hands of firms and/or resource owners will expand output and reduce the threat of recession.

A wide range of problems can be studied when the problem is cast in terms of aggregate income and aggregate expenditure. Figures 10–2, 10–3, and 10–4 show variations on this theme. Figure 10–2 shows aggregate expenditures made by consumers (C); consumers and investors ($C + I$); and consumers, investors, and government ($C + I + G$). The amount of expenditure, as before, is read along the vertical axis, and income, now in terms of NNP, is read on the horizontal axis. The point of intersection (E) between $C + I + G$ and the 45-degree line shows the level of income at which all output is consumed. At this level of income, the system is in equilibrium. In Figure 10–2, the equilibrium level of income is assumed to be the level at which all factors wanting employment are employed. At this level of NNP, the economy is in equilibrium at full employment.

The Deflationary Gap

Figure 10–3 is simplified. The consumption line (C) and the consumption plus investment line ($C + I$) are removed, leaving only the line desig-

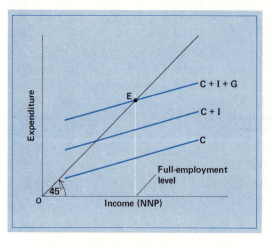

**Figure 10–2
Recapitulating the Income-Determination Model**

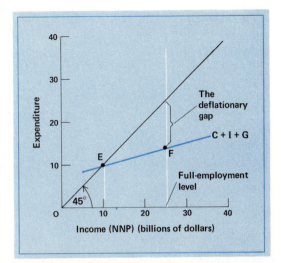

**Figure 10–3
The Deflationary Gap**

nating aggregate demand from all three sources ($C + I + G$). Moreover, $C + I + G$ has been lowered, so equilibrium occurs at a level of NNP considerably below the assumed level of full employment (from Figure 10–2). The system is in equilibrium at E; full employment is at F. In this case, aggregate demand ($C + I + G$) is insufficient to purchase all goods and services produced at the full-employment level of income (F). Even if firms were operating at full-employment levels of output, they would not be able to sell all their output. There would be pressure and incentive for firms to slow activity and cut purchases of factors. At any point where the full-employment level of NNP is higher than the equilibrium level (any level of NNP between $10 billion and $25 billion in Figure 10–3), the $C + I + G$ line lies below the 45-degree line. The vertical gap between the two lines at such a point (between aggregate output and aggregate demand) reveals the amount of pressure for economic contraction, and has traditionally been called the *deflationary gap*.

The deflationary gap is the amount by which aggregate demand must increase in order to equal aggregate supply at the full-employment level of output. It is deflationary because demanders are not willing to purchase all that is produced and firms are therefore induced to contract or *deflate* their activity.

A deflationary gap can be removed by increasing the purchasing power of firms and households. This is done by reducing their taxes or by increasing the volume of government purchases.

The Inflationary Gap

Figure 10–4 shows the opposite situation. In this case, equilibrium (E) for the economy is at a level of aggregate income considerably higher

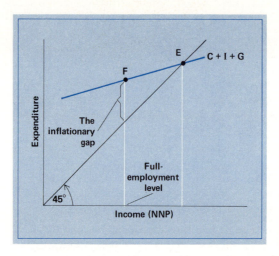

Figure 10-4
The Inflationary Gap

than the full-employment level (*F*). Consumers, investors, and government want to purchase more than the economy can produce. How much more is indicated by the vertical distance between the *C* + *I* + *G* line and the 45-degree line at the full-employment level. An economy in this situation will be pushed toward equilibrium because demands of buyers exceed the available output. Buyers will compete to purchase all that they can, and prices will rise. The *inflationary gap* shown in Figure 10-4 can be eliminated by taking money away from consumers and producing firms or by reducing the purchases and payments made by government.[1]

The inflationary gap describes the amount by which aggregate demand exceeds aggregate supply when the economy is at the full-employment level of NNP. Since demand exceeds supply, prices will rise.

The expenditure lines used to designate the deflationary and inflationary gaps in Figures 10-3 and 10-4 are composite *C* + *I* + *G* lines that include consumer expenditures (*C*), investment expenditure (*I*), and government spending (*G*). The lessons of these graphs can be emphasized by concentrating on government expenditures (*G*)—the one component of aggregate demand that can be consciously manipulated through changes in fiscal policy. If an inflationary gap is present, government spending can be reduced or taxes can be increased so that *C* + *I* + *G* will shift downward until it intersects the 45-degree reference line at a lower level of output that is consistent with full employment. In Figure 10-5, the aggregate demand curve *C* + *I* + *G'* shows that

---

[1] To be sure, inflationary tendencies could also be removed by increasing output so that the quantity of goods and services could catch up with demand. This, however, takes time, and economies in inflationary conditions can seldom wait for output to expand.

the equilibrium level of total expenditure made by all three actors is $45 billion and is well above the full-employment level of $32.5 billion. If this level of spending persists, prices will have to rise since demanders are seeking to purchase much more than producers are willing or able to supply. Fiscal policy can be used to reduce the spending level by decreasing the government component. The same goal can be achieved by increasing the taxes paid by households and firms. With an increase in taxes, the C component and the I component fall, bringing total expenditure to a lower level—ideally one that is compatible with full employment but is not inflationary in character.

If a deflationary gap is present, as in the case of C + I + G″ in Figure 10–5, the opposite prescriptions are appropriate. With a deflationary gap, the problem is too little rather than too much aggregate demand. In this situation, government may attempt to increase aggregate demand by increasing its own spending. Increased government spending will require firms to produce more and this will cause firms to use more factors of production and increase their payments to households. Or the government can choose to cut taxes and thereby increase the ability of households to buy the output of firms. In either case, the hope is that output and income will stop growing at just that point where all factors are employed and where aggregate expenditures just equal aggregate income.

Figure 10–5 Two Cases Where Fiscal Policy Will Help

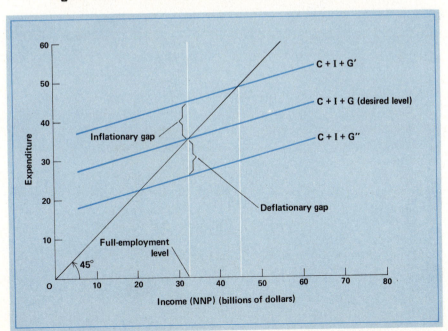

These models of the inflationary gap and the deflationary gap show how fiscal policy can be used to increase or decrease the components of aggregate expenditure in order to achieve an economic condition in which there is full employment without either inflationary or deflationary pressures. Discussion will now center on the size of the change needed in fiscal activity.

How Much Should Fiscal Activity Be Changed?

As in the case of private consumption or investment expenditure, a change in government fiscal activity produces amplified, or multiplied, results. The multiplied results stem directly from the multiplier introduced in Chapter 9. As an increase or decrease in income spreads through the economy, its effects become amplified. Figure 10–6 shows the multiplier effect working in response to changes in fiscal activity. Two parallel

Figure 10–6 Fiscal Policy and the Multiplier

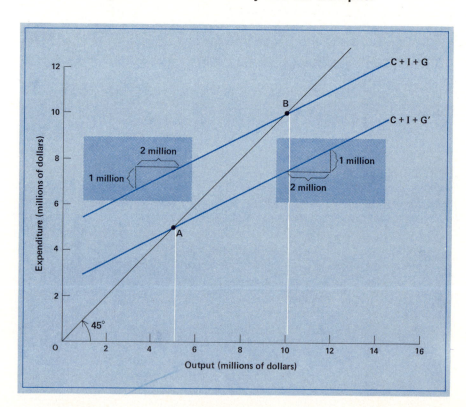

aggregate demand lines—each including expenditures made by consumers, investors, and governments—are shown. If an economy starts at equilibrium position B (with an aggregate output of $10 million), but fiscal authorities desire an equilibrium at output level A (aggregate output of $5 million), the correct prescription is to drop C + I + G by an amount equal to the vertical distance between the two aggregate demand lines ($2.5 million). A reduction of $2.5 million in government spending will bring with it the desired $5 million drop in output. How can this be? The insert on the C + I + G line tells the story. In traveling down the C + I + G line, a one-unit reduction in the volume of expenditures (vertical change) is accompanied by a two-unit change in the value of output (horizontal change). Expanding this to a much larger scale, a $2.5 million reduction in expenditures (vertical change) brings a $5 million decrease in output (horizontal change). To get from B to A, then, government needs to reduce spending activity (on the vertical axis) by much less than the desired reduction in aggregate output (on the horizontal axis).

The process works in reverse. An economy starting at A but wanting to use fiscal policy to reach output level B will have to add to its spending an amount equal to the vertical distance between the two aggregate demand lines. This $2.5 million increase in spending will increase aggregate output by $5 million. The insert on the C + I + G' line shows why. An increase in expenditure of one unit (vertical change) brings with it an increase in output of two units (horizontal change). Expanding this principle leads to the situation depicted in the graph where $2.5 million of added government expenditures yield a $5 million expansion in aggregate output. This happens as a result of the multiplier process also. Each dollar of government spending is spent and respent in accord with the recipient's marginal propensity to consume. The result is a multiplied chain of expenditures.

A very disarming question remains: How much should taxes and spending be changed? Unfortunately, the answer to this question is largely unknown. Economic planners and policy makers may feel that the economy needs to move from A to B, and may therefore instigate fiscal changes aimed at increasing spending or decreasing taxes. However, if the marginal propensity to consume—and hence the multiplier—is not known, the size of the needed change in taxes and spending can only be estimated. Similarly with a change from B to A. The direction of the desired change may be known, but the required magnitude remains troublesome. So it is with all fiscal policy. It is a relatively dependable tool in that it will elicit the desired *direction* of change, but it is unreliable with respect to the *magnitude* of the response. In the spring of 1975, President Ford used an income-tax rebate to return $8 billion to individual taxpayers. Although this was a controversial step, Ford's hope was that the $8 billion would be *multiplied* sufficiently to liven a sluggish economy and employ some of the 6.5 million persons who were out of work.

Automatic Stabilizers

Not all fiscal policy is discretionary. Some fiscal policies automatically begin to force money into the economy whenever employment or incomes lag and automatically begin to remove purchasing power when inflation threatens. The major automatic stabilizers are unemployment compensation and progressive income taxes.

Unemployment Compensation

Nearly all industrial economies are occasionally plagued by unemployment. The early capitalistic societies in Western Europe were troubled by the unemployment caused by the Enclosures and by the Industrial Revolution. In more recent experience, unemployment has been related to heavy immigration, technological change, and fluctuations in business activity. From the time people began to break away from the soil, unemployment has been a worrisome problem for public officials. As early as 1601, Great Britain attempted to aid the unemployed through the Poor Laws, which were based on a complex set of taxes and payments left to the discretion of local officials. The original laws were somewhat ineffective but were continually modified and eventually became Great Britain's general unemployment relief laws.

The Enclosures

Great Britain went through many changes between the fifteenth and nineteenth centuries. Not the least of these was the Enclosures—the partitioning and fencing of what had previously been common property. The partitioning became necessary as agricultural technology changed and as the labor force switched from pastoral employment to industrial employment. The small, fenced plots of land took the place of the large common area. An individual decided how each plot was to be used, what crops would be grown, and what land was to lie idle.

The change was not easy, since it required some workers to leave the land and seek employment in industry. With the Industrial Revolution barely under way, finding an alternative to farming was not always possible.

Although the Enclosures began in Great Britain as early as 1450, the process took over 400 years.

The Enclosure movement is especially interesting today, since now, in the highly industrialized 1970s, the world's advanced nations are trying to reverse the pattern. They want to make more common space available for pent-up residents of metropolitan areas. And "defencing" land is proving to be at least as troublesome as fencing it was.

Unemployment compensation laws impose modest taxes on workers while they are employed, but pay dividends (in lieu of wages) to them when they are unemployed. An unemployment insurance program of this kind is *automatically* doing what fiscal policy should do. When employment is high, payments from government to workers stop because no one is qualified to receive unemployment insurance. When unemployment increases, so do insurance payments, so that injections into the income stream are automatically made when they are needed. The program collects taxes during periods of full employment but adds to the purchasing power of households during times of distress. In 1966, when approximately 3.6 percent of the U.S. civilian labor force was unemployed, unemployment compensation checks totaling $1,891 million were delivered to people temporarily out of work. By contrast, in 1975 when unemployment levels reached 8.5 percent of the labor force, checks valued at nearly $12 billion reached qualified recipients. These billions of dollars helped maintain the individual families who received them and also helped improve the performance of the sluggish economy of the mid-1970s.

The Progressive Income Tax

After all the discussion of the conscious use of taxes to perform specific functions in managing the economy, it may seem contradictory to call tax receipts an *automatic* stabilizing influence for the economy. Both claims are true.

The tax systems used by the federal government and by 39 of the 50 states include a *progressive income tax*.

A progressive income tax is one that collects proportionately larger amounts of money from the wealthy than it does from the poor.[2]

In addition to this advantage, a progressive tax acts to stabilize the economy as the nation goes through periods of recession and inflation. The mechanism is very simple. In times of inflation the incomes of households increase. As incomes increase, however, the progressive income tax takes away an increasingly larger part of that income. The tax system automatically absorbs some of the increase in purchasing power and reduces the threat of inflation. By contrast, in times of recession economic activity falls, the circular flow slows, and payments to factors drop. During such periods the tax bite drops, too, taking proportionately less income for tax purposes. Again, the progressive tax system is operating to counteract the problem of recession in the economy.

---

[2]It is fully recognized that the tax system as practiced in the United States is full of loopholes that seem to favor wealthy people. Nonetheless, in principle, the progressive income tax is intended to tax the wealthy more heavily than the poor.

Discretionary Stabilizers

While the automatic stabilizers do work, they are not effective enough to cope with serious fluctuations in economic activity by themselves. Taxes help reduce purchasing power as income rises, and unemployment payments provide purchasing power when income and employment fall. But progressive income taxes take only a part of increased income, leaving much behind to be spent during an inflationary cycle. Similarly, unemployment checks go to many families during a recession, but there are still many classes of employees not covered by unemployment programs.

The automatic stabilizers are supplemented by a major group of policies that are discretionary; that is, they are put into effect only through deliberate efforts of economic planners. Major discretionary policies include public works programs, welfare payments, and changes in tax rates.

Public Works

When a highway is built or a dam constructed or a library opened, the nation adds to its stock of *social overhead capital*.

Social overhead capital includes those forms of capital that do not necessarily produce a salable product, but that contribute to the production of other goods or services. Social overhead capital includes things like roads, fire departments, museums, and flood-control dams. Since these forms of capital are not easily sold in organized markets, they are most often installed by government.

The process of creating this capital is called *public works*. Public works includes all activities that add to the stock of productive capital owned by the public. Hence, the construction of highways, government-sponsored irrigation projects, airfields, and city streets are public works. Also included are some temporary activities that perform useful functions but do not necessarily add to the economy's stock of capital. Efforts by VISTA volunteers to organize and teach minority groups and the work of the Job Corps to clean public campgrounds do not add to productive capacity, but they do qualify as public works.

Public works can be used to reduce the severity of economic fluctuations. They change the amount of purchasing power in the circular flow. The clearest examples come from a generation ago when, during the Great Depression of the 1930s, thousands of men were hired by the federal government to build Shasta Dam in northern California, plant windbreaks in Kansas, and blaze trails in the Maine woods. All of these public-works activities and hundreds of others added purchasing power to an economy that was struggling to recover from very low levels of aggregate demand.

Public-works projects have an advantage that many fiscal measures do not enjoy: they can be geographically selective. If local economies in Nevada or Tennessee show signs of weakening, specific programs can be used to expand aggregate demand in those areas. In the 1930s, the Tennessee Valley Authority was used not only to fight the general depression but also specifically to aid the seven states in the Tennessee Valley. Similarly, in the years just after World War II, the construction of huge hydroelectric plants was undertaken in the Pacific Northwest to create employment for returning veterans and to give the Pacific Northwest the important advantage of lower electric power rates—an advantage that was well used as that area became industrialized. More recently, selective public-works policies have been used to revitalize Appalachia.

Public-works programs suffer two significant disadvantages. First, the administration of a public-works activity is painfully slow, and aggregate demand may have to be stimulated rather quickly in order to maintain acceptable performance in an economy. Public works on a major scale —even if previously planned—can require weeks, months, or years to get started. The government does not decide to build a dam today and start construction tomorrow. Such a venture needs careful planning, complete approval in Congress, and the appropriation of money before it can begin. Federal agencies participating in public-works programs can diminish the planning problem to a limited degree by developing a backlog of projects already approved by Congress. Even then, though, starting up is often so slow that the original economic problem could be solved by other means before the proposed project is under way.

The Steps Required to Build a Dam

For decades, the development of natural resources has been an important part of public-works programs in the United States. Activities related to natural resources were extensively used to put people to work and to get purchasing power into their hands during the depressed decade of the 1930s. Public development of a major natural resource cannot be turned on and off at will, however. Such projects require months or years of planning. In the case of a large dam, four major steps and untold numbers of other steps and procedures must be taken before the first shovel of dirt is moved. The major steps are:

1 *Initiation.* The first step is initiated by local people or by developmental agencies in consultation with the congressional delegation from the state(s) in which the project will be located. A public-works project is undertaken only in response to a clearly identifiable problem.

2 *Feasibility.* To make sure the proposal is economically, socially, and environmentally sound, reports and surveys must be made, reviewed and revised. These reports must comment on all aspects of the proposed development. Reports are voluminous and can easily take years to complete.

3 *Authorization.* Authorization is a congressional gesture that says all interested and affected groups have agreed that the proposal is good and that the dam can be built. After authorization, it is permissible to start constructing the dam if money can be found.

4 *Appropriation.* Appropriation provides money to construct the dam. This, too, is a congressional act, but it may (and often does!) come years after authorization has been received.

A second disadvantage associated with public works is that they are difficult to stop. A period of unemployment may stimulate many public-works projects—highways, flood control activities, VISTA programs—in several states. These efforts may no sooner have begun than the nation's economic misfortunes reverse themselves and require a completely different type of fiscal policy. While it makes good economic sense to stop unneeded public-works activities that are under way, it is hard for the public to accept half-completed highways (that do no good), half-completed flood control efforts (that do no good), or VISTA programs that are stopped before they have time to show results.

Welfare Payments

Since the 1600s, most Western nations have made some attempts to provide for families that have no reasonable means of support. In the United States, welfare payments are made to the aged, the infirm, families with young children but no income, and a number of other disadvantaged groups.[3] Payments are most often made by individual states, but large amounts of federal money are transferred to states to help finance the state programs. By adjusting the amount of money transferred to a state and by manipulating eligibility requirements, economic planners can use welfare payments to meet fiscal objectives. In times of high employment, high wages, and inflation, welfare payments can be reduced to keep from adding excessively to aggregate demand. In times of unemployment and recession, welfare payments can be increased to stimulate aggregate demand.

In practice, three things prevent welfare payments from being a powerful fiscal tool. First, the number of people eligible for welfare payments is quite low. Even if all eligible persons were reached through the welfare system, the number of dollars added to the income stream would not be sufficient to make a demonstrable change in aggregate demand. Second, since the activist era of the 1960s, welfare payments have become an almost permanent government obligation and have lost their discretionary characteristics. No rational politician would dare attempt to manipulate welfare payments beyond certain limits. Finally, public sentiment regarding welfare payments runs contrary to the discretionary needs of a fiscal policy. In good times, the public becomes magnanimous and makes large welfare payments to the needy. In bad times—just when added money should be injected into the income stream—public senti-

[3] Welfare payments are not to be confused with unemployment compensation. Welfare payments are grants (gifts) made to people who are not regular members of the labor force. Unemployment compensation payments come from insurance programs financed by employers and employed workers for the benefit of unemployed members of the labor force.

"It's the welfare department. Hide everything."

ment often calls for "tightening the belt"—meaning smaller rather than increased payments to those who are unable to become part of the mainstream of economic life.

Changes in Tax Rates

The progressive nature of the personal income tax has been mentioned as an automatic force in dampening business fluctuations. It is true that this kind of tax acts to offset changes in economic activity, but no economic swing can be stopped by the automatic features of the progressive income tax alone. The taxing mechanism can be strengthened by exploiting its discretionary features. By changing the rate of taxes absorbed from all levels of income earners, fiscal authorities can alter the amount of money left in the pockets of consumers and investors. Table 10–1 uses hypothetical data to illustrate this process. A progressive tax schedule appears in the second column. The increased rate shows that as income increases, the proportion taken for taxes increases too. If increased taxes are to be used to reduce buying power, the higher tax rates shown in the third column might be used in the place of the old, lower rates. The new

---

The Council of Economic Advisers

The Employment Act of 1946 was a historic piece of legislation. It did not cure any economic ills, nor did it make provisions for large-scale changes in aggregate demand. It did establish some required goals for the economy, it set up the Joint Economic Committee in Congress, and it called for the formation of the Council of Economic Advisers (The CEA).

The CEA is made up of three economists appointed by the President to serve as his personal advisors on economic matters. The three, together with their staff, aid in the preparation of legislation, coordination of economic affairs, and promotion of the President's economic plans. Members of the CEA have most often, but not always, come from the academic world.

Since its formation thirty years ago, the CEA has continued to grow in stature and importance. At its inception, few citizens could name Edwin G. Nourse as the first chairman of the CEA. Now, the name of Alan Greenspan is almost a household word.

The decade of the 1960s was a particularly active time for the CEA. Its members worked very hard to insure passage of the Tax Reduction Bill of 1964 and the tax-increasing legislation of 1968. Much of the credit for these legislative successes goes to Walter W. Heller, who, as chairman of the CEA from 1961 to 1964, helped instigate a number of broad economic programs. More than anything else, however, he taught economics to the citizens of the United States.

Table 10-1 Hypothetical Changes in Tax Rates

Household income level	Original tax rate	New tax rate (increase)	New tax rate (decrease)
$ 0 – 5,000	10%	11%	9%
5,001 – 10,000	12	14	10
10,001 – 15,000	18	21	15
15,001 – 20,000	25	29	21
20,001 – 25,000	33	38	28
25,001 and above	50	56	45

tax schedule will reduce the amount of money available to households, while maintaining the progressive nature of the tax. It will force high-income groups to pay still more than was required by the original tax schedule. If the objective is to raise purchasing power, on the other hand, the lowered rates shown in the last column will leave each family with increased capacity to buy.

The executive and legislative branches of government did not use taxing powers extensively for stabilization purposes until very recent years. By 1963, however, Keynesian economic policies had become well enough understood to permit President John F. Kennedy to suggest —after much persuasion by his Council of Economic Advisers—that a tax cut would stimulate the economy sufficiently to yield a major reduction in the 5.7 percent rate of unemployment. President Kennedy did not live to see his recommendation become law. In 1964 President Lyndon B. Johnson convinced Congress that a tax cut would indeed do as the macroeconomists promised: it would add to the purchasing power of households. The untaxed income would be spent, forcing output to increase and unemployment to drop. When it was passed, the tax cut called for individual income tax rates to drop from a range of 20 to 90 percent of taxable income to a range of 14 to 65 percent.[4] Corporate income taxes were cut from 52 percent to 47 percent of taxable profits, and small businessmen who had business incomes of less than $25,000 saw their corporate-profits tax rates drop from 30 to 22 percent. This daring and controversial fiscal move paid off. Unemployment dropped from a high of 6.7 percent in 1961 to 3.8 percent in 1966 and declined further to 3.5

---

[4] A range of 20 to 91 percent means that 20 percent of the first taxable dollars must be turned over to the federal government. As income increases, so does the amount that must be paid to the government. At very high levels of income, 91 cents of each added dollar of taxable income goes to the government. Reducing the range to 14 to 65 percent leaves much more money in public hands.

percent in 1969. There is little doubt that the Kennedy tax cut accomplished its purpose. It showed that a tax cut can achieve economic objectives other than simply reducing the dollar intake of government.

More recently, fiscal policy has been used to reduce aggregate demand and slow the rate of inflation. In the late 1960s, U.S. military involvement in Southeast Asia resulted in inflation for the domestic economy. In 1969, President Richard M. Nixon asked Congress to impose a 10 percent *surcharge* on all income taxes.

A surcharge is an extra fee imposed on top of a regularly established fee. In 1969, the decision to raise taxes was made quite late, so the increase was calculated very simply: an individual calculated his tax and then added 10 percent. The 10 percent was a surcharge, or an added fee. The term is not common in macroeconomics.

The surcharge was to last only two years. The request was granted, and it indeed reduced aggregate demand. Unfortunately, a variety of other influences kept the measure from being more effective. Inflation continued, to be accompanied later by very high rates of unemployment.

Conclusion

The discretionary fiscal policies—public works, welfare payments, and tax-rate changes—are powerful tools, but they have disadvantages when used to control the economy. Their strength comes from the fact that they can be manipulated in time, in magnitude, and to some extent, in place. The weaknesses stem from the inability of Congress to act quickly, the inability to stop programs once they have been started, and, again, lack of knowledge about how large a change is needed to accomplish a specific objective.

How much has fiscal policy been used since it achieved widespread acceptance as a macroeconomic tool? A rough indication can be gained by looking at the extent of government spending over the years since Keynesian economics emerged. In 1930, the federal government made expenditures of $3.3 billion—3.5 percent of GNP. By 1940, expenditures had increased in both actual dollars and as a percent of GNP. In that year, 6.9 percent of all goods and services produced by the nation were produced in response to government action. Increases were sustained through 1950 ($43.1 billion; 12.2 percent of GNP), 1960 ($92.2 billion; 18.3 percent of GNP), 1970 ($184.5 billion; 18.9 percent of GNP), and on to 1975, when federal expenditures amounted to $361 billion and accounted for 21.3 percent of GNP. Apparently, as time has passed and the message of Keynesian economics has become more widespread, the U.S. government has increased its use of fiscal measures to aid in managing the economy. This has not been without cost. It has meant that the nation has had to revise its ideas about the role of government, taxing and spending, government's role in capital formation, the setting of a budget, and most particularly, the national debt.

Summary

1. Fiscal policy is based on the power of government to tax and spend. By using these powers carefully, government can decrease or increase the amount of purchasing power held by firms and households.
2. Some fiscal policies operate more or less automatically to adjust the amount of purchasing power in the system. Unemployment compensation and progressive income taxes are examples.
3. Other fiscal policies are discretionary and can be used only after explicit action by one or more agencies of government. Public works, welfare payments, and tax-rate changes fall into this category.
4. Fiscal policy has the tremendous advantage of being amenable to change and the lesser advantage of being geographically selective.
5. The disadvantage associated with fiscal policy is that it is seldom known exactly how much fiscal policy should be used, exactly when it should be started, or exactly when it should be stopped.

Exercises

1. Explain these important terms and concepts:
   - fiscal policy
   - fiscal activity
   - deflationary gap
   - inflationary gap
   - automatic stabilizers
   - unemployment compensation
   - progressive income tax
   - discretionary stabilizers
   - public works
   - social overhead capital
   - welfare payments
   - Council of Economic Advisers
2. Assume that the economy is functioning at levels of NNP below the full-employment level. The Council of Economic Advisers estimates that a $50 million increase in aggregate demand will raise performance to acceptable levels. An increased spending program is suggested as the means of increasing aggregate demand.
   a. If the MPC is .80, how much additional spending will be needed? (Recall Chapter 9.)
   b. If the spending is financed using tax revenues, does it matter who pays the tax or what monies are used for the tax?
3. What are the major strengths and weaknesses of the following fiscal policies, and when might each be most appropriate?
   a. An increase in unemployment benefits.
   b. Building a new highway.
   c. Reduced taxes for the wealthy.
   d. Reduced taxes for the poor.
   e. Cutting military expenditures in half.
4. Correcting an inflationary gap requires that $C + I + G$ be lowered. Is it easiest to work with C or I or G? Why?

A Contemporary Problem

The Defense Budget

Few things in the United States are so controversial as the military and the huge expenditures required to maintain the vast army, navy, and air force that we now have. Defense is by far the largest single item in the public budget. At no time since 1960 has defense expenditure dropped below 30 percent of the federal budget, and it has sometimes been very close to 50 percent. The massive scare of the Cold War and heavy U.S. involvement in Southeast Asia have kept military spending quite high.

The end of the war in Vietnam caused many people to wonder if defense expenditures could be lowered. Some were motivated by the desire to have their own taxes lowered; others thought the money could be better spent in other ways. But lowering defense spending is a hazardous move. Reducing the size of the armed forces would place many young men in the already saturated labor market and would cause a reduction in the number of workers needed to produce aircraft, guns, tanks, and uniforms. Reducing military expenditures by a significant amount would have economy-wide consequences. Critics of the capitalist system have been quick to wonder whether it could survive the shock.

Fortunately, this problem can be analyzed objectively. The analysis hinges on fiscal policy, aggregate demand, and the marginal propensity to consume (and, hence, the multiplier). The annual defense budget now hovers around $100 billion. If it were to be cut in half, $50 billion would continue to be used to maintain a military establishment. The other $50 billion would be available for other purposes. Taxes could be reduced by $50 billion, or other public functions could absorb the money.

If taxes were cut, the $50 billion would become a part of every taxpayer's disposable income. It might be used to purchase autos, new blankets, and kitchen appliances. But would these expenditures generate the same amount of aggregate demand as the military expenditure? Probably not, because part of the money would be saved and would, hence, not remain part of the income stream. If 10 percent were saved, $45 billion would return to the circular flow. The increase in consumption expenditures then would not quite offset the reduction in government expenditure.

An alternative is to substitute peaceful expenditure for military expenditure. There is no end to the list of things this economic society needs: energy research, cancer research, recreation facilities, urban renewal, health services, youth programs. The $50 billion would have no trouble finding its way into worthy efforts.

Cutting defense spending would bring serious adjustment problems for the many colonels, technical sergeants, and aircraft workers who have spent their lives in the direct or indirect employment of the military. The transition to civilian jobs would be very difficult. But, by making the transition a slow one and using fiscal policy judiciously, there is every reason to believe that defense expenditure could be significantly reduced without adversely affecting the functioning of the economy.

11

The Public Debt

A possible outcome of an active fiscal policy is increasing public debt. The very thought of debt strikes ominous chords in most people's minds. Debt is commonly thought to be highly undesirable, if not morally wrong. Children are trained to live within their allowances. Families try to balance their budgets. Businesses incur debts only after carefully studying their prospects for repaying the loans. Yet in spite of this strong moral stigma, the federal government becomes increasingly indebted. The public debt rises, interest payments soar, and from time to time the press cries in outrage that the country is on the brink of disaster, bankruptcy, and ruin.

The public debt is probably the most misunderstood attribute of the U.S. domestic macroeconomy. Even though the government now owes nearly $650 billion, it is not on the brink of disaster and ruin. This chapter explains the relationship between the budget and the debt, the debt itself, and the problems associated with the debt.

CHAPTER ELEVEN

202

The Public Budget and the Public Debt

Each year, the federal government prepares a budget. The budget is a plan for future incomes and expenditures, and its preparation begins about 18 months before the *fiscal year* in which it is to be effective.

A fiscal year is a twelve-month period used for accounting purposes. It may or may not coincide with the calendar year. For decades, the fiscal year used by the federal government ran from July 1 of one year to June 30 of the next. In 1976, the federal fiscal year was changed. It now begins on October 1 of each year and runs to the following September 30. The fiscal year is designated by the year in which it ends. Thus, fiscal year 1979 begins on October 1, 1978, and ends on September 30, 1979.

The budget originates in the executive branch but must be approved by the legislative branch of government. Usually, the President sets out rather flexible guidelines, then asks each agency to estimate how much it will spend in the coming fiscal year. Agencies use estimates of the economy's performance and estimates of federal revenues to make their internal decisions. After a lot of give-and-take among agencies, the President and his budget office present a finished budget for congressional approval.

The public budget is closely intertwined with the public debt. When government income exceeds its expenditures, there is a budget surplus, and when expenditures exceed revenues, there is a budget deficit. A surplus reduces the size of the public debt; a deficit adds to it.

For many years, the U.S. Government and its citizens thought that all budgets should be balanced. A balanced budget means that government cannot spend more than it receives or receive more than it spends. It can collect only that amount of money needed to dispatch its duties. This would place severe limitations on the economic policies stemming from Keynesian economics. For these policies suggest that aggregate demand be expanded or contracted in accordance with the needs of the economy, and changing government spending is one of the surest ways to alter aggregate demand. If the budget must remain in balance, however, spending cannot be used to add purchasing power in a recession or reduce purchasing power in a period of inflation.

Fortunately, the public's attitude toward budgets, deficit spending, and the debt has changed to accommodate the requirements of fiscal policy. The prevailing attitude now toward these matters is described as *functional finance*.

Functional finance is an approach to government budgeting that emphasizes the results achieved by a given set of government activities rather than the relationship between the activities and a balanced budget. Functional finance holds, for example, that in times of high unemployment, money should be given to those who are out of work even if these payments add considerably to an already high public debt.

Functional finance allows the government to tax and spend with an eye toward adjusting aggregate demand, rather than with concern for the size of the debt.

When the government needs to spend more than its current income will allow, it must rely on borrowing. A government borrows money in much the same way as a major corporation does. Once the federal government ascertains that it will need more money than current tax receipts will produce, the U.S. Treasury arranges to sell bonds, treasury bills, and other types of securities. The securities vary in the time they take to mature (90 days to 20 years), minimum size of purchase ($18.75 to $1,000), and availability for purchase (some can be purchased only by banks, some by individuals, and some only by other federal agencies).

The securities are sold by commercial banks or auctioned in bond markets like corporate bonds. Any qualified purchaser can enter the market and buy securities issued by the federal government. They provide a safe investment for those wishing to buy securities and a way for the federal government to obtain funds that might otherwise be idle. The act of selling a bond provides government with the money needed to carry out its fiscal operations. At the same time, it adds to the amount of money owed by the government. It expands public debt.

The Public Debt

The economy of the United States has withstood many shocks in the past half century. Most of them have added to the public debt. The Great Depression, three major military involvements, heavy investment in social overhead capital (highways, schools, hospitals, and the like), large com-

Debt at All Levels of Government

The federal debt, or public debt, is not the only governmental debt in the United States. Counties, cities, states, school districts, and myriad other special "governments" also borrow money so that they can occasionally spend beyond their current incomes. The nearly annual "school-bond election" is a local vote that gives the school board power to borrow money to expand its building or improve its teaching. If passed, the school-bond election adds to the indebtedness of the people in the school district. Similar mechanisms add to the indebtedness of flood-control districts, towns, cities, and states. In 1973, total indebtedness of state governments stood at $59 billion and local governments had debts of $129 billion.

mitments to foreign nations, and recessions (1958–1960 and 1974–1976) have all required budgets to be unbalanced and spending to exceed income (Figure 11–1). Large deficits have come in response to war. There were deficits exceeding $40 billion each in 1943, 1944, and 1945, and $25 billion in 1968. But the largest, a deficit of nearly $52 billion in 1976, has been the result of deliberately trying to increase aggregate demand. Surpluses have appeared during periods of favorable economic conditions like 1956–57 and in 1969, when policy makers chose to extract income from the circular flow to slow an overheated economy. Twenty-nine federal budget deficits in thirty-seven years have left a debt accumulation of nearly $650 billion. The pace of this accumulation since 1940 is shown in Figure 11–2.

Why Increase the Debt?

No debt of $650 billion can be ignored. To an individual or household accustomed to looking at debt as a threat or even as a sin, $650 billion is almost beyond comprehension. Those who fear the public debt often describe their concerns in highly individual and personal terms:

Each new baby in the United States is born owing over $3,000!
Each household, instead of just owing on the house, car, and refrigerator, also owes $9,000 on the public debt.
We are saddling future generations with insurmountable obligations to pay for things we are presently doing.

"Today's problems should have been paid for in the 1950s, but in the 50s we were paying for the problems of the 20s, and in the 20s we were paying for the problems of the 1890s . . ."

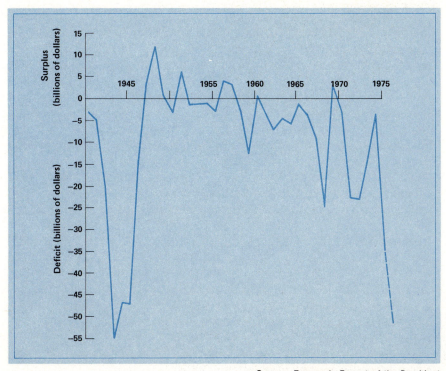

Figure 11-1
Federal Budget Surpluses and Deficits, 1940-1975

Source: *Economic Report of the President*

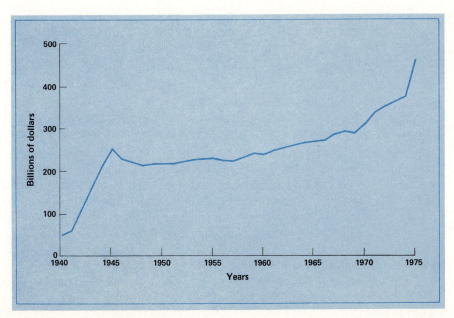

Figure 11-2
Growth of the National Debt, 1940-1975

All of these are misleading statements, since they do not indicate what has been accomplished by increasing the debt. To understand the public debt, it is necessary to start at the beginning and ask why the debt was incurred and what it stands for. It is commonly believed the debt was caused by fighting wars, carrying out reckless spending policies, and pork-barreling by politicians. Certainly the majority of the debt has been incurred during wartime. Any war effort requires expansion of a nation's productive capacity, and this expansion requires funds beyond those available through current income, so the warring government must borrow. In peacetime, however, deficits are used to increase aggregate demand by enhancing purchasing power and to finance public works. By adding to the public debt, the nation was able to expand its transportation network in the 1950s and 1960s. By adding to the public debt, the nation acquired large stocks of social overhead capital—new universities, libraries, federal office buildings, and scientific laboratories devoted to a better understanding of outer space. If the nation wishes to perform some function or achieve some goal that cannot be met using current income, it must borrow. But by borrowing, the nation increases its debt.

The Other Side of the Ledger

In either of these situations, wartime or peacetime, the public debt is comparable to one incurred by an individual or by a firm. An individual incurs debt to pay for a capital, or long-lasting, item—a car, refrigerator or boat, for example. The capital item itself becomes part of the assets used to "back" the debt. If he defaults on the debt, the individual may be embarrassed when the bank repossesses the refrigerator, but society still has the refrigerator.

The Chrysler Corporation incurs debt to build a new factory. It may borrow from a large bank, or it may sell bonds to gather funds from people who are allowing part of their incomes to stand idle. The debt of the Chrysler Corporation is thereby increased, but that increase in debt is backed by the new capital (the new plant). If Chrysler should default, it is embarrassing to Chrysler, but society still has the factory. The debt of the U.S. Government is comparable. It is incurred by using funds borrowed from thousands of individuals and firms who voluntarily loan their money to the government. The borrowed money is used to build new public facilities or to invest in human beings (by financing their education, for example). The debt is backed by vast amounts of capital created during the deficit-spending process. The existence of this capital guarantees that the public has something to show for its debt, and it eliminates the argument that deficit spending is merely pouring money down a hole.

In 1975, Congress did not want to spend a great deal of money, but the high unemployment rate demanded federal aid of some kind. Deficit spending totaling $70 billion was proposed. When newly created debt is used to finance welfare payments, these payments must be examined from another vantage point. Welfare payments made to people outside the mainstream of economic life do not add to the capital plant of the nation. If payments go to able-bodied workers, they represent a potential increase in productive capacity, but most welfare payments go to people outside the labor force. They go to aged, infirm, and incapacitated persons. Payments to these groups cannot be described as capital formation, but in this era of increased concern for human dignity and equal opportunity, the use of borrowed public monies to increase the purchasing power of welfare recipients is generally consistent with the mood of the nation and need not be classified as reckless spending.

The public debt is incurred to perform some necessary fiscal functions. While the debt is often feared, it must be realized that incurring it often yields significant increases in the productivity of the nation. When viewed in this way, the public debt looks very much like debts held by major corporations. The important clue is that incurring debt allows an individual, a household, a firm, or a government to do things and perform functions that might otherwise be impossible.

Problems of the Public Debt

Once the public debt is understood, it is hard to imagine why the uproar over it has been so persistent unless there are some real problems associated with it. To be sure, there are. The principal problems are the size of the debt, repayment of the debt, and interest on the debt.

The Size of the Debt

Figure 11–2 shows that the debt has grown consistently since the 1950s. Many observers wonder if this growth can go on indefinitely. The answer requires examination of the debt from still another perspective. Figure 11–3 holds a surprise. Even though the magnitude of the public debt has grown, the debt *as a proportion of GNP* has actually fallen quite steadily since 1950. As the nation has grown, it has been required to borrow a smaller and smaller proportion of its product. When an individual's income doubles, no one would argue that his capacity to bear debt does not increase too. It is the same with governments: as their incomes grow, they are able to carry a larger burden of debt.

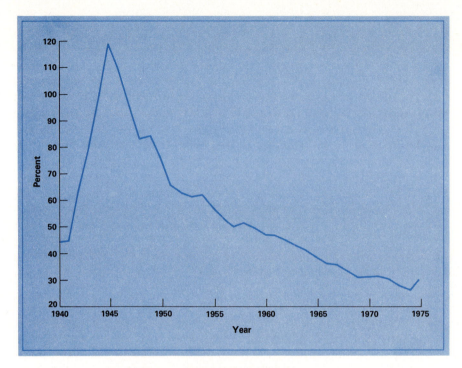

Figure 11-3 The Public Debt as a Percentage of GNP, 1940-1975

The real limit on debt is the willingness of people to lend money to the public. No one knows the exact limits of this willingness. We do know that throughout its recent history, the U.S. Government has had no difficulty borrowing whatever funds it needed to carry out an active fiscal policy.

Repayment

Like all debts, the public debt must be repaid. The public debt is, however, unlike a private debt, in one important aspect: To whom is the debt owed? It is owed to bondholders who purchased government bonds. And who are the bondholders? The public! The public debt is owed to the public. This paradox can be explained by comparing a family debt to the national debt.

Internal and external debt. Figure 11-4 shows some possible lending arrangements open to a family. Much lending and borrowing goes on *within* a family. Daughter borrows 50 cents from mother; son borrows

$50 from daughter; father borrows 85 cents from son. These are borrowing activities just as surely as the government's borrowing $20 million from the Federal Reserve System. The only difference is that within the family no one really forecloses, because the family is a single decision-making unit; it owes the money to itself. When the extended family is considered, the situation does not change much. Aunts and cousins and nephews borrow among themselves. Even in these cases, there is no real threat, since the family is still roughly the same decision-making unit, having the same concerns, and the money is still owed by the family to the family.

The situation changes quite demonstrably when the family borrows funds from a bank. A bank is external to the family. If the family borrows $20,000 to buy a house, two separate decision-making entities are involved. If the family does not make good its promise to repay, the bank can foreclose and take possession of the house. The house remains, but ownership changes hands. The existence of this kind of threat makes the family uncomfortable and to a large extent lies behind the moral objection to debt. When sums of money are owed to some external decision-making unit, the possibility of external control or domination emerges.

Fortunately, the public debt in the United States is internally owned. Only about 12 percent of the bonds sold by government are purchased by foreign governments or foreign nationals. This means that in every essential way, the public debt is like money owed by father to son. Both lender and borrower are parts of the same decision-making unit. If the entire $650 billion debt were to be paid tomorrow, it would merely mean a big reshuffling of money and paper.

Income redistribution aspects. One of the consequences of paying off the public debt would be a redistribution of income. Redistributing income has become an important theme in recent years as major efforts have been made to make more income available to the poor. Paying the

Figure 11–4 A Family Owing to Different Groups

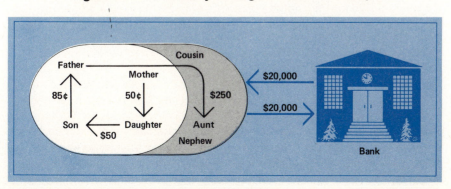

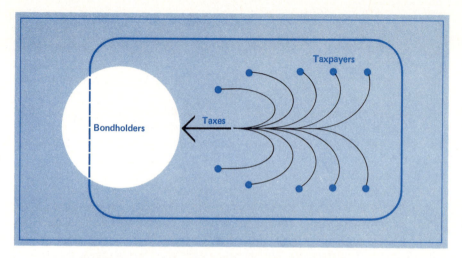

Figure 11-5 Taxpayers Paying Off the Debt

debt, however, would probably not result in an income redistribution of this type. Working through the mechanisms of repayment will show why. In Figure 11-5, the two overlapping shapes represent two sub-groups within the economy. The large area represents all families and firms in the United States who contribute to federal revenues. These are the taxpayers and include nearly every family and every corporation in the nation. If the debt were to be paid off, taxes would have to increase enough to raise the needed $650 billion. All taxpayers would likely share the burden of this increase, so all would share the burden of payments. The smaller area to the left represents the bondholders. Most bondholders (individuals, firms, banks) are also taxpayers, so most of the bondholder area falls within the taxpayer area. A few bondholders—like banks in foreign nations or children who own one or two government bonds—do not pay taxes to the U.S. Government, so they fall outside the oval. When the public debt is liquidated, taxes are collected from the many and transferred to the few. Since bondholders are generally among the middle- and higher-income groups, repayment causes a redistribution that is in a direction away from the goal of most redistributive efforts currently being employed in this economy.

Interest

Lest the public debt appear too easy to live with, a serious disadvantage must be pointed out. Interest on the debt must be paid. Prior to World War II, the federal debt was so small that interest payments were almost negligible. In 1931, for example, interest on the $16.8 billion debt was only $600 million. By contrast, in 1975 the $538 billion debt required interest payments of $31.3 billion. Certainly, such costs are quite high and could become a real burden to all taxpayers. Since 1950, however, interest payments have remained about constant at 8 to 9 percent of all government expenditures and 1.5 percent of GNP. Even though interest on the public debt is a major item in the budget, paying it does not appear to be driving the nation to bankruptcy.

Who Sacrifices?

A final observation on the debt relates to the familiar comment of politicians, orators, high school valedictorians, and small-town newspaper editors when they refer to the debt as a heavy burden of obligation left to future generations. A moment of reflection will serve to dispel this erroneous view of who does the sacrificing and who is saddled with a debt. The single most notable period of debt accumulation in this nation occurred in the early 1940s, when huge sums were expended to provide materials needed for World War II. During that time, huge campaigns were mounted to persuade people not to purchase consumer goods but

---

Refunding and Paying Off

The discussion of how paying the debt will lead to an undesirable redistribution begs a question: Will the debt ever be paid? The likely answer is "No, why should it be?" Here, the curious difference between the expectations people place on government and those they impose on their own businesses causes difficulty. No one ever seems to question General Motors, A T & T, Safeway Stores, or the Boeing Company about going into debt. Moreover, these companies and the thousands of others like them generally have no reasonable expectation of ever paying off their obligations. They do and will continue to issue bonds as a means of obtaining funds to add to their capital, expand their plants, and pay their expenses. Private debt in the U.S. economy now stands at over $2 trillion and no one notices. The government is not treated with the same indifference; it is expected to pay the debts.

Large business corporations commonly use a process known as "refunding" to manage their debts. Refunding is nothing more than selling new bonds to obtain the funds needed to pay off old bonds as they come due. This is a rather continuous process, and keeping it up depends only on a firm's ability to maintain a productive capital plant and to keep up public confidence in its future profitability. The same option of refunding is available to the government and is frequently used. Some government bonds issued in 1970 will mature in 1980. To pay the obligation incurred by the maturing bonds, the government generally sells more bonds, gathering in savings from here and there and using the funds to pay off maturing debts.

to buy bonds issued by the federal government instead. The sale of bonds, of course, added to the size of the debt. The real sacrifice associated with the public debt was made by those who bought bonds and went without goods and services during the war. The descendants of the war generation, far from sacrificing and far from being overwhelmed with repayment obligations, have actually had their purchasing power, and perhaps their well-being, increased as a result of the funds made available to them by the government when the bonds matured.

Summary
1 The public debt is a huge sum of money owed by the federal government to the millions of persons, firms, and institutions who choose to invest their savings and surplus funds in government bonds.
2 Government debt arises when the government engages in deficit spending, the practice of spending more than is currently generated by tax revenues.
3 The bonds sold by government are secured by the billions of dollars of capital assets owned by the federal government. These assets either add directly to the productive capacity of the nation (dams, highways, libraries) or allow life to be lived more comfortably (justice, education, health research, welfare payments to the needy).
4 The public debt is owed by citizens to citizens.
5 Two real difficulties related to the debt are the redistributive problems associated with its repayment and the size of the interest payments that must be made on it.

Exercises
1 Explain these important terms and concepts:
   fiscal year   federal budget
   balanced budget   functional finance
   public debt   refunding
   budget deficit
2 The previous several chapters have dealt with government activity aimed at supplementing the working of a market economy. This chapter has discussed government borrowing and spending. It is hard to imagine borrowing and spending practices that have no net effect on the economy. Taxing takes money forcibly from some and (usually) makes payments to others. Deficit spending gathers money from those who have surpluses (purchasers of bonds) and makes payments to entirely different groups. With this in mind, describe the *likely* effects of the following situations:
   a The economy is in a period of full employment and reasonably stable prices. Contented citizens want more parks and recreation areas. Political officials are reluctant to increase taxes, since that is politically unpopular. The parks are financed through deficit spending (selling bonds). What is the effect on employment? On prices of goods and services?

b A modern economy has a heavy commitment to technology and technologically based industries. This commitment often means that laborers with technical skills can find employment while those who are low-skilled cannot; the highly skilled are well paid, the low-skilled are not. A deficit-spending program will gather money from the highly skilled population and perhaps make transfers to the low-skilled population. What will be the effect on consumption? On capital creation? On the distribution of income?

c If a fire in the U.S. Treasury Building suddenly wiped out all records of the public debt, who would be affected and in what ways? Owners of bonds? Common taxpayers? The economy as a functioning entity?

3 One bad feature of the public debt is the redistribution of income that comes when the debt in repaid. The repayment goes to bondholders, who are ordinarily among the wealthy. The money to repay comes from all taxpayers, a group that includes rich and poor alike. Imagine a map of the United States, and suppose that taxpayers are arranged on the map in exactly the same way that the population is spread (many people on the Atlantic, Pacific, and Gulf coasts; few people in the heartland). If all bonds are owned by people in Nebraska, how will repayment affect income distribution? If all bonds are owned by banks centered in New York, Dallas, and San Francisco, how will income be redistributed?

4 The nature of the tax system has a great effect on the redistribution of income that comes with repaying mature bonds. The following table shows the incomes and the value of mature bonds held by each of ten families. Using the specified tax rates, calculate the tax bills and the income after repayment for each of the families. How does each taxing system affect the distribution of income?

		Proportionate tax		Progressive tax		
Current taxable income	Value of mature bonds held	Taxes paid with 5% tax rate	Income less taxes paid plus repayment	Progressive tax rate	Taxes paid	Income less taxes paid plus repayment
$10,000	$ 1,000			9%		
3,000	250			0		
22,000	10,000			25		
15,000	900			17		
19,000	1,400			20		
11,000	1,150			12		
4,000	500			2		
1,000	200			0		
8,000	700			8		
7,000	700			3		

A Contemporary Problem
What to Do in Case of Peace

In the late 1960s, a few writers were beginning to venture opinions about what might happen if peace came to Southeast Asia. Most worried about social adjustments and rebuilding the capital plant of war-devastated nations. One writer, Edwin L. Dale, began to wonder what would happen if suddenly all the financial resources committed to active U.S. military involvement were made available for peacetime spending. After discussing various plans of the Nixon administration, Dale addressed the possibility of raising the incomes of the poor, sharing federal incomes with the states, and expanding federal expenditures along "traditional" lines—that is, spending more on existing programs. Toward the end of one article, Dale inquired about the possibility of using some of the extra money to reduce the national debt:

> [This suggestion] will come as a surprise to many. Certainly, it is agreed by practically all economists that there is very little merit in reducing the debt, as such.
>
> But wait. There is a new development in the American economy—arising in part out of our social and urban problems—that will probably make Federal debt reduction, in rising amounts over the years, both good economics and good social policy.
>
> It is now entirely clear that a large part of our unmet needs should be and will be "debt-financed"—that is, through mortgages and non-Federal public bond issues. The new Housing Act alone, plus family formation, will generate, over a time, as much as $15-billion in new mortgages to finance housing both for the lower-income groups and for those who can afford ordinary housing—an increase of 60 percent over the $25-billion now invested in mortgages each year. New plans for college dormitories and academic facilities, sewage plants and other needs will generate an already predictable multibillion-dollar addition to the $10-billion, net, of present borrowing by state and local governments and public authorities through tax-free bonds.
>
> Where is all this capital to come from? Who is going to buy all these bonds and mortgages? The American economy generates an enormous and growing amount of savings—including such indirect instruments as life insurance and pension funds—but our present high interest rates are, in some part, a reflection of the fact that the demand for these savings is already very large in relation to supply. The price of borrowed money has gone up.
>
> The problem, with major social implications, is to find a new source of investment capital, which means essentially a new source of savings. But new sources of savings do not grow on trees. Without such a new source of capital, some housing projects for lower-income families simply cannot be built, some new sewage plants to clean up our rivers cannot be financed.
>
> The problem of high interest rates, a reflection of the over-all shortage of capital, affects even tax-exempt state and local bonds, though their rates are still below those on the bonds of, say, corporations. Foreseeing real difficulties for local governments as their borrowing costs inevitably rise, the [Johnson] Administration proposed an "Urban Development Bank" to take over a good part of the state and local need. It would float Federally guaranteed, taxable bonds and relend the money to the localities at low interest rates, with the difference to be made up by a Congressionally appropriated annual subsidy.

"Well, some peace is good for the economy, but not too much peace."

It is an ingenious idea, and it may well be taken up by the Nixon Administration. But it does not solve the over-all problem of simply too many bonds and mortgages for the supply of savings. The new Urban Bank bonds would just substitute for others that would have come along.

Is there an answer to this dilemma—a potentially very acute one for solving our problems of water pollution, higher education and, above all, housing? The answer may be: a large and growing Federal budget surplus with a consequent reduction in Federal debt. The money used to pay off—retire—Federal bonds could be invested in the new bonds and mortagages.

The concept is really quite simple. If the Federal Government spends less than it takes in, and uses the excess revenue to pay off some of its debt, it becomes, in effect, a saver. It adds to the supply of private savings. If some of the revenue dividend is not used in this fashion, some needs will almost surely go unmet—not to mention the likelihood of perpetually high interest rates. An added bonus of reducing the national debt, of course, is lower Federal interest costs, freeing a modest amount of funds to be used elsewhere.[1]

Analysis. The Dale argument is an intriguing idea. He correctly notes that vast amounts of savings will soon be needed if the nation is going to attend to its many social needs. The supply of savings is limited, but it could be increased if the federal government collected large sums through taxation, then used these funds to pay off the public debt, thus putting "savable" income into the hands of individuals, banks, and other bondholders. The scheme will work only if most of what is currently saved continues to be saved. If the money paid to bondholders on redemption is then used to purchase consumer goods (or to pay the now-higher taxes), the supply of savings will not be expanded and new bond issues will not be sold. The Dale idea is fascinating but precarious. It rests on the assumption that saved money will remain in savings; it assumes the MPC to be near zero.

---

[1] Edwin L. Dale, Jr., "What Will We Do with All That Extra Money?" *New York Times Magazine,* 16 February 1969, pp. 32ff. © 1969 by the New York Times Company. Reprinted by permission.

12

Money, Symbol of Mutual Trust

Money is the grandest example of the trust people have in each other and in their government. The days when money was gold (and gold was money) are long past. Today, the U.S. Government, through its elaborate Federal Reserve System, issues coins and currencies that have value. They have value because they are scarce and because they can be exchanged for things like food, housing, clothing, and entertainment. They keep their value because everyone agrees that the alloyed, layered, and sandwiched metal coins and the beautifully engraved pieces of paper are a sensible and convenient way to pay for things, to describe the value of things, and to store and maintain purchasing power over reasonable lengths of time. They are money.

Money is an important part of any modern economy. As an economy becomes more interdependent, the role of money intensifies. In the U.S. economy money has great importance in facilitating trade among individuals—it greases the wheels of industry. Money may be even more important in an aggregate sense. Like fiscal policy, money and the policies designed to regulate it have a role in determining the aggregate level of output (GNP) and the general level of prices.

This chapter and the next two are discussions of money. This chapter defines money, explains its historical development, and shows how it is created for use in a modern economy. Chapter 13 describes some con-

"In a way I feel bad—taking all these coins out of circulation."

flicting views about the relationship between money and the performance of the economy. Chapter 14 tells how the supply of money can be altered through the monetary policies of the nation's banking system.

The Evolution of Money

When every family was self-sufficient, money was not needed. It quickly developed, however, that universal self-sufficiency is not a very productive kind of social organization. Specialization made more goods and services available, and even the very early forms of specialization had to be accompanied by trade. Primitive trading depended on the *barter* process. The hunter who had surplus meat traded some of it to the witch doctor in exchange for his healing services.

Barter is a system of trading in which one good is exchanged directly for another without the use of money. Bartering is done by primitive people and by children exchanging the artifacts of youth (marbles, baseball trading cards, and the like) without resort to prices and money.

As specialization, mechanization, and industrialization grew and then flourished, the barter process became increasingly awkward. The farmer who had surplus corn and who needed a harness for his horse had to find a harness maker who had a spare harness and who *at the same time* wanted corn. The search for this "double incidence of wants" could be long and painstaking. In a barter economy, it could easily take longer to trade the goods than to produce them. A more streamlined method of transaction had to be found. Money was the answer.

The switch from a barter economy to a money economy required that something be selected *and be widely agreed on* as (1) a medium of exchange, (2) a store of value, and (3) a standard of value. A medium of exchange must be recognizable, divisible into small units, and convenient to handle—even in large quantities. An effective store of value has to be durable, in constant demand, and not subject to violent changes in supply. The standard-of-value role is what makes it possible to measure and compare the "worth" of different goods. Any substance or artifact that passes the tests as a medium of exchange and a store of value could easily become a unit for measuring value.

Early Forms of Money

Through time, many things have been used for money, but some are more suitable than others. Bananas would make poor money because they spoil. They fail the store-of-value test. Large stones make poor money because they are inconvenient and hard to divide into small units. They fail the medium-of-exchange test. Animals fail both tests because they are not easily divisible into small units and they also tend to multiply and to die, so that their supply is not stable.

In the Western world, then, slaves, shells, stones, wine, olive oil, and dozens of other things served as "money" at various times before a few precious metals were settled on as common mediums of exchange. Gold and silver were prominent among these because they were available,

---

Debasing a Coin or Currency

Minting coins (minting is the process by which Lincoln's profile is impressed on a blank copper coin) brought unique opportunities to the enterprising rulers of medieval fiefdoms and kingdoms. The preferred metal for most coins in past centuries was gold, but gold by itself is so soft that a strengthening metal had to be added before a coin could be minted. A coin may have been 80 percent gold and 20 percent "base" metal.

In a time of financial desperation, a frantic king could call in all gold coins, melt them, add more base metal, and reissue them *at the same face value.* If the coins were now 60 percent gold and 40 percent base metal, the king would have issued four new coins for each three that had been turned in. An easy way to pay the bills!

The process of adding more base metal is called *debasing* a currency.

they kept their value, they were easily recognizable, and they could not be counterfeited. Even so, the early use of metals as facilitators of trade caused problems. The metals had to be weighed each time they were traded—how else could a businessman know he was obtaining the correct amount?

The weighing of metals was much superior to the barter system, but it still entailed a considerable amount of bother. The same metal was weighed, reweighed, and weighed still again as it passed from purchaser to purchaser. To reduce this inconvenience, governments made coins of uniform weights. The coins eliminated the weighing ritual, but brought abuses. Small slivers could be cut from them, or the edges could be filed to obtain flakes of the metal. If the price of uncoined metal rose high enough, it became profitable to melt the coins and sell the metal. In spite of such abuses, metallic monies were in widespread use until the time of the Industrial Revolution.

The Introduction of Paper Money

The industrialization of Europe greatly increased the volume of goods and services changing hands. Coal was purchased by the thousands of tons; iron ore was shipped in huge quantities; and hundreds of laborers had to be paid their wages. Trading activities on this scale required metallic monies in large amounts—amounts so large as to be cumbersome and difficult to transport and to guard. Those who were heavily involved in trade ceased to use the actual metals specified in trading agreements. Instead, they devised a more convenient method based on the use of warehouse receipts. The use of these receipts was a primitive form of banking. Merchants with large amounts of gold deposited it in a very secure warehouse. The warehouse operator issued a receipt stating that a certain volume of gold was now in his possession. The merchant paid for goods and services by giving such warehouse receipts to his sup-

---

Warehousemen or Goldsmiths?

In all likelihood, it was the goldsmiths of industrializing England who issued the receipts that could be used like paper money. Goldsmiths were dealers in gold. They used it for artistic and ornamental purposes and were accustomed to keeping large quantities of it in stock. When merchants began to use gold in the conduct of trade, it seems only natural that they would have turned to the goldsmiths to store it in their strongrooms and safes. Because their receipts were being transferred among merchants and traders, the goldsmiths were the first bankers.

pliers. The suppliers could use the receipts to claim gold, or they could pass them on to other merchants, who in turn might or might not want to claim the actual gold. The warehouse receipt was an early form of paper money and the warehouseman was the forerunner of the banker.

Money Grows

At first the warehousemen who stored gold treated it as they might have treated cotton, hides, or whale oil. A receipt for 1,000 ounces of gold meant that exactly 1,000 ounces of the metal was being held in a warehouse and could be redeemed by presenting the receipt to the keeper. With the growing acceptance of gold as money and warehouse receipts as the circulating medium of exchange, the stocks of gold held in warehouses increased. In time, the keepers of the gold noted that receipts were seldom redeemed. Merchants passed the papers to each other in their transactions, but very seldom used them to actually claim the gold. And even when some gold was withdrawn, new deposits replaced it. Warehouses were filled with idle and apparently useless gold, while the pieces of paper certifying its availability did the work of a medium of exchange.

Knowing that the gold would not be withdrawn, the warehousekeepers issued receipts for more gold than they actually had. They loaned the additional receipts to people who needed financing for their businesses. The creation of these new claims on the stored gold caused the quantity of circulating money to expand.

This practice of issuing money worth more than the gold backing it became known as a *fractional reserve system*: only a fraction of the real value of the money supply was kept on reserve at any one time. Although gold is no longer used as backing for money in the United States, the fractional reserve principle remains an important feature of this nation's banking system.

Money in the U.S. Economy

The money supply in the United States today is a logical extension of the fractional reserve (or fractional deposit) system. Instead of gold, each bank accepts deposits of money to keep in its vaults. These deposits, like the gold deposits of earlier centuries, are generally not withdrawn all at one time. Knowing this, the modern banker loans the unclaimed money, within limits imposed by law. The bank earns its keep by providing a safe place for deposits and loaning the otherwise idle reserves at interest to qualified borrowers. By making loans, banks place more money in circulation than they have on deposit. The system is safe as long as everyone is confident that the banker is living within the rules. Bankers operating in this milieu deal with three kinds of money: coins, currency, and demand deposits.

Coins

Coins are very important to individuals—to drivers who must feed parking meters, or to commuters who drop quarters in fare boxes. In terms of the total supply of money, though, coins are rather insignificant. In 1975, "minor coins" valued at $7.4 billion were circulating in the United States. (Minor coins include pennies, nickels, dimes, quarters, and half-dollars. Dollar coins are in a separate class called "cupronickel clad dollars." About 250 million of these dollar coins were circulating in 1975.) At one time, minor coins contained metals worth approximately the face value of the coin. Thus, the silver quarter contained silver worth approximately 25 cents. In the 1960s, world prices of silver rose rapidly, so that the silver contained in U.S. coins was worth more than the minted coins. As a result, millions of minor coins were illegally withdrawn from circulation, melted, and sold at a high price as raw silver. Since 1965, the United States has minted layered coins whose metal content is worth only a fraction of their face value. Popularly referred to as "sandwich coins," they are known in official circles as "clad coins." These coins have not lost their value in exchange because citizens still have confidence that the money is exchangeable for goods and services. These coins are *fiat money*.

Fiat money is money whose face value is greater than the value of the metal it contains. Fiat money also includes paper money that is not backed by an equivalent value of precious metal. All money circulating in the United States today is fiat money.

Gresham's Law

The appearance of layered coins a decade ago provided a vivid illustration of the working of Gresham's Law. Stated simply, Gresham's Law says that bad money will always force good money out of circulation. A person who holds two coins and suspects one to be counterfeit will spend the counterfeit coin first. When dimes with no silver in them appeared in 1965, people used them and saved the silver dimes. "Bad money" drove "good money" from circulation.

This phenomenon was apparently noticed by Copernicus, a Polish astronomer, in the fifteenth century, but it was first formally stated by Sir Thomas Gresham, a British financier and government official, around 1550.

Paper Money

Any adult's wallet or purse usually contains a collection of green slips of paper used as legal tender (money). In the United States, in the not too distant past, some of the bills in a person's possession could have been bank notes, some silver certificates, and some Federal Reserve Notes. The bank notes were "warehouse receipts" issued by private banks, the silver certificates were similar evidence (issued by the U.S. Treasury) that the Treasury was holding silver in its vaults, and the Federal Reserve Notes were special bank notes issued by the twelve Federal Reserve Banks. Now bills are issued only by the Federal Reserve System. They are easily recognized, come in several denominations, and are quite hard to copy. Since there is no precious metal stored in a vault to back them, these bills, like coins, are fiat money. In 1975, bills valued at nearly $62 billion were circulating in the U.S. economy. Over half of this value was in bills of $20 or less in denomination.

Coins and paper money taken together are described as *currency* in the technical language of economics and the official language of banking.

Currency is the money printed and distributed by the U.S. Treasury. It includes both coins and paper money. In 1976, approximately $75 billion of currency was in circulation in the U.S. economy.

Demand Deposits

Not many decades ago most transactions involving monetary payment were consummated using paper money. Now the most popular form of payment is the personal check. About 40 billion checks are written in the United States each year. These checks pay phone bills, tuition, grocery bills, and rent, and can be converted into cash at banks or at stores where the check writer's identity and reputation are known. Approximately 80 percent of all money transactions in the United States involve checks rather than currency or coin, for checks are a kind of money too.

A check is an order for a bank to transfer dollars from one person to another. Checks can be written only by a person who has deposited money in a bank checking account, which is a flexible account designed for this purpose. Because of the safety and convenience of writing checks, U.S. citizens do much of their business this way.

Checking accounts are important to economists, since about 80 percent of all money in the U.S. economy is checkbook money. In technical language, checkbook money is called *demand deposit* money—banks hold money for one person and pay it *on demand* to others.

A demand deposit is a bank account containing money that can be transferred on demand by writing a check.

"I'm afraid that despite the term 'free checking', you still have to deposit funds in your account."

Because most payments in the U.S. economy are made by check, demand deposits are considered to be part of the money supply. In 1976, the nation's banks held demand deposits valued at $225 billion.

The Modern Banking System

There are now approximately 15,000 *commercial banks* in the United States. These banks hold billions of dollars in demand deposits for customers who trust the bankers to keep their money safe.

A commercial bank is a financial institution that has the privilege of holding checking accounts and savings accounts as well as performing a number of other functions related to money. The privileges come from the state or federal government, either of which may grant a charter to the bank. In addition to granting these powers, the charter also requires that the individual bank maintain a specified volume of assets, follow certain practices, and agree to be inspected at periodic intervals. Banks chartered by states are called *state banks* while those holding federal charters are called *national banks*.

The demand deposits placed in banks, coupled with the fractional reserve principle, give bankers the power to alter the supply of money in the economy.

The process is quite simple. When a customer deposits $1,000 in her checking account, experience tells the banker that the most this customer will ever try to withdraw at any one time is $50. To be safe, the banker decides to keep $200 on hand. The remaining $800 can be used to grant loans and to earn income for the bank. A prospective borrower now enters the bank. He borrows $800 and immediately puts the entire amount into his own checking account. Demand deposits in the bank automatically increase by $800. The banker has used the $800 surplus from the first depositor to *create* new demand deposits for the second customer. Since demand deposits are counted as part of the supply of money, the bank has added to the total money supply. If the bank refuses to loan to a prospective borrower or chooses to keep the extra $800, the money supply will be maintained at its original level. Although a bank may choose to keep more than $200 as a precaution against withdrawals, it will seldom, if ever, keep all the original deposit on hand.

The capacity of a bank to create demand deposit money traces to the fractional reserve system. The fraction that must be kept is specified by law and is called the *required reserve*. Required reserves are kept as a kind of insurance that a bank will not lend out all its deposits, leaving none to service its depositors. All other reserves are called *excess reserves*. They are "excess" in the sense that they need not be kept in the bank but can be used at its discretion. The excess reserves form the basis for the banker's lending activities.

Expanding the Money Supply

In the creation of money, as in so many other aspects of economic society, there is a multiplier effect at work. If a banker is required to keep only part of all demand deposits on reserve, a multiplier effect will permit the money supply to expand to many times the size of the original deposit. If the reserve requirement is set at 25 percent, for example, the multiplier will work as follows: Someone deposits $1,000, increasing the banker's required reserves by $250 (25 percent of $1,000). But the banker now has $750 in excess reserves to use for other purposes. If the $750 is loaned out, it becomes new money in the hands of the borrower.

The borrower of the newly created $750 may withdraw the money and deposit it in another bank. This move requires nothing more of the first bank than bookkeeping entries. After all, it is *expected* that the borrower will withdraw the $750 almost immediately. (Why borrow except to use the money?) When the money is deposited in a second bank, this bank obtains demand deposits of $750. Like the first bank, it must increase its required reserves by 25 percent of the deposit, or $187.50, and may use the remaining $522.50 (excess reserves) to loan out, thereby creating more new demand deposits. The process continues in exactly the same way increased spending continues to add to national income through round after round of economic activity. This operation of the multiplier effect is portrayed in Table 12-1, which shows how a deposit of $1,000 will move from bank to bank, requiring each to add to *required* reserves but also permitting each to use the newly created *excess* reserves to make new loans. Ultimately, the original deposit permits the money supply to increase by $4,000.

Deposit expansion multipliers. The one-to-four relationship between the original deposit and the total expansion of the money supply is no accident. It is directly related to the proportion of the original deposit that must be kept as required reserves. Intuition tells us that a low reserve requirement permits more money to be loaned and therefore means that the accumulated sum of all loans deriving from an initial deposit will be high. A high reserve requirement, on the other hand, will force banks to keep more of a new deposit on hand as required reserves and will not allow such a large expansion of the money supply. The amount of expansion in the money supply is defined by the *deposit expansion multiplier.*

The deposit expansion multiplier is the relationship between an original deposit and the potential addition it can make to the total money supply. The numerical value of the deposit expansion multiplier is found by the following formula:

$$\text{Deposit expansion multiplier} = \frac{1}{\text{Legal reserve requirement}}$$

In the example reported in Table 12-1, the reserve requirement is 25 percent, so the multiplier is $1/.25 = 4$. If only 10 percent of all deposits were required to be held in reserve, the multiplier would be $1/.10 = 10$; if the reserve requirement were 50 percent, the multiplier would be $1/.50 = 2$. As the reserve requirement goes down, the capacity of the banking system to expand deposits goes up; as the reserve requirement goes up, the capacity of the banking system to expand deposits goes down.

The deposit expansion multiplier is related to required reserves, but it is the *excess reserves* that provide the money used by the banker in creating new deposits. The total value of excess reserves times the deposit expansion multiplier yields the total amount by which commercial banks can expand the money supply.

A monopoly bank. The example in Table 12-1 is expressed in terms of six banks, and it illustrates how money is created as deposits move from bank to bank. It is not necessary to have more than one bank in order to increase the money supply. Even if only one bank existed—a monopoly bank—the result would be the same. A client would deposit $1,000 in an account, required reserves would be increased by $250, and the banker would have $750 in excess reserves. The excess reserves would be

Table 12-1 The Banking System Creating Demand Deposits
(reserve requirement: 25 percent)

Bank	Original deposit	Reserves Required	Reserves Excess	Loaned out	Accumulated increases in demand deposits
A	$1,000.00	$250.00	$750.00	$750.00	$1,000.00
B	750.00	187.50	662.50	662.50	1,662.50
C	662.50	165.62	496.88	496.88*	2,159.38
D	496.88	124.22	372.66	372.66*	2,532.04
E	372.66	93.15	279.51	279.51*	2,811.55
F	279.51	69.88	209.63	209.63*	3,021.18
All other banks	1,305.10	326.28	978.82	978.82*	4,000.00

*All figures begin to creep away from their exact values because of rounding errors. While these errors do build up, they are not large enough to damage the major argument associated with demand deposit creation in local banks.

loaned and deposited in another client's account, thus increasing the money supply. The borrower would spend the money and the recipients of these expenditures would probably make their own deposits in the bank. If the mechanism worked perfectly, the entire $750 would eventually find its way back into the bank and provide the basis for another round of lending and expansion of the money supply. A monopoly bank would be just as effective as a series of banks in expanding money supplies.

Contracting the money supply. While this discussion has centered on expanding the money supply, it should be noted that the process can operate in reverse too. Demand deposits are destroyed when withdrawals from banks occur. An extreme example makes the point: If a depositor in a bank suddenly withdraws $1,000 and buries it, several things follow. First, the usable money supply is reduced by the now-buried $1,000. Second, the bank is relieved of the responsibility of keeping $250 in required reserves. Third, the bank also no longer has the $750 in excess reserves as a basis for lending activity. In reality, the effect goes much deeper, since, as we have seen, the $750 could have been used as reserves behind another $3,000 in demand deposits. In this case, the demand-deposit-creation activity is operating fully in reverse. The multiplier works in both an upward and a downward direction.

Monetizing debts. The process of creating money in this fashion is often called *monetizing debts*. When a bank loans money, it is exchanging the money for a promise to pay. It is exchanging money for a debt. This scarcely seems important, but if the notion is carried past the superficial level, an interesting phenomenon can be observed. The banker loans because he is quite sure his client will repay. If this does not happen, the banker can seize the client's assets and sell them to recover his money. The statement that the newly created money is backed by a debt is only partially true; it is also backed by other assets owned by the borrower. The pragmatic importance of this observation cannot be overemphasized, since it explains why the U.S. banking system does not need large amounts of gold to back its money supply. The money supply is backed by the tremendous collection of assets—buildings, machines, dams, houses, and skills—that this nation has accumulated over the past two centuries.

Weaknesses of a Fractional Reserve System

A fractional reserve system of banking is not without its weaknesses. A bank that creates more demand deposits than it has reserves to back faces a very real problem: What would happen if all depositors simultaneously attempted to convert their deposits into cash? The requests could not be honored, since the deposits are only fractionally backed. This does not happen as long as the economy, the government, and the individual bank's integrity are in good standing. But when stresses beset the economy or the government, or when the banking public suspects that a bank has overextended itself, depositors are apt to demand that their deposits be converted to cash. In this circumstance a bank cannot honor all the requests, so it must close its doors. Its business is ruined and its depositors all lose, since only a fraction of their deposits can be returned to them.

The possibility of this occurring in the 1970s is quite remote, but throughout the nation's history banks have occasionally closed because they could not meet the public's requests to withdraw money. The Panic of 1893 saw closure of banks in all major cities, and the Great Depression of the 1930s brought widespread bank failure. People simply lacked confidence in the system and wanted their money in gold coin rather than in bank deposits. The banks could not respond.

During the eighteenth century, bankers in the Western world were operating in unstable social and political settings. National governments were not strong and could not guarantee that banks would remain open or that money would retain its value. As nations became more settled, and as the use of money spread, governments established central banks that were responsible for maintaining the solvency of banks and the integrity of the money supply. One of the most important means of doing this was to regulate the degree to which banks could issue money in excess of the quantity of gold held in their vaults. This is an important function of the U.S. Federal Reserve System, which will be examined in Chapter 14.

Enlarging the Definition of Money

While no one disputes that coins, paper currency, and demand deposits are a part of the nation's money supply, a number of economists are not content with this restricted definition. They feel that savings accounts, sometimes called *time deposits,* as well as demand deposits should be included as part of the money supply.

A time deposit is a bank deposit that cannot be withdrawn without the depositor giving the bank adequate advance warning. Most banks do not enforce this rule on ordinary savings accounts.

This expanded definition would include not only savings deposits in commercial banks but also deposits in savings banks, savings and loan associations, mutual savings agencies, postal savings unions, and co-operative credit unions. Including these savings as money does make sense, since money in these places is easily turned into cash and is easily shifted from one institution to another. Including these kinds of savings as money would increase the total money supply in the United States from approximately $300 billion to approximately $680 billion.

A very small group of economists would not be satisfied with even this expanded definition. This group wants to include $450 billion of *near-monies* in the total money supply.

Near-monies are U.S. Government bonds held by individuals and businesses. The bonds are called "near-monies" because they can be easily converted into cash, and hence people holding them behave nearly as they would if they were holding cash.

The arguments about whether or not near-monies should be included as part of the money supply are extensions of the arguments surrounding the inclusion of savings as part of the money supply. Yes, they should be included, because near-monies affect people's behavior and they can be converted into cash rather quickly. No, they should not be included,

"Plastic Money"

In the past decade, U.S. citizens have made increasing use of credit cards, or "plastic money." A few years ago, only the major oil companies and large department stores extended credit by giving cards to preferred customers. In the 1960s, several large banks—most notably the Bank of America—issued credit cards that enabled holders to purchase items from certain merchants. The acceptance of credit cards since then has been overwhelming. By the end of 1975, nearly 2,000 commercial banks were issuing credit cards and $20 billion of credit was being used by card holders. The credit card had become a kind of money substitute.

In a technical sense, the credit card is a combination of a demand deposit and a small-loan service. It makes business easy for card holder, banker, and merchant. While the cards may actually encourage some purchases that otherwise would not have been made, their main function is providing convenience. It is doubtful that plastic money will replace the conventional coins, currencies, and checks.

because they are not held in commercial banks and they cannot be *instantly* converted into cash.

Certainly, refined economic analysis requires refined definitions. Individual economists performing exacting studies of the behavior of the macroeconomy will have differing uses for these various definitions of money. For purposes of gaining a basic understanding of the role of money in macroeconomic behavior, however, the straightforward definition including only coins, currency, and demand deposits is sufficient. Although it is restrictive, this definition permits an explanation of the role of the banking system and of the necessity of maintaining a flexible money supply.

Summary
1. Money is anything that is widely accepted as a medium of exchange, a store of value, and a standard of value.
2. Many things have been used as money. Because of their limited supply, convenience, and durability, a few precious metals have become preferred by most nations.
3. Modern paper money is the descendant of warehouse receipts for gold used centuries ago.
4. The money of today is not backed by precious metals and is, thus, fiat money.
5. Coins, currency, and demand deposits make up the nation's supply of money.
6. The nation's commercial banks can add to the money supply by making loans and creating demand deposits. Similarly, the banks can maintain the money supply at present levels by refusing to loan money.

7 The volume of money a commercial bank can create is related to the proportion of demand deposits that must be kept as required reserves.
8 A single, monopoly bank would have the same power to create money as a large series of banks.
9 Near-monies, time deposits, and other monetary holdings are sometimes considered money.

Exercises

1 Explain these important terms and concepts:
    barter system   fractional reserves
    Gresham's Law   medium of exchange
    store of value   demand deposit
    debasing   near-monies
    fiat money   demand deposit multiplier
    required reserves   excess reserves

2 Money is anything that serves as a medium of exchange, a standard of value, and a store of value. Name the advantages and disadvantages associated with using each of the following as money:
 a Gold.
 b Paper money backed by gold.
 c Farmer Jones's pregnant cow.
 d Round stones washed up on Atlantic beaches.
 e A share of stock in a major oil company.
 f Tickets to an inaugural ball.

3 The United States and Canada share a very long frontier. On either side, minor coins of the two nations are used interchangeably, and tourist dollars are quite often accepted at par or face value. Officially, the exchange rate has fluctuated from time to time. In 1965, a Canadian dollar could be purchased for 92 U.S. cents. If a room in a tourist motel cost $20 per night and the innkeeper did not care whether the payment was made in Canadian or U.S. dollars, which would you use?

4 How does question 3 relate to Gresham's Law?

5 If all holders of demand deposits suddenly attempted to convert their deposits to cash, they would be turned away at the bank. Why? Why don't such attempts occur in the United States today?

6 How might each of the following affect the supply of money?
 a An increase in the reserve requirement.
 b A bank's own decision to increase its reserves.
 c A decline in public confidence in banks.

7 Would a 100-percent reserve requirement make banking "safer"? What effect would such a requirement have on the supply of money?

8 If a federal law required that 10 percent of all demand deposits be kept as required reserves and if, at the same time, a local banker thought it prudent to keep an extra 10 percent of demand deposits on reserve, how much could the total supply of money increase in response to a new demand deposit of $1,000?

A Contemporary Problem
Government Grants and the Local Bank

For many years, Professor Kenneth Boulding, an economist at the University of Colorado, has commented that with the proliferation of grants made by one unit of government to another, and by government to individuals, the United States is rapidly becoming a "grants economy." There is nothing especially right or wrong about this kind of economy, but some of the regulations surrounding the grants have important side effects. One is the free money local commercial bankers obtain as a result of some granting procedures.

Grants from the federal government to state or local governments are most often made on a cost-reimbursable basis. This means the local unit of government pays the bill, then asks the federal granting agency for reimbursement. Occasionally, however, a federal agency will grant money in advance of the activity. If that money is invested and earns interest, all the interest earned must be turned over to the U.S. Treasury, along with an explanation of why the money was invested rather than used. Small governments (towns, counties, mosquito-control districts, and the like) are not prepared to deal with interest payments in this way, nor do they want to. When a local government obtains a grant in advance of the time it wishes to use the money, it is most likely to simply put the money—$500 or $30,000 or $250,000—into its checking account at a bank. This is most convenient for the local government.

The banker takes a different view. Since the grant increases the bank's demand deposits, the bank is in a position to make interest-earning loans. The grant money is "free money," since the bank does not have to pay interest to either federal or local authorities. Moreover, because of the fractional reserve system of banking, the bank can lend some multiple of the deposit, with each loan bringing more money to the bank in the form of interest paid by borrowers.

In this period when governments at all levels are starving for revenue and the public is asking for even more services, this practice seems strange. A simple rule change permitting local governments to earn interest on the unused portion of a federal grant would give those governments access to more money without taking more from the federal government, and would cut down the size of the free-money revenues earned by private bankers as they use public money.

13 Money and the Performance of the Economy

How important is money to the performance of the economy? No one will argue about the importance of money in facilitating trade. Its role as a medium of exchange is beyond question. But what of other matters? Just how much does money influence price levels, employment, GNP, and "overall performance"?

For many years money was thought to be the prime mover of economic affairs. The classical economists and their immediate followers believed that the economy could be controlled by manipulating the stock of money. Then, in the 1920s, a number of other factors began to appear more important in explaining the economy's performance. In the mid-1960s, it became clear that the policies and theories based on nonmonetary variables as regulators of the economy were not adequate, so attention turned again to money. The *monetarists* regained prominence and the relationship between money and economic performance again became an urgent concern. That concern remains strong in the late 1970s.

Monetarists are economists who feel that fluctuations in economic activity are closely related to variations in the money supply and that policies regarding economic growth and economic stabilization should be related primarily to changes in the supply of money.

The question, "How important is money?" brings different answers from different economists. At one end of the spectrum is the view that all macroeconomic problems are related to money and can be corrected by changing the money supply. At the other end is the belief that money is not important at all and macroeconomic problems must be solved by fiscal policies related to changes in spending (C + I + G). Not many economists take either of these extreme stands. Some say money has some importance, and others say money is most important, but both groups admit that monetary and nonmonetary factors together determine the behavior of the macroeconomy. Very heated arguments arise, however, over the proper emphasis.

This chapter explains the monetarist view of the macroeconomy, as it has developed from the somewhat crude quantity theory of money to a much-expanded view that is more helpful in explaining the way in which money affects the macroeconomy. The chapter is arranged into sections dealing with money and prices, the desire to hold money, and changing the supply of money.

Money and Prices

In the thinking of most classical economists, the economy was divided into the real sector and the money sector. Real-sector activities had to do with the allocation of resources (how much of Manhattan should be used for office buildings and how much for parking space?) and the distribution of income (should revenues from sales go to the workers or to the capitalists who provide the machines?). Money-sector activities had to do with prices of goods but not with goods themselves. Prices of all goods and services could go up or down without much effect on real activities.

The classical economists reasoned that an economy has a tendency to settle into equilibrium with all factors of production fully employed. At this equilibrium, the real economy produces Lincoln Continentals and Chevrolet Vegas and other commodities in quantities determined by consumer demands and relative production costs. The real sector of the economy allocates resources between the two kinds of automobiles in accord with demands of the public. The quantities demanded and costs determine relative prices. Perhaps one Continental turns out to be equal in price to four Vegas. If a fuel shortage occurs, lowered demand for the gas-consuming Continentals may cause their price to drop and increased demand for fuel-conserving Vegas may cause their price to climb. The relative prices have now changed and the real economy will adjust its allocation of resources to produce fewer Continentals and more Vegas.

The real economy has responded to changes in *relative* rather than *absolute* prices. What matters is whether the ratio of the prices of the two cars is 4 to 1 or 2 to 1, not whether their absolute price is $7,000 or $14,000. If all relative prices remain unchanged, money wages, the price of cars, the price of lawn furniture, and the price of rides in hot-air balloons will all stay in the same ratios. Nothing will have changed except the value of the currency. Surely, the argument runs, no one cares whether wages are $100 a week and the price of bread is 10 cents, or wages are $500 weekly and bread sells for 50 cents.

The classical economists also reasoned that while the quantity of money in circulation might not influence the real economy, it would influence the general level of prices. An increase in the money supply would cause general prices to increase and a decrease in the money supply would cause general prices to decrease.

Doubling the quantity of money would double all prices, but in equilibrium, it would also double all wages and other sources of family income. This would not disturb *relative* prices, and so would not change activities in the real economy. If this were true, money would be neutral in the conduct of economic affairs. It would affect the price level, but it would have no effect on the performance of the macroeconomy.

The Quantity Theory of Money

The mechanism described above, linking the quantity of money to price levels, is the *quantity theory of money.*

In its elementary form, the quantity theory of money states that as the supply of money in an economy changes, the general price level changes by the same proportion and in the same direction.

The logic of this elementary theory depends upon full employment in the economy. When resources are fully employed total output cannot expand, so any new money in the economy must be used to bid up the prices of existing goods and services. The theory is generally stated using four terms:

M = the dollar volume of money in the economy
V = the velocity with which money circulates
P = the general level of prices
Q = the quantity of goods and services available

By definition, P multiplied by Q yields GNP. At any moment in time, M is known, but it can be altered by commercial banks when they create or destroy demand deposits. Normally, M will be lower than GNP, so each dollar will be used more than once while GNP is being purchased.[1] The

---

[1] Although the money supply is almost always less than GNP (in the U.S. economy of the middle 1970s, the stock of money is about one-fifth as large as GNP), it does not need to be. If the money supply is larger than GNP, each dollar will be used less than once in the purchase of GNP.

number of times each dollar is used is the "velocity" with which money circulates. When GNP is $1,000 and M is $250, V is $1,000 \div 250 = 4$. The quantity theory equation can be stated more compactly as $MV = PQ$. In fact, this quantity equation is an *identity*.

An *identity* is a construct borrowed from mathematics. It is a relationship that is necessarily true for all values of a set of variables. For example, total sales × price = total revenue no matter how large or small either price or sales should be. An identity is more a definition than an explanation. A three-barred equality sign ($\equiv$) designates an identity. The quantity equation is an identity and is properly written $MV \equiv PQ$.

The identity shows that regardless of the separate values of M, V, P or Q, MV will always equal PQ. If, as the classical economists thought, GNP settled at the full-employment level of output, Q could not increase. At the same time, if the customary methods of paying laborers and settling accounts with merchants kept velocity from changing, any increase in M had to be accompanied by a proportionate increase in the general level of prices, P. Prices have to rise, since no other variable can respond.

According to all observations available to the classical economists, the quantity theory was a reasonable hypothesis about the working of the system. From the fourteenth century until comparatively recent times, precious metals were the accepted money. As nations increased their supplies of these metals, the money supply expanded and prices in-

The Preclassical Quantity Theory

The quantity theory of money actually predated the classical economists by nearly a century. The late seventeenth and early eighteenth centuries were times of severe economic fluctuation in Western Europe and in the Americas. Prices rose and fell, output rose and fell, and employment was never entirely secure as the face of the industrial order changed in response to new sources of power, new methods of production, and new institutional regulations. During this turmoil, scholars tried to find a relationship between the supply of money and the level of economic activity. Among the more successful were John Locke (English political philosopher, 1634–1704) and John Law (Scottish financier, 1671–1729). They reasoned that since total money payments must always equal total money receipts, the number of dollars in circulation times the frequency with which each dollar is spent must equal the volume of output times its price. Any change in the number of dollars would, other things being equal, yield a change in price. This is clearly a version of the quantity theory.

Other preclassical contributors to the early quantity theory were Richard Cantillon (Irish economist, 1697–1734) and David Hume (Scottish philosopher, 1711–1776).

creased. Moreover, those centuries during which the quantity of precious metals increased most rapidly coincide with the periods of time during which prices rose most rapidly. The elementary quantity theory seemed to be a satisfactory explanation of how prices are related to the supply of money.

Limitations of the Elementary Quantity Theory

Although the quantity theory had considerable predictive power during times of full employment, it lost some of its incisiveness at other times. As long as some resources were unemployed, a massive injection of money into the economy could affect either output (Q) or prices (P). The quantity theory by itself did not provide clues to which would change first or by how much. Since modern economies were seldom characterized by full employment, modern economists began to speculate that the impact of money on the performance of the economy is related to the *demand* for money and that knowing *why* firms and households want to hold or spend money would provide insights into the effects of changes in the money supply.

The Desire to Hold Money

A household's or firm's decision to spend or hold money is closely bound up in habits, law, and perhaps even the psychological make-up of the people involved. Dismissing those cranks who just like to look at money piled in a vault, the desire to hold money basically derives from the need for money to consummate transactions, the desire to be prepared for unusual events, and the desire to use money in speculation about the future. These three desires are called *the transactions demand, the precautionary demand,* and *the speculative demand,* for money.

The Transactions Demand

The role of money as a medium of exchange and the high degree of specialization in the U.S. economy require that firms and households use money on an almost daily basis. Customs, laws, and historical accidents cause most of a household's income (from wages, rents, profits, or interest) to arrive at well-defined intervals. Wages are paid weekly or monthly; dividends come from corporations at three-month intervals; the farmer's income from his cotton crop comes once each year. Expenditures, however, must be made almost daily. Ten cents goes to the parking meter on

"But my dear, a false sense of security is better than no sense of security."

Monday, five dollars goes to the barber on Tuesday, ten dollars is used for groceries on Wednesday. The sequence may or may not be the same next week. Because income streams and expenditure streams are not perfectly synchronized, a household must keep some of its income as money for transactions purposes. Moreover, when incomes rise, the amount spent between pay periods rises, too, so the demand for dollars held for transactions purposes increases. When income falls, fewer dollars are available to bridge the gaps, so the transactions demand falls.

Firms face a similar timing problem between their incomes and expenditures. Their incomes are derived from daily sales of products, so they are fairly regular. They make payments only on paydays or when obligations come due. In order to synchronize these two streams, firms demand money for transactions purposes. As the volume of business grows, payments, too, must grow, so the transactions demand for money increases. When the business volume diminishes, fewer dollars are needed for payments, so the demand for money drops. In firms as well as in households, the demand for money for transactions varies directly with the volume of economic activity. At high levels of income, the transactions demand is high. At low levels of income, the transactions demand is low.

The Precautionary Demand

In addition to holding money as a means of synchronizing income patterns with expenditure patterns, firms and households hold money as a hedge against emergencies. Firms always run the risk that buyers will not pay for goods. There is always the possibility that their retail outlets will not mail payments to the home offices on time or that a worker will slip on a banana peel and slow production enough to delay deliveries. Even when these emergencies arise the firm must still pay wages, rent, and insurance premiums. Most firms keep a reserve of cash on hand to guard against these events. They take precautions.

Households also keep money in case of unforeseen needs—a few dollars for unplanned purchases or doctor bills. And a university professor keeps a few dollars in his desk to pay for lunch when former students appear on surprise visits.

As the income of either a firm or a household increases, its activities become more complex and more things can go wrong. The low-income family may find twenty dollars an adequate emergency fund, whereas a wealthy family may keep hundreds of dollars around for this purpose. A large industrial firm will keep thousands or tens of thousands of dollars in a "discretionary fund" to meet unanticipated expenditures. Like the transactions demand, the precautionary demand for money increases with income.

The aggregate of transactions and precautionary demands for money is shown in Figure 13-1. Unlike a demand curve for eggs or gasoline, the demand curve for money has a positive slope. This is because the demand curve for money is not being related to price. Demand stems from the number of dollars the firm or household *thinks it needs* in order to carry on trade (transactions) or meet emergencies (precautions). This number of dollars increases as GNP increases.

Figure 13-1 Transactions and the Precautionary Demand for Money

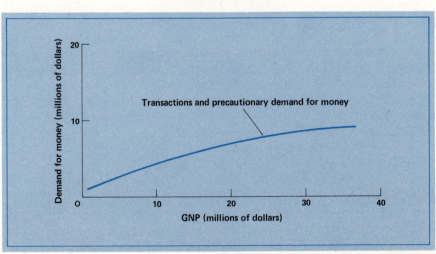

The Speculative Demand

One of the major functions of money is to act as a store of value. As long as prices vary in an uncertain fashion, however, money is not a *perfect store of value.*

A perfect store of value maintains the same purchasing power relative to all other goods through all time. If some quantity of a perfect store of value bought two loaves of bread or three gallons of gasoline today, it would maintain these same ratios in all future time periods.

The purchasing power of money rises and falls as prices of various commodities change. Some people, noting this, have used money for speculative purposes. When its purchasing power rises, they wish to hold money because the amount that will buy one pair of shoes today may purchase two pairs tomorrow. When the purchasing power of money is falling, they wish to hold goods whose values are not falling, so they exchange money for goods. Thus, money moves among households and firms as their expectations about its future purchasing power change.

Speculation of any kind requires quick and decisive action. Those who speculate on the future purchasing power of money must be prepared to exchange cash for noncash assets or noncash assets for cash on an instant's notice, and they must hold a stock of cash on reserve to use in such exchanges. These exchanges have important consequences with respect to the performance of the macroeconomy. They influence the rate of interest, and this in turn has some impact on investment. Although speculators trade money for stocks, bonds, Treasury bills, and promissory notes, the relationship between money and the interest rate is best learned by considering a bond such as a municipal bond.

Bonds are issued by public and private groups (or individuals) in order to raise money. The sellers of a bond agree to pay an annual rate of interest on its face value and to redeem the bond (buy it back) for the face value at the end of a specified number of years. Individuals, groups, and corporations who have idle money may purchase bonds as a source of income or as a store of value. Bonds are bought and sold in highly organized markets, and their prices respond to the laws of supply and demand.

Even though the bond's market price varies with respect to the laws of supply and demand, the interest earnings of the bond owner are calculated with respect to the bond's face value and its stated rate of interest. If a bond has a face value of $100 and a stated interest rate of 7 percent, the company or government entity issuing the bond pays whoever owns the bond seven dollars per year ($100 $\times$ .07 = $7) regardless of how much the owner paid for it. If the bond was purchased for $50, the company or government agency still makes the same seven dollar interest payment. The buyer is the winner, for he is receiving a 14 percent return rather than the stated return of 7 percent (7/50 = .14). If prices in the bond market rise very rapidly and a buyer must pay $200 for the same bond, the new buyer still receives the $7 annual return. The return to him is 3.5 percent (7/200 = .035).

Speculators make a choice. If they think money will command a higher purchasing power in the future than bonds, they will keep their money in a *liquid* form—they will keep it in cash.

When used in connection with money, the term *liquid* means "easily used for transactions purposes." Cash is the most liquid of all assets; demand deposit money is probably next. Liquid assets are assets that can be turned into cash on a moment's notice.

When they think that the purchasing power of money is dropping, speculators shift to bonds as a "safer" way of holding assets. When there is a shift to bonds, the demand for them increases. Following the law of supply and demand, this increased demand causes bond prices to increase. Since interest is paid with respect to face value, the effective interest rates fall with the rise in bond prices. If at another time speculators think money is a safer way to hold purchasing power, they will convert their bonds into money by placing them on the market. Subsequently, the supply of bonds increases, bond prices fall, and the effective rates of interest rise.

The choice of holding money instead of bonds is referred to as *liquidity preference*. This preference has much to do with the rate of interest as well as the quantity of money held.

Liquidity preference is the desire to hold cash or demand deposits rather than interest-earning assets. It is closely related to income, the rate of interest, and expectations for the future.

Liquidity preference is shown in Figure 13–2 as a negatively sloped curve. When interest rates are generally high (as at point A), the "cost" of holding idle money is high, since the same dollars could be used to purchase bonds having high annual yields. At such times, very little money is held as cash; it is transformed into bonds. When rates of interest

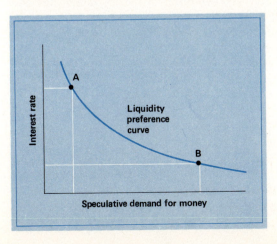

**Figure 13–2
A Liquidity Preference Schedule**

are low (as at point B), little income is given up by holding cash. Larger stocks of money are held, since it is not worth the loss of liquidity and the broker's fee to purchase bonds. The liquidity preference curve shows a relationship between cash holdings and the interest rate. As incomes or future expectations change, the desire to hold cash (remain liquid) may also change. Thus, the entire liquidity preference curve may shift up or down, or it may become steeper or flatter.

There is a great deal of controversy in macroeconomics about the slope and position of the liquidity preference curve, but almost everyone agrees about the potential *result* of a steep or a flat curve. A steep liquidity preference curve indicates that changes in the rate of interest will be accompanied by only modest changes in the amount of money held. A flat liquidity preference curve indicates that even small changes in interest rates will bring large changes in the amount of money held. This responsiveness of the liquidity preference curve is important in determining how much money will be held and how much will continue to be used to purchase the economy's factors and products.

The Total Demand for Money

The three demands for money can be summarized in two general hypotheses. The first says that as income increases, the demand for cash balances increases, too. The amount of money demanded for transactions purposes and for precautionary purposes is rooted in money's value as a medium of exchange. When income increases, aggregate demand increases and more money is needed to serve these purposes. The second hypothesis says that as the interest rate rises, the demand for money in the form of cash will fall, because the rewards of "putting the money to work" are too high to ignore. This hypothesis concerning the speculative demand for money centers on money's function as a store of value. The first hypothesis is illustrated in Figure 13–1 and the second in Figure 13–2. Although the demand for money is still not perfectly understood, the shapes of the curves are quite certain. When income changes, so does the demand for money for transaction and precautionary purposes. As the rate of interest changes, so does the quantity of money that will be held because of liquidity preferences.

The Supply of Money

All this has been preparatory to asking a very fundamental question: Does the quantity of money affect anything except prices? The old quantity theory of money still does a reasonable job of showing that the gen-

"How do we know when to stop?"

eral level of prices can be influenced by manipulating the supply of money. Can aggregate output (GNP) and the level of employment be similarly influenced? The answer seems to be Yes, because of the demand for money as a liquid asset.

If an unexpected surge in the quantity of money should occur, firms and households would find that they had more cash than they really wanted and would seek to convert cash into noncash assets—they would purchase bonds and other interest-bearing securities. The increased demand for bonds and securities would cause interest rates to drop. The lower interest rates would not provide sufficient incentive to give up all liquidity, so some of the added money would be kept as cash. The drop in interest rates would have the added effect of increasing demands for many kinds of investment and consumer expenditures like housing construction, new cars and refrigerators, and vacations. The interest payment on the monthly BankAmericard statement would no longer be such a formidable obstacle to increased buying.

All the new expenditures that come in response to a reduction in the interest rate are injections into the income stream and are similar in every way to the government injections described in Chapters 8, 9, and 10. They are multiplied in the course of their passage from original purchaser to retailer to wholesaler to manufacturer. If a deflationary gap exists, an increase in the quantity of money has the potential capacity to remove it.

A decrease in the supply of money has the opposite effect. When money is scarce, firms and households try to become more liquid. They need cash to satisfy transactions, precautionary, and speculative demands. To obtain cash, they sell bonds and securities. The sudden rush to sell bonds causes bond prices to fall, just as a sudden rush to sell hammers or stoves or Dodge Chargers will cause the prices of these items to fall, too. However, the price of bonds has a direct effect on the interest rate. As the price of bonds falls, the rate of interest rises. Now, purchases of those consumer and investment items that respond to interest rate changes will be decreased. The new house will not be built and the new washer will not be purchased. Money will be extracted from the income stream in order to maintain transactions, precautionary, and speculative balances. These withdrawals mean less activity for buyer, retailer, wholesaler, and manufacturer, so a modest reduction in incomes is multiplied. The withdrawn dollars do double duty in removing an inflationary gap.

In sum, the supply of money has an important effect on economic activity. The early economists were, in a way, correct when they formulated the quantity theory of money. At full employment increases in the money supply cannot affect output, but they do have a direct effect on the general level of prices. This theory was too elementary, however, to explain the role of money in an economy frequently plagued by unemployment and inflation. Economists of this century have constructed a more elaborate theory recognizing that people (firms and households) hold money for many reasons. Some is held for transactions purposes, but people also maintain cash balances for precautionary reasons and as a means of speculating. The volume of money held is a determinant of the rate of interest. When money holdings are converted into bonds, interest rates fall. When bonds are sold so cash can be held, interest rates rise. These fluctuations in the interest rate bring changes in the volume of interest-sensitive transactions. A drop in the rate of interest increases the level of investment, while an increase in the rate of interest causes investments to fall. Thus, changes in the supply of money have an important influence on the broad scope of aggregate economic activity. The expanded theory of money helps explain the level of output as well as the level of prices. Chapter 14 is devoted to explaining how the quantity of money can be monitored.

Summary
1 While economists agree that money is important in regulating the performance of an economy, they disagree on *how* important it is. Some say money is the most important variable affecting performance, others say money has only modest importance.
2 The classical economists explained money's role using the quantity theory of money. This theory did an adequate job of relating the money supply to price levels, but it was inadequate in explaining changes in the level of output.

3 Contemporary economists place considerable credence in various explanations of the demand for money. Money is demanded for transactions, precautionary, and speculative purposes.
4 Transactions demands and precautionary demands are related to money as a medium of exchange. Speculative demands are related to money as a store of value.
5 As the rate of interest increases, the cost of holding money increases, so money is released to be used for investment purposes.
6 As the rate of interest falls, the cost of holding money drops, so money is held as cash rather than being reinjected into the income stream.

Exercises

1 Explain these important terms and concepts:
   quantity theory   liquidity
   monetarists   liquidity preference
   bonds   transactions demand
   $MV \equiv PQ$ velocity
   precautionary demand   speculative demand
2 In the very recent past, the U.S. economy had its first modern brush with "double-digit" inflation. The classical economists would have claimed this rapid rise in prices to be neutral with respect to the real economy. In fact, the inflation has not been neutral. Why?
3 What motives explain the following holdings of cash?
   a A bank account containing a college student's summer earnings.
   b Money stashed in a cookie jar.
   c Cash in the vault of a savings and loan association that anticipates a fall in bond prices.
   d Minor coins in a child's piggybank.
   e Large cash holdings in the wage account of Kennecott Copper Co.
4 As the price of a bond *increases,* its interest yield *decreases.* Why? As the price of a bond *decreases,* its interest yield *increases.* Why? Be sure you understand this inverse relationship between bond prices and their yields.

A Contemporary Problem
How Potent Is Monetary Policy?

Economics, like all sciences, has its fads. What seems perfectly correct one year may appear foolishly absurd in another. The reason is not that economists are bad scientists but that the economy changes. The priorities of the public and of policy makers change, and different theories apply at different times.

One of the continuing battles among economists is the importance of monetary theory. No one denies that changing the quantity of money will have some effect on the performance of the economy. The controversy is whether the effect will be great, so-so, or very minor. The polar views are as follows:

The anti-monetarist view. The anti-monetarists argue that money matters very little and that monetary policy is likely to prove weak when it is needed most. Their argument entails two basic points:

1 Business or other types of investments, they say, are not highly responsive to reductions in the interest rate. If a business is highly risky, a small reduction in the interest rate is not likely to make the difference between attractiveness and unattractiveness of an investment in that business. In effect, an increase in the money supply is an offer to make money available on easy terms. But if business prospects are not promising, who will want to borrow it?

2 The anti-monetarists argue that interest rates will not fall very far in response to increases in the money supply and that there is a lower limit to interest rates. After this lower limit is reached, further increases in the money supply will be largely ineffective in stimulating investment, home building, and consumer buying. If this is true, expanding the money supply becomes a limited tool to use in managing the economy.

This extreme position has not held up very well under the experience of recent events. For example, investment in home and commercial construction has been extremely responsive to the interest rate, and interest rates have proved to be influenced by the Federal Reserve System and its decisions to expand or contract the money supply.

The extreme monetarist position. The other end of the spectrum is occupied by those who hold that fiscal policies do not really work, so that only money matters to any substantial degree. Curiously, most monetarists argue that even monetary policy is effective only in the short run!

The monetarists begin by arguing against fiscal policy. They say that in order to conduct a fiscal policy such as public works, government must either tax money away from people or borrow money to use in the spending program. But taxing or borrowing just to spend is merely a transfer, not an increase in real activity. In order for the fiscal policy to yield a net gain in economic activity, the activity must be financed, but not with tax or borrowed money. Even in fiscal policy, the government must be printing money. In that case, the effect will be to stimulate the economy, but the stimulation, the monetarists say, comes from the printing of money, not the public works.

The extreme monetarists go on to say that even this will work only for a while. The increased money supply will stimulate employment, but it will soon begin to raise prices. Rising prices erode the purchasing power of money, finally eliminating it altogether. When this occurs, the community finds itself back at the initial money supply in terms of purchasing power. Thus, say the monetarists, in the long run it is possible to keep employment at an "artificially" high level only by continuing to expand the money supply, and this will bring accelerating inflation. In the long run then, the extreme monetarist position is that nothing can help employment—neither fiscal policy nor money really matters.

The facts seem to offer little support to either of the extreme views. Since the mid-1930s, a combination of monetary and fiscal policy seems to have helped the United States to maintain unprecedented levels of employment. Even in the severe recession that began about 1973, the rate of unemployment did not approach the levels frequently reached in earlier decades. In sum, the evidence seems to suggest that a judicious combination of monetary and fiscal instruments constitutes a powerful and helpful weapon that can be used as part of an effective policy to deal with the problems of unemployment and inflation.

14 The Federal Reserve System

Money is a necessity in a specialized market economy. Nearly everyone in the United States comes in daily contact with it, yet money is still the object of love, hate, fear, attraction, ignorance, and misunderstanding. Desperate people rob service stations for money, while others wager it freely on the speed of horses, the roll of dice, or the chance holdings of certain combinations of playing cards. Men have sought power by using money and they have sought money through the abuse of power. The economy that has too little money is driven to recession or even to bartering. The economy with too much money suffers wildly inflated prices.

The power of the banking system—even of a single bank—is enormous. In their daily activities related to lending money and holding assets, banks create and destroy demand deposits. In doing so they cause the money supply to fluctuate, and, as Chapters 12 and 13 showed, this can have important effects on the tempo of economic activity. Because of their potential effect on the performance of the macroeconomy, banks in this nation are subjected to close supervision and management through monetary policies formulated and carried out by the Federal Reserve System. This chapter is about that system and its monetary policies, its relationship with the U.S. Treasury, and the effectiveness of monetary policy in general.

CHAPTER FOURTEEN

250

Creation and Organization of the System

Few conscientious observers doubt that the quantity of money in circulation helps to determine the way the macroeconomy will behave. This extremely important variable, though, is left in the hands of approximately 15,000 private banks that, by granting or not granting loans, can expand or contract the supply of money. If the macroeconomic impact of money is to be harnessed, the activities of bankers must be coordinated with those of other macro policy makers. Regulating 15,000 individual and independent banks is not a simple task. Although the nation tried for many years to operate without central banking control, the Federal Reserve System was finally established in 1913 as a means of maintaining some control over the creation and destruction of money.[1] "The Fed," as the system is commonly known, consists of twelve regional Federal Reserve Banks designed to help carry out monetary policies that affect the macroeconomy.

When the System was established, it was ruled by a seven-member body called the Federal Reserve Board. During the 1930s, in one of several minor reorganizations, the name of the body was changed to the Board of Governors but it remains a seven-member group with each member appointed by the President of the United States to serve a fourteen-year term. Much of the work of the central banking system is conducted by an elaborate set of committees, of which the Open Market Committee is the most important. Another committee, the Federal Advisory Council, maintains contact between the board and the twelve regional Federal Reserve Banks.

The regional banks are located in the 12 cities shown in capital letters in Figure 14–1. The other cities named on the map contain branches of the twelve banks, maintained primarily for the convenience of commercial banks in the district.

Each of the twelve regional Federal Reserve Banks is owned by individual banks in the region. A commercial bank may buy part ownership of the Federal Reserve Bank in its district. Once a part owner, the member bank has the privilege of using the name "national bank," may keep a portion of its required reserves on deposit in the Federal Reserve Bank and borrow from the bank, and agrees to follow suggestions and policies made by the Federal Reserve System. This type of ownership allows the member banks some control over banking activity. At this time, nearly 6,000 banks in the United States are member-owners. Although this is

---

[1]Soon after the United States won independence from England it established a central bank. The First Bank of the United States lasted from 1791 until its charter expired in 1811. After five years without a central bank, the nation set up the Second Bank of the United States in 1816. It, too, lasted twenty years. From 1836 until 1913—77 years—the nation was without central banking authority.

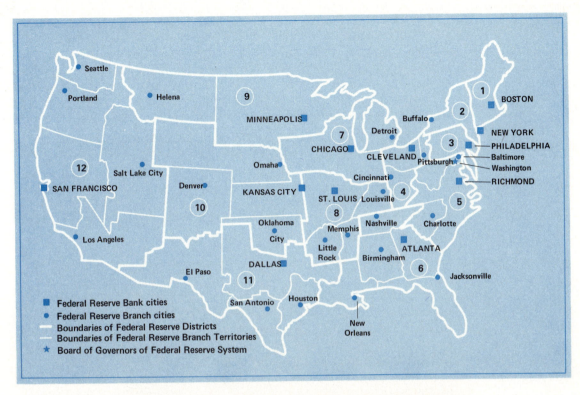

Figure 14-1 Federal Reserve Map of the United States

less than 40 percent of all U.S. banks, those belonging to the system are generally the larger banks. Currently, about 75 percent of all banking activity in the United States is conducted through banks affiliated with the Federal Reserve.

Even though the system is privately owned by its many member banks, the Board of Governors is responsible to the President and, indirectly, to the Congress. The board is in charge of supervising the activities of the twelve regional banks and is obliged to coordinate its own monetary policy with the activities of other agencies responsible for managing the macroeconomy.

The member banks do not join the System simply for the honor of belonging. They buy into the Fed to obtain its services as a bank for bankers. The 12 regional banks hold deposits for members, just as commercial banks hold deposits for their customers. The System distributes small coins and currency to member banks, just as banks supply them to individuals. The System provides facilities for "clearing" checks: If a check is written in a town 500 miles from the bank on which it is drawn, the check must be returned to its home bank so that the proper accounts can be credited and charged. The Federal Reserve System performs this function without charge to member banks.

An extremely important function performed by the system is the issuing of paper currency—not just the distribution mentioned above, but the actual issuing of new paper money. Most paper money in circulation today is in the form of Federal Reserve Notes. The value of these notes is guaranteed by the System. To insure the value of currency it issues, the Fed holds large stocks of government securities or other "safe" securities in much the same way that commercial banks hold stocks of required reserves to insure, or back, their deposits.

In sum, the whole central banking system includes nearly 6,000 commercial banks that keep at least part of their required reserves on deposit in the twelve Federal Reserve Banks. The twelve Federal Reserve Banks, in turn, use these reserves to purchase huge volumes of government and other securities that are eventually used to insure the value of paper money issued by the system. The Board of Governors directs this network and is charged with the responsibility of managing the money supply. Although the board is government-appointed, ownership and administrative control of the System reside in the private sector of the economy.

Altering the Money Supply

The Federal Reserve System uses three major instruments and a host of minor ones to adjust the money supply to the needs of the economy. Major policy instruments include altering the discount rate, buying or selling bonds in the open market, and changing the fraction of deposits required to be kept by banks as reserves.

Changes in the Discount Rate

The Federal Reserve System was created to help guard against the possibility that individual banks would overextend themselves by lending out all their excess reserves. A bank that is "loaned up" is incapable of responding to the needs of its customers. The Federal Reserve System has the power to circumvent this possibility by loaning additional excess reserves to member banks. When a member bank's excess reserves are exhausted and it has customers wanting to borrow money, the bank can borrow from the Fed. In this capacity, the Federal Reserve System is truly a banker's bank.

Borrowing reserves is not free of charge. Just as every commercial bank charges interest on loans made to individuals, so the Fed charges interest on the loans it makes to its members. Because the interest on a loan from the Fed is deducted at the time the loan is made, the loans are said to be *discounted;* the rate of interest is called the *discount rate.*

The discount rate is the interest rate charged member banks when they borrow money from the Federal Reserve System. The term *discount* refers to the Fed's practice of collecting interest when the loan is made rather than when it is repaid.

Just as the interest rate influences how much money an individual or firm will borrow, the discount rate affects bankers' behavior. When the discount rate is high, bankers are reluctant to borrow. When the rate is low, they are willing to borrow.

During an inflationary period the task of the banking system is to reduce the volume of purchasing power available to society. At such times, therefore, the Fed makes every effort to reduce the capacity of commercial banks to create demand deposits. One way to do this is to make borrowed reserves very expensive: raise the discount rate. During deflationary or recessionary periods, the banking system endeavors to increase the banks' ability to create demand deposits in order to *increase* purchasing power. This can be done by lowering the discount rate, making it easy for member banks to obtain additional reserves should they be needed.

Early in the history of the Federal Reserve System, the discount rate was an important control on the ability of commercial banks to expand and contract the supply of money. In the past thirty years, however, this control has lost some of its strength. Individual banks seldom run short of excess reserves, and when they do the Board of Governors discourages extensive borrowing of reserves. Now changes in the discount rate are announced with much fanfare because they do have a psychological effect and they do cause commercial banks to change their own rates of interest. In large measure, changes in the discount rate *follow* the use of other tools.

Buying and Selling Bonds in the Open Market

The Federal Reserve System is a major buyer of government securities available for purchase through the U.S. Treasury. In 1975, the Fed purchased Treasury bills and U.S. Government bonds valued at more than $21 billion. In the same period of time, the System sold bills and bonds valued at nearly $5.6 billion.

A Treasury bill is a short-term security with a maturity of 91 (sometimes 182) days. Because they have short terms to maturity, the bills seldom gain or lose value because of inflationary or deflationary pressures. They are liquid assets, sought after as bank reserves.

Even though the banking system does this huge business with the Treasury, there is no assurance that the securities will be kept by banks that purchase them. The bonds, Treasury bills, and other securities can be resold to member banks, nonmember banks, firms, agencies, or individuals. Similarly, the Federal Reserve System need not buy its entire portfolio of securities from the Treasury. It can buy and sell bonds and securities from agencies, other banks, firms, or individuals. This process of buying and selling bonds has an enormous effect on the capacity of individual banks to create demand deposits and alter the money supply.

Security transactions performed by the Federal Reserve System are carried out in the public market on recommendation of the Open Market Committee. In times of inflation, when the appropriate monetary objective is to reduce purchasing power and relieve pressures on limited supplies of goods and services, the Open Market Committee recommends the sale of government securities. In selling securities, the central banking system collects funds and thereby reduces the volume of money in the hands of consumers. With less money at their disposal, individuals lower their demands for many items, thus relieving inflationary pressures.

It is particularly important to note that commercial banks are the major purchasers of bonds and securities placed on the market by the Federal Reserve System. Since commercial banks use excess reserves to purchase these bonds and securities, the reserves they have available for use in extending bank credit are reduced whenever they make a purchase. The process is demonstrated in Figure 14–2. If the reserve requirement is 25 percent and a bank has $10 million in excess reserves,

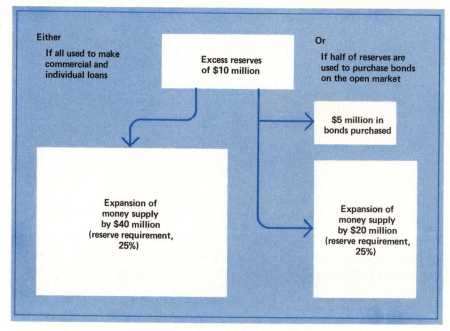

Figure 14–2 The Effect of Open-Market Selling on Expansion of the Money Supply

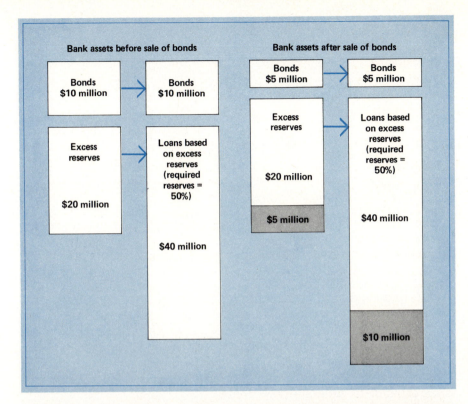

Figure 14-3 Expanding Lending Capacity by Selling Bonds and Securities

the bank can ultimately increase the money supply by $40 million. If, however, half of this $10 million is used to purchase securities, the bank's capacity to expand demand deposits is reduced to $20 million. Selling bonds to banks therefore depletes their reserves and reduces their ability to expand the supply of money.

Even if the bonds are not purchased by banks, the Federal Reserve's act of selling in the open market reduces the amount of money in circulation. When individuals or corporations purchase securities, their hoards of cash are depleted. If they pay for the securities by check (demand deposit), reserves available to their banks will be curtailed and the banks' capacity to extend loans will be reduced.

If the Federal Reserve Board senses that the economy is slowing, the above process can be reversed: by buying bonds and securities on the open market the Fed can expand the supply of money. In these transactions it is trading money for securities, and the money thus placed in the hands of people and institutions will be used for additional purchases. Money banks receive from selling bonds to the Fed can be used as excess reserves and form the basis for loans many times the actual value of the bonds. Even if commercial banks do not sell securities to the Federal Reserve System, chances are quite high that those who do sell—firms, individuals, or corporations—will deposit revenue from the sales in commercial banks, thus adding to the banks' capacity to make loans. The process is shown in Figure 14-3. A bank originally has bonds and securities valued at $10 million and excess reserves of $20 million. If the

> **Open-Market Operations in Capsule Form**
>
> 1. When the Federal Reserve System buys securities
>   a. Money goes from Federal Reserve to commercial banks (securities go from banks to Federal Reserve).
>   b. The money acts as excess reserves for making loans and for monetary expansion.
>
> 2. When the Federal Reserve System sells securities
>   a. Money goes from banks to the central banking system (securities go from Federal Reserve to commercial banks).
>   b. Reduced reserves limit the banks' ability to make loans.

reserve requirement is 50 percent, the banking system can use the $20 million as a basis for loans of $40 million. This starting position is shown on the left side of the figure. If half the bonds and securities are sold, the value of bonds and securities drops to $5 million, while cash reserves increase to $25 million. These new millions of dollars can be used to generate loans of $10 million, thus greatly expanding the banking system's capacity to generate new money.

When the Federal Reserve System *buys* securities, it places money in the hands of people who can use it. Since this money provides the base for lending an even larger sum, buying bonds and securities in the open market is a highly expansionary activity. When the Federal Reserve *sells*, it exchanges bonds and securities for money. In taking money out of circulation, the central banking system dampens the lending capacity of commercial banks and exerts a contractionary effect on the money supply.

Changing the Reserve Requirement

The most powerful of all the Federal Reserve's tools of monetary policy, its ability to change reserve requirements, is used very infrequently. When the reserve requirement is changed, changes also occur in the deposit expansion multiplier. If a bank is required to hold 5 percent of its deposits on reserve, the money supply can be expanded to twenty times the amount of excess reserves (deposit expansion multiplier = $1/.05 = 20$). If the reserve requirement increases to 20 percent, the money supply can be expanded by five times the amount of reserves ($1/.20 = 5$), and if the requirement reaches 100 percent no expansion is possible, since every dollar deposited must be kept in reserve ($1/1.00 = 1$). Changing the reserve requirement alters the volume of excess reserves, and these excess reserves are the key to a bank's ability to create demand deposits.

If the Board of Governors feels that a state of economic emergency is approaching, reserve requirements might be altered. An increase in the reserve requirement decreases the amount of money that can be used for lending; a decrease in the reserve requirement increases the amount. Because this is such a powerful tool, Congress has placed restrictions on how much the requirements can be changed by the Fed. Large banks, those with demand deposits in excess of $400 million, have reserve requirements that can be changed but must remain between 10 and 22 percent. The smaller banks with demand deposits up to $400 million have reserve requirements that must stay between 7 and 14 percent. For many years, the larger banks were found only in large cities and acquired the name *reserve city banks*. The smaller banks were in predominantly rural areas and were called *country banks*. Although the geographic distinction has had no meaning since 1972, the names have remained as informal indicators of bank size. Higher required reserve ratios for the larger banks make a good deal of sense. First, small banks (country banks) often deposit some of their required reserves in banks of the larger cities. This is done for convenience in clearing checks and so that the reserves will be earning interest. Because of this connection between country banks and reserve city banks, a run on small banks would put a severe strain on the reserves held in the reserve city banks. To ease this threat, reserve city banks are required to keep a higher proportion of their deposits on reserve. Second, in a large city even a modest drop in public confidence in banks could bring thousands of depositors through the doors to claim their deposits in the form of currency. Again, the larger reserve requirement keeps enough money on hand to cope with such events.

Changing the reserve requirement is such a powerful tool of money-supply management that when it is used, every bank must alter its behavior. The Federal Reserve System resorts to it only when problems seem too severe to be solved using the more common open-market operations. Reserve requirements for all banks changed several times during the "stagflation" of the early 1970s. Between 1968 and 1973 the requirement was raised, but on February 13, 1975, the rates were dropped to allow expansion of the money supply. At that time, the following rates and their respective deposit expansion multipliers applied to various sizes of banks:

Demand deposits (millions of dollars)	Reserve requirement	Deposit expansion multiplier
0– 2	7.5%	13.33
2– 10	10.0	10.00
10–100	12.0	8.33
100–400	13.0	7.69
over 400	16.5	6.06

Minor Controls

The major tools of money supply management are supplemented by a host of minor controls used to alter behavior of individual bankers and to change the amount of money in circulation.

Ceilings on interest paid to savers. Commercial banks are highly competitive and will go to great lengths to gain the opportunity to serve a particular client. They compete mostly by offering personal services like banking by telephone or mail, or small fringe benefits including gifts to customers who open new accounts. The possibility of competing by raising and lowering interest rates is kept to a minimum by Federal Reserve System regulations. This provision was intended to prevent depositors from shifting deposits from one bank to another in response to modest changes in the rate of interest paid. Economists have increasingly viewed this regulation as a restrictive device that allows banks to keep from paying depositors the full value of their earnings. This control is seldom mentioned in the newspaper, but it does have a stabilizing influence on banking behavior and practices.

Limits on installment credit. The power of the central banking system to place limits on installment credit has been used only during or immediately following periods of war or international conflict. The limits may be lenient or strict. The Federal Reserve System can instruct its member banks to be very selective about the manner in which they dispense credit. Controls can be placed on the total volume of installment credit, the interest rates charged, the minimum size of down payments, and the maximum length of time that can be allowed for repayment. This con-

"As a matter of fact, the small monthly payment isn't *all*. There are large weekly payments that go with it."

> ## The Meaning of "Minor" Controls
>
> Minor controls are minor only in the sense that they do not have the massive power associated with the discount rate, open-market operations, or changes in reserve requirements. Minor controls may be more important than the major ones to a bank manager faced with the responsibility of living with the minor controls. Their effects are generally so selective that even using them repeatedly could never accomplish a major national money-management goal. Minor controls are oriented more toward maintaining the integrity of an individual bank.

trol affects the expansion or contraction of purchasing power available to consumers and, hence, aggregate demand.

Control of the housing market. Nearly all private housing in the United States is financed using borrowed money, and much of the borrowed money comes through commercial banks. The ability to regulate mortgage lending influences both the volume of money circulating in the economy and the number of people employed in the building trades. At one time, the Federal Reserve System attempted to control the housing market by establishing controls on down payments, interest rates, and lengths of repayment periods. These limits had some influence, but their major effect was to encourage borrowers to bypass commercial banks in favor of other financial intermediaries in seeking money for homebuilding. There are about 5 million savings and loan associations in the United States, and they make mortgage loans amounting to approximately $50 billion.

Stock market margin requirements. The stock market is one of the strangest and most incomprehensible market institutions in the U.S. economy. It provides opportunities for new firms to obtain financing, for older firms to refinance, and for individuals to put idle money to work by using it to purchase part ownership in the nation's productive enterprises. Because of the psychology of the market and because information on prices, purchases, and sales is readily available, the market sometimes moves very rapidly from high to low and back to high. No one completely understands its workings. Even though more than 20 million shares of stock are sometimes exchanged in a single day, very little money changes hands. Most of the buying and selling is done on a credit basis. Purchases that are made using credit are said to be made "on the margin." The margin represents the proportion of the sale price that must be paid in cash. A 25 percent margin requirement means that a down payment of at least 25 cents on the dollar is needed to make a purchase. A 50 percent margin requirement means that half the total price must be paid in cash. By raising or lowering the margin requirement, the Federal Reserve System can simultaneously regulate activity on the stock market *and* in the money-lending market. Since 1960, margin requirements have varied from 50 percent to 90 percent of the purchase price. The margin requirement has been 50 percent since January 1974.

Moral suasion. The term *moral suasion* must have an appealing lilt. This power of the Federal Reserve System seems to be remembered by students and referred to by newspaper editors more often than is warranted. Moral suasion is nothing more than a good, tight administrative practice. When a member bank (or a group of member banks) is not violating any specific rule but is not behaving in a fashion consistent with the objectives of the system either, its manager (or president) is called on the carpet and told to make certain changes in the bank's behavior. This is an important activity in any complex administrative hierarchy, and the Federal Reserve System is no exception. In this case, though, the persuasive power of authority has some control over the capacity or willingness of a bank to loan money. In time of recession the Fed will "suggest" that a bank make more money available for loans. In an inflationary period, it will "suggest" that loans be harder to obtain.

Moral suasion need not be confined to the Federal Reserve family of banks. The Board of Governors can exhort other financial agencies to fall into line, or it can ask certain industries to behave in a fashion consistent with the policies of the central banking system. In the early 1950s, the Federal Reserve System used its persuasive influence to enlist the aid of all financial institutions in stopping inflation. In the early 1970s—in conjunction with the Nixon administration's Phase I and Phase II programs—the board again used persuasion but extended it to industries outside banking. Moral suasion, however, like so much of monetary policy, depends for its effectiveness upon the fish actually taking the bait.

In summary, the Federal Reserve System is charged with the responsibility of maintaining a flexible and dependable money supply. Flexibility is essential in any highly specialized market economy, if for no other reason than that more money is required at some times of the year than at others. In the United States and in other capitalistic economies, there is some evidence that the supply of money has a direct influence on the performance of the economy. Because of the possibility of a strong connection between money and performance, the supply of money cannot be left entirely unmanaged. The Federal Reserve System, with its Board of Governors, twelve Federal Reserve Banks, and nearly 6,000 member banks, has the power to control the availability of money in the economy. It does so by making changes in the discount rate, engaging in extensive open-market operations, changing reserve requirements, or using any of several minor devices to influence the behavior of commercial banks.

The Federal Reserve System and the U.S. Treasury

Although the Treasury and the Federal Reserve System have no formal administrative or functional ties to each other, they are related in purpose as well as through some of their activities.

The U.S. Treasury is the fiscal agent for the federal government. In this capacity, it collects taxes and pays bills.

These functions are colossal, considering the fact that the annual federal budget is nearly $300 billion, there are over 2.7 million employees to be paid, pensioned, and insured, and there are countless purchases—tons of paper, new buildings, and thousands of miles of highway, not to mention staples and pencil sharpeners. Payments for these and thousands of other items must be made each day. The money comes from taxes, fees, borrowing, and dozens of minor sources.

Like most major corporations and private business firms, the federal government does not always have enough cash on hand to meet its daily obligations. In these instances, the government borrows by selling bonds or special-purpose securities. Selling bonds provides the Treasury with ready cash, but it also means that the government is in debt and must pay interest on this debt. The process of repaying bonds and paying interest presents no real problem either to the Treasury or to those who have purchased the securities. The amount of interest charged on the debt does. The government as borrower naturally wants interest rates to be as low as possible. Since altering the discount rate is a major tool of money management used by the Federal Reserve System, the Fed cannot commit itself to interest rates that are perpetually low. It must have highly flexible rates so macroeconomic problems can be met when they arise. The possible conflicts between a Treasury demanding low rates and the central bank demanding freedom to change the rates have become very real on more than one occasion. In the late 1960s, the war in Southeast Asia required large amounts of money. Since it was politically impossible to raise taxes at that time, the federal government had to borrow considerable sums. At the same time, the war-excited economy began to display many signs of inflationary pressure. To combat inflationary tendencies, the Federal Reserve System tried to raise interest rates to discourage borrowing, thus reducing the money supply. The low rate desired by the Treasury conflicted with the high rate desired by the banking authorities. Such conflicts arise, because the two agencies have different kinds of obligations to fulfill. Most such conflicts are settled by "accords," or informal agreements between the two agencies, but, in the main, the Federal Reserve System goes about its business keeping in mind only the basic monetary needs of the economy.

The Use of Monetary Policy

Monetary policy is a set of tools used to control the volume of money in the U.S. economy. Although some economists feel that monetary policy is the key to understanding and manipulating the rate of growth in an economy, others say that its value is limited. Regardless of the disposition of an individual economist or policy maker, the use of monetary policy is rooted in the idea that changing the quantity of money will have an effect on prices, output, and employment.

The whole of monetary policy is seriously weakened by its asymmetry. The major tools of monetary policy—changing the discount rate, buying and selling bonds and securities on the open market, and changing reserve requirements—may do an excellent job of making money tighter or easier to obtain, but there is never any assurance that the public will respond in the fashion anticipated by monetary authorities. Money can be made easy to obtain, but there is no guarantee that this money will actually be borrowed and spent. Monetary policy is more effective when *decreases* in the money supply are desired. When inflation appears imminent, money is tightened by increasing the discount rate, selling bonds and securities in the open market, or increasing the proportion of demand deposits that must be kept in reserve. Tightening the money supply generally has some influence. In the late 1960s and early 1970s, for example, extremely high rates of interest made mortgage lending and installment purchasing almost prohibitive. In either case, expansion or

contraction, monetary policy must be indirect. Banks and the banking system can make money available, but an anxious public may pay no heed.

One of the advantages of monetary policy is that it can be implemented very quickly, although its total effects may be slow in coming. Since monetary policy is controlled by only a few people, (the Board of Governors and its companion committees) who are not restricted by an elaborate system of checks and balances, today's idea can become tomorrow's policy. In a recessionary period, the order to expand the money supply can go out instantly. The only lags are in the system's recognizing a policy change and in the public's response to the increased availability of funds. In times of inflation, the order to restrict lending today can be put in force tomorrow. This speed is not enjoyed by fiscal policy or other means of adjusting the performance of the economy.

Summary

1 The Federal Reserve System (or the "Fed") is a central banking authority charged with coordinating the borrowing and lending activities of the nation's commercial banks.
2 The system includes twelve regional banks that are owned by some 6,000 commercial banks. A seven-person body called the Board of Governors, and several subcommittees within it, watch over the performance of the economy and regulate the quantity of money in circulation.
3 The System uses three major tools to adjust the capacity of commercial banks to grant loans. These are changes in the discount rate, open-market activities, and changes in the reserve requirement.
4 A number of minor controls are used to influence the behavior of individual banks or certain groups of customers. These include ceilings on interest paid to savers, limits on installment credit, controls on mortgage lending, stock market margin requirements, and persuasion.
5 The Fed and the U.S. Treasury are sometimes in conflict, with the Treasury pressing for low interest rates and the Fed insisting on very flexible rates.
6 Monetary policy is fast. By working its way through a small board, today's idea can become tomorrow's policy.
7 Monetary policy is also asymmetrical. While it is effective in contracting the money supply, it cannot by itself insure that the money supply will expand.

Exercises

1 Explain these important terms and concepts:
    the Fed   monetary policy
    reserve city   Open Market Committee
    Board of Governors discount rate
    member bank   country bank
    minor controls

2 The ability to expand or contract the money supply is closely related to both the reserve requirement and open-market operations. Reserve requirements can be raised or lowered. Open-market operations can be either buying or selling. Does raising the reserve requirement have the same effect as buying or selling bonds on the open market?

3 In 1939, the Federal Reserve Board (forerunner of today's Board of Governors) issued a statement saying that the Federal Reserve System was capable of making money available to anyone at reasonable rates of interest but the system could not force the public to borrow. How does this lack of power affect monetary policy?

4 Why does the Treasury want interest rates to be low and why does the Fed want them to be flexible?

5 Suppose banks were required to maintain 100 percent of their deposits as reserves. Would there still be a need for a Federal Reserve System? Could there be a monetary policy?

6 Raw numbers can bring misunderstanding. Only about 40 percent of the nation's banks are members of the Federal Reserve System, so only 40 percent are directly affected by the Fed's monetary policy. The other 60 percent of the banks can do as they please. What keeps them from destroying the effectiveness of the Fed's policies?

7 If there is an inflationary gap of $10 billion and the reserve requirement is 10 percent, how many dollars worth of bonds will have to be sold on the open market to reduce the inflationary gap to zero?

A Contemporary Problem
Bank Lending

Since 1964, the Federal Reserve System has conducted quarterly surveys of banking practices among the nation's largest banks. In 1975, the survey contacted 123 banks and asked many questions about the way they used their lending powers. Here is what was learned.

For much of 1974 the slowing of the economy was hidden from bankers by the heavy borrowing of businesses that were willing and able to pay high rates of interest for bank loans. By late 1974, however, it was becoming increasingly apparent that the economy was in a severe economic downturn. The optimism of the banking community was rapidly replaced by a cautious and restrictive lending policy that lasted through 1975.

Loan/deposit ratios had risen sharply in 1973 and 1974 under the pressure of inflation-induced business borrowing, and bank liquidity had been permitted to erode. Consequently, 1975 was a year when large banks became concerned about their own reliance on borrowed funds to finance loans. They increased their holdings of liquid assets and reduced their dependence on borrowed funds. While demands for loans declined throughout 1975, banks generally maintained or tightened their previously adopted restrictive loan policies to restrain *business* loan growth and improve earnings. On the other hand, easing of lending policies toward *consumers* was apparent in the surveys, and this availability of bank financing contributed to increased consumer spending in 1975, which was an important element in the recovery of the economy.

As the recession continued through the year, demand for business loans deteriorated. Even though the decreased demand for this type of loan eased pressure on loanable (excess) reserves, most banks retained a restrictive policy on other types of loans.

When the survey was updated in November, inflows of deposits to banks had accelerated, the banks themselves had made considerable progress in improving their liquidity positions, and there were some signs that lending policies toward business had been eased. In addition, there had been a further easing in consumer loan policies; for the year as a whole, banks appeared to have become increasingly more willing to make such loans.

Far from being completely in control of their own futures, banks—even the very large ones—are extremely sensitive to conditions in the economy. Making too many loans puts the banks in a precarious position. Making too few loans results in intolerably low bank earnings. The banks themselves try to maintain a suitable balance between liquidity and earnings. In 1975, the shift between business and consumer demands made this very difficult.[2]

[2]Adapted from the *Federal Reserve Bulletin,* April 1976.

15 Economic Instability and Macroeconomic Policy

Economic instability is the price of specialization and decentralization. Centuries of records pertaining to the U.S. economy and other free-enterprise nations indicate that this form of economic organization has a strong tendency to be unstable: Periods of inflation follow periods of recession. No one completely understands these swings in economic activity, but because they bring changes in the allocation of resources and the distribution of income, U.S. economic policy at home is geared largely to maintaining economic stability. This chapter deals with business fluctuations and the policies economists recommend to combat them. It draws heavily on the fiscal policy lessons of Chapters 9 to 11 and the monetary policy lessons of Chapters 12 to 14. In some respects it shows how the two types of policies have been synthesized, but in other respects it emphasizes their differences.

Business Fluctuations and Their Causes

Records kept by the Cleveland Trust Company show that the direction of economic activity in the United States has changed approximately 250 times in the last century. Early observers thought that economic swings were very regular and spoke of them as cycles, like the eternally repeated intake-compression-ignition-exhaust cycle of a running gasoline engine. Later it was noted that the "cycles" were not always regular. Sometimes, the "up" side of the swing was longer than the "down" side. Sometimes the downswing lasted much longer than the upswing. The swings did recur, but they were not so regular as a true cycle should be, so they began to be called *business fluctuations.* Both terms are now used in the popular and the formal language of economics.

Business fluctuations (or cycles) are recurring patterns of changes in the direction of business activity. The pattern includes phases of prosperity, recession, depression, and recovery.

An imaginary set of business fluctuations is shown in Figure 15-1. The fluctuations go through four distinct stages. Starting with prosperity, when per capita income, employment, and the rate of economic growth are high, the economy stumbles into recession. During recession, economic indicators begin to show signs of increasing unemployment, decreasing income levels, and lowered profits. More important, during a recession firms and households slow their rates of investment and consumption expenditures. Future expectations are bleak. The recession

Figure 15-1 Business Fluctuations

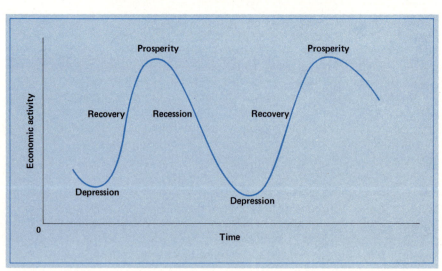

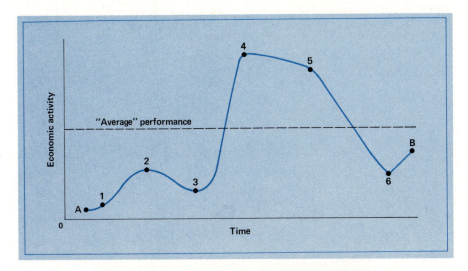

Figure 15-2 Changes in Business Activity

leads to depression—the lowest portion of the cycle. During depressions there are high levels of unemployment, per capita output is very low, investment slows or stops altogether, and some downward adjustments in consumption take place. Recovery begins when investment and consumption pick up, unemployment drops, and output, income, and optimism are high. Recovery continues until the cycle begins anew with another recession.

The symmetry of Figure 15-1 and its precise definitions of the four-stage cycle are deceptive. In reality, there is no well-defined turning point between depression and recovery or between prosperity and recession. The economy is either going up, going down, or standing still. Even while it is going up or down, the *rate* of movement may change perceptibly. An economy growing at 10 percent per year may suddenly begin to grow only 2 percent per year, or the rate of unemployment may continue to fall but at a slower pace. A more realistic but still hypothetical picture of business fluctuations is shown in Figure 15-2. The dashed line through the middle of the graph shows "average" or "desired" performance; the blue curve shows the actual performance of the economy from time *A* to time *B*. Each numbered point on the performance curve shows a change in the rate of economic activity. At points 2, 3, 4, and 6, the economy "turns around" by switching from expansion to contraction (points 2 and 4) or from contraction to expansion (points 3 and 6). At point 1, an expanding economy begins to expand more rapidly and at point 5, the rate of contraction increases. Economic science has not developed sufficiently to predict *when* any turning point or change will appear. Indeed, it is not known for sure whether the next change will be up or down, large or small. Thus, in 1974 and 1975, the newspapers commonly ran two

"What bothers me is that we all look so successful."

stories side by side, one saying that an upswing had started and the other that the downswing would continue.

Economists have proposed many different hypotheses about the causes of business fluctuations. A number of them describe forces that work together to generate fluctuations, some explain the causes of a single historic fluctuation, and others attempt a general explanation of all cycles. Hypotheses about fluctuations can be divided into two groups. The first group insists that fluctuations result from something happening outside the economic system; the second group assumes that fluctuations stem from events inside the system.

Exogenous Theories

Several plausible explanations of business fluctuations depend on events that have no basis in the economic system itself. They are *exogenous* theories.

Exogenous means "external or outside." An exogenous theory is a theory of economic behavior that depends on something outside the economic system. If men from Mars suddenly handed everyone a crisp new $100 bill, the money supply would be increased by an exogenous force.

One such explanation is related to inventions. A significant invention or technological breakthrough can cause a major increase in economic activity. The introduction of the steam locomotive in the nineteenth century and that of the automobile in the twentieth both brought vast amounts of investment. Railroads meant building engines and cars, laying tracks, moving mountains, constructing stations, and hiring section gangs. The advent of automobile travel changed dirt roads to paved highways, created subsidiary industries, built Detroit, led to huge investments in service trades, and even caused changes in residential building to include attached garages or carports. Such major inventions, some feel, are the driving force behind fluctuations in economic activity. A time when many inventions appear will be prosperous; a time of low inventiveness will be depressed and stagnant.

A second exogenous theory of economic fluctuations relates to political and social activity. To be sure, the line between social and political life and economic life is often vague. Nonetheless, great political upheavals like wars and revolutions do significantly alter economic conditions and bring changes in economic fortunes. The four major U.S. military conflicts of this century (the two World Wars, the Korean War, and the war in Vietnam) were all accompanied by prosperity and, with the exception of the Korean War, each time of prosperity ended in a business and economic crisis. On a smaller scale, the massive grain sale in 1972, which reopened trade between the United States and Russia, disrupted grain and feed prices in the United States sufficiently to cause rapid inflation of meat and other food prices in this country. Similarly, the contraceptive pill and the planned lowering of birth rates may eventually cause significant changes in investment patterns that could bring shifts in the business cycle.

Inventions and Business Activity

The argument relating inventions to economic activity sounds as if it might explain a large number of things, and the record shows that truly major inventions have happened at the beginning of generally prosperous times. The railroads had their greatest expansions in the post–Civil War years. From 1870 to 1900, there were more good years than bad. The great growth in automobiles came in the 1920s—a prosperous decade. More recently, space technology advanced during the 1960s, another decade of general prosperity.

The invention theory may be losing its impetus now because most inventions today are made and patented by the research and development departments of major industrial firms. In good times, the firms expand these departments and reap the benefit of many new patents. In poor times, the R & D departments slow their activity and contribute fewer inventions. In the 1970s, because of institutionalized research, the rate of invention may be a result rather than a cause of economic fluctuations.

Another exogenous theory was in fact among the first modern scientific hypotheses about economic fluctuations. In the 1860s, W. Stanley Jevons, a pioneer in using mathematics to solve economic problems, noted a very close relationship between the incidence of sunspots (magnetic storms on the surface of the sun) and the business cycle. Great sunspots appeared at 10.45-year intervals, and a century and a half of records showed that business cycles in England lasted an average of 10.46 years from boom to boom. Jevons reasoned that sunspots caused weather changes, the weather changes altered rainfall patterns, rainfall affected crops, and the varying crop yields caused economic activity to rise and fall. Closer investigation of sunspot data and more scientific knowledge about the causes of weather proved Jevons' theory to be quite wrong. However, from time to time there will appear a small item, buried in the back pages of a major newspaper, about some scientist who has "rediscovered" the sunspot theory and is working diligently to prove that these massive solar electrical disturbances do indeed influence the way the economy is working.

Endogenous Theories

A number of theories of the business cycle emphasize relationships that are inside the economic system and are therefore *endogenous* theories.

Endogenous refers to something that is occurring within. An endogenous economic theory is one that depends on economic variables. A theory relating aggregate demand to the money supply is an endogenous theory, since both variables are part of the economic system.

> ## The Study of Business Cycles
>
> For many years, business cycles have been studied by specialists called economic historians. Some of the best work on cycles has been done by economists who did not use cause-and-effect models but who methodically and carefully pored over masses of data about business activity and searched for patterns. The patterns were few in number. Some prosperous times seemed to be related to consumer demand, others to investment, and still others to the psychological conviction that "now is the time" to behave in a certain way.
>
> Two noted U.S. economists who made valuable contributions studying cycles were Wesley Clair Mitchell and Arthur Burns. Mitchell was born in Illinois in 1874 and studied at the University of Chicago. He became so interested in cycles and in empirical research that he helped establish the National Bureau of Economic Research in 1920. The NBER became a vast information-gathering agency aimed at the better understanding of economic fluctuations.
>
> Arthur Burns (born in Austria in 1904) was a student of Mitchell's. He began his career by coauthoring a book about business fluctuations with Mitchell. In 1969, Arthur Burns was appointed to serve a 14-year term as chairman of the Federal Reserve System's Board of Governors.

One such theory says that cycles occur because from time to time people simply do not consume enough and when demand is too low, plants must let workers go and hold inventories until more favorable times. This theory, like others, is plausible, but the contemporary record shows that consumer expenditures do not cause enough variation to have created 250 switches in the direction of economic activity in the last century. A companion theory says cycles appear because investment changes. The upswing is started by a massive increase in investment and the downswing appears when investment falls. A third endogenous theory relates to money. It says that the economy heats when more money is introduced into it and cools when money is removed.

All endogenous theories seem plausible but none answer the nagging question, Why? Why do consumers stop buying? Why do investors start investing? Why does the banking system produce too much or too little money? The answers to these difficult questions lie in psychology and sociology as well as in economics. Much more needs to be known about how business people view the future, how they respond to that outlook, and how their individual views combine to form the collective view of economic society. Until all this is known, economists, policy makers, and citizens must be content to respond to the symptoms of cycles rather than cure the actual disease.

The history of economic stabilization policy has been a history of waiting. Minor shifts in the economy's performance are ignored in the hope that they will reverse themselves, or at least not grow worse. When major problems of instability develop, the forces of monetary and fiscal policy are brought into play as economic policy makers try to do what the system is not doing for itself.

Monetary vs. Fiscal Policy

Since business cycles do exist and do cause hardship for those who must endure them, some policy for stabilization is needed. Two broad types—monetary policy and fiscal policy—are available, but the two are not equally attractive to all economists. The monetarists place heavy emphasis on controlling the supply of money; the Keynesians, or neo-Keynesians, prefer to emphasize fiscal policy. As was mentioned in the previous chapter, most economists agree that some combination of fiscal and monetary policy is needed to achieve economic stability. There is, however, much disagreement on which is more important.

The Monetarists

In general, the monetarists strongly believe that a free-enterprise economy is self-correcting—that there may be times of inflation and times of recession, but by and large, each fluctuation will be a temporary phenomenon and will diminish in severity if the system is left essentially alone.

Monetarists do not deny the existence of fluctuations in economic activity. In their view, the swings have been caused by alterations in the supply of money. Two noted monetarists recently used data from nearly a century (1867 to 1960) to demonstrate a close relationship between the money supply and the level of economic activity. During this period major depressions were accompanied by actual reductions in the money supply; minor recessions came when the rate of growth in the money supply slowed. In the Great Depression of the 1930s, the money supply dropped by 35 percent, while the nation's real output was dropping by 50 percent.

The relationship between the money supply and economic activity is undeniable: As one rises, so does the other. There is considerable dispute, however, over which variable is cause and which is effect. Does rising business activity bring rising money supplies, or is it the other way around?

In blaming inflationary and deflationary gaps on the rate of change in the money supply, contemporary monetarists are adhering to the dictates of the quantity theory of money. A change in M brings with it some change in P or Q.

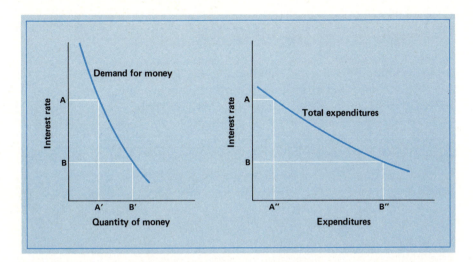

Figure 15-3 The Monetarist View of Changes in the Money Supply

The monetarists argue that changes in the money supply are translated into changes in the volume of business activity through the interest rate and investment mechanism. Private expenditures for investment and consumption are, in their view, extremely sensitive to interest rate changes. An increase in the supply of money will thus depress the interest rate and expand aggregate expenditures. These relationships are shown in Figure 15-3. The demand for money is shown as a very steep curve, with the interest rate very responsive to a change in the quantity of money. A small rise in the money supply from A' to B' will cause a substantial drop in the interest rate—from A to B. Total expenditures are in turn very responsive to changes in the interest rate, so the drop from rate A to rate B on the right-hand side of the figure brings with it an increase in investment and consumer expenditures represented by the horizontal distance A'' to B''.

If this link between money, the interest rate, and economic activity is a secure one, the monetarists could be expected to advocate a *countercyclical policy* of stabilization that calls for adjusting the money supply to fit the needs of the cycle—expand during recession, contract during inflation.

Countercyclical policy is economic policy that runs in cycles opposite the general fluctuations. A countercyclical policy seeks to expand while the general economy is contracting and to contract while the general economy is expanding.

Surprisingly, this is not the case. The monetarists hold the opinion that monetary policy is so powerful that it cannot be used in combating the small swings that plague aggregate economic activity in a decentralized

Lags in Monetary Policy

Monetarists speak of two kinds of lag—*inside* lag and *outside* lag. Inside lag occurs within the Federal Reserve and the private banking system. It refers to the time required for an actual change in policy to be felt at the local bank level. Outside lag is the delay that comes because individual citizens and corporations are slow in responding to a policy change. In general, when the central bank (the Fed) is following a policy of contraction, it has only to contend with inside lag. When the Fed is attempting to expand the money supply, both inside and outside lags must be considered.

economy. They argue that there is a lag between the time a policy is made and the time its effects begin to be felt. Since the length of this lag cannot always be predicted, the economy may reverse its course before monetary policy becomes effective. If there is a chance that a powerful force unleashed today will not be felt for several months, it should not be unleashed!

Milton Friedman: The Nation's Leading Monetarist

The University of Chicago has long been the intellectual capital of the monetarists. A major figure currently upholding this tradition is Professor Milton Friedman. Friedman is a versatile and capable economist who has made outstanding contributions to consumer theory, methods of economic research, and the study of the economic role of government in a free-enterprise economy. His most famous works, though, relate to money.

Long a critic of the policies of the Federal Reserve System's activities, Friedman endorses the simple monetary policy of allowing the money supply to grow at a constant rate. He has been particularly critical of the Fed's potential use of discount rates in managing the money supply because of the possibility of long lags occurring between changes in the discount rate and actual changes in the level of banking activity.

In the late 1960s and early 1970s, Friedman was instrumental in causing economists to reevaluate monetary policy and accord it more importance than it had enjoyed in the earlier post-World War II period. He appeared frequently on television news and commentary shows and in many popular news magazines. His name is still prominent in business-related journals and in the business section of major newspapers, and in 1976 he was awarded the Nobel Prize in economics.

Like all monetarists, Friedman is criticized because of his steadfast reliance on the self-correcting aspects of the modern economy and because he cannot name the "correct" rate at which the money supply should grow.

If monetary policy is too strong to be used countercyclically, how should it be used? The monetarists believe that the money supply should be directly related to some long-run growth plan for the economy. If the economy is to grow at 4 percent per year, for example, the money supply should be expanded at this same rate and the rate should not be changed when modest swings appear around the long-term growth rate. This position is based on a strong reliance on the self-correcting nature of the economic system and a belief that altering the money supply will have certain effects. Make the system grow but leave it alone to correct its own minor problems. The major weakness of the monetarist position is that by itself it says nothing about what the "proper" rate of economic expansion should be. That apparently is to be left to political or social forces.

The Keynesians

The "Keynesians" are described in many ways. They are called "Keynesians" after John Maynard Keynes. They are called neo-Keynesians (the prefix *neo* means "new") because they have modernized the work of Keynes, and they are called advocates of the New Economics because they harbor a set of views that are sharply divergent from those of the monetarists and those of most earlier economists. The Keynesians are more diverse in their views than the monetarists, but their view of the role of money is a common thread holding Keynesians together.

Like the monetarists, the Keynesians have a special disposition about how changes in the quantity of money lead to changes in aggregate economic activity. They believe that the demand for money is intimately bound up in the speculative motive and is very sensitive to changes in the interest rate. Thus (1) large infusions of money cause interest rates to fall; (2) with falling rates, the speculative motive induces people to hold money rather than to invest or spend their new funds. In their model, the demand curve for money is responsive to changes in the rate of interest, but the aggregate expenditures curve is unresponsive. The relationships are shown in Figure 15–4. Because of a sensitive demand relationship, a decrease in interest rates from A to B will cause the demand for money to increase quite considerably—from A' to B'. The level of aggregate expenditures, however, is *unresponsive* to changes in interest rates, so the large drop in interest rates brings only modest increases in aggregate expenditure—from A'' to B''. If aggregate expenditure is unresponsive to changes in the money supply and changes in interest rates, altering the money supply is a weak tool of macroeconomic policy, and some other means must be used to stabilize the economy. That other means is fiscal policy.

Fiscal policy is a policy of active intervention. The Keynesians suggest that when an economy is not functioning well, it is the obligation of fiscal authorities to take corrective action. They believe this to be true especially in times of recession or depression because, while monetary policy may influence large corporations, it does not attend to the needs of the poor, small businesses, or individual households. The Keynesians mount direct attacks on altering the level of $C + I + G$. This is done through changes in taxing, spending, or some combination of the two. Quite often, the Keynesians paint with a fine brush and in so doing are described as *fine tuning* the economy.

Fine tuning is the process used by fiscal authorities to make very selective changes in the performance of the macroeconomy. A program aimed at employing minority workers in the central cities is fine tuning. This term was very popular during the economically activist federal administrations of the 1960s.

The major weaknesses of the Keynesian position center on the role of government and on psychological factors related to economic activity. Active fiscal policy requires freedom for government activity. When the need arises, the government must be able to use newly created money to solve deflationary problems or to destroy money to solve inflationary problems. It must be able to start and end programs. It must be able to play a Robin Hood role by taking from some and giving to others. The U.S. economic society places heavy reliance on individualism and the work ethic. If government, through massive attempts to alter aggregate demand or through fine-tuning fiscal activities, damages individual incentives to invest or work or even spend, the policies may actually exacerbate existing problems. Although it cannot be known for sure, the heavy government spending activities of the mid-1970s may be doing this.

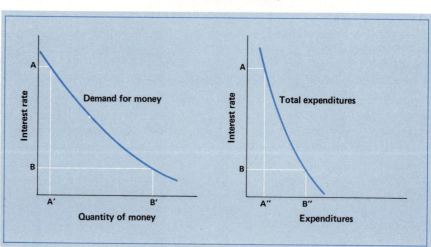

Figure 15–4   The Keynesian View of Changes in the Money Supply

Two Contemporary Keynesians: Paul Samuelson and Walter Heller

The universities of the United States are filled with Keynesian economists. Most do credit to their positions by simply teaching college students about fine tuning and the possible role of government in managing the economy. Two, however, stand out because of their contributions to the general public's understanding of the Keynesian message. They are Professors Paul A. Samuelson of the Massachusetts Institute of Technology and Walter Heller of the University of Minnesota.

Paul Samuelson is truly one of the great economists of the era. Trained at Harvard in the late 1930s, he was among the first wave of Keynesian economists in the United States. He was the first to incorporate the Keynesian theories in an introductory economics textbook, and his book has handsomely survived nine revisions and remained extremely popular for thirty years.

Samuelson's many contributions to economics center on the use of mathematical models to analyze macroeconomic problems. His insights into this problem were sufficient to earn him the 1970 Nobel Prize in economics.

Although Samuelson has not been in constant public view, he gained much popularity in the early 1970s for a series of public debates with monetarist Milton Friedman.

Walter Heller is a convincing and dynamic advocate of Keynesianism. Trained at the University of Wisconsin, Heller became an early proponent of revenue sharing. He was asked to serve as chairman of President John F. Kennedy's Council of Economic Advisers in 1961. After he had accepted, Kennedy gave him a simple charge: "Teach the people economic awareness." Because of Heller's efforts, the citizens of the United States know more than ever before about the operation of their economic system.

A strong Keynesian himself, Heller did not play down the importance of monetarism during his tenure with the Council of Economic Advisers. Indeed, it is perhaps because of his efforts that monetarism has enjoyed such an increase in popularity.

The Middle Ground

It would be wrong to assume that in the real world the disputes between monetarists and Keynesians have drastically affected the course of U.S. macroeconomic policy. In point of fact, their arguments become most intense during periods when countercyclical policy is least needed and abate during times of true economic distress.

In an economic catastrophe marked by rapid inflation, monetarists and Keynesians would both advocate contractionary policies. The monetarists would deviate from the rule of constant growth in the money supply and would insist that the Fed become contractionary and make money hard to obtain. At the same time, the Keynesians would advocate cutting back government spending and increasing taxes as a means of reducing aggregate demand. If the combined policies of the two groups were successful, each would take credit for the success and the argument would continue.

In a deflationary catastrophe, all policies would be reversed. The monetarists would encourage the Fed to expand the money supply, and the Keynesians would work toward increasing government spending. Again, each group would claim the credit for success, and blame the other for lack of success. So it is with intellectual disputes.

In spite of significant differences of opinion on cause, effect, and emphasis, those who formulate economic policy generally agree on what needs to be done. Only in rare instances, such as the stagflation of the 1970s, does the dispute actually become problematic. In this case, a policy that corrects one problem makes the other problem worse. In this setting neither economist nor fortune teller has devised the correct approach to solving the economy's problems.

Summary

1 Business fluctuations seem to be the price of maintaining the free-enterprise form of economic organization.
2 A complete business cycle goes through four stages: prosperity, recession, depression, and recovery. Not all cycles are complete, and even when complete, cycles vary in length and severity.
3 Business cycles are sometimes explained by exogenous events like wars, inventions, and social changes; sometimes by endogenous events like low consumption and overinvestment; and sometimes by a combination of the two.
4 Most macroeconomic policy is designed to reduce the severity of fluctuations. It is countercyclical policy.
5 The monetarists and the Keynesians disagree on which policies should be used to correct cycles. The monetarists would establish a long-term policy and permit small fluctuations to work themselves out. The Keynesians are more active interventionists and advocate a continuing stream of macro policies to fine tune the economy.
6 In times of severe economic collapse, monetary policies and fiscal policies would be directed at the same goal and the only conflict would be one of emphasis.

Exercises

1 Explain these important terms and concepts:
business cycle (fluctuation)   endogenous causes
four stages of the cycle   monetarist policy
exogenous causes   Keynesian policy
inside and outside lags

2 In the course of a business cycle, consumer purchases of some kinds of things are affected more than others. How would expenditures on each of the following be affected by a *downturn* in economic activity?
  a Refrigerators
  b Food
  c Fur coats
  d Houses
  e Well-made, functional work clothes
3 Do your responses to exercise 2 give any clues about the relationship between an item's *durability* and the stability of the industry that produces it?
4 How would you expect each of the following to respond to downturns in the business cycle?
  a Unemployment checks mailed by the state
  b The birth rate
  c Personal bankruptcies
  d Business failures
  e Purchases of industrial equipment (investment)
5 Trends for each of the items in exercise 4 can be found in the *Statistical Abstract of the United States.* Check your responses. A reasonable time period for checking is the "cycle" lasting from roughly 1957 to 1965.
6 The arguments between the monetarists and the Keynesians are mainly over what is cause and what is effect. Using knowledge about inflationary and deflationary gaps, the quantity theory of money, and the demand for money, formulate what you believe to be a defensible position on the "great debate."

A Contemporary Problem
Monetarists and Keynesians—The Dispute Continues

The conflict between the Keynesians and the monetarists is not new. Since Keynes's ideas first became public in the 1920s and 1930s, his efforts and explanations have been sharply criticized by the monetarists. Some writers have thought the differences were not deep-seated ones about economics, but only disagreements about the role of money, tempered by the time period in which the particular economist wrote. J. H. Wood uses this approach to compare and contrast the theories advanced by J. M. Keynes and Milton Friedman. His comments were originally made in a 1972 lecture given at the University of Birmingham (England) but were later reformulated and published by the Federal Reserve Bank of Philadelphia. The following comes from the published version.

There are no fundamental theoretical differences between Keynes and Friedman. As with such controversies, the differences between Keynes and Friedman on the employment of fiscal and monetary policies to achieve economic stability hinge on differences in economic conditions existing at the times that each economist wrote and from dissimilar political philosophies rather than from any theoretical differences over money's influence on output.

Keynes wrote during a time of extraordinary upheaval. Between 1914 and 1920 prices tripled, then dropped by nearly one-half by 1932. He pointed out that the arrangements of the nineteenth century could not work properly if money, the assumed standard, is not dependable.

If businessmen are to develop their productive capacity and if the savings of households are to be converted into investment projects, then businessmen must be able to foresee with a reasonable degree of assurance the prices of the products coming out of their new plants and the costs of the inputs from which those products will be made.

To Keynes, the overriding determinant of investment is price expectations. Expectations of price increases encourage investment; expected deflation discourages investment. Uncertainty is the worst offender. If rapid monetary changes have occurred in the past and are expected to be repeated in the future —in which direction no one knows—businessmen will refuse to bear the risk of investment. . . .

Keynes came to the conclusion that in a world of rapidly fluctuating prices, uncertainty on the part of businessmen would be so great that the state would have to undertake the investment necessary for growth and economic stability. . . .

Reading Milton Friedman and Anna Jacobson Schwartz's *A Monetary History of the United States* is a frustrating experience. . . . But if we carefully examine the way in which Friedman handles the data in this and other historical discussions, we can get an inkling of how, in his view, money matters.

In comparing the two periods 1865–1879 and 1879–1897 as well as other lengthy intervals, Friedman and Schwartz conclude that over long periods "generally declining or generally rising prices had little impact on the rate of growth [of output], but the period of great monetary uncertainty in the early nineties produced sharp deviations from the long-term trend." . . .

. . . Surprise is the key word in all this. To the extent that changes in money and prices proceed smoothly and are foreseen, money does not influence economic activity. But sudden and unforeseen monetary disturbances produce fluctuations in output. . . .

Both Keynes and Friedman, therefore, fear monetary instability. They both desire a stable growth rate in the money supply as a way of minimizing fluctuations in prices, output, and employment. But they part ways in approach and emphasis on how to achieve the benefits of monetary stability.

Keynes, on the one hand, was pragmatic. He was a man of a thousand plans. If one was impractical, he would try another. To him monetary policy was important but not the "be-all and end-all." And so he moved from a reliance on monetary to fiscal policy when he thought it unrealistic on political or other grounds to expect a stable growth in the money supply.

Friedman, on the other hand, has less confidence than Keynes in the willingness or ability of the authorities—monetary or fiscal—to make the economy work smoothly. That is why Friedman wants to tie both the monetary and fiscal authorities to certain specific rules—not because the people who would make the rules are more intelligent than those who formulate and implement discretionary policies, but because, whatever the rule, it will be known. People can formulate plans on the basis of what they can expect the future money supply and price level to be. In such a way, Friedman hopes, as Keynes did with fiscal policy, that money *can be made* not to matter.[1]

---

[1] Excerpted from J. H. Wood, "Money and Output: Keynes and Friedman in Historical Perspective," *Business Review,* Federal Reserve Bank of Philadelphia, September 1972, pp. 3–12.

16

Macro Policy in Action

There is no time like a troubled time to study macroeconomics. In times of crisis or even uneasiness, macroeconomic policy becomes active, people become concerned with what the Fed is doing, and the President's proposed budget provokes anxiety on all sides. The mid-1970s are providing ample opportunities to inquire about macro policy. Although trouble had been brewing for months, the economic affairs of the nation nearly tumbled into chaos during the final toilsome months of the Nixon administration. Tight money policies (contractionary) by the Federal Reserve System appeared simultaneously with expansionary deficits in the federal budget. Taxpayers voted to cut back on many government programs and at the same time wanted more jobs, better police protection, and extended welfare benefits. It was a confusing and perplexing time for the new administration of Gerald R. Ford and for hundreds of economists who for the most part could not seem to grasp the enormity of the problem. President Ford, seeing the turmoil, called an "economic summit conference" for late September 1974. At the conference, economists from government, business, and universities discussed problems and policies that might be used to relieve pressures on the unstable economy.

Art Buchwald, the syndicated newspaper humorist, wrote the following editorial about the conference:[1]

Economics Made Simple

I listened to the economic summit for two days and it was a great inspiration to see so many learned men from all walks of life tell us why the country is in such a mess. Although there was some disagreement, this is what we now know for sure.

The Republicans are responsible for inflation because of their tight money policies, high interest rates and giving in to big business at every turn.

The Democrats are responsible for inflation because of their large welfare programs, reckless government spending and catering to the interests of labor.

In order to cure the upward spiral of prices, we have to make more money available for business investment.

We must make bank loans more difficult for business investment.

Arthur Burns of the Federal Reserve Board is responsible for the recession we are in.

George Meany is responsible for the recession we're in.

There is no recession.

We cannot solve our economic problems until we bring down the cost of fuel, particularly oil and natural gas.

The only way we can get more fuel is to raise the price of oil and gas to encourage the oil companies.

Congress is responsible for the crisis because of the large amounts of money it has voted for unneeded government programs.

Congress has to vote new funds to keep the country from going into a depression.

Unless we have a tax cut, the economy will never recover from the doldrums it is in.

The only way to lick inflation is to raise taxes and keep the dollar from being devalued.

The Arabs are responsible for all our troubles.

There is no inflation. Our main problem is stagflation.

We must stop selling agricultural products abroad so we can bring down the price of food at home.

We must increase our food exports so we can have a more favorable balance of payments.

Labor has to show more responsibility when asking for wage increases.
Labor is being penalized for the mistakes of management.

We must have wage and price controls to ward off disaster.
Introduction of wage and price controls would be a disaster.

[1]*Los Angeles Times,* 3 October 1974, Sec. IV, p. 2.

The people who are suffering the most from inflation are the poor, the sick and the old.

The people who are suffering the most from inflation are the brokers.

We cannot lick inflation overnight.

Summit conferences are the best way to resolve differences in economic philosophies.

Calling back Nixon's economists to tell us how we can win the battle against inflation is like asking the Italian general staff to tell us how to win World War II.

Fortunately not all periods are this confusing, nor do all meetings of economists yield such contradictory results. More often, the lessons of macroeconomics have helped lead to policies designed to provide an economy with relatively full employment, relatively stable prices, and modest but satisfactory rates of economic growth.

The purpose of this chapter is to present the recent record of economic performance in this nation and to match it with the record of macroeconomic policy. In some respects this is an impossible undertaking. If monetary and fiscal policy were totally effective, economic growth would be steady and unemployment low, and prices would vary only within extremely narrow limits. In this perfectly controlled world, macroeconomic policy would move rapidly. Planners and policy makers could make quick decisions to correct the economy for changes in technology, weather, demand, and international affairs. But even then it would be difficult to judge the effectiveness of corrective policy.

There would always be the question, Would the problem have corrected itself without the policy? So it is with aspirin and a mild headache. The headache is experienced, the aspirin is taken, and the headache disappears. Would the headache have gone away by itself? No one can say for sure.

For decades, U.S. economic policy makers have been reluctant to follow a policy of laissez faire because that might permit another catastrophe like the one experienced during the 1930s. Instead, policy has pursued certain goals for the economy, and so the policy must be judged by how closely these goals have been approached. With this in mind, it is possible to examine recent economic policy and ask if it has been consistent with the desire to alleviate the nation's economic ills.

Accurate records of the performance of the U.S. economy have been available since the 1930s. It is sometimes interesting to trace records back to that era, since the 1930s and 40s displayed both the best and the worst behavior of a market economy. Here, however, the record is picked up in 1950. By then, the nation had recovered from the Great Depression and was well on its way to settling down after World War II. The Employment Act of 1946, which required the federal government to maintain high levels of employment, appeared to be working and the interventionist message of the Keynesians was beginning to reach government officials and officers in the Federal Reserve System. How well did they respond to the needs of the economy?

The Record

Since World War II, the three major goals of U.S. economic policy have been (1) to achieve rates of economic growth that allow continued increases in well-being, (2) to maintain prices at reasonably stable levels so that neither fixed- nor variable-income groups will be unduly harmed, and (3) to maintain employment at high enough levels that any able-bodied person can find work. Although it is true that terms like "well-being," "reasonably stable," and "unduly harmed" have no clear-cut meanings, these three objectives—growth, price stabilization, and employment—continue to be the backbone of national economic policy.[2] Although environmental protection and increased well-being are often mentioned as goals for the economy (see Chapter 5), they are not yet considered major parts of economic policy and thus are not discussed in this chapter.

Growth

Figure 16–1 summarizes the growth of per capita GNP in the United States from 1950 to 1975. The current-dollar curve shows that growth occurred in every year except the recession year, 1958. Growth has been sometimes slow (1956–1960) and sometimes fast, but the overall record looks remarkable. When per capita GNP is corrected for price changes and all years are compared using 1958 prices, a different picture emerges. Prices have generally risen for the past 25 years. Therefore, the real value of GNP before 1958 is higher than GNP expressed in current-dollar terms. Since 1958, real value is lower in comparison to current-dollar GNP. More important, real GNP per capita has fallen six times since 1950. The record of real growth is not so impressive. In 1950, the economy provided each man, woman, and child a collection of goods and services valued at $2,342 in 1958 prices. By 1960, production was $2,699 per person, and by 1975—the closing year for the series—output was valued at $3,637 per person.

---

[2]It is important to note that all nations, regardless of their form of economic organization, follow goals similar to these. The Japanese (archetypical capitalists) follow policies devoted to employment, growth, and stability. The Scandinavian nations (economic middle-of-the-roaders) do the same, and China, largest of the collective economies, attempts to grow, to maintain stability, and to keep people employed.

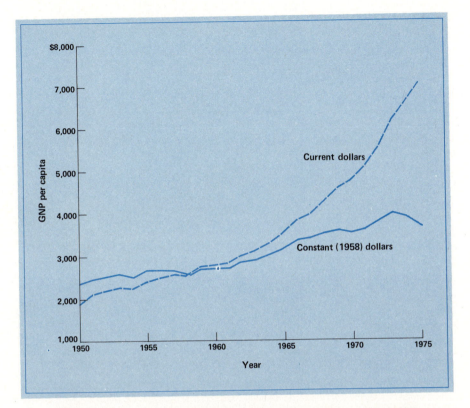

Figure 16-1 Actual and Real GNP Per Capita, 1950–1975

Price Stability

The record of growth, even in deflated GNP, gives no indication of the inflation that characterized this period. Figure 16-2 shows how prices rose, eroding the purchasing power of the dollar. The index described by the vertical axis considers changes in the prices of ordinary things a consumer would buy. The base year for the index is 1958. From 1950 to 1965, the increase in the consumer price index was quite gradual—certainly within tolerable levels. In the mid-1960s, prices began to climb at an uncomfortable rate, reaching 135.2 (35.2 percent above 1958 levels) in 1970, then climbing even more rapidly to 184 in 1975. The price rise of the mid-1970s was the most rapid in peacetime in this century, and was clearly intolerable to much of the public.

Employment

The third stated goal of economic society is to keep unemployment low. The U.S. unemployment record is charted in Figure 16-3. Wide variations

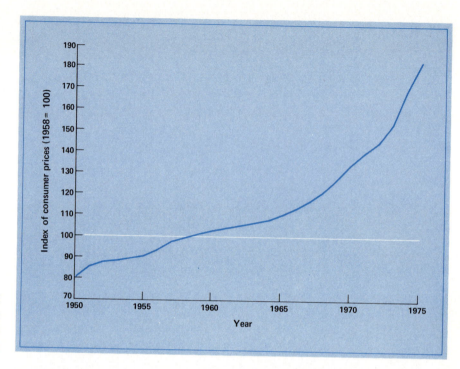

**Figure 16-2
Consumer Price
Index, 1950-1975
(1958 = 100)**

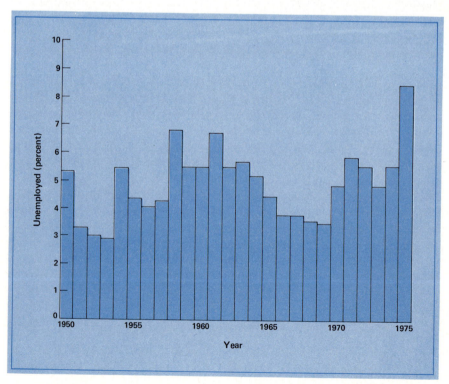

**Figure 16-3
Unemployment
as a Percent of
the Civilian Labor
Force, 1950-1975**

make unemployment appear to be more sensitive and changeable than either GNP or price levels, and so it is. The unemployment record also tells more about human happiness and misery, since it deals directly with whether or not people are working.

The decade of the 1950s saw ups and downs in unemployment, but each time unemployment rose, it reached a peak higher than the previous one. A high for the decade, 6.8 percent, was reached in 1958. In the 1960s, unemployment was reduced—dropping below 4 percent for four consecutive years 1966, 1967, 1968, and 1969. The 1970s started on a poor note, with 5 percent of the labor force unemployed. By 1975, nearly one of every ten members of the labor force could not find employment.

Policy Indications and Responses

When the GNP per capita chart and the unemployment chart are examined together, some clues to the appropriate economic policy emerge. *Generally speaking,* the dips in real GNP per capita were accompanied by increases in unemployment. The drop in per capita GNP in 1954 occurred simultaneously with a surge in unemployment. The drop in per capita GNP in the late 1950s was also accompanied by high levels of unemployment, and in the 1970s the same conditions coincided once again.

Using only information related to changes in GNP, unemployment, and prices, an economic policy calling for injections of money and purchasing power into the system would have been appropriate in 1950, 1954, 1957–1958 and 1969. However, this prescription may have been difficult in the late 1960s, when high rates of inflation called for removing money from the system. A policy for extracting money (purchasing power) from the system might also have been appropriate during the early 1950s and again in 1966–1969, when unemployment was very low and growth was moderately high.

To deal with the stagflation of the middle 1970s, changing the volume of money in the economy through either monetary or fiscal activity would probably not have been appropriate. During this time unemployment was very high, but conventional means of dealing with it would have made the inflation problem even worse. To attack inflation by removing purchasing power would have made the unemployment problem worse. The stagflation was puzzling because no one really knew how to approach it. Because of this, the monetary and fiscal policies of the mid- and late 1970s were often confusing or even contradictory. Other explanations and other policies were called for, but no economist was entirely sure what they might be.

The economy's record of performance in output, prices, and employment is accessible and can be viewed, discussed, and modified using monetary and fiscal policy. There is increasing evidence that a fourth goal of economic performance will be (or has been!) added: the quality

Unemployment and Per Capita GNP: Cause and Effect

Drops in per capita GNP or in the rate of increase of per capita GNP are most often *accompanied by* increases in the rate of unemployment. The fact that one *accompanies* the other does not imply that one *causes* the other. In point of fact, the two changes are jointly caused by economic forces operating in the economy at large. When managers' sixth sense tells them that business will not be as good next year as it was this year, they cut back on output (they do not want to produce products that will not sell) and *simultaneously* reduce purchases of factors from households. Thus, both output and employment drop when expectations are poor.

When business executives use this same sense and decide that business and economic conditions will be good, their reaction is to produce more (increasing GNP) and to use larger quantities of factors of production (reducing unemployment). In this way, changes in GNP and in employment accompany each other, but they are both caused simultaneously by other forces.

of life.[3] At this moment, there is very little solid evidence that the overall quality of life in this nation has increased or decreased since 1950. Los Angeles is definitely more polluted and Lake Erie is less polluted than a decade ago. More money than ever before is currently being spent to clean up industry's waste, but it is also true that more industrial wastes are being noticed and hence need to be cleaned up. More is now being spent on education and on recreation than ever before. Spending to maintain penal systems and narcotics abuse programs has also reached record highs. Has well-being increased? No one can say. The status of society and the effectiveness of fiscal and monetary policy will for the moment have to be judged with respect to nonqualitative measures—rates of growth, price changes, and levels of unemployment.

A summary view of the 1950–1975 period indicates that in a general way, economic conditions in the 1950s could have been helped by an expansionary policy of easy money and more jobs. In the 1960s, the unemployment problem lessened in severity but the rate of inflation began to increase. Mild contractionary policies were warranted—especially by the end of the decade. About 1970, macroeconomic policy issues be-

[3]Many economists object strenuously to including the quality of life as an economic goal. There is justification for this objection. The quality of life cannot be measured in economic terms, so economic theory and practice should have little to say about it. In point of fact, however, economists more than any other scientists and/or policy advisors are being called upon to bend their attentions to problems relating to this theme. More germane to this chapter, economists are continually asked to demonstrate how specific fiscal policies will affect the quality of life.

came very complex. The high rates of inflation could be reduced by increasing taxes, reducing spending, and tightening money. But any of these moves would aggravate the unemployment problem. Economic policy makers are at a loss.

Fiscal Measures

The record shows that fiscal authorities have tried to follow the correct policy prescription. In the 1950s, a budget deficit was incurred five times (Figure 16–4), generally in response to periods of high unemployment. From 1960 to 1965 the budget was nearly balanced, but increased government expenditures (primarily for highways, space exploration, and education) aided in bringing unemployment down. There was no extraordinary pressure causing prices to increase during these years. At the end of the decade, the confusing high unemployment/inflation combination struck the economy. The immediate response was to run a deficit and pump additional money into the economy to solve the unemployment

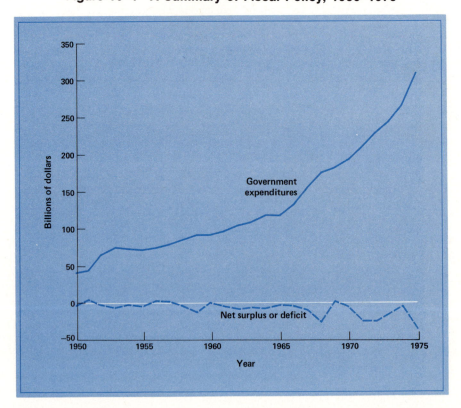

Figure 16–4 A Summary of Fiscal Policy, 1950–1975

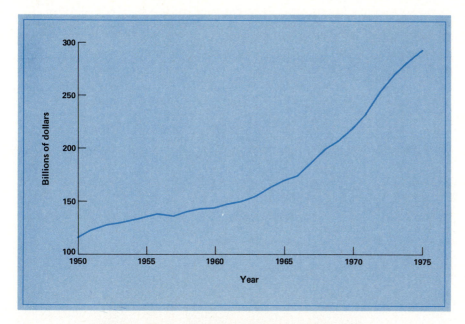

Figure 16-5 Supply of Money, 1950-1975

problem, while relying on direct price controls to fight inflation. When the general price controls proved politically unpopular and economically ineffective, macroeconomic policy fell into a somewhat confused condition. A huge fiscal deficit and a general easing of credit combined to yield unanticipated results—the rate of inflation slackened slightly but the rate of unemployment remained very high.

Monetary Measures

In general, monetary policy followed suit, although there is no simple measure or index that can be used to summarize monetary activity. The money supply continued to expand throughout the period, but the low *rates* of expansion may have hindered economic growth in the late 1950s and early 1960s (Figure 16-5). By the end of the 1960s, the efforts to encourage growth by expanding the money supply led to increases in the money supply that were not accompanied by increases in output. The result: increased volumes of purchasing power adding to inflationary pressure.

Although the discount rate is no longer an important tool of money supply management, the intentions of the monetary authorities can be understood by examining discount-rate changes. In the early 1950s, discount rates (Figure 16-6) were low and unchanging. Price increases and dropping rates of unemployment brought contractionary increases

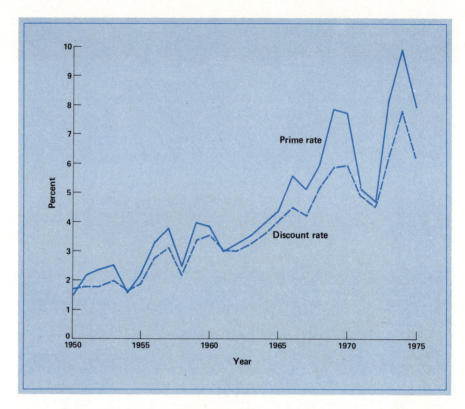

Figure 16-6 Prime Rate and Discount Rate, 1950–1975

in discount rates in 1953. The huge increase in unemployment in 1954 was a signal that monetary authorities had gone too far. The discount rate dropped precipitously, so that individual bankers could borrow inexpensive money and use it to make more loans to their customers. In the mid-1960s, unemployment was headed downward and prices were beginning to creep up at an increasingly rapid rate. Monetary authorities in the Federal Reserve System responded by gradually increasing the discount rate, making money more difficult to obtain.

The late 1960s brought low rates of unemployment combined with high rates of inflation. The situation called for tight money policies that would make money difficult to obtain. Monetary authorities chose to oblige by increasing discount rates sharply. After a cooling of the economy in the early 1970s discount rates were lowered, but the problem of rising prices continued.

The discount rate is a weak tool of monetary policy, but when it is changed, the change is announced with much fanfare. When the discount rate changes, there is usually an accompanying change in the *prime lending rate* charged by private banks.

The prime lending rate is the interest rate that the best ("prime") customers of major banks must pay. It is lower than a household would ordinarily pay, because prime borrowers are generally industrial firms borrowing millions of dollars. In addition, the risk of a prime borrower defaulting on a loan is very low. The prime rate is an important indicator of how banks view business conditions.

Figure 16–6 shows that the prime rate and the discount rate have moved together in most years. When they did not move together, as in 1969–1970, the change in each was very modest. The private banking system was apparently following the lead of the Fed in trying to accomplish goals related to the macroeconomy.

Conclusion

Macroeconomists truly walk a tightrope. They are expected to know how to maintain a stable economy within which markets can do an effective job of allocating hundreds of thousands of goods and services among thousands of households. This economic stability requires that there be just enough growth to keep expectations high, not a great deal of unemployment (ideally only the amount that results from people changing jobs), and no more price changes than can be tolerated by people with fixed incomes. If one of these conditions begins to waver from the ideal goal, efforts to correct that situation may deflect the economy from one of the other goals.

The tools for regulating a macroeconomy are well established. In fact, there are two sets—monetary policy and fiscal policy. However, economists are not yet sufficiently skilled at forecasting to know which set to use, or whether to use both, to accomplish a given macro objective. For some years it seemed that fiscal policy would provide sufficient power for regulation. More recently, especially after fiscal policy's generally unspectacular showing in the late 1960s, monetary policy seems to be gaining in popularity and in authority, and the Federal Reserve System is becoming more responsive to the economic needs of the society.

Even fiscal and monetary policy together have not been strong enough to offset the pressures of inflation and unemployment in the 1970s. It is not yet clear exactly why such an odd collection of phenomena should be striking the U.S. economy at one time. Growth has stopped, employment is low, and inflation is unacceptably high. Fiscal policy is being applied in only weak ways, but monetary measures are being used quite regularly. Still the problems persist. It will be up to the next generation of economists and voters to find the right combination of policies to use in providing the type of macroeconomic base that this highly complex, interdependent society must have if it is to enjoy a high level of well-being.

Summary

1. Judging the effectiveness of macroeconomic policy is very hard to do. It must be done with respect to the performance of the economy and how well the several goals of the economy have been met.
2. In the past quarter century, the U.S. economy has grown in both current and real terms, but it has been plagued by inflation and periods of widespread unemployment.
3. Although for brief periods other conditions may have prevailed, in general the problem of the 1950s was unemployment, the problem of the 1960s was inflation, and the problem of the 1970s has been a combination of the two.
4. There has been an active fiscal policy during this period. Because unemployment was unacceptably high during much of the period, budget deficits were incurred.
5. Monetary policy has in general been to increase the supply of money. The rate of increase has seemed to accelerate during the last quarter century.
6. Interest rates, both the prime rate charged by banks and the discount rate set by the Fed, have varied with economic conditions, increasing when inflation threatened, decreasing in time of recession.
7. Macroeconomists have a difficult job in trying to match policy with the performance of the economy. They are hindered by a lack of knowledge about factors affecting economic performance.

Exercises

1. Explain these important terms and concepts:

    macro policy
    fiscal policy
    monetary policy
    GNP in current dollars
    GNP in real dollars
    prime rate
    discount rate

2. Here is a table showing major economic indicators for each month in 1975:

Month	Personal income (dollars)	Unemployment (percent)	Consumer Price Index (1967 = 100)
Jan.	1195.7	7.9	156.1
Feb.	1203.2	8.0	157.2
Mar.	1205.0	8.5	157.8
Apr.	1209.0	8.6	158.6
May	1217.2	8.9	159.3
June	1245.2	8.7	160.6
July	1244.0	8.7	162.3
Aug.	1212.4	8.5	162.8
Sept.	1278.7	8.6	163.6
Oct.	1287.4	8.6	164.6
Nov.	1295.9	8.5	165.6
Dec.	1300.2	8.3	166.3

a Did real personal income increase or decrease during the year?
  b If monetary and fiscal policies could be implemented on a monthly basis, what policies would have been appropriate during 1975?
3. The last time a budget surplus occurred in the U.S. economy was in 1969. Even then, the surplus was so small as to be negligible. Can the United States continue to run budget deficits? Explain why or why not.
4. Why do attempts to solve unemployment problems have a strong tendency to add to inflation problems?
5. Why do attempts to cope with inflation problems have a similar tendency to worsen problems of unemployment?
6. With all this confusion about the proper role of economic policy, what hope is there for the economist? Why don't economic solutions seem to work?

A Contemporary Problem
Recovering from Stagflation

The problem of stagflation has been mentioned time and again over several chapters. It is a curious problem because, until very recently, most economists did not think the two major economic problems of a modern market economy—inflation and recession (stagnation)—could exist simultaneously. In mid-1976, the economy began to show indications that some aspects of the stagflation were abating, and a mood of cautious optimism prevailed. Some politicians wanted the problem to end quickly, but most economists were skeptical of a hasty recovery, since a quick burst of economic activity or a quick burst of consumer demand would likely touch off another round of inflation.

In mid-July of 1976, the *Wall Street Journal,* the prestigious and widely circulated business-oriented daily paper, conducted a survey to find out how economists felt about the brief recovery. Most economists were conservative. Some thought a Democratic administration would increase spending in order to speed the creation of jobs. But most thought the increase would be slight. The economists surveyed thought that most economists were becoming more conservative, preferring slow and balanced recovery to a burst of activity.

Surprisingly, the economists gave the Federal Reserve System very high marks. The Fed had earlier announced that it would maintain a monetary policy intended to support further growth in output and employment while avoiding the excesses that would aggravate inflation. The Fed backed its stated intentions by slowing the rate at which the money supply was being expanded and allowed interest rates to edge up when inflation threatened in early summer.

When viewing the overall growth of the economy, the economists themselves thought the U.S. economy would expand slowly until about the end of 1977. At that time, the productive capacity of the nation would be approached, unemployment would drop, and the threat of inflation would increase. The appropriate policy rests in the hands of the Fed—tighten the money supply.

The same group saw no real escape from inflation and expected prices to rise at rates between 5 percent and 7.5 percent over the next months. The rate may increase by the end of 1977. Some economists, especially those employed by businesses, expect inflation to be less of a problem; those employed by banks felt it would become more serious—perhaps reaching 9 percent.

Unemployment, which stood at 7.5 percent of the civilian work force in June 1976 is expected to drop slowly to 6 percent in the summer of 1977.

In sum, when economists were asked about the near-term future of the economy's performance, they showed amazing consistency in what they expected to happen, but few ventured guesses on how it would happen or why it would happen. None wished to comment on fiscal policy and only a few made comments on monetary policy. The "projections," then, appear to be "feelings" about what will happen. The "feeling," or the "educated guess," is not haphazard, nor should it be ignored, but it should help to demonstrate one more time that understanding the problems of the macroeconomy and making suggestions about improving its performance are very difficult jobs.

PART THREE
MICROECONOMICS

17 The Demand for Economic Goods

Just as a microscope allows us to observe the details of tiny organisms, microeconomics enables us to view the individual parts of economic society. Microeconomics deals with the problems of scarcity and choice as they affect individuals, firms, corporations (large or small), and government agencies. Microeconomics is the study of scrabbling to make a living, trying to make a business profitable, deciding whether a health program or a new airport is a better use for tax dollars, and deciding whether strawberries or Sara Lee cheesecake will bring greater satisfaction to a family. It is the study of single decision-making units and how they should respond to signals received from markets, regulatory agencies, and other decision-making units.

Some people say that microeconomics is not economics at all, but merely a form of logic applied to economic questions. In a sense they are correct, since once a firm's or household's objectives are known, microeconomics is simply the logic of pursuing these goals. Others say that without microeconomics there would be no economics. This statement also contains some truth, for how can the study of scarcity and choice be meaningful without considering the entities that choose? Either way, microeconomics remains that branch of economics concerned with allocating scarce means within a single decision-making unit. It is a fundamental study and its theories are necessary to an understanding of rational choice.

The following 11 chapters are designed to provide an understanding of the scope, logic, and usefulness of microeconomics. This chapter and Chapters 18 and 19 expand the discussion of the market mechanism and demand, supply, and equilibrium relationships that was begun in Chapter 4. Although either demand or supply could be studied first, Chapter 17 concentrates on the study of demand.

The Market System

If the market system had not evolved but been purposefully invented, it would have been one of the most important inventions in history. The market system is an institution used to organize economic activity. In a sense, it is nothing more than an elaborate system of voting. Goods and services that are in high demand receive many votes, while goods and services that are not demanded receive no votes at all.

Market voting differs from political voting in two important respects. First, the "election" is constantly in process. Candidates—goods and services—are continuously coming onto the market and continuously being selected or rejected. Second, there is no rule in market voting about how many votes each person may cast. The votes are dollars, and the system is indifferent as to whether a given person has many or few; it does not care that one person is able to cast 15,000 dollar votes for a sports car, while a second person does not even have enough dollar votes to provide food for the family.

Like all voting processes, market voting both affirms and refutes. Wing-tipped shoes are voted out; patent leather platform shoes are voted in. Gas-consuming, powerful cars are voted out; economical compacts are voted in. Dresses are voted out; pantsuits are voted in. Producers of products voted out must suffer the consequences, for the market guarantees them nothing. Producers of products that are voted in face the happy problem of rearranging their productive activities to satisfy the voters' needs.

In this sense, the market is a huge machine that gathers and dispenses information. It gathers information about the day's voting and translates it into demands for goods and services. Simultaneously, it gathers information about what candidates are for sale and translates these offerings into supplies that are available. The market tries to fit demands and supplies together to yield a balance in which both voters (buyers) and candidates (sellers) are satisfied. This chapter expands the discussion of demand begun in Chapter 4. Major sections are devoted to the concept of demand, individual and aggregate demand, and elasticity.

The Demand Curve

The demand curve is a graphic portrayal of information about the quantity of a good that will be demanded at each of several prices. The following hypothetical information relates to the price of eggs and the quantity of eggs demanded at each price:

Price per dozen	Quantity demanded (dozens)
47¢	50
52	35
58	25
68	15

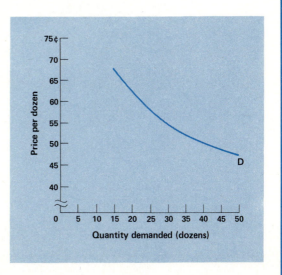

This information is graphed here, with price on the vertical axis and quantity on the horizontal axis. The resulting curve is the demand curve.

The Concept of Demand

The law of demand is one of the most fundamental and one of the most consistent laws of economic behavior. It states simply that as the price of a good falls, the quantity purchased of that good will increase, and if price rises the quantity purchased will fall. The law is ordinarily presented using a graph in which the demand curve appears as a curve sloping downward to the right in a quadrant with price on the vertical axis and quantity demanded on the horizontal axis.

Diminishing Marginal Utility

The demand curve is based on the notion of diminishing *marginal utility*, which says that each additional unit of a good that is acquired provides less utility or satisfaction to the user than the previous unit.

In economics, *margin* refers to a very small change in the magnitude or importance of a variable. Thus the marginal loaf of bread is an increase or decrease of one loaf of bread from the total number originally pos-

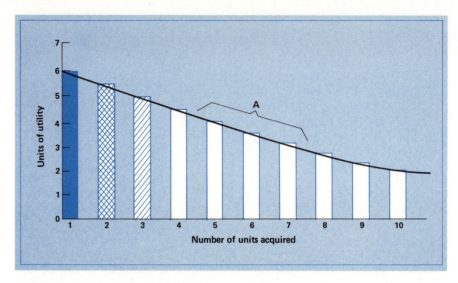

Figure 17-1 Diminishing Marginal Utility and the Demand Curve

sessed by the consumer. Marginal utility is the added usefulness resulting from the acquisition of a marginal unit of a good. This utility is most often measured in terms of the money given up to obtain the extra unit of the good.

This relationship between goods and the utility they provide is thought to be quite regular and is sometimes referred to as the law of diminishing marginal utility.

The law of diminishing marginal utility is described in Figure 17-1. The first unit of the good brings 6 units of utility, as shown by the solid bar. The second unit of the same good brings 5 1/2 units of utility (crosshatched bar), and the third unit brings 5 units (hatched bar). As more units are acquired, marginal utility continues to drop, so that the tenth unit brings only two units of utility.[1]

Even though all goods are purchased for the utility they provide, the term *utility* is highly subjective and therefore hard to measure. A drop in utility can perhaps be recognized, but up to now, no one has been able to quantify satisfactorily the decrease in the capacity of a good to satisfy wants as more units of the good are made available. Even though

---

[1] "Utility" can certainly become negative. The small boy eating green apples finds that the first brings great joy and the second brings a measure of delight, but by the time the seventh or eighth apple is consumed, joy has turned to misery and utility is negative. For most products, utility can be assumed to approach zero but perhaps never quite reach it. Even if your own demand for automobiles is completely satiated, total utility can be increased by accepting still more automobiles, selling them, and using the money to purchase items that add to your satisfaction.

utility defies measurement, the law of diminishing marginal utility is almost universally applicable, and very few goods or services that violate it can be named.[2]

When the subjective term *utility* is replaced by the observable measure *price,* the diminishing marginal utility curve becomes a demand curve. As a good's capacity to satisfy diminishes, so will the price that one is willing to pay for added units of it. Thus, if units of utility trade one-for-one for dollars, the first unit in Figure 17–1 can be sold for $6.00, the second for $5.50, and the third for $5.00. These price/quantity relationships can be connected as shown to yield a demand curve.

The demand curve is not just a wild dream of some economist. Like diminishing marginal utility, the demand curve is a very real description of human behavior as it relates to markets. Demand curves for particular commodities and services have been analyzed, described, and drawn. Since economists are limited in their observations to those price/quantity relationships that have actually occurred, however, *empirical* demand curves are limited to a very narrow segment of the entire curve—say, segment A in Figure 17–1. No economist or statistician has yet been able to measure and plot a demand curve that runs the full range from its intersection with the vertical axis to its intersection with the horizontal axis. The intersection of the demand curve with the vertical axis would occur at a very high price, at which no one would buy the product. The intersection with the horizontal axis would occur at that quantity which would completely satisfy all consumers, the quantity beyond which another unit could not be given to them even at a price of zero.

Changes in Demand

Even when a segment of a demand curve is isolated, it must be interpreted with great care. The curve is based on evidence collected at one period of time during which consumers have a given level of income and certain tastes, and prices of other commodities are at a given level. If any one of these conditions changes, the location and/or slope of the demand curve is almost certain to change as well. The following example will illustrate this.

Condition. A (hypothetical) empirical study shows that 40 percent of the women in the United States will purchase one pair of multicolored sandals when these shoes cost $18 per pair. This empirical study was conducted when average family income was $12,000 per year, the aver-

---

[2]The violations of the law of diminishing marginal utility are very exceptional cases. A miser who is compelled to add to his collection of gold coins may not feel that these coins provide progressively less satisfaction (utility). Similarly, a stamp collector who has all but one stamp may find that acquiring that last stamp doubles or triples the real and psychic value of the whole collection. The marginal utility of that additional stamp is, therefore, quite high.

age woman was exposed to 10 minutes of TV shoe advertising per week, and women's plain white pumps cost $12 per pair. This study isolates a single point on a demand curve.

Change A. Family income drops from $12,000 to $8,000 per year. This change causes considerable shifting among priorities. A $4,000 reduction in income makes money much more dear and causes women to reconsider their opinions regarding multicolored sandals. Under these altered circumstances, plain white pumps may look like the better buy, and the original point on the demand curve may no longer be valid.

Change B. Advertising increases in intensity. The average woman is now subjected to *twenty* minutes of shoe commercials on TV every week, plus newspaper ads and full-page color advertisements in leading magazines. Suddenly multicolored sandals become almost a necessity, and even if the price remains at $18 per pair, 75 percent of all women will buy them. Again, other factors have not remained constant, so the point on the original demand curve must change.

Change C. The price of white pumps increases to $18 per pair. Now the price of a competing item has changed enough to have some influence on demand. If both styles of shoes are $18 per pair, many people who purchased the plainer shoes to save money will be induced to switch to the more fashionable shoes. Again, the original point shifts.

A demand curve is an elusive construct. Once its location is determined, it is likely to shift in response to the ever-changing forces in a complex economy. This fact in no way invalidates the *concept* of the demand curve or diminishes its usefulness. It must be remembered, however, that the empirical demand curve is surrounded by limitations. While it may be an excellent reflection of market behavior at the time it is isolated, it cannot be expected to remain accurate over any great length of time.

Individual and Market Demand Curves

Up to this point, demand curves have been considered rather generally. It has not been made clear whether they apply to the demands of a person or of a state or nation or world market. In reality, a demand curve can apply to any of these. It is possible to ascertain an individual's demand curve for a product. (How much will Smith buy at each price?) It is also possible to determine Chicago's demand curve for sugar or the nation's demand for polyester clothing. When the term *demand curve* is used

Alfred Marshall and the Development of Microeconomics

In the closing years of the nineteenth century, Alfred Marshall, one of the greatest of the Cambridge economists, gave economics a new start. He formulated a method of economic analysis based on a very simple principle: All questions except the one being asked should be ignored. If one is interested in the behavior of the price of eggs, one assumes at the start that the price of chickens, the price of chicken feed, and the price of milk will not change. Everything except the price of eggs is assumed to be constant. After the question regarding the price of eggs has been answered, the next question (perhaps the relationship of the price of eggs to the price of chickens) can be asked. The method became known as *partial equilibrium analysis* because it studies only a part of the system at a time. It is as important to microeconomics as the circular flow model is to macroeconomics, and much of the material in this and the following chapters is rooted in partial equilibrium analysis.

Marshall was originally trained as a philosopher and mathematician. Therefore it is not surprising that he used mathematics as a tool of economic analysis. He was the great synthesizer. With crisp logic, he put established economic theories into terms that could be functionally and mathematically related to each other. For example, scores of economists before him had puzzled over why diamonds, which no one really needs, were so valuable, and water, which no one can do without, was so cheap. Marshall explained that diamonds are scarce *relative to the demand for them*, while water is plentiful. Earlier economists had struggled to learn whether demand or supply was more important in setting the price of a good. Marshall supplied a pragmatic answer: Demand and supply act simultaneously to set prices. Over short periods of time demand may be more important, and over long periods of time supply may be more important, but the two must always act simultaneously to set a price.

From the time of Marshall to the time of Keynes—roughly 1890 to 1936—nearly every young economist was trained to be a microeconomist, and there seemed to be an endless number of problems capable of keeping any number of economists happily employed. Then came Keynes' theories, which attracted the fancy of most young economists in the 1930s, so that microeconomics enjoyed less popularity after the end of World War II. By the mid-1960s, some of the excitement aroused by the Keynesian message had begun to fade, and attention turned again to those micro units that make daily decisions about how and when to use scarce resources. Now, in the 1970s, microeconomics is perhaps more prominent than it has been in nearly half a century.

In 1977, the important questions in microeconomics are the same as they were in Marshall's time: supply, demand, equilibrium, price, and firm-industry relationships.

Table 17-1 Quantity of Mystery Novels Demanded by Four Individuals at Four Prices

Price per book	Individual				Total for market
	A	B	C	D	
$2	10	14	4	7	35
4	9	11	2	4	26
6	8	7	1	2	18
8	7	4	0	1	12

without modifiers, it usually refers to the entire society's response to changes in the price of a commodity. There is, however, a unique relationship between an individual demand curve and a market demand curve. The market demand curve for a good or a service is found through the "horizontal summation" of the individual demand curves of the many persons who are purchasing, or who may decide to purchase, it. This horizontal summing process is shown in Table 17-1 and in Figure 17-2. Table 17-1 gives imaginary information on how many mystery novels each of four persons will purchase at four different prices. Person A buys nine books at four dollars and seven books at eight dollars. Person C buys four books at two dollars and only one at six dollars. From the information in this table, a demand curve can be constructed for each of the four individuals. The four individual demand curves in Figure 17-2 have the characteristic downward slope, showing that as price falls, each individual purchases more mysteries.

The behavior of the four individuals can be aggregated to show the behavior of this *group* of people who together make up our market for mystery novels. The purchases of persons A, B, C, and D at each price are added to find how much the entire *market* will purchase at each of the several prices. If the price is four dollars per book, the market will require 9 + 11 + 2 + 4 = 26 mysteries. The results of all such additions can be used to draw the market demand curve shown in Figure 17-2.

Elasticity of Demand

Firms are also interested in the demand curve because the varying relationships between price and quantity demanded tell the total revenue that the firm will receive at each price. Since a lower price may entice many more buyers to purchase the product, a drop in price does not necessarily bring a drop in revenue. Increased sales may offset the effect of the lower price. The demand curve in Figure 17-3a shows that at the beginning price of $6 per unit, 25 units are sold, yielding a total revenue

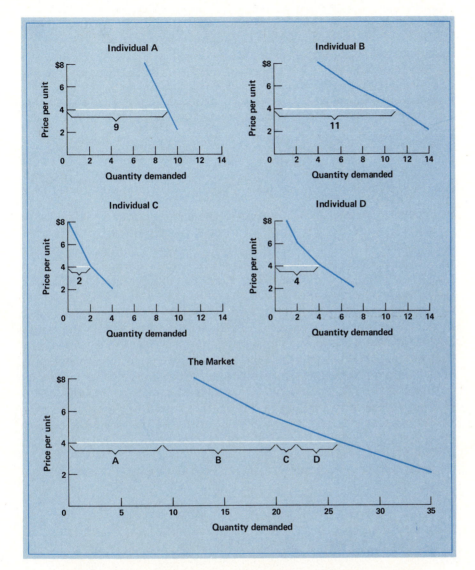

Figure 17-2 Constructing an Aggregated Demand Curve

of $150 for the firm ($6 × 25 = $150). If the price falls to $4 per unit, demand grows because more people are interested in buying the product and original buyers now buy more of it. At $4 per unit, 50 are sold and the firm's revenue increases to $200 ($4 × 50 = $200). The drop in price causes a reduction in the revenue earned by each of the 25 original units, but this loss is more than offset by an expansion in sales. The loss and gain are shown in the figure.

In Figure 17-3b, the beginning price is $8 per unit and 25 units are sold, yielding total revenues of $200 ($8 × 25 = $200). When price drops to $6 per unit, 30 are sold, but now total revenue is only $180 ($6 × 30 = $180). In this case, losses from the drop in price are not compensated by the increase in sales.

The technical term *elasticity of demand* is used to describe the various relationships between changes in price, changes in quantities purchased, and changes in the firm's total revenue. The name sounds formidable but the concept is extremely useful.

Elasticity of demand is a measure of responsiveness. If quantity demanded is very responsive to a change in price, demand is elastic. If quantity demanded is not very responsive to a change in price, demand is inelastic.

In general, luxuries have very elastic demands. A change in price will cause the quantity purchased to change quite demonstrably. By the same token, necessities like salt, matches, gasoline, eggs, and heating oil are all demanded in such rigid quantities that even severe price changes will not persuade buyers to purchase much more or much less. Beginning in the summer of 1973, gasoline prices in most parts of the United States began to climb quite rapidly. In response to the rise in price, families reduced the number and length of trips taken and began to plan more efficient ways of using their automobiles. But the number of cars entering and leaving cities at rush hours did not change demonstrably. This leads to the conclusion that there must be two demands for gasoline. One is for gasoline to get to work. Demand for this gasoline is not overly responsive to price changes. The other is for gasoline for pleasure driving. Demand for this gasoline apparently is quite responsive to price change. Demand for the first is *inelastic;* for the second, *elastic.*

Figure 17–3 Two Examples of Elasticity

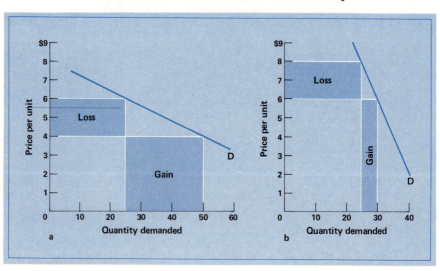

"Until this moment, I never realized we needed a food chopper with a built-in transistor radio."

Elasticity says something about the relationship between price and total revenue. If demand is elastic (responsive), a drop in price will be more than offset by the increase in quantity, so total revenue will increase. Price and total revenue move in opposite directions when demand is elastic. If demand is inelastic (unresponsive), a change in price will not cause significant changes in the quantity purchased. Price and total revenue will change in the same direction. In the unusual circumstance where a change in price causes a change in sales but no change in total revenue (offsetting changes), elasticity is described as *unit,* or *unitary.*

The term *unit elasticity* derives from a formula used to calculate the coefficient of elasticity. The formula relates the percentage change in quantity to the percentage change in price and is often written

$$\text{elasticity} = \frac{\text{percentage change in quantity}}{\text{percentage change in price}}$$

If the value of this coefficient is greater than one, a price change will be accompanied by changes in quantity large enough to offset any effects of the change in price. In such a case, demand is very responsive to price change, or elastic. If the coefficient is less than one, a price change will be accompanied by small changes in quantity—changes not large enough to offset the effects of the price change—so demand is not very responsive, or inelastic. The middle ground, where the price increase is exactly offset by the quantity decrease, yields a coefficient of one and is called unit, or sometimes unitary, elasticity.[3]

[3]Since the demand curve slopes downward, the percentage change in price will always be a negative number. With a negative number in the denominator, the elasticity coefficient will be negative, too. Since the coefficient is an indicator of responsiveness, the minus sign that should accompany it is most often omitted.

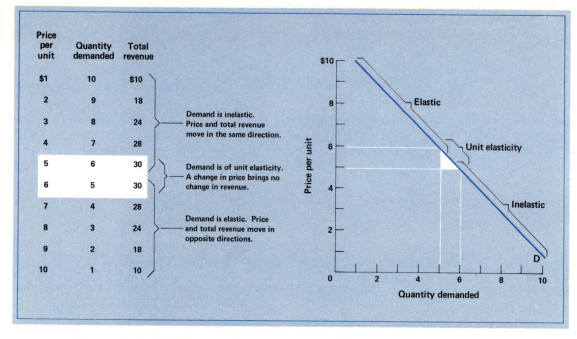

Figure 17-4 Elasticity Changing Along A Straight-line Demand Curve

Even with all these rules, a casual attempt to estimate the elasticity of demand can be deceiving. A glance at a demand curve will not always reveal whether demand is elastic or inelastic. Figure 17-4 describes an imaginary situation in which a product's price varies from $1 per unit to

Two Exceptions to the Straight-line Rule

This chapter makes the strong point that a straight-line demand curve will not have the same elasticity over its entire length. There are, however, two kinds of straight-line demand curves that *do* have the same elasticity throughout—a vertical curve and a horizontal one.

A horizontal (flat) demand curve is *perfectly elastic.* Regardless of what quantity comes onto the market, it will be purchased at the going price. It retains this elasticity throughout.

A vertical demand curve is *perfectly inelastic.* No matter how much price changes, the quantity demanded remains the same. Because quantity in this case is not responsive to changes in price, the vertical straight-line demand curve maintains the same elasticity over its entire length.

Elasticity is a measure of responsiveness. If quantity demanded does not respond to price changes, elasticity remains the same.

Who Uses Demand Curves?

Any firm or household seeking to buy or sell a factor or a product can use the information a demand curve provides. Its picture of price/quantity relationships is helpful in deciding how much of a factor or product to sell and when to offer it for sale. In many large corporations, market research departments employ economists to learn as much as possible about the demand for the firms' products. The Ford Motor Company produced the Mustang and the Pinto only after receiving fairly good indications that these vehicles would be demanded by the public. Other companies work equally hard to learn something of the shape and location of the demand curves for their products.

Skeptics will be quick to point out that Ford's research department did not do so well years ago when the Edsel was placed on the market and proved a miserable failure. The Edsel experience underscores two features of demand studies: (1) they can be wrong; (2) even if they are correct when conducted, they may lose their reliability within a short time span.

"Survey or no survey—we're not giving the American people a 6-wheeled, twin-engined, all-chrome convertible."

$10 per unit. As we would expect, the quantity sold varies inversely with price: At $1 per unit, 10 units are taken; at $10 per unit, one unit is purchased. At low prices ($1 per unit to $5 per unit), a price increase brings an increase in total revenue. But at high prices ($6 per unit to $10 per unit), a price increase causes total revenue to drop. If the price/quantity relationships are plotted on a graph, the demand curve D emerges. This demand curve is properly drawn as a straight line, yet one part of it is elastic and another part is inelastic. Again, remember that the shape of a demand curve can be deceiving. Even if it is a straight line, its elasticity will change from one segment to another.

The concept of demand is a powerful tool of economic analysis, for demand is one of the two forces that make the market mechanism work. But demand curves have been estimated for only relatively few goods, and those that have been derived are likely to change as the world on which they are based changes. There is no assurance that incomes, tastes, values, and prices of other products will remain the same.

Summary

1. The market system is an assimilator of information. The market gathers information about demand and supply and tries to rationalize it so demanders can obtain what they want and suppliers can sell those products that they have on hand.
2. The demand curve is based on the diminishing marginal utility of goods and services. It is shown as a curve that slopes downward to the right, indicating that as price falls, more units of a good will be purchased.
3. A demand curve will shift and twist with changes in tastes, incomes, prices of other products, or any other attribute of economic society. A demand curve is constructed with the assumption that all else remains constant.
4. Demand curves can be drawn for individuals, areas, or whole markets. The market demand for a commodity is the horizontal summation of demands expressed by all individuals in the market.
5. *Elasticity* is a term used to describe how responsive a demand curve is to a change in price. If demand is elastic, a small change in price will bring a large change in quantity demanded. If demand is inelastic, large changes in price will bring only small changes in quantity demanded.

Exercises

1. Explain these important terms and concepts:
   - demand
   - demand curve
   - elasticity of demand
   - horizontal summation
   - marginal utility
   - individual demand
   - market demand

2. For many years, air fares have been determined by an agency of the federal government. Even though air fares are "set," major airlines use a number of devices to alter the prices charged to transport people from one place to another. The New York–to–Miami run has always been a popular route to tamper with. If you were the vice-president in charge of finance for a major airline serving this route, you would be interested in the following figures:

Fare per round trip	Number of passengers per week
$100	1,500
200	1,300
300	1,100
400	1,000
500	900
600	800
700	700
800	500

   a. Draw a demand curve for passenger traffic on this route.
   b. Over what range of prices is demand elastic? Inelastic?

    c What fare would you suggest if your fleet were capable of handling 1,500 passengers per week? 1,000 passengers per week?
3 Classify the following as either movements along a demand curve or shifts to a new curve. (Review Chapter 4 or the following Contemporary Problem to refresh your memory on this distinction.)
    a The federal government relaxes rules imposing limits on the price of fuel.
    b A new, low-cost electric car causes sales of Chevrolets to plummet.
    c The apple crop fails, so people buy more oranges.
    d Because of import restrictions, foreign automobiles go up in price.
4 Because of high unemployment in the inner cities, many baseball teams decided to lower prices for tickets to games during the 1975 season. They reasoned that the lower prices would attract more people, thus giving them something to do while they waited for a job. If the lowered prices brought increased revenue, would demand for baseball games be elastic or inelastic?
5 You operate a barbershop near a large university campus. Over the last decade, the trend toward longer hair and home haircutting has driven many of your competitors out of business. Now the university students adopt a new dress code calling for men's hair to be trimmed to three inches or less in length. Should you raise or lower your price?

A Contemporary Problem
Shifts and Changes in Demand

Demands, and the shape and position of demand curves, are affected by hundreds of forces. The shifting of demands will in turn cause some firms to flourish and others to fail. Those that are doing well are commonly the ones whose products are in high demand. Those that fail are those facing decreased demands and dropping sales. Some homely examples show how demand can change.

    (1) In recent years, firms producing substitutes for petroleum products or petrochemicals have done quite well, while firms producing items that require much petroleum have not done well at all. The gas-saving small cars have succeeded; the huge gas-consuming luxury cars have failed.

    (2) With the advent of the automobile, the demand for horses and their trappings diminished. It was not merely a case of utility falling for the last few horses (low marginal utility on the right-hand end of a demand curve), but rather a case of a drop in the utility of *all* horses. The whole curve shifted in response to a change in technology, and as it shifted, resources—land, labor, and capital—were forced out of horse-oriented activities and into automobile-oriented ones.

    (3) As family incomes have increased, the demand for air-conditioned houses has increased. At any given price, more air-conditioned homes are demanded now than formerly, simply because family incomes are now high enough to permit more people to indulge in this luxury. The

shift in the demand curve for air conditioning has caused more resources to be devoted to their production.

Knowledge of demand shifters can often help individual firms adjust to changes. If Amtrak knows that rail travel will increase in importance, it will put on more trains; if several reservoirs in an area are expected to go dry, boat salesmen will move to other areas. Some important shifters of demand are described below.

Income. When income increases, price becomes a less vital consideration in the purchase of many commodities. Marginal utility need not change, but the ability and willingness to pay for this utility increases. As a result, demand curves for many items shift upward to the right, indicating that a higher price will be paid for the same amount.

Tastes. As a society develops, or changes, its tastes for various things change, too. Nowhere is this more apparent than in the market for apparel or for "fad" commodities. A change in tastes can shift a demand curve up—as for double-knit fabrics in the early 1970s—or downward—as for white shirts and narrow ties in the same period.

Technology. As technology has developed, many new commodities have become available. The availability of low-cost electricity to virtually every home in the nation brought increased demands for electric lights, stoves, heaters, and electrical gadgetry (although much of this is related also to income). In the 1880s, when electricity was available in only a few cities, the demand for lightbulbs was very low. Now, with nearly universal power availability, the want-satisfying capacity of lightbulbs has increased, and the demand curve for this product has shifted to the right.

Interrelationships with other products. Some products come in groups or are used only in groups. Using more gasoline always requires using more tires. A person who buys a stereo will be purchasing records, too. If the U.S. Corps of Engineers builds a dam, the dam will create a lake, the existence of the lake will increase the demand for boats, and the increased demand for boats will raise the demand for water skis.

All these types of shifts are shown in Figure A. In each section of the figure the demand curve labeled I can be considered as a starting point, and curve II is the result of a shift. The shift shown at the top comes in response to generally expanding demands—the same quantity can be sold at a higher price or an expanded quantity can be sold at the original price. Such an expansion in demand may come from increasing population or from increased income. The second change, a rotation in the demand curve, means that the responsiveness of the curve is changing. For some reason, a change in price will bring about either a greater or a smaller change in quantity than formerly. A change in technology or a

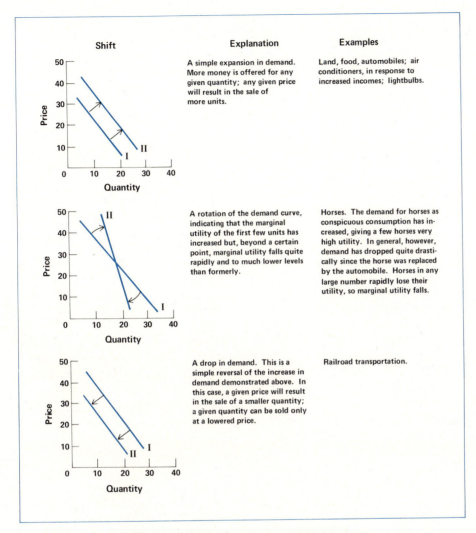

Figure A Shifts in the Demand Curve

change in the way a good is used can cause this to happen. Before the invention of the automobile and the tractor, horses were important means of transport and power. When this was the case, a demand curve for the animals might have been somewhat flat—lower prices would bring a large response among horse users. After the horses were technologically displaced, some people still demanded these beasts as luxuries—for recreation and the life style of "horse people." Such users are few in number, however, so it can be expected that decreases in price will not bring with them large increases in quantity sold. The demand curve rotates in a clockwise direction. The decrease in demand shown at the bottom could be the result of forces opposite to those causing the increase in demand. A decrease in population is unlikely in the closing years of the twentieth century. A more likely cause of diminished demand is, again, technology. The emergence of first the automobile, then air transport, may well have caused the demand for rail transport to drop.

Thus demand curves change position in response to a number of forces, some of which are understood well and others not at all.

18 The Supply of Economic Goods

Doña Rosa has lived all of her nearly 75 years in a small village in Oaxaca, Mexico. She is a potter who makes beautiful black Madonnas from a clay, found only near her village, that turns dark in the firing process. For years, local residents bought the little figures to use as religious ornaments, and the business provided only a modest living for Doña Rosa and her family. Then, many tourists discovered the state of Oaxaca. The subtle beauty of the black Madonnas immediately caught their fancy, and suddenly Doña Rosa was selling all she could possibly produce. The price doubled, then tripled, then quadrupled, as tourists bid for the privilege of buying. Doña Rosa trained her friends and neighbors to make the figures and now has a flourishing business. A few Madonnas are still sold to visitors in the village, but most are sent to Acapulco, Mexico City, and even gift shops in foreign countries. Each Madonna, though, still bears the carefully written signature of Doña Rosa—they are all authentic.

Doña Rosa operates a firm. Even when she produced only a few figurines each year, her operation was a firm, since she used inputs (clay, fire, ovens, labor, and time) to produce her art. Now the firm is large. It supplies a large quantity of objects to a large clientele. The firm responded to demand by increasing the quantity supplied.

All firms respond to demand by offering either more or less of a product. This response is termed *supply*. The concept of supply is the subject of intense economic theorizing and inquiry. This chapter deals with supply. After supply is defined, the topics of costs are introduced. These costs lead to construction of a supply curve for a product.

Supply and the Costs of Production

The concept of supply is more complicated than demand. It seems intuitively correct that when the price of a good rises, more units will be placed on the market. With more people casting dollar votes for a product, sellers increase its availability. Such a view implies that a *supply curve* is positively sloped (in contrast to the negative slope of a demand curve), as shown in Figure 18–1.

A supply curve is a positively sloped line showing the quantities of a good that will be placed on the market at each of several prices. The curve is plotted in a quadrant having price on the vertical axis and quantity supplied on the horizontal axis.

The supply curve is determined by producers' expectations, technology, and the costs of producing goods and services. Expectations of individual businessmen are difficult to analyze and the advance of technology is impossible to predict, so most discussions of the supply curve center on costs of production. In large measure, a firm's costs dictate how much it will place on the market at each price. The best way to understand the relationship between costs and supply is to consider the costs incurred by an individual firm.

Classes of Production Costs

A firm incurs two types of costs during the production process, *fixed costs* and *variable costs*.

Fixed costs do not change with output. They include insurance, taxes, depreciation, and a variety of other expenses that must be met whether the firm produces zero output or at maximum capacity. Real estate taxes on the factory are a perfect example of a fixed cost. These taxes must be paid, but the amount of the tax does not change if production stops or if it doubles.

Variable costs rise and fall as output rises and falls. When a factory expands its output, it incurs higher variable costs. If only one unit of output is produced, X laborers must be hired; if two units are produced, $X + Y$ laborers must be hired; if three units are produced, $X + Y + Z$ laborers must be hired. When GM reduces its output of Buicks, Vegas, and trucks, it lets workers go, purchases less steel, and uses less electricity. Each of these changes in the use of factors brings a change in variable costs.

In addition to fixed and variable costs, economists and businessmen alike are interested in the cost of producing one extra unit of output. This is the *marginal cost* related to a single unit of output.

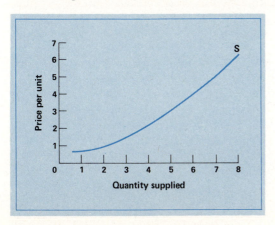

**Figure 18-1
A Supply Curve**

Marginal cost is the additional cost associated with the production of one more unit of output. If producing nine tons of steel requires expenditures of $1,750 and producing 10 tons requires $1,900, the marginal cost of the tenth ton is $1,900 − $1,750 = $150. A similar process can be used to determine the marginal cost associated with any level of output.

The relationships among fixed costs, variable costs, and marginal costs are referred to as the *cost structure* of the firm.

Other categories in the cost structure of a firm are *total costs* and *average costs*.

Total costs are the sum of fixed costs and variable costs. Average costs, or average costs per unit of output, are total costs divided by the number of units produced. Average costs are often broken into two parts—average fixed costs (fixed costs ÷ quantity produced) and average variable costs (variable costs ÷ quantity produced).

Table 18–1 shows hypothetical costs in each of these categories for 10 different levels of output. The same cost data are graphed in Figure 18–2. The average fixed cost (*AFC*) curve is perhaps the most confusing. Although the total amount of fixed costs remains the same, the amount per unit of output changes when output changes. If only one unit is produced, that single unit must bear the burden of all fixed costs. If two units are produced, each unit bears exactly one-half of total fixed costs, and if three units are produced, each unit is charged with one-third of the total. This is a never-ending sequence. So long as output expands within the same fixed plant, fixed costs continue to be spread among more and more units of output, and average fixed cost continues to drop.

Table 18–1 Costs Incurred at Different Levels of Output

Quantity produced	Total fixed cost	Total variable cost	Total cost	Average fixed cost	Average variable cost	Average total cost	Marginal cost
1	$40.00	$ 85.00	$125.00	$40.00	$85.00	$125.00	$125.00
2	40.00	145.00	185.00	20.00	72.50	92.50	60.00
3	40.00	187.50	227.50	13.33	62.50	75.83	42.50
4	40.00	226.00	266.00	10.00	56.50	66.50	38.50
5	40.00	265.00	305.00	8.00	53.00	61.00	39.00
6	40.00	307.00	347.00	6.67	51.16	57.83	42.00
7	40.00	355.00	395.00	5.71	50.72	56.43	48.00
8	40.00	408.00	448.00	5.00	51.00	56.00	53.00
9	40.00	469.00	509.00	4.44	52.11	56.55	61.00
10	40.00	549.00	589.00	4.00	54.90	58.90	80.00

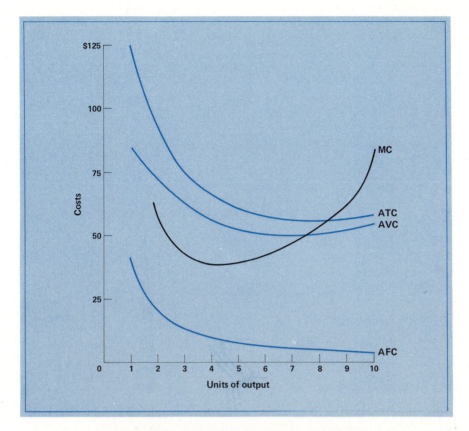

Figure 18–2 Costs over a Range of Output

The average variable cost (AVC) curve in Figure 18–2 has a characteristic U shape that will be repeated many times in the next few chapters. As output increases, the firm becomes more efficient in the way it transforms factors into products. Laborers become more specialized and more skilled, tasks become mechanized, and underemployed parts of the factory, farm, or mine begin to be used. Each of these changes increases the efficiency of the firm and reduces the cost per unit. Such reductions in costs per unit are called *economies of scale.*

Economies of scale are the reductions in unit costs that come from increasing output. They result from more advanced technology, more specialization of labor, and sometimes from the ability to purchase large quantities of inputs at discount prices.

Eventually, all economies of scale are realized and costs per unit of output begin to rise. This occurs because machines are run too fast, foremen find it more difficult to control activities, and bottlenecks appear in the production process. The rising costs per unit correspond to *disecono-*

> ### How's Your Geometry?
>
> In a geometry text, the path taken by the average fixed cost curve would be called a *rectangular hyperbola*. That is, the curve traces a path such that any rectangle drawn under it must have the same area. With cost per unit on the vertical axis and output on the horizontal axis, this is exactly what the average fixed cost curve should show—a given volume of cost being divided among an increasing volume of output. The two rectangles in Figure A each have the same area, and each represents the same volume of fixed cost (average fixed cost × units produced). Any other rectangle that can be drawn under the curve also has this same area. The fact that the curve has a definite and constant geometric description has no real economic meaning, but it is an easy way to describe and to remember the shape of an average fixed cost curve.
>
>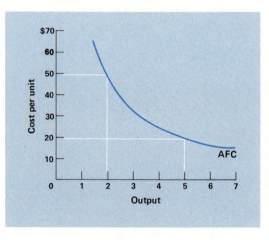
>
> **Figure A**

mies of scale and combine with earlier efficiencies to yield a U-shaped variable cost curve.

The average total cost (ATC) curve is the vertical summation of average fixed costs and average variable costs at each level of output. The U shape of the average total cost curve is explained by the combination of two forces—the spreading of fixed costs and the U shape of the average variable cost curve. At low levels of output, average total costs per unit are driven down as output increases and the massive fixed costs are spread among more and more units. At higher levels of output, these drops in fixed costs become less pronounced and there comes a point when the further spreading of fixed costs cannot counteract or offset increases in the variable costs per unit. Eventually, diseconomies in the use of variable inputs cause average total costs to increase.

The marginal cost (MC) curve is of special interest. Table 18–1 shows marginal costs dropping from $125, the cost of the first unit of output, to $38.50 for the fourth unit, but after the fourth unit is produced, marginal costs begin to creep upward, eventually reaching $80.00 for the tenth unit. The marginal cost curve, too, has a U shape, for largely the same reasons that explained the drop and rise in average variable costs.

Opportunity Costs

A firm pays wages for the labor it must hire, and it pays the going price for fuel and electricity used in the production process. If the firm is rational, it will also pay itself wages for the labor it owns and rent for the use of its own buildings. These "payments" made to owned factors reflect opportunities that are given up by not using resources in some other way (recall Chapters 1 and 2). By keeping $10,000 tied up in inventories, a firm denies itself the opportunity to earn a 5 or 7 or even 9 percent return that would result from putting that money in the bank. This potential earning is an opportunity that is given up when a business makes the decision to keep its funds in their present employment. Since these costs are revenues given up by the firm, they must be calculated as costs of doing business, and they should be included in the cost structure in the same fashion as the cost of labor or rent for the garage.

In a production process, the opportunity costs of the firm's own capital are often called normal profits that should be earned by that capital. Normal profits are the profits necessary to keep capital and other factors of production in their present occupations. If a parking lot does not earn enough to pay wages, taxes, and upkeep and still yield a normal return to its owner, the land should be used for something else. If normal profits are not being earned by a particular productive activity, it would be advantageous to dissolve that activity and use the funds in an alternative capacity.

Marginal Cost and the Supply Curve

Recall that in the case of demand, decisions regarding how much to purchase center on the amount of utility that accompanies each newly acquired unit. If a person feels that the marginal utility afforded by another unit of a good is greater than its price, he will purchase that added unit. Therefore the marginal utility curve becomes the individual's demand curve. The marginal cost curve has the same close relationship with supply. If a manufacturer can produce another unit of output for $40 and the selling price is $50, that unit should be produced—or so it seems.

Figure 18–3 shows the marginal cost (*MC*) and average total cost (*ATC*) curves for a softball manufacturer. If this business can sell softballs at three dollars each, the marginal cost rule above says the business should produce and sell about seven balls. Below this level of output, each ball can be sold for more than its marginal cost; at each unit above this level, *marginal revenue* is exceeded by marginal cost.

Marginal revenue is the addition to total revenue provided by selling one more unit of a good or service. If the price of softballs is four dollars

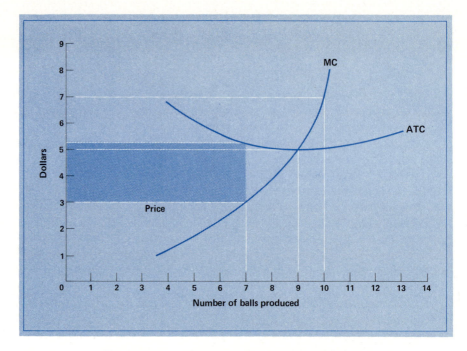

Figure 18-3 Costs of Producing Softballs

apiece and the company finds one more ball to sell, that ball can be sold for four dollars and the marginal revenue produced by the sale is four dollars.

Apparently, the seven units of output that equate marginal revenue with marginal cost are the output that maximizes the firm's profit.

A closer look reveals the folly of this decision. Even though marginal costs are covered when seven balls are produced, the average costs of production are not. At this level of output, the firm loses money equal in volume to the shaded area in the graph. Each ball sold brings three dollars but each one costs slightly more than five dollars to produce.

When the price of softballs rises to five dollars each, the marginal cost rule indicates that nine should be produced and sold. At this level of output revenues generated by sales (9 × $5 = $45) are just sufficient to cover costs incurred during the production process (also $45), and the firm breaks even. As the price per ball reaches levels above five dollars, the rule of equating marginal cost with marginal revenue (price) does provide an adequate guide to the number of balls the firm should place on the market. At seven dollars per unit, for example, 10 should be produced and sold. In sum, for all levels of output above the level at which marginal cost intersects average total cost, the marginal cost curve becomes the supply curve of the firm.

Any firm bent on maximizing profits must equate marginal cost with marginal returns. If it does not, it is not taking advantage of all profit-making opportunities. However, as a rule for firm behavior, equating marginal cost with marginal returns is subject to one qualification: If marginal cost equals marginal returns at levels that do not cover average total cost, the firm loses money on each unit produced. Only when marginal revenue equals marginal cost *at or above average total cost* does the rule become sufficient. That portion of the marginal cost curve lying above the average total cost curve tells how many units of output should be placed on the market at each price. It thus becomes the supply curve for the firm.

This supply curve for the firm is analogous to the demand curve for an individual; it too is a very fragile construct. Any change in variable costs will alter the cost structure of the firm and have an impact on supply. An increase in the price of labor will raise the cost of production and subsequently raise the marginal cost. A drop in the cost of fuel will lower the marginal cost, and a technological advance could cause a change in the shape or location of the curve. Just as changes in tastes, in time, and in prices of other goods affect the individual demand curve, changes in costs affect the firm's supply curve. Since such changes occur almost daily, isolating a supply curve for beans, books, or glass-bottomed boats is a very difficult and precarious task.

To this point, the discussion of supply has centered on the supply curve of an individual firm. Unless the firm is a perfect monopoly (a subject considered in Chapter 21), there will be other firms producing the same product. In 1972, for example, approximately 536,000 farms produced wheat, 303,000 restaurants produced meals, and over 9,000 firms produced lumber for the U.S. economy. To obtain the industry supply curve for each of these products, the supply decisions and cost structures of all the individual firms in the industry must be taken into account. In the case of demand, aggregation was relatively easy. Demand curves could be horizontally summed because at a given price, the quantity demanded by one person could be added to the quantity demanded by a second person without one affecting the other. But adding up the supply curves appropriate to all firms does not yield an accurate picture of the industry supply curve. The supply curve for a single firm is a still picture of one firm's responses to changes in the product price. That picture holds still only so long as the cost structure of the firm remains the same. It remains so only as long as all other things remain equal. If the industry is expanding output in response to an increase in product price, firms in the industry will find it necessary to compete with one another for factors of production. This competition for factors will cause factor prices to rise. As the price of wheat climbs, wheat farmers will compete for land with potato growers and with developers. Restaurants will compete for locations when profits increase in the restaurant business. When lumber prices soar, lumber companies will compete with one another for trees.

This competition will drive factor prices up. As factor prices rise, cost structures of individual firms change, and so do their individual supply curves. A horizontal summation of the supply curves of individual firms can only provide a rough estimate of the supply curve of the industry, since expansion in industry output will bring about changes in prices of factors.

In spite of its limitations and the fragility of the supply curve, the law of supply is a straightforward, reasonable, and highly useful concept: As the price of a factor, good, or service increases, more of that factor, good, or service will be placed on the market.

Supply and Technology

Supply curves are intimately related to technology. As technological progress occurs, costs of producing things change. When costs change, a producer's conclusion about how much to offer for sale also changes. Technology has greatly lowered labor costs in many production processes and has allowed vastly larger quantities of goods to be placed on the markets. It has also created entirely new methods of producing many products. A supply curve shifts in response to these changes. Two examples are shown in Figure 18–4. The downward shift of the supply curve indicates that a larger quantity of product will be offered for sale at any given price. The shift may be the result of an improvement in technology—the use of low-cost machines rather than high-cost labor. The upward shift of the supply curve indicates that any given quantity will be placed on the market only if a higher price is offered. This may be the result of a change in the price of factors used in the production of the commodity in question.

Regardless of how or when (or even *if*) a supply curve shifts, the relative steepness of the curve shows how producers respond to changes in

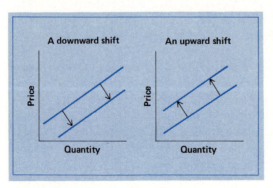

**Figure 18–4
Shifts in a Supply Curve**

> ## Elasticity of Supply
>
> Just as it is possible to calculate a coefficient of elasticity for a demand curve, it is also possible to calculate an elasticity coefficient for a supply curve. Elasticity of supply is found by dividing the percentage change in quantity by the percentage change in price. When the resulting coefficient is greater than one, supply is elastic. A small change in price will bring about a large change in the quantity placed on the market. When the coefficient of elasticity is less than one, a change in price will bring only a small change in the quantity supplied.

price. A vertical, or totally unresponsive, supply curve is possible. Such a curve would indicate that one quantity of the product is available and, regardless of how high or how low the price may go, that quantity and only that quantity will be offered for sale. The supply curve for the Hope diamond is vertical. No change in price will bring more than one Hope diamond onto the market or even into existence. Its supply does not respond to price changes. Similarly, the supply curve for land is vertical. Since the quantity of land is not influenced by price, the same quantity is available regardless of whether the price is zero or very high.[1]

At the opposite extreme from a vertical supply curve is one that is perfectly responsive to price changes. Such a supply curve is horizontal and shows that any desired quantity (within the bounds of reason) will be forthcoming at a given price. The two extreme cases of the supply curve—unresponsive (vertical) and perfectly responsive (horizontal)—are interesting, but most supply curves lie between these extremes.

Supply and Time

Firms respond to price changes by offering to sell more or less of the product they produce. A rise in price signals an increase in output; a drop in price signals a decrease. Although a firm can lower its output to zero in a moment, it requires time to increase the amount it will offer for sale. A modest increase in output might be achieved by running machines faster or hiring a few more workers. A major increase in output

---

[1]This is actually not quite true, for two reasons. First, it is *possible* to alter the supply of land through drainage, filling of bogs or flooding existing land. This has been done in many areas—such as San Francisco and Boston—where land has taken on extremely high values. Second, the supply of land for any one *purpose*—housing, highways, farming—may, within limits, respond to price changes.

most often requires obtaining new space, installing new facilities, and training new personnel. These actions require time. In economics, the relationship between supply and time was standardized by Alfred Marshall in his monumental *Principles of Economics.* He considered three time periods during which choices could be made and supplies altered. They are the market run (or the short short run), the short run, and the long run. These time periods are best understood by referring to the production of a perishable commodity.

A fisherman who earns his income by catching fish to be sold on the commercial market is a firm. He has one fixed and limiting resource, a boat. He also has fishing gear, market arrangements, and supplies. He and a small crew leave port, fish their favorite areas, and return to port with their catch. The fish must be sold within a very short time after returning. And, once in port, the firm cannot alter its supply. It is operating in the *market run* or *short short run.*

The market run (or short short run) is that period of time during which supply cannot be increased. In some industries, the market run is only days in length, in other industries it is months or years long.

If fish prices are especially high, the fisherman may want to supply more. In the short run, this can be done by adding more variable inputs to the fishing boat—more fuel so the vessel can go farther out to sea, more ice so the vessel can stay out longer, or more laborers so nets can be emptied and returned to the water more quickly. In the *short run,* supply can be expanded by using fixed equipment more intensively.

The short run is that time period during which supply can be altered by changing the amount of variable inputs applied to a given set of fixed inputs. Output can change within limits of the existing plant.

If the fisherman expects prices to rise and remain stable at a high level, he will consider adding to his fixed plant by building another boat. Boat building takes time. The time required to alter the fixed plant of the firm is the *long run.*

The long run is the time required for all resources to become variable. In a restaurant, it is the time needed to add seating capacity or expand the kitchen. In shipbuilding, it is the time needed to build more drydocks and launching facilities, and train more shipwrights.

These three lengths of run will vary from industry to industry and from firm to firm. Regardless of industry or firm, their effects on supply remain much the same. As time passes, supply becomes more elastic. That is, as opportunities to expand and contract increase, so does a firm's responsiveness to price changes. This is shown in Figure 18–5. The market-run supply curve for fish indicates that three tons reach the dock when the boat lands and no variation in price will change that amount. Neither a very high price nor a very low price will change the

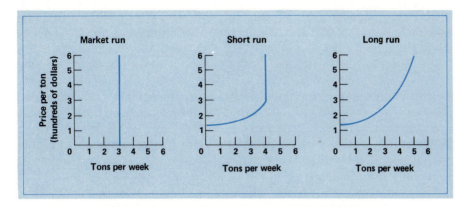

Figure 18-5 Supply in Three Time Spans

quantity of fish on the market. The short-run supply curve shows that modest price changes will bring a response in the quantity supplied. No fish at all will be caught if the price per ton is below $150. As the price rises from $150 to $300 per ton, the supply increases to four tons per week. At this level of output, the fishing boat's capacity is reached and no further additions of variable input will allow it to catch more. Beyond four tons per week, supply becomes unresponsive to changes in price.

In the long run, the boat is no longer limiting. A low price for fish will cause the fisherman to obtain a smaller, more efficient boat. A high price for fish will bring expansion in the number of boats. The supply curve becomes responsive to changes in the price of the product.

Conclusion

The supply curve is a useful device that summarizes the behavior of people who have factors or products to sell. Their behavior may be highly responsive to changes in price, indicating that a modest price change will bring forth a huge change in the quantity offered for sale. Or sellers may act in an unresponsive way, with large changes in price bringing only modest changes in the quantity offered. To understand markets, it is necessary to know something about prices, quantities offered, and responsiveness. Thus, supply is a crucial tool of economic analysis.

As in the case of demand, a final qualification must be made. Any known supply curve applies only under certain highly restricted circumstances. It applies to a given time, a given place, and a given set of conditions. A change in tastes, technology, factor prices, or individual behavior will shift or twist the curve and invalidate it as an empirical observation. In spite of this limitation, the supply curve does describe economic behavior and is a useful device for organizing thoughts about the market.

Summary

1 The supply curve shows the quantities that will be placed on the market at each of several prices. With price on the vertical axis and quantity on the horizontal axis, the supply curve will slope upwards to the right.
2 The supply curve is closely related to the cost structure of the firm. That part of the marginal cost curve that is above the average cost curve is the firm's supply curve.
3 The cost structure of a firm includes fixed costs, variable costs, total costs, and marginal costs.
4 Although the relationship is very complicated, the industry supply curve can be approximated by horizontally summing the supply curves of many firms.
5 The supply curve is related to technology. When technology changes and allows a new method to be used to produce a product, the supply curve shifts or twists.
6 Supply is related to time. In the short short run, or market run, supply cannot respond to price. In the short run, supply can respond within limits imposed by the fixed plant; in the long run all costs are variable, so supply is more elastic.

Exercises

1 Explain these important terms and concepts:

supply curve — economies of scale
fixed cost — normal profit
variable cost — elasticity of supply
marginal cost — short run
average cost — long run

2 A firm reveals the following information about its cost structure:

Output	Total cost
0	25
1	35
2	41
3	45
4	47
5	49
6	52
7	57
8	65
9	79
10	100

a Calculate each of the following for each level of output (Hint: Recall that fixed costs are costs that must be incurred even if production is zero.):
  (1) Fixed costs
  (2) Average variable cost
  (3) Average fixed cost
  (4) Average total cost
  (5) Marginal cost
b Plot ATC and MC.
c What is the appropriate level of output if price is
  (1) two dollars?
  (2) five dollars?
  (3) eight dollars?
3 How did Henry Ford's pioneering work in the use of production-line methods alter the supply curve of early automobiles?
4 Agriculture uses a great deal of fuel. Since 1973, fuel prices in the United States have risen quite significantly. How has this increase in input prices affected the price of food?
5 The supply curve for land in cities is virtually inelastic (for example, Manhattan Island has only so many acres), yet more business and more people continue to crowd into the nation's metropolitan areas. What technological advance has given the supply curve for city space some responsiveness?
6 Why does the firm's supply curve start with the intersection of *MC* and *ATC*?

A Contemporary Problem
Bigger Is Not Always Better

Early in this chapter it was mentioned that supply results from a combination of three things: costs, expectations, and technology. Few industries have been more responsive to these three than the airlines. In recent years the jet, then the jumbo jet, and now the prospect of a very long range mini-jumbo have presented a tantalizing picture for boards of directors who want to dazzle the public with an ever-widening array of gleaming hardware. These have come, however, at a time when passenger loads have decreased, costs of operating planes and ground facilities have soared, and foreign competition has become keener by the month. The fate of Pan American is illustrative.

Of all of the United States' international air carriers, Pan American has long stood out as the luxury line serving the world. It was begun in the 1930s by men who enjoyed the experience of flying more than the numbers in the accountant's book. After years of sending planes into new places and making respectably high profits from travel-hungry Americans, Pan Am faced a severe jolt in mid-1968 when profits suddenly turned to losses. The losses have continued through 1976, and now the accumulated losses of these years are nearly $425 million.

One big reason for the losses is Pan Am's fascination with planes. In 1966, after experiencing a decade of growth and profits, Juan Trippe, one of the line's founders, agreed to purchase 25 Boeing 747 jumbo jets at a total cost of $600 million. The fully loaded Boeing 747 is a thing of financial beauty. Its size and efficiency enable it to carry people long distances at very low costs. A half-filled 747 is a miserable failure; it loses money. Trippe's purchase plus some others by Pan Am officials have pushed Pan Am's capacity to nearly 40 billion seat miles per year. Unfortunately, only 20 billion of those seat miles have been used, and at a time when costs have been soaring.

"Supply" is controlled by the managers of firms. One large firm—Pan Am—read signals that made business appear to be good and as a result became overcommitted to aircraft and to routes that generated little revenue. To cut back on supply will require a very long time (what airline will want to buy airplanes when only half the seats will be occupied?), and the prospect of lowering the cost of either flying or maintaining ground facilities will not be reduced in the near future. The cost of misreading signals is near bankruptcy for a pioneer U.S. flying firm.

19

Demand, Supply, and Equilibrium

Kitchen ranges come in many shapes and sizes. Some have four burners, others have two burners and a grill. Some have a single oven suitable only for warming things. Some have two regular ovens, a microwave oven, and four huge burners. On the more complicated models, there are buttons, dials, buzzers, warning lights, and timing devices. Many of these "kitchen stoves" not only bake, boil, and fry but are decorative elements and status symbols as well. If a visitor from a primitive jungle tribe encountered one, he might wonder if it flew, floated, or told fortunes. He would not suspect that it cooked.

For all its splendor, though, the modern range only tells the time when it has access to an energy supply. Without electricity or gas it is of no use to someone who has to make breakfast. In this respect, a kitchen stove is like a demand curve. The demand curve must have its companion, the supply curve, before it can be fully utilized. It is an interesting object, but it must have its fuel before it can be used to best advantage. Demand and supply together provide the information used by firms and households. Together they form "the market" and yield market prices. This chapter is about the use of supply and demand. Its purpose is to show how the two concepts together contribute to an understanding of how the market works. In doing this, it deals with the market, market prices, equilibrium, and the process of adjustment.

CHAPTER NINETEEN

The Market

From the beginning of this book the market has been characterized as an information feedback system that gathers and dispenses information about what is available, what is desired, and what sets of prices will bring buyers and sellers together. The market system is not the only way to organize an economy, but it is the only way that emphasizes individual choice and permits individuals to allocate their resources to those activities that yield the most profit, utility, or satisfaction. Because of specialization, the constituents of modern market economies usually have one thing to sell and others they wish to buy. The selling activity is supply; the buying activity is demand. The market's chore is to match varied supplies and suppliers with the wide array of demands and demanders. When supplies and demands are finally joined, a price is set and the law of supply and demand causes the market to move toward *equilibrium*.

In microeconomics, equilibrium refers to a combination of price and quantity exchanged that will satisfy both buyers and sellers. At equilibrium there is no net force toward change in either the quantity exchanged or the price paid.

Newspaper editors, barbers, farm operators, and economists frequently discuss the law of supply and demand. This much talked of and much abused law of market behavior derives from the separate law of supply and law of demand. When the supply and demand curves are shown in a single diagram, as in Figure 19-1, they intersect at one price/quantity combination. This intersection shows the only combination of price and quantity that will simultaneously satisfy buyers and sellers. In Figure 19-1, the intersection appears where price is $5.00 per unit and 800 units are offered for sale. Sellers are willing to place any quantity on the market as long as they receive a price at least as high as that designated by the supply curve S. Thus, if price is $2 per unit, suppliers will be willing to sell 500 units, and if price is $7 per unit, they will supply 1,000 units.

Demanders are willing to purchase any quantity shown on the horizontal axis so long as the price is no higher than that designated by the demand curve D. When price is $3 per unit, demanders will want to purchase 1,200 units. If the price doubles to $6 per unit, on the other hand, the good is considered relatively expensive, so only 600 units are demanded.

The point of intersection between the two curves (price = $5.00; quantity = 800 units) simultaneously satisfies buyers and sellers because both are getting what they asked. Since both suppliers and demanders are satisfied with this price, there is no automatic tendency to move away from this condition and the market is in equilibrium.

At any higher price—say $7 per unit—demanders are dissatisfied and will not continue to purchase 800 units. Some potential buyers drop out of

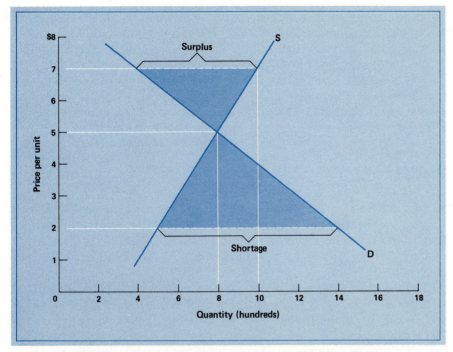

Figure 19-1 Supply, Demand, and Market Price

the market, and those remaining purchase only 400 units. The $7 price, however, makes suppliers enthusiastic over the prospect of high profits and they gladly place 1,000 units on the market. The resulting surplus (1,000 supplied − 400 demanded = 600 unsold units) can be sold only when prices drop toward the old equilibrium level. Analogously, at the very low price of $2 per unit, suppliers see little opportunity for profit and only a few (500) units are offered for sale. Buyers, attracted by the offer of much utility at bargain prices, are willing to purchase 1,400 units. The resulting shortage (900 units) is relieved only when price increases back toward the original equilibrium price.

This market is a self-correcting one. When surpluses appear in the market, forces to remove them automatically come into play. Shopkeepers who have acquired too much of a product drop the selling price; wholesalers make the product available at below cost, and the market begins to clear.

Clearing the market is a term used to describe the process of removing all of one commodity (or service) from all marketplaces. The market for wheat is "cleared" when this year's crop has found its way to millers, feeders, and distillers. The market for winter clothing is "cleared" when manufacturers, wholesalers, and retailers finally dispose of unwanted inventories and clear their shelves.

When shortages appear because price is below the equilibrium level, potential buyers bid against each other, and shopkeepers hold back goods for favored customers. Since not all buyers can be satisfied, prices begin to rise. In the process, the shortage is removed.

This automatic, self-correcting mechanism is a highly desirable attribute that gives a market economy the capacity to allocate or reallocate resources in response to the changing demands of purchasers and changing abilities of suppliers to meet demanders' needs.

A Change in Equilibrium

As was pointed out in Chapters 17 and 18, there are almost continual forces at work causing demand and supply curves to shift and twist. Incomes and tastes change, causing the position of the demand curve to change. Technology and institutions change, causing supply curves to shift.

Each of these shifts, and any others that may occur, causes equilibrium to be disrupted. Consider the plight of the fuel industry and the automobile industry in the 1970s. Since the beginning of the gasoline crisis in 1973, a number of shifts have occurred in the supply and demand for gasoline and in the supply and demand for automobiles. Figure 19–2 shows a hypothetical demand and supply situation for gasoline. It as-

Figure 19–2 Hypothetical Market Curves for Gasoline

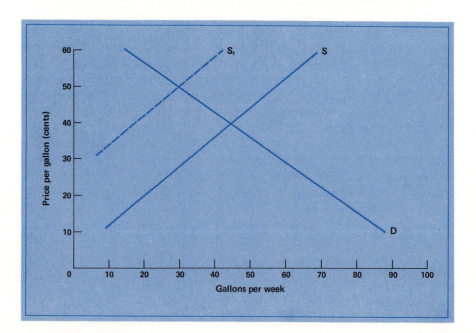

"Now listen again. This is one of a line of seven compacts. Four of the seven are large compacts. This is the smallest of the four."

sumes that before the oil-exporting nations decided to raise the price of exported crude oil, the gasoline market in this country was in equilibrium at 40 cents per gallon. At this price, each family purchased 45 gallons of gasoline per week. This equilibrium is shown by the intersection of the solid supply and demand curves S and D.

When the price of imported crude petroleum suddenly rose from $1.62 per barrel in January 1973, to $3.15 per barrel in October 1973, then to more than $11.00 per barrel in 1974, the supply curve for gasoline moved to a higher level. Suppliers would supply the same quantity as before only if they received prices high enough to cover the increased costs. This new supply curve is shown by the supply curve S_1. The new supply curve did nothing to change consumers' dispositions about demand; it merely increased the price. Consumers, following the wishes demonstrated by their original demand curve, purchased 30 gallons per week at 50 cents per gallon. The market was again in equilibrium.

If gasoline consumption is going to be very expensive, the huge, gas-hogging muscle cars become less attractive and the small, gas-efficient, modest cars become more attractive. Figure 19–3 shows demand and supply curves in the markets for two types of automobiles. The market for gas hogs is on the left; the market for the smaller, more efficient cars is on the right.

Even though the abrupt jump in the fuel supply curve did not affect consumers' dispositions about buying fuel, it did change their demands for automobiles. Prior to the rise in gasoline prices, 40,000 large cars were sold each year at an average price of $5,500 per car (curve D in the left-hand graph) and 35,000 small cars were sold at the lower price of $4,000

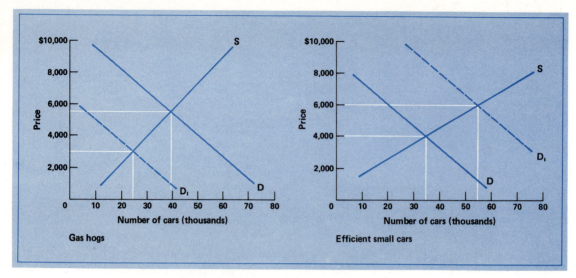

Figure 19-3 Changing Demands for Two Classes of Cars

per car (curve D in the right-hand graph). The rise in gasoline prices, though, changed buyers' dispositions. If gasoline is very expensive, the larger car is less desirable, so demand falls to demand curve D_1. This shift does not affect supply. Auto manufacturers still have the same disposition about how many cars should be placed on the market at each price, and they have the same technical capacity as before the change in demand. The change in demand does, however, lead to a lower equilibrium price/quantity relationship. Now, even at the considerably lower price of $3,000 each, only 25,000 large automobiles are sold.

Things are different in the market for small cars. Since the cars use so little gasoline, drivers want to purchase them and are willing to pay high prices for them. In the short run, manufacturer's dispositions do not change, so there is no change in supply. A new equilibrium price appears when the demand curve D_1 intersects the existing supply curve. The new price is $6,000; the new quantity, 55,000 cars.

Shifts in the *supply* of one commodity—crude petroleum—are thus transmitted through the market in such a way as to alter the *demand* for another—automobiles. As time passes, and if gasoline prices remain high, the firms that produce gasoline may respond by expanding output in hopes of capturing high profits. At the same time, firms that produce large automobiles may be expected to slow their assembly lines, or close them entirely, as Chrysler did with its luxurious Imperial line of cars in the spring of 1975. Manufacturers of Pintos and Vegas and Pacers may expand their activities in response to sharp increases in demand, and importers of some of the highly efficient foreign models may expand, too. So it is, with changes in supply and demand ricocheting through the system: a change in one price sets off a chain reaction that moves from product to product, price to price, and household to household. The market always moves toward equilibrium, but in fact there may be sufficient forces for change to prevent that resting place from ever being reached.

The Cobweb

The preceding section describes a straightforward movement of a market toward equilibrium. In the dynamic and complicated world of long production periods, shortages of materials, labor disputes, crop failures, technological changes, and equipment breakdowns, getting price/quantity relationships to move toward equilibrium is not always so direct. The production of hogs, and the "hog cycle," provide an example. Data kept by the U.S. Department of Agriculture for more than a century show that, on the average, the price of hogs rises for two years, falls for two years, then rises again in a remarkably stable pattern. Such a pattern means that hog producers are reading market signals. They observe high prices and respond by raising more hogs for the market. This increased number of hogs can be sold only at reduced prices. As prices drop, the lowered incentive to raise hogs causes cutbacks in production. But hog production cannot be turned off in the same way an automobile assembly line can be stopped. It takes many months to raise baby pigs to salable size and cut breeding herds in number. During these months of contraction, price

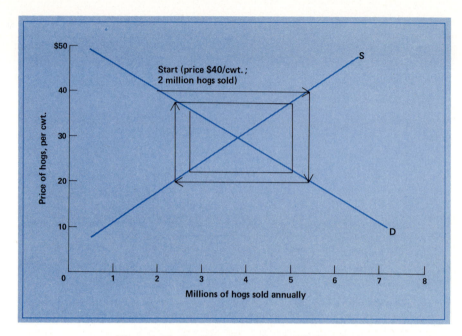

Figure 19-4   The Hog Cycle Cobweb

gradually rises again, eventually signaling more resources to enter this unstable industry.

In graphic terms (Figure 19-4) the hog cycle makes a beautiful "cobweb." At the starting price of $40.00 per hundredweight, supply far outstrips demand, so price must fall if the market is to come into equilibrium. In order to sell the quantity made available by suppliers, the price tumbles to $20.00 per hundredweight. With this price as a signal, producers cut supplies from 5.4 million head to 2.4 million head. Cutting supplies takes two years. During those two years, price is driven up again to $37.50 per hundredweight, calling on suppliers to supply more but setting in motion still another cycle from boom to bust.

In a market like the hog market, the equilibrium price may never be reached. Price continues to fluctuate from levels above equilibrium to levels below equilibrium, never settling—as the rule book says it should—on that one price indicated by the intersection of the supply curve and the demand curve. Market forces—many of them automatic—are at work in the hog market, but the reaction to them is exaggerated because production periods are long and adjustment is slow. Plans made on the basis of today's prices have two effects: first, they drive the price toward equilibrium, second, they set in motion plans (regarding the breeding herd) that ultimately *prevent* future equilibrium in the market for hogs.

A Final Comment

In 1969, Joan Robinson, one of the foremost economists of the twentieth century, wrote that she was disappointed in microeconomists for their inability to accurately estimate the location or slope of the demand curve or the supply curve for many important commodities. She argued that since such curves had not been isolated, a major tool of microeconomic analysis and policy could not be fully utilized. The law of demand, the law of supply, and the equilibrium price were concepts devoid of empirical content. They can be discussed in terms of direction of change, but the magnitude of change is not known. Robinson aptly described the curves as "smudges" rather than well-defined lines like those in the diagrams of this and the two preceding chapters. Far from discrediting microeconomics, this expression of doubt should encourage the next generation of economists to work even harder to put empirical content into the basic tools of micro analysis.

Summary

1. The market is an important institution used in making decisions regarding what should be produced, how it should be produced, and for whom it should be produced. The market depends on individuals being left alone to make independent decisions.
2. Supply curves and demand curves for a commodity can be examined together to ascertain an equilibrium market price, the price satisfying both buyers and sellers.
3. If price deviates from equilibrium, surpluses or deficits occur and set in motion a series of actions that tend to bring the market back into equilibrium.
4. Shifts in supply and demand continually force markets out of equilibrium, but when the market is working well, a deviation from equilibrium will be followed by events that lead back toward equilibrium.
5. Disequilibrium in one market is often transmitted to other markets.
6. In some cases even a correct response to market signals will not yield an equilibrium price.

Exercises

1. Explain these important terms and concepts:
   - equilibrium (in microeconomics)
   - law of supply and demand
   - surplus
   - cobweb market
   - shortage
   - clearing the market
   - self-correcting market
2. Draw a hypothetical demand-supply-equilibrium price diagram for beef. Make both curves somewhat responsive to price changes. How would

each of the following affect the equilibrium price and equilibrium quantity? A shift in supply? A shift in demand? Both?
    a A severe blizzard kills many beef animals in the Plains States.
    b The price of crude oil imported from Venezuela drops from $11 per barrel to $7 per barrel.
    c In an austerity move, the President rules that no beef can be eaten on Mondays or Thursdays.
    d A huge grain deal sends much domestic feed grain to other nations.
    e Canada raises the price of natural gas coming into the Lake States.
3 How might decisions about crude-oil prices affect the decisions of tire makers in Akron, Ohio?
4 From 1933 until very recently, the U.S. Government placed a floor on prices of several agricultural commodities. This price floor was intended to increase the income of farmers and, when coupled with restrictions on acreage planted, to reduce the production of crops that were in surplus. Farmers responded by reducing acreage and applying more fertilizer, water, and other nonland inputs to the land that remained in production. The result: still higher output being sold at supported prices. Some observers said that this government action violated the law of supply and demand. Others said it proved the law was working. Who was right? (Hint: Draw a diagram including supply curves and demand curves *and* the designated price of about $2.00 per unit sold.)

A Contemporary Problem

Office Space on Manhattan Island[1]

When Robert Tishman, president of Tishman Realty and Construction, announced last December [1974] that his company was taking an extraordinary pretax loss of $51 million, he set off shock waves in the real estate industry far greater than even that substantial figure would imply. The slashing move by New York's foremost developer meant that the bills were falling due for the colossal office-building binge that has transformed the skyline of Manhattan over the past several years. The vacancy rate in Manhattan is now up to 18 percent, the highest since 1939.

Manhattan now has too much empty office space. To the nearly 150 million square feet already standing in 1965, builders have added almost 80 million square feet, most of it since 1970. More than 30 million feet—or one square mile—is excess space, built at a cost of about $2 billion.

All of that investment is not a dead loss, to be sure, since many tenants have moved from old buildings to new ones. But when viewed in a broader context, such moves simply spread the loss around. The basic problem, surplus space, is not going to disappear for ten years or more, even if New

---

[1] Excerpted from Eleanore Carruth, "The Skyscraping Losses in Manhattan Office Buildings," *Fortune,* February 1975, pp. 78–166.

York's office jobs start growing strongly again—and the prospects for that are dim.

[The current problem is not a new phenomenon for Manhattan Island.] Following the overbuilding that began in the late 1920s and ended with the Depression bust, the New York financial community set up in effect a tight "production control," which for nearly forty years prevented a repetition of the fiasco. Developers traditionally borrowed from the banks to finance projects. But traditionally the developer could not get a full mortgage commitment from institutions without pretty firm leases in hand from solid, reliable tenants for about 75 percent of the planned space—and he couldn't get all the bank money needed to erect a building without such a mortgage commitment.

Over the years, however, this control weakened, and in the late 1960s it all but collapsed. Because of an extraordinary boom in white-collar employment from 1965 to 1969, both interim and permanent lenders thought the demand for new space was a sure thing, even without tenants on the dotted line. They began competing furiously for the right to finance new building. The result of this blithe approach was that flood of nearly 80 million square feet of space, 55 million of which reached the market after white-collar employment peaked in 1969.

Competition [for tenants] is now interacting everywhere—new versus old space, landlord versus sublessor. The key, says John Dowling, executive vice president of Cushman & Wakefield, the biggest rental agents in town, is this: "Rates on sublease space will continue to go down, and as they do, it will be a significant pressure on landlords of new buildings. As the squeeze comes, something has got to happen."

"Today, the rental market is a horror," says Harry Helmsley. "It's worst in job-depressed downtown, where leasing is minimal and rents remain around $7 per square foot, compared to $9 in 1969. Some buildings take what they can get," says Richard Seeler, executive vice president of Cross & Brown.

All strategies are based on the belief that if they can keep their buildings going, rental rates will turn up again. But an examination of supply-and-demand trends does not reveal much reason for even that bleak kind of optimism. To be sure, the developers no longer have to contend with a flood of new construction. But for the last twenty years, new construction has never fallen below 2,200,000 square feet annually.

As for demand, developers can count on a little lift from a continuing trend of corporations to allot more space per employee. A number of studies, however, indicate that this trend is slowing and will add perhaps only half a percent per year to demand in the future. So, if white-collar employment does not pick up, new supply and demand might just about balance out, and the vacancy rate would stay at that high 18 percent.

But it will take a great increase in jobs to put the industry back on a sound footing. If the growth in white-collar employment gets back to the average increase since 1959—1.5 percent a year—all the surplus space would be absorbed in a decade. Vacancies in 1985 would then be below a normal 4 percent, and the market would be strong again. But that seems too much to expect in the light of the city's economic outlook and employment trends over the past five years.

Analysis. With 18 percent of all office space currently unoccupied and the prospect that it will remain unoccupied for several years, it is clear that the market for office space in Manhattan is out of equilibrium. The disequilibrium is the result of changes on both the supply and the demand side of the market. Although it is hard to analyze rents paid by firms occupying the space, there is some evidence that rents have started to drop—the correct move if disequilibrium is to be removed. What led the market into disequilibrium? Identify factors affecting change on both the demand and supply side of the market. Will future changes eliminate the glut of office space in the United States' largest "office city"?

20 Competition

The United States possesses an amazing array of productive capital—from factories, dams, office buildings, and stores to nuts and bolts. This capital is organized and used in a variety of combinations with labor and natural resources to produce the economy's vast output of goods and services. In automobile production, for example, enormous amounts of labor, materials, and machines must be coordinated so that the bumper arrives at the right moment and the driver is on the spot the second the new car rolls off the assembly line ready for the storage lot. This intricate and gigantic manufacturing operation works best in very large firms. Hence, the American automobile industry consists of only four huge producers. Running at capacity, these four firms employ 800,000 workers and can produce as many as 7.5 million cars per year.

The agricultural industry—surely one of the most important in the economy—is also made up of firms that combine land, labor, and capital in order to produce their output. By contrast with the auto industry, however, there are almost 3 million individual farms buying seed, planting, and irrigating the crops. The agricultural industry, when operating near capacity, can harvest hundreds of different products that, taken together, have had an annual value in recent years of more than $90 billion.

How can two major and vital industries be organized so differently? One is dominated by four firms; the other includes 2.8 million. When one automobile firm ceases production, the remaining firms feel an immediate effect. Yet farms come and go, and no one notices. Why? The answer lies in the technologies appropriate to the two industries.

Automobiles are best produced in large, centralized, capital-intensive plants. These plants have high fixed costs, so as output expands, costs per automobile continue to drop rapidly over a very wide range in output. Economies of scale, then, dictate that there will be a few large firms, each capable of producing thousands of autos in a week. In agriculture, the need for large amounts of geographic space, the single production period each year, and the decision-making process that is part science, part art, and part tradition dictate that one family operate one farm without much help except during the planting and harvest seasons. A family and its land make a farm. Whether this is right or wrong is not at issue. What is at issue is how technology and capital structures affect the economic organization of a major industry. While firms in other industries have merged, substituted machines for labor, and adopted assembly line techniques, agriculture remains an industry made up mainly of small, competitive firms. In farming, the decision maker and capitalist is most often the laborer, too.

Hence, 2.8 million micro units grow this nation's food supply, and production is organized quite differently in agriculture than in the automobile industry. In the auto industry, the low point on the average cost curve may be found when hundreds of thousands of units are being produced each year. Agriculture is organized so that a single firm reaches the low point on its average total cost curve when only a few units are being produced.

Firms in some industries reach the low point on their average cost curves at low levels of output, while in other industries firms have costs that continue to decrease over a very wide range of output. This characteristic, along with the quantity of the product demanded by society, does much to explain the relationship between firm and industry. It helps explain why autos are produced by four firms, books are published by 6,500 firms, and corn is grown by 1,085,000 firms.

The economic organization of firms and industries is explored in this and the following three chapters. This chapter concentrates on industries like agriculture—industries that are made up of many small firms. The following chapter is devoted to monopoly, and Chapters 22 and 23 describe the in-between kinds of economic organization.

Firms and Industries

A distinction must be drawn between a *firm* and an *industry*. The firm is the basic building block in the production/distribution chain. It owns or purchases factors of production, and makes choices regarding how to use these factors. It reaps the benefits of correct choices and bears the burdens of incorrect ones. Because of this, a firm is usually assumed to order its activities so as to maximize profits.[1]

A firm is an individual producing unit that is responsible for its own behavior. The firm's choices are usually made with respect to some goal. In economics, the goal is assumed to be the maximization of profit or the minimization of loss.

A firm may be as small as a one-man upholstery shop or as large as General Motors. Regardless of size, what makes a firm is its capacity to make independent decisions about how much to produce, what to produce, how to produce it, and to whom to sell it. The firm is a primary actor in economic society. Through the circular flow, a firm purchases factors from households, sells products to households, and interacts with government in a number of ways.

Just as a university may have several campuses, a firm may have several plants. The du Pont Corporation is a firm with headquarters in Wilmington, Delaware, but there are du Pont plants all across the nation. A du Pont plant is part of the du Pont firm. Although the plant manager may make choices about whom to hire and whom to fire, he receives instructions from the main office on major production decisions.

An industry is the aggregation of all firms that produce similar products. The nation's 2.8 million farms comprise the agricultural industry, and its four auto makers combine to form the auto industry. The industry is of special interest, since its organization determines the way supply emerges, how supply interacts with demand, and how much control buyers or sellers have over the price of a product.

The Competitive Industry

Competition is a technical term in economics. Its technical meaning must not be confused with more popular uses of the word. Unfortunately, economists use the word in a *number* of ways that are different from the ways other people use it. Sometimes *competition* is used to refer to the intense rivalry that develops between banks or grocery chains or car dealers. Sometimes *competition,* or the *competitive system,* is used as shorthand to describe a decentralized market system like the U.S. economy. Certainly these are legitimate uses of the word but the economist's technical definition of competition is restricted to describing one form of

---

[1] This statement regarding profit maximization is still subject to the qualifications outlined in Chapter 3. It may be that the firm's objective is to do good (a hospital or a school can be a firm), but most often a firm's objective is to do well!

economic organization for an industry. Thus, an industry may be a competitive industry or a noncompetitive industry.

Individual firms in a *competitive industry* have cost structures that permit them to reach the low point on their average cost curves while still producing only an insignificant part of the industry's total output. An individual firm in a competitive industry may be very efficient, but by itself it still cannot come close to satisfying the market's demand for the product of that industry.

A competitive industry is characterized by many firms—so many that none can be large enough to have any impact on price—producing identical products. A single firm can leave a competitive industry and no one will notice. Another firm can join the industry and no one will notice. In competition, the single firm is always an extremely small part of the industry.

There are only a few competitive industries in the United States today. Surely the automobile industry is not competitive. If GM, Ford, or Chrysler

But in Some Parts of Agriculture ...

Agriculture is a huge industry made up of tiny firms. The statement that no one farmer can affect the price of his product is a bit too general. Some highly specialized crops, like spices, exotic fruits, and novelty foods, may be produced by only a few farms. These farms can and do influence product price as they move into and out of production and as they increase or decrease output. The major part of the industry, though, does consist of many firms that offer a homogeneous product, so that no one of them can have any noticeable influence on price.

were to leave the industry, the effect would be quite noticeable. The same is true of steel, soap, communications, medicines, tobacco, and scores of other industries. Two major industries, agriculture and commercial fishing, may qualify. Even the largest wheat farmer could discontinue production without a noticeable repercussion in the national wheat market. This is true even though the largest producers control thousands of acres of land and produce millions of bushels of wheat. By comparison to the total output of wheat, even the output of these giants is insignificant. Similarly, commercial fishing along the coasts and in the Gulf of Mexico is carried out mainly by small operators who own only a few fishing vessels. These owner-operators enter and leave the occupation and the output of the industry is not noticeably affected.

Why Are Industries Competitive?

Both agriculture and commercial fishing have peculiarities that make the competitive form of organization reasonable. In agriculture, land is required and no single farmer or farm corporation has been able to amass enough of it to control the industry. In fishing, the vessels that fish the coastal waters are small and have been largely unaffected by technological developments. This, coupled with the part-time nature of the job (one fishes only during certain seasons), has made the fishing industry one of many small producers. In both industries, each firm produces a *homogeneous product* (or undifferentiated product).

A homogeneous product is one for which the producer is not easily identifiable. Wheat is graded into several qualities, but a buyer cannot go to the warehouse and purchase wheat from the Smith farm in Gove County, Kansas. The buyer is as likely to get the same quality wheat grown on the Jones farm near Rapid City, South Dakota. Wheat is homogeneous.

Adding Precision

A perfectly competitive industry has these characteristics:

1. **Many buyers and sellers.** No one buyer or seller can have any appreciable influence on the price of its product.

2. **A homogeneous product.** All producers sell an undifferentiated product.

3. **Freedom of entry into the industry.** There are no unreasonable barriers to starting production.

4. **Freedom to exit from the industry.** Production can be stopped quickly, and the resources can be shifted to some other employment.

5. **Perfect information.** Anyone can find out about prices, technologies, credit, and other factors that affect the business.

6. **Perfect mobility of factors.** There are no restrictions on factors moving into or out of the industry. Any of the factors of production can easily be purchased or sold by any firm in the industry.

A moment's reflection indicates that 6 is merely an extension of 3 and 4, so an industry with perfect competition is an industry of many changing firms.

Price for the Industry

Because no single firm can influence price, the firms in a competitive industry behave in a peculiar way—they must each accept the price arrived at by thousands of sellers (suppliers) interacting with thousands of buyers (demanders). The process is described in Figure 20-1, where the numbers yield the following situations:

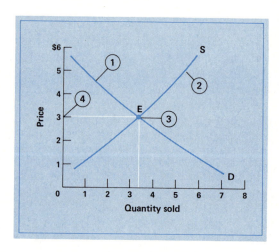

**Figure 20-1
Price Determination in a Competitive Industry**

1 The demand curve (D) is an aggregation of the individual demands expressed by all firms or households interested in and able to purchase the product. As price drops, demanders increase the quantity they purchase. When price rises, the quantity demanded falls.
2 The supply curve (S) results from aggregating the supply curves of individual firms producing the product.
3 The curves intersect, yielding the equilibrium price/quantity relationship.
4 This equilibrium price must be accepted by each firm in the industry. Each firm in a competitive industry can be referred to as a *price taker*.

Price, Cost, and Firm Supply

The price-taking firm (perhaps a wheat farm or the owner of a commercial fishing vessel) has information enabling it to make decisions about how much to produce. The rule says that the firm should extend production until marginal revenue is equal to marginal cost. Put another way, output should be expanded as long as the revenue added by the sale of the last unit of output (marginal revenue) exceeds the costs of producing that output (marginal cost).

Since each firm must accept the going price regardless of level of output, the market price is also the average price received by the firm and the marginal revenue received for the sale of each unit of output. When the market price is $2.50 per unit, the single firm in a competitive industry can expect to receive $2.50 for the first unit it sells, $2.50 for the 100th unit, and $2.50 for the 1,000th or 10,000th unit it places on the market. In a graph depicting the options open to a single competitive firm, the marginal revenue curve (MR) will be shown as a horizontal line intersecting the vertical axis at the market price. (See Figure 20–2.) This same curve

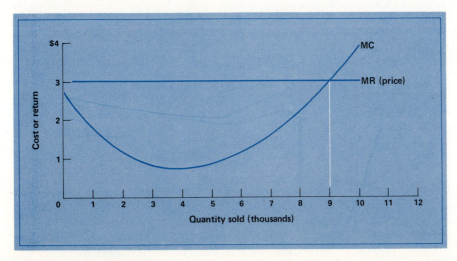

**Figure 20–2
Optimal Output for the Competitive Firm**

can be called the average revenue curve, the price line, or the demand curve facing the firm. The last designation applies because any amount produced by the firm will be absorbed (demanded) by the market at this same price.

Since the competitive firm is not exempt from the law of diminishing returns (Chapters 4 and 18), the short-run marginal cost curve (MC) for the firm takes its characteristic downward plunge, then rises over some considerable range. The point of intersection between MR and MC defines the firm's optimal level of output. In Figure 20–2, the market price of $3.00 per unit is accompanied by an optimum output of 9,000 units. At any lower level of output marginal revenue exceeds marginal cost, so the firm has incentive to expand output. At higher levels of output, marginal cost exceeds marginal revenue, causing the firm to lose money on the marginal units. These forces combine to make 9,000 units the optimal output when the price is $3.00.

Profits or Losses?

While the optimal level of output is immediately ascertainable as 9,000 units, a question remains: Is the firm earning profits or incurring losses at this level of output? This question cannot be answered without reference to the average cost of production. The marginal cost curve defines costs associated with one added unit of output; the average cost curve tells the cost of producing each and every unit at any given level of output. Three average cost curves (AC_1, AC_2, and AC_3) and three marginal cost curves (MC_1, MC_2, and MC_3) are shown in Figure 20–3.

Figure 20–3 Cost Curves for Three Firms in a Competitive Industry

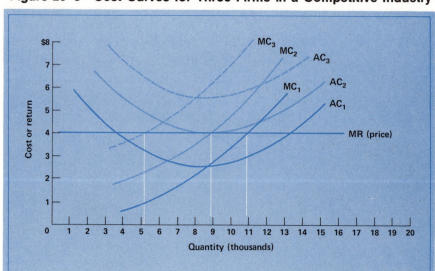

"First thing we'll do with this windfall is raise the ceiling."

In the diagram, AC_1 and MC_1 are assumed to show costs incurred by Firm number 1. AC_2 and MC_2 represent Firm 2, while AC_3 and MC_3 come from Firm 3. All three firms are involved in the same competitive industry, so they produce the same product and no one of them can influence its price. The positions of the cost curves show that Firm 1 can produce the product more efficiently than either Firm 2 or Firm 3. At any given level of output, the average cost of production for Firm 1 is below that of the other two firms. If Firm 1 wishes to maximize profits, it will follow the rule equating marginal cost with marginal revenue and produce 11,000 units of output when price is $4 per unit. At this level of output, Firm 1's average cost per unit is considerably below the price the firm receives when it sells its product. This firm thus earns *supernormal profits* of $11,000 ([price per unit − average cost per unit] × 11,000 units sold). (Remember: Included in the cost curve is the normal profit needed to keep factors of production in their present employment. Any profit greater than this is defined as supernormal.)

Supernormal profits are any profits in excess of normal profits. They are sometimes called "windfall gains."

Firm 2, following the same rule, equates marginal cost with marginal revenue and produces approximately 9,000 units of output. Since its average cost of production is just equal to the price it receives at this level of output, it earns only the normal profit needed to keep factors in this occu-

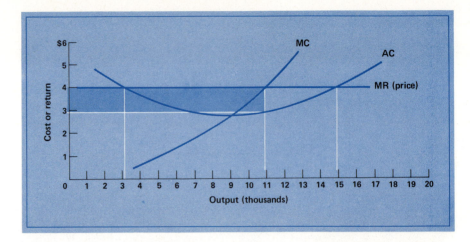

Figure 20-4 The Competitive Firm Earning Supernormal Profits

pation. Firm 2 breaks even. Using the $MC = MR$ rule, Firm 3 would elect to produce 5,300 units. At this level of output, however, Firm 3's average cost of production is well above the average revenue for each unit sold, so the firm loses money on each unit produced and sold. Moreover, Firm 3 cannot help itself. There is no level of output attainable by this firm that will permit its costs per unit to drop below revenue per unit. Firm 3 is committed to losses as long as it chooses to remain in production. Its best course of action is to stop production.

Entry of new firms. Added insight can be gained by separating the three firms. Figure 20-4 shows that Firm 1 is efficient and profitable. At any level of output between 3,250 units and 15,000 units, this firm's average cost (AC) per unit is below the price it can expect to receive for each unit sold. Thus, any output within this range yields profits for the firm. If one firm in a competitive industry is able to earn large profits over a considerable range in output, there is no reason why other firms cannot enter the industry and also earn large profits. A competitive industry like agriculture or commercial fishing is an "open" industry. There are so many firms that none has any chance of hiding its intentions or the results of its efforts. And when one firm's profits are as extensive as those indicated by the dark blue area in Figure 20-4, new entrepreneurs are likely to enter the field to capture some of this profit.

If many new firms enter a competitive industry, it will affect that industry's supply curve. More firms mean more total product at each price, and so the industry supply curve shifts to the right. As the supply curve shifts to the right, price falls, reducing the volume of supernormal profits and making the industry less inviting to new entrepreneurs. The process, described step by step below, is shown in Figure 20-5. The circled numbers in the figure refer to the steps outlined in the text.

1. The industry supply curve (S)—arising from the behavior of individual firms in the industry—intersects with the demand curve (D) to determine an equilibrium price (P). This price must be accepted by each firm in the industry.
2. If, at this price, some firms are earning more than normal profits (designated by the dark blue area in the firm diagram), other firms will be attracted to the industry in hope that they too can earn supernormal profits.
3. The entry of new firms causes an expansion of output, shifting the supply curve to the right. The new industry supply curve is shown by the dashed curve S_1.
4. This shift of the supply curve causes a reduction in the equilibrium price. The lowered price P_1 does not *eliminate* supernormal profits, but reduces them to the amount indicated by the darkest blue area. Since profits above normal continue to exist, still more firms are attracted to the industry and the supply curve shifts still further to the right.
5. Eventually, a new supply curve S_2 emerges and interacts with the demand curve to determine a market price (P_2) low enough to discourage additional firms from entering the industry. Supernormal profits are eliminated. The firm's marginal cost curve (MC) crosses the marginal revenue curve (or P_2) at exactly the low point on the average cost curve (AC). Marginal cost, average cost, and marginal revenue are all equal, and each firm earns only enough to keep its resources in their present employment. Profits are not high enough to attract resources away from other industries. Both firm and industry are in equilibrium.

Figure 20-5 Relationship Between the Competitive Firm and the Competitive Industry

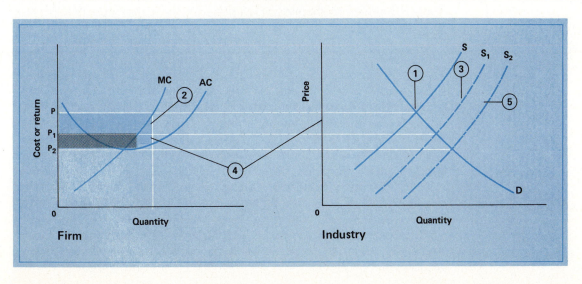

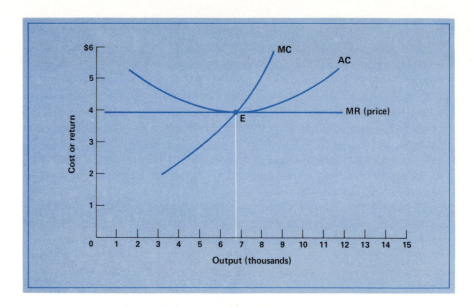

Figure 20-6 A Competitive Firm in Equilibrium

Competitive equilibrium. An industry whose firms have cost structures like those of Firm 2 in Figure 20-3 must be in equilibrium. This is shown once again in Figure 20-6. At $4 per unit, the firm equates marginal cost with marginal revenue when producing 6,800 units of output. This output allows the firm to earn just enough to cover average costs, including normal profits. No supernormal profits and no losses occur; the firm is in equilibrium with the industry. Equilibrium is attained where MC, AC, and MR all intersect. In a situation like this, existing firms will not be driven out of the industry, but neither will new resources be lured into it. The industry supply curve remains constant, as does the price that must be accepted by individual firms.

Firms leaving the industry. An industry represented by Firm 3 in Figure 20-3 is shown in Figure 20-7. In most respects this case is the opposite of Firm 1. The firm's entire average cost curve lies above the marginal revenue curve. No matter what level of output is chosen, the decision maker cannot cover costs. A competitive industry with many firms like this will be losing money and relinquishing resources to other industries. When air travel gradually replaced intercity train travel in the 1940s and 1950s, the railroads lost money on passenger service. Gradually, the downtown ticket offices, travel agents, and other travel-related facilities shifted from serving railways to serving airlines. The resources left the unprofitable industry.

The interesting relationship in this situation is the one existing between firm and industry. In Figure 20-7, the following steps in that relationship are shown.

1. At the outset, the industry supply curve S intersects the demand curve D, yielding the price (P) that must be taken by each firm in the industry.
2. At this price the firm loses money, since the average cost of production (from AC) is greater than average revenue earned from selling the product regardless of the firm's level of output.
3. Since this firm—and any others with similar cost structures—continually loses money, it is senseless for it to remain in the industry. When it and similar firms begin to drop out of the industry, the industry supply schedule begins shifting to the left. This shift to supply curve S_1 means that at any given price, there will be fewer firms and smaller amounts of the commodity reaching the market.
4. The shift to the left yields a new equilibrium price/quantity relationship for the industry (E_1). Because of increased scarcity, the new price (P_1) is higher. But it is still the price that must be accepted by individual firms.
5. If enough firms leave, the supply curve can shift far enough to cause a significant rise in price. The price rise shown is just sufficient to enable the firm to produce where $MC = MR$, and to cover average costs. It can remain in the industry and earn normal profits on its resources.

The outstanding feature of a competitive industry is the role of the firm as price taker. The firm must be a price taker, because no firm can become large enough to have any influence on price. Because firms in a competitive industry are small and many, it is hard for them to keep secrets. Profits are visible, and anyone with enough funds can buy into the industry. When losses are observed, resources transfer to other uses. A competitive industry is one of shifts and changes, comings and goings, as firms and their managers struggle to take advantage of opportunities for profits or to avoid losses.

Figure 20-7 A Firm Losing Money in a Competitive Industry

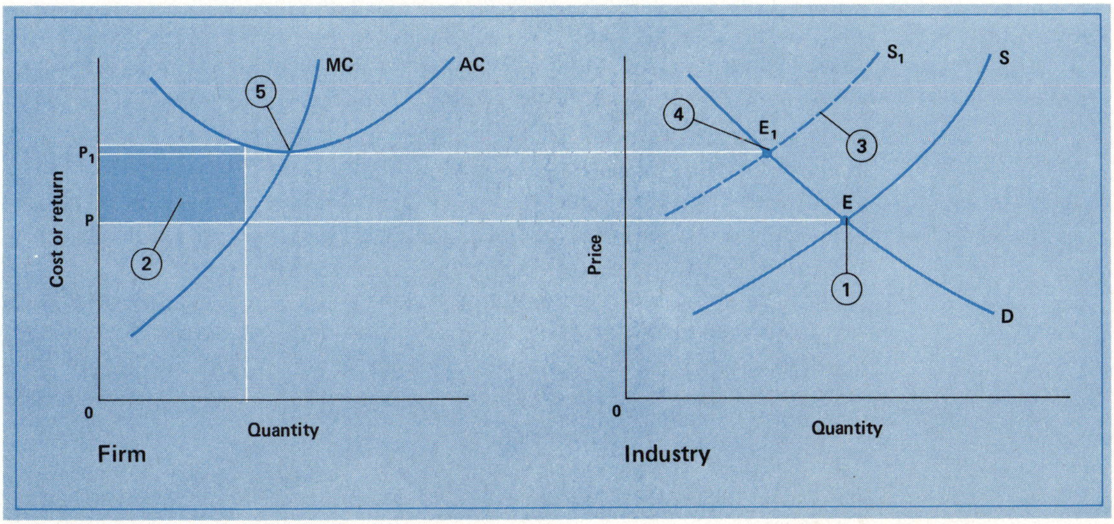

Competition: Norm or Model?

A distinction is often made between positive economics and normative economics. Positive economics is the study of what *is;* normative economics stresses what *ought to be.* Positive economics says that scores of businesses close their doors and go through bankruptcy each year; normative economics says that many firms *should* close their doors so the resources they command can be diverted to more profitable uses. When introduced to economics, many people come to regard the competitive form of industrial organization as a norm and describe it in terms of what should be. Many serious students of economics conscientiously believe that most industries should be organized in a competitive way. The reason is not hard to find. The competitive industry—if it behaves as described here—automatically allocates resources so that all earn their normal profits. In equilibrium, all resources earn just enough to keep them in their present employments and no more. There are no surpluses or losses; there are no excess profits to be usurped by entrepreneurs. If surpluses or losses appear, market mechanisms come into play to eliminate them. This automatic adjustment and lack of supernormal profits has some appeal, but this too-simple picture of industrial organization should scarcely become a pattern for all productive activity. An economy that requires all firms in an industry to produce a homogeneous product and to be so small so as not to be able to influence the market price would be an economy unable to take advantage of mass production techniques, modern technology, and economies of scale.

Rather than a *norm,* the competitive industry should be viewed as a simplified caricature of one small part of an economy. It should be a *model* designed to allow insight into the working of more complex systems. The competitive model shows in the simplest possible terms the workings of an industry that (1) produces a homogeneous product, (2) is made up of firms so small that not one can influence price, (3) is open, so that resources and information can pass freely among firms in the industry and to resource owners who could become part of it. Once this model is understood, its assumptions can be dropped one by one, and more complex systems can be analyzed. The competitive model is not an ideal, but it provides a starting place for study. It is an indispensible tool of microeconomic analysis.

Summary

1. Industries are organized in a variety of ways, depending on production techniques, the size of the market, and custom or tradition. In some industries (automobiles, household cleansers, and steel, for example), only a few firms produce nearly all of the nation's output. In other industries (like agriculture and commercial fishing), thousands of firms engage in the production of similar products.
2. A competitive industry is one in which many firms produce a homogeneous product. The number of firms is so large that no one of them can influence market prices and firms are free to enter and leave the industry at any time.

3 Because firms in competition cannot affect product price, they must accept the market price. If the market price is high, firms earn high profits and more resources are attracted to the industry. If the market price is low, firms lose money and resources find employment in other industries.
4 A firm in a competitive industry is in equilibrium when $MC = MR = AC$. The only level of output at which this can be true is that level designated by the low point on the average cost curve.
5 A competitive industry in equilibrium is one in which resources earn only their normal profits.

Exercises

1 Explain these important terms and concepts:
   firm   price taker
   industry   supernormal profit
   competitive industry competitive model
2 Most firms in the U.S. economy fall into one of the following categories: mining, manufacturing, agriculture, transportation, retail trade, wholesale trade, public utilities, and construction. Name some products in each of these industries that could possibly be produced in a competitive industry. (Remember: To be competitive, an industry must have many firms, a homogeneous product, freedom of entry and exit, and perfect information.)
3 Even though the number of farms has halved in the past quarter century, agriculture is still probably the economy's most competitive industry. Why? How does this relate to the cost structures of individual firms and to the size of the market for agriculture commodities?
4 Why does equilibrium in a competitive industry require $MC = MR = AC$? (Recall that the $MC = MR$ rule is universal. What, then, is peculiar about adding the requirement that MC and MR also equal AC? Note the role of normal profit.)
5 Explain how persistent losses in a competitive industry will lead to a shift in the location of the industry supply curve. Will the supply curve of each individual firm be affected by firms moving out of the industry?
6 What is the role of demand in a competitive industry? How does the aggregate demand schedule affect the individual firm? What is the shape of the demand curve facing the individual firm? Why?

A Contemporary Problem

Agriculture in a Mechanized Economy

Agriculture has always been an important part of the U.S. economy. This importance stems partly from a natural endowment of millions of acres of rich farmland and partly from a cultural heritage that admires the small, freeholding farmer. The agricultural industry is often described as a competitive one in which each farm is small in comparison to the total market for agricultural commodities. Firms and resources move into and out of agriculture with relative freedom, and with the exception of a few farms that produce specialty crops, the output of the industry is very nearly homogeneous. Grade A milk in Los Angeles is the same as Grade A milk in Rochester, New York; apples in Idaho are the same as apples in Georgia.

Farms have been declining in numbers for forty years. From 6.3 million farms in 1930, the number dropped consistently, especially during the 1950s and 1960s. By 1975, only 2.8 million farms remained. In spite of this, there seems to be little danger that the agricultural industry will be anything other than competitive for a long time. However, the *process* by which 3.5 million farms were liquidated is typical of what can happen in any competitive industry.

In 1930, the nation's 6.3 million farms averaged 151 acres. They were basically family units in which the farm family and its draft animals provided most of the labor and power. They broke ground, planted, tended crops, and sold the harvest. The cost structure of one corn-producing farm looked much the same as the cost structure of another. The situation was similar for other kinds of farms.

Beginning in the 1920s, mechanization, industrialization, and modernization began to catch up with agriculture. Tractors replaced horses and mules, new varieties of seed greatly increased crop yields, and chemical fertilizers replaced manure and "soil-building" crops. The new technologies shifted the supply curve to the right and simultaneously lowered the average cost curve of the more modern farms. Their increased supplies were sold at lower prices, but these prices were still sufficient to cover costs. Farmers who could not (or would not) follow suit were left facing lower prices. Unless they had been earning supernormal profits before, they were forced to abandon farming because their resources could not earn normal profits.

The continuing stream of agricultural technology has caused this pattern to persist for half a century. A new method appears, those who adopt it cause output to increase, and those who cannot adopt it leave the industry. The result has been (until very recently) increasingly inexpensive food for the U.S. consumer, a concentration of farmland in the hands of fewer people, and a great migration of farmers and farm workers to the cities.

Analysis. By definition, a firm in a competitive industry does not have market power; nor does it have a surplus of funds to use for inventing new ways to do things. Its revenues are exactly offset by its costs, and it responds to events imposed on it from outside. Agricultural firms have responded to many cost-reducing technologies. They have purchased more machinery, more chemicals, and more information. In doing so, they have expanded the output of agricultural commodities, and since the nation's collective stomach can hold only a certain amount, the price of agricultural products has had to fall. The falling prices have stranded less flexible and less innovative farmers and forced them to leave the farm. Society should ponder several questions. First, in an era of high unemployment, should farmers continue to be forced to quit the farm only to join the unemployment and welfare roles? Second, should the number of farms be allowed to decrease even more, creating the danger that some farmers might gain enough power to be able to control the output of food? Third, in a food-short world, should technological advance be spurred even more, so that more food will be available?

21

Monopoly

Beginning in 1840, thousands of families left the eastern and midwestern states to head west on the Oregon and Santa Fe Trails. Their motives were many. Some were searching for gold and silver, some wanted fertile land to farm, and others simply wanted to escape the turmoil of the rapidly industrializing East. The trip by either route was hard. For many, disease, Indian attack, and starvation lay between the Mississippi and their intended destinations.

One obstacle faced by the pioneers was the ferries and toll bridges controlled by some of their fellow migrants, who charged the wagon trains exorbitant fees to cross rivers or streams along the routes west. The tollkeepers were the only ones who provided the service. There was no other way to cross the water, so there was no way the wagon trains could avoid paying. Like the wicked troll in "The Three Billy Goats Gruff," the tollkeepers had physical and economic control over a needed service. They were monopolists.

The word *monopoly* derives from Greek words meaning "alone to sell." The technical meaning of the word in economics is not much different. Monopoly is a form of economic organization in which a single firm comprises the entire industry. More than this, the monopoly firm produces a commodity for which there are no close substitutes. The monopoly need not be concerned about the activities of other firms because there are no other firms!

Do Monopolies Exist? – Yes and No

In the previous chapter, it was admitted that a perfectly competitive industry is a rare thing. The same is true of monopolies. Although many industries are composed of only a few firms, it is hard to name an industry that includes only one firm. Moreover, those few industries made up of only one firm are most often regulated by some level of government, so they cannot charge exorbitant prices for their products. The truly free, unregulated monopoly is probably a construct confined to pages of economics textbooks. However, the hypothetical unregulated monopoly must be understood before the need for regulation can be discussed effectively. Hence, in this chapter, the monopoly and the monopolist are described as if they were actually prominent parts of the American economic scene.

This chapter is about monopolies. It deals with cost structures and revenues, the allocation of resources by monopoly firms, the effects of monopoly on income distribution and the advance of technology, and the discriminating monopolist. An appendix shows the cost structures of some special kinds of monopolies.

Cost and Revenue Structures

The monopoly—or monopolistic firm—faces the same rules of production that any firm must face. The monopoly has sets of fixed and variable cost curves like those elaborated in Chapter 18 (see Figure 21–1). In the monopoly firm, average fixed costs decline as expanding output spreads fixed costs over more units of product. Average variable costs drop as the firm becomes more efficient, but eventually rise as bottlenecks occur and the monopolist must bid higher and higher to attract needed factors from other firms. Average total costs are the vertical summation of fixed and variable costs. Over some range in output, the drop in fixed costs per unit is enough to pull average total costs down, but eventually a point is reached where—even though fixed costs per unit continue to drop—the rise in average variable costs is sufficient to cause average total costs to rise. In Figure 21–1, average total costs begin to rise at about 500 units of output.

What Makes a Monopoly?

If the cost structures of monopoly firms are similar to those experienced by competitive firms, what makes a monopoly? A monopoly firm is a single firm that is able to turn out enough of a product to satisfy market demand for it at prices sufficient to cover the costs of production. A firm attains monopoly status through any of three conditions.

Indivisible inputs. A firm can become a monopoly if its production process requires huge, expensive, and *indivisible inputs* that permit the firm's fixed costs to drop rapidly over a wide range of output.

An indivisible input is one that cannot be purchased in small units. A flood-control dam is an indivisible input. Either the whole dam or none at all is available. For a gas company, the distribution system (gas lines to every house) is an indivisible input. There is either the whole system or none at all. Labor, on the other hand, is divisible and can be purchased by the hour. Most classes of inputs are divisible and producing firms can choose to buy as much or as little of them as they need.

If market demand for the product is limited, it is senseless for more than one firm to incur the huge costs of installing indivisible capital equipment. Public utilities like the telephone system or the water works or the bus system are examples of this type of monopoly. The telephone company makes huge investments in switchboards, offices, and lines. These indivisible investments are required even if only a few telephones are connected to the company's lines. Once these fixed and indivisible facilities are installed, more phones can be added at very little cost. When an addition is made, average fixed cost drops but the marginal cost of added phones is near zero. Because of the technological advantages of using large indivisible equipment in a phone system (or sewer or bus company),

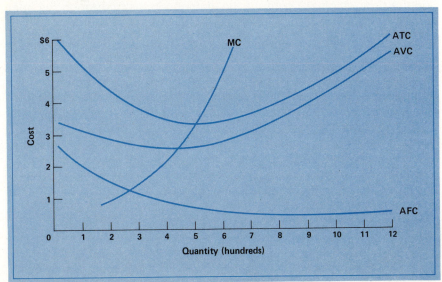

Figure 21-1 Cost Curves of a Monopolistic Firm

these public utility firms are almost always allowed to exist as *natural monopolies,* but they are closely regulated so they cannot arbitrarily charge outrageous prices or restrict use to only those few who can afford the service.

A natural monopoly is a firm put in a monopoly position because huge investments are required in order to start production. More than this, once the huge investments are in place, many customers can be served using the single plant. In these industries, average costs decrease over a wide range in output.

Patent ownership. A firm might also be a monopolist because it possesses a patent on a unique piece of equipment. A patent insures that for a time, at least, no other firm can gain access to the production process. For many years, IBM held unique patents on various kinds of calculating machines and bookkeeping equipment. These patents allowed IBM to monopolize the electronic accounting field. Similarly, the United Shoe Machinery Company held patents on machines used in the nation's shoe repair shops. The company became a monopoly in shoe repair machinery.[1]

Control over resources. A third way for monopoly to develop is for a company to have complete control over access to a specialized input or resource. Until the early 1940s, the Aluminum Company of America (ALCOA) was a monopoly firm in aluminum production because it had exclusive access to all domestic supplies of bauxite, the ore from which aluminum is derived. ALCOA was eventually ordered to relinquish its control over the aluminum industry, and other firms (notably Kaiser and Reynolds) began to produce aluminum and aluminum products. A contemporary example of monopoly by resource control is DeBeers, Ltd., of South Africa, which still controls the diamond industry through resource control.

The Monopolist as Price Searcher

Regardless of the reason for the existence of a monopoly, the unregulated monopolist is assumed to behave so that profits are maximized. In pursuing this goal, the monopolist follows the general rule of equating marginal cost and marginal revenue. Adhering to this rule is not such an easy task for the monopolist, since the marginal revenue curve is no longer the constant "price" that emerges automatically in a competitive industry. *The firm is the industry,* so each time the monopoly firm tampers with the quantity placed on the market, it also changes the price obtained in the market.

---

[1] Eventually, the U.S. Supreme Court intervened against the United Shoe Machinery Company and the privilege of manufacturing equipment of this kind was awarded to other companies, too.

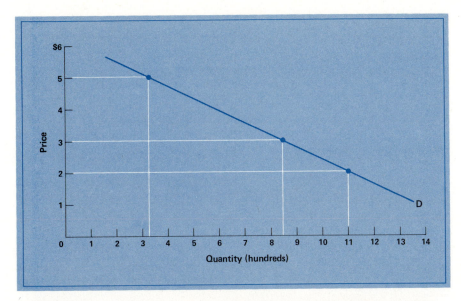

Figure 21-2 Demand, Price, and Quantity Relationships for the Monopolist

The monopolist faces the familiar downward-sloping demand curve. Since the single firm is the industry, however, each time the quantity placed on the market changes, another point on the demand curve becomes appropriate and the monopolist must charge a different price. A monopolist facing the demand curve in Figure 21-2 could place 315 units on the market at $5 per unit. If 840 units were placed on the market, price would have to be lowered to $3 to sell all the units; to sell 1,100 units, the price per unit could not exceed $2. Unlike the price-taking firm in a competitive industry, the unregulated monopolist can manipulate price by altering the quantity placed on the market. The monopolist searches for the price that will realize the most profits for the firm.

Being a price searcher does not invalidate the decision rule. To maximize profits, marginal revenue and marginal cost must still be equated. Production should expand to the point where the cost of the added unit is exactly equal to the revenue collected from its sale.

A complication arises for the monopolist because the demand curve and the marginal revenue curve are not the same. In order to sell more, the monopolist must drop the price on every unit sold, not just on the expanded output now placed on the market. This important feature of monopoly results in a marginal revenue curve that is lower than the price (average revenue) per unit. Figure 21-3 provides an explanation.

If a monopolist places one unit of product on the market, it is sold at $10 and the firm's total revenue is $10 (shown by the dashed lines in the figure). In order to sell the second unit, the price must fall to $9 *per unit.*

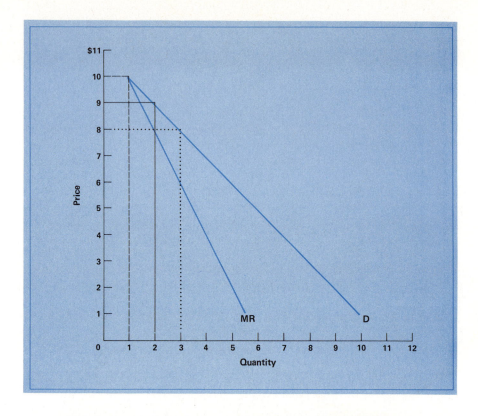

Figure 21-3   Calculation of the Marginal Revenue Curve

The new, lower price applies to all units placed on the market. When the second unit is marketed, total revenue thus becomes $18 (2 × $9) (outlined by the solid black lines). *While the price of the second unit is $9, its contribution to total revenue is only $8.*

Dropping price to $8 per unit in order to sell three units brings the same general result (shown by the dotted lines). At $8 per unit, total revenue rises from $18 to $24 (3 × $8). The third unit sells for $8 too, so the addition to total revenue is only $6 ($24 − $18). In each case, marginal revenue is lower than price. The general rule may be stated as follows: When a firm faces a downward-sloping demand curve and must lower price in order to increase sales, its marginal revenue curve is steeper than, and lies below, the demand curve.

Optimal Level of Output

Once marginal revenue and marginal cost curves are known, the optimal level of output for the monopolist can be determined (Figure 21-4). Marginal cost and marginal returns are equal at 300 units of output. At this level of output, marginal cost of production is $3.20 per unit and average cost of production is approximately $3.75 per unit. These costs—marginal cost and average cost—are set by the firm's technological makeup, its business practices, and the prices that it must pay for inputs. The price charged for the product is whatever the monopolist wishes, but it would be foolish to charge any price lower than that defined by the demand curve. In Figure 21–4, the maximum price at which 300 units can be sold is $5.50. Profits are maximized when 300 units are produced and sold at $5.50.

The difference between price and average cost per unit is profit accruing to the monopolist. (See the shaded area in the figure.) Since normal profits are included in the average cost curve, all monopoly profit is a supernormal profit. If the firm were competitive, the existence of supernormal profits would attract more resources and more entrepreneurs into the industry. In the monopolistic industry, technological conditions, patent protection, or control of resources prevent other firms from entering, so all supernormal profits remain for the monopolist. These supernormal profits have been the source of much controversy about monopoly and monopolists.

Figure 21–4 Optimal Output for the Monopoly

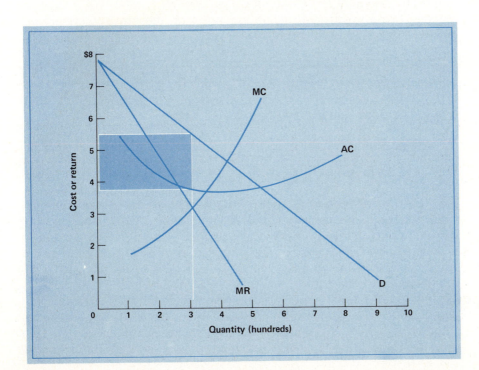

Controversies About Monopoly

The monopoly firm/industry follows the same rules as the competitive industry in determining the optimal level of output. Why, then, have people in the United States held the monopolist in such disfavor and passed so many laws to regulate or eliminate monopolies? At first glance, the monopoly firm is behaving correctly. It equates marginal cost with marginal revenue, thus insuring that neither too little nor too much is produced. It sets its price using consumers' demands as its guide. Why all the fuss? There are three main reasons—one related to the allocation of resources, one to the distribution of income, and one to the advance of technology.

Allocation of Resources

Economists as early as Adam Smith raised strenuous objections to monopolies because monopolies had the power to control markets. Even if this power is not overtly used, the monopolist's behavior is still considered objectionable because the monopolist does not produce at the low point on the average cost curve. In a competitive industry, the rivalry of the many firms makes them serve as regulators for each other. High profits attract resources and increase output, while low profits cause output to decrease and resources to move into other activities. All adjustments lead toward the industry being in equilibrium, with $MC = MR = AC$ and production being maintained at the low point on the firm's average cost curve. Since costs are just offset by revenues, production is efficient.

The monopolist follows the same rule of equating MC and MR, but since MR is below the demand curve, production is stopped short of the point where MC, MR, and AC are all equal. The point is made in Figure 21–5, where a *constant-cost industry* is shown in equilibrium under both competition and monopoly.

A constant-cost industry is an industry that produces at the same average cost per unit of output over a very wide range of output. If the 100th unit costs $25.00 to produce, so do the 1,000th and the 10,000th.

If the industry shown in Figure 21–5 were competitive, thousands of small firms would contribute to its output. Each firm would accept $4.25 per unit as its marginal revenue, and industry output would expand to 4,000 units. Marginal cost would equal price, and each unit placed on the market would bring enough revenue to pay for the resources used in its production.

If the same industry were in the hands of a monopolist, the single firm could adjust output and thus manipulate price. The single firm would respond by equating its (constant) marginal cost to marginal revenue, so it would produce 2,000 units of output each to be sold at approximately

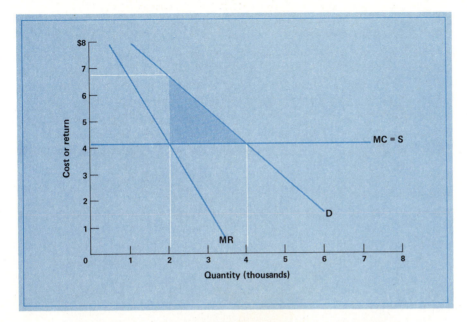

Figure 21-5 Comparing Monopoly and Competition in a Special Case

$6.80 (read from the demand curve). The monopolist earns supernormal profits, and the consuming public must pay more for each unit than the cost of production incurred by the firm.

The shaded triangle brings the problem into sharp relief. As output increased from 2,000 units to 4,000 units, consumers would be willing to pay more than the cost of producing each additional item. However, since additions to output (and subsequent reductions in price) cause the monopoly industry's marginal revenue to fall below its marginal cost, the monopolist refuses to produce these units. From the public's view, therefore, the monopoly is inefficient in the way in which it allocates resources.

The Distribution of Income

A monopolist, like any producer, must enter the circular flow to purchase factors of production. In this case, factors valued at (purchased for) $1,000 are transformed into products that eventually sell for more than $1,000. The surplus over the factor price is retained by the monopolist as a supernormal profit. The failure to return all factor earnings to factor owners is a forceful antimonopoly argument. By retaining supernormal profits, the monopoly firm redistributes income from factor owners to itself.

The way income is distributed among residents of the United States has always been a controversial topic. Clearly, income distribution today is unsatisfactory, because it leaves many people poor and keeps very few wealthy. Just as clear, though, is the fact that there is no "correct" or "ideal" way to distribute income. (Income distribution is the main theme of Chapters 24 and 25.) Some people favor one distribution; others another. In general, most people agree that redistributing income from rich to poor would be an improvement. If this is a desirable goal, the existence of monopoly may run counter to it. Although data on corporate ownership are not complete, it is commonly believed that most corporations and companies enjoying some monopoly power are owned (or partially owned) by families in upper income brackets. If this is true, the tremendous profit-earning potential of these companies places even more money in the hands of the well-to-do. The extent of such a transfer is not known, but the *possibility* that it may be large has reinforced antimonopoly sentiment and contributed to relatively easy passage of antimonopoly legislation.

The Advance of Technology

The effects of monopoly on the development of new technology is a controversial argument. It sounds reasonable to say that monopolists can sit back, earn especially high profits, and enjoy their sheltered position without ever making technological changes or improving their production processes. There may be thousands of *local monopolies* throughout the United States that behave in just this fashion.

A local monopoly is a firm that enjoys an exclusive market in a restricted local area. The only bank in a rural county is a local monopoly, as is the only tavern at a desert crossroad. The "company store" of a Western lumber town or a Pennsylvania mining town is an extreme form of a local monopoly.

They continue to produce their special goods and services using antiquated equipment and costly processes. Surely, if some of these firms were not monopolies but were threatened by other firms producing the same or similar goods and services, they would be forced to modernize and use more efficient techniques.

On the broad scene, a different picture emerges. The monopoly—because of its great capacity to earn profits—can afford to spend large amounts of money on research and development that can improve the monopoly's service or perhaps benefit society in some other way. There is no better example of this than the case of the Bell Telephone Laboratories. The Bell Laboratories are among the most sophisticated and most productive in the world. They have been responsible for development of the transistor, the coaxial cable, and the laser beam, as well as thousands of more pedestrian items. Research and development activities of the Bell

It's a fantastic breakthrough . . . remarkable . . . if I could just find it. . . ."

Telephone Company have been supported largely by profits gleaned from the company's monopoly position in the communications industry. Similar but less dramatic testimonials can be given to the Du Pont and General Electric laboratories—also financed with money garnered from some monopolistic activities. A degree of monopoly power in the marketplace gives a firm the opportunity to undertake research and development activities.

Firms operating in a competitive industry cannot enjoy the luxury of major expenditures for research. Because they operate at profit levels barely sufficient to keep resources in the industry, nothing is left to use in conducting research. Consider agriculture. In the mid-1880s, when many industrial firms were beginning to conduct research using profits from their monopolistic, or near-monopolistic, activities, no one farmer was able to gather enough surplus funds to conduct any research. As a result, the comparative position of farmers began to decline. Farmers were having to pay more for the items they purchased but—because of the way the agricultural industry was organized—they were unable to retaliate. The federal government noted this, and in 1862 established the land-grant colleges to train students in "agricultural and mechanical arts." The activities of these institutions took an explicit turn toward research in 1887 with the passage of the Hatch Act and the establishment of agricultural experiment stations in the states. These stations conducted research on plant and animal breeding, production technology, and marketing practices. Their establishment was direct recognition that if research was to be conducted for the benefit of those in a competitive industry, funding for the research had to come from some source other than the industry itself.

In the end, the question of monopoly's effects on technological advance remains unsettled. It is certain that some monopolistic industries have used at least a portion of their profits to conduct research that has led only to higher profits. While it is useful to question each industry's use of research, it seems unwarranted to build a case against monopoly solely on the grounds that the monopolistic form of business organization inhibits progress or stymies the advance of technology.[2]

The Discriminating Monopolist

While the firm in a competitive industry is a price taker, the monopolist can charge any of a number of prices. The knowledgeable monopolist selects the price that will maximize profits and charges this price for each unit of output sold. In some instances, the good or service that a monopolist sells is unique, so that the seller can carry price-making behavior to extremes and charge what the market will bear for each individual unit of output. This behavior is depicted in Figure 21-6, where a "demand curve" is shown as a series of dots rather than as a continuous curve. The dots represent the price each successive unit can command in the marketplace. The pattern follows the law of diminishing marginal utility. If only one unit of good is placed on the market, that unit provides sufficient utility to make some person willing to pay $7 for it. The second unit provides somewhat less utility, so the highest bidder will pay only $6. The highest bid for the third unit is $5; for the fourth unit, $4.

If the usual practices of price setting are followed, the correct monopoly price may be $2 per unit and the profit-maximizing output, six units. Total revenue is $12 ($2 × 6). If, however, the monopolist can keep his customers from talking to each other and can produce a commodity that can easily be handled one unit at a time, he may be able to *discriminate* among buyers and charge the first buyer $7, the second $6, the third $5, etc., until all possible opportunities are exhausted. If this practice is followed, total revenue for six units of output will be $27 ($7 + 6 + 5 + 4 + 3 + 2)—considerably above the $12 earned through use of a single-price policy. These added earnings are shown by the portions of the vertical bars lying above the $2 price line in Figure 21-6.

A perfectly discriminating monopolist is one who is able to use a differential pricing system to extract from his customers the total value of all

---

[2] The question of distribution of the benefits is a legitimate one. Are those who provide the necessary profits to Bell, Du Pont, and GE also the ones who receive the benefits from the research activity? The answer seems to be sometimes Yes and sometimes No. When the research yields a transistor that is consumed in some form by nearly every household in the United States, those who pay for the research are also the beneficiaries. When research yields highly sophisticated and very specialized medical-care equipment, only a few may ever benefit from its use.

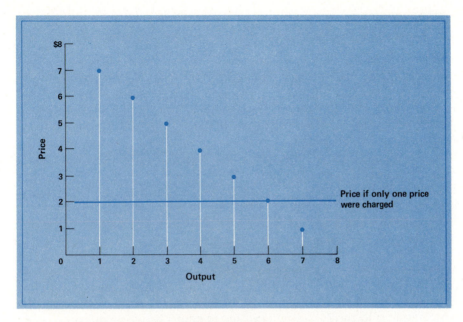

Figure 21-6 Prices Charged by the Perfectly Discriminating Monopolist

utility associated with each added unit of output. It is doubtful that there is actually a *perfectly* discriminating monopolist, but some price discrimination is present in each of the following practices:

1 A physician or dentist charging wealthy patients more than poor patients. (This is probably less prevalent now than in the past, when doctor-patient relationships were much more intimate and doctors knew more about the patients and their incomes.)

"I understand Dr. Sykes has made a major breakthrough. He raised his house-call fee to $30."

The Morality of Price Discrimination

While many economists have tried to establish economics as a discipline free of moral judgment, the question of morality still arises from time to time. Is it "moral" for a monopoly firm—because of its unique market position—to charge one person one price and another person another price for the same good or service? The answer is Yes if one believes that every buyer should always be asked to pay the full amount he is willing to pay for a good or service. If the demand curve shows one person willing to pay $50 and another person willing to pay $10, why shouldn't the seller make separate contracts with each, so that each pays the full amount he is willing to pay?

Price discrimination seems immoral—or at least highly objectionable—to those who feel that justice is best served when equal products have equal prices regardless of who the buyer may be. An airplane ticket from San Francisco to New York should cost $200 to anyone occupying a seat regardless of age, income, or urgency of the trip.

The moral question surrounding price discrimination goes even deeper. By charging one person more than another, the discriminating monopolist is effecting a transfer of income from one group of consumers to another. Should the monopolist have the power to dispense this kind of economic justice—justice at his own discretion? Most observers think not.

This question can be formalized by reference to Figure A, in which the price of a good is defined by the intersection of the supply and demand curves. This equilibrium price, P, may be charged all consumers of the good. If it is, a number of consumers are getting more than their money's worth, since they would have been willing to pay a higher price in order to secure the good. These are the consumers whose desires make up that portion of the demand curve lying above the horizontal price line. This excess willingness to pay is the darker area in Figure A. Although it cannot be effectively measured, this area is called *consumers' surplus*. Consumers' surplus is the difference between what one is required to pay and what one is willing to pay. For all consumers taken together, consumers' surplus is designated by the area above the price line (what one must pay) but below the demand curve (what one is willing to pay). The whole question of the morality of price discrimination centers on who should get this surplus. If price discrimination takes place, the monopolist gets at least part of it. If no discrimination exists, consumers enjoy the full amount.

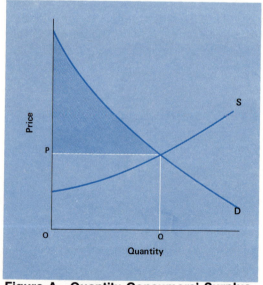

Figure A   Quantity Consumers' Surplus

2 Lower travel fares and theatre admission charges for children, even though a child occupies as much space as an adult.
3 Higher tuitions at state universities for out-of-state residents, even though the education offered is the same for all.

In each of these cases, the demand for the product can be divided into identifiable and nontransferrable portions, thus permitting some units of output to be sold at higher prices than others.

Antimonopoly Measures

This society, at least, seems to think that monopolies are objectionable. Since 1890 it has passed a continuous stream of antimonopoly legislation. Economists have objected to monopoly because it encourages firms to maximize profits at a level of output less than that which would be offered by a competitive industry. Legislators have objected because the monopolist has power—power to influence prices and power to keep other firms from entering certain types of economic activity. Regardless of whether the economist's or the legislator's frame of reference is used, the objection is the same: A monopolist is in a position to hamper the flow of factors into their best uses.

Possible Solutions

The problem of misallocating resources can be approached in either of two ways. One centers on expanding the monopolist's output, while the other centers on taking away the monopolist's supernormal profits. A monopolistic industry can be brought under government control and forced to expand output as shown in Figure 21-7. This expansion does two things: (1) It requires the monopolist to expand purchases of factors, thus offsetting the monopoly firm's tendency to use too few resources and produce too little. (2) It causes price to fall. The market will not absorb 9,500 units at the old price of $5.50. In order to sell the added 3,300 units, price must fall to $3.75. At this level of output, all costs of production—including a normal profit—are still being met. Indeed, this solution appears most desirable, since it forces the monopolist to produce at the low point on the firm's average cost curve—the point at which production would take place in a competitive industry. Most agencies responsible for regulating monopolies attempt to follow a scheme that forces the firm to serve all reasonable demands and charge a price close to that which would be charged by a competitive industry. The competitive price is preferred because it is high enough to allow the monopolist to cover all costs but not so high that it prevents all but the wealthy from purchasing the good or

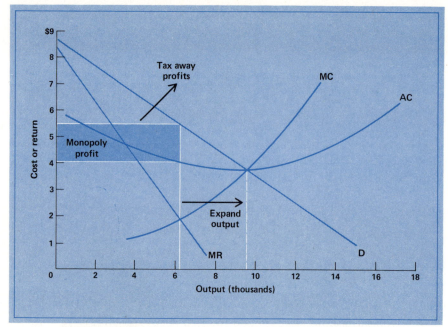

Figure 21-7 "Solutions" to the Monopoly Problem

service. Railroads and airlines, for example, are regulated by federal agencies. The agencies allow fares to be high enough to yield what is considered a "fair" return on the company's investment.

A second possible solution is designated in the upper portion of Figure 21-7. The monopolist is allowed to produce the profit-maximizing quantity (6,200 units) and charge the profit-maximizing price ($5.50), but once all the revenues are collected and all the expenses have been paid, the government taxes away any excess over normal profits earned by the firm. This method insures that the monopoly firm will still earn a return sufficient to keep its factors producing the same product, and also insures that the monopolist will not receive rewards due to its monopoly position. They will, instead, go into government coffers whence they can be drawn upon to meet other kinds of commitments. This approach is in fact unsatisfactory, because it allows the price to remain well above marginal cost and thus does nothing to relieve the problem of misallocated resources; it merely prevents a monopoly firm from accumulating the vast profits that come from its unique position. (Obviously, the cost and revenue curves in Figure 21-7 are arbitrarily placed to illustrate possible answers to some difficult problems. Examples of other cases are shown in the brief appendix to this chapter.)

Each of these solutions requires that someone—an economist? an accountant? a public official?—ascertain the nature of the average cost curve for the offending monopoly firm. This is not an easy task, so the solutions recommended by economists must often give way to more expedient solutions suggested by legislators.

Legislation

Politicians in the United States have been very unkind to monopolists. Beginning in the 1880s, the monopolistic power and price-setting tendencies of several railroads and of the Standard Oil Company began to concern legislators interested in the welfare of their constituents.

The railroads. In the case of the railroads, it was clear that many routes could profitably support only one railroad line. The rural areas of the Plains states and the West simply could not guarantee enough railroad business for there ever to be any semblance of competition among roads. The railroads themselves noticed this and developed intricate price discrimination schemes to exploit their respective monopoly positions. The public, however, demanded that railroads be forbidden to carry out such practices, and through the early 1880s, state legislatures attempted to pass laws regulating freight rates charged by railroads.

When state laws proved ineffective, the federal government was moved to establish a federal regulatory commission, which eventually became the powerful Interstate Commerce Commission (ICC). This commission forbade railroads to engage in discriminatory practices, required publication of rate structures, prohibited railroads from negotiating fares with clients, and declared that all rates should be "fair and just." Enforcement was left in the hands of the commission. Apparently early efforts at enforcement were too lax. Discriminatory pricing and price negotiation continued into the 1890s. Then, however, the economic recession and the resulting panic of 1893, coupled with rigid control by the ICC, forced 192 railroads into bankruptcy by mid-1894. By 1898, about one-third of the total mileage of track in the United States had gone through bankruptcy. The ICC may have gone too far in its zeal to relieve the pressures of monopoly power—the cure may have been worse than the disease.

The Standard Oil Company. The Standard Oil Company—source of the tremendous Rockefeller fortunes—was a problem of another sort. Standard Oil started in Ohio, but in order to expand it had to gain access to lands in other states, a practice strictly forbidden by Ohio state law. To circumvent this obstacle, John D. Rockefeller I established a group of "trustees" and turned the ownership of non-Ohio properties over to them. Eventually, all the Standard Oil properties—even those in Ohio—were given over to nine trustees and the original owners—the Rockefellers and the owners of 40 small oil companies—were given *trust certificates*.

A trust certificate is a document that certifies involvement with a large industrial complex. The trust certificate shows who controls the company rather than who owns the assets. Those who control the company issue a trust certificate to show that they will manage the assets in a particular fashion.

The nine trustees of the multi-state Rockefeller firm had tremendous power. They controlled the vast holdings of Standard Oil, which were widely recognized as among the most successful business ventures in the land. Because of this success, many other firms adopted the "trust" form of control. Scores of trusts appeared in many fields of industrial endeavor. This trend toward concentration of economic power again called for antimonopoly legislation. In 1890, the Sherman Antitrust Act was passed. The wording of the act itself is vague, but its intentions against "monopoly," "restraint of trade," "conspiracy," and "combination" are very clear. It legitimized the fight against monopoly and paved the way for more sophisticated legislation in later years.

The Natural Monopoly

Are monopolies all bad? Perhaps not. One class of monopolies seems to be inevitable. These are the firms that use huge fixed plants but very small quantities of variable inputs to provide services for large numbers of people. Public utilities like the phone system, the water system, the gas company, and city bus companies fit this description. Each of these services requires a large investment, but once it is made, many customers can be served at zero or nominal marginal cost. Since fixed costs make up such an important part of the total cost package in these industries, average cost per unit decreases over an extremely wide range. If many firms were encouraged to enter the business of providing phone services, domestic water, or sewage disposal, each individual firm would be forced to operate at a low level of output and average costs would be extremely high. In such cases it is wise to have only one firm produce the special class of good.[3]

Because goods produced by natural monopolies quite often have high and inelastic demands, those who control them are in a very powerful position. Given the chance, for example, the electric company could extract high monopoly profits from a captive clientele. In such cases the public has nearly always stepped in to regulate natural monopolies as a

---

[3] An additional, noneconomic consideration sometimes favors natural monopolies. If a dozen phone companies were permitted to operate in a city, the streets and alleys would become clogged with telephone poles and wires—scarcely an attraction to a society that seems increasingly bent on protecting beauty and keeping nature as uncluttered as possible.

means of protecting both buyers and sellers. The public grants a license to a single producer—a monopolist—to (1) protect it from the possibility of a second firm performing the same activity (and so having to duplicate very expensive forms of capital) and (2) protect the public from being charged exorbitant fees for the service.

Monopoly is a fascinating form of economic organization. It is a firm but also an industry. Unlike a firm in a competitive setting, the monopolistic firm can have some influence on price. It can have a conscious price policy, and it can be a price setter rather than a price taker. Monopoly is subject to severe criticism because the profit-maximizing monopolist restricts production to an amount lower than would be produced in a competitive industry. It is also objected to because the monopolist earns supernormal profits—returns not usually shared with the factors that contributed to the production of the product.

In addition, monopoly is criticized because it concentrates economic power and can either restrict the behavior of others or dictate terms of sales. Adverse opinion against monopolies has resulted in the imposition of restrictions on them. Only natural monopolies are allowed to function in the United States, and these are under close public supervision.

It is not likely that—with the exception of that business done by the natural monopolies—much business activity in the United States is conducted by monopolies. However, so long as businesses are separated in space so that at a moment in time a client must buy at the one store or go without, some element of monopoly power is present. To the extent that this power does exist, the simplified model of the monopoly firm has relevance.

Summary

1 The monopoly is a single-firm industry.
2 Like the entrepreneur in a competitive industry, the monopolist attempts to maximize profits by equating marginal cost with marginal revenue. Since the whole industry is wrapped into one firm, the monopolist faces a downward-sloping demand curve and a marginal revenue curve that lies below it.
3 Equating marginal cost with marginal revenue causes the monopolist to stop producing at some point less than the largest output that can be produced without loss.
4 This reduced level of output causes concern, since it leads to a misallocation of resources and concentration of economic power, characteristics that have led to public outcries against monopoly.
5 Some monopolies have to exist. It is senseless for a small town to be served by more than one water system, for example.
6 When natural monopolies exist, public control is most often used to protect the public from overpricing and to protect the monopoly from the threat of undue competition.

Exercises

1. Explain these important terms and concepts:
   - the monopoly firm/industry
   - indivisible inputs
   - natural monopoly
   - monopoly by patent or by resource control
   - price searcher
   - objections to monopoly
   - local monopoly
   - discriminating monopolist
   - consumers' surplus

2. A monopolist can select either the price he wants to charge or the quantity he wants to sell, but not both. Why is this statement true? (Hint: Refer to an imaginary demand curve for a product.)

3. Southwestern University is located in an extremely remote town whose permanent population is smaller than the university's enrollment. The students complain that merchants in the town exploit their monopolistic positions and charge very high prices for many ordinary goods and services. The merchants respond that the remoteness of the town increases the costs of supplies and inventories. Should the merchants charge higher prices? Explain why, ignoring the question of justice and morality.

4. Antimonopoly legislation has been directed only at the huge monopolies that have nationwide influence. Although the laws apply also to local monopolies—like the only service station on a 150-mile stretch of highway or the only bank in a rural county—these monopolies are never broken up by law enforcement officials. Why not? What economic problem is at work here?

A Contemporary Problem

Monopoly or Not in Hawaii

The State of Hawaii has two major inter-island airlines: Aloha, which flies orange and yellow Boeing 737s to several towns on the five major islands, and Hawaiian Air, which flies red and magenta DC-9s to nearly the same airports. The two airlines have fought for dominance for thirty years. Since fares between island cities are set by the Civil Aeronautics Board, the only way the two lines can compete is through frills and through convenient arrival and departure times.

In 1970, the two lines sought to merge and to become a monopoly in order to reduce the costs associated with competing through fancier service for very-short-haul patrons. The attempt failed, and each airline sued the other, claiming "bad faith." Aloha sued Hawaiian Air for $23 million, claiming that Hawaiian Air used illegal scheduling procedures to capture the market and reduce Aloha's profits. Hawaiian Air counter sued for $30 million, making exactly the same accusation about Aloha.

In April 1975, a jury awarded the decision to Aloha and asked Hawaiian Air to pay them $4.5 million. The payment has not been made, Hawaiian Air is claiming the verdict is "just not right," and Aloha is hailing the verdict as one that will "preserve competition."

During all these legal entanglements and awards, Aloha placed orders for two new Boeing 737s. The planes were needed to meet competition coming from Hawaiian Air's jet fleet. The talk of a merger and the prospect of a monopoly airline caused Aloha's officers to cancel the order and even to sacrifice $1.5 million in prepayments that had been made for the planes.

At present, the struggle continues. Two small airlines serve Hawaii's airports. Each earns profits and each struggles to outdo the other, but it is quite possible that each secretly wishes it could merge with the other and stop the interminable feuding.

If the merger had occurred, inter-island fares and changes in schedules would still be subject to CAB approval and control. The monopoly airline, though, would not need to lure passengers; they would either fly the one airline or not travel from one island to another. The costs of advertising, the "extras" at the terminals, the expensive jet aircraft, and the maintenance of service all hours of the day to all major islands could have been stopped. The single airline could have lowered costs, kept fares high, and earned monopoly profit. Apparently Aloha knew all this, because it first tried to "compete" by buying new planes, and then, when merger was very close, it decided that the old planes were satisfactory. The merger would have been worth at least the $1.5 million sacrifice of prepayments.

Appendix

Monopoly, Demand, Revenues, and Costs

Throughout Chapter 21, the monopoly firm was presumed to equate marginal cost with marginal revenue and in doing so, to earn supernormal profits. Earning supernormal profits, however, requires that the demand curve be quite high in relationship to average costs. In reality, this is often not the case. The following sequence shows how the profit position of a monopolist may change, depending on the relative locations of the cost and revenue (demand) curves. Only the essentials are shown in the figures.

Figure A shows the cost structure of a firm. It could be a dairy farm, a fishing vessel, or a monopoly firm; the cost curves would look the same. The curves in Figure A, however, are assumed to belong to a monopoly. The demand and marginal revenue curves reiterate what has been said in the chapter: The monopolist equates marginal cost with marginal revenue, charges the price allowed by the demand curve, and earns a supernormal profit, designated by the shaded area.

If the costs of production are somewhat higher, as shown in Figure B, the monopolist bent on maximizing profits will still equate marginal cost with marginal revenue (at five units of output) and will still charge the price permitted by the demand curve ($10 per unit). Now, however, because price and average revenue are equal, the monopolist earns only normal profits. This return is sufficient to keep resources in their present employment, but there is no incentive for other firms to enter the industry or for this one to leave.

Figure C shows a case common in many public goods. The average cost curve is above the demand curve. The profit-maximizing monopolist will again try to equate marginal cost and marginal revenue. When this is done—at five units of output—average costs are $10 per unit, but since the demand curve lies below the average cost curve, the monopoly firm incurs losses equal to the shaded area. Many city bus companies and mass transit companies operate under these kinds of circumstances. The huge fixed investments—buses, terminals, repair shops, and waiting benches—drive costs so high that they are above any revenues that the service can ever hope to recover through its fare boxes. The bus service may be a crucial and necessary service to the community, and clearly, "breaking up" the monopoly bus company will not help. Many firms cannot succeed where one fails. In most instances, monopolies providing a needed public service but unable to cover costs are paid a subsidy to make up their losses. Goods and services of this kind are called *merit wants*.

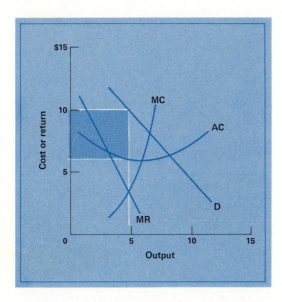

Figure A The Optimizing Monopolist—Case 1

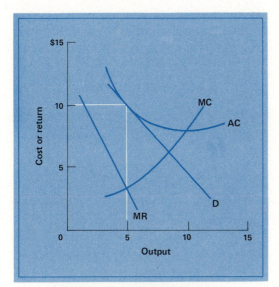

Figure B The Optimizing Monopolist—Case 2

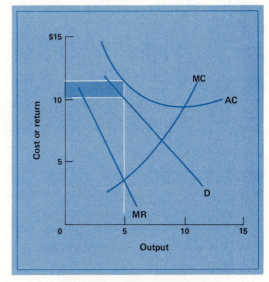

Figure C The Optimizing Monopolist—Case 3

A merit want is a good or service provided on the basis of its merit rather than because consumers reveal a willingness to pay for it. Education, pollution control, defense, flood protection, and smallpox vaccinations are among the many merit wants in the U.S. economy.

22 Monopolistic Competition

Chapters 20 and 21 presented models explaining the price and output decisions made by firms in competitive industries and firms in monopolistic industries. Those two models, however, do not explain the behavior of *all* firms that produce the nation's output. In fact, only a small fraction of all goods and services are produced by wholly competitive or wholly monopolistic firms.

Although accurate information is not available, a common estimate says that over 90 percent of all goods and services in the United States are produced in industries that have some of the characteristics of both monopoly and competition. The three major steel companies are like a competitive industry because they all produce rolled steel—a very homogeneous product. At the same time, they are like a monopoly because there are almost insurmountable barriers to entering the steel business. Small restaurants are like monopolies because each has its own location, its own menu, and its own decor. But the restaurant business resembles competition, too, since resources can move into and out of the industry with relative ease. Most output in the U.S. economy is produced by in-between firms like these.

Economists have struggled for decades to build models "explaining" the behavior of the many firms and industries that fall somewhere between competition and monopoly. These industries are so different from each other, however, that no single model will cover them all. It sometimes seems that each industry requires its own special model, but two major models are used to describe how firms in these industries make price and output decisions. One explains market situations in which a few firms dominate—so few that the behavior of one firm has a pronounced and noticeable effect on the behavior of other firms in the industry. This situation is called *oligopoly,* and is the subject of the next chapter. The other in-between form of market organization is *monopolistic competition.* In this form of organization there are so many firms that no one of them can influence the market. When a firm enters the market to sell its wares or when the manager of a firm retires and closes his store forever, the industry scarcely notices. This characteristic is similar to the many buyers/many sellers quality of competitive industries. At the same time, each firm in monopolistic competition sells a product that is unique and can be distinguished from the output of other firms in the industry. The firm has monopoly control of this uniqueness even though other firms in the industry produce similar products.

Monopolistic competition is a form of market organization in which many firms produce slightly differentiated products. No one firm dominates, and firms can enter or leave the industry without disrupting the plans of other firms.

This chapter is about monopolistic competition. It is divided into sections dealing with the nature of this form of market organization, the behavior of the individual firm, special characteristics of the industry, and the role of advertising.

The Nature of Monopolistic Competition

Since the definition of monopolistic competition is quite broad, it is hard to say exactly what proportion of all goods and services is produced by firms of this type. Data from 1972 suggest that the industries shown in Table 22-1 have all the characteristics needed to be described as monopolistically competitive. Each of these industries includes many separate firms. Even though the 50 largest firms in an industry may do a considerable part of its business, they do not dominate entirely.

Over 2,000 firms produce soft drinks. Many of them are so small that their existence goes virtually unnoticed by other firms in the industry, and they make independent decisions without fear of reprisal by other soft drink firms.

Because of their small size and low capital requirements, soft drink manufacturing firms (as well as short-order restaurants, travel agencies, barber shops, clothing manufacturers, and dozens of other kinds of retail

Table 22-1 Output Produced by the Largest Firms in Selected Industries

Industry	Number of firms	Percent of output produced by		
		4 largest	20 largest	50 largest
Soft drinks	2,271	14	32	44
Women's dresses	5,294	9	18	28
Plastic products	6,762	8	21	34
Commercial printing	8,160	4	15	24
Newspapers	7,416	17	43	60

Source: *Statistical Abstract of the United States*

or service establishments) can come and go with relative ease. Resources move into or out of the industry without great hindrance.

Each soft drink firm produces a unique product, even though there are many close substitutes. Only one firm produces Coca-Cola, but many others sell similar products to fill the demand for cola drinks. Each cola has its own characteristics. Some are sweeter than others; some more effervescent than others; some come in bottles; some come in cans. The subtle differences give each cola producer an element of monopoly control over the market for its product.

The monopoly-like quality means that each firm in the industry faces a demand curve that slopes downward. If one firm lowers its price, consumers of similar products will switch to the less expensive substitute. Coca-Cola and Pepsi-Cola are very much alike. If the price of one is lowered, many consumers will simply choose the less expensive of the two. Analogously, if one cola producer raises its price, it can expect to lose customers to the others. The products are so similar that consumer loyalty is not strong, and a small change in the price charged by one firm brings large adjustments in the quantity of the product that it sells.

In Figure 22-1, the demand for colas produced by a single firm is represented by the straight line *D*. If the firm charges 30 cents per quart, it will sell 8,000 quarts. If it raises the price to 40 cents per quart, buyers will shift to other colas.

At 40 cents per quart, sales drop to 2,300 quarts per week. The abrupt decrease in sales occurs because close substitutes are available and buyers do not have strong preferences among the several drinks that satisfy the same want. If the firm suddenly drops its price to 20 cents per quart, purchasers of close substitutes now find this cola more attractive. They change to take advantage of its lower prices, and sales increase to more than 13,000 quarts per week.

The demand curve slopes downward because products of individual firms in an industry are close but not perfect substitutes. They are *differentiated products*.

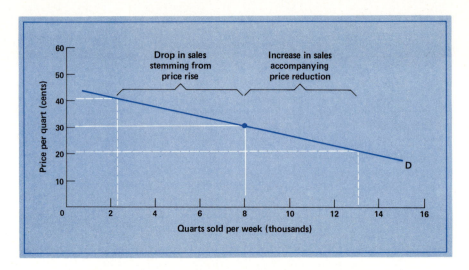

Figure 22-1 Demand Curve for a Cola Firm

Monopolistic Competition: Portland, Oregon, 1977

The 1977 telephone directory for Portland, Oregon and its immediate environs lists 559 gas stations. Of these, 311 (55.6 percent) are affiliated with one of five major national oil companies (ARCO, Chevron, Mobil, Shell, or Texaco) and 248 are "independent." Some independents sell gasoline without a brand name, while others operate using the name of local or regional chains.

Regardless of the name or brand of gas, the stations are all in one business—selling fuel to auto owners. The services they provide are very much alike. Any major brand station will have attendants who are quick to clean windows and check the level of oil in the engine and air in the tires. A trip to the "U-Serve" yields gasoline and very little else.

Most consumers agree that all gasoline is the same. The automobile engine cannot recognize the difference between Shell and Exxon. But one station may be closer to home or work; one may be cleaner or its pump attendants more courteous. Portland's 559 gas stations sell the same things, yet they are different—they are in a monopolistically competitive industry.

If one station raises its price a cent or two per gallon, its location, cleanliness, and courtesy may enable it to keep most of its customers. If it raises its price by three or four cents per gallon, even steady customers are sure to switch brands. Similarly, a significant drop in gasoline prices will attract customers even to a poorly located station. Each firm in the industry knows it is selling a product just like everyone else's, but each firm also knows that it is selling a product that has some distinguishing qualities. This is monopolistic competition.

A differentiated product is one that is recognizable as the product of one particular firm but for which many close substitutes are available. Firms in monopolistic competition go to great lengths to differentiate their products so that buyers will ask for their products by name. Differentiating is most often done through sales campaigns (advertising), distinctive packaging, or slight modification in form.

Most retail outlets (grocery stores, drug stores, department stores, and filling stations) sell only slightly differentiated products. The same is true among wholesale dealers, repairmen, and professionals like doctors or lawyers. Since people do most of their buying from sellers in these kinds of trades, most *final transactions* in the U.S. economy involve monopolistic competition.

A final transaction is the transaction that places a finished good in the hands of its final consumer. A homemaker buying the weekly groceries is consummating final transactions.

Equilibrium of Firm and Industry

How are resources allocated and production decisions made in an industry where many firms produce similar products? As in competition and monopoly, the firm in monopolistic competition enters the circular flow to purchase inputs. As output increases, the average cost of production falls at first, but eventually the firm becomes inefficient and the average cost rises. The average and marginal cost curves for such a firm retain the same general shape as in any other form of market organization. (Note: The firm need not be a manufacturing firm for this rule of production to apply. A retail store purchases inventories, hires clerks, and turns on the heat. If only a few customers are served, the cost per transaction is very high. As more customers use the store, the cost per transaction drops. The same clerks are doing more work. When the store is overflowing with customers, the cost per transaction again increases as breakage is high, shoplifting becomes a problem, and harried clerks make errors.)

The relationships between the cost curves and the demand curve of a firm in monopolistic competition are shown in Figure 22–2. In the first graph, the four curves (demand, marginal revenue, average cost, and marginal cost) represent a firm that should equate marginal cost and marginal revenue at approximately 3,700 units of output and sell this output at $30 per unit. (Remember, changing the form of market organization from competition or monopoly to monopolistic competition does not alter the decision rule. It is still advantageous for the firm to expand production until $MC = MR$, *but no further*. Stopping short of this level means that some profitable units are not being produced; expanding

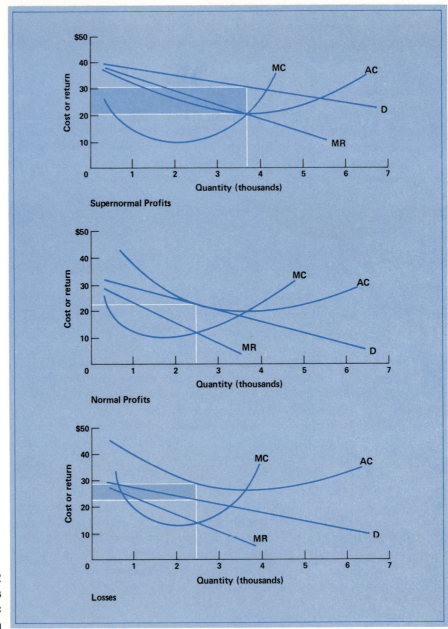

**Figure 22–2
Three Situations
in Monopolistic
Competition**

beyond this level means that some units will cost more than they return.) Because the demand curve lies well above the average cost curve at 3,700 units of output, the firm earns supernormal profits.

As in competition, supernormal profits are a signal for additional resources to enter the monopolistically competitive industry. There are generally no legal, resource control, or patent-protection barriers preventing new firms from entering. Therefore, if gasoline stations, for example, are very profitable, more people will build, furnish, and operate them. If grocery stores or barber shops are extremely profitable, more resources will be attracted to these lines of employment. When more filling stations, grocery stores, or barber shops appear, the limited number of buyers spread their purchases among the increased number of outlets, reducing the volume of business conducted by any one firm. When business volume drops, the demand curve facing a single firm shifts downward to the left, so that at any given price the firm does less business.

Eventually, enough new firms enter the industry to cause the individual firm's demand curve to shift until it is tangent to the average cost curve. This is shown in the second graph of Figure 22-2. The firm still follows the rule equating marginal cost with marginal revenue, but now produces only 2,500 units and sells them at $22 each. At this quantity, average cost is just equal to average revenue, so the firm no longer earns supernormal profits. The entry of new firms has eradicated all supernormal profits, and there is now no incentive for resources to move either into or out of the industry. The firm is in equilibrium, and the industry is using the correct volume of resources to produce the product.

If too many resources are attracted to a monopolistically competitive industry, industry sales will be spread so thin that the demand curve facing a single firm will drop below its average cost curve. When this occurs, there is no available level of output at which the firm can cover its costs. If it produces at all, it must lose money. This is a common experience and one that results in a very high mortality rate among small businesses. Some small-scale entrepreneurs, for instance, apparently feel that their own very good cooking is enough to assure success in the restaurant field. Many learn too late that one more restaurant in town spreads a limited amount of business just a bit too far, which insures that at least some of the eating establishments will fail. They will earn less than normal profits. When profits below normal profit levels are encountered, as shown in the third graph of Figure 22-2, resources leave the industry and seek employment in other industries.

A market-oriented economy allocates resources reasonably well in industries that are monopolistically competitive. When supernormal profits appear, land, labor, capital, and entrepreneurial skill rush to the industry that is doing well. Thus, in the 1960s, when universities and colleges were growing very rapidly, large numbers of students sought to become professors, supply firms and service firms located branch offices near campuses, and publishers mobilized to produce high-quality and innovative texts in all principal fields of academic pursuit. With the recession of the mid-1970s and the accompanying pressure on university budgets, fewer students are seeking careers in academe. Branch offices of typewriter companies and office supply houses are closing and many publishers have either cut back their staffs or gone out of the college textbook busi-

"Given the downward slope of our demand curve and the ease with which other firms can enter the industry, we can strengthen our profit position only by equating marginal cost and marginal revenue. Order more jelly beans."

ness. When too many resources enter industries in which many firms sell slightly differentiated products, supernormal profits can quickly turn to losses. Monopolistic competition—especially in retail and small-scale industrial pursuits—is characterized by rapid shifts in uses of resources and the composition of output. It responds to signals from the market.

Three Peculiarities

Industries that are part competitive and part monopolistic have three peculiarities that influence price, output, or the allocation of resources. One is the fact that equilibrium of the firm does not occur at the low point on the average cost curve. The second is the firm's never-ending struggle to differentiate its products from those of others in the industry. The third is the use of nonprice competition.

Equilibrium

In monopolistic competition, equilibrium is defined as that combination of price and output that yields normal profits—no more and no less. Any price/output combination lying along the average cost curve is consistent with this definition of equilibrium, since average cost curves include all production costs and normal profits. In monopolistic competition, equilibrium is attained when the demand curve is tangent to the average cost curve. There is only one *attainable* price/output combination that yields sufficient revenue to cover all costs, and that combination occurs where the D curve is tangent to the AC curve. *Since the demand curve slopes downward, the point of tangency must come where the average cost curve is also sloping downward.* With both curves sloping downward, the tangency must take place to the left of the low point on the average cost curve. The firm depicted in Figure 22-3 is in equilibrium (E) when output is 2,500 units and price is approximately $6.50 per unit. To reach the lowest possible cost per unit, output would have to expand to 5,000 units. Remember that the low point on the average cost curve represents the most efficient level of output that can be attained. At this level, the smallest possible commitment of resources is used to produce each unit of output. Many people argue that production of nearly everything should be at or near this lowest possible cost. One of the major advantages of a competitive industry is that it comes to equilibrium at the lowest possible level of average costs. One of the major complaints surrounding monopoly is that it does not.

Why doesn't the firm in Figure 22-3 expand its output? Notice the relationship between the demand curve (D) and the average cost curve (AC). If the firm expanded output, the price it could receive would drop faster than costs. If 5,000 units were placed on the market, these could be

Figure 22-3   Equilibrium in Monopolistic Competition

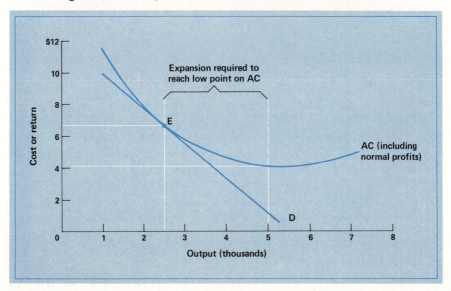

sold only if price dropped to $1 per unit. With costs at $4 per unit and price at $1 per unit, the producing firm would incur losses on each unit it sold. Since the firm would incur greater and greater losses as output approached 5,000 units, it refuses to expand beyond the normal-profits level of output—2,500 units. If the firm in Figure 22–3 reduced output below the equilibrium level of 2,500 units, it would find that average costs of production increased along AC, while the price it could charge increased along D. Costs would increase faster than returns, which would result in losses for the firm. Therefore, equilibrium at the point of tangency is a rigid condition. Any deviation from it causes the firm to lose money.

It seems reasonable to expect that society would want production carried out at the lowest possible average cost and would therefore oppose a situation where many firms operate at levels of output lower than those consistent with the low points on the average cost curves. Society, however, has not insisted on this point. There are no laws that even encourage firms in monopolistic competition to increase output and lower price. If such a fuss has been made over monopoly, why is the same fuss not made about monopolistic competition?

There are three fundamental reasons. The first is the number and diversity of firms. It is relatively easy to control the telephone company, because there is only one per town and there are only a few in each state. controlling retail outlets like grocery stores, drug stores, or Portland, Oregon's 559 service stations would be a formidable task. The cost of attempting to force firms to produce at the lowest possible cost per unit could easily be greater than the savings.

The second reason for not controlling monopolistic competition is that forcing the firms to operate at the low points on their average cost curves would also force them to earn less than normal profits. If the industries in monopolistic competition are at all responsive to signals received through the market, they will increase activity when profits are above normal and reduce activity when profits are below normal. This adjustment process will continue until all opportunities for supernormal profits or all chances for loss have been eliminated. Forcing the industry to act in any other way would inflict losses on the firms.

Finally, monopolistic competition remains free of control because this form of organization fosters variety through product differentiation. It is true that the week's groceries could be less expensive if there were only one brand of coffee, one brand of cornflakes, and one brand of canned peas, and if all these items were sold in only one store. But consumers in the United States value variety and are willing to pay for it. The prices of table lamps may be higher than necessary, but they are tolerated so that many firms, *none of which is operating at its lowest possible level of costs,* will continue to make lamps in many different sizes, colors, and styles. What at first appears to be a waste is actually a price willingly paid for the sake of a wide choice.

Product Differentiation

A downtown restaurant must somehow make its meals "different" in order to attract customers. Dress manufacturers continually modify necklines and hems in order to keep customers buying. Gas station operators provide little extra services to make their stations popular. The restauranteur, dress manufacturer, and gas station operator all try to differentiate their products so that their demand curves will have a greater slope.

Product differentiation brings a variety of problems. First there is the matter of increased costs. Changing dress patterns, styles, and trimmings requires constant changes in resource mixes and highly skilled labor. These constant changes raise the cost of the clothing.

Product differentiation leads to the desire for differentiated retail outlets. A town may have 30 shoe stores, varying from the serve-yourself discount sandal outlet to the very exclusive shop that handles only custom-made footwear. Each shoe shop could probably serve more customers than it does, but since there are so many, each will have relatively few patrons. These stores are underutilized and the underutilized facilities represent a cost to society. Finally, there is a subtle cost associated with having too much choice—confusion on the part of the buyer. Faced with dozens of styles, he or she may give up in dismay and not purchase any shoes at all.

The variety that monopolistic competition provides through product differentiation is a mixed blessing, and any argument based on it must end on a weak note. Some variety is surely good, but too much may be very wasteful, expensive, and confusing. How much is too much? No one can say for sure, but a large number of economists believe that monopolistic competition is enough like competition to make this only a small worry. Apparently legislators and staunch antimonopoly advocates agree, because the many firms and industries in monopolistic competition have escaped the scrutiny and legislation directed at monopolies.

Nonprice Competition

Since all firms in a monopolistically competitive industry sell products or services that are very much alike, they are reluctant to compete with each other through changes in price. A drop in price could bring retaliation from other firms; if the firm is in equilibrium, its prices would drop faster than its costs. Since altering price is too dangerous, most businesses and many professionals in the United States must resort to nonprice competition, an attempt to influence the attitude of the potential buyer without changing the price and without changing the form of the product or service itself. Grocers do have "special" prices, but they also lure customers with promises of the freshest meats and vegetables in town. A hardware dealer might offer patient, helpful advice on how to "do it yourself." Some taverns have a variety of games patrons can play while drinking beer. Even dentists sometimes rely on nonprice competition. They may all have comparable skill, but many attract patients by means of their decorator waiting rooms, electronic-age gadgetry, or stereophonic music.

Nonprice competition takes so many forms that it is difficult to generalize about it. Surely it is sometimes overdone. TV commercials frequently insult the viewer's intelligence. And sometimes it is underdone. The promise of fresh produce alone is not enough to cause shoppers to switch grocery stores. Since nonprice competition is such a prominent part of monopolistic competition, however, most firms in these industries can be expected to make major expenditures on attempting to change people's attitudes toward their products. In 1973, U.S. firms spent $25 billion on advertising. It was not all spent by monopolistically competitive firms, but much of it was used to induce consumers to switch from one cola to another, from one restaurant to another, or from one cigarette to another—to lure customers to switch to another product without changing either the form or the price of the product.

Mr. Chamberlin and Mrs. Robinson

The 1930s was a tumultuous period in microeconomics as well as in macroeconomics. While Keynes was breaking new ground in describing the performance of whole economies, a number of other scholars were making intense explorations into the behavior of single firms. Outstanding among them were Edward H. Chamberlin (1899–1967) of Harvard University and Joan Robinson (b. 1903) of Cambridge University. These two pioneers bent their considerable talents to explaining the role of selling costs, demand creation, and the cost structures of firms. They emphasized that existing models were incomplete, and succeeded in breaking microeconomists away from the spellbinding symmetry of the competitive model and the rigorous exercise in logic associated with the study of monopoly. They showed how firms producing the same products could have vastly different profit-and-loss statements. Economists since Chamberlin and Robinson have taken different approaches to the problems of monopolistic competition. Numerous empirical studies of such industries exist, and scores of additional studies are underway at this moment. Studies of market shares, internal decision making, and selling strategies have suggested more avenues of study for future generations of economists. Even though the behavior of the many firms and industries still cannot be predicted accurately, the work done by Chamberlin and Robinson has made it possible to formulate the right questions about prices, about outputs, and about the allocation of resources.

"I like to think our false and deceptive advertising is falser and more deceptive than any other agency's false and deceptive advertising."

Advertising the Product

Firms in monopolistically competitive industries almost always advertise. Unlike competitive firms, which sell homogeneous products and so cannot entice customers, or monopolies, which are the *only* suppliers of their products, monopolistic competitors constantly attempt to keep the public interested. They *must* advertise. But advertising is a complicated topic. It has moral and psychological dimensions in addition to its economic consequences. At the same time, it is so important to monopolistic competition (and to oligopoly) that its economic effects, at least, must be analyzed.

Advertising is people management and thought management. It is an attempt—subtle or blatant—to persuade people to think in a particular way. If it is well done, it is called informative and useful. If it is overdone it is called brainwashing, unethical, and garish. Because of the way the industry is organized, a firm in monopolistic competition must struggle to maintain contact with customers so that their attention will not wander to the very similar products of other firms. Monopolistic competitors must try through advertising to convince customers that their particular product is different and preferable. Bayer aspirin users must be reminded that the pill they take is not just aspirin alone and Bubble-Up drinkers must be reminded that they are not drinking 7-Up.

Although advertising is almost universal in monopolistic competition, it is hard to analyze whether or not it actually changes people's minds. Does a 15-second radio spot actually bring more people into a store? Does a TV soap commercial at 8:30 P.M. cancel the effects of a rival soap advertisement aired an hour earlier? The answers are not clear. Because of the uncertainty surrounding the effectiveness of advertising, arguments for and against it are legion. Those in favor of advertising (generally the ad men themselves) say that it is good because (1) it provides information, (2) it supports many forms of communications, (3) it provides employment, (4) it stimulates the production of new (differentiated) products, and (5) it helps expand the advertiser's output to a lower point on his average cost curve.

Arguments against advertising are just as convincing. There are those who deplore advertising because (1) it attempts to coerce rather than to inform, (2) it misallocates resources to unsightly billboards, ridiculous TV commercials, and sensational magazine centerfolds, (3) it stresses the importance of private goods to the exclusion of public goods, (4) its effectiveness is negated by counter-advertising, and (5) it may actually aggravate business fluctuations because advertisers increase expenditures during booms and curtail expenditures during recessions.

The *possible* effects of advertising are shown in Figure 22–4. The lower cost curve reflects a firm operating in monopolistic competition but not attempting to differentiate its product by advertising. Its demand curve, D, is tangent to the cost curve when price is \$15 per unit and output is 4,000 units. The firm decides to engage in advertising as a means of attracting more customers. As a result of these efforts, the demand curve shifts upward and to the right, to D_1. The advertising has been successful in at least this one aspect. However, advertising costs money. The firm must incur

Figure 22–4 The Effects of Advertising in Monopolistic Competition

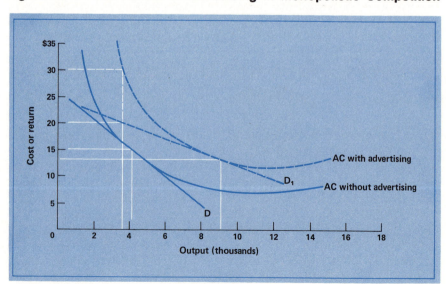

ing the finished good is relatively easy. Each year hundreds of new firms appear; each year hundreds of disappointed entrepreneurs close their shops after learning that they cannot earn enough to feed their families by selling their beautifully handcrafted and durable garments.

Clothes making is a monopolistically competitive industry. Easy to get in, easy to get out. There are many sellers. Products are differentiated so that each seller has his own niche. This kind of industry seems designed expressly for people who want to become their own bosses and gradually work their way to wealth and fame. At the same time, this kind of industrial organization invites failure—many jump in, but few survive.

Monopolistic competition is good because it provides opportunity, variety, and challenge. It is bad because of the waste and the frustration accorded to those who try but fail. On balance, should this form of organization, which produces half of all U.S. output, be encouraged, tolerated, or discouraged?

23

Oligopoly

In 1972, 136 firms in the United States manufactured automobile tires and tubes. One hundred of these firms combined produced only 3 percent of the industry's output, while the four largest firms produced 73 percent of the total output.

For all practical purposes, only four firms manufacture automobiles in the United States. One of them—American Motors Corporation—manufactured only 4 percent of all cars made in 1974.

Cigarettes are manufactured by 13 firms. The four largest account for over 84 percent of the industry's output.

Nearly 600 firms manufacture soap and detergents. Four giant companies produce 62 percent of the industry's output. Fifty (one sixth of all firms) produce 92 percent of all soaps and detergent products in the United States.

The four largest manufacturers of primary aluminum (aluminum ingots) produced over 98 percent of the nation's aluminum, making this industry one of the most concentrated in the U.S. economy.

Industries as concentrated as these worry economists, policy makers and citizens. Their concern is legitimate. When four firms control 73 percent of tire production, or 100 percent of automobile output, or 98 percent of primary aluminum output, or 84 percent of all cigarette production, the power these firms command must be questioned.

A decision made in the board room of General Motors or Kaiser Aluminum can have a very real effect upon the daily lives of millions of Americans. When the automobile giants refused to make small cars, 20 percent of the market was eventually taken over by imported cars. When the Ford Motor Company finally responded by introducing the Pinto, it was an instant success. The Pacer, introduced by American Motors in 1974, gave vital breath to that company and promised its thousands of workers at least a few more months of employment. Had the board members of these two companies voted not to produce the small cars, production lines would have slowed and the demand for steel and for design engineers would have dropped.

These firms, and the people who run them, wield enormous economic, social, and political power. Because only a few firms are involved in such concentrated industries, this type of market organization is called *oligopoly,* which, loosely translated from the Greek, means "few sellers."

Oligopoly occurs when the number of firms in an industry is so small that each must consider how the other firms will react if it changes its price or output levels.

Most individual consumers do not have much direct contact with oligopolies because consumer goods are not usually purchased directly from firms like General Motors, Kaiser Aluminum, or Lever Brothers. The existence of oligopoly has a profound effect on all consumers, however, since most production processes and many retailing processes rely on the output of industries that are dominated by a few firms. Agriculture—the most competitive of all major U.S. industries—depends upon oligopolies for seed, fertilizer, farm equipment, fuel, shipping, and numerous other inputs. Auto manufacturing, oligopolistic itself, depends on other oligopolies for glass, aluminum, rubber, steel, and upholstery fabric. Retailing (generally characterized by monopolistic competition) depends on oligopolies for its supplies of cigarettes, gasoline, fabric, soap, and scores of other items. Various estimates suggest that approximately 40 percent of all the nation's output is produced by industries that are oligopolistic.

This chapter is devoted to understanding oligopoly. It opens with a section describing the importance of oligopoly in the U.S. economy, then turns to hypotheses about how oligopolists make decisions, and closes with a section on the legality of oligopoly.

Why Oligopoly Exists

The basic techniques for producing most goods or services are not secret. Automobiles could be produced, conceivably, in the workshops of tinkerers or craftsmen—certainly in a few dozen relatively small firms.

Concentration Ratios in U.S. Industry

Economists and politicians have always shown intense concern for industries whose firms are concentrated into the hands of a few owners. The economists are worried that the concentration will impose imperfections on the market—that what is to be produced and who is to be hired to produce it will be dictated by people in board rooms across the nation rather than by the impersonal but highly responsive laws of supply and demand. Politicians have a similar worry. They worry about big business and the control that size might exert on the nation's domestic and international policies.

These concerns have been combined by the U.S. Senate Subcommittee on Antitrust and Monopoly. For years, this subcommittee has studied combinations of businesses, mergers, and business affiliations, using the *concentration ratio* to measure the extent of oligopoly power. The concentration ratio is the proportion of an industry's total business volume that is consummated by a small number of firms. Ratios used by the committee (and subsequently by most economists) refer to volume of business done by the largest four firms, the largest eight firms, and the largest 50 firms in any one industry.

"Tooling up" and organizing the production process is complex, however, and once arrangements are made to produce the first car, or airplane, or light bulb, the maker can lower costs considerably by producing a second, tenth, hundredth, and thousandth unit.

Economies of large-scale production are the harbingers of oligopoly. Thus for many items production has become concentrated in a very few firms. Most of the output of oligopoly firms is produced using modern technology, advanced production and assembly techniques, and enormous, costly plants. Steel, for example, is refined in enormous blast furnaces and processed in huge assemblies designed to handle the molten metal. Railroad spurs carry the ores in and the finished products out. Soap is manufactured in high-speed processes that mix, mold, dry, wrap, and package millions of bars per hour. Aircraft are constructed in buildings that cover 40 acres, and tested on specially designed machines that are even more sophisticated than the planes themselves. Firms that are large enough to afford large-scale operations, and to develop new assembly line techniques for them, can generally manufacture all of a good that the market for it can absorb. They also enjoy such widespread economies of scale that they can produce each unit at relatively low average cost.

Many of today's oligopolies have developed as a result of mergers among firms producing the same or similar products. Chevrolet, Pontiac, Oldsmobile, Buick, and Cadillac (along with several other firms) merged to become General Motors, and Standard Oil of New Jersey became one of the nation's largest oil producers by acquiring 14 rival firms between 1956

"My plan is that we form a merger with around 25 of the country's largest corporations, create a joint executive committee, and take over the government."

and 1963. Merging is done for pecuniary and nonpecuniary purposes. The financial rewards of a merger can be high. The parent firm enjoys profits formerly earned by the acquired firm, and the two acting as one may be more efficient in production or may be able to buy inputs at lower costs.

In today's uncertain world, nonpecuniary motives for merging may be just as high. One firm may absorb another to insure future access to raw materials. Thus, 19 of the nation's 20 largest oil refining companies merged with crude petroleum producers between 1956 and 1968. These *backward mergers* may not be profitable in themselves, but may insure the survival of the parent firm.

A backward merger occurs when a producing firm buys another firm that is a supplier of inputs. Conversely, a forward merger occurs when a manufacturer purchases retail outlets for its own products. In the 1930s, major oil companies were active in backward mergers. More recently, especially since oil shortages and embargoes began, the same companies have become very interested in retailing their own gasoline and as a consequence have engaged in forward mergers.

Regardless of the reasons, the "urge to merge" has been strong among large firms, and has intensified the concentration of productive activities.

The relentless forces of a downward-sloping cost curve and the drive for economic, social, and political power have combined to yield two types of oligopolies. One, the homogeneous oligopoly, produces a single, undifferentiated product. Even if 20 firms are producing the product, the product remains the same. The oligopolies in steel and in aluminum are homogeneous. Rolled steel is always rolled steel; aluminum ingots are always aluminum ingots. Differentiated oligopolies are industries dominated by a few firms producing products that are close substitutes. The automobile oligopoly and the cigarette oligopoly are differentiated. Each auto firm produces cars, but a Dodge is not quite the same as a Chevrolet or a Mercury. In general, oligopolies that produce inputs for other firms tend to be homogeneous, but those producing goods used by consumers are differentiated.

How the Oligopolist Makes Decisions

Chapters 20, 21 and 22 described models that can be used to show how decisions should be made and how resources should be allocated in industries that are competitive, monopolistic, and monopolistically competitive. In each of these types of industries, the model determined an equilibrium in which the firm equated marginal cost with marginal revenue and the industry neither attracted nor relinquished resources. These models provided guides to firm behavior.

There is no comparable model for oligopoly. Oligopoly is too diverse. It includes industries where two or three firms battle over how much of the total market each will supply, and it includes industries in which 12 or 15 firms struggle to find the "correct" price to charge their many customers. Some oligopolies are homogeneous; others differentiated. Some oligopolies prevent other firms from entering the field; others are not so restrictive. These variations make it difficult to develop a single model that is applicable to all oligopolistic industries. The auto industry behaves differently from the soap industry. Neither has much in common with the photographic equipment oligopoly. A model for one does not help understand the others.

In addition to being diverse, the firms in oligopoly are highly dependent on one another. This causes significant analytic complications. In pure competition, marginal revenue will always equal market price for an individual producer. A monopolist who knows the shape and location of the demand curve can determine the slope and location of the marginal revenue curve. But, a firm in oligopoly is never sure of the marginal revenue because it depends on how rival firms are acting or reacting to industry problems. If one oligopolist decides to lower its price, marginal revenue will drop. If rival firms decide to retaliate and drop their prices even more (as they may well do!) the first company's marginal revenue will drop even more. Without reliable information about marginal revenue, the oligopolist cannot use the same rules as firms in other kinds of industries. Instead of carefully inspecting its own cost data and adjusting output so that marginal cost will equal marginal returns, the oligopoly firm becomes a

Breaking into the Auto Business

In the late 1930s, automobile manufacturing was not quite so concentrated as it is today. Studebaker still made autos, as did Hudson, Packard, and Willys. The industrial upheaval caused by World War II forced changes in the industry. At war's end, the same old companies tried to come back into production, but only GM, Ford, Chrysler and American Motors survived. One by one, the formerly successful firms dropped by the wayside.

Two entrepreneurs noticed this and tried to fill what they thought were gaps in the industry. One was Preston Tucker and his ill-fated "Tucker Torpedo." The other was Henry J. Kaiser, an industrialist who had just made millions building ships for the U.S. Navy. Tucker and Kaiser each wanted to make cars.

The Tucker Torpedo was futuristic in every aspect of advanced exterior design. The car also had front-wheel drive, power accessories, and automatic features that were well ahead of its time when the car was designed in 1948. Tucker was a good inventor and designer, but he could not put together a production and distribution system capable of getting his clearly superior auto on the market. Although he had a plant at his disposal and had sold franchises to hundreds of potential distributors, he ran out of money after manufacturing only two automobiles. Preston Tucker simply could not amass the capital needed to compete successfully with the established firms.

Kaiser was only slightly more successful. He had industrial know-how, huge financial reserves, and a partner, Joseph W. Fraser. Together, Kaiser and Fraser manufactured good, but not imaginative, automobiles. The cars came in several models and sizes, but did not offer any spectacular advantages in either engineering or design. Production started in 1946 and continued through 1953. Kaiser's best year was 1948, when he produced barely 5 percent of domestic new car sales in a market dominated by three giants.

watcher of its rivals. The firm manager must always be alert to the changes and *possible* changes occurring in other firms, but systematic analysis is impossible, since the changes may not follow given rules. A rule telling Kodak how to respond to Land's introduction of the Polaroid camera would not help Chrysler respond correctly to the (unsuccessful) Edsel or the (successful) Pinto.

Oligopoly Prices

Firms in oligopolistic industries do have two distinctive characteristics. First, their prices are considerably more stable than prices in other kinds of markets. In competition, changes in prices attract and repel resources. In monopoly, shifts in demand bring shifts in prices. In oligopoly, however, prices tend to remain quite stable even though the firm's profits may rise or fall. Second, when oligopoly prices do change, the prices charged by all firms in the industry tend to change together. When the price charged by U.S. Steel rises, for example, so do the prices charged by Bethlehem and Republic.

Why this stability in an otherwise dynamic and volatile economy? This question has puzzled economists for decades, and their attempts to answer it form the basis for several hypotheses about oligopolistic behavior. Prominent ones relate to kinked demand curves, joint profit maximization, and price leadership.

The Kinked Demand Curve

In the 1930s, during a period of general reappraisal of microeconomics, Paul M. Sweezy formulated a popular and controversial hypothesis about price stability in oligopolies. This hypothesis stems from the interdependence among oligopolists. It says that the individual oligopoly firm makes decisions with reference to the demand curve it faces and that the demand curve for the product of that particular firm will be determined by whether or not its actions are imitated by rival firms in the same industry.

Mellow Purr is a wholly imaginary firm in the equally imaginary international tail pipe oligopoly. Mellow Purr, which we shall call simply MelPur, manufactures a tail pipe and muffler assembly that causes cars to make a distinctive sound not unlike the contented purr of a well-fed lion. Until recently, MelPur was a small firm that made price and output decisions after careful examination of its books and sober contemplation. In the last year, MelPur acquired Vibrant Roar, another muffler-producing firm specializing in somewhat more spirited sounds. The combined firms (selling only under the name MelPur) account for 20 percent of all muffler assemblies sold in the U.S. market. Now price and output decisions are more complicated.

When the firms first merged, the manager of MelPur tried to continue the policy of totally independent decisions. MelPur's initial price/output combination is shown as point P in Figure 23–1. Price is $22 per unit and 8,000 units are produced. What is the shape of MelPur's demand curve? When MelPur was a very small producer, this was an interesting question. Now that the firm is a giant, it is a necessary question. MelPur must know something about how its sales will change with a change in price. This relationship depends upon how rival muffler-producing firms react to MelPur plans. With rival firms following every action made by MelPur, MelPur's demand curve may look like D_1. As the industry price falls, more will be purchased from each firm, but MelPur itself will not make spectacular gains in sales because the increases must be shared with other firms. Likewise, if the other firms are acting just like MelPur, a price rise will cause a reduction in each firm's sales and MelPur must share this reduction, too. When oligopoly firms all behave in the same way, the demand curve facing each firm will be steep and unresponsive to price change.

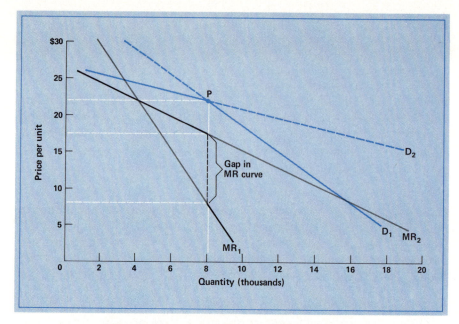

Figure 23-1 The Kinked Demand Curve

If rival firms choose to ignore MelPur's price changes, the demand for MelPur mufflers becomes much more elastic (responsive). Now, a slight drop in price will attract buyers' attention. Noting that MelPur's price is low relative to those of other mufflers, they will switch and purchase the resonant and deep-throated product of this firm. MelPur will prosper at the expense of other firms in the industry. Should MelPur alone decide to raise its price, buyers will switch to other, quite similar brands that are now less expensive. When only one firm in an oligopoly raises its price, its quantity sold will drop precipitously along a demand curve like D_2.

But in a world filled with economic rivalry, inside information, and corporate distrust, how will MelPur's price rivals behave? Will they match or ignore MelPur's changes? Sweezy suggests that rivals will match the price reductions but ignore the increases.

This strategy is a reasonable one. If MelPur alone raises prices, it will be out of line with other producers. Those retaining lower prices will now share the sales lost by MelPur, whose reduction in sales will follow D_2. If, however, MelPur lowers prices, its rivals will not stand idly by. They will not allow one firm to capture the market through price reductions, so they will feel compelled to follow by lowering the price charged for their own mufflers. When MelPur and the other firms lower price, MelPur's sales expand but only modestly, along the original curve D_1. The mixed response of rivals thus yields a demand curve for MelPur that follows the bent blue line. Paul Sweezy called this a "kinked demand curve." (The upward-sloping marginal cost curve has been omitted from the diagram for simplicity's sake.)

A kink in a demand curve would be only mildly curious were it not for the relationship between demand and marginal revenue. Each demand curve has its own marginal revenue curve showing that, as price falls, the marginal revenue obtained from the sale of one more unit drops even faster than price. The steeper demand curve (D_1) has a very steep marginal revenue curve (MR_1), and the shallow demand curve (D_2) has a somewhat flat marginal revenue curve (MR_2). When MelPur is operating at point P (still in Figure 23-1) and its rivals are matching price reductions but ignoring price increases, any increase in price above $22 will increase marginal revenue along MR_2, but a decrease in price will bring decreases in marginal revenue shown along the lower end of MR_1. The kink in the demand curve causes a gap in the marginal revenue curve.

This gap has important consequences. In Figure 23-1, the gap at 8,000 units of output extends vertically from $8 per unit to $17.50 per unit. If a firm's marginal cost per unit of output changes but remains within the gap, it will have no compelling incentive to change either its price or its level of output. An oligopolist attempting to equate marginal cost with marginal revenue will produce 8,000 units as long as marginal cost is in the $8 to $17.50 range. Sweezy argued that the kinked demand and the accompanying gap in the marginal revenue curve explained price stability in oligopolies. It was an hypothesis about firm behavior. More than this, it was consistent with economic models used to explain behavior of firms in nonoligopolistic industries. Under the Sweezy hypothesis, the entrepreneur still tries to equate marginal cost with marginal revenue but, in so trying, might be locked into one price and output combination.

Many economists have been unhappy with the Sweezy argument. Some argue that the hypothesis is lacking because it does not explain how price got to be $22 per unit in the first place and if it is to fit with the other models, it must explain price. What economic and institutional forces came into play to instruct MelPur to establish price at $22 per unit? Other economists, notably George Stigler of the University of Chicago, suggest that empirical evidence does not support the Sweezy hypothesis—that prices among oligopolies are not entirely rigid. Regardless of objections, the Sweezy hypothesis remains an important suggestion about why oligopolists behave the way they do.

Joint Profit Maximization

A second hypothesis assumes that oligopolists do not like the prospect of constant vigilance and constant fear of retaliation so they choose to act in *collusion* with one another.

Collusion is an agreement or conspiracy among rival firms not to engage in price competition or other kinds of competitive activities that could disrupt the relationship among firms. Since collusion is illegal in the United States, collusive agreements must be secret. Several court cases in re-

"Well, gentlemen, how much do we raise the cost of living this *time?*"

cent years have been difficult to prosecute because the alleged collusion was based upon "gentlemen's agreements" consummated on the golf course or at cocktail parties.

When oligopolistic firms decide to maximize their profits jointly, they agree to work together and behave like a monopoly. Therefore, the model used to analyze the price and output decisions of a collusive oligopoly is the same as that used to analyze monopoly. The whole industry now equates marginal cost with marginal revenue, charges the price P indicated by the demand curve, and earns supernormal profits as shown by the darker area in Figure 23–2. Collusion has significant advantages for

**Figure 23–2
Joint Profit Maximization in a Collusive Oligopoly**

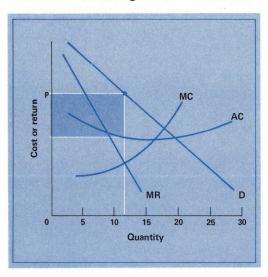

the individual firm. There is relative certainty about the demand curve, there is no fear of price cutting by "cooperators," and supernormal profits are maintained at the highest possible level.

The advantages of collusion, though, are offset by a list of reasons why it may not work. Most center on the issue of whether or not there is honor among thieves. If the collusion is to work to maximize the industry's joint profits, there must be rigid arrangements about price and about the proportion of market demand each firm is to supply. There must be production quotas to insure that the industry's output does not exceed the output that equates marginal cost with marginal revenue. As the number of colluding firms increases, enforcing the quotas becomes more difficult. The only two producers of tin cans can agree in one phone call on how their market will be shared. It is quite another thing for the thirteen cigarette producers to establish production quotas. The prospect of 136 tire manufacturers reaching output agreements is almost too much to contemplate.

By far the most difficult aspect of collusion is the possibility that there *is* no honor among thieves. One oligopolist, even though he has a gentleman's agreement with his rivals, may choose to sell to a preferred customer at a slightly lower or "shaded" price. This price concession ordi-

Collusion in Electrical Equipment

Electrical generators, heavy-duty electrical switching devices, and transformers are manufactured by a very few firms and are generally sold by sealed bid to only a handful of purchasers. The industry has all the qualities needed for reasonably effective collusion. Apparently, the industry itself noted this and during the 1950s participated in some of the economy's most famous collusions. Although many of the guilty firms' executives eventually pleaded guilty to charges of price setting and market sharing rather than expose themselves and their companies to trial, the case made public much information about how oligopolists work together to share markets and set prices.

Beginning in the early 1950s, officials of General Electric, Westinghouse, Allis-Chalmers and Federal Pacific met regularly and exchanged weekly memos to keep each other informed about sales, prices, and possible future contracts. The goal was to give GE 35 percent of the business, Westinghouse 25 percent, and each of the other firms 10 percent. This "arrangement" lasted until 1957, when the intercompany price stabilization plan began to deteriorate. High officials of the companies then began to hold secret meetings across the nation.

The meetings eventually were noticed and their purpose revealed. In 1960, action by the Department of Justice brought indictments to 29 corporations and 45 individuals. The judge levied nearly $2 million in fines, sent seven corporate executives to jail, and gave suspended sentences to 25 others. In this case, the price of collusion was quite high!

narily applies to sales above those allowed by the quota and, hence, will add to the one firm's profits but reduce the volume of business shared by rival firms. Oligopolists retaliate against firms caught cheating on agreements through price wars that can leave the entire industry in disarray.

Price Leadership

Price leadership occurs when some firms watch the prices charged by others and imitate any price changes. Price leadership is ordinarily thought to be present when overt collusion is absent. Without collusion, price leadership becomes a perfectly legal maneuver or strategy. (Note: Although price leadership is by itself legal, strict adherence to a leader-follower pattern is almost certain to be noticed by the Justice Department. Price leaders are nearly always under investigation to see if collusion is or is not present.)

Either of two conditions will allow a firm to emerge as a price leader. One is dominance in the industry; the other is efficiency, and hence, low production costs. In some oligopolies, a single firm is so powerful that its prices are accepted by others as their own. General Motors, selling about 52 percent of all U.S.-produced autos, is a price leader in the four-firm auto industry. Each fall, a small article appears in the nation's daily papers telling that GM has announced a price increase of 5 or 6 percent for its next year's models. A second article soon appears to indicate that Chrysler and Ford have announced similar price increases for similar models.

Surprises can and do occur in price leading and following. For years U.S. Steel has dominated the steel industry, but in recent years it has not set prices for the industry. More often, the smaller steel firms make the first move, with the giants quickly falling into line. In this industry, efficiency is the important factor in price leading. The more efficient firm has lower average costs, so it can drop prices to lower levels and still earn sizable profits. Since oligopoly is an interdependent form of organization, all other firms must make suitable countermoves. The giant, inefficient firm is forced to follow the price lead of the small firm in order not to lose its large share of the market.

In the absence of collusion, the stability of an oligopoly will ordinarily weaken during a recession and strengthen during full employment. A recession lowers sales and renders much of the oligopolist's plant idle. Since the firm is so large, this idle capacity is extremely costly and the management is tempted to offer price concessions or use any other gimmicks to increase sales. The formal and informal agreements and any other relationships among firms began to weaken. When over one-fourth of the automobile industry's capacity was idle in 1974, first GM then the other companies made $300 to $500 "rebates" available to purchasers of new cars. This was nothing more than an attempt to stimulate sales and utilize idle plant capacity. Although all firms eventually were led to a rebate program, the depressed condition of the industry moved each firm to act alone in trying to make profits.

In a period of full employment, all firms will be operating at or near full capacity, all will be earning reasonable levels of profit, and none will want to disrupt the tenuous equilibrium by violating agreements or acting in an untoward fashion. Thus, a full-employment economy is conducive to stability as the oligopolists act in concert to maintain their positions.

Other Explanations of Oligopolists' Behavior

The three hypotheses above are not the only available explanations of the relative stability in oligopolistic industries. Past and present economists have developed a long list. Some of their hypotheses focus on prices, some on quantity produced, some on market power, and some on the psychological and sociological dispositions of company owners and managers. Some of the more prominent and interesting are listed below.

Revenue maximization. In 1961, Professor William J. Baumol of Princeton University argued that large, oligopolistic firms strive to maximize total revenue from sales rather than total profit. Baumol's argument is that huge firms are motivated by their own large size. The success of their managers is measured in terms of the flow of money through the firm. The argument is persuasive *so long as profits are high enough to prevent a stockholders' revolt.* "Sales"—the number of dollars coming into the firm—is a widely recognized and easily understood measure of activity. Firms are often ranked with respect to total sales, and officials as well as salespersons are often compensated with respect to the volume of sales they generate. Small wonder, then, that some firms, especially oligopolies, are inclined to make decisions with respect to this goal.

Simple mark-ups. Some retail chains are large enough and dominant enough to be considered oligopolistic. Sears, Wards, and Penneys, for example, dominate department store sales in many areas. These firms, dealing as they must in thousands of different items, may choose the simplest possible way to decide on prices: All goods in the store will be sold at cost plus 20 percent. This is easy to carry out in a firm that has scores of outlets scattered over all 50 states. Simple mark-ups do not necessarily lead to either the highest possible profits or the highest possible sales. The strategy is chosen because of its one advantage: simplicity.

Economic power or prestige. Although it is hard to recognize and harder to prove, some oligopolists may use their firms as means of gaining or exercising economic power. In the late 1800s, the magnates operating competing rail lines derived a diabolical pleasure from driving other rail owners into bankruptcy. One railroad would cut shipping rates, knowing that rivals would have to follow suit or lose all their business. The original price cutter might suffer unbelievable financial losses during the ensuing price war, but if the rival capitulated, it would all be worth it—the remaining entrepreneur would be recognized as having more power. There are no recent nationwide instances of this type of behavior, but local examples abound in the thousands of neighborhood shopping districts and small towns.

A strategy of games. In 1944, John von Neumann and Oskar Morgenstern published a highly technical book called *The Theory of Games and Economic Behavior.* The book pointed out that managers, especially those in interdependent situations, may make decisions using models more like

John Kenneth Galbraith and the Theory of Countervailing Power

John Kenneth Galbraith is one of the most colorful and versatile of all contemporary economists. Born in 1908 and trained as an agricultural economist at the University of California, Galbraith went immediately to Harvard University and on to a distinguished career as an economist, novelist, diplomat, and iconoclast. When still young, Galbraith took controversial positions regarding the importance of conventional models used by microeconomists to explain the operation of a modern industrial society. In 1956, after studying the problem for a decade, Galbraith published *American Capitalism: The Concept of Countervailing Power.* The book argued that industrial output had been wrested from small firms through the relentless march of technology. Economies of scale simply prevented small firms from competing with large producers, so small firms ceased to exist and oligopolies came to dominate the U.S. economy.

But domination by oligopolies did not—as Adam Smith and Karl Marx had predicted—cause the economic structure of the U.S. to crumble. Rather, Galbraith reasoned, it forced the rise of huge groups of laborers (unions), then huge groups of consumers, who made collective demands on the system and prevented oligopolies from exploiting either group. One huge power structure "countervailed" against another.

Galbraith went on to write *The Affluent Society* (1958), *The New Industrial State* (1967), and *Economics and the Public Purpose* (1973). This trilogy expanded the basic notion of countervailing power and argued persuasively in favor of a stronger role for government in U.S. economic affairs.

Few economists agree fully with Gailbraith's assessment of economics or of the economy, but most are haunted by the possibility that he may be correct. Now retired, Galbraith remains a very active critic of the American economy and of economics as it is practiced in the United States today.

those of a bridge player or a military man than those of a calculating economist seeking to equate marginal cost with marginal revenue. "Game theory" has become a popular approach to understanding the oligopolist who sits and asks, "If I do this, how will my rival react?" and the further question, "If he reacts that way, how should I respond to his reaction?" Game theory likens oligopoly to a game of bridge, where each player is pondering what cards his opponents hold. The object is to play your own cards so that you maximize your own advantage or minimize the advantage of your rival.

In sum, oligopoly is an important but complex form of economic organization. While it accounts for as much as 40 percent of all economic activity in the United States today, economists have not been able to put forth any definitive, systematic explanations of why oligopolists behave the way they do.

Summary

1. An industry in which production is centered in a few large firms is an oligopoly. "Few firms" in this case is defined by interdependence—each of the firms in the industry must constantly watch its rivals.
2. In the United States, automobiles, light bulbs, detergents, heavy electrical equipment, and steel are produced in oligopolies.
3. Oligopolies are usually formed in industries that can make use of large-scale production technologies. In these industries, large firms merge with small ones until a few giants prevail.
4. Economic models used to explain price and output under oligopoly are not comparable with the models for other forms of market organization.
5. Some economists argue that oligopolies are stable because their demand curve is kinked. Others suggest that oligopolists use illegal "agreements" to maximize their profits jointly. Still others indicate that leading firms emerge and the prices that they set are immediately adopted by other firms.
6. A variety of other, sometimes noneconomic hypotheses attempt to explain oligopoly behavior in terms of sales, good will, and power.

Exercises

1. Explain these important terms and concepts:
   - interdependence
   - concentration ratios
   - forward merger
   - backward merger
   - kinked demand curve
   - joint profit maximization
   - collusion
   - price leadership
2. Monopolistic competition and oligopoly are both forms of "imperfect competition." What distinguishes one from the other? Is the differentiation a necessary or even a useful concept?
3. The steel industry is a clear-cut example of oligopoly. A few firms produce a high proportion of the industry's output. From time to time

someone or other will suggest breaking the steel industry into many firms to make it competitive by the economist's definition. What would such a move accomplish? What would it do to the price of steel? To resource allocation?

4 Two concepts are very important to the existence and understanding of oligopoly: interdependence and stability. What does each mean and how do they influence the allocation of resources?

5 An oligopoly firm may come into equilibrium in the sense that there are no forces toward change, but the equilibrium may have nothing to do with normal profits. What effect does this have on resource allocation?

6 No major firm has tried to break into the auto industry since 1950. No new steel company has appeared since 1941, and no new aluminum manufacturer has appeared since 1955. These are all oligopoly industries. Do the existing firms *prevent* new firms from entering, or are other factors responsible?

7 Which of the following products are likely to be produced under conditions of oligopoly?

steel beams eggs
mainsprings for watches air travel
greeting cards thimbles
fashion clothes ready-to-wear clothing
candy cigarettes

A Contemporary Problem

Oligopoly in Oil

Since about 1973, all firms, enterprises, industries, and agencies having any relationship to energy have been watched very carefully by U.S. Government officials. Those firms manufacturing petroleum products have been more subject to government control because petroleum plays an important role for consumers and producers.

In 1970, the top four petroleum companies (Exxon, Texaco, Shell, and Standard of Indiana) produced about one third of all domestic crude oil, maintained about one third of the gasoline-refining capacity, and sold about one third of all gasoline purchased by consumers at filling stations. These four firms were each vertically merged. They controlled the petroleum from the time it left the earth as crude oil until it reached the automobile gas tanks where it was finally converted into usable energy.

Whatever the causes, gasoline prices began to rise very rapidly in 1973. The production and retailing of gasoline became so profitable that most major companies tried to expand their own retailing activities and cut back on the volume of business done by independent service stations. The large firms imposed quotas on how much they would sell to independents, and by mid-1973 over 1,200 independent gasoline stations had closed. At that time, the U.S. Department of the Interior stopped counting the stations that had failed.

In 1973, Congressman Les Aspin (a professional economist) and Senator James Abourezk introduced legislation into the U.S. House and Senate attempting to force the vertically merged firms to break apart. If passed, the bill would have allowed a refiner to own no more than 25 percent of his source of crude oil and to sell no more than half his own gasoline. The bill was intended to keep more firms in all aspects of the oil business—drilling, refining, and retailing. It was based on the idea that competition, as the economists know it, would produce more gasoline at lower prices. The Aspin-Abourezk bill was a challenge to an oligopoly that has existed for many years.

Although the oil crisis seems to have been temporarily solved, it is certain to return as the U.S. economy continues to use larger and larger volumes of petroleum products, and a major part of the world's crude oil supplies continues to be dominated by leaders of a handful of nations in the Middle East. When the crisis comes again, there will be more attempts to legislate against oligopoly. Why will this occur? Will it benefit the consumer in any way? Or will it be nothing more than a "moral objection" against bigness?

24 Selling the Factors of Production

In 1942, the International Harvester Company placed the first mechanical cotton picker on the market. Many other machines had been introduced on the farm over the previous hundred years, and this one did not look much different. The steel plow, the reaper, the combined harvester, the continuous churn, and the gasoline-powered tractor, to name a few, had caused employment problems in some regions because each machine did the work of several men. But no one could foresee the sweeping social and economic change that the cotton picker would bring. From its beginnings in Egypt around 3,000 B.C., cotton cultivation had been toilsome. The seed, with its heavy coat of fibers, had to be picked by hand. Then the fibers had to be stripped from the seed before carding, spinning, and weaving could take place. This long process yielded a durable cloth that was warm and could be easily worked into clothing, tents, or other products.

By 1900, all U.S. cotton production processes except picking had been mechanized. The picking was done by millions of low-skilled people residing in the South. Many of these people had descended from slave and plantation families, and remained in the South only because they were sure of income during the cotton picking season. The mechanical picker gradually released laborers from the land and sent them north to find markets for their skills in industrial areas.

In 1977, very little cotton is picked by hand. The descendants of workers once tied to the crop and to the soil have become machinists, production line workers, telephone operators, and airline captains. They found these jobs by entering the labor market—by supplying their labor to anyone who might wish to demand it. Like all markets, this market responds to a variety of forces. If supply exceeds demand, price is likely to fall or some labor will go unsold. If demanders want more labor than can be supplied, price will be bid up and currently unoccupied homemakers and grandfathers will go back to work.

The labor market is just one of the markets for factors of production. Land and capital are also sold in reasonably orderly markets, and these markets for land, labor and capital form the *factor markets* in the U.S. economy.

The factor markets are markets in which land, labor, and capital change hands. These markets transmit information about the demand for and availability of factors. The Help Wanted section of the classified ads is part of the factor market, as is the casual cocktail party remark that an office in the Lincoln Building will soon be available for rent.

This chapter is about the specialized markets in which factors of production are bought and sold. It provides insight into the demand for factors, supplies of factors, and imperfections in the market. The later sections deal separately with the individual factors.

The Demand for Factors

Factors of production are never demanded on the basis of their beauty or because they are esthetically pleasing. They are demanded entirely because they add to the output of a firm. To decide how much, if any, of each factor should be used in its production process, the firm must know something about the way inputs are transformed into outputs in its production process.

The Production Function

In the early years of this century, biological scientists working in the field of food production studied the physical relationships between such things as water or fertilizer application (resource inputs) and plant growth (a product). Their research yielded estimates of *production functions* for a variety of crops.

A production function is the relationship between quantities of factor inputs and the yield of a particular kind of product. Although the function can be written in mathematical form (for example, $Y = a + bX_1 + cX_2$, where Y = corn yield, X_1 = hours of labor, and X_2 = pounds of fertilizer used), it is often shown in graphic or tabular form. A production function is drawn on a graph with the quantity of output on the vertical axis and the quantity of one variable input on the horizontal axis. Output can be measured in either physical or monetary terms.

A hypothetical production function for barley is described by Table 24-1. The only variable is the amount of fertilizer. The quantities of all other inputs—land, water, labor, tractor fuel, and the like—are assumed to remain constant. The table assumes that if no fertilizer is used, no barley will be produced, as shown in the first column. With the application of one unit of fertilizer, productivity jumps to 11 sacks of barley. *Total product* is 11 sacks, the *marginal product* of the first unit of fertilizer is 11 sacks, and the *average product* is 11 sacks of crop. A second unit of fertilizer brings total product to 24 sacks of output. The marginal product of the second unit is, then, 13 sacks and the average product for the first two units of fertilizer is 12 sacks.

Total product is the entire output produced by a given collection of inputs. Average product is the total product divided by the number of units of input used. If total product is 50 sacks and 10 units of labor used, average output per unit of labor is $50 \div 10 = 5$. Marginal product is the change in output associated with the addition (or deletion) of one unit of a factor. If adding one more unit of labor increases total product from 50 to 54 sacks, the marginal product of the added input is 4 sacks.

The most important columns in Table 24-1 relate to total product and marginal product. The total product column shows that total product rises until 6 units of fertilizer have been applied. After that, additional units of fertilizer become destructive to the plant and total yield falls. This is restated in the next column, where the marginal product associated with the additional unit of input is recorded. Marginal product starts at 11 sacks

Table 24-1 Barley Crop Yields with Added Units of Fertilizer Input
(all other factors constant)

Units of fertilizer	Total product (sacks)	Marginal product (sacks)	Average product (sacks)
0	0	0	0.0
1	11	11	11.0
2	24	13	12.0
3	38	14	12.7
4	50	12	12.5
5	58	8	11.6
6	61	3	10.2
7	59	-2	8.4
8	55	-4	6.9

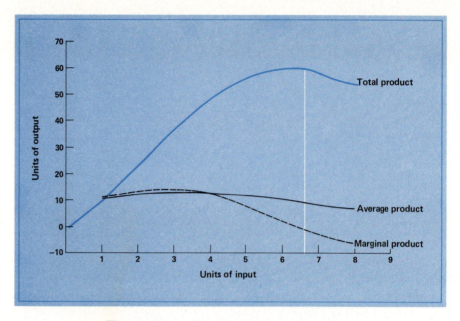

Figure 24-1 The Production Function

because the first application of fertilizer increases output from zero to 11. The second unit of fertilizer is even more efficient. It raises total product from 11 to 24 sacks, so it has a marginal product of 13 sacks (24 − 11 = 13). Eventually, though, the fertilizer ceases to do its work. The sixth unit increases output by only three sacks. The seventh unit of input actually decreases total product so that it has a negative marginal product.

The tabular information is graphed in Figure 24-1. The total product curve rises steeply, falls over to the right, and finally declines after 6.5 units of input. The marginal product curve rises, falls, and eventually—also after 6.5 units of input—becomes negative. In this example, the average product curve remains fairly stable, but does show a tendency to drop as the final units of input are added.

Production in Terms of Revenue

While Figure 24-1 is shown in terms of physical product, it can be easily converted to value terms by assuming the price of the product to be $1 per sack. Now, one unit of fertilizer yields a product valued at $11, four units of fertilizer yield a crop valued at $50, and six units of fertilizer increase the total value of the crop to $61. With these values in mind, the original question can be asked: How many units of the input should be employed? That primary rule—equating marginal cost with marginal revenue—provides the answer. When the vertical axis of the graph is changed from measuring the size of the output (number of sacks) to measuring the revenue earned by the output (by making each sack worth one dollar), the total product curve becomes the total revenue curve, the marginal product curve becomes the marginal revenue curve, and the average product curve becomes the average revenue curve. Of these, the marginal revenue curve is most useful. It shows the revenue produced by the increase in output associated with each successive unit of input. The question of how much input to use is answered by determining when the revenue produced by the last unit of input is equal to the cost of that input. Figure 24–2 shows how the optimal level of factor input can be ascertained. The numbered paragraphs below correspond to the circled numbers in the figure.

1. The marginal revenue product (*MRP*) curve rises as the input becomes more efficient, but eventually falls when the input becomes destructive.

2. The cost of input is assumed to be $7.50 per unit. The input cost line shows the *marginal* cost the firm must pay to obtain an additional unit of input. Since the firm can buy any reasonable quantity of the input at $7.50 per unit, the line is horizontal.

3. The intersection of input cost with marginal revenue product (*MRP*) shows the most profitable amount of input to be purchased and utilized. The intersection appears at about 5.6 units of input. At levels of input below this amount, marginal revenue exceeds marginal costs, so expansion of input use is in order. At quantities of input above this amount, marginal input price is greater than marginal revenue, so contraction is in

Figure 24–2 Equating Marginal Input Cost with Marginal Revenue

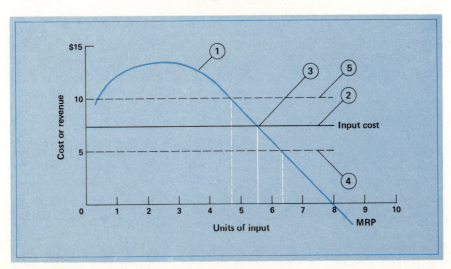

order. Just as there are automatic forces compelling supply to draw toward equilibrium with demand in product markets, there is an incentive driving factor users to apply that amount of input which will equate marginal input cost with marginal revenue. The incentive is that too little input causes profits to be foregone; too large a quantity of input drives profits down, too.

4. If input cost falls to $5.00 per unit, the intersection of the new input cost line with the *MRP* curve will shift to the right so that approximately 6.4 units of input will be purchased. This makes sense. As the cost of the input is lowered, it becomes profitable to apply a larger quantity.

5. If the cost of the input increases from its original $7.50 per unit to $10.00 per unit, the intersection of the input price line with the *MRP* curve moves to the left. High costs of inputs cause the profit-maximizing level of input use to drop to 4.75 units. If less is added, *MRP* is greater than the marginal input cost and more inputs should be used. If more than this amount is used, the cost of the marginal unit of output will be above its capacity to earn income and lower profits will result.

Demand and input costs. The lessons of steps 3, 4, and 5 combine to form a firm's demand curve for a factor of production. This demand curve (Figure 24-3) displays all the characteristics of a demand curve for any finished good or service. The only difference is that the demand curve for a factor obtains its downward slope from the law of diminishing returns rather than from the law of diminishing marginal utility.[1] The price of an input must drop in order for it to be profitable for an entrepreneur to use added quantities.

[1] The two laws describe analogous phenomena. The law of diminishing marginal utility points out that an individual's capacity to enjoy a good diminishes as more units of the good are made available. The law of diminishing returns says that as more of a single *input* is utilized (holding all other inputs constant), each subsequent unit will make a smaller contribution to output than the previous one.

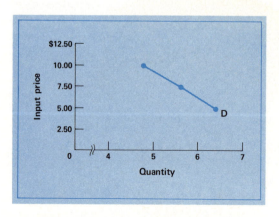

Figure 24-3
Demand Curve for a Factor of Production

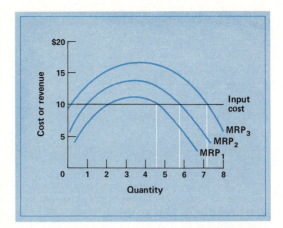

**Figure 24-4
Changes in Input
Associated with Changes
in Product Price**

Demand and product prices. Changing the price of the *product* can also cause an increase in the demand for an input. In Figure 24-4, the three marginal revenue product (*MRP*) curves are derived from the same physical production function. The physical productivity of the factor input does not change, but the value of the marginal product does, since the price of the product changes. MRP_1 corresponds to the case where the product is selling at a low price. The low price means that each unit of output brings only a small reward. If demand for the product rises, its price will also rise and a new marginal revenue product curve will emerge even though there is no change in the marginal physical productivity of the input. A second rise in product price causes a further rise in the marginal revenue product curve. With the low product price, MRP_1 = marginal input price at 4.6 units of input. When product price is at its intermediate level, equating marginal cost with marginal revenue requires 5.8 units of input, and when product prices rise higher still (MRP_3), the entrepreneur should use 7.2 units of input. As product price increases, the most profitable level of input utilization increases, too. When the prices of automobiles rise, it pays GM, Ford, and Chrysler to use more labor, steel, glass, and plastic.

The phenomenon described in Figure 24-4 is described as *derived demand*.

Derived demand refers to the demand for factors of production. If the price of the product is high, the demand for factors used to produce it will be high and factor users will be willing to pay high prices for them. If product prices are low, production will not be especially profitable and entrepreneurs will not be willing to pay high prices for large quantities of factors. The demand for factors is derived from the demand for the product.

Even though the price of the factor remains constant, the quantity demanded changes in response to changes in product price.

The demand for factors is intimately bound up in technology, availability of substitutes, and product prices. The concept of factor demand is

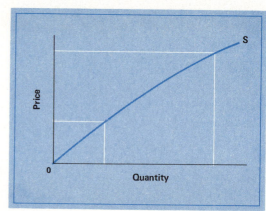

**Figure 24-5
The Supply Curve for a Factor of Production**

comparable to the demand for a product. The only difference is that a product is demanded directly for the satisfactions it will produce, while a factor is an *indirect* producer of satisfactions, and is demanded only for its ability to produce products.

The Supply of Factors

Except for a few unusual cases, the supply of inputs, like the supply of products, will increase when their price rises. Dump trucks are factors of production. If the price of dump trucks goes up, companies supplying these capital items will be happy to oblige the market and produce more. When plotted, the relationship is a positively sloped supply curve for dump trucks: As price rises, more dump trucks are placed on the market. A typical supply curve for a factor of production is shown in Figure 24-5.

Some factors have special properties that cause their supply curves to take on peculiar shapes. If factors are grouped using the land, labor, capital, and entrepreneurship categories, it is plausible that factors in the capital category (dump trucks, office buildings, and crude oil, for example) have positively sloped supply curves. If a higher price is offered, more of each factor will be forthcoming from the firms that produce them.

The argument is similar for entrepreneurial skill. If the rewards to risk taking in the furniture business increase, the number of persons willing to take risks and enter that business increases. In the case of both capital and entrepreneurial skill, the quantity supplied responds positively to changes in price. An increased price increases the quantity placed on the market; a decreased price decreases the quantity placed on the market. The cases of land and labor are not so simple.

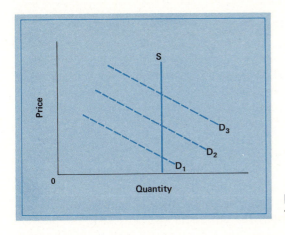

Figure 24-6
The Supply Curve for Land

Land and Natural Resources

The earth's land area is fixed at approximately 58.5 million square miles.[2] In economic language, the supply of land is perfectly inelastic. The supply curve for land is a vertical line at 58.5 million square miles on a graph showing the price on the vertical axis and the quantity on the horizontal axis. No increase in the price of land can ever bring more onto the market. As shown in Figure 24-6, when demand increases from D_1 to D_2 to D_3, the price of land increases but the quantity remains fixed—it does not respond to changes in price.

[2]This is not *entirely* true. The supply of land can be increased by draining swamps, by building walls to hold out the sea, or by filling bogs, inlets, and lakes. These activities may make significant differences locally, but in a worldwide setting, they are negligible.

"Oh, oh—a lump of coal with a note attached!"

Henry George and the Supply of Land

Henry George (1839–1897) is one of the most interesting and peculiar figures in American economic history. He had no formal training in economics, and was not embarrassed to suggest that he did not need any. He started his career as a lecturer-scholar in California, but gradually gravitated toward New York, where the rigors of running for governor caused him to fall victim to a heart attack. His main recommendation for society was to tax only land. Land was a gift of nature, he reasoned, and anyone who owned this gift should be taxed quite heavily. His argument was based on the idea that land is limited in supply, and therefore any increase in demand for land causes its earnings (rents) to increase. The owner does not need to do anything at all to earn these rents, but gets them simply by virtue of holding the land. The unearned reward, then, should be taxed away. Henry George felt so strongly about this matter that he advocated a single tax on land, and argued that this be the only tax used to support governmental functions.

There are still people who adhere to the Georgian single-tax idea, but most are prepared to dismiss it—not because it was a bad idea but because (1) there is no guarantee that the revenues from such a tax would be adequate to cover all government expenses; (2) other factors besides land earn rents, and therefore should also be taxed; and (3) the administrative problems that would arise as a result of taxing all these forms of rents would be outrageously expensive.

Although land area is a specific case of perfectly inelastic supply, recall that in Chapter 3 "land" was defined to include all natural aspects of the environment—water, petroleum, minerals, fresh air, wind, and tides, as well as soil and geographic area. Unlike geographic territory, the supply of many natural resources can be increased by investing more capital in

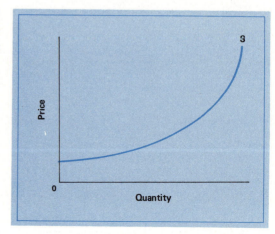

Figure 24-7
The Supply Curve
for Natural Resources

their production. Thus, the supply curve for them is not truly vertical. However, the responsiveness of their supply must be attributed to the capital and labor that make more available rather than to a change in the quantity provided by nature. The supply curves for natural products like oil or gold look much like the curve in Figure 24-7. When prices are low, small quantities—perhaps the amounts nearest the surface of the ground—are produced and placed on the market. If product prices rise, producers will place more of the resource on the market because they can now afford to spend more money searching for the material and exploiting natural deposits.

In recent years the public has become more aware of the fact that all natural substances are in finite supply. There is a point where the supply curve for any resource turns sharply upward, and a very large increase in price is required to obtain even a small increase in output. The 1970s have seen a sudden scarcity of some resources that have been plentiful and readily available for years. Petroleum and petro-chemicals, for example, have become expensive because supply is limited and unresponsive to small changes in price. As demand for scarce resources continues to grow, prices will surely rise very rapidly. Since the supply curves for natural resources are unresponsive, many experts fear that the world is entering an era of severe resource scarcity.

Labor

The supply of labor has some peculiarities stemming from the way people behave and how they value money as opposed to leisure. An individual has only two choices about how to spend time: in work or in leisure.

As the price of labor (the wage) rises, the cost of leisure increases, since each hour away from work represents a larger sacrifice of income. At some wage, leisure becomes too expensive to enjoy, so the laborer

"Now that we've settled the minimum wage, we'd like to discuss the maximum wage."

offers more hours to productive rather than leisurely pursuits. As the wage rises still more, the cost of leisure continues to increase but a different set of incentives comes into play. At very high wages a worker may feel his total income is high enough to permit him to enjoy all the reasonable things he can want. Instead of offering more hours of labor services he offers fewer, being content to live with less than he could earn but having considerable leisure. The result of this behavior is a peculiar supply curve like the one shown in Figure 24-8.

There is some evidence that this backward-bending supply curve for labor holds for the number of hours of work an individual will offer in the labor market and also for the number of entrants into the market. In the latter case, the explanation centers on second jobs, overtime labor, or more than one person in the household working. As the price of labor rises, it becomes too expensive for a homemaker to stay home. Her time is too valuable. At some wage rate she enters the labor force and contributes to the family's total income. However, as the wage rate continues upward, the primary wage earner may be able to earn an income high enough to satisfy the family's needs. The homemaker drops out of the labor force, causing the supply curve to bend back on itself. There is evidence that the supply curve for labor does have this peculiar shape. However, an important area of investigation for economists interested in labor is determining the point at which an increase in the price of labor will bring with it a reduction in the volume of labor placed on the market.

In sum, the markets for factors of production and the markets for goods and services are guided by the same forces—supply and demand. Different forces affect factor demand and supply, but the interactions of supply and demand curves yield equilibrium prices for the factors in the same way. The resulting price/quantity relationship determines the amount of money that will be transferred from firm to household.

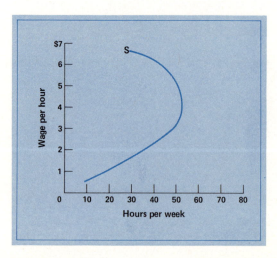

**Figure 24-8
A Supply Curve for Labor**

A Household's Sale of Factors

In Chapter 4, it was argued that all factors of production are owned by the households in the U.S. economy. To be sure, many or even most of the nonlabor factors are turned over to others to manage. A household owns capital and natural resources, but these are in the form of stocks in some major corporation. The corporation makes decisions about how factors will be used and when they will go onto the market. If the factors bring high returns, the managing company sends a reward, or dividend, to the household.

Some conscious choices must be made about marketing the resources that remain in the hands of the households. In general, these factors will be placed on the market when the market price exceeds the value of utility received by keeping them unemployed. No one will deny that leisure or just having resources available is worth something. For this reason, people cherish their vacation time each year. At some point, though, the marginal utility of leisure is exceeded by the marginal reward associated with giving it up. When this happens, leisure, which represents an idle resource, is sold.

Imperfections in the Factor Markets

A perfect market is one in which information is freely exchanged, anyone can buy or sell, and no one buyer or seller can have an appreciable influence on price. Few markets live up to these requirements. Imperfections plague the factor markets, and impede the movement of land, labor, and capital into those uses that would yield the highest return to society or to individual factor owners.

Land

In nearly every purchase of land, there is some contingency clause that prevents the buyer from being totally free to do what he likes with it. Zoning provisions and city codes prevent a land owner from raising chickens in the suburbs. Building codes insist that structures be built in a certain way, and regional plans insist that residences cannot be mixed with industrial activity in the local industrial park. These kinds of restrictions may prevent a land owner from engaging in a very profitable form of enterprise. Similarly, easements must be given to utility companies so they can maintain and repair their underground pipes and wires. (An *easement* is a right to use land for a very restricted purpose, such as to drive across it or dig into it. Nearly all urban land has some kind of easement on it.) Provisions like zoning and easements make the market for land and other natural resources imperfect, since they cause resource owners to forgo many opportunities for profits.

Labor

The labor market is more demonstrably imperfect. Labor is infrequently sold directly by the owner (worker) to the user. Instead, the arrangement between workers and employer is negotiated through a union that operates as a broker for many workers. There are many unions in the United States, and more groups are seeking to unionize each year. The advantages are clear: a group of 100 or 1,000 or 10,000 workers can negotiate with an employer more effectively than each worker operating alone. Unions have sought and obtained tremendous improvements in wages, working conditions, and fringe benefits for the majority of the workers in industry, trades, and crafts in the nation today.

With all these benefits accruing to them, it is legitimate to ask why unions are listed as an "imperfection" in the labor market. First, unions involve power in exactly the same fashion that a monopoly involves power. A labor union—quite apart from the will of many of its members—can strike. In so doing, it can disrupt the plans of its individual members with respect to how much labor they wish to sell and at what price they wish to sell it. Second, the union is often felt to make wages inflexible, especially in a downward direction. This violates the rules of demand and supply and can prevent the market from achieving its natural equilibrium.

Capital

The imperfection in the capital market is somewhat indirect. Much capital investment takes place using funds borrowed from banks, insurance companies, and other financial intermediaries. In its efforts to control the economy, the Board of Governors of the Federal Reserve System places limits on interest rates charged by lending agencies. These limits prevent the forces of supply and demand from operating to effect an equilibrium price.

Summary

1. Households earn income by selling factors of production. The factors are sold in markets that, to ranging degrees, respond to the laws of supply and demand. In this market economy, they help direct resources into their most profitable uses.
2. Factors of production are demanded because of the things they can produce; a factor is in demand if it helps produce a good that is in demand. Therefore, factor demand is derived from the demand for finished goods.
3. Production functions show the relationship between quantities of inputs and quantities of products.
4. If an input price drops, more of the input will be demanded. This is consistent with the demand curve as defined earlier.
5. Factors are supplied either directly by their owners or indirectly through managers. Corporations often act as managers of factors for people who own the corporation.
6. The supply of land (natural resources) is generally unresponsive to changes in price.
7. The supply of labor is peculiar because higher wages call forth more labor only to a certain point. After this point is reached, higher wages may *reduce* the amount of labor coming on the market, and the supply curve for labor may "bend back" on itself.
8. The markets for many kinds of factors have imperfections that prevent them from working with complete effectiveness.

Exercises

1. Explain these important terms and concepts:
   - production function
   - derived demand
   - inelastic supply of land
   - backward-bending supply curve
   - market imperfections

2. Assume that the following data came from a toaster factory. Since toasters are largely handmade, changes in the input of labor are accompanied by changes in output.

Men at work	Toasters made per day	Marginal product	Marginal revenue
0	0		
1	5		
2	14		
3	21		
4	26		
5	30		
6	33		
7	35		
8	36		
9	36		

   a. Calculate the marginal product produced by each *added* worker.
   b. If the price of toasters is $10 each, what is the value of each additional worker?
   c. If each worker receives $20 per day, how many should be hired?
   d. How many should be hired at $30 per day? $10 per day?
   e. Can this information be used to generate a demand curve for labor?

3. The demand for air travel has increased considerably since 1973. Air travel is a *factor;* it takes people to destinations where they can do or enjoy other things. Why has demand increased? Does the same explanation apply to the increases in demand for electric power? For medical services?

4. In earlier discussions of demand for goods and services, the demand curve was described as applying to one time, one place, one set of other prices, and one set of tastes. Do the same restrictions apply to the demand for factors? Why?

5. Hewlitt Packard moves to town. Its new plant will employ up to 5,000 persons, 2,500 of whom will be trained on the job to assemble components of various electrical devices. Both women and men may apply. The wages are reasonably high, working conditions are excellent, and the plant managers are getting along very well with union officials. What will the plant's arrival do to the local supply of labor? What will it do to the supply curve for labor? (Note: The difference is an important one.)

A Contemporary Problem

A Young Man Enters the Labor Force

Jerome Jeffries is a black 17-year-old from Butler Springs, Alabama. He and his six older brothers and four older sisters were born on a small parcel of land owned by their father. The land was not good; only a few crops could be grown each year. Even in the 1970s, the family saw and used very little cash. They grew food on the land in the summer and preserved for the other months. Jerome's father could read, but his mother could not.

Despite their own lack of education, the elder Jeffries tried to convince their children that education was the key to future job opportunities. Jerome watched the older children leave home for jobs or training schools, or to start families of their own. By 1976, the lure of a job and money became irresistible. Jerome quit high school in the middle of his junior year and headed north.

In February, Jerome arrived in Columbus, Ohio. He had $95 and a suitcase filled with work and school clothes. He was ill-prepared for the devastating cold, but after finding a room in a shabby hotel, he started to look for work. He tried the large plants whose signs he recognized, but the recruiting officers always had the same answer: "You're too young and have no skills." Jerome thought—but would not say—that he was not hired because he was black.

Soon his money dwindled, so he asked for jobs anywhere. Busboy in a restaurant? Grocery boy? Sweeper with the sanitation department? Still no work. At just the time his money ran out, the saddened Jerome Jeffries put all his information together. Although he could not state the problem with any sophistication, he reached these conclusions:

1 In 1976 jobs were very hard to find.
2 Fewer jobs were open to the young than to older applicants.
3 Blacks had a more difficult time finding employment than whites.
4 Education—at least a high school diploma—was important in obtaining even the most menial jobs.

Since Jerome was young, uneducated, and black, he stood virtually no chance of finding employment. To make the situation even more difficult, his childhood in Butler Springs has not prepared him for life in Columbus, Ohio. He knew nothing of welfare agencies, unemployment insurance, or even where to go for help. He returned home to Butler Springs in defeat.

Analysis. Jerome Jeffries' story begins almost like Ben Franklin's. Jeffries, like Franklin, headed for a new territory to find wealth and fame. He arrived penniless and started the search . . . but the similarity ends there. Franklin had opportunity in a labor-short land. Jeffries had little to sell, and as a result was forced to return to the life he had struggled to escape. While many of Jeffries' problems stemmed from the state of the economy, some were also related to imperfections in the labor market. Sort out the problems into these two categories and estimate their importance in the U.S. economy today.

25 The Distribution of Income

In his confirmation hearings prior to being named Vice President of the United States, Gerald Ford's personal fortune was announced as $256,378. Some months later, in an identical situation, Nelson Rockefeller told the same group that his fortune was $62.6 million.

The family of a migrant worker in Washington State's Yakima Valley includes four adults, four children, and two dogs. The head of the family reports they "do very well" on an annual income of $3,760.

A highly skilled machinist with several years' experience suffered a drop in income from $245 per week to $65 per week when he lost his job with the Chrysler Corporation during the recession of the middle 1970s.

In 1975, the average net income of all farmers in Arizona was $37,594. In West Virginia, it was $897.

A bellhop in a Honolulu hotel works for the minimum wage, but tips bring his annual income to "above $30,000."

The United States may or may not be a land of equal opportunity, but it is certainly not the land of equal income. Family incomes range from very high to very low. Since household incomes are earned through factor markets, the factors that families have to sell must vary substantially too. This, in fact, is true. Some families—the Rockefellers, Vanderbilts, and Revsons, for example—own large amounts of land and capital that are turned into large volumes of money in the factor markets each year. At the

"Aerospace, banking, chemicals, aluminum—we feel this neighborhood is a real melting pot."

other extreme are families that are very poorly endowed with factors and turn these into subsistence incomes.

Economists have always been concerned about the distribution of income, because when it changes, other things change too. Economics as a study of choice and choosing, however, has little to say about the distribution of income. Factor owners make choices about when and where to sell their factors, but beyond that, other forces and events determine how returns will be divided among them. Income distribution is important because it is closely related to people's sense of justice and to the kinds of decisions discussed in Chapters 1 and 2.

This chapter is about income distribution. It includes major sections on what some important economists have thought about the income distribution problem, on how income actually is distributed in the United States, and on the possible consequences of changing the distribution.

Economists Grapple with the Problem

Long before economics was even heard of, philosophers, intellectuals, and politicians worried about who should have how much income. If the ruling class took too much, the peasants were likely to revolt; if the ruling class gave the peasants a large share of all income, the class difference between the ruler and the ruled would be eroded. If some people were allowed to have very high incomes while others were forced to accept low ones, the high-income group could supply the volume of savings needed for investment and growth. If all people (or families) had the same incomes, it was possible that no saving at all would take place and economic growth might be stymied by lack of funds for investment. (Remember the concepts presented in Chapter 9. A high rate of income is accompanied by a higher marginal propensity to save than a low rate of income.) The controversy seemed endless.

After economics had become established as a scientific discipline, Adam Smith (1723–1790), then Karl Marx (1818–1883) had important things to say about income distribution. Smith, writing in an era when most people were poor and the world was just beginning to feel the rumblings of the Industrial Revolution, opined (1) that a generous wage would cause population to increase, (2) that the wage ought to be related to a worker's productivity, and (3) that a growing economy would provide more favorable opportunities for the poor than a declining or even stable economy.

Smith, David Ricardo (1772–1823), and the other classical economists approached income distribution in a systematic way. They supposed that society was divided into three large classes: workers, capital owners (whom they called *capitalists*), and landlords. This division led to the classification of factors as labor (what the worker has to sell), capital (what the capitalist has to sell), and land (what the landlord has to sell). The returns earned through sale of these factors were the incomes of the three classes of society. Smith and Ricardo predicted that as time passed and society progressed, landlords would outdo the capital owners in their shares of income. Karl Marx, the sociologist and economic theorist, concluded that as time passed, the capital owners would get the lion's share and the workers the smallest.

"*One day, my boy, when communism works, nothing will be yours.*"

These debates focused on the share of income that would go to each class of factors, and the resulting distribution came to be known as the *functional distribution of income.*

The functional distribution of income shows how much is earned by each of the major classes of factor inputs. Land earns rent, labor earns wages, capital earns interest, and entrepreneurship earns profits. The sum of these earnings is national income, which was defined in Chapter 6 as the return to the factors of production.

In more modern times, John Bates Clark (1847–1938) and Vilfredo Pareto (1848–1923) have contributed to the body of economic thought devoted to income distribution. Clark, in a monumental book entitled *The Distribution of Wealth,* subscribed to the Puritan ethic: Work begets income. Income must be earned by placing factors on the market and letting market forces allocate them to the most productive uses. Once allocated, factors are to be paid with reference to their marginal productivity. Very productive factors should earn high returns; factors of low productivity should earn low returns. Thus, the unskilled laborer earns $2 per hour while the highly skilled neurosurgeon earns $125,000 per year and Johnny Bench earns nearly $200,000 per year, all because of the marginal values of the activities they perform.

This method of determining income is not restricted to labor. It covers the services of other factors as well. Households owning land or capital can sell rights to use these resources, but they should still be rewarded on the basis of the resources' marginal productivities. According to Clark's view, justice is done when all of a household's factors are receiving payments equal to their marginal productivities. If a household has nothing to sell, it receives no income. If a household has much to sell, it receives much income. For decades, the marginal productivity approach to income distribution has served as an explanation or a rationalization of income distribution in the United States.

In his discussion of productivity and income distribution, Clark made a very useful distinction. He was careful to point out that *income* and *wealth* are not the same thing. Income is a *flow,* with dollars always flowing in from sales and flowing out to pay for purchases. Wealth, though, connotes a stock (or collection) of factors owned and having a value determined by the market.[1] Great wealth may or may not lead to high incomes; high incomes may or may not lead to great wealth. A wealthy person may be unable to pay his bills because he cannot turn his resources into cash on short notice. Similarly, a person of high income may never accumulate wealth.

---

[1]The market value of a stock of wealth may change demonstrably from time to time. This is particularly true of wealth held in the form of common stocks. One thousand shares of IBM stock were worth $365,000 in January 1970. Five years later the same shares were worth $170,000.

Vilfredo Pareto, an Italian economist, was a near contemporary of Clark's. He took an entirely different approach to income distribution. Rather than concentrating on the income earned by factors, Pareto studied the income earned by people regardless of their status as workers, capitalists, or landlords. The evidence available to Pareto suggested to him that the *size distribution of income* was very uneven in all nations regardless of their degree of development or the form of their economy.

The size distribution of income refers to the way in which the total value of a year's output is distributed among persons. Since it is a relatively new way to describe income distribution, the terms denoting it are not entirely settled. Some authors will use *personal distribution,* others *family distribution,* and still others *money distribution.*

This nearly universal income inequality intrigued Pareto, and he spent much of his intellectual life trying to learn what "laws" governed income distribution. He was unsuccessful, finally concluding that the determinants of income distribution were so complex that they might never be understood.

While Pareto could not find an *explanation* for the way income is distributed, he did draw attention to *describing* it. Where Clark would have asked, "How much labor does Jones have to sell and what can it earn at the margin?" Pareto asked, "What is the Jones family's income?" The former is a very useful question in the study of resource allocation; the latter is very useful in studies of human welfare and wage and income policies.

The Functional Distribution of Income

The functional distribution of income for five-year intervals starting in 1950 is shown in Table 25–1. The table entries are percentages of national income, the one income account designed specifically to show rewards to factors. In 1950, and for many years before, employee compensation

Table 25–1 The Functional Distribution of Income (percent)

Type of income	1950	1955	1960	1965	1970	1974
Employee compensation	63.9	67.7	70.8	70.0	70.6	74.9
Corporate profits	15.8	14.2	12.3	13.1	10.2	8.1
Proprietors' profits	15.8	12.7	11.1	10.3	10.3	9.3
Rental income	3.7	4.2	3.9	3.4	3.6	2.3
Net interest paid	0.8	1.2	1.9	3.2	5.3	5.4

(wages) amounted to approximately two-thirds of national income. Changes in the past quarter century would have surprised the classical economists, who thought that land's share would increase, and also Marx, who thought the share going to capital would grow. Since 1950, labor's share has gradually crept upward in response to minimum-wage legislation, general pressures for higher wages, and increases in the number of persons employed in *service industries.*

The service industries are those that provide a useful service rather than a tangible product that can be sold and resold. Since 1950, service industries in the U.S. economy have grown very rapidly. Among the fastest growing are government service and personal care.

The share of interest payments has also increased, but even in 1974 it was less than 6 percent of all income. These increases in the shares of wages and interest have come at the expense of rents and business profits.

The Size Distribution of Income

In the last generation, economists and citizens have switched attention from the functional distribution to the size distribution of income. The new approach centers attention on the degree of inequality among family incomes. The U.S. Department of Commerce provides data on the size distribution of income. Some of these data are shown in Tables 25-2 and 25-3. The tables are best understood if a base point is kept in mind before reading them. A suitable base is average family income. In 1953, average family income in the United States was $4,738. By 1963, it had grown to

Table 25-2 Personal Income of Families by Income Class (percent)

Income class	Percent of families					
	1950	1955	1960	1965	1970	1974
Under $1,000	11.5	7.7	5.0	2.9	1.6	1.3
1,000–1,999	13.2	9.9	8.0	6.0	3.0	1.3
2,000–2,999	17.8	11.0	8.7	7.2	4.3	2.7
3,000–3,999	20.6	14.6	9.8	7.7	5.1	3.6
4,000–4,999	13.6	15.5	10.5	7.9	5.3	4.1
5,000–5,999	9.0	12.7	12.9	9.3	5.8	4.4
6,000–6,999	5.2	9.5	10.8	9.5	6.0	4.7
7,000–9,999	5.8	12.9	20.0	24.2	19.9	13.8
10,000–14,999	3.3	4.8	10.6	17.7	26.7	24.3
15,000 and above		1.4	3.7	7.6	22.3	39.8

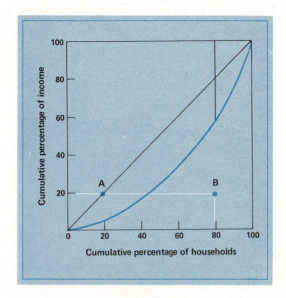

**Figure 25-1
A Lorenz Curve for the Mid-1970s**

$6,998, and by 1973 it had nearly doubled to $13,622 per family. (*Caution:* The 1953 to 1973 period was characterized by rapid inflation, so the growth in real family income appears to have been larger than it actually was. When all incomes are inflated to reflect their 1973 purchasing power, average family income becomes $8,200 in 1953, $9,386 in 1963, and $13,622 in 1973.)

Table 25-2 shows the percent of families in each of several income classes since 1950. Although the presence of inflation weakens the argument somewhat, the table shows that in the past quarter century many families have moved from the lower to the higher income classes. In 1950, over three-quarters of the population earned incomes below $5,000, and only 3.3 percent of all families had incomes above $10,000. In 1974 only 13.0 percent of the families were in income classes earning $5,000 or less, and 64.1 percent had incomes over $10,000. Even after correcting for changes in purchasing power, the general population had more purchasing power in recent years than in the immediate post-World War II years.

The income class scheme of Table 25-2 is only one way to present the size distribution of income. Figure 25-1 uses a Lorenz curve to show how income is divided among families. The Lorenz curve is a special kind of diagram used to show the relationship between two cumulative series of percentages. In describing the distribution of income, the cumulative percentage of income is shown on the vertical axis, while the horizontal shows the cumulative percentage of population. The black diagonal line is similar to the 45-degree reference line encountered in the chapters on macroeconomics. All of the points on this line represent equality. If the distribution of income among families were equal, 20 percent of the population would receive 20 percent of the income and this equality would be

Distribution of Wealth

The connection between income and wealth is a clear one. Wealth comes from the possession of resources, and income comes from their sale or the sale of their use. The U.S. Department of Commerce measures income and the distribution of income each year. Measurements of the distribution of wealth are much less common. In 1962—15 years ago—the Federal Reserve System studied the distribution of wealth. The results are given on the right.

Over 8 percent of families in the U.S. had negative *net worth*. Net worth is the number of dollars a person or family (or company) would have if all its assets were sold and all its debts were paid. A family or company with negative net worth owes more money than it could possibly amass. Only 7.5 percent of families could claim net worths of over $50,000.

The Board of Governors also found that in 1962 the wealthiest 1 percent of the population owned 26 percent of the nation's private assets, the wealthier 20 percent owned 75 percent of all assets, and the poorest 25 percent had none at all. The distribution of wealth in the United States is even more unequal than the distribution of income!

Net worth class (thousands of dollars)	Percent of population
Negative	8.1
0– 1	17.3
1– 5	17.3
5– 10	14.2
10– 25	24.4
25– 50	11.2
50–100	5.1
100–200	1.0
200–500	0.9
500 and above	0.5

indicated by point A on the line. But if 80 percent of the population was receiving 20 percent of the income, the result would be shown as point B. In this way, all information about the distribution of income can be presented below the line of equality.

The unequal distribution of income in the U.S. yields an actual Lorenz curve like the one shown below the equality curve in Figure 25-1. In 1974 the low-income 20 percent of the population taken together received 5.4 percent of all income. The next fifth (21–40 percent) received 12 percent, and the high-income fifth (81–100 percent) received 41 percent of all income. The Lorenz curve displaying the actual distribution of income traces a bow under the line of equality.

The kind of data used to construct a Lorenz curve are shown in Table 25–3. Although there has been some shifting of income between 1955 and 1974, the distributions in these years are amazingly consistent. True, the low-income fifth increased its share from 4.8 percent in 1955 to 5.4 percent in 1974, but the gain came from the second and third quintiles, not

Table 25–3 Distribution of Income among Fifths of the U.S. Population (percent)

Group	1974	1965	1955
1 (low-income fifth)	5.4	5.2	4.8
2	12.0	12.2	12.2
3	17.6	17.8	17.8
4	24.1	23.9	23.4
5 (high-income fifth)	39.9	40.9	41.8

from the high-income group, which consistently earns approximately 40 percent of all income.

A quick look at Table 25–2 shows that U.S. families are getting richer. The message of Table 25–3 is more sombre. Even though all incomes have gone up, the low-income 20 percent of U.S. families still earn only 5.4 percent of the nation's income—not significantly more than the 4.8 percent they earned two decades ago. The high-income 20 percent continues to earn over 40 percent of the income. There has not been a transfer of income from rich to poor. Even the massive income transfer programs of the 1960s and 1970s (welfare, unemployment, Aid to Families with Dependent Children, food stamps, and the like) have not helped the nation's low-income groups to gain ground on the high-income groups.

Recent social and economic foment has brought about some change in income distribution. Women are coming closer to men in their drive to receive equal pay for equal work. More significantly, nonwhites are gaining ground. In 1955 the median nonwhite family income was 55 percent as high as the median family income for whites ($4,685 for nonwhites; $8,495 for whites). In 1965, nonwhite family income was still only 55 percent of the income earned by whites, but in 1974, after a decade of civil rights movements and racial activism, nonwhite family income rose to 62 percent of white family income.

The Effects of Change

Any change in the way income is distributed will also change the composition and distribution of the nation's total product. If income is taken from the very poor and given to the very rich, the demand for things purchased by the poor will diminish, while the demand for things purchased by the wealthy will increase. Demand for stout wool coats, inexpensive automobiles, and ground meat will fall. Demand for furs, luxury automobiles, and lavish restaurants will increase. If income is transferred from rich to poor (moving the Lorenz curve closer to the line of equality), demand for steak and lobster tails will change to demand for rib steak, and demand for hamburger will change to demand for rib steak too. The formerly rich will be able to afford fewer luxuries, and the formerly poor will buy more and better things. In either case, a change in distribution causes changes in what is being produced, in the value of factors, and in the marginal returns to factor owners.

Although the effects of income transfers on income distribution are not completely understood, society has demonstrated little fear of their general economic consequences. In 1974 the federal government made payments of $30.1 billion—an amount larger than the defense budget—for income security. Included in income security programs were unemployment compensation, social security, welfare, and many other special kinds of payments to insure the incomes of special groups. These payments were made without regard to possible ill effects, simply because the cost of *not* making the transfers was *known* to be too high.

Perfect Income Equality?

From time to time someone proposes that every family, or even every person, should receive the same income. If national income is $1,054 billion and 211 million people reside in the United States, each person should receive $4,995. Under this scheme, monies would be gathered by some central agency, then doled out to citizens so that everyone, regardless of age, sex, race, ability, or need would receive the same amount. While such a scheme may be appealing on account of its equity and simplicity, it has significant problems. Equal sharing of national product would surely damage the incentive to work especially hard or to engage in risk taking. If hard-earned income is going to be scattered among those who do not work, there is no particular incentive to work more than absolutely necessary. Similarly, if there is no chance of large gain, no one will want to undertake the risk associated with a new business venture. It is quite possible that, under such a system, no one would even bother to invent a more efficient automobile or become a neurosurgeon.

A more insidious problem of perfect equality in the size distribution of income concerns the act of saving. Saving is one of the main requirements of economic growth and progress. Unless society produces a surplus that can be saved, it has no extra funds to invest in the machines, factories, or services that will enhance future production. In the U.S. economy, most income classes do some saving, but the majority of the saved funds come from the upper-income groups. If income were taken from them, this traditional source of saving would be weakened, thus diluting society's capacity to generate investment funds.

The question of income distribution and redistribution is an important one in the U.S. economy, and economists acting *as economists* cannot indicate the best distribution. They stumble on fundamental questions: Best for whom and best for what purpose? Early theorists thought that income should go to those who had the capacity to earn it, so that those who possessed large volumes of usable resources would have high incomes and those who had little to sell would be able to earn only low incomes. Owning salable factors is still the key to earning very large incomes, but the views of economists, legislators, and the general populace have gradually shifted to place emphasis on the income needed by a family rather than on the income it is able to earn. Even so, there are still many families in the United States who have very low incomes and very slim chances of improving them.

Summary

1 Although most segments of the U.S. population now have higher incomes than before, income is still distributed very unevenly among families.
2 Economists are unable to specify the *best* or the *correct* income distribution.
3 J. B. Clark described a family's income by referring to the factors the family owned and the ability of these factors to earn money.
4 Vilfredo Pareto approached income distribution by asking who *has* it, not necessarily who *earns* it.
5 Although income has gone up, the proportions earned by each fifth of the population have remained essentially the same for many years.
6 Changing the distribution of income brings many changes in the allocation of resources.

Exercises

1 Explain these important terms and concepts:
    classes in society   size distribution
    functional distribution   inequality
    income (as opposed to wealth)   Lorenz curve
                                   income transfer
2 Classify the following as either income or wealth:
  a One hundred shares of Union Pacific stock
  b An unemployment insurance check
  c The ability to lay bricks
  d A gift certificate from a department store
  e A dividend check from Union Pacific
3 Changing the *geographic* distribution of income can have significant effects on allocation and efficiency. Comment on the possible consequences of the following redistributions:
  a Taxing people in Nevada, then transferring the revenues to people in Wisconsin

b Sending money from Michigan to Appalachia
c Taking money from New Englanders and giving it to the poor in Southern California

4 There is an intimate connection between income distribution and unemployment. A policy to raise incomes of the poor will often also result in increased employment. Why? (Hint: In responding to this question, recall the lessons of the marginal propensity to consume and the multiplier from Chapter 9. Real-life examples are the tax cut in 1964 and the income tax refund in 1975.)

5 Past Congresses have proposed, discussed, then defeated several bills aimed at providing rental allowances (partial payment of rents) for poor people. The motivation behind these bills has been humanitarian: Poor people residing in cities need subsidies to help pay the very high rents. The opponents have argued that the benefits of the program would eventually fall into the hands of slumlords, thus aggravating the uneven distribution of income. Which view is correct? Which is the more acceptable to you? To the U.S. public?

A Contemporary Problem

Food Stamps in the U.S. Economy

During the New Frontier programs of the Kennedy administration and President Johnson's War on Poverty, the federal government tried several methods of increasing the volume and quality of food available to the nation's poor. The food stamp program is one of the few survivors of that affluent, socially conscious era.

The program is simple. A qualified and certified poor person (or family) purchases food stamps at the local post office or other designated outlet. If the purchaser has a very low income, he pays approximately $45 for stamps that can be used to purchase food valued at $100. The intent of the program is to redistribute income by placing more purchasing power in the hands of the poor. The stamps are used like cash in buying most foods. Over the years, they have allowed many families to upgrade their diets through either quantity or variety. In 1973, the program had 12.2 million participants, who paid $1.8 billion for stamps worth $3.9 billion in food purchases.

The food stamp program has been controversial because it places only modest restrictions on the user. The stamps can be used on hot dogs or New York cut steaks, soda crackers or caviar. Grocery lines are filled with customers using stamps to purchase food that costs nonstamp users much more in cash. The problem centers on visibility and choice. For decades this society has kept its poor well hidden from the public eye. When welfare was absolutely necessary, it was doled out in offices away from the mainstream of commerce and industry, or in the quiet of a church rectory. The benevolent rich, in effect, "bought" the privilege of not having to see the poor. The food stamp program has brought welfare recipients into the open and given them the opportunity to select what they want

"Well, why the devil don't *you* accept food stamps?"

to buy and eat. Many people have objected to the kinds of things they see the poor putting into their grocery carts. "Nobody on welfare should eat such expensive food" is the theme of many common complaints.

On the other hand, it is exactly in this criticism that a very important advantage of the food stamp problem can be seen. Rather than forcing the poor into a lock-step cycle of handouts and begging, the program allows low-income families free choice. They now have purchasing power that can be exchanged for food of their liking. True, some have gone to excess and spent outrageous sums for the fleeting pleasure of an expensive cut of meat or a rare cheese, but such extravagance does not increase their capacity to purchase the stamps. It means only that fewer stamps are left for milk, bread, and vegetables. The stamps are actually an increase in income to the users, who may spend it as they wish. In doing so, they help society to allocate resources into the production of things consumers want to buy. The program aids the economy in two ways: First, the low-income families receive food; second, the economy becomes more efficient.

26 When the Market Fails

At this moment approximately 22,000 small towns in the United States are actively seeking industries to help bolster their sagging economies. Any industry will do. The towns want payrolls. They want the church pews filled. They want children romping merrily in the streets, and they want to hear the happy ring of the cash register. Somehow the world has passed these communities by, and now they are trying to catch up. Only about 1,500 industrial relocations take place each year, however, and in many of them an industry moves from one large city to another—from Akron, Ohio to Santa Fe, New Mexico. Left behind are Lyons, Kansas; Davenport, Washington; Mahoney, Pennsylvania; Saludu, South Carolina, and over 20,000 others.

Occasionally one of these towns does succeed in its quest for industry. What happens then? Certainly many of the original objectives are fulfilled, but there are often unexpected and unwanted results too. Clean air turns gray and smelly. Traffic problems snarl the main street at rush hours. Thousands of new workers move into town and everyone's rent goes up. The arrival of the industry is a mixed blessing.

Many of the unwanted aspects of industry—like smoke, odor, and noise—are not accounted for in any market transactions. Neither the buyer of a product nor its manufacturer considers the effects of noise on people living close to the factory. These people have an interest in the exchange, since the factory affects their daily lives, but the market fails to acknowledge that interest.

"The air today is smoother to the touch, but it doesn't taste very good."

This chapter is about market failure. It opens with a look at its causes, describes some common types of market failure, then turns to the economist's disposition toward market failure. Some ways of dealing with the problems are mentioned, and the chapter ends with a discussion of beneficial market failure.

The Causes of Market Failure

A market fails because it cannot take account of all parties who are affected by a particular transaction or economic process. Such failures abound, and they appear in a wide range of complexity. Take a simple instance: A suburbanite purchases a power mower. The seller gets a fair price for the mower and the buyer obtains the necessary amount of utility from the expenditure. Neither buyer nor seller, though, considers the "costs" imposed on the neighbors, who must now suffer the noise and fumes on Sunday mornings. The market fails to count these costs because no one—buyer, seller, or disturbed neighbor—is willing to go to the trouble of collecting payments for the damages.

A more complicated case occurs in a model economy consisting of a factory, a household that supplies labor to the factory, and a second household that has no direct connection to the factory. A hypothetical map of this little economy, showing the locations of the actors and some of the effects they must endure, is shown in Figure 26-1. The factory produces an industrial product (steel or autos or railway spikes) and must purchase labor from a nearby household. A sure market relationship exists between the two. The household receives wages in return for its labor. There exists, however, a third party—a household downwind that has no economic relationship to the factory but must absorb the polluting discharges from its chimneys. The factory is taking away clean air from this household, but the household cannot make the factory compensate for the effect. The market fails because there is no way for the injured parties to make the factory pay for damages it incurs.

The effects on the third-party household are external to any transactions engaged in by the factory. Hence, such market failures have come to be called *externalities.*

An externality is an incidental effect produced by economic activities but not accounted for by the market system. Such effects do not enter the cost or benefit decisions of either buyer or seller, and are thus considered external. Externalities can be either harmful or beneficial, but the harmful ones attract more attention by far. Externalities are sometimes called "nonmarket effects" or "third-party effects."

Figure 26-1 A Common Externality

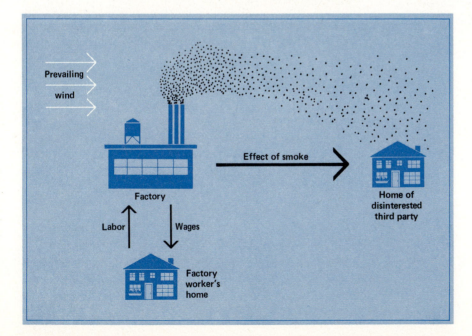

Kinds of Market Failure

Several attempts have been made to facilitate analysis and policy making by classifying market failures into neat boxes. But in every case, even the casual observer can usually find an exception. For that reason, the kinds of market failure are best described through examples. In the case of the lawn mower cited earlier, the market mechanism cannot determine the value of the neighbor's sleep, nor can it devise a way for the neighbor to pay to have the lawn mower quieted. If one neighbor bribes the mower owner to stay in bed, all other neighbors will benefit too. Who, then, should pay?

Now consider a factory that dumps industrial wastes into Lake Erie. The lake waters are "free." No one has rights to them, so people can do with them as they please. The factory avoids the costs of waste treatment by simply dumping the wastes into the lake. Other "owners" of the lake (the general public) cannot find a way to provide a market for clean water in Lake Erie.

Suppose a service station moves into a residential neighborhood. The station does a good business and is a real help to people in the vicinity, but its existence causes property values to fall. There are no regulations that prevent a landowner from putting up a service station, so neighboring owners suffer harmful externalities.

It is natural to think of all externalities and all market failures as undesirable, since the most dramatic ones—smoke, smog, sewage, and noise—are. But the economy is filled with favorable results of market failures as well. Since they are favorable and no one is inclined to eliminate them, they are not in the news. The following are some examples of "good failures":

1. *Bees.* When one farmer contracts with a beekeeper to put bees in his orchard, the farmer next door benefits, too. The bees do not know that the neighbor is not helping to pay for their services, so they pollinate his trees as well. The market fails to collect for this beneficial effect.
2. *Paving sidewalks.* When a homeowner paves the sidewalks bordering his property, all the people in town benefit because they no longer have to walk in the mud. There is no way for the homeowner to collect from the many sidewalk users.
3. *Educating the population.* An educated populace is worth something. Educated people supposedly choose more wisely and direct resource use with more precision. Because of these good aspects of education, society has declared that everyone must complete at least some schooling. Society has had to do this through government intervention and financing, because there is no effective way to recover the benefits accruing to the rest of the group as a result of one person's education, and a market for public schooling has failed to develop.

The Economist's View

External effects and market failures have been noticed since economics began. However, the emphasis on these problems has changed significantly over time. When Adam Smith was writing his important message regarding the source of a nation's wealth, there was little doubt that specialization added to the output of material objects and any increase in output increased society's well-being. In Smith's day, the emphasis was on *more.* Little attention was paid to the fact that the process of producing more things for the market incidentally produced effects that the market showed little desire for. Smoke, industrial waste, and congestion made an early appearance in industrializing Europe. They were recognized as bad, but they were presumed necessary adjuncts to progress.

John Stuart Mill wrote nearly three-quarters of a century after Smith. Like Smith, Mill lived in an era that needed and venerated growth. Even in Mill's time, people in Europe were starving and living in squalor. They clamored to get to the New World, only to find that it too was a harsh place and did not provide easy access to unlimited supplies of goods and services. When Mill published his major economics work in 1848, most people were still living a hand-to-mouth existence, and asked no questions about propriety when it was necessary to violate nature in order to survive. Mill saw the human race on a treadmill, going nowhere. As soon as more goods and services became available, more mouths appeared to consume them; as soon as technology allowed production to expand, the existing population simply extended its wants so as to consume whatever was available. He was forced to ponder the question: Why struggle for more if the struggle must only become more and more intense and occupy time that might otherwise be spent enjoying life? John Stuart Mill was raising basic questions about any economic system that depends upon, or even thrives on, growth. He was among the first economists to suggest that growth might have some damaging qualities. Although he did not carry his reasoning to analytical extremes, he did pose important questions. His questions went unremarked for 75 years.

Early in this century, an economist at Cambridge University in England began to investigate the problem of the economic system from another point of view. Rather than following Mill's tradition and examining the macro consequences of growth, A. C. Pigou (1877–1959) pondered the questions of humanity's total happiness under the label "welfare economics." While the main burden of his arguments centered on the size, distribution, and stability of income, Pigou also asked about the costs unwittingly imposed on society as a result of economic activity. He reasoned that two kinds of costs accompanied all economic activity: *private costs,* those paid for factors of production; and *external* or *unpaid costs* imposed on others. A steel mill pays for land, labor, and raw materials. It

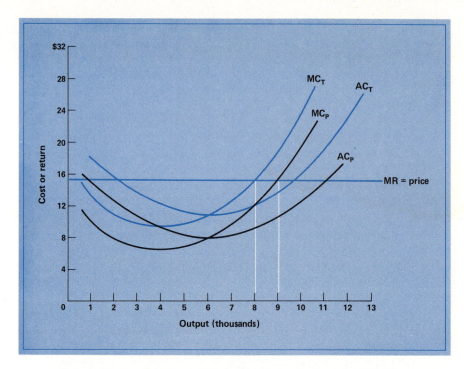

Figure 26-2 Effects of Unpaid Costs on Level of Output

does not pay to have people's sooty draperies cleaned, or for ears damaged by noise, or for repainting the houses near the mill.

The prices paid through factor markets are called private costs, since they are actually paid by the private producing firms. Other costs directly attributable to the production process are called unpaid costs, or sometimes external costs. Together, the costs make up *social cost,* the cost society must bear in order to insure production of certain outputs.

Pigou suggested that unpaid costs arise primarily because firms are not required to bear all of the costs associated with their productive activities. Smoke is belched into the atmosphere without cost to the offending firm. The air that absorbs the smoke is free and there is no way to charge for its use. When a firm can use the atmosphere as a sewer, it avoids paying some costs of production by shifting them to the general public. If it can avoid some costs, it has a tendency to produce more than the socially optimal amount of product.

Two sets of cost curves are shown in Figure 26-2. The lower set, AC_P and MC_P, show the private costs that accompany the firm's productive activity. A higher set, AC_T and MC_T, show the total or social costs of productive activities. If the firm pays only private costs, its optimal level of output will be 9,000 units. If society is making the output decision, however, output will be cut back to $MC_T = MR$ or 8,000 units. Society, because it must count filthy air, polluted streams, and occupational disease as very real costs, will wish to produce less than the firm that is not required to pay for all the resources it uses.

All costs avoided by the firm add up to the vertical distance between AC_P and AC_T in Figure 26-2. This vertical distance shows the dollar value of unpaid (external) costs incurred during the production process. If these costs were included in the firm's decision making, the firm would elect to produce a lower volume of output. If a firm is not required to pay *all* costs, it will expand output to a level beyond the socially optimal level. It will allow its neighbors to help pay some of the costs. The question is, what can be done to correct market failures?

Means of Correcting Market Failures

In the last 15 years, economists, lawmakers, public officials, and citizen groups have tried to find ways of bringing harmful externalities under control. These efforts are so new that the methods used are not consistently effective. Three popular ways of coping with market failure are internalization (or merger), tax and subsidy plans, and legal restrictions.

Internalization or Merger

In a market failure, the transaction does not take account of the interests of all parties affected. Factories pollute streams without regard for who might suffer the consequences of dirty water. Rural areas educate their children only to see them flee to the cities for employment. In the former case, the downstream water user is not compensated for his loss; in the latter case, the urban resident does not help educate the migrant from the rural area.

Say that the stream polluter is a firm that produces lettuce picking machines, while downstream there is a firm using the water to irrigate lettuce fields. The manufacturing firm finds it profitable to forgo expensive waste treatment facilities, and dumps its wastes directly into the stream. Because the firm disregards these costs, its cost curves are low and the picking machines can be offered for sale at a low price. However, the wastes fill the stream with chemical elements that interfere with plant growth. Thus, as more lettuce picking machines are built, the pollution problem increases and lettuce production drops. One possible solution is for the lettuce-producing firm to merge with the firm that manufactures picking machines. The merger would yield a single firm with one cost and revenue structure and one set of profits to attempt to maximize. This

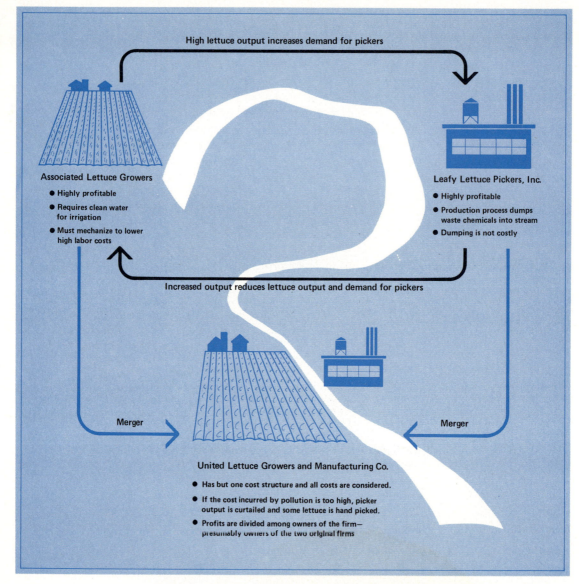

Figure 26-3 Internalizing an Externality

scheme is depicted in Figure 26–3. Before merging, a mutually destructive relationship exists between the two firms. High lettuce output leads to increased demand for picking machines. If this demand is filled, however, the resulting increase in water pollution reduces lettuce output. Low lettuce output leads to diminished output of pickers since fewer machines are needed. Combining the firms allows one decision maker to make one decision that is optimal for the combined productive activities. Merging internalizes the externality.

For decades, the nation's rural areas have sent their youth to the city. As technology in rural-based industries—agriculture, forestry, and mining, for example—has caused capital and machines to be substituted for labor, new entrants into the rural labor force have been forced to seek employment in larger towns and cities. The children of the rural United States leave for the city as soon as they have completed their mandatory local schooling.

Providing education for a group of people who will not make a notable contribution to the local economy is an expensive externality borne by rural residents. Cities gladly accept ready-educated laborers, but make no voluntary move to reimburse rural school districts for the cost of training these laborers. The market fails, since one group—the rural taxpayers—pays the costs of education while another group—the students and their city employers—reap the benefits. This externality could be internalized by developing a tax and subsidy scheme like the one in Figure 26-4.

In the top portion of the figure, a rural school district is bearing the total cost of education, while some part of the outside world is receiving the

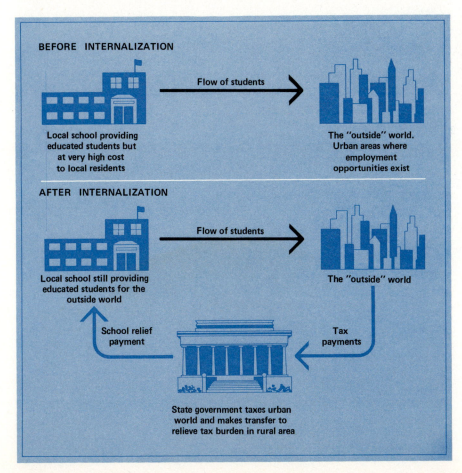

Figure 26-4
Internalization Through a Third Party: The School Funding Case

educated students. In the lower portion of the figure, a state taxing authority has intervened to tax the urban area and make a monetary transfer back to the rural area. Such policies are now in effect in many states.

Taxes and Subsidies

Perhaps the most common externality problem arises when an industrial firm uses the atmosphere, a stream, or a lake as a dumping ground for waste materials. Lake Erie is a notable case. For decades, the industries around Lake Erie used it as a receptacle for raw sewage and industrial waste. By the mid-1960s the lake was nearly incapable of supporting life of any kind. Now, in the late 1970s, it is slowly coming back to life, but only because tremendous sums of money are being spent by polluting firms and public agencies to repair the damage. The smog over Los Angeles and New York have resulted from scores of industries and millions of private autos using the atmosphere as an open sewer. In each case, users of the resource (the lake or the air) do not pay the full social cost associated with their use. These external effects are not counted in the price of the products.

One way to correct this problem is to force polluting firms to pay a tax based on the volume of pollutants they put into the atmosphere, a lake, or a stream. Such a tax can induce a firm to install anti-pollution devices or otherwise to clean up its own mess so that third parties are not forced to suffer the effects of an impure environment. How a tax of this type works is shown in the cost curves of Figure 26–5. The pre-tax output of a polluting

Figure 26–5 Taxing a Polluting Firm

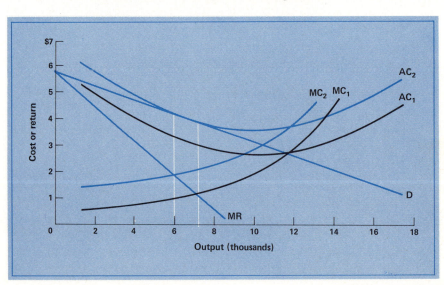

firm enjoying some monopoly power would be about 7,200 (derived from the intersection of MC_1 and MR). This output is sold at approximately $4 per unit. The production process causes some deterioration in the quality of the environment, since wastes are allowed to flow into a nearby stream. If the government (local, state, federal, or some combination) imposes a tax on pollutants equal to the vertical distance between MC_1 and MC_2 (also between AC_1 and AC_2), the firm's immediate reaction will be to reduce output. Following the $MC = MR$ rule, output is reduced to about 6,000 units (to $MC_2 = MR$) bringing $4.30 each on the market. Even though price has increased, the firm's profits have diminished because of its higher costs. The firm will either (1) be satisfied with lower profits, (2) reduce the amount of pollutants dumped into the stream, or (3) go out of business. Option 1 requires no action other than paying the tax. The tax does not directly affect the amount of pollution in the stream, but the tax collecting agency can use the tax revenues to finance its own cleanup program. Option 2 can be accomplished in either of two ways: The firm can reduce output and thus reduce the amount of tax it has to pay. This is not wise, since by itself this action does not change the location of either the marginal cost or the marginal revenue curve. Tax avoidance of this kind is not economical since it forces the firm into a situation in which MR exceeds MC. A second way to accomplish option 2 is to install anti-polluting equipment. Like the tax, this move would raise costs and would, hence, alter the optimal level of output. Since the cost of this alternative is not shown in the figure, its effect upon price and output is not known.

Those who advocate control through taxing argue that a tax scheme is manageable; it requires only monitoring polluting firms and applying the tax. They also argue that the penalty is assessed precisely where it should be—on the offending party. Opponents argue that such a tax will immediately be passed on to purchasers of the final product, and that no one knows for sure how high the tax should be. Purists argue that the tax does not eliminate the problem, but only slaps the wrists of those who make the mess.

Many scholars and lawmakers do not endorse taxes on pollutants (or on polluters). They feel that paying this kind of tax is nothing more than purchasing the right to pollute, or buying a "license" to pollute. This view is a hard one to dispute. Indeed, the industrialist who pays the tax *can* continue to pollute the atmosphere, river, or lake. Three arguments can be marshalled in favor of a tax. First, a taxing scheme would be easy to enforce. A paper mill would pay a certain sum, and a feedlot a different sum, but each rate would be related to the volume and type of pollutants emitted by the offending firm. Second, the tax could be set high enough to virtually insure that all offending firms would install equipment to clean up the mess. Third, the funds raised through the tax might be used to finance some other mode of relieving the problem.

Subsidies are the opposite of taxes. Whereas the tax discourages a firm from behaving in a certain way, the subsidy *encourages* particular kinds of activity. A subsidy might be designed to encourage a polluting firm to install pollution-controlling equipment. The government might allow large tax credits (a subsidy) for the installation, or it might even pay some portion of the installation cost.

Subsidies are not limited to pollution-related externalities. The National School Lunch Program is designed to provide nutritious, low-cost lunches to needy schoolchildren. Since school personnel cannot effectively screen students to separate the needy from those who are not, the program is made universal. Any child attending a participating school can purchase a large noonday meal at low cost. The nation feels that the general population receives some benefit from having well-fed children, so it subsidizes the program through direct financial assistance and by making some surplus foods available to the schools at very low cost.

Subsidies must always be used with care. The U.S. Government has always been cautious in its use of subsidies because they smack of "something for nothing," which runs counter to the Puritan work ethic and the general mood of the nation's reward structure. The school lunch subsidy is sanctioned because even the most cautious conservative cannot speak out against feeding needy children. The huge subsidies paid to farmers between 1935 and 1970 were unpopular because the general public did not like being taxed to support an industry that was producing a then unsalable product. It remains to be seen how effective subsidies can be in removing some of the externalities associated with congestion, industrialization, and economic growth.

"We must consider the health of the community, we must consider our image, and we must consider the fine of $25,000 a day."
Reproduced by special permission of *Playboy* Magazine; copyright © 1971 by *Playboy*.

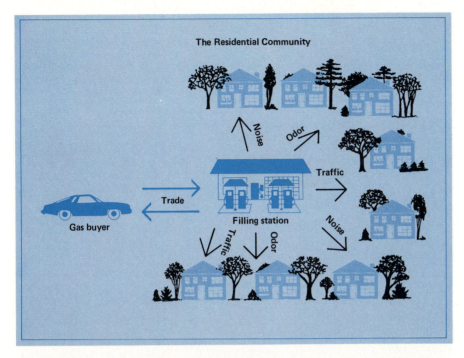

Figure 26–6 Externalities Solved Through Noneconomic Institutions

Legal Restrictions

Some external effects are so far removed from the market that no market-oriented institution or rule can be used to remedy them. A filling station in the center of a residential district may be convenient for nearby residents and very profitable for its owners, but it may lower the values of adjacent residential properties. There is no manageable economic solution to this common problem. Cities use zoning laws to protect property values against the adverse effects of a business being located in a residential neighborhood. This problem is shown graphically in Figure 26–6. The filling station and its customers are two parties to an economic transaction. They may carry out their transaction in a residential area, but neither of them needs to have any other connection with the area. The operator may live blocks away; the customer, miles away.

The gas station is odorous and noisy, and causes traffic problems at certain hours of the day. These effects are so diverse that no taxing device or internalizing arrangement can be expected to compensate the owners of nearby land for losses in the value of their properties, so zoning ordinances are instituted to prevent people from opening filling stations in residential neighborhoods. The community uses a law or legal restriction to avoid lowered property values and hostile voters. The zoning law is not an economic law, but it has economic consequences.

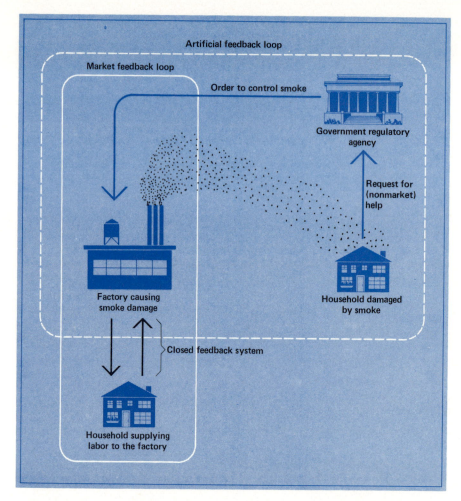

Figure 26-7 A Market and an Artificially Closed Feedback Loop

Legal or regulatory solutions to externality problems have become popular methods of augmenting the market. It is now illegal to put up certain kinds of signs along certain highways because their external effects impose upon drivers using the highway. It is illegal to exceed certain noise levels because the sound may damage the hearing of people nearby who have no direct way to prevent the noise. It is illegal to dump raw sewage, pile up solid waste, or allow large quantities of sulphur dioxide to flow into the air. It is even illegal for one of Seattle's most famous restaurants to broil salmon over alderwood fires, because the smoke emitted into the air violates state and federal clean air standards.

In the 1960s and 1970s many environmental protection laws have been passed to reduce the harmful effects of externalities that had developed as a result of market failures. This use of codes and laws does close market feedback loops, although indirectly. Such a closure is illustrated in Figure 26-7. This figure differs from Figure 26-1 in that now the household affected by smoke has sought and obtained help through an institutional restriction. The governing institution imposes legal limits on the polluter, who must now reduce the volume of pollutants emitted into the air. The rule is a clear-cut case of using the law to eliminate a deficiency of the market system.

Beneficial External Effects

In a pollution-conscious era, it is easy to overlook the possibility of favorable external effects or favorable market failures. There is no reason to believe that favorable externalities will occur either more or less frequently than unfavorable ones. From a purist's point of view, both the good and bad externalities represent the failure of market transactions to close completely. In a practical view, favorable externalities do not usually cause objections or find their way to the courts. When one family living in Providence, Utah decides to spray its backyard to cut down the number of mosquitoes, the next-door neighbors receive some of the benefits, since the mosquito population around their house is diminished, too. Since the neighbors did not help to pay for the spray materials, they received something beneficial without going through the market. The market failed to assess them correctly. Similarly, when a car owner installs a new muffler, all the people nearby are relieved of the engine noise. They receive a beneficial externality even though they do not help pay for the improvement.

If Pigou had concentrated on beneficial externalities, his social cost diagram might have been called a "social benefit" diagram, and it would have looked like the one in Figure 26-8. The private costs now paid by the firm are represented by the solid AC and MC curves. MC equals MR at 5,600 units of output. At this output, average cost equals average revenue, so the firm is earning only normal profits. In its production activity, however, the firm produces benefits for society that cannot be sold in ordinary markets. Since the benefits cannot be sold, the firm is not credited with them. A contrived example would be a firm that emitted waste into the air in the form of an odorless, colorless, and tasteless substance that repelled mosquitoes but had no effect on any other form of life or any other activity. By making the surrounding area mosquito-free, the firm would reduce irritation, lessen the incidence of malaria, and make for a happier populace. The firm would be producing social benefits.

If these benefits could be counted, they would be equal in value to the vertical distance between the solid AC and the dashed AC_1, and the marginal cost of production would now be the dashed MC_1. The new optimal

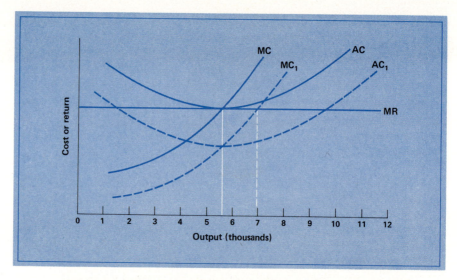

Figure 26-8 A Firm Producing Beneficial Externalities

level of output would be found by equating MC_1 with MR, and this level would be 7,000 units of output. A firm that produces beneficial externalities has a tendency to produce less than the socially optimal level of output.

A firm that produces adverse externalities has a tendency to overproduce. A firm that produces beneficial externalities has a tendency to underproduce.

Examples of beneficial externalities are not difficult to find. In many parts of the nation, ground water close to the surface prevents a productive agriculture from developing, or requires individual farm operators to install expensive drainage facilities before crops can be grown. If a city puts wells down in such an area, the wells may draw off water and eliminate the need for drainage. Usually, the city receives no credit for providing the service.

Another example comes from the clustering of industries. When many industries producing essentially the same product appear in the same general area, a specialized labor force appears to accommodate those industries. Boeing, Cessna, and Beech all produce airplanes in Wichita, Kansas. If only Boeing were there, it would have to search out engineers, draftsmen, and technicians when it wanted to expand. The search costs would have to be added to the total cost of airplane production. Since the three companies are in one city, that city is a logical place for aeronautical technicians to look for work. A reliable supply of labor thus exists in Wichita for the three producers, and the expense associated with recruiting and moving workers is eliminated. This "externality" lowers the cost of each firm's doing business,[1] but there is no way for the costs saved through this cumulative or "agglomeration" effect to be paid through the market.

In sum, the market price does not always include all costs or benefits associated with a transaction. The incidence of external effects will undoubtedly increase as an economy grows in complexity, and it is unreasonable to expect that the market, left to its own devices, can solve all emerging problems. Several partial solutions can be suggested, but if market failures are to be adequately cared for, a superstructure of nonmarket institutions will have to supplement the market in making decisions regarding allocation and choice.

Summary

1. Some kinds of market transactions are accompanied by external or third-party effects not compensated in the usual buyer/seller exchange. These effects are results of market failure.
2. As the economy has become more complex and interrelated, the incidence of market failure has increased.
3. No one solution can be suggested as the answer for all externality problems. Economists have suggested solutions that depend upon mergers or internalization, taxes or subsidies, and direct (legal) control.
4. Internalization makes all parties affected by the externality part of the same decision-making unit.
5. Tax and subsidy solutions are feasible, but they require establishing specific rules for the taxes or subsidies.
6. Taxing externalities is sometimes viewed as providing a license to continue producing the harmful externality.
7. In situations where the external effects of an action are widely distributed, no economic solution may be feasible and a legal approach may be required.
8. There is every reason to believe that favorable externalities occur as frequently as unfavorable ones.
9. If strict economic logic is applied, a firm producing harmful externalities will produce more than the socially optimal amount, and a firm producing beneficial externalities will produce less.

Exercises

1. Explain these important terms and concepts:
    - market failure
    - externality
    - private cost
    - social cost
    - internalization
    - taxes and subsidies
    - a license to pollute
    - legal restrictions

[1] A phenomenon similar to the Boeing-Cessna-Beech one explains why so many consulting firms spring up around college campuses. The consulting firms require talent on an intermittent basis, and can hire university faculty to perform short-term functions.

2 Private costs are paid by producers when they purchase land, labor, capital, and entrepreneurial skill. These costs are recovered by producers when their products are sold on the market. The buying public (which includes the producer!) often must pay additional costs. They must pay the costs of pollution, they must bear the discomfort of smog, and they must insulate their houses to keep out noise. Why is the total cost of production called *social cost*? How does social cost relate to opportunity cost? Is there any reason to believe that social costs increase whenever private costs do?

3 Under what circumstance is it possible for social costs to be less than private costs?

4 Three major ways to cope with market failure are internalization (merger), tax/subsidy plans, and legal enforcement. In each of the following examples, identify the market failure, then decide which method should be used to eliminate it.

   a Your neighbor puts his trash burner close to your property. The smoke and odor bother you.

   b An industrial giant puts a piano-manufacturing facility (a "clean" industry) into a town of 1,000 people. The 500 new employees and their families cause the town to expand and put increased burdens on public services.

   c Increased use of electricity in city A causes an increase in smoke and fly ash in city B, where the generating plant is located.

A Contemporary Problem

Selling "Pollution Certificates"

Many conservative economists and citizens believe that pollution-related externalities could be solved through market means by arranging a market for privileges to pollute. This would work the same way a city dump works: You must pay for the privilege of dumping. A comprehensive plan might be developed as follows:

A regional pollution control agency would calculate the volume of wastes dumped into the region's air, streams, and dumping grounds. Since the wastes come in many forms, they would need to be converted to ton equivalents or some other measure, and a conversion table would have to be prepared (one smoking chimney equals two leaking sewers, etc.). The control agency would then decide how many units of waste the local environment could absorb, and "pollution certificates" in that amount would be printed. Any polluter—factory, city disposal plant, or the like—wanting to use the atmosphere or local waterways for waste disposal would be required to purchase the appropriate number of pollution certificates. The pollution control agency could use the revenue to install cleaning devices of its own, or it could develop compensating amenities—man-made devices that would take the place of clean air and water.

Over time, population growth and increases in the number of industrial plants operating in the region would drive up the price of pollution certificates. The higher price would provide added incentive to cut down pollution. A car owner who drove a car requiring a single $250 pollution certificate might switch to a low-pollution car if the certificate price rose to $400. If local people desired a lower level of pollution, they could use a voting process to either reduce the number of pollution certificates or increase their price. In either case, pollution loads would probably diminish.

This market system for pollution certificates would also offer conservation groups, anti-pollution associations, and interested citizens the opportunity to fight pollution by purchasing certificates and holding them off the market. Buying-and-holding would have two effects. First, the amount of polluting materials emitted in the region would be reduced by the amount of certificates purchased and held; second, the holding action would drive up the price of remaining certificates so that only the most profitable (or wealthy) polluters could afford the luxury of purchasing them. The extremely high price would provide added incentive for polluters to "be clean." If they were not, some might be forced to close their plants (thus adding to unemployment and requiring the general economy to go without some things that it is used to having).

This price-based method of pollution control would allow the regional pollution control agency to circumvent its own general lack of power. It would substitute a negotiable set of certificates for elaborate rules, regulations, and policing activity, and it would permit the market for certificates to allocate the privilege to pollute among all possible polluters.

Analysis. The pollution certificate market has the same general appeal as the market method for allocating anything: It is efficient, automatic, and impersonal. These are desirable attributes in a society that places great importance on freedom. Such a system has some notable disadvantages, however. First, there is the difficult technical task of determining how heavy a pollution load the local environment can withstand, and the accompanying problem of converting all varieties of pollution (solid waste, smoke, effluent, noise, congestion, and the like) to a single unit so that they can be reckoned in the same terms. Second, there is the problem of distribution. Who would receive the first allocation of certificates? Present polluters? The highest bidder? New, low-pollution plants? Some other group? And third is the certificate system's own set of externalities. If a conservation-oriented group purchased all available certificates, industry, commerce, and transport in the region could grind to a halt, leaving thousands unemployed, without income, and on the welfare roles.

On balance, the system of pollution certificates is attractive because it uses the market system to eliminate some of the system's own problems. It does this, though, by substituting one set of problems for another. Which is more correct, just, and equitable? No one can say for sure, but as society, science, and technology advance the problem is sure to become more prevalent and more severe.

27 When There Is No Market At All

The market exchanges examined in Chapter 26 were feedback systems in which buyers and sellers interacted with one another. In such transactions, each brings something to the exchange and takes something from it. Buyer brings money and takes goods; seller brings goods and takes money. When markets work perfectly, all affected parties are direct or indirect contributors to this final transaction. When markets fail, someone is left out of the decision-making or compensation scheme, and the feedback system does not close completely. Incomplete closure causes problems that are external to the market transaction. Many externalities are too inconsequential to even notice. Apartment dwellers are annoyed when their neighbors cook sauerkraut, but the annoyance is not usually sufficient to cause objection so the market for sauerkraut continues to allocate resources to producing this food. The neighbor's complaint is not recognized by the market.

Not all externality problems are as trivial as the odor of sauerkraut. If cooking sauerkraut produced lethal fumes, someone would have to protect the neighbors. But who? Should each neighborhood or apartment house have a sauerkraut alarm system? If so, how are the resources to be allocated to this purpose and how should the service be priced? One thing is sure: There is no easy market solution to this kind of problem. The externalities are so great and so diffuse as to prevent markets from ever developing.

In the real world, consumers do not come to a market with money to exchange for national defense, yet 27.2 percent of the federal budget is used for this purpose. Merchants do not stand on street corners asking passers-by to purchase the privilege of using the sidewalks, but sidewalks are built and paid for. Neither lawyer nor felon enters into market transactions to purchase justice. No markets develop for defense, sidewalks, or justice, yet each of these is produced in the U.S. economy.

This chapter deals with goods that are produced and consumed in a market economy but do not themselves have markets. The purpose of the chapter is to show how such goods are evaluated, how resources are allocated to their production, and how the goods are financed. These purposes are accomplished through three extensive examples. The first deals with lighthouses, the second with sidewalks, the third with income redistribution programs.

Lighthouses-Pure Public Goods

The hulks of over a thousand ships are known to lie in the shallow waters off Cape Hatteras, North Carolina. If the captain of any of the sunken vessels had been aware of his proximity to the treacherous coastal waters, he would have immediately turned toward the open sea to avert disaster. In the dark of night, though, there is no market where such information can be purchased, and as a result the best of captains lose their ships. As early as 1775, navigators of ships plying the waters near Cape Hatteras requested a lighthouse to guide them away from the rocks. None appeared until 1798, when the fledgling U.S. Government built the Cape Hatteras lighthouse, whose light has aided mariners continuously since that time.

Surely, the Cape Hatteras light had value in 1775, but no entrepreneur stepped forward to invest time, money, bricks, and glass in a tower that would send beams of light out to sea. The light continues to have value in 1977 and it will still have value in 1990, but if bids were let for private operation of such a light, no investor would respond. How can such an important and useful instrument be overlooked by an economic system bent on producing goods and services that have obvious economic value? The answer lies in the nature of the light's service and in the way that service is consumed.

The beams flashed from the Cape Hatteras lighthouse are pure *public goods*. Any number of ships can use them without diminishing the amount available to others. Unlike books or bread or playing cards, a beam of light cannot be claimed solely by one person. Once produced, the light is automatically available to all possible users.

A public good is a good or service that can be used simultaneously by any number of people. One person's use does not diminish the quantity available, nor does it interfere with the capacity of others to use the good. Moreover, once a public good is produced, there is no way of stopping anyone from using it. Public goods are sometimes called collective goods.

Since the light cannot be possessed, it cannot be exchanged, and therefore no market can develop for it. When no market exists, there is no way for a private entrepreneur to determine if too few, too many, or just the right amount of resources are being devoted to lighthouse building. This causes a terrible dilemma in a market economy. A valuable good is needed and desired, but no market information is available to allocate either factors or products.

The economic theories and policies applicable to pure public goods differ somewhat from those applicable to private goods because the latter are competitive in use while the former are shared. The remainder of this section will examine the economic implications of sharing in the production, distribution, and financing of public goods. The examination will center on lighthouses and will deal with demand, pricing, and financing.

The Demand for Lighthouse Services

Even though no market exists for lighthouses, there is a demand for their services. Shipowners and captains need the facilities and are willing to pay to have them installed. There is every reason to suspect that demand for lighthouse beams follows the law of diminishing marginal utility. The first beam received is extremely valuable. Following beams have some

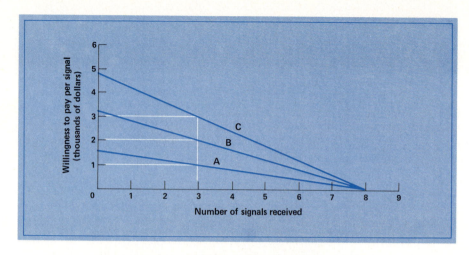

Figure 27-1 Three Individual Demand Curves for Lighthouse Services

value but not so much, since the ship's captain has already received the warning. Each shipowner or captain has a downward-sloping demand curve for lighthouse services.

It is also logical to think that different shipowners and captains will have different dispositions about the value of the protective beams. The captain of a luxurious but cumbersome passenger liner will have a very high demand for the protection afforded by a light. The owner of a small and highly maneuverable fishing vessel will have a much lower demand for the same beam.

Three individual demand curves are shown in Figure 27-1. They represent three vessel operators with high, average, and low demands for lighthouse services. The three individual demand curves aggregate to the market demand curve shown in Figure 27-2. Aggregating the demand for light beams is different from aggregating the demand for shirts or for pork and beans, because each demander is simultaneously using (sharing) the same light. Rather than adding the number of beams A, B, and C will each buy to obtain the quantity desired by the whole market, point X in Figure 27-2 is found by asking how much shipowner A will pay for the third signal, then adding to this the amount B would pay for the same three lights, and then adding how much C would pay—again for the same lights. The result is a vertical aggregation of the individual demand curves shown in Figure 27-2. This vertical summing shows how much the three users are willing to pay for each of several signals. Together, they are willing to pay $6,000 for the third signal (point X), $3,500 for the fifth signal (point Y) and $1,200 for the seventh signal (point Z).

The total value of the lighthouse is shown by the triangular area under the aggregate demand curve. (The total value is ascertained by measuring the total amount all users would be willing to pay for each level of service. If the first beam could command $10,000, the second $8,000, and the third $5,000, total willingness to pay and hence total value would be $10,000 + $8,000 + $5,000, = $23,000.) This area provides a significant clue to answering the question: Should the light be built? If the area under the total demand curve exceeds the magnitude of total costs, then the total benefits of the lighthouse are greater than total costs incurred to build it, and it has passed a major economic test. It will add more to society's benefits than to society's costs.

After the lighthouse has been built and is operating, another question arises: How should its services be allocated among users? The answer is found in the nature of its operating costs. It costs exactly the same amount of money to operate the lighthouse whether its warnings are used by 10 passing ships or by 10,000. Neither construction nor operating costs vary with the number of ships that use the service. In the formal language of microeconomics, the marginal cost of an added viewer of a beam of light is zero. If another ship can use the services of the lighthouse at zero marginal cost, this is what should be charged for them—zero. The allocation of the pure public good becomes very simple: Let everyone who wants to use the services use them free.

If the optimal price charged for the service is zero, and if it costs money to provide the collective good produced by the lighthouse, problems of financing are bound to arise. Whoever establishes the light and charges

Figure 27–2 Aggregate Demand Curve for Lighthouse Services

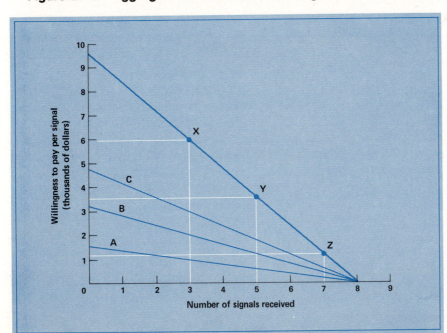

the zero price will have no revenue with which to pay the costs. Although the general evaluation showed that the lighthouse would provide benefits in excess of costs and should, therefore, be constructed, that decision was independent of how the installation was to be financed. Once the decision to provide the lighthouse is made, the question of how to pay for it cannot be ignored.

Generally speaking, the best way to finance pure collective goods is by taxing each user. When individual users can be identified, as in the case of a lighthouse, there should be a "lighthouse tax" imposed on that segment of the population. When, as in the case of clean air or national defense, the benefits are dispersed over the whole population, a general tax is warranted and should be levied. The economic advantages of a tax in financing pure collective goods are that (1) all beneficiaries must pay and (2) payment does not affect the amount used. If shipowners have no choice but to pay $2,500 each per year for the lighthouse, they obviously will use it to the full extent.

In sum, a pure collective good is evaluated by comparing benefits with costs. If it is produced, it should be allocated at zero price so that all users will use it to the fullest extent possible. And it should be financed by taxes on everyone who benefits, directly or indirectly, from the good. This completes the discussion of the allocative and pricing aspects of collective goods, but it is not yet completely clear why the market mechanism fails to provide an optimal quantity of this public good automatically. This question is the subject of the next section.

Public Goods and the Free Rider

The lighthouse may be reconsidered in order to explain the failure of the market to allocate resources properly to the production of public goods. Assume that individual shipowners A and B decide to form a consortium of all shipowners to build the lighthouse through private means. Two facts are apparent: (1) as the number of users increases, the net benefits of the lighthouse increase; (2) as the number of shipowners contributing to the expense of the lighthouse increases, the average cost to each user decreases. Both facts stem from the fixed-cost nature of the lighthouse. Therefore it will be in the interest of everyone to have as many shipowners as possible join the consortium.

But will all shipowners join? It is very unlikely. Once the lighthouse is built, any shipowner will be able to enjoy its benefits without joining. There is no way, short of using torpedo boats, for the members of the consortium (who have incurred the expense) to prevent nonmembers from enjoying the fruits of their efforts. Nonmembers can thereby obtain a "free ride" on the backs of members. Because of this potential opportunity for a free ride, it is unlikely that the lighthouse will be privately built, even though it would create substantial net benefits to society as a whole. Each individual shipowner will be tempted not to join the lighthouse-building consortium, hoping that "others" will build it. Each will want to get all the benefits from the lighthouse without having to pay any of the costs. Since everyone is playing the free-rider game, no one will actually build the lighthouse. And ships will continue to crash on the shoals.

The lighthouse has been used as an example because it represents a kind of collective good least subject to free-rider problems. The private interests involved (shipowners) are few in number, and the benefits and costs are obvious to all. Yet even under these elementary conditions, the free-rider game can lead individuals to behave in an irrational manner—that is, against their own interests. To insure that society does obtain the many benefits accruing to the lighthouse, some unit of government undertakes the responsibility of building it.

The lighthouse is only one example of a beneficial public good. Other examples are national defense, flood control, city beautification, and hurricane warning systems.[1] In each case, the problem is the same: Once the good exists, it is available for all to use. There is no way to prevent anyone from participating in the enjoyment of the good, but, for exactly this reason, there is no way to make anyone pay for it. Free riders prevent a market from developing.

City Sidewalks–Uncollectible Revenues

Most cities have sidewalks. Sidewalks are serviceable fixtures that separate motor traffic from foot traffic, keep people dry, and allow easy access to shops and yards. Most people take sidewalks for granted.

On a rainy day in Tulsa, Oklahoma, when the gutters are deep with muddy water, ask the thousands of pedestrians what the sidewalks are worth. If a sidewalk were like a toll road, some would gladly pay 10 cents a block, others 25 cents, and still others only 5 cents. Walkers with these dispositions have economic demands for sidewalks just as they have economic demands for eggs. But neither the city, nor the entrepreneurs whose shops line the walks, nor whoever else may own the sidewalks charges for the use of a particular walkway. It would be impractical.

Many public services resemble sidewalks in this one important regard: Users would be willing to pay for them but there is no efficient way to collect such payments. Streets, highways, public parks, swimming holes,

---

[1] Each of these examples comes from the technological world. Another large class of public goods exists in nature. Any number of people can simultaneously enjoy the same beautiful sunset, the same flock of whooping cranes, or the same riverside recreation area. In the natural world as in the technological world, the free rider has caused innumerable problems. Free riding on nature has been the source of much of the contemporary interest in ecology and the environment.

and meat inspection all qualify. They are not quite public goods, because one person's enjoyment of a road or sidewalk can interfere with another person's capacity to use the same facility. However, these types of service are most often provided by some level of government because it is impractical for a private entrepreneur to negotiate with each user to extract a price or to obtain what the user is willing to pay. (An exception: If it is impractical to charge for the use of streets, roads and sidewalks, how can the Kansas Turnpike, the Golden Gate Bridge, and the Pennsylvania Turnpike charge motorists for their services? The answer lies in the limited number of access points to these facilities. If only a few toll stations must be attended, it is easy and sometimes quite profitable to make users pay. It is only on the downtown and residential streets that collection becomes impractical.)

Even though a "sidewalk use market" cannot develop, sidewalks do appear in all up-to-date business districts and in most residential districts in the United States. They appear because city and town councils are certain that benefits accrue to street and sidewalk users even though there is no efficient way to make the users pay. Since the market will not entice cement, gravel, and labor to be turned into sidewalks, town councils intervene and command that resources be used for this purpose. A public body usurps the power of the market.

Once it is in place, there is still a question of who should use the walk. Since use contracts cannot reasonably be negotiated with each walker, and since most of the time an additional walker can be accommodated at no increase in cost, the walk is open for anyone to use free of charge.

Income Redistribution Programs

A market society is very efficient in showing producers how much bread should be produced, or how much structural steel should be used to construct a bridge across the Missouri River. This type of society is generally lacking in compassion, however, and has no sense of responsibility toward those who are unable to earn their daily bread. Welfare payments, old-age pensions, unemployment checks, and disaster relief are not marketable commodities or services. Markets exist for factors that have immediate uses, but if a family has no factors to sell, the market guarantees it no income. As we have seen in Chapters 24 and 25, the market is a ruthless mechanism that responds to supply and demand, but not to need and desire.

Since the 1930s, state and federal lawmakers have tried to find efficient ways to provide relief for individuals and families who are unable to obtain incomes through factor markets and who have no other means of support. Retirement programs and medical care are now available to the

"I'd just like something to tide me over until the guaranteed annual income takes effect."

aged, public assistance programs are available for the needy, and a variety of government agencies have taken responsibility for aiding families whose breadwinners are temporarily out of work. Through some sense of compassion or duty, the public has bypassed the market to attend to the needs of millions of individuals.

Even so, welfare programs must be subjected to economic analysis. What resources do they require? Who should receive the benefits? Who is to pay the costs? Should people be able to receive benefits for unlimited periods of time? These are difficult questions that cause conflict in society's conscience. One part of the social conscience declares that all U.S. citizens should be well-fed, warm, and dry. Another part says that, except in very unusual circumstances, people should work to earn what they receive. But all cannot work all of the time. The automatic cotton picker threw thousands of farm workers out of work. Accidents and illnesses leave children with no one to support them. Dial telephones took the jobs of telephone operators. Age and retirement sometimes leave families with little or no income to use in meeting daily expenses. The self-regulating market responds slowly (if at all) to these kinds of circumstances, so the voting public has agreed to supplement the market through programs and policies.

In sum, there are some things a market society does very poorly or cannot do at all. Therefore the mix of goods and services produced by the market is not always in harmony with the desires of society. Society may wish to change the kinds of things being produced, the mix of goods, or the distribution of goods. In the United States a democratic voting process is used to provide signals about the direction and magnitude of a desired change. Voting through the ballot box supplements voting with dollars.

A Note of Caution

A quick reading of this chapter might leave the impression that when a free and unrestricted market does not do an adequate job of allocating factors and distributing products, government need only step in and, through judicious use of voting and microeconomic policy, insure that some new things are done and some old things are stopped. In reality, this is not so simple. It is relatively easy to decide why the market is not doing a thorough job, and it is relatively easy to determine whether society wants larger social security payments or more national parks. It is *not* easy to determine how much more of these things should be produced, or how they should be financed if they are produced. Specific policies must be designed to accomplish specific goals. The integration and coordination of such policies is a formidable task. The problems of ascertaining the public will, translating the public will into policy, and then managing that policy are so complex as to insure that at any moment the collection of goods available through the market and the public sectors combined will not be entirely in agreement with public desire or public need.

Making Decisions: Benefit/Cost Analysis

It is not easy to make reliable decisions about public goods, goods for which revenues are uncollectible or goods related to compassion or obligation. Even when accurate information about demand and costs is available, planners and lawmakers must weigh the pluses and minuses attending each possible decision. Although several techniques are available to assist in making public decisions, most governmental bodies (and some private firms) use some variation of a method called *benefit/cost analysis.*

Benefit/cost analysis is an old and reasonably sophisticated method used to evaluate public facilities and programs. There is no dependable record of its first use in this country, but it seems likely that the U.S. Army Corps of Engineers used the technique early in the nineteenth century to determine the value of navigation developments along the eastern seaboard.

Benefit/cost analysis is especially popular in decisions related to natural resources. The flood-control efforts in the Ohio and Mississippi River basins were evaluated using benefit/cost analysis. The massive hydroelectric dams on the Columbia River were evaluated using the same procedures, as were the public investments in many small irrigation projects in Southern Idaho, Utah, and Colorado.

A diagram of the technique is shown in Figure 27–3. On the left is an abbreviated version of the circular flow. In order to produce a public good (perhaps a flood-control dam protecting St. Louis and New Orleans), the public sector dips into the circular flow and gathers together resources needed to carry out the project. Land, steel, labor, cement, and a host of other factors are diverted from private uses into the flood-control activities. The diversion of factors causes a reduction in the output of private goods, so it is a measure of the cost of flood control. This cost can be stated in terms of dollars required to buy the land, steel, labor, and other factors, or it can be thought of in terms of the private goods sacrificed when resources are moved from the production of automobiles, canned soup, and winter coats to the production of the desirable but unmarketable collective good—flood control. (Flood control, like lighthouse beams, is a collective good. If a valley is protected from flooding, everyone in the valley automatically receives protection. If one person is kept dry, all stay dry. Moreover, additional people can move into the area and enjoy its protected status without diminishing the amount of protection available to previous residents.)

The diversion of factors from private to public production activities lessens flooding. The lessened flooding returns to the circular flow (from right to left across the top of the diagram) as a benefit to society. Although the dollar benefits of protection are hard to define, the protection afforded by flood-control activities can be described in dollar terms by thinking of costs saved by not having to rebuild front porches swept away by high water, costs saved by not having to clean mud out of basements, and

Figure 27–3 Schematic Presentation of Benefit/Cost Analysis

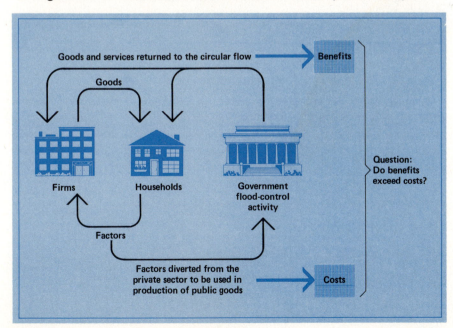

costs saved by not having to rebuild bridges each year. After flood control is available, factors that would have been used for these tasks are "released" and can be used to produce autos, canned soup, winter coats, or other private goods.

Benefit/cost analysis is based on a comparison of benefits (saved front porches) with costs (steel and cement). If the *benefit stream* is larger than the *cost stream,* diverting productive inputs into flood control increases the well-being of the nation.

Since flood control is a capital investment with a long expected life, the benefits and costs associated with it are referred to as *streams.* A benefit stream is the time path of benefits accruing to the facility over its entire life. A cost stream is the time path of costs for the same facility.

If costs exceed benefits, the public project would not pay its own way and it would not be undertaken.

When benefit/cost analysis is employed, each proposal is examined to see if the value of the goods and services returned to the circular flow exceeds the value of the goods and services taken from the flow. Many critics object to this simple test, claiming that public sector evaluation techniques should be just as critical and just as incisive as evaluation techniques used by private firms. This is an understandable disposition, but it ignores an important point: The public sector is being called upon to produce goods and services that the private sector will not or cannot produce. The private sector has the rules of the market to use in solving allocation problems. However, the public sector becomes an active producer of economic goods only when private sector rules fail. It seems untoward to apply the rigid private sector allocation rules. Benefit/cost analysis becomes a surrogate rule.

It is legitimate to criticize benefit/cost analysis because of its *project* orientation.

As it applies to government activity, a project is a single effort designed to accomplish a particular purpose. Each dam along the Tennessee River is a project. The urban renewal activity in Denver is a project, and a single small town may have a community beautification project. A *program* is ordinarily a series of projects that, taken together, accomplish some broad goal. Thus, there is a whole flood control program, a welfare program and a disaster relief program.

The method is generally applied to single proposals, and asks only if these single proposals will yield more than they cost. As it is now used, the method does not have the capacity to examine all aspects of a program simultaneously. Again, an example from the natural resource field clarifies the point. In Figure 27–4, Unsafe City is a city of 50,000 people. For years the denizens of Unsafe City have been plagued by the periodic flooding of the Deluge River system. By 1975, city, county, and state governments had cooperated in building Dam I on the North Fork and Dam II on the

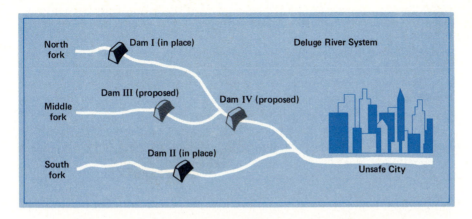

Figure 27-4 Flood-Control Efforts on the Deluge River

South Fork of the system. These dams were well designed, and considerably lessened the extent and frequency of flooding in Unsafe City.

Capricious rains along the uncontrolled Middle Fork of the Deluge, however, continued to occasion uneasiness among Unsafe's inhabitants whenever clouds darkened the sky. In response to this disquiet, the local chamber of commerce joined forces with the local chapter of the Sierra Club and invited the area's Congressional delegation to inquire into the flooding situation. Subsequently, a study was undertaken by state and federal agencies to evaluate two possible sites for new flood-control dams. The Dam III site on the Middle Fork and the Dam IV site just below the confluence of the Middle and North Forks were possibilities. They were both feasible from an engineering point of view, and they would each contribute to effective control of the river. Close examination revealed that Dam III had a benefit/cost ratio of 2.5. For each dollar invested in Dam III, benefits valued at $2.50 would be produced and returned to the income stream. This dam would be a worthwhile investment. Dam IV was found to have a benefit/cost ratio of 1.8—not so high as Dam III but *still* quite acceptable. Planners immediately suggested building *both* structures.

Unfortunately, those involved in financing and constructing the two dams learned too late that many of the benefits counted for Dam III were exactly the same benefits as those counted for Dam IV! When the two dams were studied together, they were found to have a combined benefit/cost ratio of only 1.01—barely acceptable by any standard.[2] Had the

---

[2] One of the most frequent criticisms leveled at major federal agencies that use benefit/cost analysis is that when examining a new proposal they do not count as a "cost" the reduction in benefits produced by facilities already in place. A new birth control information clinic in the slums of Chicago may have "benefits" amounting to 250 patients per day. What is not considered is the fact that perhaps half of these patients are diverted from other clinics and come to the new facility simply because it is more convenient. In such a situation the "net" or "true" benefits of the clinic are the 125 *new* patients who had not been involved in treatment prior to establishment of the new clinic.

two analyses been carried out as one, such an error could have been averted.

Developing substitutes for the market is difficult business. Benefit/cost analysis is one reasonably successful substitute that has been used for many years, especially in the natural resource field where it has been used to evaluate public goods like flood control, recreation, and water quality as well as privately used goods like navigation and hydro power. As time passes, more goods and services are likely to be produced in response to nonmarket demands. Economics must be able to expand its horizons beyond the logic of the market in order to answer those basic questions: What should be produced? How should it be produced? For whom should it be produced? Benefit/cost methods represent one such expansion.

Once Produced, Who Pays?

The production of goods by public entities presupposes the existence of a public budget and a way of obtaining money for it. In the U.S. economy, a variety of taxing procedures at local, county, state, and federal levels are used to obtain funds for public purposes. Taxing is a complex theme, because so many special cases and special taxes are used to accomplish particular ends and solve particular problems. As has been seen, a special tax on shipowners can be used to provide lighthouses. Special taxes in local areas may also be used to support very local services. However, very general taxes must be used to provide benefits like defense, education, and national parks. The tax system in the United States is thus a complex mixture of special and general taxes. Two general philosophic bents surround the complex process of taxation. One says that people should be taxed according to benefits they receive. The other says that they should be taxed according to their ability to pay. Many heated arguments develop over which is preferable, the benefit principle or the ability principle.

Both principles are currently used to justify taxes employed in the United States. State and federal gasoline taxes are based on the benefit principle. Tax revenues collected from the sale of gasoline are used to improve transportation systems. A person using vast quantities of gasoline pays heavy taxes but also receives the benefits of new road surfaces, improved traffic control, and expanded highway networks. Similarly, in many states, a small portion of liquor tax revenues is earmarked for use in rehabilitation programs for alcoholics or for educational programs regarding alcoholism. Those who use alcohol are paying to alleviate an alcohol-related problem, and the benefit principle applies.

When taxes are based on ability to pay, there is no necessary connection between the source of the tax revenue and its ultimate use. The ability tax is based solely on some measure of an individual's wealth—usually income or property. Public schools in the United States are most often financed by a tax on real property within local school districts. Those having much property pay high taxes, and those having no property pay no taxes regardless of whether or not they have children in the school system. Nearly all economic activities carried out by the federal government are financed using taxes related to either personal or corporate income. These taxes are clearly based on the ability principle: Individuals having high incomes are required to make high tax payments. This general tax is collected and the revenues are used without reference to who uses the service provided.

Which principle is better? No one can say. Each is fair in some cases and unfair in others. Each is adequate in some case and inadequate in others. Each is easy to administer in some cases and difficult in others. The argument over taxes need not, however, end on a weak note. The decentralized market economy that has been developing in the United States for two centuries depends upon specialization, interdependence, and exchange. Specialization requires education, skill, innovation, risk taking, communication, the protection afforded by a legal code, and many other qualities provided largely by the public. Interdependence insists that people be each other's keepers through welfare, social security, programs related to social justice, and other goods and services produced through the public sector. A mark of a mature economic society is its capacity to recognize its own need for nonmarket goods and services. While it is useful to know if a particular tax is based on the benefit principle or on the ability principle, the important issue remains whether or not sufficient public funds can be gathered to produce the needed volume of lighthouses, city parks, and welfare aid that the society needs.

Summary

1. A large number of desirable goods and services cannot be bought and sold because markets for them fail to develop. Reasons for the absence of markets include the existence of public goods, the inability to collect revenues, and income redistribution plans.
2. If goods and services of these types are to be produced, they must be produced by the public sector.
3. General dispositions about what nonmarket goods to produce are obtained through the balloting process. More specific determinations are made through the use of tools like benefit/cost analysis.
4. Benefit/cost analysis is a common method of organizing information about the appropriateness of a public expenditure. The method was pioneered by the natural-resource-related agencies in the federal government.
5. When it is decided to produce public goods, it must also be decided which taxes will be used to pay for which public-sector activities.
6. Taxing can be done with reference to the ability principle or the benefit

principle. Arguments can be marshalled in favor of either principle, but the mark of a mature economy is its ability and willingness to tax enough to finance the large volume of public goods and services needed.

Exercises

1. Explain these important terms and concepts:
    - public good
    - free rider
    - uncollectible revenues
    - benefit/cost analysis
    - benefit principle of taxation
    - ability principle of taxation

2. Develop a case for or against government (public) production of the following kinds of goods or services:
    - elementary education
    - freeways through a city
    - residential streets
    - the annual corn crop
    - navigation on the St. Lawrence Seaway
    - smallpox vaccinations (Hint: Do you obtain any benefit from your neighbors' being vaccinated?)

3. Here are some goods or services that are or could be available in the United States. They are not listed in any particular order.
    - below-cost postal service
    - Aid to Families with Dependent Children
    - police protection for public figures
    - aid to victims of crime and violence
    - public parks
    - polio innoculations
    - Medicare and Medicaid
    - air traffic control

    a. Rank the above with respect to their importance.
    b. What can economics say about allocating resources to these purposes?
    c. How should allocation decisions be made?

4. Hell's Canyon, the rugged area along the Idaho-Oregon border, is one of the few true wilderness areas remaining in the United States. It is scenic and remote, and it provides refuge for several endangered species of animals. The area also provides the few remaining sites for high dams that could be used to produce inexpensive hydroelectric power. For 20 years a three-way battle has raged: Should a private company build a high dam and spoil the canyon? Should the federal government build a high dam and spoil the canyon? Or should all dams be prohibited so the area can be saved as a natural wonder? What does economics contribute to answering these questions? Should the dam (or dams) be built? If energy becomes even more scarce, will the answer change?

5. What is the relationship between the externalities arguments of Chapter 26 and the "no market at all" arguments of this chapter?

6. Each of the following taxes is based on either the benefit principle or the ability principle. Define which principle applies, and defend your choice.
    - a state sales tax
    - the cigarette tax
    - a room tax on hotels
    - the federal income tax
    - a bridge toll
    - a business license tax

A Contemporary Problem

Public Goods and the Budget Crunch

The mid-1970s have been particularly difficult times. High rates of inflation, high unemployment, and uncertainty about the economic future have led people to become cautious and cut back many economic activities that were very popular only a few years ago. The crunch has not been limited to private activities. Government budgets, already under extreme inflationary stress, are being carefully watched by a public that is adamantly against tax increases.

The pressure on public budgets has required reevaluation of the production of many public goods—goods for which there is no market at all. Although many public activities have come under close scrutiny, only two—day care centers and air traffic control—are mentioned here.

Day care centers are a product of the affluent 1960s. In that decade a generally wealthy and socially conscious constituency used large amounts of public monies to construct facilities where small children could be cared for while their mothers worked at part- or full-time jobs. The centers were established in predominently low-income areas where no market could develop for this kind of service.

In the mid-1970s, budget-conscious state and local officials saw closing the day care centers as a possible way to save money and relieve strain on their inadequate budgets. In cities across the nation, day care services were terminated or reduced in size and quality. With no care available, mothers were required to give up jobs, and family incomes were reduced. The decision to close a public facility had a direct impact on the welfare of thousands of (especially) low-income families.

During this same general period (1974–1976), air traffic controllers at the nation's airports made some unfortunate mistakes. Several near-collisions between fully loaded aircraft, and at least one well publicized crash, were blamed on controllers who, because of increases in air traffic, were under intense pressure in an already tense line of work. Public response to the air traffic control problem was quick: Make more money available to increase the number of controllers and to increase their average rate of pay (thus attracting and retaining more capable people). The strains on public budgets seemed less severe when it came to finding money for this service.

The comparison raises an important question: Why, in a time of generally tight public money, must one service be terminated and another expanded? Who does the choosing? Is there wisdom in the choice? Can you argue in favor of restoring day care centers at the expense of air traffic control? These are very real questions facing public decision makers who have no genuine market signals to guide them. They choose, but do they choose well? How can economics help in making these kinds of choices?

28

Microeconomic Policy

Perhaps the most important role of parents is socializing their children—teaching them how to behave toward others. This involves establishing limits to behavior, which vary from family to family and among societies, but in general concern amounts and kinds of activity. There is a set of minimum standards about clothing, nutrition, and personal cleanliness. There is a set of maximum standards about how much one can interfere with others. And there are some actions, like murder, larceny, arson, and robbery, that are simply forbidden.

It would be a mistake to say that the economic system is the child of government, or that government is solely responsible for designing the behavior of an economic system. Comparing parent and child to government and economic activity is apt, though, because government does place bounds on the economic behavior of firms and households. These bounds are designed to supplement market activity by insuring that some desirable things left undone by the market get done. The bounds also prevent the free market from doing some undesirable things or ruthlessly exploiting people or groups.

Placing limits on the economic behavior of firms and households is called *microeconomic policy*. This chapter defines microeconomic policy, and deals with antimonopoly policy, protection of natural monopolies, limiting behavior, and enhancing the welfare of individual households.

What Is Micro Policy?

It is hard to imagine a public policy that does not have economic effects. War has not been waged recently expressly for economic purposes, but maintaining a huge defense system has many economic consequences for those who supply defense materials and those whose employment is related to the defense establishment. The liberalization of divorce laws in many states was not motivated by economic considerations, but it has had economic effects on the parties to divorces, on the lawyers who no longer need argue so long, and on the whole judicial system. The decision to open a new section of an existing cemetery may seem devoid of economic content, but such a move transfers land from one use to another and causes a change in the capital resources needed to maintain the property.

Although all government acts, policies, and programs seem to have economic consequences, they cannot all be called a part of microeconomic policy. Microeconomic policy is deliberate. It encompasses those laws, policies, and programs designed specifically to alter the behavior of micro units in the economy.

Microeconomic policy is geared to effect microeconomic change. Like many other aspects of microeconomics, it divides rather sharply, with one set of policies directed toward firms and another set directed toward households. Policies concerning firms have generally been coercive. They have tried to make firms engage in activities not ordinarily called for by market signals, or to prevent firms from following the dictates of some market signals. The policies directed toward households have generally been supplementary, and aimed at giving specific households advantages they might not otherwise have.

Figure 28-1 is a schematic diagram of how microeconomic policy works. At the top of the scheme are the policy makers. These are the local, state, and federal officials, as well as the large agencies that make rules governing the economic behavior of micro units. In the center are the firms and households acting as economically motivated entities. They respond to supernormal profits, they exploit all economic opportunity, and they do not engage in any uneconomic or noneconomic behavior. The consumer/voters appear at the bottom of the figure. They are essentially the same people who are found in the firms and households, but in acting as consumers and voters they take some noneconomic views of the world around them.

Policy influences the behavior of firms and households. Policy rules require, for example, that firms not sell spoiled meat, or not behave like monopolies, or run the buses on Sundays even though it is not profitable. Rules made by policy makers also require laborers to help pay for unemployment insurance and wear hard hats, and require physicians and

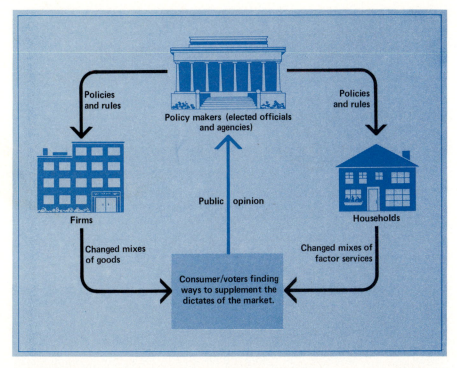

Figure 28-1 The Formation and Effects of Microeconomic Policy

druggists to be licensed. Such rules imposed on firms and households result in a different mix of goods and services available to the consuming public.

Policy makers do not operate entirely by their own lights. They must respond to the interests of their constituents or they will be removed from office. Microeconomic policy is made because consumer/voters want it to be made. Surely it is not always perfect policy, and on occasion it falls short of correcting the problem at hand. In this day of Ralph Nader, consumer advocates, antimonopoly drives, and damaging rates of inflation, the communication from consumer/voters to policy makers is an important force helping to guide the creation of micro policy.

Regardless of how the policy is formed or whether it is firm- or household-oriented, it is sometimes difficult to distinguish between micro and macro policy. Often, the federal government directs policy at individual firms—a micro orientation—hoping that when all firms have responded there will be some noticeable macro result.[1] Much time can be wasted

---

[1] An investment tax credit falls into this category. Investment tax credits induce firms to invest more in new plant and equipment by allowing them to "write off" the investment when income taxes are paid. The policy is directed at individual firms (micro), but the anticipated result is an economy-wide increase in investment (macro).

trying to classify each economic policy as being either micro or macro, a problem that was noted in Chapter 15. The emphasis here will be on policies that are clearly directed at firms or households. Their aggregated effects will not be considered.

Antimonopoly Policy

Chapter 21 and its appendix described a number of policies and rationales related to the prevention of monopoly in the United States. By most standards, monopoly can be considered harmful to economic affairs. It allows exploitation of some consumer or producer groups and it allows the concentration of economic power into the hands of a very few. Monopoly also allows firms to charge high prices and earn supernormal profits. In the absence of monopoly power, more resources would enter the industry and prices charged consumers would fall. Because of these problems the U.S. Government has always been openly committed to antimonopoly and antitrust legislation.

Recall that a *trust* and a *monopoly* are not the same. A monopoly is a firm that produces a unique product that has no close substitutes. Buyers are at the mercy of the firm if they wish to buy the product. A trust is a way of controlling firms. A small group of individuals are the "trustees" for resources used by many firms. They thus have great power over what is produced and on what terms it is sold.

Since 1890, when the first major piece of antitrust legislation was passed by Congress, scores of antimonopoly laws have been introduced. Some of the most important are described below.

    1. The Sherman Antitrust Act (1890) made it illegal to monopolize trade, form business combinations, or enter into conspiracies that restrain trade. This Act was enacted against the *process of monopolizing;* it did very little to break up the many monopolies already in existence in the late nineteenth century.

    2. The Clayton Act (1914) outlawed price discrimination, *tied contracts,* and *interlocking directorates.*

A tied contract is an arrangement whereby a producer forces a retailer (or another producer) to deal exclusively with it. Retailers can sell one producer's brand only if they promise not to sell any other brand. Interlocking directorates are complex interconnections among firms allowing a few people to sit on many boards of directors and thus control many firms.

The law emphasized prevention but also permitted prosecution and punishment for officers of firms violating its provisions.

3. The Robinson-Patman Act (1936) broadened the portion of the Clayton Act dealing with price discrimination. Robinson-Patman forced buyers to treat all sellers equally and sellers to treat all buyers equally. Under this law, a small, unfavored local buyer can seek redress against firms that give price advantages to large and powerful buyers.

4. The Celler-Kefauver Anti-Merger Act (1950) closed an important loophole in the Clayton Act. The earlier act specified that mergers by *stock* acquisition were not permissible. That is, one company could not buy a majority of a second company's stock, then vote the purchased company out of existence. The later act outlawed mergers by asset acquisition, too, thus eliminating the possibility of one company's buying another outright if such a purchase would significantly reduce competition in the industry.

These and scores of lesser acts make up the present body of antitrust or antimonopoly legislation. Law by itself is of little consequence in the American legal system. Violators must be prosecuted before the law becomes effective. Although antimonopoly sentiment has always been a part of economic lore in the United States, legislators have been slow in passing laws and prosecutors have been even slower in taking action against offenders.

One reason for the latter has been ambiguity in the laws themselves. The Sherman Act and the Clayton Act appeared at a time when monopolies, trusts, and other concentrations of corporate power were rampant and visible. Prosecutions were few because the intent of the law was unclear to federal prosecutors. Should an existing monopoly that was not using its power in a damaging way be prosecuted? Or should only those companies *seeking* monopoly *power* be reproached? This ambiguity apparently kept authorities from prosecuting more than a few cases per year in the years immediately after passage of the acts. More recently, as loopholes have been closed and public sentiment against monopoly has increased, public prosecutors have been taking 45 to 50 major cases to court each year, and federal investigators have worked diligently to maintain surveillance of the nation's industrial giants.

The history of antimonopoly activity makes interesting reading. Pages could be filled with cases that cause emotions to run high. The government can be described as moving against "harmless" monopolies, and the government can be shown to have been thwarted in its attempts to break up some clearly objectionable trusts. This has been the longest and the most active part of microeconomic policy in U.S. economic history. Its major thrust has been at preventing the development of monopolies or breaking existing monopolies that act in restraint of trade and prevent resources from being used in the most efficient possible way. In a word, antimonopoly legislation has been passed so that the public would not be forced to contribute to supernormal profits being earned by a few giant corporations.

Some Noteworthy Cases

Among the many cases that have been brought into court under the antitrust laws, a few stand out because of their size, their complexity, or the public interest they have generated. Here are some examples:

United States v. *Standard Oil of New Jersey* was among the first cases prosecuted under the antimonopolization section of the 1890 Sherman Act. In 1911, Standard Oil was found to be "predatory" in its attempts to drive other oil companies from the industry. The courts required it to divide into 11 smaller companies.

United States v. *Aluminum Company of America* was a strange case reaching the courts in the late 1930s. Alcoa was indeed a monopoly, since it controlled access to nearly all the bauxite in the Western world. (Bauxite is the principal ore from which aluminum is extracted. Some of this ore is found in Arkansas, but the U.S. aluminum industry depends upon imports from Surinam and Jamaica.) However, Alcoa had acquired these properties without coercion, and apparently with no objective other than to supply the needs of its own plants. Alcoa was not thought to be gouging the public or restraining trade when the case came to court. Nonetheless, the monopoly was broken up because the possibility of future malfeasance existed.

United States v. *E. I. du Pont de Nemours and Co.* Beginning in the late 1930s, Du Pont purchased a large number of shares of General Motors common stock. At approximately the same time, Du Pont was becoming a major supplier of GM's paint, finishing materials, and upholstery. By 1949, Du Pont owned 23 percent of GM's stock. At this point the government intervened, saying that the large holding kept GM from trading with other potential suppliers. Du Pont was required to sell its GM stock.

Standard Oil, Alcoa, and Du Pont were giants. Breaking them into several smaller firms noticeably reduced the concentration of economic power in each industry and reduced the possibility that a few men could control the economic livelihood of whole industries.

A more unusual antimonopoly case came before the courts in 1960. In that year, Von's Grocery Company in Los Angeles was ordered to sell its recently acquired interest in Shopping Bag Food Stores because the two combined controlled $7\frac{1}{2}$ percent of the Los Angeles retail grocery trade. They were divided because even with only $7\frac{1}{2}$ percent of the trade, they "displayed a threatening trend."

By far the most celebrated antimonopoly case occurred in 1961 and involved a number of manufacturers of heavy electrical equipment. This equipment (generators for municipal plants, dynamos, transformers, and high-capacity switching devices) is built by a very few firms and sold to very few buyers. The industry is ripe for collusive activity. In 1961, the Department of Justice found that prices of this heavy equipment had been rigged, and that the market had been deliberately shared among 29 producing companies. The companies were found guilty and eventually paid fines totalling nearly $2 million. Individual executives were fined up to $12,500, and 32 executives received prison sentences. Seventy years after the war on monopoly had started, top executives in top companies were finally shown that at least one judge meant business.

Protecting Natural Monopolies

On its surface, microeconomic policy seems inconsistent with respect to monopolies. On one hand, the law forbids Du Pont to become an active owner of General Motors and refuses Alcoa the opportunity to extend its control over the West's supply of bauxite. On the other hand, the law refuses to let more than one telephone company operate in a given area, and it takes over the nation's railroad passenger service so that it can be run as a monopoly.

The monopolies that have the endorsement (or protection) of public policy are the natural monopolies—those industries that provide necessary services but which often cannot by themselves earn even normal profits. Far from being broken up, the natural monopolies are protected, nurtured, and even subsidized by policies of local, state, and federal governments. There are two broad classes of natural monopoly: those that are protected and controlled and those that are protected and nurtured.

Protection and Control

The telephone system in the United States is a monopoly that is protected but at the same time controlled. In 1972, the Bell System owned or managed about 81 percent of all telephones in the country. The remaining 19 percent were controlled by nearly 1,800 small companies. Some of the non-Bell companies (especially General Telephone) were quite large, but even in the early 1970s many other telephone companies were little more than small, independently owned switchboards. At present, very few cities or towns are served by more than one telephone company. The reason is that a second company requires a second set of poles, wires, switchboards, operators, trucks, and repairmen. Duplication of a service is not necessarily bad, but since the separate systems would have to be tied together anyway (to enable customers of one system to communicate with customers of another), it has always made sense for one town to be served by only one telephone company. The community (or county or state) gives the company a license to do business, then agrees to protect it by not granting a license to any rival firm.

Since demand for telephone service is relatively unresponsive (inelastic) to changes in price, the protected company is in a favored position. It can double its rates and make much more profit, or it can charge businesses higher rates than it charges residential users, or it can freely discriminate on an *ad hoc* basis. To prevent this from occurring, the unit of government granting the license insists that all telephone rates be regulated. Regulation of telephone rates is handled by the powerful Federal Communications Commission (FCC) and numerous local commissions. The rates for local and long distance calls are designed to enable the company to earn a "fair and just" return on its investment. In the language of economics, rates are set to enable the telephone company to earn normal profits.

The arrangement between government and natural monopoly is convenient for each. The natural monopoly need not worry about rival firms encroaching on its market, and users of the service pay fees that bring only a regulated volume of profits to the firm. This arrangement works well in encouraging while at the same time regulating those natural monopolies that provide telephone service, natural gas, water, garbage collection, sewage disposal, and a wide variety of other municipal or semiprivate functions.

Protection and Nurture

While the populace may demand protection from a ruthlessly profiteering natural monopoly, it may also need to develop a micro policy insuring the provision of some services. Public transportation is a notoriously difficult problem for most metropolitan areas. Urban residents want a public transportation system, but they seldom are willing to use it sufficiently or to pay fares high enough to make the system profitable. (In 1973, there were 1,020 municipal bus companies operating in U.S. cities. Together, they had fare box revenues of $1.8 billion and expenses of $2.4 billion. The loss was made up from local, state, and federal subsidies.) The cost curve for municipal bus transportation is above its demand curve over the relevant range of riders.

Most cities reason that many people depend upon public transportation. Moreover, those depending on public transportation include the poor, the elderly, the infirm, and those who do not have easy access to other forms of transportation. In order to aid these groups, cities invite the creation of a monopoly firm and guarantee that the firm will remain solvent even if its costs are not met through fare collections. The guarantee is a subsidy, paid to insure that the factors of production committed to public transportation will earn normal profits and thus remain in the industry. The subsidy or guarantee can take many forms. It can be cash payment, the granting of tax-free status, or provision of some part of the equipment or facilities needed to operate the system.

The point remains that governments regulate different monopolies for different reasons. The most common reason is that monopolists are in a unique position to charge extra high prices, prevent resources from being allocated correctly, and earn high profits on their own resource commitments. Some natural monopolies are, however, encouraged because they provide a useful and desired service but could not earn sufficient profits without some form of protection.

Who Regulates Whom... and for What Purpose?

Early in the U.S. economy's antimonopoly campaign, it became clear that "commissions" or "boards" should have responsibility for regulating individual industries that had the potential of becoming monopolistic. A Civil Aeronautics Board (CAB) was established to watch the airlines, the Interstate Commerce Commission (ICC) was set up to watch the railroads, and the Federal Trade Commission (FTC) was named as a general monitor of wholesale and retail trade relationships.

When the commissions were first established they were staffed by experts in the particular fields that were to be regulated. Railway experts found seats on the ICC, and air travel authorities made up the CAB. At first, their chore was singular: Prevent the monopoly (or near-monopoly) from using its power to charge exorbitant prices or restrict economic activity. As time passed, board members and commissioners seemed to become more interested in the industries they were regulating than in the public they were supposed to protect. The emphasis seemed to turn from eliminating supernormal profits to guaranteeing at least normal profits.

Nowhere is this more evident than in the air transport industry. Time and time again, some airlines have asked for lower fares so that they could attract more passengers and fill their planes. Other airlines have countered by simultaneously requesting higher fares to pay rising costs even if their planes are half full. Those in charge of setting fares have consistently taken a conservative stance: Let fares keep up with costs; don't tamper with fare reductions.

Who is being served? The public or the air carriers? No one can be entirely sure, but it seems that in this era of consumerism, the consuming public will not be so patient as it has been in the past.

"The FCC says 'yes,' the FTC says 'maybe,' and the SEC says 'no.'"

Placing Bounds on Behavior

The market is an amazing assimilator and transmitter of information. It tells sellers what will sell and it tells buyers what and where to buy. However, like all nonreasoning systems, the market gathers, digests, and dispenses partial and erroneous information just as easily as it transmits complete and correct information. Water-filled hams can be sold as "hams" just as quickly as slow-smoked Kentucky hams. Meat from diseased animals, and vegetables canned using improper techniques sit on shelves side by side with higher priced but safe foods from more careful packers. The market does not differentiate on any basis other than price. The situation is no different in the factor market. A laborer can respond to a well-worded job advertisement, only to find that the job demands operating a machine surrounded by highly dangerous spinning gears and loose belts.

In each of these cases, the whole truth has not been told to one of the parties entering into an economic transaction. It is unlikely that meat cutters will ever be entirely truthful about what they are selling, and it is unlikely that industrial employers will ever give each prospective worker complete information on how dangerous the job really is.

A type of consumerism dating from well before Ralph Nader fills this information gap. There are microeconomic policies that force firms to take some measures to protect their customers and their employees. Food crossing state lines must be inspected, and must meet quality standards set by the U.S. Department of Agriculture. The safety of employees is guarded by the Occupational Safety and Health Administration, an agency of the U.S. Department of Health, Education and Welfare.

These agencies can only do partial jobs. It would be impossible to examine all cucumbers that pass from neighbor to neighbor, and it would be impossible to insure that every drill press operator wears goggles each time the drill is running. Over the years, though, the laws have tightened so that consumers can be reasonably sure of quality, and laborers can be reasonably sure of safety. A microeconomic policy has succeeded in supplementing the information and incentives coming through the market system.

Policies Affecting Households

While policies affecting firms have been geared to regulate, protect, or encourage, microeconomic policies directed at households have nearly all been aimed at transferring incomes from one group to another or at providing mandatory insurance protection against times of unemployment or for retired workers. At present, both federal and state governments are involved in household-related policies. In general, the federal government is responsible for maintaining income transfers to individuals after they retire from the labor force. The individual states are responsible for unemployment compensation and *public assistance* before retirement age is reached.

Public assistance is the catch-all category of income transfers. It includes aid to the disabled and blind, Aid to Families with Dependent Children, special grants to families with severe health problems, and a variety of selective programs. Public assistance is administered by the individual states, but part of the funds for the programs comes from the federal government.

Old age is a universal risk. Everyone who exercises moderate caution and does not contract a dread disease must one day grow old. For centuries, the extended family cooperated in taking care of its young and its old. When parents died, their children were raised by grandparents. When a man was disabled, his brothers contributed to support him and his family. Not too many years ago, three and four generations commonly lived under one roof, sharing the incomes earned by the working household members. There were no pensions, insurance, or large amounts of public assistance, because society was organized to circumvent the need for them.

With the emergence of the industrial economy, large numbers of workers were uprooted from their rural homes and brought together in congested industrial areas like New York, Chicago, and Birmingham. They left parents and grandparents behind, breaking the centuries-long tradition of extended family care. There was no longer an easy way to care for those who had been left behind. As harsh as it may sound, the out-of-sight, out-of-mind attitude seemed to prevail as the new generations of workers used their incomes to support themselves and let their parents get on as best they could.

The concentration of population continued through the early decades of this century, placing increasing stress on those who could not participate directly in the economic affairs of the nation. When the economy entered the Great Depression of the 1930s, the stage was appropriately set for social reform. One of President Franklin D. Roosevelt's prime interests was the organization of a social institution that would provide incomes for people with no visible means of support.

Retirement insurance. In August 1935, the Social Security Act was signed into law. Under it the federal government adopted compulsory insurance programs designed to prevent income interruption due to unemployment or old age. The old-age component was kept for administration by federal authorities. Other parts of the program were turned over to the states. On

January 1, 1937, a federal old-age benefit tax of one percent of wages was levied on employers and workers in some industries. These tax receipts were used to accumulate a fund that would later be used to pay old-age benefits. By 1940, sufficient funds had been collected to enable payment of the first federal old-age pensions.[2]

At first, the old-age and survivors insurance programs were quite limited. Only workers who had been employed in industry, commerce, or the trades were eligible to receive benefits. In the 40 years that have passed since the law's inception, coverage has been extended to many more groups. Now only a few classes of persons, mainly those in the service occupations and in government, are not automatically covered by some part of the social security program. In 1974, the federal retirement system made payments of $34.6 billion to 19.3 million persons. Another $19.4 million went to survivors and disabled persons, and Medicare—the medical aid program started in 1965—extended $7.7 billion to purchase health care for aging people.

Unemployment insurance. Although it was quickly turned over to the states for administration, the unemployment compensation program started on January 1, 1936, when a 1 percent payroll tax was levied against all employers having more than eight employees. This tax was quickly raised to 2 percent in 1937 and then to 3 percent in 1938.

On August 17, 1937, Wisconsin became the first state to issue an unemployment check. Efforts to extend unemployment coverage included emergency provisions to provide unemployment or "transition" insurance for veterans of World War II and the Korean conflict. In 1954, employers of four or more workers were required to participate in the program; in 1970, any employer of one or more became a participant.

Unemployment insurance is an extremely important part of this nation's microeconomic policy. In 1974, payments of $6.3 billion were paid in response to 13.3 million claims. Nevertheless, the varying laws among the states, plus the severe increases in unemployment in more recent years, must lead to the conclusion that the able-bodied worker in the U.S. economy is far from secure. A person who is in the correct job has access to unemployment compensation, but even then the weekly payment may be very low and may last only a few weeks. A worker who is not in a job covered by unemployment insurance has few options.

Public assistance. The third part of household-oriented micro policy is public assistance. Public assistance is used to fill gaps in the welfare system. It gives purchasing power to families who have no incomes and who

---

[2]The term "old-age pension" is too restrictive. In reality, the portion of the program kept for federal management included pensions for survivors of workers, aid for children whose parents had been killed or disabled, and, eventually, payments for medical care needed by the aged.

do not qualify for either social security or unemployment compensation. Like unemployment compensation, public assistance is a state responsibility, and again rules vary from state to state. The most important component of public assistance is Aid to Families With Dependent Children, but emergency aid, grants for medical care, and other incidental items may be included in a state's overall public assistance program. In 1974, $8 billion in public assistance went to families with dependent children and another $13 billion was used for other kinds of grants.

Even though the provisions of the microeconomic income-transfer programs are numerous and appear to be complete, there are still large numbers of families in the United States with incomes well below the *poverty line.*

The poverty line is a level of income below which people cannot attain a satisfactory level of living. Because prices differ from place to place and from time to time, the poverty line is constantly being adjusted. In 1974, the poverty line for a family of four was $5,038—approximately one-third of the average income of all four-person families.

In recent years efforts to help these families have centered on negative income tax plans and family assistance programs.

Negative income tax plans are based on the existing bookkeeping system of the Internal Revenue Service. Family size, income, and special circumstances are used to determine if a payment should be made to a low-income family. These plans are easy to administer, but have the potential of damaging incentives if earned dollars replace dollars that come through the welfare program. Recent versions of the negative income tax plans have allowed recipient families to keep a portion of earned income in addition to receiving full program benefits. In this way, aid continues to flow to the families, and work incentives remain intact.

Ideas for family assistance plans are numerous, but to date none has been implemented. They are basically the same as the negative income tax scheme but do not necessarily build on the existing bookkeeping framework. Both kinds of plans suffer the same problems: How is eligibility to be documented? How will incentives be retained? Should there be time or dollar limits to a family's participation?

The history of microeconomic policy related to households is relatively short. The economic trauma of the Great Depression was needed to encourage enactment of laws providing a minimum of economic protection for families with no visible means of support. In the 40 years since the first laws were passed, numerous modifications have expanded the proportion of the populace that is covered by the programs and increased the types of coverage enjoyed by U.S. citizens. There is, however, much to be done in providing institutions that give uniform and adequate protection to those households that are temporarily or permanently outside the mainstream of economic affairs.

Summary

1. In a modern market economy, the government must develop policies to induce firms and households to carry out some activities and prevent them from doing others. Since this kind of policy is directed at the individual decision-making unit, it is called microeconomic policy.
2. The part of micro policy aimed at firms has most often been regulatory. It has prevented monopolies from forming or has protected natural monopolies.
3. Antimonopoly legislation began in 1890, and has been prominent since that time.
4. An important problem with antimonopoly legislation has been the inconsistent mood of the U.S. Justice Department and the Supreme Court.
5. Natural monopolies are nearly always protected from rival firms. Some must be regulated so that they will not earn excessive profits. Others may need to be subsidized if they are to survive. Telephone companies are in the former group, public transport in the latter.
6. Microeconomic policy directed at households relates almost entirely to income transfers to families that cannot participate actively in economic affairs. These policies stem from the great economic upheaval of the 1930s.
7. The major household-related programs include the federal old-age and survivors' insurance and the state-managed unemployment compensation and public assistance programs. While these programs do provide much security, they are far from adequate in terms of relieving hunger, alienation, and anxiety.

Exercises

1. Explain these important terms and concepts:

micro policy	controlling monopolies
a trust	public assistance
Sherman Antitrust Act	the poverty line
protecting monopolies	

2. Many people are appalled at the breakdown of the family as an institution in U.S. society. It is true that families are no longer as close-knit as they once were, and they do not seem to care for each other as much as they once did. How has this breakdown of an institution contributed to the development of welfare programs? In your opinion, has this been good or bad?
3. Some monopolies should be controlled because they have the power to earn especially high profits. Other monopolies should be encouraged because they provide needed services that could not be sustained under any other form of market organization. Here is a hypothetical list of monopolies or potential monopolies. Which should be controlled and which should be nurtured? Why?

door-to-door milk delivery	the gas company
trunk-line air transport	a national wool fabric monopoly
main-line rail transport	the postal service

4. A very serious problem arises in many industries that can gain efficiencies in production only by becoming giants. The huge size might enable them to offer their product to the public at a low price, but it might also bring the threat of antimonopoly prosecution. If you were a company executive facing this problem, how would you respond to it?
5. Natural monopolies are often protected by boards or commissions. These groups have the task of maintaining the firm and also preventing it from overcharging the public. If you were called to sit on the board that regulates phone company rates, what objectives would you have in mind and what information would you need to meet them?
6. Microeconomic policies aimed at households almost always deal with transferring income to low-income households. A serious problem arises when it is recognized that payments to households may become substitutes for income earned by selling labor. That is, welfare payments, if they are high enough, can damage the incentive to work. Devise a plan that would give needy families more income but would at the same time encourage them to move back into the mainstream of economic activity.

A Contemporary Problem
The Taxis in New York

For many years the number of taxicabs in New York City has been limited by a city licensing agency. Limiting the number has been necessary in order to maintain some control of traffic, insure that vehicles used as taxis are safe, and keep resources (cabs and their drivers) from moving into and out of the business of transporting people. A licensed cab can be distinguished by a large medallion attached to the right-hand side of the vehicle's hood. The licensing process is microeconomic policy instituted by New York City.

A limited number of medallions are issued by the city at a nominal fee. Once the medallion leaves City Hall, however, it can be resold to anyone who has the money to buy it, and the owner can sell it for whatever price he can obtain. In recent years medallions are known to have been sold for as much as $30,000.

The policy of limiting cabs in the city had very straightforward objectives, but the consequences of the policy have been diverse. The policy was designed to help regulate traffic, but it has resulted in a few people becoming very wealthy simply because they were fortunate enough to obtain a medallion from the city. This kind of danger exists in many micro policies. Unintended consequences bring problems of a different sort.

If you were on the city licensing board, what would you suggest? You might suggest the city sell medallions to all buyers at $30,000 each, but this could result in the number of cabs doubling or tripling very quickly. You could suggest that more and better *buses* be provided, so that cab profits and the value of a medallion would drop. But this would require an increased subsidy to the bus system. You could suggest much higher rates for cab users. This would do one of two things: either increase the profits to cab owners, thus driving up the price of the medallion, or prevent people from using cabs so much and drive the price down. A final possibility is increasing the availability of parking space for private autos. This would take profits away from cab owners but it would increase the traffic congestion on New York's streets.

Microeconomic policy is never as easy as it seems. Correcting one problem may bring dozens more, and information is seldom adequate to allow the best choice of policies.

29 An Introduction to the World Economy

In an age when men have viewed the earth from the surface of the moon and daily weather photos show movements of cloud systems over whole continents, it seems quite appropriate to speak of a world economy encompassing all the world's production, exchange, and consumption activities. These three functions define the workings of an economy, and they take place throughout the world, so there *must* be a "world economy." In a sense there is, but the world economy is intractable and cannot be managed or measured. One can only guess at the magnitude of gross world product, the distribution of income among the world's 4 billion people, or the rate of unemployment among the world's laborers. Few people know the relative profitabilities of growing rice in Alabama or Burma or Algeria, and rice-producing resources (even those not attached to the land) cannot flow to the most profitable locales. Most important, there is no integrated policy-making group keeping track of the world economy and making recommendations about the world money supply, world antitrust policy, and world economic growth rates.

Although there is world production, world exchange, and world consumption, there is no well-defined world economy. Economic activities are carried on in a collection of national economies. Each national economy is composed of and defined by producing units and consuming units that agree to follow the same rules when trading with each other and with

Who Does the Trading?

"International trade," "exports," and "imports" are terms commonly used to describe economic transactions among nations. These are aggregate terms, and they obscure the fact that the individual transactions are made by independent businesses, investors, and individuals. Macy's department store decides it wishes to carry a product line including German-made cutlery. Macy's itself deals with the German manufacturer. The Hallmark shops decide to stock elegant knick-knacks from Ukrainian Russia, so Hallmark deals with the Russian artisans. These are private firms making private decisions to carry foreign goods. These private activities, along with thousands of others, are aggregated and referred to simply as "U.S. imports." The total value of imports reported in the national income accounts hides the process of individuals searching, bargaining, and marketing.

"It's a good buy. A pot like that costs $45 at Bloomingdale's."

other national economies. Thus, for example, firms and households in the United States all use the same kind of money to pay for foreign-produced goods, and must all subject their imports and exports to the same inspection routines. Similarly, Japan's 46 prefectures follow the same Japanese laws, and the Republic of Ireland's 26 counties and 5 boroughs follow one set of Irish laws when entering into exchanges with other nations.

Nations trade with each other for a simple reason: to exchange their surpluses for goods they do not have. Goods having low marginal utilities to domestic citizens are exported, while goods with high marginal utilities are purchased from other nations. Argentina trades home-grown, low-cost beef to West Germany for machinery. Since Argentina has many cattle, meat has low marginal utility to most Argentinians, but since the nation has scanty supplies of minerals and metals, it must look abroad for mechanical equipment. West Germany has great industrial capacity but little land on which to raise livestock. West German equipment and tools are traded for Argentine beef, and each nation is better off after the trade. The Central American nations trade tropical fruits for medicines and industrial equipment. The United States trades its relatively abundant food and its technical know-how for mass-produced clothing, high-quality electronic gear, and automobiles. The economies of the world produce everything from A to Z, exchange everything from A to Z, and consume everything from A to Z.

This chapter and the four that follow explain the relationship between the United States economy and the other economies in today's world. They explain international trade. The present chapter includes an historical account of U.S. trade with other nations and a description of some problems now faced by the world's economies. It is filled with definitions, diagrams and brief explanations of complex problems. Chapter 30 goes into some detail to show why nations trade, Chapters 31 and 32 talk of international flows of money and payments among nations, and Chapter 33 describes some particular problems faced by developing nations.

Trade Among National Economies

The domestic economy of the United States has already been described as a system in which firms, households, and governments interact to produce and exchange goods and services. The interaction yields one of the highest levels of living in the world. In the U.S. economy, firms carry out productive activities and final consumption takes place in households. The two are interconnected by market exchanges and make up a circular flow like the one shown in the center of Figure 29–1. (To simplify the figure, the role of government is omitted.)

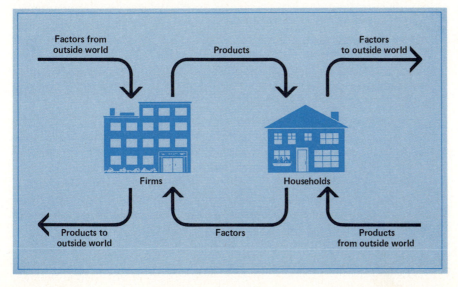

**Figure 29–1
The Basic Multi-economy Circular Flow**

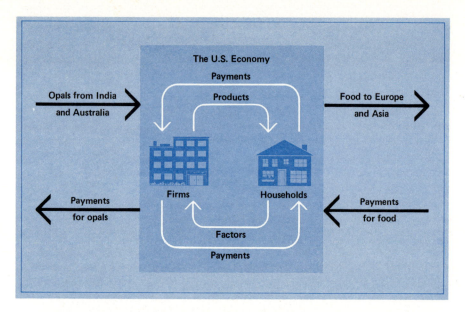

Figure 29-2 The United States Trades with Other Nations

If an economy includes only one or a very few firms and households, it is unlikely to be self-sufficient. In order to obtain needed goods and services it engages in trade with firms and households that are parts of other economies (other circular flows). Factors and products are sent to and purchased from other economies. These various possibilities are shown by the arrows pointing to and from the main circular flow in Figure 29-1.

Much the same process applies when the United States trades with other countries. The domestic economy produces most of its own goods and services. There are, however, some things it wants but cannot produce. For example, some U.S. citizens like to adorn themselves with black opals, which are not found in gem quality in any of the 50 states. To obtain these precious stones, the United States must trade with India or Australia. Other nations need food. The agricultural industry in the United States is one of the world's most productive, and U.S. farmers are happy to sell part of their crops to foreign nations.

The U.S. economy is represented in the center of Figure 29-2. Domestic activity is carried out in the usual circular fashion, but the domestic economy has trading ties with other nations. Some transactions result in U.S. money being exchanged for Indian and Australian opals, and other transactions result in foreign money being exchanged for U.S. food. The exchanges give people access to things they cannot produce for themselves and thus increase the level of their satisfaction.

When U.S. citizens buy or sell in other countries, they are still initiating and responding to market forces. When international market forces bring buyers and sellers together, decisions are made about what to produce, how to produce it, and for whom it should be produced. The allocative purposes and mechanisms of economics do not honor national boundaries. An international market is more complicated than a local market because of problems associated with time, distance, and the risk of making decisions based on faulty information. However, it is known that De-Beers of South Africa has diamonds to sell, Lloyds of London has insurance to sell, and Sony of Japan has electronic equipment to sell. It is known that U.S. consumers will buy high-quality small cars, it is known that Great Britain will buy the raw materials needed for industrial production, and it is known that U.S.-made fashion clothing is in great demand in Japan. Demand and supply information is transmitted through markets, and, within national economies, resources are allocated in response to the international market signals. When U.S. consumers decided to purchase 2.6 million imported autos in 1971, automobile manufacturers in Japan, West Germany, Italy, and the Scandanavian nations took note and devoted more factors to producing autos for the export trade.[1] Similarly, when Canada and Western Europe demand increased quantities of U.S. products, domestic manufacturers are quick to respond.

Although the economics of trade among nations is much like the economics of trade among domestic households and firms, it is nearly always complicated by political alliances and the problems of economic growth and of money. Some nations choose never to trade with each other. For years, the United States Government forbade all trade between its citizens and the People's Republic of (mainland) China and allowed only very limited trade with the other centralized economies of the Communist bloc. While this policy may have been politically and diplomatically correct, it deprived U.S. citizens of access to raw materials (especially ores and minerals), textiles, hides, and even the sight of the frolicsome panda bear. At the same time, the no-trade policy prevented Chinese industrialists from buying U.S. tools and kept Chinese airlines from purchasing U.S. commercial aircraft.

The primary difficulty in international trading is not related to politics or tariffs or panda bears. It stems from the fact that each nation has its own monetary system, its own monetary units, and its own internal monetary policy. This is the way it must be. Nations use their own monetary systems as powerful tools to control the intensity of economic activity within their own boundaries. They increase and decrease money supplies and subsequently increase and decrease product prices. Changing domestic prices also changes relative prices among nations. When Japan's monetary policy causes the price of Toyotas and Datsuns to rise, U.S. manufacturers of Pintos and Vegas take note, and automobile dealers become

---

[1] In 1971, imported automobiles accounted for 23.5 percent of all new automobile sales in the United States. Since then, imported autos have represented a gradually diminishing share of the U.S. market.

"What does Confucius say about foreign policy based on a couple of pandas?"

wary about whether to buy or sell. The need for domestic flexibility causes international uncertainty in a world filled with French francs, Italian lire, Canadian dollars, and Indian rupees.

These chapters on international trade must unravel a number of problems. They must show why nations trade, the extent to which trade can be profitable, the problems of money in international trading, and the effects of political restrictions imposed on trade. In some respects the lessons will be easy, because economics, even in its international dimensions, remains the study of wise choosing. In other respects, however, international economics is confusing because it must deal in a world of multiple currencies (and the way they are related), uncertainty, and flexibility. Nevertheless, it is extremely important, in this era of close relationships among nations, to understand their economic components.

The United States as a Trading Nation

The part of North America that eventually became the United States was trading with Europe even as it was being settled. The first settlers coming from Western Europe were fleeing from religious and political oppression, but in addition to freedom from persecution, the rude new land provided only land and natural resources. The settlers needed tools, labor, *working capital,* and organization.

> Working capital is cash used to pay current bills and obligations. A factory owner uses working capital to pay laborers, the electric bill, and other expenses directly related to the production process.

They had to maintain trading ties with Europe in order to insure that their food and forest products could be traded quickly for the machines and capital they needed.

The settlers arriving in the late seventeenth and early eighteenth centuries were not necessarily fleeing oppression, but were coming to join a *colony*.

> A colony is a geographic territory subservient to another nation's government. Most European nations—especially England, Spain, Portugal, and France—had vast colonial holdings. The colonies were expected to be producers of raw materials and consumers of finished goods. Thus, England expected to purchase wood, hides, cotton and foodstuffs from its North American colonies. In return, the colonies were expected to purchase machines, shipping and protection from England.

They may have been looking for a better life and for more opportunities, but most also realized that they were subjects of a European government and that one of their tasks was to produce raw materials for the parent country. Moreover, when the settlers needed to buy things, the purchases, insofar as possible, were to be made from the mother country. Trade between the colonies and Europe was guaranteed, and it was important.

North America produced very well for its various parent countries. The colonists turned the abundance of natural resources into forest products, agricultural products, and minerals that could be sent to England, France, and Spain. Industrial equipment, manufactured goods, investment capital, and more immigrants made the return trip.

Once the United States was independent and extended all the way to the Pacific, it lessened its trade relations with other nations. Only those things that were particularly abundant (primarily agricultural commodities and minerals) were exported, and growing industrial capacity in the northeastern states reduced the need to import machinery and small capital items. The United States was emerging as a powerful and diversified economy.

In more recent decades, U.S. trade relationships have gone through several distinct periods. Early in this century, foodstuffs and raw materials were exported to Europe to help the nations of that continent prepare for World War I. During the war, the United States exported large volumes of food, armaments and other war-related materials, and afterward U.S. agricultural products were exported to nearly all of the ravaged European continent (including Russia, which, in addition to participating in the World War, had also been through a devastating revolution).

During the world-wide economic depression of the 1930s, U.S. imports and exports diminished to very low levels. Individual firms and households could not find the money to purchase desired goods within their own economies, and there was virtually no money for international trade. Both international trade and internal trade in most domestic economies nearly ground to a halt.

The 1940s brought an end to the depression and a resurgence of trade among nations. Europe was again girding for war and needed U.S. food and industrial products. U.S. farmers, who had produced vast surpluses of food beginning in the 1920s, were happy to find foreign markets. Arms manufacturers sold planes, guns, and munitions, and tools makers sold every conceivable kind of machine to manufacturers in other nations. At the end of the war, the devastated European countries again purchased, or received as gifts, the food, clothing and implements needed to restart their own production of peacetime goods and services.

During the last quarter century, international trade has grown demonstrably, and the world's economies have become much more interdependent. All nations have engaged in more trade and have capitalized upon and exploited their own capabilities. New Zealand has recognized that it can do very well by selling lamb and importing automobiles. Japan has exported automobiles and imported saw logs, and Chile has sought to obtain machinery in exchange for its tin. In 1958, exports from all trading nations had an aggregate value of $103 billion. By 1968, the nations of the world traded goods having a total value of $240 billion and by 1974, the value of international trade reached $775 billion.

Since one nation's exports must be another nation's imports, the total value of goods passing among all nations can be measured by counting *either* all exports *or* all imports. Thus, the $103 billion in *exports* measures total international trade in 1958.

For the United States the most rapid increases in foreign trade came from increased trading of manufactured goods, minerals, and agricultural products. In 1960, the United States sold manufactured goods valued at $10,816 million. By 1974, U.S. exports of these goods were valued at $40,151 million. In 1960, U.S. farmers and food processors exported foods valued at $3,167 million. By 1974, the value of food exports had increased to $15,232 million. The U.S. experience is not unique. In the past 25 years, all industrial and most developing nations have increased dramatically the number and value of things they export to other nations. These increased exports have in turn led to increased imports of the things the exporting nations cannot or do not want to produce for themselves.

The U.S. economy continues to grow with respect to international trade. Because the United States now produces more GNP than all other industrial nations combined, anything that happens here is very likely to have international repercussions. A prolonged strike by U.S. auto workers is felt by Fiat, Toyota, and Saab. The completion of the Alaska pipeline will affect U.S. relationships with the OPEC (Organization of Petroleum Exporting Countries), and a crop failure through the Plains States will cause the prices of bread and flour to rise in Western Europe and the Far East.

The diversity of the U.S. economy makes it unique, too. No other major nation presently has such a rich variety of usable natural and capital resources. These endowments make the nation capable of becoming a *closed economy.*

A closed economy is one that is self-sufficient and carries on no trade with other nations. Although some modern economies have the capability to sustain themselves as closed economies, none of them does.

In 1973, GNP in the United States was $1,294 billion. The nation's international trade activities included goods and services valued at only $70 billion—about 5 percent of GNP. By contrast, some European nations (notably Belgium and The Netherlands) regularly export over one-third of their GNP, and others (Denmark, Switzerland, Norway, and Sweden) annually trade more than 20 percent of their GNPs. Even the powerful West German economy must trade goods valued at about 20 percent of its GNP each year in order to provide a reasonable variety of goods and services for West German citizens.

Since such a small amount of the U.S. product enters international trade, the U.S. economy is relatively immune to shocks and disturbances that may arise in the economies of other countries. But "relative immunity" and "complete immunity" are quite different things. Even though the U.S. economy could probably be self-sufficient, it still depends upon other economies to supply some important goods and services that cannot be produced easily by the domestic economy. For example, the United States has rather large petroleum deposits, but they are not large enough to satisfy domestic needs. Purchases of petroleum products from foreign nations are valued at nearly $8 billion each year. Similarly, the United States produces more than 35 percent of the world's aluminum, but less than 5 percent of the world's bauxite (the ore from which aluminum is derived) is produced domestically, so bauxite must be imported. Without these imports and others like them, the size and *quality of output* in the United States would be altered.

Quality of output refers to the mix or "menu" of goods and services produced.

The story is much the same with respect to the things exported to other nations. Although only 5 percent of domestic production leaves the nation, several industries depend heavily on foreigners to make large annual purchases. The wheat farmers of the Pacific Northwest sell a large proportion of their product in the Orient. Without this foreign market, the price of the region's specially grown soft white winter wheat would be much lower. World production of soybeans is only about 58 million tons, but 85 percent of all soybeans entering foreign trade comes from U.S.

farms. And, although the United States is generally an importer of minerals, two-thirds of all molybdenum mined here is sold to foreign economies.

These exceptions do not change the general rule that the U.S. economy is a giant compared to other economies. They only point out that, while the economy is generally self-sufficient, some parts of it are highly dependent upon trade with other nations. If trade stopped, the quality of output in the United States would change.

With Whom Does the United States Trade?

Carol Kennicott, the physician's wife in Sinclair Lewis's 1920 American classic novel, *Main Street,* was a city girl who did not adapt well to life in Gopher Prairie, Minnesota. "Carrie," as her husband called her, did not shop for the lowest prices or necessarily for the highest quality merchandise. She shopped by custom, preferring one drug store because the proprietor appealed to her, and preferring one grocery because the obviously poor store needed her business. Carrie arranged informal but special trade relationships in Gopher Prairie. Her preferences were not necessarily economic, since they also included social choices (the pleasant druggist), need (the destitute grocer), and the habit of trading with one person in one spot.

Nations behave in much the same way when they establish international trade relationships. Once individual traders have established successful relationships with each other, some inertial force causes these relationships to be maintained. Table 29–1 shows the remarkable stability of imports and exports flowing between the United States and each of

Table 29–1   Percent of U.S. Trade with Each of Several Groups of Nations

Nation or group	Exports				Imports			
	1960	1965	1970	1973	1960	1965	1970	1973
Canada	18.5	20.5	21.0	21.1	19.8	22.6	27.8	25.2
Latin American Nations	17.4	13.8	13.2	12.5	24.1	17.2	12.0	11.0
European Economic Community	19.3	19.1	19.5	17.7	15.4	15.5	16.5	16.2
European Free Trade Association	12.0	10.5	10.4	8.8	11.1	11.5	9.6	9.5
Communist areas in Europe	0.9	0.3	0.8	2.5	0.5	0.6	0.6	0.8
Japan	7.0	7.6	10.8	11.7	7.8	11.3	14.7	14.0
East and South Asia	10.7	11.3	9.3	9.3	8.6	8.1	8.5	10.0
Australia and Oceania	2.5	3.5	2.7	2.4	1.8	2.1	2.2	2.2
Africa	3.9	4.5	3.7	3.2	3.6	5.8	2.8	3.4
Other	7.8	8.7	8.6	10.8	7.3	5.3	6.3	7.7

several groups of nations. For the past 15 years, exports to Canada have hovered close to 20 percent of all U.S. exports. Europe has purchased about one third, and the other nations quite stable proportions, of this nation's total exports. The import record is similar, except for substantial recent increases in the proportions of imports coming from Canada and Japan.

To be sure, trade patterns are circumscribed by what is demanded and what is supplied by each trading nation, but the influence of custom cannot be denied. The United States buys wool sweaters from Ireland and Hong Kong. Similar wool sweaters could be purchased from Italy or Malaysia or New Zealand, but the trade patterns are set. Macy's buyers know how to place orders in Ireland, and Irish mills know how to arrange shipments of sweaters to Macy's stores. The cost of continuing to do business with the same nations is low compared to the cost of making new arrangements in other nations, so reasonably stable international trade patterns have developed.

Problems of World Economics

A glance at any issue of the *Wall Street Journal, The Economist, Fortune, Business Week,* or other business-oriented periodicals will indicate that the world economy is not just an expansion of the national firm–household–government feedback system. It is, rather, a complicated system of interrelationships in which questions of prices and commodities are often made subservient to politics and people. Pride often supersedes rationality, and custom prevents beneficial choices from materializing. A number of very serious problems confront the world economic order. Some will be elaborated in later chapters; several are mentioned here.

The Expansion of World Trade

Individuals, families, communities, and nations improve their well-being by trading. In general, an increase in trade increases the satisfactions of those who engage in it. If Switzerland were restricted to eating only its own cheeses and wearing its own watches, the Swiss would be punctual and filled with protein. But time and protein alone do not make a happy, healthy life. If Iowa had to consume all its own corn, it would be a rather dull place, and Japan could not possibly improve its well-being by driving all its own Toyotas and Datsuns. The trades must take place so Iowans can have Datsuns and Swiss cheese, and the Japanese and Swiss can utilize Iowa corn and soybeans. Merchants and manufacturers in Iowa, Switzerland, and Japan, however, do not always know how to go about trading with other countries, and once they find out, they learn of many complicating rules and regulations. In spite of all the natural and man-made hindrances, international trade must continue to expand if the inequities caused by the uneven distribution of the earth's resources and its people are to be redressed.

Population

There are now slightly more than 4 billion people living on this planet. Some sets of projections suggest that by the year 2000 there will be 7 billion, and by 2050, 13 billion people on earth. While questions of population growth are not entirely economic, they certainly have economic consequences. Population growth is perverse. It seems to happen fastest in those areas least able to cope with it. The nations struggling to develop find their increases in output consumed immediately by additions to the population. The developed nations, while they have not yet reached the much talked-of Zero Population Growth, have generally experienced falling birth rates and a slowing in the rate of population growth.

Growing populations raise economic questions: Who will feed the new arrivals? Where will they live? How will health and sanitation facilities be provided? How many resources should go for heat and how many for transportation? These questions must be answered. In some nations, the answers come by dictum—a central agency decides. In others, voting schemes help make some choices. In a very few, the market is the primary arbitrator.

The increasing populations of developed nations lead to increased trade. With more people, Switzerland needs more of Iowa's corn and Iowa needs more of Switzerland's cheese. Canada needs more U.S. steel and the United States needs more of Canada's natural gas. The real pressure, though, is on the developing nations. They have only a limited number of things to sell, and they need to purchase many more things. Peru sells metals to other nations, but must import large quantities of food. Currently, the United States buys 30 percent of all Peru's exports and supplies 30 percent of that nation's imports. A major labor dispute in some metal-using U.S. industry could hinder Peru's ability to sell metals. If Peru cannot sell metals, it will not be able to earn the money needed to buy food—an especially difficult problem since Peru's population is growing at a rate of 3.1 percent per year.

Income Distribution

Population, "gross world product," and world trade have all grown very rapidly in the past two decades. Nonetheless, advanced nations seem to advance faster than underdeveloped nations and the gap between rich and poor seems to widen. Some of the differences could be removed by more sophisticated trading or more sophisticated production processes in the less developed countries. So far, however, the way to transfer information and methods from rich peoples to poor ones has remained a puzzle.

Technology does not transfer easily from the United States, to Mexico, then to Zaire, then to Bangladesh. Therefore the traditional means of production and exchange dominate and will probably continue to do so in the developing nations. At the other end of the spectrum, the technologically advanced nations seem willing to send advanced technical skills to developing nations, but to date they have been less willing to send products. The developing nations cannot adapt to one kind of aid, and the developed nations will not offer the other. This impasse has increased the severity of income differences and political tensions in the world economy.

Artificial Barriers to Trade

Nations, like individuals, have a good deal of pride. Spain's was irreparably damaged when the slapdash English navy destroyed the formidable Spanish Armada in 1588. The pride of the United States was severely injured when, in 1956, Russia thrust Sputnik, earth's first artificial satellite, into space. Although military and technological exploits provide dramatic examples of the importance of a nation's self-esteem, that esteem spills over into other critical parts of a nation's existence. Understandably, no nation wants to be dependent on others for all of its needs, or even for most. Nations want to be able to control their own economic destinies, and to do this they must become relatively self-sufficient.

Similarly, nations take great pride in the specialities they export. French champagne, Irish lace, Brazilian coffee, Australian wool, Scandi-

navian glass, and West German tractors all bring great satisfaction to their producers. To encourage self-sufficiency and keep other countries from encroaching on the markets for their special products, governments sometimes establish artificial barriers in international markets. They may impose taxes on imported goods that compete with home-produced goods, or subsidize domestic producers, or protect domestic industries by allowing only a certain volume of a good to be imported. Although these barriers are a hindrance to trade and violate the strict economic rules of allocation and efficiency, it is understandable that some nations—even the economically powerful ones—sometimes use trade barriers to protect their own industries.

Multiple Currencies

Trade among nations would be much simpler if they all decided to use one currency—the dollar or the bhat; the yen or the lira. Settling on one would be a formidable task. The Germans like their marks and the French like their francs. Sixty million West Germans would not like changing to another currency simply to accommodate world trade. Nor would 215 million U.S. citizens willingly accept some new currency especially when only 5 percent of their GNP is traded using money other than dollars. Why make such a large change for such a small part of all economic activity?

Multiple currencies developed for a number of reasons. The pound sterling used in England came from carefully weighed and measured amounts of metal. The U.S. dollar came from similarly measured substances in the Low Countries. All national currencies were designed to give nations their own monetary identity and their own monetary policy. Converting to an international currency would be advantageous when Peru tried to trade with Nepal, but it would make the management of domestic economies all the harder.

In sum, nations trade because resources are unevenly distributed among them. Some can grow wheat, some can make sweaters, and some can catch fish. Trading brings variety and increases the number and quality of things available to the traders. Trading requires elaborate relationships among economies. Arrangements have to be made to insure that factors and products move smoothly and that things are eventually paid for. This requires interconnections among a number of national circular flows. Trading is not new, so many international trade relationships are based upon habit, convenience, and tradition. Nonetheless, international trade causes resources to flow out of some lines of production and into others. However beneficial it may be, the trading among nations is hindered by political considerations and the problems associated with the very poor nations, population growth, and multiple kinds of currencies used by the trading nations.

Summary

1 The idea of a world economy sounds useful, but at present it lacks practical and analytical value. The "world economy" is actually a loose collection of many national economies.
2 National economies trade with one another. They sell goods that are plentiful to them and buy things that are scarce to them. This trade expands people's options, and opens opportunities to the citizens of the trading nations.
3 International trade sets up flows of goods, services, and payments that connect the circular flows of national economies.
4 International markets have been established for goods exchanged among nations. Like domestic markets, international markets provide signals that help buyers make choices and help sellers make decisions about how to use productive resources.
5 The United States began as a nation very dependent upon trade with other countries. At present, it is a nearly self-sufficient economy with only 5 percent of its GNP entering international trade.
6 International trade among all nations has grown rapidly since 1950.
7 International trade patterns tend to be quite stable from year to year.
8 Expanding world trade, population growth, the distribution of the world's income (product), artificial barriers to trade, and the world's many currencies have proven to be problems to trading nations.

Exercises

1 Explain these important terms and concepts:
   world economy   colony
   international trade   world exports = world imports
   tariff   closed economy
   reasons for trade   trade barriers
2 In October and November 1975, record-breaking cold spells ruined much of the Brazilian coffee crop. Although this caused a rapid upward spiral of retail coffee prices in the United States, it could also have reduced the number of goods and services available to Brazilian citizens. How could this occur? (Hint: Draw the circular flow of the U.S. and Brazilian economies and think through the linkages that connect them.)
3 The limitations on U.S. trade with Communist countries have gradually been removed since 1973. Although U.S. trade with, say, China and Cuba is not nearly so extensive as U.S. trade with Canada and Western Europe, it is beginning to grow. Who are the likely beneficiaries of opening trade with these nations?
4 How did the U.S. economy switch from a position of complete dependence (primarily on England) in 1700 to a position of dominance in world trade in 1977? Does this country provide a pattern for behavior for emerging nations today?
5 Does the economic logic of international trade differ from the economic logic of trade between two individuals, or between General Motors and Du Pont?

6 Is the process of exchange between nations different from the process of exchange between individuals? If so, in what ways and for what reasons is it different?

A Contemporary Problem
A "Trade Visit" from China

In the following extract, Louis Kraar, a reporter describes his own reactions to a group of 10 Chinese trade officials who were visiting U.S. manufacturers in the fall of 1975. The primary objective of the tour was to cultivate trade relationships between China and the United States.

Business dealings between Communists and capitalists . . . have brought forth a new form of commercial intercourse that might be called the red-carpet tour. By now just about every American chief executive worth his salt has been invited to trek through one or more Communist countries, or has played host here to a squad or two of senior Communist trade officials. The trips are arranged by commercial organizations, but governments hover in the background as matchmakers.

The theory of the grand tour is that if chief executives and comrades are thrown together in congenial surroundings, difficulties can be ironed out, bargains will be struck, and detente served.

But how well does this theory work out in practice? To find out, I jumped at a chance to tour America this fall with the first high-ranking trade group ever sent to this country by the People's Republic of China.

MONDAY: The Peking delegation and its U.S. hosts pay a courtesy call on President Ford. The President tells them he is looking forward to visiting China. His studied courtesy reinforces my impression that the relationship [between the U.S. and China] remains fragile and cautious, though both sides obviously want to give the appearance that it's progressing.

TUESDAY: At a Washington meeting, the group's leader, Li Chuan, who is vice chairman of the China Council for the Promotion of International Trade, assures his American business hosts that "trade relations are quite normal." Actually, the two-way volume is expected to dip from more than $900 million in 1974 to an estimated $450 million this year, largely because a bountiful harvest in China has curtailed purchases of U.S. grain. Li says that his country will continue buying wheat in the future but cautions, "Only if you buy more things from China will it be possible to buy more from you."

WEDNESDAY: Perhaps nothing is more alien to the revolutionaries in Mao jackets than their first impressions of New York. They stay at the unproletarian Plaza Hotel and are taken straight to the World Trade Center. Li says the twin towers, the city's highest buildings, "look like a pair of chopsticks."

He and his comrades find it even more difficult to relate to a zippy slide presentation by Young & Rubicam, "Ten Essentials to Achieve Marketing Success." Li, ignoring the thrust of the talk, pops questions about the profit margins of wholesalers and retailers, as well as the government's tax bite. Apparently, he is appalled at the U.S. markups on Chinese goods.

THURSDAY: Like millions of tourists before them, the visitors long to see the Empire State Building. Instead, they are hauled back to the World Trade Center and talked at all day by importers of Chinese goods. The dull briefings drone on about everything from U.S. customs procedures to food and drug regulations. The delegates often doze.

FRIDAY: A visit to J. C. Penney's headquarters begins with breakfast at the company cafeteria. Soon, the Chinese are marched off to a conference room to huddle with Penney executives, who plead for help in purchasing more goods from China. The department store chain has ordered several million dollars' worth of apparel and handicraft items, but deliveries have been slow and supplies uneven. Penney executives lead them into a men's clothing showroom and hand Li a sample cable-knit sweater just received from China. A long, loose thread is dangling from it. "We will fix that," says Li. Charles White, a merchandise manager, explains that the original pattern was sent to China two months ago, and will take another three months to get set up for production.

Holding up a second sweater, White adds: "In another country in your part of the world, we sent a buyer over and got samples within a week. It will be in our stores within just two months of that—in time for the fall season." The competing sweater is from Taiwan, though the Penney official avoids saying so. But the Peking traders get the message immediately, and one delegate declares: "Bring your samples, and we can make it anytime."

SATURDAY: At the Seventy-ninth Street Boat Basin, on the Hudson River, [the visitors] board the handsomely appointed yacht of a Coca-Cola executive for a trip around the tip of Manhattan and up the East River to La Guardia Airport. At the airport, a jet owned by Bandag Inc. awaits them. The company hopes to buy petrochemicals from Peking and sell its tire-retreading process to the Chinese.

Their visit to the agricultural heartland is choreographed with care and finesse.

SUNDAY: The day's highlight is a visit to the 1,000-acre corn and cattle farm of Orville Hein and his son, Darel, near Wallcott, Iowa. A Chinese-language folder, which Deere [Corporation] officials had prepared, tells how the farmers each work sixty to seventy hours a week, have only one full-time employee, but use farm equipment worth $200,000.

In the fields we watch a demonstration of the Heins' machinery. On this occasion, one of the few in their entire tour, the Chinese all take notes—on crop yields.

MONDAY: The Chinese visit plants of International Harvester and Deere, but ask few questions. An American attorney who has worked closely with Peking on trade deals confides to me that the Chinese sense of cultural and political superiority prompts them to act as if there's really not much to be learned from the West.

TUESDAY: While most of the group goes sightseeing in Chicago, several of the key Chinese trade officials fly to Dearborn on a Ford Motor Co. plane. Among them is Cheng Chi-hsien, fifty-six, deputy managing director of China National Machinery Import and Export Corporation. His company has purchased eight ammonia plants from M. W. Kellogg Co. and ten Boeing 707 passenger jets.

Cheng had expected to see Ford manufacturing facilities, but the company concentrates on a straight sales talk about its line of trucks and tractors. While a Ford executive flips through product-display charts, he asserts that the heavy-duty trucks have an "on-the-road life span" of seven years. Cheng frowns, confers with his technical aide, and finally asks, "After that, it cannot be used?" A Ford executive replies, "It is consumed, and in our economy is not considered useful after that." The frugal Chinese look incredulous.

[A Ford Motor Co. vice-president] confides to the visitors that Henry Ford has been invited to China. He presents the guests with chrome Cross pens, saying that they were "not for the purpose of signing a purchase order today, but for later." "We have pens, too, in Kwangchow," Tien replies. Kwangchow, known to Westerners as Canton, is the site of the biannual Chinese Trade Fair, and Tien is suggesting, not too subtly, that Ford buy from China as well as try to sell it trucks.

Later, at dinner with G. M. executives, the company's overseas manufacturing manager, Jack Trible, declares, "Maybe we'll do business with China one day on the basis of a joint venture or joint operations." The notion of foreign investment is so repugnant to Peking that his remark is not even fully translated.

WEDNESDAY: The Chinese receive a flamboyant Texas welcome to Houston. Anthony J. A. Bryan, president of Cameron Iron Works, Inc., greets the Chinese saying that the visit "is for your pleasure and knowledge of America. We are not attempting to make commercial presentations." Then an official of the *Oil & Gas Journal* gives them a long briefing which stresses that Houston has 869 oil-field supply and service companies.

Oil proves a sensitive subject to the Chinese, who are just beginning to tap potentially vast reserves and are even exporting some of it to Japan and Southeast Asian countries. Just prior to the trade delegation's visit, major U.S. newspapers had prominently reported on a study concluding that by 1988 China might approach Saudi Arabia's present petroleum production.

[The Chinese] go to Cameron Iron Works, which makes drilling and production equipment for the oil industry, and pointedly ask its president for a price list.

THURSDAY: Another helicopter ride takes the trade team to Brown & Root, Inc., which shows off the mammoth platforms it makes for offshore oil production, and hands out company brochures.

FRIDAY: They seem tired on arrival in San Francisco. After only a brief rest, the Chinese are taken to dinner with 180 people at the baroque Bohemian Club. A. W. Clausen, president of the Bank of America, gives an earnest speech proposing that U.S. companies finance some of Peking's industrial development and help prospect for its off-shore oil. The Chinese must be puzzled, if not astonished. They have made it amply clear they will accept no credits and do not want foreigners drilling for their oil.

SATURDAY: At the Greater San Francisco Chamber of Commerce, leaders of the National Council meet the Chinese for a final business session. The U.S. organization proposes several steps to facilitate trade. Specifically, the Americans want an exchange of industrial survey missions, annual meetings with their Chinese counterparts, trade exhibitions in both countries, and permanent offices in Peking and Washington. Politely, but firmly, Li declines to commit China to any of the moves. Basically, the Chinese want to preserve their freedom to deal with many different private organizations, such as local chambers of commerce and various industry and trade associations.

The Chinese, in other words, will insist on remaining free to tap all channels into the U.S. economy, where companies actively compete and commercial information is freely available. But American companies that deal with China will have only one route, through the state trading corporations—and then only on invitation.

TUESDAY: Then to Boeing, a company well known to the Chinese. It has trained about a hundred Chinese pilots and maintenance engineers in Seattle to handle the ten 707 aircraft it sold Peking. Boeing would like to sell China some 747 jumbos.

It is the last night of the Chinese visit, so they host a small dinner in the Olympic Hotel and offer toast after toast with Mau Tai. The Chinese seat me beside one of the most articulate, English-speaking members of their team. Our conversation is exceptionally candid, though he specifically asks not to be quoted by name. China, the official says, is unlikely to have very much oil to export within the next ten years.

What did the Chinese learn here? "We were most impressed with your farming, the high degree of mechanization and productivity."

I notice that he is drinking water, instead of the dizzying Chinese liquor. My impression is that he is a high-ranking party member who has been assigned to answer questions that his colleagues had earlier often ducked.

WEDNESDAY: The Chinese trade team departs for home. Assessing the visit, Christopher Phillips, a former deputy representative to the United Nations, says: "We have gone a long way toward creating an atmosphere of trust and understanding, which is a lot considering the twenty-five year gap in our relations."

But it is not entirely clear just what this tour contributed toward that laudable goal. During the visit, the Chinese did buy some aluminum ingots and began discussing the purchase of computers and oil-drilling equipment. But for the most part it seems that [on the tour] we have all been role playing in a piece put on by politicians—part of the drama of detente. Detente implies increased trade, and red-carpet tours are highly visible demonstrations of good commercial intentions, whether there is any follow-through or not. Future delegations from China will be friendly, cool, or hostile, as the political climate requires, and the Chinese will continue to be quite selective and very shrewd purchasers of U.S. goods. To think otherwise is to fail to understand the revolutionary principle of self-reliance in the People's Republic.[2]

[2]Excerpted from Louis Kraar, "A High-Level Sales Pitch for Shoppers from Peking," *Fortune*, November 1974, pp. 108–113, 187–190.

30 Why Nations Trade

The Creator surely had some grand design in mind when creating heaven and earth. All 4 billion of us in the world today might well wonder if the rewards will be apportioned as unequally in the Hereafter as they are in the here and now. An even distribution of goods, services, and wealth does not seem to be the pattern on which the world is based. Intelligence, skill, and strength are not distributed equally among people, fish are not distributed evenly in the oceans, and fertile soil is not distributed equally among the continents. Indeed, if there is a Grand Plan, it seems to be one of inequality and maldistribution.

This apparent inequity extends to the nations of the world. Much of the United States has fertile soil, a long growing season, and ample rainfall in the early weeks of summer. It is ideal for producing corn, soybeans, potatoes, and other crops. Egypt, Greece, and Israel have good climates but generally poor soils. Iran and Libya have poor soils and arid climates, but there is oil underground. Japan has a highly trained work force but few raw materials. Siberia has dense forests but no one to cut them. Bolivia has tin; Chile has copper; Wales has coal.

There is no reasonable way to rearrange the natural resources of the world so that people everywhere can enjoy relatively similar collections. Nor is there an easy way to rearrange the people so that everyone will have comparable access to wider ranges of goods and services. The population of Japan will have to get along without land, Iranians will have to get along without water, and people in the United States will have to get

"Who crossed our irrigation system with our oil pipeline?"

along with only skimpy deposits of nickel. But there is a way to redress the imbalance. Natural resources and raw materials can be converted into products, and these products can be traded among nations. Even if the forests cannot be moved, wooden furniture can.

The question is: What should be produced and what should be traded? Should the United States trade away all its corn? Should Iran trade away all its oil? Should Iceland trade away all its fish? These are ageless questions in the field of international trade. Fortunately, economics provides realistic and practical answers. This chapter is about production and exchange between nations. It introduces a model that has been used for 175 years to explain why nations should trade, then it moves into sections dealing with the gains from trade and the impact trade can have on the remainder of an economy.

The Law of Comparative Advantage

In 1776, Adam Smith wrote his treatise on the wealth of nations. An important part of that comprehensive volume was its treatment of specialization. Smith reasoned that some people should be lawyers, some should be craftsmen, some bankers, and some educators, according to their particular talents. The products of their skills should be exchanged to obtain those things best produced by others. Smith went to some lengths to show that the total output of an economic system will be larger if each worker specializes than if all must produce everything they need. That was sound advice.

About four decades later, David Ricardo, a British financier and economist, applied the same reasoning to nations. He concluded that the world's output could be increased if each nation specialized in what it could do best and traded with other nations to obtain other goods and services. Ricardo used rather homely examples to make his point. He wrote of Great Britain specializing in manufactured goods while another nation produced agricultural products. This was a reasonable argument in 1815—about the time Ricardo was writing. In the previous century Britain had become an industrial giant among nations. Machines were turning the once tranquil and productive English countryside into factories; the work force was leaving agriculture to be employed in the mills and shops. While the output of textiles and other manufactured goods soared, the nation's agricultural production fell. The volume of foodstuffs needed to feed the British people could be maintained only by trading with other nations. Ricardo's model showed the limits of such trade.

Like all great thinkers, Ricardo had the ability to reduce a problem to its barest essentials before attempting to solve it. (See Chapter 2.) In trying to answer questions about Britain's international trade problems, Ricardo first made a simplifying assumption about production in Great Britain and the other trading nations. He assumed that there were no economies of scale, so that all per-unit costs of production were constant. Under this assumption, if it costs one man-day of labor, one pound of raw cotton, and one spinning frame to make the first yard of cloth, it will also cost one man-day of labor, one pound of raw cotton, and one spinning frame to make the 10th, or the 100th, or the 1,000th yard of cloth. These assumptions violated the law of diminishing returns, but they allowed the case to be presented much more simply.

Here, the model representing trade between nations will include two nations, each of which can produce two products. The countries will be the United States and Great Britain; the products are textiles (a manufactured good) and wheat (an agricultural commodity). Each is assumed to be produced by a single factor, labor.

If one man-day of U.S. labor is available and used for growing wheat, it can produce 60 bushels of wheat per day. If the same man-day of U.S. labor is used for producing textiles, it can produce 20 yards. Thus, one yard of cloth exchanges for three bushels of wheat. Alternatively, one yard of cloth *can be transformed into* three bushels of wheat by shifting the laborer out of manufacturing and into agriculture. All possible combinations of wheat and textiles that can be produced using one man-day of labor make up the straight-line production-possibility curve shown in Figure 30-1.[1] If all labor is devoted to wheat, the total product is 60 bushels. If all labor is devoted to cloth, the yield is 20 yards. If the U.S. laborer's time is divided equally between wheat and cloth, he can produce 30 bushels of wheat *and* 10 yards of cloth—a combination shown by point M.

In Great Britain, conditions are somewhat different. Since the land is not well suited to wheat production, a full man-day of labor will yield only 20 bushels of wheat, and since textile production is carried out using primitive tools, a day's labor at the mills yields only 10 yards of cloth. In Great Britain, one yard of cloth exchanges for two bushels of wheat. Alternatively, in Great Britain one yard of cloth *can be transformed into* two bushels of wheat by shifting a laborer out of manufacturing and into agriculture. These productive capabilities, plus all other possible combinations of wheat and cloth that can be produced by a British laborer working a single day, are shown by the production-possibility curve in Figure 30-2. A full day in the fields yields 20 bushels; a full day in the mills produces 10 yards. If half a day is spent in each activity, a lone British worker can produce 10 bushels of wheat and 5 yards of cloth, as shown by point N. Other distributions of time would yield other combinations of the two products.

So far, the information from the two figures relates only to how many units of each commodity a laborer can produce. It takes on economic dimensions when the *tradeoffs* between wheat and cloth are considered.

[1] The assumption of constant costs forces the production-possibility curve to be a straight line. If diminishing returns were allowed, the curve would bow outward from the graph's origin.

**Figure 30-1
Production Possibilities
Open to One U.S. Laborer**

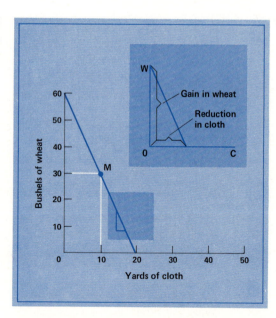

Opportunity Cost and Trade

When the United States or Britain moves up its production-possibility curve, it chooses to give up the opportunity to produce cloth and opens the opportunity to produce wheat. This is a restatement of the important notion of opportunity cost: When one thing is chosen, the other is lost forever. The concept is important in international affairs. In the late 1940s, West Germany decided to produce millions of VW "Beetles." This choice gave West Germany an exportable commodity, but forced it to give up the opportunity to produce many other kinds of goods. In the early 1970s, the United States chose to stop exporting military aid to Southeast Asia. In doing so, it gained the opportunity to produce more things at home.

"Our new model must be roomier, faster, and have an easier name for Americans to write on their order blanks."

A tradeoff is a result of choosing and is therefore the proper concern of economics. A tradeoff includes two acts, the act of selecting one thing and the act of rejecting a second. It is closely related to the notion of opportunity cost.

In the United States, a one-unit reduction in the output of cloth (a movement to the left on the horizontal axis of Figure 30-1), releases enough labor to produce three bushels of wheat (a rise along the vertical axis of Figure 30-1), so one yard of cloth exchanges (or trades) for three bushels of wheat in the domestic economy.

In Figure 30-2, the production-possibility curve has a different slope, so when one yard of cloth is sacrificed the labor that is released can be transformed into two bushels of wheat. One yard of cloth exchanges (or trades) for two bushels of wheat.

Great Britain and the United States can trade profitably with one another precisely because of their different abilities to turn labor into cloth or wheat. If Britain sends one yard of cloth to the United States, U.S. producers will be happy to return as much as three bushels of wheat—more than the British could produce at home with the labor released from producing one yard of cloth. If the United States sends two bushels of wheat to Great Britain, Great Britain will be happy to send back one yard of cloth because two bushels is as much as could be produced if Britain chose to give up a yard of cloth and use more of its own labor in wheat production.

If the United States has to give up *more* than three bushels of wheat to obtain a single yard of Great Britain's cloth, the transaction will not take place. The United States can make its own yard of cloth by giving up the production of three bushels and transferring the released labor to cloth production. Similarly, if Great Britain cannot obtain more than two bushels for each yard, no trade will be made. Instead, a domestic transfer of labor from cloth production to wheat production will take place.

The two technical ratios—1 yard : 3 bushels (United States) and 1 yard : 2 bushels (Great Britain)—define the technical or economic boundaries on exchanges between the two nations. At any exchange ratio between these boundaries, (say 1 : 2.5 or 1 : 2.9 or 1 : 2.1), profitable exchange can take place. But who will trade what for what?

In the example used here, Great Britain is a relatively poor producer of wheat. Poor soil, short growing seasons, and a lack of fertilizers keep wheat yields very low. Because of the relatively high labor cost of wheat, Great Britain will find it advantageous to trade cloth for wheat grown in the United States. Admittedly, the cloth can be produced elsewhere with the same amount of labor, but *comparatively speaking,* more can be saved by producing cloth and trading it for wheat. Britain has a *comparative advantage* in the production of cloth.

Comparative advantage is the term used to describe the relative efficiencies of two (or more) nations producing two (or more) products. In the example, Britain must give up two bushels of wheat to release enough labor to produce one yard of cloth. The United States must give up three bushels to attain the same objective. Thus, by having to give up only two bushels, Britain has a comparative advantage in cloth production.

Because of comparative advantages in the contemporary world, the United States buys coffee from Brazil, Libya buys lumber from the Scandinavian nations, and the Philippines buys diamonds from South Africa. Differential resource endowments give almost every nation a comparative advantage in some product, so almost every nation will find some trade to be advantageous.

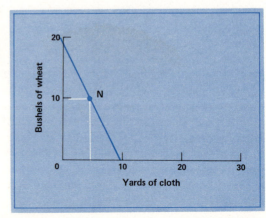

Figure 30–2
Production Possibilities Open to One British Laborer

A Domestic Example

The law of comparative advantage is most often presented in terms similar to those used in this chapter: One country produces wheat; another produces cloth.

The principle of comparative advantage can also be used to explain many of the specialized activities within a domestic economy. Some U.S. states are now easing the shortage of health-care personnel by allowing paraprofessionals to perform tasks formerly reserved for physicians. Paraprofessionals are trained to suture wounds, give inoculations, and diagnose common illnesses. In most instances, a paraprofessional is assigned to work with a physician and works under close supervision.

In theory, the physician—because of training and experience—should be able to perform all tasks better than the paraprofessional. In practice, the minor tasks should be turned over to the less-well-trained person, because that releases the physician's time for the more difficult tasks associated with the practice of medicine. Both paraprofessionals and physicians are thus allowed to pursue the activities in which they have a comparative advantage.

The Gains From Trade

Carried to its logical extreme, the law of comparative advantage says that at least some nations should do only those things that they do best. If the principle were strictly followed, all of Costa Rica's resources would be used to grow bananas, and all of Ceylon's would be used on tea plantations. If such complete specialization took place, the world's output could be maximized and the individual nations could derive the highest possible benefit from trading.

Figure 30-3 uses the exchange relationships considered earlier to show the maximum advantages that can possibly accrue to the United States and Great Britain if they produce and trade wheat and cloth. The left side of the figure represents United States; the right side, Great Britain. Notice that the scales along the axes are different in the two graphs. (If the scales were the same, the graph for Great Britain would be so tiny that no reasonable changes could be recognized and no explanations could be shown!) In the U.S. graph, a black production-possibility curve connects 60 bushels of wheat and 20 yards of cloth. This is the ratio at which U.S. wheat can be transformed in U.S. cloth. Since the comparative advantage of the United States lies in the production of wheat, it is reasonable to expect that all U.S. labor will be devoted to producing this product. At the outset, then, each laborer produces the 60 bushels of wheat designated by the intersection of the production-possibility curve and the vertical axis.

Now, however, the United States has two options. It can divert labor from wheat to the production of cloth, or it can trade with Great Britain for

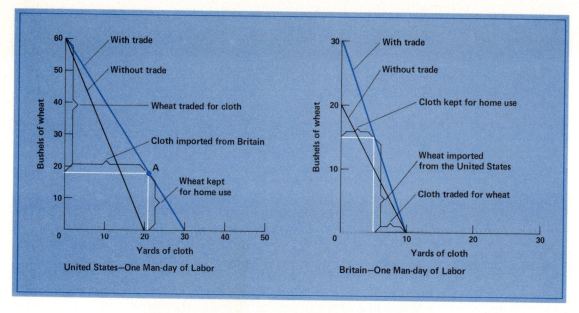

Figure 30-3 The Possible Gains from Trade

British-made cloth. If the former option is chosen, the original production-possibility curve will be followed. When three units of wheat are given up, one unit of cloth is gained. If, however, the trading option is chosen, a yard of cloth can be obtained by exporting two bushels of wheat to Great Britain. Under this option, if all U.S. wheat is sent to Great Britain, 30 yards of cloth will be obtained in exchange. If 30 bushels of wheat are sent, 15 yards of cloth will be obtained in exchange.

Trade offers a new production-possibility curve to the U.S. economy. The new curve is higher and farther to the right, so it represents larger collections of goods and services than are available in the absence of trade. Point A is representative of any point on the new curve. To reach point A, the United States uses all its labor to produce 60 bushels of wheat. It trades 42 bushels to Great Britain and keeps 18 bushels for home consumption. Great Britain sends 21 yards of cloth back to the United States, completing the transaction and leaving the United States with a combination of goods (21 yards of cloth and 18 bushels of wheat) that it could not have obtained by itself.

A similar line of reasoning applies to Great Britain. Since that country has the comparative advantage in cloth, all of its resources are assumed to be used for that purpose. It produces 10 yards of fabric. Great Britain now has the choice of following its internal production-possibility curve (the black line), gaining two bushels of wheat each time it gives up one yard of cloth. Or it can trade, and gain three bushels of wheat for each yard of cloth it exports to the United States. When the latter action is chosen, Great Britain follows the blue production-possibility curve and reaches combinations of cloth and wheat that could not have been enjoyed without trade.

So Ricardo reasoned in 1815, and so it is today. The United States trades *X* tons of steel for *Y* tons of Brazilian coffee, because producing coffee domestically would require many more resources than producing the steel that is traded. Brazil is happy with the arrangement because by trading coffee beans it avoids huge investments in steel mills. Sweden exports lumber and imports oil. All of these exchanges arise because of comparative advantage—the result of uneven distributions of resources.

The Rate of Trade

In the left side of Figure 30-3, the United States is assumed to trade wheat to Great Britain at a rate of two bushels per yard of cloth. On the right-hand side, Great Britain receives *three* bushels of wheat for one yard of cloth. In a world market, only one price (rate of trade) exists at any moment in time.[2] Which is it? In our examples, it is known that the price of a bushel of wheat will be somewhere between two and three yards of cloth if trade between Great Britain and the United States is to occur. The exact rate at which the two commodities will trade cannot be specified because it is determined by the combination of supply and demand in the world markets. If wheat is plentiful and cloth is scarce, Britain will benefit because of its comparative advantage in cloth. The world price will rise toward the extreme—one yard of cloth trading for three bushels of wheat. If wheat is scarce and cloth is plentiful, the United States will benefit as the price of cloth drops toward its lower limit—one yard trading for two bushels of wheat. As the actual rate of trade between the two commodities changes, the production-possibility curve (with trading) will move closer to or farther from the production-possibility curve without trade. The blue production-possibility curves in Figure 30-3 represent the *best possible* rates of trade for each of the two nations. In reality, the gains from trade will be somewhat more modest and will change as relative prices change.

Do Nations Specialize?

Even though the rules of the game seem to say that nations should specialize in those things that they do best, nations in fact never specialize completely. Even though the Philippines does best at producing rice and pineapples, it still produces some steel and other manufactured goods.

---

[2]The term "rate of trade" is used to emphasize that the discussion is still being conducted in physical terms. When money enters the discussion, the term "rate of trade" will be replaced by the more specific "rate of exchange." This is a topic in the following chapter.

Even Equador, a very poor nation with very few natural endowments, has a pharmaceutical industry. Why?

Several answers are possible. One continues from Chapter 29 and centers on national pride. No nation ever wants to be limited by dependency on another. Until very recently, nearly one third of all U.S. imports came from Canada, and approximately 30 percent of all U.S. exports were shipped to that nation. Canadians were understandably alarmed, because this high rate of economic integration gave Canada colony-like status with respect to the United States. This status was objectionable to many Canadian citizens.

A second reason is the sheer need to survive. If Ghana is completely dependent upon France for medicines and the ship bringing the pills sinks just as an epidemic hits, Ghana is thrown into a very precarious situation. Even though Ghana cannot produce *all* of its own medicines (and would not want to), it does want some emergency capacity in case of contingencies.

Artificial Barriers to Trade

Nations are sometimes quite fearful of being limited by or dependent upon other countries. To prevent this from happening, they ignore the law of comparative advantage and establish artificial barriers around their own economies. The most common barrier is the protective *tariff*.

A tariff is a tax on an import. It may be levied with respect to the value of the imported item (an ad valorem tariff), or it may be a flat charge on each unit of the product brought into the country. Tariffs are often referred to as "duties" or "import duties."

Tariffs are justified (or rationalized) by using a number of arguments related to infant industries, diversified economies, and the protection of domestic labor forces. While each argument has a germ of truth, each can be carried to ridiculous extremes.

Infant Industries

The infant-industry argument is used by developing nations to justify tariff protection for domestic industries that are just beginning to emerge. If India suddenly aspired to enter the very competitive business of manufacturing automobiles, those given the task of establishing the new factories would correctly reason that India simply could not compete with the experience and capital facilities of the United States, Germany, Japan, and Italy. They might ask for tariff protection to make imported Chevrolets, VWs, Toyotas, and Fiats *artificially* expensive relative to the newly produced India autos.

Protecting new industries through the use of tariffs does sound like a good idea. Its weakness lies in the fact that industries that are protected in this fashion often come to depend on the tariff, and lose the incentive to grow into efficient domestic concerns capable of competing with similar imported products. The continued existence of a protected industry yields only higher prices for consumers.

Diversified Economies

Even though the law of comparative advantage suggests that Honduras should specialize in producing bananas, Honduras would like to have an economy that is not totally dependent upon one fruit. A one-crop or one-industry economy is extremely vulnerable to the vicissitudes of weather, the possibility of disease, and the outside chance that people will suddenly stop buying that crop. Honduras may then want to develop some light manufacturing, some mining, a handicraft industry, and a tourist trade. To do this, Honduras simply places high tariffs on imported items. The high tariffs bring in revenue, but they also raise domestic prices. Entrepreneurs noticing the high prices will begin to devote resources to products other than bananas, and a diversified economy will emerge.

There are two fundamental objections to using tariffs to force diversification. First, the tariff, like any tax, raises the prices that must be paid by the ultimate consumers of the product. Second, diversification may be very expensive, since it may push the diversifying nation into many activities for which it is not well suited. It is hard to imagine, for example, that Honduras would ever produce large volumes of consumer durables like refrigerators, stoves, and kitchen mixers, yet these are the kinds of products that are easily singled out for tariff "protection."

Protecting the Labor Force

In the years immediately following World War II, and to some extent even today, tariffs were recommended as a means of protecting the United States from "cheap foreign labor." How can U.S. manufacturers who must pay minimum wages of $2.50 per hour compete with imports made by Hong Kong laborers who are paid 50 cents a day? This argument sounds plausible but breaks down under close scrutiny. Production of any item uses combinations of resources. Capital, land, and entrepreneurial talent *as well as labor* must be used to produce all items. If labor is the only factor used, certainly Hong Kong's 50-cent-a-day workers can produce an inexpensive product. However, if the job can be done using some

"This is, without a doubt, the earliest piece of pottery found on the North American continent which was used for ornamental purposes and was made in Hong Kong."

combination of people and machines, the superior efficiency of the U.S. machines will offset the inexpensive Hong Kong labor and a competitive product can be made in the United States. Imposing a tariff does little more than raise product prices and encourage inefficiency in domestic production.

In sum, tariffs can be and are used to protect domestic economies or to protect special segments of economies. There is little reason to believe that many nations will forgo the use of tariffs and immediately go to a "free-trading status." If tariffs are considered desirable, it is best to think of them as short-term measures used during periods of adjustment. If they are extended over long periods of time, they have a tendency to become firmly entrenched in the fibers holding economic society together, encouraging inefficiency and increasing the prices consumers must pay for some products.

Comparative Advantage and Diminishing Returns

Early parts of this chapter presented the law of comparative advantage under very special circumstances—constant costs of production. This assumption overlooks an important fact related to production. The production-possibility curve faced by a nation (or a region or firm within a nation) is arched outward from the graph's origin in a manner similar to the curve shown in Figure 30–4. When most resources are committed to wheat production, as at point A on the curve (55 bushels of wheat, 18 yards of cloth), the curve is relatively flat, showing that the costs of wheat production have increased so much that, to obtain even a small increase in wheat production, many resources must be diverted from cloth production. As point B (40 bushels of wheat, 35 yards of cloth) is approached, the costs of wheat production are not quite so high. Transferring resources from cloth to wheat production yields a significant gain in the output of wheat. Moving on to point C (10 bushels of wheat, 48 yards of cloth) changes cost relationships still more. At C, very little wheat is produced, so transferring even a few resources from cloth to wheat has a noticeable impact on the total output of wheat. A small reduction in cloth output is accompanied by a large increase in wheat output.

The arched production-possibility curve is more realistic. It also shows why nations do not specialize completely. Put very simply, complete specialization becomes too expensive. Transferring those last few resources to wheat production (at the top of the curve) does not increase wheat output enough to make the transfer worthwhile. Similarly, investing the last few resources in cloth production (at the bottom of the curve) is not practical because the resources are not very efficient. It takes too many of them to produce a yard of cloth. Thus, even if it seemed perfectly wise to allow Japan to produce the whole world's TV sets, the technical conditions of production dictate that no nation should specialize completely in any one thing.

A degree of specialization combined with trade allows all people to have more things. If each nation does what it does best and trades with other nations, the total number of goods and services available to all peoples will increase. Rather than carry the arguments for specializing to extremes, however, most nations choose to produce some mix of commodities.

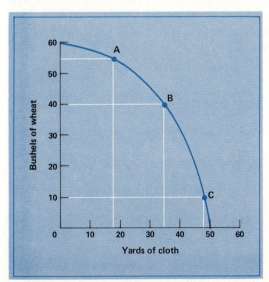

Figure 30–4
The Production-Possibility Curve Reflecting Diminishing Returns

Summary

1. The resources and population of the world are arranged in a very unequal way. This unequal distribution encourages nations to specialize in the things they do best.
2. By specializing and trading, the total product of the world can be increased.
3. The law of comparative advantage is a guide to how each nation should specialize, but by itself it cannot tell exactly how the output will or should be shared.
4. Nations most often choose not to specialize completely because they do not want to become dependent on other parts of the world for important goods and services.
5. Nations use tariffs to protect infant industries, to encourage their domestic economies to diversify, and to protect their own labor forces. The tariffs also prevent total specialization in the domestic economy.
6. Tariffs often have advantageous effects in the short run, but in the long run they yield higher prices for consumers and misallocation of resources. Tariffs are very hard to remove, once they have become established.
7. In the absence of tariffs, the law of diminishing returns will prevent an economy from specializing completely in the production of any one product.

Exercises

1. Explain these important terms and concepts:
   - specialization
   - constant costs
   - comparative advantage
   - gains from trade
   - rate of trade
   - tariff
   - infant industry
   - diminishing returns
2. New Mexico and Connecticut trade beef and insurance policies, respectively. Spain trades almonds and filberts to Germany for machines and automobiles. Trade between New Mexico and Connecticut is very easy. Trade between the two nations is not. Why?
3. Is there a rule of comparative advantage among individuals? If so, is it different from the rule among nations?
4. Assume that Iceland and Newfoundland each use only labor to produce fish or handknit sweaters. The production-possibility curve for each can be derived from the following information:

	One unit of labor yields	
	Iceland	Newfoundland
Fish	20	40
Sweaters	10	30

Which area should specialize in which product? Why?

5 What good reason can be advanced for having tariffs? Are tariffs likely to go up or down during a period of domestic unemployment?
6 How do tariffs affect product prices? Resource allocation? If tariffs on imported automobiles were to increase to extremely high levels, who would be helped and who would be hurt?
7 Even though the United States is very efficient in steel production, it still imports about 15 million tons of the metal annually. Why? How does this fit with the law of comparative advantage?

A Contemporary Problem
Multinational Corporations and Diversification

The *multinational corporation* (see Chapter 32) has grown in prominence in the past quarter century. Tax laws, local zoning problems, sources of raw materials, and labor supplies have enticed profit-minded corporate executives to locate plants in other countries. This is nothing more than moving resources around to compensate for nature's inhospitality.

At first blush, the multinationals seem to bring diversification to a local economy. When General Motors establishes a plant in Spain, Spain automatically becomes more industrialized. The low wages in Hong Kong, Taiwan, Haiti, Mexico, and Venezuela are inviting industries to those areas, creating jobs for local peoples and goods for the nations to export. By most definitions, this is progress. The multinationals are helping these areas realize their comparative advantages.

For some areas, the multinationals are, however, mixed blessings. Being motivated by profits, they have little concern for their lasting impact on countries where their plants are located, and most often only a few of the laborers in these countries receive benefits from the corporation. Multinationals have brought a dramatic increase in manufacturing in Latin America, yet manufacturing employs a smaller percentage of the work force now than it did a half century ago. Diversifying the economies through multinational activity does not seem to give more people more things, or more things to do.

The tie-ins between multinational activity and domestic (U.S.) economic problems are interesting too. The large international firms seek to increase their profits by abandoning high-cost domestic facilities and re-establishing new plants in low-wage areas. While Detroit was suffering its worst recession and unemployment ever in the fall of 1974, Ford and General Motors were increasing their investments abroad. Ford plans to produce thousands of compact cars in its new plant in Valencia, Spain for export to the United States!

Perhaps the most ironic twist in the law of comparative advantage goes back to the kind of example Ricardo used. An increasing number of U.S., Japanese, and Middle Eastern concerns are "going international" in the field of agriculture. The world food supply is short and food production is profitable. Huge firms are buying or renting more and more land, and deciding in thickly carpeted corporate board rooms, with the company's balance sheet in mind, what to produce and where to sell it. Because of comparative advantage, it has become profitable to use a poor nation's good soil to produce luxury export crops while the local population starves. In Columbia—scarcely an affluent nation—a hectare of land needed to produce food for local people can produce wheat valued at 12,500 pesos. When the same land is used to produce exportable carnations, the return is 1 million pesos. Surely the multinational corporations per se should not be blamed for the switch from wheat to carnations, but their sheer size and power does seem to exert an inordinate pressure on production activities within nations and on trade relationships among nations.

Analysis. The multinational corporation is apparently a permanent fixture in economic affairs. The corporations should not be faulted for trying to find profitable ways of producing goods and services. It does seem reasonable to ask if the multinationals have any "social responsibility" to the various nations in which they operate. Does the Ford Motor Company owe something to Detroit or to Valencia? Do the Colombian carnation growers owe something more than wages to the citizens of Columbia? These are difficult questions but ones which economists will be asked to help answer.

31

Money and International Trade

Chapter 30 showed that profitable trade can develop between nations that have different factor endowments. While trade can be conducted in yards and bushels, such arrangements are terribly inconvenient. The nations of the world have all removed this inconvenience from their domestic economies by choosing mediums of exchange to use within their own boundaries. The United States uses dollars, Great Britain uses pounds sterling (designated by the symbol £) and Chile uses escudos (E^0) to consummate domestic transactions.[1] These different currencies make domestic trade very easy, but they cause serious problems when nations engage in international trade. This chapter is about those problems. It introduces money into the international economy. Since money is virtually universal, the discussion centers on the toilsome process of exchanging one kind of money for another. The chapter opens with a brief example of uncomplicated trading between two firms in dif-

---

[1] Most monies or monetary standards can be traced to some specific amount of precious metal. The British "pound sterling," for example, comes from the 8th-century practice of dividing a pound of sterling silver into 240 pieces. In large transactions, the small pieces were not even counted; the metal was weighed out in pounds. Hence, "pounds of sterling" or "pounds sterling." The U.S. dollar is less unique. The word comes from the German word "thaler" and is a shortened form of "Joachim's thaler"—a 16th-century coin bearing the image of St. Joachim. "Thaler" took many variations (daler, daalder, tallero, etc.) and has been used as a general term for a unit of money.

ferent nations, then gradually adds complications to describe unbalanced trade, money markets, and exchange rates. It closes with a discussion of some attempts to make trading easier and to allow each nation to profit from its comparative advantages.

British Automobiles and U.S. Machinery

The British have a long history of fine craftsmanship in automobiles—especially sports and luxury cars. For years, U.S. buyers have purchased large numbers of these cars, partly because there are no U.S. cars of comparable quality and partly for the "snob appeal" of these beautifully crafted British autos. The United States has, meanwhile, developed the capacity to produce well built, heavy-duty machinery that is very serviceable and inexpensive compared to similar machinery built in other parts of the world.[2] British manufacturers have become accustomed to buying this U.S.-produced machinery for their plants. The stage is set for trade between the United States and Great Britain.

The trading could go something like this: An automobile importer in New York City gathers estimates and predictions about the coming months and, using the best information available, guesses that he can sell 100 British sports cars. He places the order, and some weeks later the 100 cars arrive. At their time of arrival, each of the cars is valued at $3,000. To pay for them, the dealer goes to his New York bank and purchases British money—pounds sterling. If the *rate of exchange* between pounds and dollars is £1 = $2.50 then £1,200 = $3,000.) The dealer pays the bank $300,000 and receives a *bank draft* for £120,000. He sends the bank draft to the British automobile manufacturer, who deposits it in his own (British) bank account. The manufacturer can then use the pounds sterling to pay for the British labor and materials used in the production process.

The rate of exchange is the domestic price of a foreign currency. In this example, a single pound sterling costs a U.S. citizen $2.50. Therefore the rate of exchange is £1 = $2.50. In Britain, the rate would be £0.4 = $1. Four-tenths of a pound would be required to purchase one U.S. dollar.

A bank draft is a special kind of check often used in international transactions. It is much like a personal check, except that payment is guaranteed in whatever currency is specified by the sender of the draft.

---

[2]"Machinery" is a very broad category of exports. It includes all kinds of tools and assemblies that might be used by other manufacturers or producers. The machinery going to Great Britain includes drill presses, air hammers, computers, lathes, stamping machines, commercial duty sewing machines, and thousands of other items. In 1974, the Western European nations (including Great Britain) imported U.S.-made machines valued at $5.5 billion.

This transaction has reduced the amount of pounds sterling held on deposit by the U.S. bank and increased the amount in the British bank. But where did the U.S. bank obtain its supply of pounds sterling? The machinery trade provides the answer.

At the same time the automobile purchase is being negotiated, a British importer surveys his marketing opportunities and decides that selling U.S.-made sewing machines to British clothing manufacturers would be a profitable enterprise. He orders 100 commercial-duty machines that have an aggregate value of £120,000. (If the exchange rate remains at £1 = $2.50, the sewing machines would be valued at £1,200 or $3,000 each). To pay for the sewing machines, the British merchant sends a bank draft for £120,000 to the U.S. manufacturer. The U.S. manufacturer cannot use pounds sterling to pay workers or buy supplies, so he sells the draft to a U.S. bank for $300,000. The British bank has lost £120,000 but the U.S. bank has gained them. The U.S. bank calls this deposit of pounds sterling *foreign exchange.*

Foreign exchange is currency (or other financial instruments) that can be used to pay international debts. Thus, in the United States, pounds sterling are foreign exchange because they can be used to pay debts in Great Britain. In Great Britain, dollars are foreign exchange. In Paris, both dollars and pounds sterling are foreign exchange.

The automobile and sewing machine transactions are diagramed in Figure 31–1. The line across the top of the figure shows 100 U.S.-made

Figure 31–1 Trade Between the United States and Britain (£1 = $2.50)

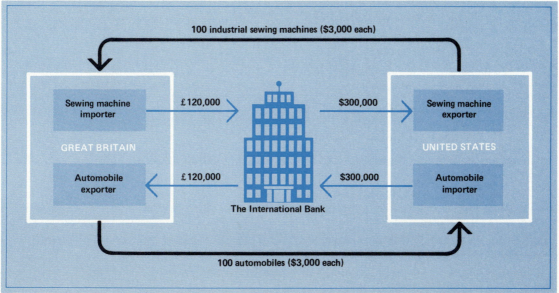

industrial sewing machines moving from the United States to Great Britain. Across the bottom, 100 British-made cars are shown moving from Great Britain to U.S. markets. This figure is like any other circular flow, except that payments are not made until dollars are exchanged for pounds and pounds are exchanged for dollars. The changing of one money into another is done by a large commercial bank—one large enough to do business in several nations. The bank in the center of the figure could be in New York City (where most U.S. international financial dealings are consummated), or it could be in London (which plays a similar role for Britain). Such banks buy and sell currency. A buyer wanting pounds can present dollars and get pounds; a buyer wanting to change pounds to dollars can do so, too.

The important point is that in order to import anything at all, U.S. buyers must be able to obtain foreign currencies. The only way to acquire these currencies is by selling things abroad. In order to buy British sports cars, U.S. citizens must have access to pounds sterling; to get these pounds, something, like sewing machines, must be sold abroad.

In the foregoing example, U.S.-made industrial sewing machines valued at $300,000 (£120,000) were exchanged for British-made sports cars valued at $300,000 (£120,000). International transactions were in equilibrium. Of course, actual international exchanges will not be this tidy. In a given year, U.S. buyers may wish to purchase British sports cars valued at £500,000, while British importers want to buy sewing machines valued at only £100,000. The large difference will place a strain on the bank that buys and sells foreign exchange. U.S. importers will come to the bank insisting that their dollars be converted to pounds sterling that can then be used to purchase British automobiles. But since no one in Great Britain wants dollars, Britishers will not supply their pounds sterling to be used as foreign exchange. U.S. importers will not be able to obtain the pounds sterling needed to make their purchases.

Always Pounds for Dollars?

It is easy to understand that in order to buy, one must first sell. However, if the United States wants to purchase British automobiles, is it necessary that U.S. exports go to England? The answer is No. Exports can go to Japan, Australia, Mexico, or anywhere. In each case, the United States is acquiring foreign exchange. If it needs pounds, the foreign exchange from Japan, Australia, or Mexico can be used to purchase pounds. Many cities in the world have large banks that specialize in converting the currency of one country into that of another, enabling the United States to buy from a country even though it does not sell directly to that country.

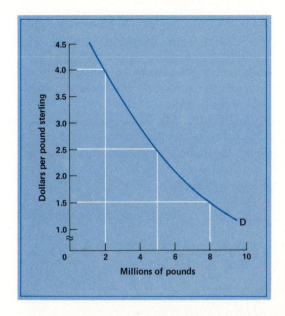

Figure 31-2
Demand for Foreign Exchange

If the problem is temporary, no real harm is done. The British car manufacturer simply lends money (British pounds sterling) to his U.S. customers in the same way that Sears extends credit to the millions of customers who hold a Sears charge card. Settlement will come next year when more British manufacturers buy U.S.-made machines and demand dollars to pay for them. If the problem persists, the rate of exchange will be affected and serious economic consequences are likely to follow. The problem becomes related to the demand, supply, and price of foreign exchange.

The Demand for Foreign Exchange

Foreign exchange is demanded by people, firms, and governments wishing to purchase things produced abroad. In the United States, yen are demanded to buy Toyotas, pounds sterling are demanded to pay for insurance purchased from Lloyds of London, and German marks are demanded to pay for Volkswagens.

A demand curve for a foreign currency slopes downward and to the right just like the demand curve for carrots or bow ties. Such a curve is shown in Figure 31-2. The price of the foreign exchange is generally reckoned in terms of the domestic currency. Thus, the vertical axis shows the number of dollars that must be paid to obtain a single pound sterling. If the price of pounds is very high ($4 per £), U.S. buyers wanting to purchase British goods must pay very dearly for the needed foreign exchange. With the price of pounds at this high level, goods imported from

Great Britain are very expensive, so that only a few are demanded. Hence, only a small volume of foreign exchange is purchased.

In Figure 31-2, when the price of a pound is $4, £2 million will be purchased. Put another way, at the high exchange rate of £1 = $4, imported goods are very expensive and U.S. importers purchase goods and services valued at only £2 million.

As the price falls to $2.50 per pound, each U.S. dollar purchases more pounds and, hence, more British goods. As British goods become less expensive their desirability goes up, so the quantity of pounds demanded goes up too. When the exchange rate is £1 = $2.50, 5 million are demanded, and as the price of the pounds falls to £1 = $1.50, £8 million are demanded. The demand for foreign currency, like the demand for any other commodity, rises as the price falls.

The Supply of Foreign Exchange

There is also a supply curve for foreign exchange. The supply of foreign exchange in the United States comes from foreigners who have purchased U.S.-made goods or services. The supply of each foreign currency is related to its price in terms of dollars.

The supply curve shown in Figure 31-3 is drawn within axes similar to those used to show the demand for foreign exchange. Like demand, the supply of foreign exchange behaves in the usual way: At low prices little is supplied, but as price rises more is placed on the market. At low prices, each pound yields only a small amount in dollars. When one pound ster-

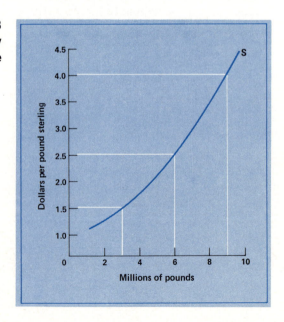

**Figure 31-3
The Supply
of Foreign Exchange**

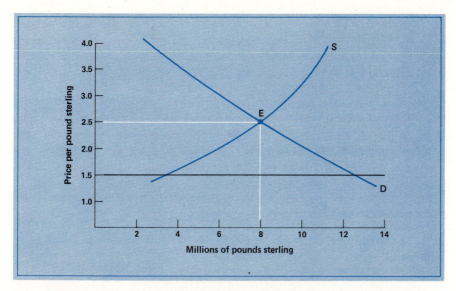

Figure 31-4 The Exchange Rate Determined by a Market for Foreign Exchange

ling can be sold for only $1.50, it does not have much purchasing power in U.S. markets, and Britishers will not be eager to make the exchange. At $1.50 very few pounds, perhaps only 2.5 million, will be made available. (See Figure 31-3.)

As the price of pounds rises, each pound sterling exchanges for more dollars and has more purchasing power in the United States. If more purchasing power can be had for each pound traded, holders of pounds are more likely to exchange their pounds for U.S. goods, thus making more pounds available as foreign exchange in the United States. Given the supply curve of Figure 31-3, when £1 = $2.50, £6 million will be supplied and when £1 = $4.00, approximately £9 million will be supplied.

The Equilibrium Price of Foreign Exchange

The supply and demand curves for foreign exchange intersect in Figure 31-4 to show the equilibrium dollar price for pounds sterling to be $2.50 = £1. At this price, both demanders and suppliers are satisifed. (Note: The average exchange rate between dollars and pounds sterling from 1968 to 1974 was £1 = $2.42. In March 1976, the exchange rate fell for the first time below £1 = $2.00. In November 1976, the exchange rate reached a record low of £1 = $1.68.)

Early in this section, it was assumed that sometimes the market for foreign exchange would not be in equilibrium—that U.S. importers would not be able to obtain enough pounds to make payments to British exporters. This circumstance is represented by the black line across the lower portion of Figure 31–4. Demanders want many more pounds at this price than suppliers are willing to supply.

If the market mechanism is working correctly, $1.50 = £1 is not an equilibrium price and market forces will begin to drive the price toward equilibrium (*E*). When the dollar price of pounds increases, Britishers find U.S. goods more attractive because each pound yields more U.S. purchasing power. At the same time, U.S. importers find British goods less attractive because more dollars have to be given up to obtain a British pound sterling. As the exchange rate comes into equilibrium, relative prices between the two nations change, and so do the quantities of goods and services traded.

As the dollar price of pounds sterling rises toward equilibrium, the dollar loses some of its purchasing power so it is described as *depreciating*. At the same time, the purchasing power of the pound sterling increases, so it is said to be *appreciating*. Between 1971 and 1972, the exchange rate between dollars and pounds changed from $2.45 = £1 to $2.50 = £1. In this period, the dollar was depreciating—it took more dollars to buy the same number of pounds. In the following year, the rate dropped back to $2.45 = £1. When this occurred, the dollar appreciated—fewer dollars were required to purchase a given volume of British goods.

Many economists and international trade experts feel that the market for foreign exchange should be free to move to any equilibrium price level. The market is automatic and it does correct its own errors, yielding higher prices during periods of shortage and lower prices during periods of surplus. There are, however, some serious disadvantages to a freely operating market for foreign currencies. Money is an important attribute of any modern economic society, and all modern nations must be concerned with how their currencies are being priced in foreign exchange markets. If the price is too high, exports will dwindle because no one will be able to afford the expensive money. Overpricing the Peruvian sol will make Peruvian sugar, cotton, and copper too expensive for other nations to purchase. Reducing exports from that poor nation will have serious effects on the incomes of the 60 percent of the population engaged in agriculture and mining. Underpricing the sol will have the opposite effect. It will make Peruvian exports very inexpensive in other nations and they will use imports from Peru rather than developing their own sugar- and cotton- and copper-producing facilities. Moreover, if Peruvian exports expand as a result of an underpriced currency, Peruvian investors may commit many of the nation's limited investment funds to farming and mining while highways, education, and health go wanting.

The biggest problem associated with freely fluctuating (market-determined) exchange rates is the great uncertainty they bring. An importer who purchases pounds sterling at $2.50 = £1 in a freely fluctuating market has no assurance that they will have the same value in a week or a month or a year. Most economists are therefore reluctant to recommend freely fluctuating rates. Instead, they generally favor some variety of fixed rates.

Fixed Exchange Rates

When economic societies want to avoid the problems imposed by a fluctuating exchange rate, they often fix exchange rates at a given level. This is done by an act of law or through a government policy stating that, beginning on a particular date, the "official" rate of exchange will be $X = £Y$ and will not change until trade officials pass new regulations. Although this interferes with the automatic action of the market, it does help avoid many of the problems that come with overpriced and underpriced currencies. Most Western countries have used fixed or official rates of exchange for the past 30 years.

The main problem in fixing an exchange rate is deciding which rate should be used. In 1975, these official rates of exchange existed between U.S. dollars and other currencies:

$1.31 U.S. = one Australian dollar
$0.17 U.S. = one Danish krone
$0.23 U.S. = one French franc
$0.12 U.S. = one Indian rupee
$0.0034 U.S. = one Japanese yen
$0.017 U.S. = one Spanish peseta

Even under fixed rates, the actual rate is generally allowed to fluctuate modestly, but the government is very sensitive to large changes in the rate of exchange.

Some of the problems that come with fixed exchange rates are shown in Figure 31–5. When the fixed rate passes through the intersection of the demand curve (D) and the supply curve (S), there are no problems. In this circumstance the fixed rate is the same as the market exchange rate would be. However, if a new demand curve (D_1) for foreign exchange should occur, disequilibrium results. If the demand curve is higher and to the right of the original demand curve (as in Figure 31–5), the fixed rate will cause a shortage of foreign exchange. Increased demands for imported goods expand demand for foreign exchange to nearly 5 million units, but at the fixed rate only the original 3 million units will be supplied. With the new demand curve, equilibrium should appear at a price slightly above $3 per unit of foreign exchange, but the price is fixed at $2.50. The market is fixed in disequilibrium.

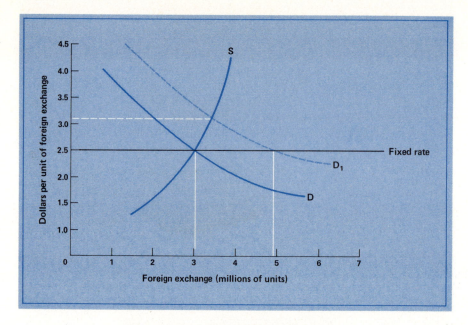

Figure 31-5 Fixed Exchange Rates

Exchange quotas. If the discrepancy is viewed as temporary, the government may choose to ignore it, thus causing hardship for a few importers and exporters but maintaining a policy that is thought to be best for the whole society. If the discrepancy is expected to last several months or even years, the government may wish to control access to foreign exchange. This can be done in a number of ways. One is through a system of quotas that makes the government the foreign-exchange broker for the nation. The government knows that 3 million units of foreign exchange will be supplied from foreign purchases of domestically produced goods and services. It also knows that domestic importers will demand nearly 5 million units of foreign exchange, so it establishes a set of rules to determine who gets the foreign money. The rules include quotas restricting the amount of foreign exchange that can be used to purchase any particular import. The quotas are used to ration or allocate foreign exchange among possible users.

Changes in the rate of exchange. When no amount of control or regulation can maintain a reasonable balance between the supply of and demand for foreign exchange, the government must consider changing the rate of exchange. This is a drastic move, since it disrupts existing trade relationships and causes the value of currencies held by individuals to change—it changes the wealth position of many people. But it must sometimes be done. If the fixed rate is too low and a government decides to raise the price of foreign exchange (say from $2 = £1 to $3 = £1) it is lowering the value of its own currency. It is *devaluing* its currency. If the fixed price is lowered to bring the supply and demand for foreign exchange into balance, the nation has *revalued* its currency.

Revaluation is a change in a fixed rate of exchange that makes the domestic currency more valuable relative to a foreign currency. Devaluation is the opposite. It makes the domestic currency less valuable.

Although all major trading nations today adhere to fixed-exchange-rate policies, there have been some significant changes in the fixed rates used by several nations. In 1949, the value of the pound sterling was changed from $4 = £1 to $2.80 = £1. The pound was thus devalued and, simultaneously, the dollar was revalued. In October 1967, the Finnish mark was devalued by 23.8 percent. In December 1971 and again in February 1973, the U.S. dollar was devalued with respect to many Western currencies. Each of these moves was an attempt to bring order to international markets which, under existing fixed rates, were badly out of equilibrium.

In sum, the problem of international trade is complicated by the existence of separate national currencies rather than an international monetary scheme. Vermont is as different from Arizona as Denmark is from Tanzania, but trade between Vermont and Arizona is very easy, while trade between Denmark and Tanzania can become very difficult. The two states use the same currency; the two nations do not. Nations have therefore had to find ways of exchanging one kind of money for another in order to engage in the exchange of goods and services. Most often, large

"I don't care if a Canadian dollar is worth more than ours. I don't take any money that's printed in fancy colors."

commercial banks do the actual exchanging of currencies but the banks follow systems and rules established by their national governments.[3]

To engage successfully in trade, a nation must try to make the volume of money flowing out to other nations equal the volume flowing in from other nations. It must seek equilibrium. This can be done by using a free market for foreign exchange. The free market will insure that the demand for and supply of foreign currencies are always equal, but the variations in the price of currencies (changes in the exchange rates) may be too severe to allow orderly trade. The alternative is fixed exchange rates. This brings order to everyday trading, but changes in the demand or supply of foreign exchange may cause the fixed rate to become an inadequate reflection of the actual market for foreign currency. The fixed rate must be adjusted when it deviates significantly from the desired rate, and changes in rates also tend to disrupt trade among nations.

Summary

1 Trade among nations is complicated because each has its own currency and its own monetary system.
2 In order to make the best of the law of comparative advantage, nations must find ways of exchanging their currencies as well as their goods and services.
3 U.S. importers demand foreign currency to use in purchasing foreign-produced goods and services. The foreign currency is supplied by U.S. exporters who have sold goods abroad and have accepted payment in foreign money. The demand and supply combine to form a market and a rate of exchange.
4 The rate of exchange may appreciate or depreciate (rise or fall) in a freely fluctuating market for foreign exchange.
5 Most nations do not allow their foreign exchange rates to vary with complete freedom. They establish fixed rates, which sometimes have to be changed to reflect changes in technology, economic structure, and relative demands.

Exercises

1 Explain these important terms and concepts:
   rate of exchange   fixed rates
   foreign exchange   revaluation and devaluation
   freely fluctuating rates $2.50 = £1
   appreciation and depreciation

2 Although the United States has official fixed exchange rates with most other nations, the exchange rate between the Canadian dollar and the U.S. dollar has always been free to change in response to market con-

---

[3] An easy place to observe the exchanging of currency is at a bank inside a major international airport. Tellers in these banks quickly exchange U.S. dollars for Japanese yen, Italian lire or Mexican pesos.

ditions. Because the two economies are so closely intertwined, the rates do not fluctuate wildly or widely, but they can be influenced by certain economic changes in either of the nations. Which of the following would cause U.S. dollars to appreciate and which would cause them to depreciate? (Hint: Think of each problem in terms of what it will do to the supply of and demand for Canadian dollars in the United States.)

  a The Alaska pipeline becomes a trans-Canada pipeline, and U.S. oil companies must build a line over large stretches of Canadian territories.
  b A number of domestic celebrations and new tourist facilities attract much interest and U.S. vacationers stay home rather than going to Canada.
  c A Canadian economic recession causes Canadians to cut imports from the United States to near zero levels.
  d Canada strikes gold and goes on a buying binge. They buy the Chase Manhattan Bank, General Motors, and the Gulf Oil Corporation.

3 Explain the apparently simple statement "In order to import, one must also export." Does this have anything at all to do with the rate of exchange?

4 What steps might a U.S. importer take in preparing to import Toyotas with a total U.S. value of $100,000? Assume that the Japanese manufacturer insists on payment in yen, and that the exchange rate is one yen = $.0034.

5 Why might a U.S. manufacturer of sewing machines refuse to accept pounds sterling in payment for these machines? Why does he insist on payments in U.S. dollars?

6 A Citroen is an expensive, high-quality French car. A medium-priced model costs about $6,500 in the United States. How many French francs will be needed to purchase the car at each of the following exchange rates:

    1 Fr. = $.15 $1 = 5 Fr.
    1 Fr. = $.18 $1 = 4 Fr.

A Contemporary Problem
Argentina Changes a Fixed Exchange Rate

In March 1976, Argentina was troubled by political and economic instability. One manifestation of this trouble was a rapid rise in prices—inflation. The internal inflation made foreign goods more attractive, since their prices were not rising as fast as those of goods and services produced in Argentina. Since imported goods were attractive, the demand for foreign exchange rose, and the older rates no longer reflected the people's disposition about how monies should exchange.

On Friday, March 6, 1976 the Argentine Economy Minister suddenly announced that the Argentine peso had been devalued from approximately 109 pesos per U.S. dollar to 140 pesos per U.S. dollar. This move was intended to make dollars less attractive so that the pesos previously

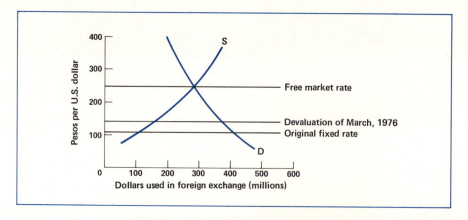

Devaluation of the Argentine Peso

spent on imported goods would be diverted and used to purchase domestic goods and services. The move was correct in its intentions and in its direction, but it seemed hopelessly inadequate in view of a free market rate of 250 pesos per U.S. dollar. The changes are summarized in the figure above. The original rate ($1 = 109 pesos) is so low that massive disequilibrium appears between pesos and dollars. The rate after devaluation ($1 = 140 pesos) is little better, but demand for foreign exchange still outstrips the quantity supplied. Only if the rate were to reach 250 pesos per dollar would the markets for currencies come into equilibrium.

Analysis. Argentine officials knew the fixed rate of $1 = 109 pesos was obsolete in 1976. They also knew that the free exchange rate was approximately 250 pesos per U.S. dollar. Why wasn't the new, devalued rate established at 250 pesos per U.S. dollar rather than 140 pesos per U.S. dollar? Possible answer: Increasing the price of dollars by 2.5 times in one instant would be highly disruptive to the Argentinian economy. Manufacturers who had placed purchases with the old 109-peso rate in mind might be able to absorb the 140 pesos rate, but they could not be expected to absorb the 250-peso rate. Because of political as well as economic instability, the Argentine government was probably wise in moving slowly toward an equilibrium position.

32
The Balance of International Payments

A homely expression says that we cannot tell where we are going unless we know where we have been. One way of remembering where we have been is to keep records, and since an enormous amount of social activity takes the form of financial transactions, account books are among the most informative records we have. In international trade, a special bookkeeping system is used to record what has been purchased from whom and what has been sold to whom. The resulting accounts show the net trade relationships among the world's economies. They tell whether, on balance, a nation exports more than it imports, or the other way around. The system is called the balance-of-payments accounting system. The record is the *balance of payments*.

The balance of payments for an economy is a summary of all economic transactions carried out between that economy and the rest of the world. It reflects all payments due, as well as all liabilities to be paid to other countries.

This chapter is about the balance of payments. It opens with a detailed discussion of the international accounting and bookkeeping scheme, then describes recent changes in trade relationships between the United States and other nations.

Table 32-1   The U.S. Balance of Payments, 1975
(millions of dollars)

Item	Debit (money outflow)	Credit (money inflow)
1. Exports from the U.S. economy		
Goods		$ 107,133
Services		23,058
Income from investments		18,219
Total		148,410
2. Imports into the U.S. economy		
Goods	$98,150	
Services	21,779	
Interest paid on foreign investments	12,212	
Total	132,141	
Trade balance (surplus)		16,269
3. Net remittances	1,727	
4. Net government transactions	2,893	
5. Capital movements		
U.S. capital outflows	31,130	
U.S. capital inflows		9,859
6. Increase in foreign currencies held by U.S. citizens		5,020
7. Errors and omissions		4,602
Total	$167,891	$167,891

Source: Adapted from U.S. Department of Commerce data.

The Balance of Payments

The annual statement of U.S. international transactions, the balance of payments, looks like a profit-and-loss statement. It records sales to and purchases from other nations, and accounts for discrepancies between the two. Although experts working on international trade problems and making international trade policy use a very detailed set of accounts, the major parts of the balance of payments can be summarized very briefly, as shown in Table 32-1.

The numerical entries are arranged in two columns. The left column shows transactions that, on balance, cause dollars to leave the domestic economy. These are called *debit entries.*

A debit entry is a bookkeeping entry showing a payment to others, a reduction in assets, or an increase in indebtedness. Any transaction, such as an import, that causes money to flow out of the economy is entered as a debit in the balance of payments.

The right-hand column shows all transactions that, on balance, cause dollars to flow into the domestic economy. Entries in this column are *credit entries.*

A credit entry is a bookkeeping entry showing a payment that has been received from others. It is the opposite of a debit entry. A credit entry reflects an increase in the amount of cash held, an addition to assets, or a decrease in indebtedness. In the balance of payments, exports give rise to credit entries.

The balance of payments is designed to show total transactions and the net credit or debt position between the United States and all other nations. The accounts are divided into several sections, representing the variety of ways that money can flow from one economy to another.

Exports and Imports

Exports and imports make up the largest part of U.S. international trade. Both exports and imports are divided into goods (items that can be seen and touched), services (performed one time and for one buyer), and transactions related to investments. Automobiles sent to Canada are exported goods; bauxite from Jamaica and clothing from Hong Kong are

"I'm afraid the imports are beginning to exceed the exports."

imported goods. When a U.S. ship is hired to transport iron ore from Bolivia to Sweden, the United States is exporting a service; when Japanese tourists vacation in Hawaii, the restaurants and hotels of that state are exporting services to Japan. Similarly, when U.S. tourists fly to Europe on Icelandic Airlines and when U.S. firms buy insurance from Lloyds of London, the United States is importing services.

The final item in the imports and exports account shows the international flow of interest on previous investments. When a U.S. firm borrows foreign money to build new factories or expand its operations, the firm must pay interest to the lender of the money. This interest payment is a debit item in the balance of payments; U.S. dollars flow to another nation. In 1975, U.S. businessmen made interest payments of over $12.2 billion to money lenders in other nations. At the same time, U.S. money lenders have found attractive investment opportunities in other nations; as a result of lending to foreigners, they earned over $18 billion in 1975. This was a credit item, since it represented an inflow of foreign currencies.

The dollar volume of exports and imports shows the *balance of trade.*

The balance of trade is the difference between the dollar volume of imports and the dollar volume of exports. It is used to show whether a nation is a net importer or a net exporter of goods and services over a short period of time.

In 1975, U.S. exports ($148,410 million) exceeded U.S. imports ($132,141 million) by $16,269 million, so the economy had a trade surplus. The goods and services sold to other nations had a higher value than the goods and services bought from other nations. On balance, U.S. trade in

Some Hidden Transactions

No one would expect a brief table like Table 32-1 to show international trading in great detail. There are, however, two groups of transactions that should be clarified. The U.S. military establishment carries on huge international trade activities. Since these activities are primarily in the goods and services categories, they are included as parts of imports and exports. When the military sells fighter planes to Israel or tanks and missiles to Germany, these are export items bringing foreign exchange into the U.S. economy.

Conversely, when the military makes large expenditures to maintain bases abroad, it is importing the services of another nation. In 1975, military-related exports amounted to $3,897 million, while military-related imports were valued at $2,232 million.

This would be of little consequence except that these purchases and expenditures are made on political rather than economic grounds. The balance of trade, then, can be seriously affected by decisions unrelated to the economic affairs of nations.

goods and services brought a surplus of foreign exchange into the domestic economy. A trade surplus is sometimes referred to as a "favorable balance of trade."

Remittances

Many Mexican citizens find temporary or permanent employment in the United States each year. Formerly, the work they did was concentrated in rural areas and in the West. More recently, Mexican professionals and skilled workers have been migrating to cities of the United States to take advantage of the higher levels of wages. Because of extended family and kinship groups, many of them feel obligated to send some money back to parents, wives, cousins, and families in Mexico. These dollars sent from the nation are "remittances." Any *transfer payment* made across national boundaries is called a remittance.

A transfer payment is a payment that is not accompanied by the exchange of goods or services. It is a gift.

Thus, U.S. money sent to the folks back home, pensions paid by Minnesota Mining and Manufacturing to a retired executive living in Samoa, and the monthly check to the college student studying in France are all remittances and appear as debit entries in line 3 of Table 32–1.

The practice of reporting only net remittances in the balance of payments disguises the fact that remittances flow both ways. Large numbers of foreign students attending U.S. colleges receive money from their home countries. Gifts from relatives continue to be sent into the U.S. economy. Even though gifts (transfers) do flow both ways, the United States is a net loser of dollars on the remittance account. In 1975, U.S. citizens sent $1,727 million more to other nations than they received in return.

Net Government Transactions

This component of the international balance of payments is the government counterpart to private remittances. It includes grants and gifts made by the United States to other nations. Over the past half century, the United States has made many extremely large loans and gifts to other nations. The entry in line 3 shows that 1975 was no exception.

Net Capital Movements

Each year a great deal of private capital flows among nations. Ordinarily, these capital flows consist of investment funds rather than physical capital. The investment funds move from one nation to another when capital owners expect that they can earn a higher return in another country. In the mid-1970s, much U.S. capital has been invested in Mexico, and a great deal of Japanese and Middle Eastern capital has flowed into the United States.

There are two general ways for capital to flow from the United States to another nation. One route is for a firm (organization) to go multinational.

A multinational firm is one that is based in one country but has business operations in other countries as well. Coca-Cola is multinational, as are General Motors and Du Pont. At this time, about 60 percent of all multinational firms have their home offices in the United States.

To become multinational, a U.S. firm must either purchase a foreign firm or build a subsidiary plant in the foreign nation. In either case, U.S. dollars are going to a foreign country, which gives rise to a debit entry in the "capital movements" rows of the balance of payments. A more common way for U.S. capital to find its way to foreign nations is through the purchase of stock in foreign companies. In 1975, U.S. investors spent $31,131 million to purchase part ownership in foreign firms.

Capital movement is a two-way street. Many foreign firms are expanding by building or buying plants in the United States. Japanese manufacturers have already invested in plants to manufacture TV sets, automobiles, and calculators in the United States. West Germany is planning to manufacture its VW Rabbit in Pennsylvania. The oil-rich nations of the Middle East are investing heavily in U.S. agricultural land and in businesses related to agriculture. Foreign investment in the United States amounted to $14,879 million in 1975.

Paying Debts Between Nations

Exports, imports, remittances, government activity, and capital movements are the major groupings of international transactions that cause money to flow from one nation to another. These flows are summarized in two ways: First, the balance of trade shows that in 1975, the value of U.S. exports exceeded the value of U.S. imports by $16,269 million—the nation had a trade surplus in that year. When the other accounts are included, a second picture emerges. Remittances sent to other nations, net government transactions, and U.S. investments in other nations all cause money to flow out of the United States. When these debit entries are taken into account (along with the small inflow of funds from other nations), the balance of payments shows that the United States spent $167,891 million in other nations while receiving in return only $158,269 million. In 1975, the United States was a debtor nation—it spent more than it received.

Paying debts between nations can be done in a number of ways, but two are used most frequently. One is by transferring gold to other nations; the other is by transferring foreign currency held by the debtor nation. Paying debts with gold has no significant effect on the operation of the domestic economy, but it has a psychological effect on citizens—people do not like to see "their" gold being shipped abroad. Paying debts using foreign currency is psychologically acceptable, but it is costly since the currencies could otherwise be used to earn interest. In 1975, the several nations owing money to the United States chose to use foreign currencies as a means of payment. They sent over $5 billion to the United States to pay the debts that had been incurred in international trade.

Errors and Omissions

Even with the inclusion of a $5,020 million payments from other nations, the balance of payments in Table 32–1 does *not* balance. The problem lies in the many international transactions that take place but are not counted or cannot be included in the usual trade categories. Some remittances are not counted because they are small or because of the way they are made. Smuggled and contraband shipments are not counted, and bad debts or defaulted accounts are sometimes missed. These omissions, and any errors in the measurement of the other accounts, are used to make the credits and debits equal. They balance the payments that flow between the United States and other economies. In 1975, errors and omissions were an unusually high $4,602 million and the balance of payments on all accounts was $167,891 million.

Continuing Balance-of-Payments Disequilibrium

During 1975, the U.S. economy experienced an overall deficit in international payments. U.S. citizens and governments spent and invested more abroad than foreign citizens and nations spent and invested in the United States. If the deficit is temporary, the economy can generally absorb it without great difficulty. However, if the balance of payments is continuously either in surplus or deficit, trade relationships among nations must change.

When a nation has a continuing balance-of-payments surplus, exports continually exceed imports and capital continues to flow in from other nations. A continuing surplus means that the nation must find things to do with the large accumulation of foreign currencies. When the United States

Restating the Accounts

The various lines that are shown in Table 32–1 are frequently rearranged into four separate accounts. In the four-way classification, imports and exports of goods and services are included in the *current account*. The *capital account* includes long-term capital (foreign investments) maturing in more than one year, and short-term credit extended by banks and other lenders to finance trade activity in the current account.

The *unilateral account* includes all personal gifts and transfers (remittances) as well as gifts, grants, loans, and aid given by one nation to another. Finally, the *gold account* reflects flows of gold or direct claims on gold (such as foreign currencies).

When this system is used, the balance of trade reflects activity on the current account and, as before, the balance of payments relates to all accounts taken together.

---

was in this position in the late 1940s and 1950s, it used the monies to aid foreign nations that were trying to recover from the devastation of World War II. In these years, West Germany, France, Italy, Greece, Great Britain, Spain, and many other countries had limited productive capacities, so they could not produce things for either domestic consumption or export. They needed food and machines. The United States sold many exports to Western Europe in these years but there was nothing to buy in exchange. The most practical solution was simply to give the foreign exchange back to the recovering nations as a unilateral government transfer.

Such a policy can only be temporary. Over the long run, the economies that engage in significant amounts of international trade must be realigned so that the trade between them is nearer to equilibrium—so that the value of exports is approximately offset by the value of imports. This can be accomplished by changing exchange rates.

If one nation has a persistent balance-of-payments deficit in relation to another nation, the change in exchange rates should make imports more expensive and exports less expensive. For example, if the exchange rate between pounds and dollars were £1 = $2 and an extensive period of U.S. deficits in its exchanges with Great Britain ensued, the appropriate change would be for the U.S. to *devalue* its currency so that a pound sterling would purchase more dollars. A new rate of £1 = $2.50 would increase U.S. exports to Great Britain and at the same time decrease U.S. imports from there. Eventually, the devaluation would remove the U.S. balance-of-payments deficit.

Generally speaking, the nations that enjoy persistent balance-of-payments surpluses do not revalue their currencies to help remove the surplus. There are two reasons. First, a surplus is generally good from the point of view of a nation that has one. It provides supplies of foreign exchange that can be used to earn interest or to purchase more goods from other nations. The processes that bring the surpluses also provide employment for laborers and add to family incomes in the surplus nations. Second, and more common, a nation with a long-standing surplus will not have the opportunity to revalue because the nations with whom it trades will devalue their currencies first.

Recent Developments in U.S. Trade

World trade emerged as a by-product of the Industrial Revolution. International trade worked surprisingly well during the nineteenth and early twentieth centuries, but the triple catastrophes of the Great Depression, World War II, and the Cold War changed that. In the Depression, no one (and no nation) had money to use for foreign trade. During this time of high unemployment, most nations imposed stiff tariffs on imports, hoping that consumers would buy goods produced at home and put domestic labor to work. While the logic of this move made sense in the short run, it went against the law of comparative advantage and greatly inhibited the movement of goods among economies.

World War II followed on the heels of the Depression and further damaged world trading opportunities. The warring nations quickly divided into three camps: The Axis powers (Germany, Japan, and Italy), the Allies (the United States, Great Britain, Russia, France, and others committed to them), and the neutral countries. Trading occurred within the Axis group and within the Allied group but, since the purpose of each side was to prosecute a war successfully, the economic consequences of the trades and shipments of goods were secondary and infrequently considered. At war's end, the devastated nations received billions of U.S. dollars to rebuild their domestic economies. This was necessary to prevent the complete social and economic breakdown of the ruined societies. Again the motives for the international transactions were noneconomic. The result was a further strain on the mechanisms of orderly international trade. More recently some European countries and Japan have become productive enough to compete with the U.S. economy in foreign markets. In spite of this, U.S. capital continues to flow to other nations. Some of this flow is in the form of unilateral government transfers (gifts) to relieve countries afflicted by natural disasters like droughts and earthquakes, but most consists of dollar transfers to *Third-World nations* that have not decided whether their political economies should be centrist like those of China, Russia, and most of Southeast Asia, or whether they should be

"It's a survey of noncommitted people. They want to know whether we're listening to the Voice of America, or Radio Moscow."

more market-oriented like those of the United States, Japan, Australia, and other members of the Western bloc.

Third-World nations are the less developed countries, primarily in Asia and Africa. Their economies are not able to provide a reasonable level of living for their populations, and they are often characterized by political and economic instability. Many Third-World nations are not aligned with either the communist or noncommunist blocs.

Dollars flowing to these nations are payments (or bribes) made to encourage the countries to become or remain part of the Western bloc.

U.S. Trade Surpluses

Since 1950, the United States has nearly always managed a *trade* surplus by selling more goods and services to other countries than it buys from them. In 1950, the United States was the only industrial economy with its capital plant in full operating condition. The others were rebuilding after the devastation of World War II. The rebuilding nations received large gifts and loans of U.S. currency. It was very easy for them to use the currency to purchase United States-made goods. Since the war-wrecked nations had nothing to sell to the United States, its exports rose while imports stayed relatively low. Thus, a trade surplus developed and remained until the mid-1970s when, for a brief period of time, the United States ran a trade deficit—its only balance-of-trade deficit in this century.

Balance-of-Payments Problems

Even though the period from 1950 to the present has been characterized by balance-of-trade surpluses, the U.S. economy has had a persistent deficit in its total balance of payments. The huge capital outflow stemming from loans and grants to other nations, plus the exodus of private U.S. capital to productive investments in other nations, has made dollar outflows exceed dollar inflows in most years since 1950. The only exceptions were 1968 and 1969, when very modest balance-of-payments surpluses were realized.

The United States at first solved these balance-of-payments deficits by transferring gold to other nations. In 1950, the United States held gold valued at over $20 billion, so payment in gold was easy and swift. By 1975, however, the gold stock had been reduced to less than $12 billion, and Treasury officials became reluctant to use more of it to satisfy international claims. Instead, they chose to use foreign currencies. During this same post-World War II period, foreign claims on U.S. dollars rose from $8 billion to $90 billion. A foreign claim on a dollar is the same as foreign ownership of that dollar and the balance-of-payments deficits poured millions of dollars into other nations. How will these annual deficits ever be reversed, and how will the claims on U.S. currencies ever be satisfied?

Possible Solutions

The causes of the balance-of-payments deficits give some clues regarding how the problems might be solved. If the United States cannot sell enough abroad to balance its international accounts, it must offer its goods at lower prices in order to increase exports and the balance-of-trade surplus. It is unlikely, however, that trade surpluses can be depended upon to eliminate the deficits caused by large capital transfers. Some economists and politicians have argued that the U.S. outflow of capital could be reduced if the nations of Western Europe would play a more active role in financing the West's mutual defense posture. Similarly, if other Western nations were to increase their aid to the developing and Third-World nations, the United States could decrease the dollars sent to them. These suggestions involve the politics and economics of several nations. They are not easily put into effect.

A more reasonable approach to the continuing balance-of-payments deficits is to enter into agreements with nations that have persistent trade surpluses against the U.S. economy. These nations sell more to the United

States than it sells to them. The agreements would ask the nations with surpluses to lower tariffs on their own U.S. imports, remove trade barriers against U.S. goods, and invest some of their trade surplus in U.S. industries, thus returning the surplus dollars to the U.S. economy.

Recent presidents, particularly President Nixon, have used their powers to help redress the balance of payments. In 1971, President Nixon imposed a 10 percent *surcharge* on all *dutiable imports.*

A surcharge is a special tax levied against only a particular item or kind of item. A dutiable import is an import on which a duty or tariff must be paid. A 10 percent surcharge on a dutiable import increases its price by 10 percent.

In doing so, he was attempting to make imports more expensive so that U.S. citizens would be discouraged from purchasing abroad. If successful, the surcharge would bring a drop in the number of dollars flowing to other nations in trade.

A final suggestion has been made before: devaluation of the dollar. Devaluation makes U.S. goods more attractive to other nations and other nations' goods less attractive to the United States. Devaluation would help bring about a balance-of-payments equilibrium by making trade surpluses offset deficits incurred through capital flows. Would these measures work? It is too early to know, but the United States has been trying them.

Even with Nixon's surcharge, the U.S. balance of payments continued to deteriorate. By December 1971, the problem had become so severe that the dollar was officially devalued. This devaluation was accompanied by the revaluation of several other currencies, and the net effect was about an 11 percent devaluation of the dollar. Even this was not enough. Early in 1973, the dollar was devalued again. Since that time, the values of many currencies and, hence exchange rates, have fluctuated widely.

Recent actions by the Executive branch of government have been complemented by actions of Congress and the general mood of the public. In recent years, Congressional support for foreign aid has been dwindling and a number of U.S. military installations in other nations have been closed. Each closure and each reduction in foreign aid lowers the number of dollars flowing to other nations and lowers the deficit in the balance of payments.

Perhaps the greatest source of encouragement is the investments other nations are making in the U.S. economy. When an Iranian oil magnate uses some of his newly earned oil dollars to purchase a U.S. firm or to buy wheat land in Kansas, he is returning dollars to the United States and helping reduce this nation's balance-of-payments deficit. The record shows that foreign investments in the United States have soared during this decade. In 1970, other nations made direct investments of $13.3 billion in the U.S. economy. In 1974, foreign investors invested a record $30 billion in the United States.

Bringing Order to the Trading World

In the past few years, a number of nations with balance-of-payments difficulties have tried to redress them by devaluing their currencies, imposing high tariffs, and exerting selective controls on their trade partners. Of these actions, devaluation and the consequent exchange-rate changes disrupt trade the most. Nevertheless, the German mark has been devalued, the dollar has been devalued twice, and the Argentine peso has been devalued.

These devaluations are needed to correct balance-of-payments deficits, but they bring chaos to individual traders in all countries. When exchange rates are fluctuating, importers and exporters do not know whether prices of goods will rise or fall, bankers do not know whether to hold dollars or pounds sterling or francs or yen, and individuals find their asset positions changing as the "value" of a currency rises or falls. Individuals, trading groups, and whole nations agree that there should be some way of managing international money matters so that changes in exchange rates will be orderly and consistent. The governments of the major trading nations have tried from time to time to develop a workable system by using an "international bank."

The Bretton Woods Conference

The first modern attempt at stabilizing international monetary problems was a meeting of the Allied nations held in Bretton Woods, New Hampshire near the end of World War II. The meeting was proposed to lay the groundwork for a viable international money system. It accomplished two major things. It committed nations to make agreements on the official prices of their currencies, and it established the International Monetary Fund (IMF). The price of a currency was declared in terms of gold (for example, the United States declared that one ounce of gold was to be valued at $35), and each nation agreed to maintain the official price of its currency within one percent of this established *par value.*

The par value of foreign exchange is the official value of a nation's currency. It is generally stated in terms of another currency (£1 = $2.00) or in terms of a precious metal (gold = $35/oz.).

The IMF was the first step toward an international banking and monetary system. Created in 1945, the IMF remains the most important agency with responsibility for managing international monetary problems. Nations choosing to belong to the IMF are required to make deposits of gold and of their own currencies in the fund. The size of the deposit is based on the size of the nation's economy. The United States maintains a very large deposit, while Costa Rica's is very small. In return for these deposits, member nations obtain the privilege of borrowing foreign exchange from the fund. The borrowing is short-term—usually no more than three years—and an interest charge is made. In this way the fund provides access to foreign currency for nations that are short of foreign exchange and feel strains on their money supplies.

In 1967, the lending capacity of the IMF, and the borrowing capacity of each of its member nations, was expanded by the creation of Special Drawing Rights (SDRs). SDRs are a relatively new kind of international reserve currency. A nation receives SDRs in relation to the size of its economy and uses them to borrow more foreign exchange than it formerly could. The SDRs are an attempt to make the IMF more flexible and more able to meet international monetary contingencies.

The Smithsonian Agreement

Even the full powers of the IMF could not alleviate the many balance-of-payments deficit problems that existed in the late 1960s. In late 1971, 10 major trading nations, all members of the IMF, met at the Smithsonian Institution in Washington, D.C. and developed the "Smithsonian agreement." Among other actions, the Smithsonian agreement called upon the United States to devalue its currency and increased the range within which a nation could let its foreign-exchange rate vary. Whereas the Bretton Woods agreement allowed only 1 percent deviations from par value, the new Smithsonian agreement permits deviations up to 2.25 percent above or below par. The overall agreement is designed to maintain stability in the international monetary system, but it allows considerably more short-term freedom than previous agreements.

At this time, the international monetary picture is a cloudy one. Inflation is gripping most industrial nations and most are also experiencing high rates of unemployment. Domestic inflationary pressures often cause goods from other nations to look attractive, but the unemployed resources in the domestic economy are a compelling argument for nations to establish tariffs that force their citizens to buy at home. The differential adoption of technology and the law of comparative advantage are telling nations and firms to specialize in what they do best and trade for whatever else they may need. But inflation, unemployment, and balance-of-payments problems argue in favor of the nation's building a trade wall around itself to keep its problems down to manageable proportions.

These myriad problems lead to only one thing: severe strains on the balance of payments. And no nation can feel entirely exempt from the strain. The international monetary system of the next decades will have to be a sophisticated one. It will have to be able to accommodate structural changes among economies and the concomitant changes in trade patterns. It will have to be able to redress differences and disparities among exchange rates. But it will have to do this so smoothly that most day-to-day traders will scarcely notice. That such a system can be created is taken for granted. The question is: When will all nations agree to its creation?

Summary

1. The balance of payments is a bookkeeping record used to keep track of international flows of currencies. The system separates the flows into debits (outflows) and credits (inflows).
2. Debits and credits arise as a result of transactions involving goods and services, private gifts (remittances), government transfers, capital investments, and flows of gold or currencies.
3. If exports exceed imports, a nation enjoys a trade surplus. If imports exceed exports, the nation has a trade deficit.
4. When all parts of the balance of payments have been considered, a nation owing money to other nations has a balance-of-payments deficit. A creditor nation has a balance-of-payments surplus. The United States has had a deficit for many years.
5. The major reason for the persistent U.S. deficit is a long history of grants and loans to other nations.
6. Balance-of-payments deficits can be removed by increasing exports, decreasing capital movements, or devaluing the domestic currency. Since 1970, the United States has tried all three.
7. Since World War II, several attempts have been made to establish more orderly mechanisms for integrating the monetary systems of trading nations. These include the Bretton Woods system and the Smithsonian agreement.

Exercises

1. Explain these important terms and concepts:
   - balance of payments
   - debit entry
   - balance of trade
   - trade deficit
   - remittance
   - capital account
   - unilateral government transfers
   - gold flows
   - Bretton Woods
   - IMF
   - Special Drawing Rights
   - Smithsonian agreement
2. Explain how a nation might have a trade deficit and a balance-of-payments surplus simultaneously. Is such a circumstance likely?
3. A nation engages in the following international transactions:

Imports	$ 250
Investment in other nations	1000
Remittances to other nations	50
Exports	325
Government grants to others	400

Other nations investing in it	875
Remittances from other nations	75
Gold flows from other nations	500

    a What is the balance of trade between the nation and the rest of the world?
    b Is the balance of payments a deficit or a surplus?
    c How large will the "errors and omissions" entry be?

4 How would each of the following affect the U.S. balance of payments? (Assume that the United States is in a debtor position.)
    a The Arab nations sell bonds worth $100 million to U.S. citizens, then use the revenue to purchase United States-produced military equipment valued at $100 million.
    b U.S. citizens anticipate a devaluation in the Mexican peso.
    c Because of massive accumulations of foreign exchange, Japan appreciates the value of its yen.
    d The Mexican peso is not devalued after all.
    e The United States sends a $50 million grant to Peru after a tragic earthquake strikes that nation.

5 Classify the following as debits or credits in the U.S. balance of payments:
    a An Iranian oil company purchases a large farm in Georgia.
    b An American student studying in Paris uses part of her allowance to buy a Japanese car.
    c Mutual of Omaha holds a board meeting in Oslo, Norway.
    d The IMF grants Brazil a large loan to be used to purchase United States-made farm machinery.
    e Standard Oil of New Jersey makes a dividend payment to a resident of Canada.
    f An estate is settled in Arkansas, and the will stipulates that $20,000 be sent to a sister now living in Spain.
    g The sister in Spain gives the money to Columbia University in New York.

A Contemporary Problem

The Common Market

Europe has always been a continent of small, independent nations. For decades, economists and political leaders in the small nations have recognized that the economies of the several nations were highly integrated. Fierce competition, occasional setbacks, and domestic crises nevertheless kept trade barriers and tariffs among the nations high. After suffering nearly complete devastation by war twice in the first half of the twentieth century and after admitting that each of the two wars had been caused at least partly by economic problems, the European nations tried to organize a single trade group or "Common Market."

    Starting in 1947, several countries gradually began to break down the barriers that had earlier set them apart. The first efforts were in coal, iron, and steel. All tariffs, quotas, and other rules of trade affecting these products were dropped. Suddenly eliminating rules that had existed for years required rather careful supervision and coordination of output and marketing plans, but it was accomplished. The effort with these products was so successful that in 1957 a tariff-free single European market for all commodities was proposed. The six original members were Belgium, France, West Germany, the Netherlands, Italy, and Luxembourg.

The six countries instantly began to discontinue tariffs, and also to permit laborers belonging to any one of them to find work in any of the others. Before long, thousands of unemployed Italian workers had moved to Germany, where there was a shortage of labor. Lowering trade and migration barriers allowed the member nations to achieve very high rates of growth in the late 1950s and early 1960s. In 1972, the Common Market was expanded to include Great Britain, The Republic of Ireland, and Denmark. In the same year, Norway held a plebiscite vote and decided not to join the Common Market.

Once tariffs, trade restrictions, and other impediments on the movement of goods, labor, and capital had been removed, the member nations turned their attention to integrating their monetary systems. Transferring from pounds, marks, francs, and lire to a single currency will be very hard for millions of people, and developing a single monetary policy where nine had been before is a formidable task. Nonetheless, the Common Market plans to have a completely integrated monetary system by the end of this decade.

Analysis. Has the Common Market worked? At this time, the answer seems to be yes. All member nations have enjoyed rather high rates of growth. Although some are now troubled by high rates of inflation and unemployment, others—most notably West Germany—are among the more stable economies in the world. An even bigger question is: Does the Common Market provide a useful model for other groups of nations like those in South America, Latin America, and Africa? Here the answer is less clear. The European nations had a great advantage when they began their community. They had experience in trading, they were all somewhat industrialized economies, and they had communications and transport networks connecting them. Since the developing nations in other parts of the world do not all have these advantages, it may be rather difficult to establish the linkages needed to made a trade community work.

33 The Less Developed Countries

The large middle class in the United States, workers in West Germany, residents of industrial areas of Russia, and a few other peoples enjoy more material goods and creature comforts than most of the world. These fortunate few live in the "developed" nations. They have mastered the process of turning resources into products, and have amassed the necessary capital to manufacture on a large scale everything from electric light bulbs to frozen orange juice.

However well-off the people in developed nations may be, the world remains a brutish place for more than 2 billion others. Each day fully half of the world's population goes to bed hungry or suffers from some nutrition-related disease. They live essentially as their ancestors lived four or five thousand years ago—close to the soil or in nomadic bands.

Progress has come to the world in an uneven way, and the world community of poverty is an increasingly burdensome problem for the wealthy nations. Leaders in developed countries increasingly respect the idea that poor peoples are restless and unlikely to be so resigned in the future as they have been in the past. The rumblings among nations in Southeast Asia, Latin America, and Africa indicate that they mean to have a share of progress too.

This chapter is about the less developed countries, how they fit into the economics of the world today, and what might be done to enhance their

"Missiles, cosmonauts, power plants—our standard of living has never been higher."

economic development. Since development is related to a combination of economic, social, and political factors, the discussion here may be unsatisfying in its lack of good answers to good questions. Nonetheless, it describes the problem, advances some possible *economic* solutions, and tells what the United States has done to help the developing nations.

World Poverty

There is no adequate definition of "poverty" for either individuals or nations. The Rockefellers are known to be rich, and many migrant farm workers in the United States are known to be poor. Among nations, the United States, Kuwait, and New Zealand are known to be rich and Ethiopia, Tunisia, Nicaragua, Jordan, and Nepal are known to be poor. But knowledge of these relative conditions does not constitute a definition. Each person must decide on his own what constitutes poor and what constitutes rich. In all likelihood, this individual determination will not be absolute, but will be relative to the position of others. Moreover, what is poor in one year may not seem poor in another.

For pragmatic reasons the United Nations must make a determination of what is developed and what is not. In recent years, it has arbitrarily declared that any nation with an annual per capita income less than $500 is a "less developed country"; those with annual per capita incomes above this level are "developed." Although the number varies from year to year, approximately 80 nations are classed as less developed. These 80 include nearly 60 percent of the world's population.

Even though there is not agreement on the separation between rich and poor, there is agreement that all the poorer nations display one or more of the following characteristics:

1. High rates of population growth, often caused by lowering death rates and lowering infant mortality.
2. A high proportion of the population employed in agriculture.
3. Such low levels of income that no savings can be accumulated for investment purposes.
4. *Underemployment* in both rural and urban areas.

Underemployment exists when laborers are not actually looking for work, but are performing no productive services or are going for long periods without working to capacity. In low-income nations, many workers, especially in agriculture, are underemployed. They work during planting and harvest but engage in no productive activity during other seasons. Underemployment is sometimes called "disguised unemployment."

5. Low levels of literacy among the adult population.
6. Heavy reliance on a few export items, usually raw or semiprocessed materials.
7. A government controlled by a small, close-knit ruling elite that does not favor economic, social, political, or technological change, which might threaten its power base.
8. A tradition-minded citizenry with a sense of helplessness about the future.

The Unfortunate Nations: What Should They Be Called?

No nation, even a poor one, wants to be called "poor." But economists, politicians, diplomats, and writers must call them something. The problem of an acceptable name did not become apparent until the United Nations was formed and sprouted many subagencies to deal with poverty and development among nations. At first, the low-income nations were called "undeveloped," but that had an understandably objectionable ring to officials and representatives from these countries. Then came "underdeveloped," an awkward term, but one with less negative overtones. The name "developing nations" was tried but dropped. Too many of the nations in question were not actually developing.

At present, the nations with low incomes are being called "less developed countries" (often abbreviated "LDCs") in both technical and popular writing. This convention will be adopted here, although it would be difficult to answer the question, "less developed than what?"

Few, if any, nations display all of these characteristics, but the poor countries each have several of them. In contrast, aggressive entrepreneurs or planners in developed nations operate in an institutional framework conducive to turning natural resources into capital goods, consumer goods, and services. The problem is how to help the poor countries get started on their way to growth and development.

The poor nations are in a vicious cycle not unlike the one that Malthus described 150 years ago. They have no savings to use in generating the capital needed to produce more things. Even if savings do occur, they are often used to increase food production, which has the single effect of increasing population. The poorer nations literally consume their own chances for progress. In spite of this strong tendency, though, some progress has occurred in the less developed countries.

Growth in the LDC's

Despite formidable odds, some LDCs have been growing. Data gathered by the United Nations, the World Bank, and the U.S. Agency for International Development (AID)[1] show that some LDCs, notably the oil-exporting nations, have done very well in increasing their per capita income in recent years.

A listing of all the nations of the world, their GNPs, and their growth rates would be very interesting but would provide more data than could be usefully assimilated. Instead, averages of *groups* of nations are used to show how the economies of the world perform. Table 33–1 uses this method to show how the world's incomes are divided.[2] In the early 1970s, over half the world's population had per capita incomes below $200 per year. These people were concentrated in Africa and Asia and, with few exceptions, lived in densely populated nations or nations that had poor collections of natural resources.

The nations at the upper end of the income scale (Group VII) produced and consumed over two-thirds of world output even though they represented less than 10 percent of the world population. In general, the na-

---

[1] AID is a semi-autonomous branch of the U.S. State Department. Although its avowed purpose is to help nations achieve their potential growth rates and improve the well-being of people throughout the world, its political goals are hard to conceal. It helps those nations that are most likely to ally with the United States. Thus, much AID assistance goes to India, Greece, and Ghana. None goes to North Vietnam, Mongolia, or Poland.

[2] The mechanisms for reporting international economic information are not so sophisticated or so accurate as methods used to gather data for the national income accounts. Data in the table are therefore somewhat outdated. Even so, the comparisons they describe are likely to be about the same in 1977 as they were in 1972.

Table 33-1 Income Differences among Groups of Nations about 1970

Group	Range of per capita income*	Number of nations	Population (millions)	Average GNP per capita	Percent of world	
					GNP	Population
I	$0–99	20	332	$ 78	0.78	9.13
II	100–199	30	1,588	138	6.57	43.65
III	200–399	45	336	306	3.07	9.23
IV	400–799	31	301	591	5.31	8.27
V	800–1,599	26	413	1,273	15.71	11.35
VI	1,600–3,199	26	306	2,244	20.57	8.43
VII	3,200 and above	10	362	4,440	67.99	9.94

* In U.S. dollars with 1972 purchasing power.   Source: World Bank, Atlas, 1973.

tions in Group VII had abundant and diverse natural resources, huge collections of capital, or both. The exceptions were the Middle Eastern nations, whose riches come from the sale of oil.

Table 33-1 is really a one-shot glance at per capita incomes in 188 nations. It says nothing about how these nations have grown or how they are performing now. Table 33-2 shows the average annual growth rates experienced by each group of nations between 1965 and 1971. The nations in Groups I, II, and III experienced low rates of growth, but the intermediate-income nations in Groups IV, V, and VI had the highest rates of all—even higher than the rates experienced by the 10 high-income nations. In the late 1960s, the 1.02 billion people whose per capita incomes were between $400 and $3,199 per year did the best job of improving themselves.

Data on growth rates suggest a powerful conclusion with important policy implications: The very-low-income nations (Groups I-III) are so poor

Table 33-2 Growth Rate among Groups of Nations

Group	Range of income	Average annual growth rate 1965–1971
I	$ 0– 99	1.28%
II	100– 199	1.14
III	200– 399	2.25
IV	400– 799	4.39
V	800–1,599	4.87
VI	1,600–3,199	4.30
VII	3,200+	3.21

that they can only expect to increase their well-being at a very slow rate. They are unable to amass capital and unable to break ties with agricultural production. The middle groups (Groups IV-VI) have apparently overcome several traditional obstacles to growth. They are on their way to industrialization. They can use some savings for investment, and will be able to employ their work forces in industry and increase their GNPs.

The high-income nations have lower rates of growth because they have exhausted their high-return opportunities and are settling on the production of goods and services that require large amounts of capital but do not necessarily yield high contributions to the collection of goods and services.

The differences in growth rates have caused some economists to contend that a nation's economic growth goes through stages, starting with primitive, no-growth conditions, working through high-growth stages, and ending in a low-growth but high-consumption stage. The evidence is not all in, but so far the stage theories seem to be a reasonable description of the process of development.

Description does little to tell why some nations are wealthy and some are poor, why some grow rapidly and others not at all. This is another of the riddles of economics. Economists do not yet know exactly why Mexico has developed quite rapidly while Brazil, with a superior collection of natural resources, has had a disappointing rate of economic growth. The following sections describe some factors that affect growth, but a blueprint for growth and development seems beyond the capacity of economics and economic policy at this time.

Factors Affecting Growth

The classical economists, the Marxists, and the many economists of the late nineteenth and early twentieth centuries had a variety of ideas about how growth and development would proceed. All stressed that in the beginning, growth depends upon combining the factors of production (land, labor, capital, and entrepreneurship) in the correct way. The following paragraphs explain how each is related to the growth process.

Land

In Chapter 3, land was defined to include all of the natural attributes in a particular region. Land includes soil, rainfall, rivers, coal, wind, and air temperature.

Most LDCs have collections of natural resources that are either worn-out from centuries of use or not used at all. The countries on the southern shore of the Mediterranean Sea and on the Indian subcontinent in times past have supported magnificent economies. Their agricultures flourished and they had surpluses that allowed the building of the pyramids, the Acropolis, and the Taj Mahal. But agricultural production was maintained in these areas for centuries without the advantages of crop rotations, chemical fertilizers, or pest control. The productivity of the soil slowly dropped, until now it can produce barely enough food to maintain the people who farm it. Other nations were mined, dug, and pillaged by imperial dynasties so that few usable resources remain. A third group of countries, mostly in Africa and Latin America, have collections of natural resources that have not ever been used effectively.

The LDCs need large doses of technical skill and capital to make use of their natural resources. A single prescription is not adequate. In some, land must be drained or irrigated (or both!). In others, roads must be built so that timber, iron ore, and agricultural products can be distributed to new markets. In still others, the energy of falling water must be harnessed to generate electricity, new resources must be found and exploited, and old resources must be reclaimed or improved.

The uneven distribution of natural resources among the world's LDCs provides differential starting places on the path to development and, more important, requires different sets of policies among nations seeking to increase their economies' well-being. Brazil needs transportation networks to open the interior. Bolivia and Peru need to rehabilitate exhausted soils. Nicaragua needs new institutions for the production and marketing of tropical crops. Ghana needs education and *social overhead capital.*

Social overhead capital is the capital needed to maintain the productivity of a nation. It includes roads, schools, hospitals, irrigation canals, flood control dams, and scores of other items that are not necessarily productive by themselves but contribute to the productivity of other factors. Most developed nations have large collections of social overhead capital. In the LDC's, collections of such capital are modest.

Labor

Most LDCs have a superabundance of people but a shortage of many special kinds of labor. Like land, labor is a composite. It includes physical ability and technical skill. The LDCs have physical ability that is often hampered by malnutrition, disease, and limited skills and ingenuity. The average farmer in Pakistan knows how to use an ox and a wooden plow to break soil. His wife and children know how to follow the plow and drop seeds into the earth. In this way, the family labor is used to produce a grain crop. The farmer has no knowledge of fertilizers, he does not know how to use a steel plow, and he has not learned about the process of irrigation. To become more productive he must be exposed to modern farming methods.

"Labor" is more than toil. It is people. In most LDCs, there is a distinct separation between what is good for the individual (family) and what is good for the nation. Neither India nor Bolivia has a well developed program for the care of the aged or the infirm. Neither has a social security program or unemployment insurance. As a result, a family in either of these countries must look out for its own aged, infirm, and unemployed. The traditional way of doing this is by having many children. In a large family, sons and daughters will contribute to the family's income after the major breadwinner retires or becomes incapacitated. A large family is the best insurance for a comfortable old age. However, when multiplied by millions of families, the need to bear more children becomes a national liability that threatens to consume any increase in output of food, clothing, or shelter. Population growth stymies economic development, but the growth in population is understandable: It is the only form of insurance available for most of the people in the world. (Note: Until very recently, the incentive for big families was as strong in the United States as it now is in the LDCs. On the American frontier the family with six sons was able to accomplish more than the family with two. This phenomenon has led Professor T. W. Schultz to refer to children as "the poor man's capital.")

The LDCs need more than physical labor. They need labor that is well-fed, better educated, and trained to perform a variety of tasks. The peasant farmer must be able to move into alternative employments where his toil can be effectively combined with other factors to yield larger volumes of consumer goods. The mechanism for making the change requires capital and skill.

Capital

Capital is a crucial variable in all economic growth processes. It is itself produced, but then it is used to produce still more. The problem is finding the surplus necessary to accumulate the early forms of capital. Capital is scarce in the LDCs. While U.S. industrial workers have machines, tools, buildings, sources of power, roads, and communication systems, the worker in an LDC may have only a single tool, no roof over his head, and no way to get his product to market.

Robinson Crusoe had a serious problem after he was shipwrecked on his tropical island. Should he give up eating roots and berries for a day while he built a fish trap? Building the trap is capital formation. It is producing an item that is not consumed but is used to produce other items for consumption. Since Crusoe had no surplus of food to use while building the trap, he would have to go hungry while he built it. Once the trap was built, however, he would not have to spend all day gathering food. He could divert attention to producing other things like clothing and leisure.

The LDCs are in a similar position. They must devote all their energies to staying alive. Once the work force produces food, clothing, and shelter, there is no physical or financial energy left to build schools, roads, hospitals, or factories. To produce capital facilities it would be necessary to cut back production of necessities. The LDC would have to go without food or some other consumer-oriented item while its energies were diverted to the production of a cement plant, a steel mill, or a school. In most LDCs there is no way to create a surplus of food and shelter to sustain the population while capital facilities are being formed.

Market economies that are reasonably well developed (Canada, New Zealand, Japan, West Germany, and France, for example) use the market mechanism to help accumulate capital. In these nations, the savings of individuals are funneled into financial intermediaries and then into investment opportunities where they are used to build more houses, add to the stock of machines, and develop new modes of transportation. The circular flow in Figure 33-1 illustrates the mechanism through which households save and transfer the savings to others for capital-forming activities.

No similar mechanism is present in the LDCs. Even in those countries that try to use the market as a method of expressing choices and allocating resources, there are no well-developed systems for moving accumulated savings from households to firms.

Figure 33-1 The Circular Flow, Savings, and Investment in a Market Economy

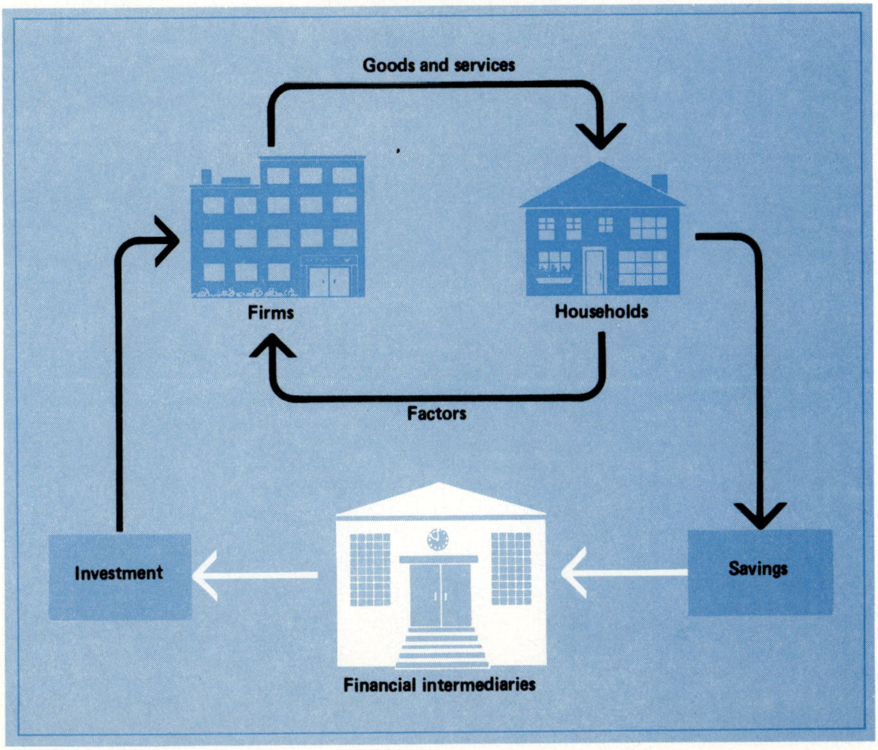

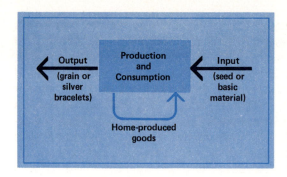

**Figure 33-2
The Firm/Household in a Primitive Economy**

In fact, two problems prevent accumulating surpluses at all. One stems from the organization of production, and the second from people's reluctance to release savings to others. In underdeveloped economies, producing and consuming are done by the same actor. Thus, the circular flow is replaced by a single unit representing both the producing firm and the consuming household (Figure 33-2). Most economic activity is conducted by and for the people in the unit. Some inputs come in and some products flow out, but the essential degree of interdependence is not present. Usually, no savings are accumulated, so no surplus is made available to firms, entrepreneurs, and governments outside this extremely local system.

Even where some market transactions take place and some interdependence has developed, the governments and entrepreneurs have a difficult time convincing the firm/households to release or lend out any savings they may have accumulated. Because of political instability, poor rules for protecting investments and general reluctance to let wealth flow beyond their own vision, the citizens of LDCs have preferred to hold any savings they amass in the form of jewels, precious metals, and land rather than let it be used to build impersonal items like hospitals and flood-control dams.

Capital, perhaps the most important single factor affecting growth and development, is very difficult to accumulate in poorly developed economies. There is little surplus to be transformed into capital, the institutional mechanisms are not always present, and there is no incentive to lend.

Entrepreneurship

The willingness and the capacity to take risks have played an important part in the progress of all developed countries. In the Western nations, risk taking is decentralized and individuals can invest in whatever economic activities they wish as long as they do not violate the law or infringe on the rights of others. As a result of opportunity plus the drive for individual success plus a moral code that venerates profit and success, a large entrepreneurial class has appeared. This group of specialized risk takers uses all varieties of resources to produce and distribute most of the output of the market economies.

In the developed *centralized* economies (Russia, China, and parts of Eastern Europe), the central government has become the entrepreneur and has assumed the function of risk taker. Rather than an individual, it is a state agency that decides to commit certain resources to egg or cabbage production. Sometimes the agency's goals are met, and other times production falls short of anticipated levels.

Regardless of who makes the decisions, who pays the costs, or who receives the rewards, risk taking is an important ingredient of economic change and progress. The LDCs often lack appropriate mechanisms and reward systems for entrepreneurs. The people in an LDC may be locked into a traditional pattern of behavior. A family may know its income will be higher if it shifts from one activity to another but refuse to make the change because of a slight chance of failure—a failure from which there is no recourse. This inability or unwillingness to take risks maintains the status quo and inhibits most kinds of progress.

Growth and development in any nation have always called for reorganizing the factors of production and reordering society. In the last few centuries, particularly since the Renaissance, some nations have managed in this way to achieve immense gains in the numbers of material things available for their citizens. England and France changed slowly from pastoral economies to industrial economies. Other countries, notably Russia beginning in 1918 and China beginning in 1948, went through large-scale internal convulsions before the process of change could begin. In all cases, the changes brought new rules, new ways of combining factors, and new mixes of outputs. A developing society is a changing one—one in which traditional roles are continually replaced by new combinations of economic, social, and political activities.

Development Strategies

Economists and politicians disagree among themselves and with each other on the best way for an LDC to start the growth process. Some argue that a nation should specialize; others say it should diversify. Some say it should become a market economy, others say the planned economies seem to grow faster. In 1977, it is safe to say that all of these contentions can be supported. The only *policy* that seems certain is one of tailoring the program to the needs of the nation. However unique their needs may be, most developing nations have to make choices about four issues: (1) the role and organization of agriculture, (2) population growth, (3) balanced or unbalanced growth, and (4) sources of capital.

The Role of Agriculture

One characteristic defining an LDC is the large proportion of the labor force that must be engaged in food production. In the early 1970s, over two-thirds of the populations of Cambodia, Sierra Leone, Tanzania, Thailand, Turkey, and North Vietnam were farmers. In another 18 nations, over half the population was so engaged. Admittedly, a nation must tend to first things first and in any society eating is high on the list of important things to do. However, the productive techniques used in primitive agricultural systems waste large amounts of labor and/or land. In some nations, the practice of dividing fields into equal pieces for all one's heirs has resulted in plots too small to cultivate efficiently. If these plots were collected into larger units, machines could replace hand- or animal-powered techniques, row rather than broadcast cultivation methods could be used, and the total output of food could increase.

In other areas, particularly the remnants of the nineteenth-century colonial empires, land is held in acreages too large to permit effective management. In these nations plantation farming of coffee, rubber, tea, and sugar cane prevents individuals from owning and cultivating land. The land is worked by a handful of managers and their low-paid farm hands. In this case too, land reform could arrange land into more efficient units.

Agriculture has the capacity to hide large amounts of unemployment. Two-thirds of the population may indeed be needed to bring in the crop each autumn, and nearly as many workers may be needed to plant the crop each spring. But harvesting and planting take only a few days. The labor force must spend the remainder of the year trying to find useful things to do. This entrapment of the labor force in rural areas is an impediment to industrial growth. Industry, especially in its formative stages,

---

Too Much Agricultural Progress?

Some people have argued that too much agricultural progress will add to the already strong centripetal forces that are causing people to concentrate in the urban areas of the world. Twelve million people now reside in the greater Mexico City area. Many of these inhabitants are recent migrants from the agricultural countryside, subsistence farmers forced from the land by the advent of irrigation to the Papaloapan River Valley. If there is no industrial need for them in the city, they become beggars and live in wretched slums.

Most LDC's do need structural changes in their agricultural industries. These changes will bring increased food production, a wider distribution of land ownership, and a larger labor force for industrial development. These potential gains can turn into liabilities, however, if no industrial opportunities are available for labor released from agriculture.

needs labor. This labor must be released from agriculture. Industrial development is, then, intimately bound up with agricultural development. One cannot proceed without the other.

Population Control

Demographers are quick to point out that the number of people inhabiting the earth is growing very rapidly and that the *rate* of population growth is also increasing. The second fact is the more ominous of the two. Prior to 1850, there were fewer than 1 billion people on earth. The second billion was reached in about 1930, the third billion in 1960. Now there are 4 billion people competing for food, space, and comfort. If population continues to grow as it has, the turn of the twenty-first century will be witnessed by 7 billion people, and 13 billion will be present in 2050.

There is little doubt that population growth and economic growth are interrelated, but the relationship is often misunderstood. Many LDCs, especially those in Asia and Africa, have very high birth rates and declining death rates. The result is high rates of population increase. Even though the increase in population puts strain on the food supply, these nations often do not wish to consider active campaigns to reduce the rate of population growth. They argue that the populations of most developed nations increased rapidly with development and that it was only after development had occurred that the rate of population growth began to slow. The facts of this argument cannot be disputed, but the whole matter represents a confusion of cause and effect. Rapid population growth did not *cause* industrialization, but was the first noticeable effect of it. Later, as industrialization began to take hold, labor forces began to value leisure and to depend on something other than large families to maintain them in their old age. At this point, family size began to drop in the developed nations. The LDCs do not need more people to spur industrial output. In point of fact, many of them have made significant increases in the output of goods and services only to see these increases spread among increased numbers of people, leaving no net gain in per capita output.

Today, population in Asia is growing at a rate of 2 percent per year. At that rate, the population will double in approximately 35 years.[3] In Africa, population grows at 2.4 percent per year and in Latin America, 2.9 percent per year. Development—the provision of more goods and services to more people—could be checked. But planned parenthood is a hard concept for an illiterate population to accept. Moreover, governments are reluctant to interfere with such a personal decision as whether or not to bear children. Although most planners and most officials know the consequences of al-

---

[3] If the annual rate of population growth is known, the number of years required for the population to double can be approximated by dividing the annual percentage increase into 72. Thus, if population is increasing by 12 percent per year, it will double in about 6 years (72 ÷ 12 = 6). If population is growing at 3.6 percent per year, it will double in 20 years.

lowing population growth to go unchecked, few are able to bring forth an acceptable method of dealing with the problem.

Balanced or Unbalanced Growth?

The economist-planner-policy-maker can become frustrated with the population problem and leave it to the demographers. The economist cannot, however, avoid the question of whether a nation should follow a path of balanced or unbalanced growth. Balanced and unbalanced growth are two different strategies for development. Choosing one or the other is surely the proper domain of the economist, but even here economists falter and disagree. Some favor one policy; others favor another.

A policy of balanced growth suggests that a developing nation should maintain somewhat stable relationships among the agricultural, industrial, and commercial sectors of its economy. This fits with the idea that as laborers are released from agriculture they should be absorbed into other industries. The other industries will make a variety of things like shoes, furniture, automobile radios, and drill presses. The mix of industries will provide a mix of goods for the country's consumers.

Advocates of balanced growth point out that as the number of things produced at home increases, a nation's dependence on international trade diminishes and it need not be so concerned about balance-of-payments problems. No nation likes to be dependent, especially in this modern era of strong national pride, and balanced growth among several industries allows the possibility of independence.

One difficulty associated with a goal of balanced growth is that it can be carried to foolish extremes. Those who favor balanced growth sometimes confuse economic sense with national pride and suggest that the domestic economy must have a well developed steel industry, plenty of hydroelectric power, first-rate universities, and a national airline complete with jumbo jets. LDCs cannot usually afford the capital expenditures needed to promote development in every industry. If they could, instant development would be within their grasp. The realistic approach is to change the mix of industries.

A reasonable variation of balanced growth proposes growth in a few very broad industries. It recognizes that an orderly transition from an agrarian society to one that produces manufactured goods and services does not require that the LDC become self-sufficient in the production of everything.

An unbalanced growth policy adheres to the law of comparative advantage. If a nation can produce tin, it should specialize in tin, become very efficient at producing tin, sell the tin to other nations, and use the foreign exchange to purchase whatever else it may need. An unbalanced growth scheme is in harmony with many other dictates of rational economic choice. It says "concentrate on what you can do best." Unbalanced growth is not as glamorous as balanced growth. It does nothing to break the nation's dependence on other nations. If the LDC's economy is based on an extractive industry, a policy of unbalanced growth may keep laborers in agriculture or mining or fishing.

The capital requirements of unbalanced growth are much lower than those of balanced growth. The risks, while of a completely different sort, are at least as high. In balanced growth, risk arises from spreading capital too thin and not developing any single industry to an acceptable level of efficiency. In unbalanced growth the risk comes from external sources. If all a nation's hopes are centered on increasing the output and exportation of copper and suddenly the world price of copper tumbles to an unprecedented low, the country suffers an unimaginable setback. It cannot sell its copper, therefore it cannot generate the foreign exchange needed to buy food, fuel, and manufactured goods.

Which policy is better? No one can say for sure. In recent years, China has performed quite well with its policy of balanced growth. In 1948, when the Revolution finally drove Chiang to Taiwan and left Mao firmly in charge, the nation was a shambles. Much of the industrial plant had been destroyed and it seemed only reasonable that unbalanced growth would start in the agricultural industry. China, however, had other ideas. Backyard blast furnaces were used to start a steel industry, schools were begun to educate the people, millions of miles of roads were built, and national output of both capital and consumer goods began to climb steadily. Considering that the nation started with nothing but labor and undeveloped natural resources, it has done very well.

Kuwait has taken exactly the opposite course. It is one of the newly rich oil producers that seems to need only drill another well if it requires more money. While Kuwait has spent lavishly on air-conditioned automobiles, expensive foods, and luxury items, it has made no real effort to expand industrial development into nonpetroleum areas or to develop its own agricultural capacity. It is content with the success it has achieved in oil, in unbalanced growth. As long as Europe remains a major importer of oil, and as long as the oil reserves hold out, Kuwait will continue to prosper.

Like China, Brazil is a huge country. It has a much smaller population than China, but its vast Amazon Basin remains one of the world's largest relatively unexploited geographic regions. In the 1950s, Brazil embarked on an unsuccessful policy of balanced growth. Internal economic strife, labor–management clashes, very high rates of inflation and an untrained labor force blocked the nation's efforts. In spite of its ambitions and rather careful planning, Brazil remains among the very poor nations of the world.

Nicaragua has gambled on unbalanced growth. The nation is in a tropical climate and has both the soil and the weather needed to produce bananas and other very specialized crops. The labor force has been engaged in agricultural production for many decades, so it knows how to cultivate, harvest, and pack these crops. Nicaragua has tried unsuccessfully to profit from this comparative advantage. Wide fluctuations in world prices, dominance by monopolist landholders, and crop diseases have kept it from earning the foreign exchange needed to make unbalanced growth work. The nation remains poor and the Nicaraguan people continue to live close to the subsistence level.

The argument over balanced and unbalanced growth is not likely to be settled very soon. China made one policy work because it was starting from point zero and because the Chinese people were willing to make sacrifices and accept firm central control over their personal behavior. Kuwait made another policy work because the nation was fortunate enough to have access to a single, very valuable resource. The experiences of Brazil and Nicaragua show that results cannot be guaranteed or transferred to other nations.

Sources of Capital

The need for capital has been discussed earlier in this chapter and repeatedly throughout the book. The *need* for capital is not at issue here. The question is: How can an LDC *obtain* the capital it needs to develop either the public or the private sectors of its economy? Two options are open. It can call upon its own citizens to generate savings to use for capital formation, or it can ask other nations to contribute capital through loans, grants, or gifts.

If a nation decides to depend upon internal sources of capital, it must ask its citizens to generate a surplus that can be taken from some individuals and given to others. After the Russian Revolution of 1918 had worked itself out and a reasonably stable government had come to the USSR, that nation imposed extreme sacrifices on all of its citizens. Consumption was cut to near-subsistence levels, and everyone was forced to produce as much as possible given the limited resources that were available. The difference between what was produced and what was consumed—the surplus—was used by the state as the basis for capital formation. The process was harsh at first but eventually resulted in a series of plans for production, consumption, and saving. These plans achieved modest success in the late 1950s and the forced-saving strategy began to pay off. Russia became a developed nation.

Forced saving can be accomplished only under dictatorial or central rule. Thus, the Eastern bloc has the option of using this method of capital formation. The Western nations do not often use force to extract savings from their citizens, though they do often use tax schemes and coercion. Spain, a Western nation under dictatorial rule, tried to use taxing to accumulate surpluses. Great Britain, though a developed nation, is now trying to extract savings from her citizens to help pay international debts and recover from severe inflationary and balance-of-payments problems.

Grants and loans from other nations appear to be a much easier way of accumulating capital. The funds can be used immediately to purchase

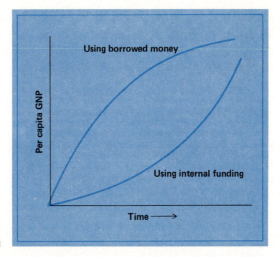

**Figure 33-3
Time Paths of Growth**

and install capital equipment, so the developing nation gets an instant boost in output and does not have to wait for several years while domestic savings are generated. This capital supplied by other nations does not, however, come free.

If the imported capital comes in the form of a loan, part of the gains in productivity will have to be used to pay it off. Figure 33-3 shows two time paths of growth in an LDC. The lower path shows slow initial growth, eventually gaining momentum and becoming quite rapid. This is the kind of growth path that may be expected when domestic sources of savings and investment capital are used for financing. The upper growth path shows an immediate spurt in growth but one that gradually tapers off. This path would be expected if borrowed funds were used for capital formation. Immediate, fast growth would be followed by a period during which the loan was being repaid so the net contribution to per capita GNP would therefore be reduced.

A developing nation may not wish to use borrowed capital because of the possibility of dependence on or control by another nation. Canadians have been wary about U.S. involvement in the Canadian economy, and now U.S. citizens are apprehensive about Japanese and Middle Eastern investment in U.S. firms and property. This is an especially serious consideration in the LDCs, where unstable governments fear political and economic takeovers and a single large foreign investment may represent a huge proportion of all investment in the nation's economy.

A grant differs from a loan in two important respects. First, a grant is a gift and does not have to be repaid. Second, a grant is frequently tied to a particular activity. Thus, the Soviet Union gave India grants to develop steel mills and cement plants. Grants are free, but they do not allow flexibility. The grants that are tied to specific purposes provide an increase in the size of a nation's capital plant, but they are restricted and often reflect the granting nation's desires rather than the developing nation's needs. It is not yet clear whether, on balance, building the Aswan dam on the Nile was good for Egypt or the Egyptian people. It was financed by a grant from the USSR because that government believed that Egypt needed flood control and hydro power.[4]

Regardless of source, capital remains the key to development, and it also poses an intractable problem in development strategy. If it is internally generated, the domestic population must suffer reductions in present income in the hope that they will be more than offset by future gains. If the capital flows in from abroad, it may lead to loss of control or be directed at purposes other than the recipient nation's needs.

U.S. Foreign Aid

The United States has exported large sums of aid to foreign nations, in the form of loans, grants, and technical aid. In the 15 years following World War II, the United States gave over $90 billion to developing and reconstructing nations. At present, foreign aid amounts to approximately $2 billion per year—less than .25 percent of GNP.

Most nonmilitary U.S. aid flows to other nations through technical assistance programs, food-sharing programs, and disaster relief. The technical assistance, often conducted under the auspices of AID, includes programs to develop public capital facilities such as highways, hospitals, and universities as well as educational programs. The food sharing is carried out under Public Law 480, a 1954 law that allows foreign nations to purchase U.S. food surpluses using their own currencies rather than foreign exchange. In 1974, food valued at $760 million was sold to other nations under this law.

The question remains: Should the United States do more? The economist is not able to answer this question. Surely the United States *could* contribute more to help Kenya, Sri Lanka, Turkey, and 175 other LDCs. In earlier years it contributed much more than one quarter of one percent of its GNP to these purposes. However, the United States is a restless nation. It is beset by internal economic problems and is having severe difficulty financing all the things it wants to do. The voters are reluctant to send more money abroad. And U.S. voters are complaining that *other* nations

---

[4] The Aswan dam has been controversial for many years. It was first designed and declared to be beneficial by U.S. engineers and economists. The United States, however, refused to fund the project. Amid much bickering over who had the right to build the facility, the USSR appropriated monies and began construction. After it had begun, public and private efforts in the United States were used to gather the funds needed to save the cultural artifacts along the river, like the Rameses Tombs. Now it is becoming clear that the dam is at best a mixed blessing, since it caused changes in the river that are a problem to farmers and boatmen.

are not doing enough to help the LDCs. Some nations, however, including Belgium, West Germany, the Netherlands, Australia, and France, use a greater percentage of their GNP on foreign aid than the United States does. It seems that the United States and Kuwait could do more, but would more be enough? How to help the LDCs is one of the most complex economic puzzles of the late twentieth century.

Summary

1 Over half the people in the world live in nations with less than $500 per capita GNP per year.
2 There is no agreement on what makes a nation poor, but all poor nations display some of the same characteristics. Among the most prominent are: a high proportion of the labor force in agriculture, rapid population growth, and scarcity of capital.
3 The very poor nations are growing very slowly, but the intermediate nations are growing more rapidly than even the wealthy nations.
4 Several factors affect the productivity and growth of the LDCs. Prominent among them are the availability of economic resources—land, labor, capital, and entrepreneurship.
5 The LDCs will probably have to reorganize agriculture to feed their growing populations and still release laborers for absorption into the industrial labor force. But if the peasants released from farming cannot be employed elsewhere, they will congregate in urban slums.
6 Population growth is misunderstood by many planners. If not checked, it could consume any growth in output, leaving a nation no better off than before.
7 Balanced growth and unbalanced growth are alternative strategies. One says that all sectors of the economy should develop together; the other relies on the law of comparative advantage.
8 Capital can be generated at home or through loans from other nations. If it is raised at home, growth may be delayed. If it is borrowed, the debt will have to be repaid at some future date.
9 The United States presently contributes less than one fourth of one percent of its GNP to foreign aid.

Exercises

1 Explain these important words and concepts:
    LDC   balanced growth
    underemployment   unbalanced growth
    poor man's capital loans and grants
    capital formation   Public Law 480
2 The world is just emerging from a period of environmental crisis and entering one of food crisis. During the environmental crisis, pesticides, herbicides, some kinds of fertilizers, and some agricultural practices were banned because they were damaging to wildlife or to the fragile ecology of a particular locale. Some of these restrictions cut back (or at

least made more expensive) the world's capacity to produce food. How should the tradeoff between a rare bird and more food be weighed? Is this disposition likely to change as one moves from a wealthy nation to a poor one? Which view is correct?

3 The world is divided into rich people and poor people. The United States is also divided into rich and poor. Can "solutions" to the U.S. poverty problem be transferred for use in Laos and Uganda? Why or why not?

4 Improved health and sanitation standards are needed in most LDCs. If such standards are implemented, death rates will drop and population will grow even faster. Can it then be argued that health and sanitation problems should be ignored?

5 What arguments can be gathered to support a program of forced saving? What counter-arguments can be suggested?

6 A technical expert from a U.S. consulting firm is called to an LDC and given this list:

steel mills
rapid transit in the cities
birth-control clinics
land reform

education in modern agriculture
a nationwide highway system
a national airline

He is told that the developing nation can have some but not all of the items on the list. How should they be ordered? Why? Would the order change from one LDC to another?

7 A poor family in the backwoods of Kentucky may earn only $500 per year. Is this family's problem much different from that of the low-income family in Ethiopia? Are they both in the same vicious cycle of poverty?

A Contemporary Problem

The Green Revolution

For about a century, scientists have been trying to improve on nature through plant breeding. Their experiments have produced hybrid roses like the delicately colored Peace Rose that is so popular in U.S. gardens. Plant breeding also gave us the seedless watermelon, the pear tomato, drought-resistant grain sorghums, and scores of common ornamental plants. The most crucial results of modern plant breeding are not flowers, fancy fruits, or uniformly shaped ornamental shrubs. They are the hybrid rices, wheats, and corns that could feed the world. These crop varieties can double and triple the yield of grain crops in the world today.

The first of these high-yielding varieties were made available to the less developed countries in the early 1960s. Their introduction triggered a "green revolution" because it was thought that the yields accompanying these new varieties would forestall starvation and allow many LDCs to start on the path to development. At first, the plant breeders who had produced the new grains and cereals were hopeful. Some 200 acres of the new varieties were planted on Asian farms in 1964. By 1968, more than 20 million acres were producing the crops; in 1973, some 39 million acres of

Asian farms were producing high-yield, high-performance hybrid corn, rice, or wheat.

The green revolution has not worked out as well as planned. The crops are as good as their developers predicted, but the agrarian societies they were put into can absorb neither the changes in farming practices nor the changes in physical yields of the crop. Problems have developed on both the input and the product side of the market.

The hybrids are very sensitive crops, much more sensitive than the traditional grains they replaced. While the traditional varieties required very little care, the new plants required skilled application of water, fertilizer, and pesticides. The LDCs needed the increased output, but they did not have the technical capacity to irrigate much farmland, to transport millions of tons of fertilizers to agricultural areas, or to teach farmers how to use the fertilizer. The proper approach seemed to be growing the new crops in new areas, away from traditional crops. Fields were irrigated and prepared for this purpose in several nations. Then an unanticipated difficulty arose. The breeders had developed very productive plants, but the plants were not immune to local plant diseases. Farmers in many areas were ruined when disease struck the crops and, since the whole area was planted to one crop, the whole area was ruined. Now, after 15 years of actual field use, a close examination of the green revolution is in order. On balance, has it been good or bad?

There is no question that Algeria, Botswana, Bolivia, Chile, Honduras, Cambodia, and Turkey all need more food. If they could have more rice, corn, and wheat, they could become more productive and could divert some labor into the production of capital facilities—perhaps roads, irrigation projects, or adult education programs. But these nations have serious problems. Even if the technical problems of water, fertilizers, and pesticides can be solved, there are cultural and economic barriers to the introduction of new crops.

Among the economic barriers are the fear of risk and the concentration of productive activity into the hands of a few people. Farmers in traditional societies fear change because there is no margin for error. The traditional means of production has kept the family alive for generations and there is no guarantee that a change will bring improvement. On the contrary, a crop failure in the first year will mean starvation. Second, nations fear that the new crops will be adopted only by the already-successful farmers who, because they can afford to take the chance, will plant their own farms and turn huge harvests into immediate and large profits. The profits in turn can be used to buy out smaller, less fortunate farmers. The result will be the rich getting richer while the poor barely maintain themselves or drop to even lower income levels as their land holdings move into the hands of others.

The proponents of the green revolution have pondered these questions for 15 years, and are now admitting that the original aims of the revolution were a bit optimistic. They did not include the second generation of problems that came with developing the social overhead capital needed to make the program work, and they did not anticipate the social problems that have accompanied the change in farming practices.

The evidence is not all in. The green revolution must be called a mixed blessing for now. Its advocates are hoping that the increased yields will buy time—time before starvation strikes the poor and hungry nations of the world. Its detractors are claiming that changing the entire mode of production will destroy the social fabric of the underdeveloped nations. Only time will tell for sure, and it seems reasonable to gamble that well-fed people will be more willing to solve problems than starving people.

34 The Migration of Labor

We have seen throughout this book that an economic system is a vast mechanism that gathers and processes data. If it is a market system, it assimilates data about prices, then makes this information available to firms and households so that they can adjust their production, purchases, and sales. Their adjustments, leading toward equilibrium, require resources to move from one production activity to another. In the macroeconomy, equilibrium occurs when aggregate expenditures are exactly offset by aggregate income. In the microeconomy, equilibrium comes when no firm is earning supernormal profits and when the marginal expenditure of a household for each item consumed yields the same contribution to the household's total utility.

Equilibrium is a temporary phenomenon, however. An industrial economy is continually responding to changes in the weather, technological advances, political instability, and consumer preferences. The resulting adjustments in production plans cause returns to some resources to increase and returns to others to decrease. When the automobile took the place of the horse, the mechanic's wages rose and the harness maker's wages fell. The village blacksmith moved from his forge and anvil in the rural community and became the mechanic in the large repair shop beside the interstate highway.

In the U.S. economy, most adjustments are small and affect only a few people. A chrome decorated automobile model is phased out and the value of chromium falls. The people who sell chromium and the people who install it suffer reductions in their incomes. But another model is soon phased in and the value of paint or vinyl increases because it is used in place of chrome. Again, a few people are affected as the price signals move out through the various sectors of the economy that depend on the chromium substitutes.

Occasionally, major change rocks the economy. The space program creates a huge demand for engineers in Florida, Texas, and California, so the universities expand enrollments and turn out more engineers. Engineers heed the price signals and move to Cape Canaveral, Houston, and Los Angeles. The contract for the U.S. supersonic transport is cancelled, so Boeing employees in Seattle are left without incomes. They adjust with their feet, moving to wherever jobs can be found. The shock of a major change can throw hundreds of families out of work. Since capital will not ordinarily move toward the unemployed, the unemployed must move to the capital if they are to have incomes. The movement of people is the harshest kind of economic adjustment.

This chapter is about the adjustments surrounding the movement of people from one area (or nation) to another. It is divided into parts dealing with the causes of migration, the kinds of migration, the effects of migration on areas that gain and on areas that lose population, and a recapitulation of the great international migrations that have influenced economic development in the United States.

Causes of Migration

Migration occurs when people can no longer cope with their present circumstances, or when they are lured to a situation they believe to be superior. The reasons for migrating may be social, political, health-related, or economic. If economics is defined to include the range of choices as well as the process of choosing, nearly all migrations can be cast in economic terms. Using this broad definition, the German Jews left Europe in the 1930s to escape the incredibly severe limitations on their choices that were imposed by the Nazis. The anti-Communists left the Cambodian Penninsula in 1974 so that they might have choices other than imprisonment.

In a more narrow conceptualization of economics, migration stems from disequilibrium—a situation in which labor is earning less in one place than it could in another. The problem is shown in Figure 34–1. The two graphs show the hypothetical demand curves for labor in two parts of the nation. The broken white lines in the left-hand graph show that there are 8,000 farm workers in the South and that they can expect to earn only $1.50 per hour. The broken lines in the right-hand graph show that in the

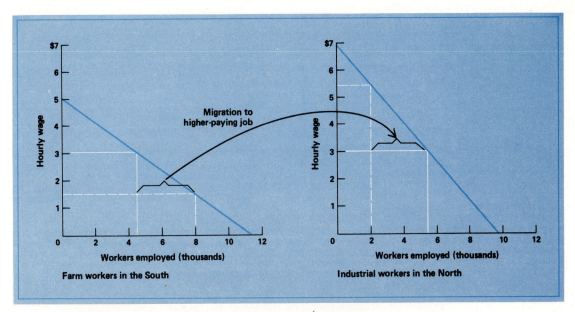

Figure 34-1 An Economic Cause for Migration

industrial North, labor is scarce and the 2,000 workers who are there earn $5.50 per hour. This large differential in wages causes workers to migrate from South to North. Labor moves from low pay to high pay. If the market is working perfectly, migration will continue until wages are the same in the two markets ($3.00 per hour) and 4,500 workers are in the South and 5,500 are in the North. The equilibrium of the two labor markets is shown by the solid white lines in either side of the figure.

Economic forces can act to "push" or to "pull" people from one place to another. The millions of Southern blacks who moved to the North in the 1940s and 1950s were pushed out of agriculture by the invention of the mechanical cotton picker. No longer needed to help bring in the region's major crop, they left an area that offered few opportunities and moved to an area that offered more. They left a region where the marginal productivity of their labor was very low, and moved to one where their labor had higher value at the margin.

The Joad family, in John Steinbeck's 1939 novel *The Grapes of Wrath,* were beset by poverty on their Oklahoma farm. In a sense, they were pushed out by drought and mechanization, but once out, they were pulled to California by the fantasy that flowers grew beside every street there, fruits and vegetables were available in every backyard, and any kind of employment could be had for the asking.

Regardless of cause (economic or noneconomic) or type (push or pull), migration is a difficult experience for most families. It requires leaving what is familiar and comfortable and stepping into something that is unknown and harsh. The person who moves must leave behind friends, the favorite rose bushes, and a social network that includes doctors, lawyers, ministers, and necessary adversaries. In a new locale there is a struggle to reestablish this network—to find a new neighborhood, school, grocery store, and doctor. All such problems are costs associated with migration.

Because so many costs are associated with migrating, some people choose to accept a lower wage instead. When a labor market is in disequilibrium because of high wages in Tulsa and low wages in Miami, workers may stay in Miami, simply because moving to Tulsa is too expensive. Similarly, rural people who till the soil, mine coal, fish, and cut timber are often reluctant to leave the rustic settings of their homes. They are a traditional people who value close contact with nature, intimate relationships with friends, and a slow pace of life. They stay in place even when they know higher earnings might be had in urban areas.

This tendency to stay in place indicates that the labor market is imperfect and does not always respond to price signals. Laborers do not flow from one area to another so easily as coal or woolen underwear or power-driven lawn mowers. In fact, moving carries so many *nonmonetary costs* that migration can be viewed as the adjustment of last resort.

Nonmonetary costs are costs not reckoned in dollars and cents. The loss of a friend is a cost, but it is not included in any demand-and-supply schedule. Moving from one town to another always involves nonmonetary costs.

Patterns of Migration

Migration takes many patterns. Some, like the migration of Asians across the northern polar cap 30,000 years ago, have had consequences so far-reaching as to be almost incomprehensible. That migration peopled the Western hemisphere. Others, like the Joneses moving from Duluth to Madison, usually have only local consequences that are easily absorbed by the two towns. Between these extremes are several general kinds of migration.

Migrating to a Frontier

A frontier is a gateway to an area that has many natural resources but few capital and labor resources to work them. The American frontier to the West in both the United States and Canada was crying for labor during the nineteenth century. In both countries there was land to be farmed, forests to be cut, and minerals to be taken from the earth, but entrepreneurs had not yet left the cities and the general comfort of the East to work the resources beyond the frontier.

Work on the frontier was hard and long, but it brought rewards that were sometimes greater than those available to the same people in the industrial cities of the East. Moreover, the frontier acted as a safety valve for social conflict in the U.S. and Canadian economies. When the cities became crowded and workers could not find jobs there, they left to become the farmers, miners, woodsmen, and traders who opened the heartland.

There are no continents left to settle and no frontiers like the Cherokee Strip are available to cause large movements of people in the world today. But *economic* fronters do exist. Australia needs more people to open its interior, and the parts of Russia lying east of the Urals are still short of people. Before the forests of Siberia can become economic goods, people will have to migrate into them and establish logging communities, sawmills, and transportation networks.

But economic frontiers do exist. Australia's vast interior has much land but no people to work it and Siberia has some of the largest forests in the world. It needs only the sawmills and the people to run them. New communities, new transportation networks and much social overhead capital will be needed to develop these frontiers. Even the United States still has some economic frontiers. The coal fields of Eastern Montana and the oil shale regions of Colorado and Utah are begging for people and capital to make use of these resources in the production of energy. The Alaska pipeline has opened a frontier on the north slopes of Prudhoe Bay. Oil workers, investment capital, and all the supporting services are moving to that area to take advantage of the opportunity to earn supernormal profits.

Rural to Urban Migration

People all over the world are migrating to cities. In ultracapitalist Japan, ex-farmers and peasants are congregating in cities to work, avoid hunger, or be close to medical care. In China, the archetypical communist nation today, people are moving from farm to city. In middle-of-the-road Italy, people are moving to town. The reason is the same in all nations: agricultural revolution.

A traditional, peasant agriculture keeps factors locked together in relatively fixed proportions. A farmer can alter the amount of seed planted or change the frequency of irrigation, but in most of the world one family is required to operate one farm. With technical change, the traditional rules are broken. A small tractor replaces labor, or changes the crops that are grown. When this occurs, fixed inputs become variable, and once they are variable the factors can move. In many nations the mechanization of agriculture has changed labor from a fixed to a variable factor and has broken the traditional tie to the soil. Once this tie is broken, there is little reason for sons and uncles and cousins to remain near the family farm, and they move out of agriculture and into the cities. Thus the greater metropolitan areas of Mexico City, Tokyo, and Calcutta each have 12 million or more residents.

The picture in industrial economies is not altogether different. Even in nonagricultural sectors, there are forces propelling firms and individuals from small towns into large towns. Very few firms in the U.S. economy are in industries that even approach competition. Instead, they are parts of oligopolies, or they are in monopolistically competitive industries. If such a firm is to succeed it must know about its rivals. To gain information, the firm might move to the city and take its employees with it, thus intensifying the concentration of population in metropolitan areas.[1]

---

[1]It is exactly this phenomenon that has given rise to concentration of industries such as the garment industry in New York City, the aircraft industry in Wichita, Kansas, the auto industry in Michigan, and the major banking industries in New York, Chicago, and San Francisco.

Following a Migration Path

Each spring, thousands of migrant workers begin the annual grain harvest in southern Texas. When the grain in Texas is harvested, the combines, swathers, and trucks associated with the harvest roll into Oklahoma, then into Kansas, Nebraska, the Dakotas, and Montana. Finally, in the late autumn months, the harvest ends in Canada's prairie provinces. The trip takes five to seven months. When the harvest is over, the equipment is driven or hauled back to Texas to wait for another spring and another crop. This migration is planned and regular. It differs from other migrations in that it is seasonal. The families in the harvest crews are not uprooted and relocated; they simply move their households, schools, and "societies" each day or each week. In an economic context, this migration has much in common with the other kinds. The move is made in response to opportunity. As opportunities close in Texas, they open in Oklahoma; when they close in Oklahoma, they open in Kansas. The migrants have huge investments in very specialized machines, which must be moved to be kept busy; so the pattern of migration is traced each year. The grain-threshing crews are the nomads of the industrial world.

International Migration

In the past three decades, more than 50 million people have moved from one nation to another, in response to technological and institutional change, differential rates of economic development among nations, political dissonance, and personal preferences. Thirty years ago, the upheaval of World War II had left millions of persons in Europe and Asia displaced and homeless. They moved from devastated nations where there was no possibility of employment to nations where they could work. Unable to find opportunity among ruins, they migrated to where factories and social overhead capital were intact and they could be reasonably productive. As the destroyed economies came back to life, they needed labor—more than their own populations could supply. In response, millions of workers moved from Italy and Greece to West Germany. The change was economically based. The migrants were moving from low-wage areas to high-wage areas.

Not all international movements of people are so orderly. When the potato famine struck Ireland in 1846, the staple food of that nation was destroyed. Had the crop failure lasted only one year, the Irish population might have survived. But the crop failed in 1847, 1848, and again in 1849. No significant potato crop was harvested until 1852. No country, old or new, peasant or industrial, can withstand six years of crop failure. The people of Ireland were literally starved into leaving. And leave they did. During the famine more than a million left—most of them bound for North American cities, where there were jobs for men in industrial shops, and where Irish women were in demand as domestic workers.

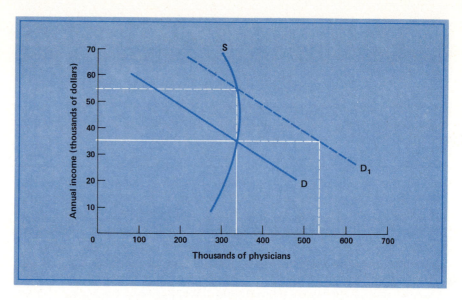

Figure 34-2 The Demand and Supply of Physicians

The Brain Drain

The United States is, by its own calculations, short of physicians and other medical personnel. This shortage has pushed physicians' incomes to very high levels. Demand for physicians and medical services has increased, but in the short run the supply of persons qualified to deliver medical services is very unresponsive to changes in price or income.

The problem is shown in Figure 34-2. Since it takes time to expand medical schools and to train new medical personnel, the supply curve for physicians is nearly vertical. The little slope that it does have is caused by physicians' decisions not to retire, or to move from administrative work back into the practice of medicine. Given the supply of physicians at present levels (slightly more than 340,000), the old demand curve, D, caused the price (income) of physicians to come into equilibrium at about $35,000 per year. But demand has increased to D_1. If the price of physicians remains at $35,000 per year, the economy will demand 540,000. This shortage cannot be removed until the supply curve shifts outward, and that requires time. The disequilibrium between the old demand curve and the new demand curve cannot be removed until more personnel are trained. During this training period, many physicians in other nations see U.S. doctors' incomes climbing to $55,000 (shown by the intersection of S and D_1 in Figure 34-2) and decide to migrate.

Their decision is economically rational. The physicians are being pulled from low-income to high-income areas, and the rules of allocation say that this is correct. However, the physicians' services may be needed much more in India or in Honduras. This capacity of the developed countries to attract highly trained workers and technicians away from LDCs has been called the "brain drain." It is a sophisticated form of migration that is understandable from the individual's point of view but has serious negative consequences for the developing world. No one has yet found how to stop the brain drain short of strict emigration quotas and casual reliance on developed nations not to steal brainpower needed in the LDCs.

Effects of Migration

Migration always shows. If only one or two families move, it shows only among their friends. If many people move, the effects multiply through the economy in a fashion similar to the multiplier effect explained in Chapter 9. If 40 families move from an area, there are 40 vacant houses, the grocer sells groceries to 40 fewer families, and the school has 40 or more fewer pupils. When 40 families move into a community, church pews fill, the golf course is more crowded, the clothier has more business, and the school board worries about adding new classrooms. The effects of emigration are quite different from the effects of immigration.

Emigration

When people leave one area to move to another, the losing area loses in more than one way. For half a century, the rural areas of the United States have sent their children away to become dentists, engineers, and architects. Because there is not enough business for these professions in small communities, the trip away to college is a trip away forever. More recently, especially in the last 25 years, farms have consolidated and the farmers themselves have left to reside in urban areas. The effects on rural areas have been calamitous. Towns have lost vitality, stores have closed, and the value of property has dropped. Storekeepers are no longer happy and eager to serve, but sullen and bitter. They are tied to their shops and are immobile. They would like to sell the store and move themselves, but who would buy a rundown store in a rundown town? Emigration may help those who can move, but it also traps those who are tied to capital.

In other areas, the emigration of one group has meant that the remaining resources are divided among fewer people so that each has a bigger share than before. When workers left Greece to seek jobs in West Germany during the late 1950s, the workers themselves benefited and those who stayed behind benefited too. Families that could barely eke a living from farm or shop were able to do much better when the older sons and daughters left home to work in the rapidly industrializing Ruhr area. Moreover, those who had left often sent money home to their families.

The tragedy of emigration is its abandonment of fixed capital. If a school is designed for 200 students but general emigration leaves only 150, the school is overdesigned and represents a misallocation of resources. If the emigrating families all lived on the same block and no one came to town to fill the houses, the opportunity costs of the houses would become zero, sidewalks would never be used, and sewer, gas, and telephone lines would stand idle. Labor, the adjusting factor, leaves all these unused resources behind, and since the resources are fixed in place there is little that society can do to reclaim them. This price is being paid by societies all over the world as population moves from country to town to city. It is particularly costly in developed nations, where each family has a significant volume of capital associated with the place in which it resides. Moving renders this fixed capital useless.

Immigration

The world is growth-oriented. The whole psyche of Western people is geared toward growth, and what is bigger is automatically considered better, too. When people move to town, the demand for housing rises and rents go up. Owners of rental property—the landlords—are among the first to benefit. Business increases in tempo, and the benefits extend to merchants. More is produced, so those who haul in raw materials and haul out finished products benefit, too.

With all these advantages it takes sober reflection to recognize that growth is not always good. As people congregate in cities, transportation systems strain, school systems bulge, and public utilities are stretched beyond their capacities. Existing capital is used too fast and new capital is hurried into place to satisfy the demands of a burgeoning population. Developers cry for more sewer and water lines, parents cry for more schools, and commuters cry for more public transportation. The result: massive and expensive investment programs, deterioration from overuse in older parts of town, and shoddy, hurry-up work in new neighborhoods.

The asymmetry is startling. When the U.S. population moves from rural to urban areas, it creates an overabundance of capital in one place and a shortage of capital in another. There is waste at both ends of the migration stream. Although the people may be bringing labor markets into equilibrium, they are simultaneously causing disequilibria in the allocation of public resources. Solving private problems intensifies public problems. To date, no satisfactory method of resolving this dilemma has emerged. When it does, it will likely include a population policy that influences where people should live and supplementary policies tending to decentralize industry so that the nation can use its fixed capital more efficiently.

The picture is no brighter in Japan, or Sweden, or South Africa. In these countries, too, migration to the cities leaves large blocks of capital idle and wasted. The sum of the private wisdom of scores of families does not yield a collective wisdom for a whole nation.

Migration and the U.S. Economy

Compared to other nations, the United States has a brief economic history. The nation was settled in the seventeenth century, gained sovereignty in the eighteenth, and industrialized in the nineteenth. It was at first a huge land with ample natural resources, but very few people and very little capital. It needed immigrants from other lands. Accurate data on people, the working force, and immigration are available beginning about 1860. Prior to that time, immigrants came, mainly from Europe, for a variety of reasons. Adverse political or economic circumstances pushed some out of Europe. Others were pulled by the opportunities offered by the new land.

Table 34-1 shows the number of immigrants coming into the United States each year from 1861 to 1920. During this time—the period of high

Table 34-1 Immigration into the United States, 1861–1920
(thousands)

Year	Number of immigrants	Year	Number of immigrants	Year	Number of immigrants
1861	92	1881	669	1901	488
1862	92	1882	789	1902	649
1863	176	1883	603	1903	857
1864	193	1884	519	1904	813
1865	248	1885	395	1905	1,026
1866	319	1886	334	1906	1,101
1867	316	1887	490	1907	1,285
1868	139	1888	547	1908	783
1869	353	1889	444	1909	752
1870	387	1890	455	1910	1,042
1871	321	1891	560	1911	879
1872	405	1892	580	1912	838
1873	460	1893	440	1913	1,198
1874	313	1894	286	1914	1,218
1875	227	1895	259	1915	327
1876	170	1896	343	1916	299
1877	142	1897	231	1917	295
1878	138	1898	229	1918	111
1879	178	1899	312	1919	141
1880	457	1900	449	1920	430

Source: *Historical Statistics of the United States, Colonial Times to 1957.*

immigration—28,592,000 people came. The table shows considerable variation in immigration from year to year. Large influxes came during good times, and the numbers tapered off during recessions. As a result of the economic panic (recession) of 1893, for example, immigration dropped from over 500 thousand in 1891 and 1892 to half that level in 1894 and 1895. The U.S. economy had temporarily lost its vigor and could not offer prospective immigrants such tremendous advantages as previously. With recovery from the panic, immigrant numbers rose again, reaching almost 1.3 million in 1907.

The origins of the immigrants changed, too. In the first half of the nineteenth century, most new arrivals came from northern Europe. The Irish, English, Scandinavians, and Germans came early and established an industrial structure in the young nation. By 1860, immigration from these nations began to taper off and large numbers of Greeks, Italians, Serbs, Russians, and Poles began to arrive.

The earlier immigrants had several advantages. Most of them either spoke or were familiar with the English language, and they all looked exactly like the people who were already in the United States. The later immigrants were not familiar with English and did not necessarily look like the original Northern European colonists. Because of these differences, immigrants arriving after 1890 found it harder to be assimilated into the mainstream of U.S. life. Nonetheless, they found work. And although they were crowded into slums, they continued to come, indicating that as bad as conditions were in the new country, it held more opportunities than the old. The migrants were following the pattern of substituting a better situation for a worse one.

In large measure, U.S. industry prospered because of the seemingly inexhaustible stream of new immigrants. They worked for low wages, increasing the profits of all they dealt with. Because they increased the size of the market, they helped industry to diversify. They required more retail trade, more transportation, and more housing so these industries grew and flourished along with the population.

Although the major industrial employers were convinced that immigration was necessary to the success of business and industry, labor unions were not. Beginning in the 1880s, the unions began to press for legislation to slow the stream of people. The first laws restricted the entry of *contract labor.*

Contract labor was a means of importing labor to perform certain tasks. A contractor would go to, say, Germany and recruit 5,000 workers to work on the XYZ Railroad. The railroad agreed to pay the immigrant's moving expenses if the worker promised to work for the railroad for a specified number of years. While the process did allow immigration, it did not provide freedom in either an economic or a political sense.

Then, after many vetoes by many Presidents, literacy requirements and other shielding laws were enacted in 1917.

Immigration into the United States has been sporadic since 1917. Since then, more than 13 million aliens have entered the country, most of them in the 1920s and the 1960s. The immigrants in the 20s were primarily from Europe; the more recent arrivals have been mainly from Asia. In 1974, nearly 400,000 new residents entered the United States from other countries. Approximately three-fifths of these were Asians who wanted to escape political subjugation in their home countries. Perhaps the biggest change in immigration is related not to the place of origin but to the destination of the immigrants. Ships filled with immigrants no longer move into New York harbor and turn their human cargoes loose to find jobs in the industrial East. Now the immigrants go to destinations all over the country. They do not form a labor pool that can be exploited by business, but are gradually assimilated, one at a time, into jobs in places like Montana, Ohio, and Alabama.

In sum, migration comes in response to disequilibrium. Since people are social creatures, many noneconomic factors tend to influence migration, but in the end the economic forces almost always win. In the less developed countries, the closing of opportunities in agriculture forces people out of rural areas. In other countries, an economic frontier attracts people hoping to exploit natural resources, or the higher salary schedules in one region will pull workers from another. The moves are motivated by changes in supply and demand—by markets that have gone out of adjustment.

Summary

1 An economic system provides signals that tell factors when to adjust to new sets of relative prices.
2 Adjustment of labor is very difficult because it requires people to move from one locale to another. It requires migration.
3 Migration has many causes, but economic conditions seem to bring about the largest movements. When conditions in one place become intolerable people are "pushed." When conditions in another place become particularly inviting, people are "pulled."
4 Migration can be to a frontier, from rural to urban areas, or from one nation to another, or it may follow a regular path. An insidious recent phenomenon has been the "brain drain," the movement of skilled technicians out of the less developed countries toward wider opportunities in the developed countries.
5 Out-migration can often leave fixed capital underutilized. This represents a misallocation of resources and a loss to society, since the fixed capital cannot be recycled for other uses.
6 In-migration often causes capital shortage problems because new people require more facilities. Many cities of the world have not been able to provide adequate social overhead capital for the number of people who are congregating in them.
7 The U.S. economy has assimilated about 60 million immigrants in the last century. They have provided labor for U.S. industry and markets for U.S. products. Until about 1920, any number of immigrants could enter the nation at any time. Since then, barriers to entry have been established and immigration has been cut to about 400,000 persons per year.

Exercises

1 Explain these important terms and concepts:
   - disequilibrium in the labor market
   - kinds of migration
   - "push" and "pull" migration
   - brain drain
   - economic frontier
   - contract labor
   - nonmonetary costs of migration

2 Few college graduates return to their home towns. Ignore all of their social reasons for not returning and describe their migration in economic terms.

3 Since the formation of the Common Market in 1958, laborers have moved freely among the nine member countries. In recent years, especially since 1973, some EEC nations have had very healthy economies while others have suffered inflation, unemployment or both. Immigrants have moved from the poor to the healthy economies. Italians have traditionally made up about three-quarters of all migrants within the com-

munity. In 1975, Italian immigrants were discouraged and the healthy economies turned to Turkish, Yugoslavian, Spanish, Portuguese, and North African workers. Why would French and West German industrialists prefer these people to the more traditional Italians?
4 What does it mean to say that the opportunity cost of capital has dropped to zero? How does this concept apply to the following:
 a small decaying towns that dot the Texas High Plains
 b vacated store fronts in an urban ghetto
 c sidewalks in a deserted part of town
5 Does the opportunity cost of labor ever drop to zero? If so, what effect does this have on migration?
6 In 1974, nearly 35,500 "professional and technical" workers entered the United States. Over 21,000 came from Asia, and another 6,000 came from Europe. Name the economic forces attracting them to the United States and discuss the social and economic consequences of their leaving other nations.

A Contemporary Problem

Trouble Near the Borders

The United States has always enjoyed good relationships with its two neighbors, Canada and Mexico. Citizens of the three nations cross common boundaries almost at will. There are cursory checks regarding citizenship and dutiable imports, and occasional searches are made just to keep honest people honest, but, in the main, crossing the border for a short visit is very easy. Crossing as an immigrant is another matter.

The move seems to be northward. Mexicans want to immigrate into the United States and large numbers of U.S. citizens would like to move to Canada. Some legal immigrations are permitted across each border each year, but problems have developed with illegal entries from Mexico into the U.S. and from the U.S. into Canada. The desire of individuals to move is quite understandable but quite different in each case. The reactions of the northern nations are, too.

In the early 1970s, the United States was heavily involved in a very unpopular war in Southeast Asia. Many young people faced conscription into the armed forces to fight an enemy they did not feel opposed to in a war they did not understand. Many young men fled to a foreign country, the prime destination being Canada because it was so easy to cross the border. Canada at first welcomed the young, generally well-trained people. They were valuable additions to the labor force. Soon, however, the numbers reached unmanageable proportions. The Canadian economy began to suffer high rates of unemployment, and U.S. citizens who were attempting to avoid a military obligation were less welcome at the borders. This migration was not motivated by economic reasons, but it did involve the matter of choice and it certainly had economic consequences. Today, thousands of young U.S. citizens are stranded in Canada. They cannot return home without facing prosecution, and they cannot find work in the highly nationalistic Canadian economy.

Things are different along the Mexican frontier. For decades, low-skilled Mexican nationals crossed the Rio Grande each year to seek employment in U.S. agriculture. They played the same role in Texas, Arizona and California that the Irish, Poles, and Italians had played in the industrial East a century before. They provided a large pool of cheap labor. Organized labor and popular sentiment were vehement. Why should a Mexican labor force be employed in a U.S. industry when U.S. citizens could not find jobs? The farm organizations were equally strong-willed. They argued that dependable domestic help either could not be found for the menial labor chores of agriculture, or the wage rate was so high as to have a significant impact on food prices and farm profits. Keep Mexican labor out of the fields and prices go up in the supermarket, they said.

Labor had its way. In 1964, laws were passed prohibiting the entry of laborers from Mexico. But the farm vote had its say, too. Even after the immigration quota law was passed, certain numbers of Mexican field laborers were allowed to enter the United States each year, provided that they have a specific job arranged before entry, that they possess a written permit indicating that they have been certified for entry, and that they not attempt to become permanent residents of the United States.

Analysis. In both the U.S./Canadian case and the Mexico/U.S. case, migration was objectionable to the receiving country. The cost of absorbing settlers is high, because in times of unemployment each immigrant competes with a domestic worker for a job. If the immigrant gets the job, the domestic goes on relief; if the domestic keeps the job, the immigrant must seek public assistance. The message is clear: People move in response to signals about their earnings, their opportunities, and their obligations. A large number of perfectly rational individual decisions can, in the aggregate, become a problem for the macroeconomy. Because of this, nations are becoming increasingly wary about permitting numbers of people to enter and become assimilated into their domestic economies.

Index

ability principle of taxation, 492–93
absolute price, vs. relative, 234–35
accounting period, 100
actual per capita GNP, 288, 289
ad valorem tariff, 544
advertising, and monopolistic competition, 403–05
The Affluent Society (Galbraith), 422
Agency for International Development (AID), 586
agglomeration effect, 475
aggregate consumption function, 134–35
aggregate demand, 89 (*see also* demand)
  altering, 90–91
  equilibrium, full employment, and, 135–37
  generated by households, 130
aggregate demand curve
  constructing, 310
  for pure public good, 483
aggregate economic behavior, 149–50
  consumer spending determinants, 150–52
  government spending determinants, 156–58
  investment determinants, 152–56
aggregate income
  and average propensities, 168–70
  and marginal propensities, 170–71
  and the multiplier, 172–78
agriculture
  as competitive industry, 353
  green revolution, 602–04
  LDCs, 594–95
  in mechanized economy, 363–65
  and technological advance, 377
Aid to Families with Dependent Children, 509
airlines, Hawaiian, monopoly issue, 386–87
Alaska pipeline, and OPEC, 522–23
Allis-Chalmers Corp., 419

Aloha Airlines, 386–87
Aluminum Company of America (ALCOA), 370
American Capitalism: The Concept of Countervailing Power (Galbraith), 422
American Motors Corp., 409, 410
anti-monetarists, and monetary policy, 246
antimonopoly measures, 381–84
antimonopoly policy, 500–02
antitrust policy, 500–02
appreciation, 558
Argentina, devaluation, 563–64
Aspin-Abourezk bill, 425
assets
  acquisition, merger by, 501
  liquid, 241
attainable price, in monopolistic competition, 399
automatic forces, 149
automatic stabilizers
  tax receipts, 191
  unemployment compensation, 190–91
automobile industry
  breaking into, 414
average cost, 324
average fixed cost, 324
average fixed cost curve, 326
average product, 429
average propensity to consume (APC), 168–70
average propensity to save (APS), 168–70
average total cost curve, 326
average variable cost, 324, 325
axis (graph), 19

backward merger, 412
balance of payments, 565–67 (*see also* foreign exchange; international trade)
  continuing disequilibrium in, 571–73
  deficit, 575–76
  errors and omissions in, 571
  exports and imports, 567–69
  and net capital movements, 569–70
  and net government transactions, 569
  and paying debts between nations, 570–71
  remittances, 569
  U.S. problems with, 575
balance of trade, 568
bank(s)
  commercial, 224, 253
  failures, 228
  lending capacity, and bond trading, 255
  local, and government grants, 232
  monopoly, 226–27
  national, 224
  reserve city, 257
  state, 224
bank draft, 552
bankers, goldsmiths as first, 220–21
banking system, 224–25 (*see also* Federal Reserve System)
  and monetary policy, 91
  and money supply, 225–28
barter economy, circular flow, 46
barter system, 218
Baumol, William J., 421
Bell Laboratories, 376–77
benefit/cost analysis of decisions on public goods, 488–92
benefit principle of taxation, 492–93
benefit stream vs. cost stream, 490
Bentham, Jeremy, 88
blacks
  family income, 453
  young man enters labor force, 443
Board of Governors, Federal Reserve, 250, 251
bond market, 240–41
bonds, open market trading, 253–56
Boulding, Kenneth, 232
brain drain, 612–13
Brazil, unbalanced growth, 597
Bretton Woods Conference, 577–78
Buchwald, Art, on economic summit conference, 286–87
budget
  crunch, and public goods, 495
  defense, 200
  public, and public debt, 202–03

surpluses and deficits, 204
Bureau of Labor Statistics, 84
Burns, Arthur, 273
business activity, and inventions, 271
business cycles, 273
business fluctuation
   and causes, 268–78
   endogenous theories, 272–74
   exogenous theories, 270–72

Cantillon, Richard, 236
capacity changes, 26–28
capital
   factor market imperfections, 441
   as factor of production, 41–42
   LDCs, 590, 598–600
   poor man's, 590
   social overhead, 192, 206, 589
   sources, LDCs, 598–600
   working, 520–21
capital account, 572
capitalism, 59, 74–75
capital movements, net, and balance of payments, 569–70
Celler-Kefauver Anti-Merger Act (1950), 501
Chamberlin, Edward H., 402
change
   in demand, 307–08
   discount rate, 252–53
   in equilibrium, 67, 158–62, 340–43
   in fixed exchange rates, 563–64
   in income distribution, 453–54
   in quantity demanded, 58
   and shift in demand, 317–18
   in supply and demand, 64–67
checks, 223
   Federal Reserve System in clearing, 251
children, as poor man's capital, 590
China
   balanced growth, 597
   no-trade policy with, 519
   trade visit from, 530–33
China National Machinery Import and Export Corp., 531
choice
   production-possibilities model of, 23–28

   and scarcity, 3–4
   specialization vs. flexibility, 2–3
choosing
   process of, 6–7
   production possibility curve as tool in, 28
   systematic, in market system, 7–8
circular flow
   barter economy, 46
   depreciation in, 103
   early model, 47
   of economic activity, 36, 45, 99
   and equilibrium, 70
   and factor markets, 70
   free enterprise economy, 46
   and governments, 38–40, 48–49, 183
   households and firms, 36–38, 43–48
   including market for loanable funds, 127
   increasing complexity of, 68
   indirect business taxes in, 102
   market economy, 591
   and product markets, 70
   and savings, 125
   and Say's law, 123
cities, migration to, 610
Civil Aeronautics Board (CAB), 505
clad coins, 222
Clark, John Bates, 448
classical model, 122
   Keynes challenge to, 129–30
   limitations, 129
   and Say's law, 122–28
Clayton Act (1914), 500
clearing the market, 339–40
closed economy, 523
clothing industry, monopolistic competition, 406–07
cobweb, hog cycle, 343–44
coins, 222
collusion, electrical equipment manufacturers, 419
collusive oligopoly, 417–20
colony, 521
Commerce Department, 97
commercial banks, 224
   and discount rate, 253
Common Market, 580–81

comparative advantage
  and diminishing returns, 546–47
  and interdependence, 40–41
  law of, 536–44
competition, 351 (*see also* competitive industry; monopolistic competition)
  and factor prices, 329–30
  and investment, 153
  vs. monopoly, in constant-cost industry, 375
  norm vs. model, 362
competitive equilibrium, 360
competitive firm
  and competitive industry, 359
  in equilibrium, 360
  optimum output, 355
  supernormal profits, 358
competitive industry, 351–53
  and competitive firm, 359
  price, cost, and firm supply, 355–56
  price determination, 354–55
  profits or losses, 356–61
  and technological advance, 377
competitive system, 351
concentration ratio, 411
constant-cost industry, 374
  monopoly and competition in, 375
constant dollars, 110
  GNP in, 110–12
consumer
  Engel's law of behavior, 152
  sovereignty, 54
  tastes, and investment, 153
Consumer Price Index, 84, 289, 290
consumer spending
  determinants of, 150–52
  and disposable income, 134, 169
  and equilibrium, 158–59
consumers' surplus, 380
consumption expenditure
  and disposable income, 169
  and GNP, 113
consumption function
  aggregate, 134–35
  household, 132
contract, tied, 500
contract labor, 617
control
  of money supply, 258–60
  of population, LDCs, 595–96
  of prices, 86
  and protection of natural monopolies, 503–04
  of resources, monopoly, 370
convenience, as product, 37
Copernicus, 222
corporate, multinational, 549–50, 570 (*see also* competitive industry; industry; monopoly; oligopoly)
cost
  input, and demand, 432
  of investment, 154
  marginal, 327–30
  monopoly revenue, demand, and, 388–89
  nonmonetary, of migration, 608
  and output, 325
  price, firm supply, and, 355–56
  private vs. unpaid, 463–64
  of production, 322–26
cost curve
  competitive industries, 356–57
  and demand curve, monopolistic competition, 395–97
  monopolistic firm, 369
cost of living, 84
cost stream, vs. benefit stream, 490
cost structure, 324
  monopoly, 368–70
Council of Economic Advisers, 196, 197, 279
countercyclical policy, 275
country bank, 257
credit card, as money substitute, 230
credit entry, 567
currency, 223 (*see also* money)
  debasing, 219
  multiple, and world economics, 528
  Special Drawing Rights, 578
current account, 572
current dollars, 110
  GNP in, 110–12
curve, graph, 21

Dale, Edwin L., 214

debasing, coin or currency, 219
DeBeers, Ltd., 370
debit entry, 566–67
debt
  and balance of payments, 570–71
  internal and external, 208–09
  monetizing, 228
  public, 202–15
decision making
  oligopoly, 413–14
  on public goods, 488–92
defense budget, 200
deficit, budget, 204
deflating a performance series, national income accounts, 109–10
deflationary gap, 184–85
demand, *see also* aggregate demand
  changes in, 307–08
  defined, 57–60
  derived, 433
  and diminishing marginal utility, 305–07
  elasticity of, 311–15
  for factors, 428–34
  for foreign exchange, 555–56
  and income, 318
  and input costs, 432
  law of, 64
  law of supply and, 338
  monopoly revenue, costs, and, 388–89
  and price, 58, 60, 433
  for public goods, 481–84
  relationship to price and quantity for monopolist, 371
  shifts and changes in, 317–20
  shifts in, 65–66
  supply, market price, and, 339
demand curve, 59, 305
  and cost curve, monopolistic competition, 395–97
  and diminishing marginal utility, 306
  for factor of production, 432
  individual and market, 308, 310–11
  kinked, oligopoly, 415–17
  monopolistic competitor, 394
  perfectly elastic, 314
  perfectly inelastic, 314
  for public goods, 482–83
  shift, 65
  users of, 315
demand deposits, 223–24
  banking system creating, 227
deposit expansion multiplier, 226
depreciation, 558
  in circular flow, 103
derived demand, 433
devaluation, 560–61, 563–64, 572, 576
differentiated oligopolies, 413
differentiated products, 393, 395
diminishing marginal utility, 305–07
diminishing returns, and comparative advantage, 546–47
discount, 253
discount rate, 295–96
  changes in, 252–53
discretionary stabilizers
  public works, 192–94
  tax rate changes, 196–98
  welfare payments, 194–96
discriminating monopolist, perfectly, 378–79, 381
diseconomies of scale, 325–26
disequilibrium
  in balance of payments, 571–73
  and migration, 607–08
disinvestment, 101
disposable income, and consumer expenditures, 134, 169
disposable personal income, 107, 151
dissaving, 147, 160
distribution of income, *see* income distribution
The Distribution of Wealth (Clark), 448
diversification
  and multinational corporations, 549–50
  and trade barriers, 545
dollar, 551, 554
  devaluation and revaluation, 561, 576
du Pont de Nemours (E. I.) & Co., Inc., 351, 502

duties, 544

easement, 439
economic activity
　circular flow, 36, 45, 99
　private vs. unpaid costs, 463–64
　round of, 176–77
　social costs, 463–65
economic frontiers, 608–10
economic growth, 86–87
economic policy, 18
economic power, oligopoly, 421–22
economics, see also world economics
　defined, 7
　and science, 14–18
　as a social science, 13–14
Economics and the Public Purpose (Galbraith), 422
economic summit conference, 285–87
economies of scale, 325
　and oligopolies, 411
economist, 5
　classical, 122
　and income distribution problem, 446–49
　view of market failure, 463–65
economy, see also world economy
　closed, 523
　competitive model, 362
　cycles, postclassical years, 129
　direct regulation, 92
　diversified, and trade barriers, 545
　empirical evidence, 97–98
　fiscal policy in managing, 182
　food stamps in, 456–57
　goal attainment methods, 89–92
　goals, 81–89
　market, 55–57, 591
　mechanized, agriculture in, 363–65
　and migration, 615–18
　mixed, 56
　money in, 221–24
　primitive, firm/household in, 592
　world, 515–17
elasticity
　of demand, 311–15
　of supply, 331

emigration, 613–14
empirical demand curve, 307
empirical evidence, 98
empirical record, national income accounts, 108–13
employment and macroeconomic policy, 289–91 (see also full employment; unemployment)
Employment Act (1946), 82, 196, 287
enclosures, 190
endogenous theories of business fluctuations, 272–74
Engel's law of consumer behavior, 152
entrepreneur, 37
entrepreneurship
　LDCs, 592–93
　and rewards to factors, 42
environmental protection, as economic goal, 87
equilibrium, 64
　aggregate demand, full employment, and, 135–37
　changes, 67, 158–62, 340–43
　and circular flow, 70
　competitive firm in, 360
　firm and industry, monopolistic competition, 395–98
　in microeconomics, 338
　in monopolistic competition, 398–400
　and shifts, 67
equilibrium price of foreign exchange, 557–59
equity, 80
errors and omissions, in balance of payments, 571
excess reserves, 225, 226
exchange quotas, 560
exchange rates, 552 (see also balance of payments; foreign exchange)
　fixed, 559–64
　freely fluctuating, 558–59
exogenous theories of business fluctuations, 270–72
expectations, and investment, 153–54
expenditure approach in measuring

economic activity, 99, 101
expenses
  of firm, 44
  of household, 43
exports, 522
  and imports, in balance of payments, 567–69
externalities, 461
  beneficial, 473–75
  internalization of, 465–68

fact gathering, 16
factor markets, 46n, 428
  and circular flow, 70
  imperfections in, 439–41
factor owners, and personal income, 105
factor price, and competition, 329–30
factors of production, 23, 41–42
  demand for, 428–34
  demand curve for, 432
  household's sale of, 439
  supply of, 434–38
family, personal income by income class, 450
family assistance program, 509
family income, nonwhite, 453
Federal Advisory Council, 250
Federal Communications Commission, 503
Federal Electric Corp., 419
Federal Reserve Bank, 250, 252
Federal Reserve Board of Governors, 250, 251
Federal Reserve System, 217
  in altering money supply, 252–60
  creation and organization, 250–52
  and monetary policy, 93
  responsiveness, 296, 297
  and Treasury, 261
Federal Trade Commission (FTC), 505
fiat money, 222
final transaction, 395
finance, functional, 202–03
financial intermediary, 46
firm
  entry into competitive industry, 358–59
  and households, and circular flow, 36–38, 43–48
  and households, in macro model, 145–47
  and households and government, in macro model, 147–48
  vs. industry, 350–51
  and industry, equilibrium, monopolistic competition, 395–98
  leaving competitive industry, 360–61
firm/household in primitive economy, 592
firm supply, price, and cost, 355–56
fiscal activity, needed change in, 188–89
fiscal policy, 89, 294–95
  and aggregate demand, 90–91
  and automatic stabilizers, 190–91
  and deflationary gap, 184–85
  discretionary stabilizers, 192–98
  and inflationary gap, 185–88
  limitation on, 93
  in managing the economy, 182
  monetarists' position on, 246
  vs. monetary, 274–80
  and multiplier, 188
  when to use, 183–84
fiscal year, 202
fishing, as competitive industry, 353
fixed costs, 323
fixed exchange rates, 559–62
  change in, 563–64
fixed income, and price changes, 84–85
food stamps, 456–57
Ford, Gerald R., 189, 285, 445, 530
Ford Motor Co., 410, 531
foreign aid to LDCs, 600–01
foreign exchange, 553
  demand for, 555–56
  equilibrium price of, 557–59
  quotas, 560
  supply of, 556–57
foreign exchange market, and exchange rate, 557, 558
fractional reserve system, 221
  and money supply, 225
  weaknesses, 228–29

free enterprise economy, circular flow, 46
free-enterprise system, 59
freely fluctuating exchange rates, 558–59
free rider, and public goods, 484–85
Friedman, Milton, 281, 282, 283
  profile, 276
frontier, migration to, 608–10
full employment, *see also* unemployment
  aggregate demand, equilibrium, and, 136–37
  as economic goal, 81–83
  and quantity theory of money, 235
functional distribution of income, 448, 449–50
functional finance, 202–03

gains from trade, 541–43
Galbraith, John Kenneth, 5
  profile, 422
game strategy, oligopoly, 422–23
General Electric Co., 419
General Motors Corp., 411, 502
General Telephone and Electronics, 503
The General Theory of Employment, Interest, and Money (Keynes), 133
George, Henry, and supply of land, 436
gold, *see also* foreign exchange; money
  fractional reserve system, 221
  par value, 577
gold account, 572
goldsmiths, as first bankers, 220–21
goods
  government vs. private, 23–24
  public, 480–93
government
  and circular flow, 38–40, 48–49, 183
  debt at all levels of, 203
  and firms and households, in macro model, 147–48
  grants, and local bank, 232

  microeconomic vs. macroeconomic programs, 88
government expenditures
  determinants of, 156–58
  and equilibrium, 159, 162
government purchases and GNP, 113
government transactions, net, and balance of payments, 569
grants
  government, and local bank, 232
  and loans, LDCs, 598–600
graphs, 18–23
Great Britain, U.S. trade with, 552–59
Great Depression, 182
  and microeconomic policy, 507, 509
  public works, 192–94
Gresham's Law, 222
gross national product (GNP), 99–104
  components, 113
  in current and constant dollars, 110–12
  in current vs. real dollars, 288
  and government expenditure, 156–57
  and quality, 115–16
  and public debt, 207–08
  and well-being, 114–15
gross private investment, 155
gross world product, 526
group choice, 6–7
growth
  balanced vs. unbalanced, LDCs, 596–98
  investment, interdependence, and, 49–50
  in LDCs, 586–93
  and macroeconomic policy, 288
  time paths of, 599

Hatch Act (1887), 377
Hawaiian Air, 386–87
Heller, Walter M., 196
  profile, 279
hog cycle, cobweb, 343–44
homogeneous oligopolies, 412–13
homogeneous product, 353

horizontal summation, 310–11
household(s)
  aggregate demand generated by, 130
  consumption function, 132
  and firms, and circular flow, 36–38, 43–48
  and firms, in macro model, 145–47
  and firms and government, in macro model, 147–48
  income and expenditure, 131
  in macro model, 144–45
  microeconomic policy affecting, 506–09
  sale of factors, 439
housing market, control of, 259
housing starts, and interest rates, 164–65
Hume, David, 236

IBM Corp., 370
identity, 236
immigration, 614
import duties, 544
imports
  dutiable, surcharge on, 576
  and exports, in balance of payments, 567–69
income, see also income distribution
  aggregate, 168–78
  and demand, 318
  disposable, 134, 169
  of firm, 44
  fixed, and price changes, 84–85
  of household, 43
  and investment, 156
  and marginal productivity, 448
  national differences, 586–87
  private, 145
  size distribution of, 449, 450–53
  vs. wealth, 448
income approach
  to GNP, 101–04
  in measuring economic activity, 99
income class, and size distribution of income, 450–53
income determination
  approaches, 161
  with consumption only, 144
  with consumption and investment, 146
  with consumption, investment, and government, 147
income determination model, 145, 148–49
  recapitulation, 184
  second approach to, 160–61
income distribution, 445–46
  economists grapple with problem, 446–49
  effects of change in, 453–54
  functional, 448, 449–50
  and income equality, 454–55
  and monopoly, 375–76
  size, 449, 450–53
  and world economics, 526–27
income equality, perfect, 454–55
income redistribution
  and income equality, 455
  programs, 486–87
  and public debt, 209–10
income tax
  corporate, 106
  cut, 1964, 197–98
  negative, 509
  progressive, 191
  surcharge, 198
income transfer, 453–54
indirect business taxes, in circular flow, 102
indivisible inputs, 369–70
industrialization and population, 595
industry, see also competitive industry; firm; monopoly; oligopoly
  agricultural vs. automotive, 349–50
  clustering, and beneficial externalities, 474–75
  concentration ratios, 411
  vs. firm, 350–51
  and firm, equilibrium, in monopolistic competition, 395–98
  service, 450
  supply curve, 329
infant industry, and trade barriers, 544–45

inflation, 70
    and economic policy, 292
    and fiscal policy, 90–91
    and jawboning, 159
    moral suasion in controlling, 260
inflationary gap, 185–88
input, 41
    indivisible, 369–70
    productive, 23
    and product price, 433
input costs, and demand, 432
An Inquiry into the Nature and Causes of the Wealth of Nations (Smith), 71
inside lag, 276
installment credit, limits on, 258–59
insurance
    retirement, 507–08
    unemployment, 508
interdependence
    and comparative advantage, 40–41
    investment, growth, and, 49–50
    market, 7–8
interest on public debt, 210–11
interest rate
    and aggregate expenditures, 277
    ceilings on, 258
    and housing starts, 164–65
    and investment, 154–55
    and money supply, 243
interlocking directorates, 500
intermediate products, and GNP, 100
internalization, in correcting market failure, 465–68
International Harvester Co., 427
International Monetary Fund (IMF), 577–78
international trade, 522, 535–36
    and Bretton Woods Conference, 577–78
    and Common Market, 580–81
    expansion of, 525–26
    and Smithsonian Agreement, 578–79
    U.S., 524–25
    U.S. and British, 552–59
Interstate Commerce Commission (ICC), 383, 505

inventions, and business activity, 271
inventory and GNP, 100–01
investment, 100
    determinants of, 152–56
    and equilibrium, 159
    growth, interdependence, and, 49–50
    and income, 156
    record, 155–56
investment expenditures and GNP, 113
investment tax credit, 499n
investors vs. savers, 128

jawboning, 159
Jevons, W. Stanley, 272
Job Corps, 192
Johnson, Lyndon B., 197
joint profit maximization, oligopoly, 417–20
Justice Department, 419

Kaiser, Henry J., 414
keeping money in circulation, 172
Kennedy, John F., 197, 279
Keynes, John Maynard, 121, 168, 182, 281, 282
    challenge to classical model, 129–30
    profile, 133
Keynesian model, 130–32
    aggregate consumption function, 134–35
    aggregate demand, equilibrium, and full employment, 135–37
    summary, 137–38
Keynesians, 277–79
    vs. monetarists, 279–80, 281–83
kinked demand curve, oligopoly, 415–17
Kraar, Louis, 530
Kuwait, unbalanced growth, 597

labor
    factor market imperfections, 440–41
    as factor of production, 41
    LDCs, 589–90
    supply of, 437–38

Labor Department, 84
labor force, see also full
    employment; migration;
    unemployment
  and trade barriers, 545–46
  unemployment as percentage of,
    83
  young man enters, 443
labor market disequilibrium, and
    migration, 607–08
laissez faire, 79–80
land
  factor market imperfections,
    439–40
  as factor of production, 41
  LDCs, 588–89
  and natural resources, supply of,
    435–37
law, 17
Law, John, 236
law of comparative advantage,
    536–44
law of demand, 64
law of supply, 64, 330
law of supply and demand, 338
legal restrictions, in correcting
    market failures, 471–73
legislation, antimonopoly, 383–84
lending capacity, and bond trading,
    255
less developed countries (LDCs),
    583–84
  agriculture, 594–95
  balanced vs. unbalanced growth,
    596–98
  capital, 590
  development strategies, 593–600
  entrepreneurship, 592–93
  factors affecting growth, 588–93
  and green revolution, 602–04
  growth in, 586–88
  labor, 589–90
  land, 588–89
  population control, 595–96
  poverty in, 584–86
  sources of capital, 598–600
  U.S. aid to, 600–01
license to pollute, taxation as, 469
lighthouse, as pure public good,
    480–84

liquid assets, 241
liquidity preference, 243–44
liquidity preference curve, 242
living costs, 84
loanable funds market, 125–26
local monopoly, 376
Locke, John, 236
long run, 332
Lorenz curve, 451–52
losses, or profits, competitive
    industry, 356–61

macroeconomic policy
  indications and responses,
    291–97
  record of, 288–91
macroeconomic problems, 15
macroeconomic model, 143–44
  households and firms, 145–47
  households, firms, and
    government, 147–48
  households only, 144–45
  summary, 148–49
macroeconomics, 80–81
macroeconomy, monetarist view of,
    234
Malthus, Thomas Robert, 122
Manhattan, office space in, 346–48
marginal cost, 323
  and marginal returns, 329
  and supply curve, 327–30
marginal cost curve, 326
marginal efficiency of investment
    (MEI), 154–55
  marginal input cost and marginal
    revenue, 431
marginal product, 429
marginal productivity and income,
    448
marginal propensity to consume
    (MPC), 170–71
marginal propensity to save (MPS),
    170–71
marginal returns and marginal cost,
    329
marginal revenue, 327–28
  and marginal input cost, 431
  oligopoly, 413–14
marginal revenue curve, monopoly,
    372

marginal utility, diminishing, 305–07
margin requirements, stock market, 259–60
market, 53, 338–40
  and artificially closed feedback loop, 472
  cobweb, 343–44
  curves, 340
  defects, 55–56
  equilibrium changes, 340–43
  interdependence, 7–8
  in isolation, 57–67
  mechanism, 53
market capitalism, 59
  Polanyi on, 74–75
market economy, 55
  circular flow, 591
  nonmarket aspects, 56–57
market failure, 459–60
  and beneficial externalities, 473–75
  causes, 460–61
  corrective means, 465–73
  economist's view of, 463–65
  kinds, 462
market price, supply, and demand, 339
market run, 332
market system, 54–55, 304
  as automatic mechanism, 55
  decentralized, 351–52
  precariousness, 69–72
  as systematic choosing, 7–8
Marshall, Alfred, 332
  and development of microeconomics, 309
Marx, Karl, 447
Mau Tai, 532
mechanized economy, agriculture in, 363–65
Medicare, 508
merger
  in correcting market failure, 465–68
  and oligopoly, 411–12
merit wants, 388–89
microeconomic policy
  affecting households, 506–09
  antimonopoly, 500–02

  defined, 497–500
  and licensing of New York taxis, 511–12
  in placing bounds on behavior, 506
  protecting natural monopolies, 503–05
microeconomic problems, 15
microeconomics, 303–04
  development of, 309
  equilibrium in, 338
migration
  and brain drain, 612–13
  causes, 606–08
  effects, 613–14
  following path of, 611
  to frontier, 608–10
  international, 611
  patterns, 608–13
  rural to urban, 610
  and U.S. economy, 615–18
Mill, James, 122
Mill, John Stuart, 122, 463
Mitchell, Wesley Clair, 273
mixed economy, 56
models, 17
  competitive, 362
  production possibilities, 23–28
monetarists, 233, 274–77
  extreme, and monetary policy, 246–47
  vs. Keynesians, 279–80, 281–83
A Monetary History of the United States (Friedman and Schwartz), 282
monetary policy, 89, 245–47, 295–97
  in altering aggregate demand, 91
  vs. fiscal policy, 274–80
  lags in, 276
  limitations on, 93
  use of, 262–63
monetizing debts, 228
money, *see also* exchange rates; Federal Reserve System; foreign exchange; interest rates; money supply
  artificial, 230
  and banking system, 224–29
  coins, 222

demand deposits, 223–24
early forms, 219–20
enlarging definition of, 229–30
evolution of, 218–19
fractional reserve system, 221
keeping in circulation, 172
paper, 220–21, 223
precautionary demand, 238–39
and prices, 234–35
quantity theory, 235–37, 274
speculative demand, 240–42
total demand, 242
transactions demand, 237–38
money supply, 242–44, 295
  and bond trading in open market, 253–56
  contracting, 227–28
  and discount rate changes, 252–53
  and economic activity, 274
  expanding, 225–27
  Keynesian view of changes in, 277–78
  minor controls over, 258–60
  monetarist view of changes, 275
  and reserve requirements, 256–57
monopolist
  perfectly discriminating, 378–79, 381
  as price searcher, 370–72
monopolistic competition, *see also* competition; monopoly
  and advertising, 403–05
  clothing industry, 406–07
  equilibrium in, 398–400
  equilibrium of firm and industry, 395–98
  nature of, 392–95
  nonprice competition in, 401–02
  product differentiation in, 401
monopolistic firm, cost curves, 369
monopoly
  and antimonopoly policy, 500–02
  vs. competition, in constant-cost industry, 375
  control measures, 381–84
  cost and revenue structures, 368–73
  defined, 367
  demand, revenue, and costs, 388–89
  elements of, 368–70
  and Hawaii's inter-island airlines, 386–87
  and income distribution, 375–76
  legislation to curb, 383–84
  natural, 384–85
  and resource allocation, 374–75
  solutions to problem of, 381–83
  and technology, 376–78
  vs. trust, 500
monopoly bank, 226–27
moral suasion, in controlling money supply, 260
Morgenstern, Oskar, 422
mortgage loans, and control of housing market, 259
multinational corporation, 570
  and diversification, 549–50
multiplier, 172–78
  differential effects, 175
  and fiscal policy, 188
  significance, 176
multiplier effect, in creation of money, 225–26
$MV \equiv PQ$, 236

nation(s)
  paying debts between, and balance of payments, 570–71
  reasons for trading, 535–36
  specialization, 543–44
national banks, 224
National Bureau of Economic Research, 273
national economies, trading among, 517–20
national income, 105
  determining equilibrium levels, 160
national income accounts, 98–99
  deflating a performance series, 109–10
  disposable income, 107
  empirical record, 108–13
  graphing, 112
  gross national product, 99–104
  limitations of, 114–16
  national income, 105
  net national product, 104–05

personal income, 105–07
summarized, 107–08
National School Lunch Program, 470
natural monopoly, 369–70, 384–85
nurture, 504
protection and control, 503–04
natural resources and land, supply of, 435–37
near monies, 229–30
negative income tax, 509
negative net worth, 452
neo-Keynesians, 277
net capital movements, and balance of payments, 569–70
net government transactions, and balance of payments, 569
net national product (NNP), 104–05, 147
net sales to other countries, and GNP, 113
net worth, negative, 452
The New Industrial State (Galbraith), 422
Nicaragua, unbalanced growth, 597–98
Nixon, Richard M., 86, 92, 198, 576
nonmarket effects, 461
nonmonetary costs of migration, 608
nonprice competition, in monopolistic competition, 401–02
nonwhites, family income, 453
norm, competitive, 362
normal profits, 327

Occupational Safety and Health Administration, 506
office space in Manhattan, 346–48
oil industry, oligopoly, 424–25
Okun, Arthur M., on national income accounts, 118–20
old-age and survivors insurance, 507–08
oligopoly, 392
decision making, 413–14
defined, 409–10
joint profit maximization, 417–20
kinked demand curve, 415–17

in oil, 424–25
price, 414–15
price leadership, 420–21
reason for being, 410–13
revenue maximization, 421
simple mark-ups, 421
strategy of games, 422–23
open market bond trading and money supply, 253–56
Open Market Committee, 250, 254
open market operations, 256
opportunity cost, 25–26, 154, 327
and trade, 539
optimizing monopolist, 388–89
Organization of Petroleum Exporting Countries (OPEC), and Alaska pipeline, 522–23
output
competitive firm, 355
and cost, 325
monopolistic competitors, 393
monopoly, 372–73
quality of, 523
and unpaid costs, 464
outside lag, 276

Pan American Airways, 325–26
paper money, 220–21, 223
Fed in issuing, 252
Pareto, Vilfredo, 449
partial equilibrium analysis, 309
par value, 577
patent ownership and monopoly, 370
Penney (J. C.) Co., Inc., 530–31
pension, old-age, 507–08
per capita GNP, 111
real and actual, 288, 289, 291
and unemployment, 291–92
perfectly competitive industry, 354
perfectly discriminating monopolist, 378–79, 381
perfect store of value, 240
personal income, 105–07
Phillips curve, 95
Physiocrats, 122
circular flow model, 47
Pigou, A. C., 463, 464
plot, 19
plotted variable, 19

Polanyi, Karl, on market capitalism, 74–75
pollution, selling certificates for, 476–77 (see also market failure)
Poor Laws, 190
poor-man's capital, 590
population, and world economics, 526
population control, LDCs, 595–96
pound sterling, 551, 554
   devaluation, 561
poverty, in LDCs, 584–86
poverty line, 509
precautionary demand for money, 238–39
prestige, oligopoly, 421–22
price
   absolute vs. relative, 234–35
   attainable, 399
   competitive industry, 354–55
   cost, firm supply, and, 355–56
   and demand, 58, 60, 433
   and discriminating monopolist, 378–81
   and inflationary gap, 186
   and investment, 153
   and money, 234–35
   oligopoly, 414–15
   and purchasing power, 240
   and quantity demanded, 310–11
   shaded, 419
   supply, demand, and, 62
   and utility, 307
price control, 86
price discrimination, 500–01
   morality of, 380
price leadership, oligopoly, 420–21
price searcher, monopolist as, 370–72
price stability
   as economic goal, 84–86
   and macroeconomic policy, 289
price stabilization, 85–86
price taker, 355
prime lending rate, 296–97
principles, 17
   generating, 16–17
Principles of Economics (Marshall), 332
private costs of economic activity, 463–64
private income, 145
product
   advertising, and monopolistic competition, 403–05
   differentiated, 393, 395
   homogeneous, 353
   interrelationships, and demand, 318–20
product approach
   to GNP, 100–01
   in measuring economic activity, 99
product differentiation, in monopolistic competition, 401
production, see also factors of production; production possibilities curve
   and externalities, 474
   and revenue, 430–34
production costs
   classes, 323–26
   and supply, 322–23
production factors, see factors of production
production function, 428–30
production possibilities
   model of choice, 23–28
   one laborer, 538, 540
production-possibility curve, 24–25
   and changes in capacity, 26–28
   and diminishing returns, 547
   moving along, 25–26
   and opportunity cost, 25–26
   as tool in choosing, 28
productive inputs, 23
production period, 100
product markets, 46n
   and circular flow, 70
product price, 433
profit, 42
   or loss, competitive industry, 356–61
   normal, 327
   supernormal, 358, 396–98
   undistributed corporate, 106
profit maximization
   joint, oligopoly, 417–20
   and reality, 37
program vs. project, 490

project orientation, benefit/cost analysis, 490
protective tariff, 544
public assistance, 507, 508–09
public debt, 203–05
  interest, 210–11
  and peace, 214–15
  and public budget, 202–03
  reasons for increasing, 205–07
  refunding vs. paying off, 211
  repayment, 208–10
  size, 207–08
public goods
  benefit/cost analysis of decisions, 488–92
  and budget crunch, 495
  city sidewalks and uncollectible revenues, 485–86
  demand for services, 481–84
  and free rider, 484–85
  and income redistribution programs, 486–87
  pure, 480–84
  taxes to pay for, 492–93
Public Law 480, 600
public utilities, as natural monopolies, 369–70
public works, 192–94
purchasing power
  and discount rate, 253
  and price, 240
push or pull migration, 607

quality
  and GNP, 115–16
  of life, and economic policy, 292–93
  of output, 523
quantity theory of money, 235, 274
  limitations, 237
  preclassical, 236
Quesnay, François, 47
quotas, foreign exchange, 560

railroads, antimonopoly legislation, 383
rate of exchange, 552, 558–64
rate of trade, 543
real dollars, 110
reality, and profit maximization, 37

real per capita GNP, 288, 289
rectangular hyperbola, 326
refunding vs. paying off debt, 211
regulation, direct, of economy, 92
regulatory agencies, 505
relative price, 86
  vs. absolute, 234–35
remittances, in balance of payments, 569
repayment of public debt, 208–10
required reserves, 225, 226
research, and competitive industry, 377
reserve city banks, 257
reserve requirements, 256–57
reserve allocation and monopoly, 374–75
resources, 23
  control, and monopoly, 370
retained earnings, 48
retirement insurance, 507–08
revaluation, 561, 572
revenue
  marginal, 327–28
  maximization, oligopoly, 421
  and production, 430–34
  structure, monopoly, 370–73
  uncollectible, for city sidewalks, 485–86
rewards to factors, and entrepreneurship, 42
Ricardo, David, 122, 447, 537
Robinson, Joan, 345, 402
Robinson-Patman Act (1936), 501
Rockefeller, Nelson, 445
Roosevelt, Franklin D., 507
round of economic activity, 173–74, 176–77

sales tax, 102
Samuelson, Paul, profile, 279
savers
  interest rate ceiling, 258
  vs. investors, 128
savings
  of household, 43
  and income, 160
  and prices, 85
  relationships, 48
  and Say's law, 124–28

savings and loan associations, 259
savings market, 125
Say, Jean Baptiste, 121, 122
Say's law, 121, 122–24
  and savings, 124–28
scarcity and choice, 3–4
Schultz, T. W., 590
Schwartz, Anna Jacobson, 282
science and economics, 14–18
self-correcting market, 339
Senate Subcommittee on Antitrust and Monopoly, 411
Senior, Nassau, 122
service industry, 450
shaded price, 419
Sherman Antitrust Act (1890), 384, 500
shifts
  in demand, 65–66
  and equilibrium, 67
  in supply, 66–67
Shopping Bag Food Stores, 502
shortage, 62, 63
short run, 332
short short run, 332
Shultz, George P., on economic policy, 93
Simon, William, 5
simple mark-up, oligopoly, 421
single tax, 436
size distribution of income, 449, 450–53
Smith, Adam, 71, 72, 122, 447, 536–37
Smithsonian Agreement, 578–79
social costs of economic activity, 463–65
social overhead capital, 192, 589
  and public debt, 206
social progress accounting, 115
social science, economics as, 13–14
social security, corporate payments to, 106
Social Security Act (1935), 507
Special Drawing Rights (SDRs), 578
specialization
  and comparative advantage, 40
  and economic organization, 35–36

vs. flexibility, 2–3
  of nations, 543–44
speculative demand for money, 240–42
stabilizers
  automatic, 190–91
  discretionary, 192–98
stagflation, 94–95
  and economic policy, 292
  and pay cuts, 139–41
  recovering from, 299–300
  and reserve requirement, 257
Standard Oil Co. (N.J.), 411
state banks, 224
Stigler, George, 417
stock acquisition, merger by, 501
stock market margin requirements, 259–60
store of value, perfect, 240
subsidy, 92
  in correcting market failure, 468–70
sunspots and business activity, 272
supernormal profits
  competitive firm, 358
  monopolistic competition, 396–98
supply, 60–61
  and demand, law of, 338
  demand, market price, and, 339
  elasticity of, 331
  of factors, 434–38
  of foreign exchange, 556–57
  of labor, 437–38
  of land and natural resources, 435–37
  law of, 64, 330
  and production costs, 322–30
  shifts in, 66–67
  and technology, 330–31
  and time, 331–33
supply and demand, law of, 338
supply curve, 60, 322–23
  for factor of production, 434
  for labor, 438
  for land, 435
  and marginal cost, 327–30
  for natural resources, 436
  shift, 66
supply/demand relationship, 61–64
surcharge, 198

on dutiable imports, 576
surplus, 62–63
  budget, 204
  consumers', 380
Sweezy, Paul, 416, 417

tariff, 544
tastes, and demand, 318
tax(es)
  and aggregate demand, 90
  in correcting market failure, 468–70
  to finance pure public goods, 484
  in paying for public goods, 492–93
  rate changes, as discretionary stabilizer, 196–98
  receipts, as automatic stabilizer, 191
  refund plan, 179
  sales, 102
  single, 436
Tax Reduction Bill (1964), 196
technology
  and demand, 318
  and investment, 154
  and monopoly, 376–78
  and supply, 330–31
Tennessee Valley Authority, 193
theories, 17
The Theory of Games and Economic Behavior (von Neumann and Morgenstern), 422
third-party effects, *see* externalities
Third-World nations, 573–74 (*see also* less developed countries [LDCs]
tied contract, 500
time, and supply, 331–33
time deposits, 229
time paths of growth, 599
time series, 134–35
timing, and transactions demand for money, 237–38
Tishman, Robert, 346
total costs, 324
total product, 429
trade, *see also* international trade
  gains from, 541–43
  and opportunity cost, 539
  rate of, 543
  U.S., recent developments, 573–76
trade barriers
  and diversified economies, 545
  and infant industries, 544–45
  and labor force protection, 545–46
  and world economics, 527–28
tradeoffs, 538–39
trade surplus, 569
  U.S., 574–75
trading
  among national economies, 517–20
  U.S. as nation of, 520–24
  who does it, 516
transactions demand for money, 237–38
transfer payments, 106–07, 569
Treasury, and Fed, 261
Treasury bill, 253
trust, vs. monopoly, 500
trust certificate, 383–84

uncollectible revenue, 485–86
underemployment, 585
undifferentiated product, 353
undistributed corporate profits, 106
unemployment, 81–82, 290, 291 (*see also* full employment)
  disguised, 585
  and fiscal policy, 184
  frictional vs. structural, 82n
  and monetary policy, 296
  and per capita GNP, 291–92
  as percentage of civilian labor force, 83
  and tax cut, 197–98
unemployment compensation, 190–91
  vs. welfare payments, 195n
unemployment insurance, 508
unilateral account, 572
unions, and factor market for labor, 440–41
United Shoe Machinery Corp., 370
United States
  balance of payments problems,

575
  foreign aid to LDCs, 600–01
  trade surpluses, 574–75
  trade with Britain, 552–59
  as trading nation, 520–24
  world trade, 524–25
U.S. v. *Aluminum Company of America,* 502
U.S. v. *E. I. du Pont de Nemours & Co.,* 502
U.S. v. *Standard Oil Co. of New Jersey,* 502
unit elasticity, 313
unpaid costs of economic activity, 463–64
utility, 306
  and price, 307

value, perfect store of, 240
variable costs, 323
variables, 18–19
VISTA, 192, 194
von Neumann, John, 422
Von's Grocery Co., 502

wages
  cuts, and stagflation, 139–41
  and national income, 449–50
  and price changes, 84–85

war
  and business activity, 271
  and public debt, 206, 211–12
wealth
  distribution of, 452
  vs. income, 448
welfare economics, 463
welfare payments
  as discretionary stabilizer, 194–96
  and public debt, 207
well-being
  as economic goal, 88–89
  and GNP, 114–15
Westinghouse Electric Co., 419
windfall gains, 357
women, income, 453
working capital, 520–21
world economics
  and expansion of world trade, 525–26
  and income distribution, 526–27
  and multiple currencies, 528
  and population, 526
  and trade barriers, 527–28
world economy, 515–17
world exports = world imports, 522
world trade, *see* international trade

Zero Population Growth, 526
zoning, in correcting market failure, 471

Glossary

aggregate demand: The total quantity of all goods and services demanded and purchased by an entire economy in a given period of time, expressed in dollar terms.

average costs: A firm's total production costs divided by the number of units produced. Average costs are often broken into two parts—average fixed costs (fixed costs ÷ quantity produced) and average variable costs (variable costs ÷ quantity produced).

average propensity to consume (APC): That proportion of disposable income that households generally spend on consumer goods and services.

average propensity to save (APS): That proportion of disposable income that households save rather than spend for consumer goods and services.

backward merger: The purchase by a producing firm of another firm that is a supplier of inputs. In the 1930s, major oil companies were active in backward mergers.

balance of payments: A summary of all economic transactions carried out between an economy and the rest of the world. It reflects all payments due, as well as all liabilities to be paid to other countries.

bank draft: A special kind of check often used in international transactions. It is much like a personal check, except that payment is guaranteed in whatever currency is specified by the sender of the draft.

barter: A system of trading in which one good is exchanged directly for another without the use of money.

benefit/cost analysis: An old and reasonably sophisticated method used to evaluate public facilities and programs. It compares the value of resources taken from the circular flow to the value of goods and services returned to the flow.

benefit stream: The time path of benefits accruing to a capital investment over its entire life.

business fluctuations (or cycles): Recurring patterns of changes in the direction of business activity, including phases of prosperity, recession, depression, and recovery.

clearing the market: The process of removing all of one commodity or service from all marketplaces. The market for wheat is "cleared" when this year's crop has found its way to millers, feeders, and distillers.

closed economy: One that is self-sufficient and carries on no trade with other nations. Although some modern economies have the capability to sustain themselves as closed economies, none of them does.

collusion: An agreement or conspiracy among rival firms not to engage in price competition or other kinds of competitive activities that could disrupt the relationship among firms. Collusion is illegal in the United States.

colony: A geographic territory subservient to another nation's government. Most European nations—especially England, Spain, Portugal, and France—had vast colonial holdings. The colonies were expected to be producers of raw materials and consumers of finished goods. Thus, England expected to purchase wood, hides, cotton, and foodstuffs from its North American colonies. In return, the colonies were expected to purchase machines, shipping, and protection from England.

commercial bank: A financial institution that has the privilege of holding checking accounts and savings accounts as well as performing a number of other functions related to money. These privileges come from the state or federal government, either of which may grant a charter to a bank.

comparative advantage: The superior productive capacity of one producer, laborer, or nation compared to all others.

competitive industry: An industry characterized by many firms—so many that none can be large enough to have any impact on price—producing identical products. A single firm can leave a competitive industry and no one will notice. Another firm can join the industry and no one will notice.

constant-cost industry: An industry that produces at the same average cost over a very wide range of output.

Consumer Price Index (CPI): A single number that compares consumer prices in one year with prices paid by consumers in previous years. A rise in the index means prices are higher than before; a drop means they are lower. The CPI is kept up to date and published at frequent intervals by the Bureau of Labor Statistics.

consumer sovereignty: The ability of consumers to use their income as they wish, and thus to influence the kind and the amount of goods produced by firms.

consumption function: The relationship between disposable income and total expenditure on consumer goods and services: As income rises so does expenditure, but not so rapidly.

contract labor: A means of importing labor to perform certain tasks by agreeing to pay the immigrant's moving expenses if he or she promises to work for a specified number of years. While the process, no longer in existence in the United States, did allow immigration, it did not provide freedom in either an economic or a political sense.

cost of living: A summary term used to describe changes in the total cost of goods and services a representative household will consume in a year's time.

cost stream: The time path of costs for a capital investment over its entire life.

cost structure: The relationship among a firm's fixed costs, variable costs, and marginal costs.

countercyclical policy: Economic policy that runs in cycles opposite the general fluctuations. A countercyclical policy seeks to expand while the general economy is contracting and to contract while the general economy is expanding.

credit entry: A bookkeeping entry showing a payment that has been received from others. It is the opposite of a debit entry. A credit entry reflects an increase in the amount of cash held, an addition to assets, or a decrease in indebtedness. In the international balance of payments, exports give rise to credit entries.

currency: The money printed and distributed by the U.S. Treasury, including both coin and paper money.

debit entry: A bookkeeping entry showing a payment to others, a reduction in assets, or an increase in indebtedness. In international terms, any transaction, such as an import, that causes money to flow out of an economy is entered as a debit in that nation's balance of payments.

deflationary gap: The amount by which aggregate demand must increase in order to equal aggregate supply at the full-employment level of output.

demand: A technical term meaning "desire backed by purchasing power." This desire is usually stated as the quantities of a good, factor, or service that will be purchased at each of a series of prices.

demand curve: A negatively sloped line showing the quantities of a good that will be purchased at each of several prices.

demand deposit: A bank account containing money that can be transferred on demand by writing a check.

deposit expansion multiplier: The relationship between an original deposit and the potential addition it can make to the total money supply. The numerical value of the deposit expansion multiplier is represented by the following formula:

$$\text{Deposit expansion multiplier} = \frac{1}{\text{Legal reserve requirement}}$$

depreciation: The loss in value or productive capacity of a capital asset, usually associated with aging, physical deterioration, destruction, or obsolescence. A machine depreciates as it wears out.

derived demand: The demand for a factor of production. If the price of a product is high, the demand for factors used to produce it will be high and factor users will be willing to pay a high price for it. If product prices are low, production will not be especially profitable and entrepreneurs will not be willing to pay high prices for large quantities of factors. The demand for the factor is derived from the demand for the product.

differentiated product: A commodity that is recognizable as the product of one particular firm but for which many close substitutes are available. Firms in monopolistic competition go to great lengths to differentiate their products so that buyers will ask for their products by name. Differentiating is most often done through advertising campaigns, packaging, or slight modification in form.

discount rate: The interest rate charged member banks when they borrow money from the Federal Reserve System. The term "discount" refers to the Fed's practice of collecting interest when the loan is made rather than when it is repaid.

disposable (personal) income (DI or DPI): A measure of the amount households have available to spend on the output of the economy; those dollars over which the household has direct control.

dissaving: Spending more than current income, as when money is taken from savings accounts or depreciation funds and used for consumption or investment purposes.

dutiable import: An import on which a duty or tariff must be paid.

duty: See *tariff*.

economics: A social science devoted to studying choice and the allocation of scarce resources among alternative and competing ends.

economies of scale: The reductions in unit costs that come from increasing output. They result from more advanced technology, more specialization of labor, and sometimes from the ability to purchase large quantities of inputs at discount prices.

elasticity of demand: A measure of responsiveness. If quantity demanded is very responsive to a change in price, demand is elastic. If quantity demanded is not very responsive to a change in price, demand is inelastic.

empirical evidence: Information based on fact or observation rather than on theory or speculation.

endogenous: Occurring within. An endogenous economic theory is one that depends on variables within the system. A theory relating aggregate demand to the money supply is an endogenous theory, since both variables are part of the economic system.

entrepreneur: One who organizes, manages, operates, and takes the risks associated with a business venture. Entrepreneurship is a special class of labor that includes the capacity and willingness to take such risks.

equilibrium: The level of price and output at which there is no net force toward changing either price or quantity exchanged. At equilibrium the money that buyers are willing to give up is just equal to the amount sellers are asking for a given quantity of the good or service.

equity: (1) The extent of a shareholder's ownership in a company; (2) fairness or equal treatment.

excess reserves: Demand deposit money that need not be kept in the bank but can be used at its discretion. The excess reserves form the basis for a banker's lending activities.

exogenous: External, or outside. An exogenous theory is a theory of economic behavior that depends on something outside the economic system.

externality: An incidental effect produced by economic activities but not accounted for by the market system. Such effects do not enter the cost or benefit decisions of either buyer or seller, and are thus considered external. Externalities can be either harmful or beneficial, and are sometimes called *nonmarket effects* or *third-party effects*.

factor markets: Markets in which land, labor, and capital change hands. These markets transmit information about the demand for and availability of factors. The Help Wanted section of the classified ads is part of the factor market, as is the casual cocktail party remark that an office in the Lincoln Building will soon be available for rent.

factors of production: Resources that are used in the process of producing a good or service. Today some economists prefer to call them *inputs*. Factors (or inputs) can be as tangible as a lump of coal or as intangible as the thought process of an inventor.

fiat money: Money whose face value is greater than the value of the metal it contains; paper money that is not backed by an equivalent value of precious metal. All money circulating in the United States today is fiat money.

final transaction: The transaction that places a finished good in the hands of its final consumer. A homemaker buying groceries is consummating a final transaction.

financial intermediary: An institution that handles money for other people (households or firms). A common function of a financial intermediary is to gather funds from many savers and make these accumulated funds available to borrowers.

fine tuning: The process used by fiscal authorities to make very selective changes in the performance of the macroeconomy. A program aimed at employing minority workers in the central cities is fine tuning.

firm: An individual producing unit, the basic building block in the production and distribution chain. It owns or purchases factors of production, and make choices regarding how to use these factors. It reaps the benefits of correct choices and bears the burdens of incorrect ones. In economies, the firm is usually assumed to order its activities so as to maximize profits, or to minimize losses.

fiscal year: A twelve-month period used for accounting purposes. It may or may not coincide with the calendar year.

fixed costs: Production costs that do not change with output. They include insurance, taxes, depreciation, and a variety of other expenses that must be met whether the firm produces zero output or at maximum capacity.

foreign exchange: Currency (or other financial instruments) that can be used to pay international debts. Thus, in the United States, pounds sterling are foreign exchange because they can be used to pay debts in Great Britain. In Great Britain, dollars are foreign exchange. In Paris, both dollars and pounds sterling are foreign exchange.

forward merger: The purchase by a manufacturer of retail outlets for its own products. Recently, especially since oil shortages and embargoes began, oil companies have become very interested in retailing their own gasoline and as a consequence have engaged in forward mergers.

fractional reserve system: The practice of issuing money worth more than the assets backing it, thus keeping on reserve only a fraction of the real value of the money supply.

full employment: In a strict sense, employment of 100 percent of the labor force, so that everyone who wants to work is working. In practice, unemployment of less than 4 percent of the civilian labor force.

functional distribution of income: The proportion of national income that is earned by each of the major classes of factor inputs. Land earns rent, labor earns wages, capital earns interest, and entrepreneurship earns profits.

functional finance: An approach to government budgeting that emphasizes the results achieved by a given set of government activities rather than balancing the budget.

gross national product (GNP): The money value of all final goods and services produced in an economy in one accounting period—usually a year.

homogeneous product: A product that is the same no matter which producer produces it. The producer is not easily identifiable.

income determination: A model of how the aggregate behavior of all individuals determines the aggregate level of income in the economy.

industry: The aggregation of all firms that produce a particular product or service.

inflation: A condition characterized by general rises in prices of most commodities.

inflationary gap: The amount by which aggregate demand exceeds aggregate supply when the economy is at the full-employment level of NNP.

interlocking directorates: Complex interconnections among firms allowing a few people to sit on many boards of directors and thus control many firms.

investment: Production that will add to further productive capacity and, hence, to the capacity to satisfy wants in the future.

laissez faire: A French phrase meaning literally "let them do." Adam Smith used the term to describe a self-regulating, market-oriented economy operating without interference from government.

law of demand: A fundamental and consistent law of economic behavior stating that as the price of a good falls the quantity purchased will increase, and as price rises the quantity purchased will fall.

law of supply: As the price of a factor, good, or service increases, more of that factor, good, or service will be placed on the market.

liquid assets: Assets that can easily be used for transactions purposes. Cash is the most liquid of all assets. Liquid assets are assets that can be turned into cash on a moment's notice.

liquidity preference: The desire to hold cash or demand deposits rather than interest-earning assets. It is closely related to expectations for the future, income, and the rate of interest.

local monopoly: A firm that enjoys an exclusive market in a restricted area. The "company store" of a Western lumber town or a Pennsylvania mining town is an extreme form of a local monopoly.

long run: The time required for all resources to become variable. In a restaurant, it is the time needed to add seating capacity or expand the kitchen. In shipbuilding, it is the time needed to build more drydocks and launching facilities, and train more shipwrights.

marginal cost: The additional cost associated with the production of one more unit of output.

marginal propensity to consume (MPC): The proportion of any increase in income that is spent on consumer goods and services.

marginal propensity to save (MPS): The proportion of any increase in income that is saved.

marginal revenue: The addition to total revenue provided by selling one more unit of a good or service.

marginal utility: The added usefulness resulting from the acquisition of an additional unit of a good. This utility is most often measured in terms of the money given up to obtain the extra unit of the good.

market: Any place where buyers and sellers come into contact with each other for the purpose of trading. A market may be a physical location, like Gimbels or Woolworths, or it may consist simply of all the possible buyers or sellers of a given product.

market economy: An economy in which decision making is broadly based and each person—buyer or seller—becomes an active part of the massive marketing apparatus. In such an economy, owners of land, labor, capital, and entrepreneurial skill are free to negotiate with potential buyers, and producers of goods and services are free to negotiate with consumers.

market mechanism: The process by which buyers express what they want to buy and sellers respond by communicating what they are willing to sell. Their combined activities yield the price at which the good or service is exchanged.

market (short short) run: That period of time during which supply cannot be changed.

merit want: A good or service provided on the basis of its merit rather than because consumers reveal a willingness to pay for it. Education, pollution control, defense, flood protection, and smallpox vaccinations are among the many merit wants in the U.S. economy.

microeconomic policy: Deliberate policy encompassing those laws, policies, and programs designed specifically to alter the behavior of micro units in the economy.

mixed economy: An economy in which some goods and services are produced and distributed under private auspices, while others are produced and distributed under the control of public mechanisms. The U.S. economy is a mixed economy, with about 65 percent of all goods produced in response to market signals and 35 percent produced through government sponsorship.

monetarists: Economists who see

fluctuations in economic activity as closely related to variations in the money supply, and believe that policies regarding economic growth and stabilization should be based primarily on changes in the supply of money.

monetary policy: Conscious policy of government and/or banking authorities to alter the supply of money, the availability of loanable funds, or interest rates.

monopolistic competition: A form of market organization in which many firms produce slightly differentiated products. No one firm dominates, and firms can enter or leave the industry without disrupting the plans of other firms.

monopoly: A form of market organization in which a single firm comprises the entire industry. The monopoly firm produces a commodity for which there are no close substitutes.

multinational firm: One that is based in one country but has business operations in other countries as well. Coca-Cola is a multinational, as are General Motors and Du Pont. At this time, about 60 percent of all multinational firms have their home offices in the United States.

multiplier: The numerical relationship between an original increase in expenditure and the ultimate change in total income that results as the money is spent and respent through various sectors of the economy.

national income (NI): The return to the factors of production sold by households.

near-monies: U.S. Government bonds held by individuals and businesses; called "near-monies" because they can be easily converted into cash.

net national product (NNP): GNP minus depreciation allowances.

nonmonetary costs: Costs not reckoned in dollars and cents. The loss of a friend is a cost, but it is not included in any demand-and-supply schedule. Moving from one town to another always involves nonmonetary costs.

oligopoly: A form of market organization in which the number of firms in an industry is so small that each must consider how the other firms will react if it changes its price or output levels.

opportunity cost: Whatever must be given up in order to gain something else. Opportunity cost is a crucial concept in economics, since it shows that economic activity is a complex phenomenon in which, usually, one thing can be gained only if another is given up.

par value of foreign exchange: The official value of a nation's currency. It is generally stated in terms of another currency (£1 = $2.00) or in terms of a precious metal (gold = $35/oz).

perfect market: One in which information is freely exchanged, anyone can buy or sell, and no one buyer or seller can have an appreciable influence on price.

perfect store of value: A product or object that maintains the same purchasing power relative to all other goods through all time.

personal income (PI): A measure of what factor owners receive, as distinguished from what factors earn; the total income persons receive from all sources.

poverty line: A level of income below which people cannot attain a satisfactory level of living. Because prices differ from place to place and from time to time, the poverty line is constantly being adjusted.

price taker: The role of a firm in a competitive industry. Because firms in a competitive industry are small and many, none can become large enough to have any influence on price. Therefore, each firm *takes* the price offered by the market.

prime lending rate: The interest rate that the best ("prime") customers (usually large industrial firms) of major banks must pay. It is lower than a household would ordinarily pay. The prime rate is an important indicator of how banks view business conditions.

private costs: The prices paid through factor markets, so called since they are actually paid by the private producing firms.

production function: The relationship between quantities of factor inputs and product yields. A production function is drawn on a graph with the quantity of output (in either physical or monetary terms) on the vertical axis and the quantity of one variable input on the horizontal axis.

production-possibility curve: A map of all the possible combinations of public and private goods that can be produced by an economy when all its resources are employed.

progressive income tax: An income tax that collects proportionately larger amounts of money from the wealthy than from the poor.

public assistance: The catch-all of income transfers. It includes aid to the disabled and blind, Aid to Families with Dependent Children, special grants to families with severe health problems, and a variety of selective programs.

public debt: Obligations incurred by government to perform some necessary fiscal functions, often yielding significant increases in the productivity of the nation.

public good: A good or service that can be used simultaneously by any number of people. One person's use does not diminish the quantity available, or interfere with the capacity of others to use the good. Moreover, once the public good is produced, there is no way of stopping anyone from using it.

quality of output: The mix or "menu" of goods and services produced by an economy.

quantity theory of money: As the

supply of money in an economy changes, the general price level changes by the same proportion and in the same direction.

rate of exchange: The domestic price of a foreign currency. For example, if a single pound sterling costs a U.S. citizen $2.50, the rate of exchange in the United States is £1 = $2.50. In Britain, the rate would be £0.4 = $1.

required reserve: The fraction of demand deposit money that must be kept on hand by a bank. Required reserves are kept as a kind of insurance that a bank will not lend out all its deposits, leaving none to service its depositors.

resources: The things society has available to use in producing the goods it desires. Resources include land, coal, machines, labor, transportation networks, technology, and the other assets that make a society productive.

revaluation: A change in a fixed rate of exchange that makes the domestic currency more valuable relative to a foreign currency. **devaluation:** A change in a fixed rate of exchange that makes the domestic currency less valuable.

Say's Law: A commentary on the symmetry between the product and factor flows, usually stated simply as "supply creates its own demand."

service industries: Those industries that provide a useful service rather than a tangible product that can be sold and resold. Among the fastest growing service industries in the U.S. economy are government service and personal care.

shortage: The quantity by which supply falls short of demand when product prices are very low.

short run: That time period during which supply can be altered by changing the amount of variable inputs applied to a given set of fixed inputs; the period in which output can change within limits of the existing plant.

size distribution of income: The way in which the total value of a year's output is distributed among persons. Since this is a relatively new way to describe income distribution, the terms denoting it are not entirely settled. Some economists use *personal distribution,* others *family distribution,* and still others *money distribution.*

social cost: The sum of private costs and unpaid costs, or the cost society must bear in order to insure production of certain outputs.

social overhead capital: Those forms of capital that do not necessarily produce a salable product, but that contribute to the production of other goods or services. Since these forms of capital are not easily sold in organized markets, they are most often installed by government.

social sciences: Those fields of learning concerned primarily with relationships among people and with institutions people use to guide behavior. Economics, sociology, political science, anthropology, and psychology are social sciences.

subsidy: A form of government financial assistance used to encourage production that otherwise would not occur. Transportation, communication, defense-related, and food-producing industries have been major recipients of government subsidies.

supernormal profits: Any profits in excess of normal profits. They are sometimes called "windfall gains."

supply: The quantities of a good, factor, or service that will be placed on the market at each of a series of prices.

supply curve: A positively sloped line showing the quantities of a good that will be placed on the market at each of several prices. The curve is plotted in a quandrant having price on the vertical axis and quantity supplied on the horizontal axis.

surcharge: An extra charge imposed on top of a regularly established fee; a special tax levied on a particular item. A 10-percent surcharge on a dutiable import increases its price by 10 percent.

surplus: The excess of quantity supplied over quantity demanded at a given price.

tariff: A tax on an import. Tariffs may be levied with respect to the value of the imported item (an ad valorem tariff), or as a flat charge on each unit of the product brought into the country. Tariffs are often referred to as "duties" or "import duties."

Third-World nations: The less developed countries, primarily in Asia and Africa. Their economies are not able to provide a reasonable level of living for their populations, and they are often characterized by political and economic instability.

tied contract: An arrangement whereby a producer forces a retailer (or another producer) to deal exclusively with it. For example, retailers can sell the producer's brand only if they promise not to sell any other brand.

time deposit: A bank deposit that cannot be withdrawn without the depositor giving the bank adequate advance warning. Most banks do not enforce this rule on ordinary savings accounts.

time series: A sequence of empirical observations made at regular intervals—weekly, monthly, quarterly, or annually—to show how a particular variable is behaving.

total costs: The sum of a firm's fixed costs and variable costs.

tradeoff: A result of choosing and therefore the proper concern of economics. A tradeoff includes two acts, the act of selecting one thing and rejecting a second. See *opportunity cost.*

transfer payments: Expenditures that involve an exchange of money but do not give rise to an increase in the production of goods or services. Pensions and welfare payments are transfers, since they are not connected with current output. The purchase of a used car is also a transfer payment because the transaction does not increase the nation's stock of automobiles.

Treasury, U.S.: The fiscal agent for the federal government. In this capacity, it collects taxes and pays bills.

Treasury bill: A short-term security with a maturity of 91 (sometimes 182) days. Because of their short term to maturity, the bills seldom gain or lose value because of inflationary or deflationary pressures. They are liquid assets, sought after as bank reserves.

underemployment: The situation when laborers are not actually looking for work but are performing no productive services or are going for long periods without working to capacity. In low-income nations, many workers, especially in agriculture, are underemployed. They work during planting and harvest but engage in no productive activity during other seasons. Underemployment is sometimes called *disguised unemployment*.

unpaid costs: Costs directly attributable to the production process but not paid through factor markets. They are sometimes called *external costs*.

variable: A characteristic whose value changes over time or from one context to another.

variable costs: Production costs that rise and fall as output rises and falls.

working capital: Cash used to pay current bills and obligations. A factory owner uses working capital to pay laborers, the electricity bill, and other expenses directly related to the production process.

INDUSTRY GROUPS IN THE U.S. ECONOMY, 1972

Industry	Number of firms	Number of employees (thousands)	Value of shipments	Capital expenditures	End-of-year inventories
			(millions of dollars)		
Food and kindred products	28,184	1,569	115,060	2,355	10,026
Tobacco products	272	66	5,920	133	2,493
Textile mill products	7,203	953	28,072	1,128	3,942
Apparel and related products	24,438	1,368	27,809	364	3,789
Lumber and wood products	33,948	691	23,816	931	2,601
Furniture and fixtures	9,232	462	11,309	306	1,750
Paper and allied products	6,038	633	28,262	1,335	2,911
Printing and publishing	42,102	1,056	30,132	1,047	2,340
Chemicals and allied products	11,425	837	57,350	2,728	7,107
Petroleum and coal products	2,016	140	28,695	1,154	2,223
Rubber and plastic	9,237	618	20,924	1,060	2,589
Leather and leather products	3,201	273	5,770	75	796
Stone, clay, and glass	16,015	623	21,538	1,196	2,491
Primary metals	6,792	1,143	58,430	2,161	9,699
Fabricated metals	29,525	1,493	51,739	1,323	8,345
Non-electric machinery	40,792	1,828	65,821	1,906	15,037
Electric machinery	12,274	1,662	53,433	1,419	9,732
Transportation equipment	8,802	1,719	94,705	2,660	15,705
Instruments	5,987	454	15,566	480	3,097
Miscellaneous	15,188	446	12,186	317	2,263